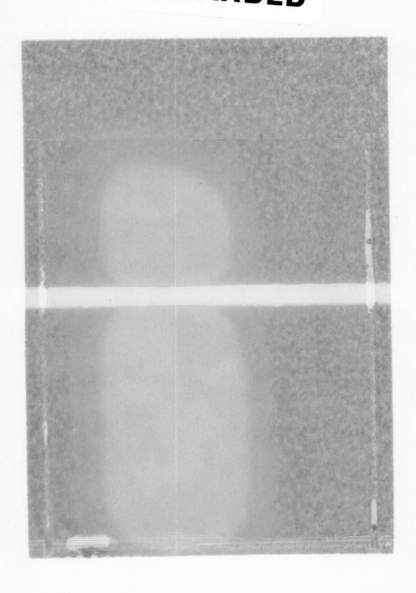

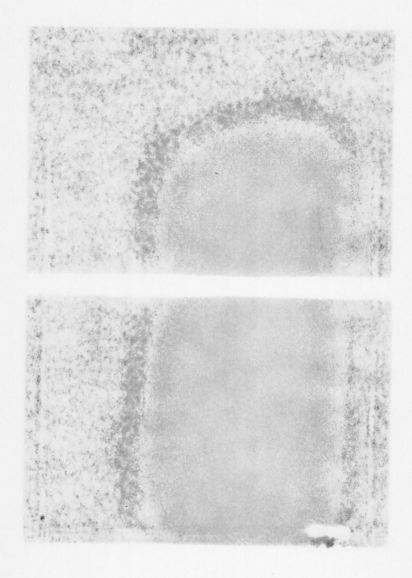

NEGRO EMPLOYMENT
IN LAND AND AIR TRANSPORT

A Study of Racial Policies in the Railroad, Airline, Trucking, and Urban Transit Industries

INDUSTRIAL RESEARCH UNIT
WHARTON SCHOOL OF FINANCE AND COMMERCE
UNIVERSITY OF PENNSYLVANIA

Founded in 1921 as a separate Wharton Department, the Industrial Research Unit has a long record of publication and research in the labor market, productivity, union relations, and business report fields. Major Industrial Research Unit studies are published as research projects are completed. Advanced research reports are issued as appropriate in a general or special series.

Recent Industrial Research Unit Studies

(Available from the University of Pennsylvania Press or the Industrial Research Unit)

No. 40 Gladys L. Palmer, *et al.*, *The Reluctant Job Changer.* 1962. $7.50

No. 41 George M. Parks, *The Economics of Carpeting and Resilient Flooring: An Evaluation and Comparison.* 1966. $5.00

No. 42 Michael H. Moskow, *Teachers and Unions: The Applicability of Bargaining to Public Education.* 1966. $8.50

No. 43 F. Marion Fletcher, *Market Restraints in the Retail Drug Industry.* 1967. $10.00

No. 44 Herbert R. Northrup and Gordon R. Storholm, *Restrictive Labor Practices in the Supermarket Industry.* 1967. $7.50

No. 45 William N. Chernish, *Coalition Bargaining: A Study of Union Tactics and Public Policy.* 1969. $7.95

No. 46 Herbert R. Northrup, Richard L. Rowan, *et al.*, *Negro Employment in Basic Industry: A Study of Racial Policies in Six Industries.* (Studies of Negro Employment, Vol. I.) 1970. $15.00

No. 47 Armand J. Thieblot, Jr., and Linda P. Fletcher, *Negro Employment in Finance: A Study of Racial Policies in Banking and Insurance.* (Studies of Negro Employment, Vol. II.) 1970. $9.50

No. 48 Bernard E. Anderson, *Negro Employment in Public Utilities: A Study of Racial Policies in the Electric Power, Gas, and Telephone Industries.* (Studies of Negro Employment, Vol. III.) 1970. $8.50

No. 49 Herbert R. Northrup, Richard L. Rowan, *et al.*, *Negro Employment in Southern Industry: A Study of Racial Policies in Five Industries.* (Studies of Negro Employment, Vol. IV.) 1971. $13.50

No. 50 Herbert R. Northrup, Howard W. Risher, Jr., Richard D. Leone, and Philip W. Jeffress, *Negro Employment in Land and Air Transport: A Study of Racial Policies in the Railroad, Airline, Trucking, and Urban Transit Industries.* (Studies of Negro Employment, Vol. V.) 1971. $13.50

No. 51 Charles R. Perry and F. Marion Fletcher, *Negro Employment in Retail Trade: A Study of Racial Policies in the Department Store, Drugstore, and Supermarket Industries.* (Studies of Negro Employment, Vol. VI.) 1971. $10.00

NEGRO EMPLOYMENT IN LAND AND AIR TRANSPORT

A Study of Racial Policies in the Railroad, Airline, Trucking, and Urban Transit Industries

(Volume V—Studies of Negro Employment)

by

HERBERT R. NORTHRUP
Professor of Industry and Director,
Industrial Research Unit

HOWARD W. RISHER, JR.
Research Associate, Industrial Research Unit

RICHARD D. LEONE
Assistant Professor of Management
School of Business Administration, Temple University

PHILIP W. JEFFRESS
Assistant Professor of Economics and Finance
Louisiana State University, New Orleans

INDUSTRIAL RESEARCH UNIT
Wharton School of Finance and Commerce
University of Pennsylvania

Foreword

In September 1966, the Ford Foundation began a series of major grants to the Industrial Research Unit of the Wharton School of Finance and Commerce to fund a series of studies of the Racial Policies of American Industry. The purpose has been to determine why some industries are more hospitable to the employment of Negroes than are others and why some companies within the same industry have vastly different racial employment policies.

Studies have proceeded on an industry-by-industry basis under the direction of the undersigned, with Dr. Richard L. Rowan, Associate Professor of Industry, as Associate Director. As of April 1971, twenty-three industry studies have been published with eight more in press or being readied for publication.

This volume is the fifth in our series of books combining industry studies and analyzing the reasons for different racial policies and Negro employment patterns among various industries. The present volume includes studies previously published as Report No. 15 (trucking), Report No. 16 (railroad), Report No. 18 (urban transit), and No. 23 (air transport), plus a final section analyzing and contrasting the Negro employment situation in these four transportation industries.

Volume I, *Negro Employment in Basic Industry*, published early in 1970, contains an introductory section which sets forth the purpose and hypotheses of the overall project and a brief overview of the position of the Negro in American industry. Volume II, *Negro Employment in Finance*, on the banking and insurance industries, Volume III, *Negro Employment in Public Utilities*, and Volume IV, *Negro Employment in Southern Industry*, have also been published. A volume on retail trade is scheduled for 1971 publication and those dealing with maritime industries, selected manufacturing industries, and building construction are in the planning stage. These nine volumes and the various industry reports should contain the most thorough analysis of Negro employment available in the United States.

Negro Employment in Land and Air Transport is the work of several persons. Part One (the railroad industry) was written by Howard W. Risher, Jr., who is now in industry and who worked with the Industrial Research Unit for several years. Mr. Risher is also completing his Ph.D. dissertation on industrial relations in the railroads under a grant from the Manpower Administration of the United States Department of Labor. The railroad industry, which he discusses so thoroughly, was once one of the largest employers of Negroes in the United States. Technological unemployment, declining traffic, and the invidious discrimination by unions, carriers, and government agencies have all tended to reduce the number and proportion of Negroes in the industry. Mr. Risher explains how these forces work slowly but surely to disenfranchise the Negro employee and greatly reduce both the numbers and proportion in the industry.

Part Two (the air transport industry) was written by the undersigned in collaboration with Professor Armand J. Thieblot, Jr., Assistant Professor of Management at the University of Maryland and a former Research Associate at the Industrial Research Unit, and Dr. William N. Chernish, who is now in industry and who also was a former Industrial Research Unit staff member. The air transport industry is the elite member of the transportation group, with professional pilots handling the equipment and a majority of its employees in salaried positions. Negroes were generally excluded from all key positions of the industry until the 1960's. In that decade a concerted attempt was made to convert the industry into an equal opportunity employer but the difficulties inherent in the long training periods and in the disadvantaged status of black citizens combined with the hiring of pilots and mechanics from the armed forces tend to make the going slow in many key jobs. On the other hand, real progress has been made in the reservation agent and stewardess positions. The progress of the industry, however, has inevitably been slowed by its current depressed condition.

Part Three (trucking) was written by Professor Richard D. Leone, Assistant Professor of Management at Temple University, and a fourth former associate of the Industrial Research Unit. Professor Leone's excellent field study of the trucking industry shows that the industry and the Teamsters' Union lag considerably in the employment of black personnel, tending to confine them to warehouse jobs or to local driving. This has occurred despite the fact that truck driving is essentially a semiskilled job for which, as Professor Leone clearly shows, there are ample qualified black personnel available. The Teamsters' Union, while making quite a demonstration of concern for the disadvantaged, has confined that demonstration largely to areas away from its basic jurisdiction of over-the-road driving. It is expected that the government will continue its efforts in this area and some progress should result now that a key case has been settled by a consent decree highly favorable to black applicants.

Part Four (urban transit) is the work of Dr. Philip W. Jeffress, Assistant Professor of Economics and Finance, Louisiana State University at New Orleans. This is an industry which has quite different problems from the other three. Despite continued decline in the industry, black personnel now comprise an ever larger proportion of the total employment. The location of the industry in the cities, the crime problem in the cities, and the industry's loss of status have all tended to induce whites to look elsewhere for jobs. The urban transit industry pays high wages and the jobs were once quite prestigious. The question of equal employment opportunity was fairly well settled in the North during World War II, in the border states during the following decade, and finally in the South once the Civil Rights Act of 1964 was enacted. Professor Jeffress predicts that the industry is moving toward being black operated and catering largely to black and other disadvantaged persons.

Part Five (concluding analysis) is also the work of the undersigned. In this section the results of the research are summarized, the industries are compared and contrasted in terms of black employment opportunities, and an analysis of the factors is made in accordance with the hpyotheses set forth in our first volume, *Negro Employment in Basic Industry*.

Many persons assisted in the writing of this book. Major editorial and research assistance was provided by Mrs. Marjorie C. Denison, Mrs. Marie R. Keeney, and Miss Elsa Klemp. Indices were prepared by Mrs. Keeney and Mrs. Margaret W. Hurst. Mrs. Margaret E. Doyle, our Administrative Assistant and Office Manager, handled the administrative details in her usual efficient manner. The manuscripts were typed by Mrs. Rose K. Elkin, Mrs. Veronica M. Kent, Mrs. Louise P. Morrison, and Mrs. Marie P. Spence.

Many others have contributed to this volume. The fine cooperation of numerous industry and government personnel made it possible to obtain material and data not otherwise available. Their request for anonymity precludes our recording individually the great debt which we obviously owe. Dr. John R. Coleman,

President of Haverford College, made the initial grants possible as a staff member of the Ford Foundation, and later Mitchell Sviridoff, Vice-President, and Basil T. Whiting, Project Officer, assured continued Foundation support and interest. Student support grants from the Labor Relations Council of the Wharton School aided the research of Dr. Leone and Mr. Risher. Numerous students added their help, questions, or discussions to improve our own understanding.

As in most previous reports, the data cited as "in the author's possession," have been carefully authenticated and are on file in our Industrial Research Unit library.

HERBERT R. NORTHRUP, *Director*
Industrial Research Unit
Wharton School of Finance and Commerce
University of Pennsylvania

Philadelphia

May 1971

CONTENTS

PART ONE

THE NEGRO
IN THE RAILROAD INDUSTRY

by

HOWARD W. RISHER, JR.

TABLE OF CONTENTS

                                                                      v

LIST OF TABLES

LIST OF FIGURES

APPENDIX TABLES

CHAPTER I

Introduction

Railroading has long been a fundamental part of the Negro heritage in America. Negro slaves worked on railroad construction and maintenance. From the era of Reconstruction following the Civil War well into the twentieth century, railroads were either the largest, or one of the largest employers of Negroes. To many Negro workers, the relatively high compensation and stable employment available on the railroads have meant better housing, improved educational opportunities, and increased status in the Negro community. In fact, until the new, young Negro leaders came to the fore, most of the leaders in the civil rights movement—Roy Wilkins, Executive Secretary of the National Association for the Advancement of Colored People, A. Philip Randolph, long-time fighter for Negro rights and retired President, Brotherhood of Sleeping Car Porters, and Lester Granger, formerly Executive Director of the National Urban League—either had worked for railroads or had come from railroad families.

On the other hand, those Negroes who took advantage of the economic benefits were exposed to some of the most blatant and pernicious discriminatory practices in American industry. Today, as the formal and informal barriers to an improved job status are being torn away, the image of the Negro railroad employee, as personified by the highly visible porter or track laborer, makes the recruitment of Negro youth very difficult.

The development of the complex railroad transportation network has been cited as the most powerful single initiator of American economic growth.[1] The rapid growth of the railroad industry in the mid-nineteenth century tied the nation together economically, opened the possibility of national markets for many manufacturers, and enabled the United States to occupy vast agricultural areas and transport their output to the cities. Less important in the nation's industrial growth were the patterns in financing and management set by the railroad magnates. By the

---

1. Walt W. Rostow, *The Stages of Economic Growth* (Cambridge, England: Cambridge University Press, 1967), p. 55.

1890's the railroad system was practically completed, with each of the major companies covering about the same territory as they did until recent mergers. Total track mileage operated by 1890 had risen to 167,000 miles from only 35,000 miles after the Civil War.[2]

The expansion during this period was attributable in no small measure to the physical effort of several thousand Negro and first-generation immigrant laborers. As early as 1830 when the first train pulled out of Baltimore to Ellicott's Mills, the same Negro workers who had built the roadbeds and laid the rails "were stationed like minutemen along . . . the route" in case of emergency.[3] The utilization of Negro workers, most of whom were slaves bought or rented by the railroads or exchanged for railroad stock, became common before the Civil War throughout the South. This practice carried over into the period after the war, when the now free Negro workers were enticed to leave the drudgery of field work for the more lucrative task of railroad building. It was reported in 1875 that 35,000 Negroes were persuaded to leave rural South Carolina and Georgia for railroad labor in Arkansas, Texas and Louisiana. One road alone is said to have employed 5,000 Negroes. Most of them were common laborers, but they were also employed as track layers, brakemen, firemen, engineers, and mechanics.[4] In the North Negroes generally were offered jobs only as waiters and porters in the pullman service. As late as 1910 the census reported that 66 percent of the 128,000 male Negro railroad workers were employed as laborers or section hands.[5]

By the turn of the century, however, the rapid expansion of the railway network had ended. Although track mileage continued to grow during the 1920's, the emphasis had shifted to the building of branch lines and the filling in of railroad systems. For the first time railroads were faced with competition for their lucrative freight and passenger business. The trend was toward

2. Alfred D. Chandler, Jr., ed., *The Railroads: The Nation's First Big Business* (New York: Harcourt, Brace & World, Inc., 1965), p. 13.

3. "Negroes in the Railroad Industry," *Ebony*, Vol. XII (April 1957), p. 34.

4. Lorenzo J. Greene & Carter G. Woodson, *The Negro Wage Earner* (Washington: Association for the Study of Negro Life and History, Inc., 1930), p. 33.

5. *U. S. Census of Population, 1910*, Vol. IV, *Occupation Statistics*, Table VI.

consolidation and merger. The industry was besieged with numerous problems from which it has never fully recovered.

Employment too reached a peak in the twenties. The decline in the work force, which continues even today, has affected all railroad occupations. Negro employees, working in the lowest occupations, were generally the first men released by the companies. Further erosion of the position of Negro workers has come about with the introduction of technological change which has reduced the need for unskilled labor. Perhaps the most conspicuous of such changes has been the virtually complete adoption of diesel locomotives, which has greatly reduced employment both among locomotive firemen and repair shop crafts.

The effect of technological change and the decreased demand for railroad services on employment will be examined both historically and currently at several points in this study. The decrease in job opportunities has served to intensify the job consciousness of the railroad unions and their typically all white membership. The attempts by labor organizations to eliminate the Negro from coveted jobs, at times with the knowledge and assistance of management and government bodies, will be an important point in the review of the history of Negro employment which follows in Chapters III and IV.

Although labor market factors and union sentiment have had a significant impact on Negro employment and upgrading, a number of other factors, such as the severely limited authority of the personnel function and the close control by government agencies, have each had a bearing on racial employment policies. The employment of Negroes in unskilled and service occupations is deeply entrenched in industry traditions and in the attitudes of industry personnel.

Even now after several years of government attempts to effectuate desired changes, institutionalized employment practices too often continue to resist modifications required by law or government. As a major carrier of government and government-contractor freight, the railroads clearly are subject to current civil rights regulations. The contracts for these essential services, however, cannot be easily revoked. Moreover, both the companies and the unions in the industry possess significant political power. Thus, the government agencies responsible for the enforcement of civil rights activities may well have less influence in the case of railroads than in many other industries.

This study then is concerned with the development and implementation of racial employment policies in the railroad industry. The long history of Negro employment problems in this industry make it an excellent introduction to an understanding of Negro employment problems in transportation, as well as in industry generally.

SCOPE OF THE STUDY

The railroad industry studied herein has been limited to Class I line-haul firms operating solely within the United States. Line-haul firms are classified under the Standard Industrial Classification (SIC) system as those which meet the following criteria:

Industry No. 4011—Railroads, Line-haul Operating

Companies primarily engaged in line-haul railroad operations. Railways engaged primarily in serving a single municipality, contiguous municipalities, or a municipality and its suburban areas are classified in Major Group 41.

Electric railroads

Interurban railways

Locomotives: building, rebuilding, and repair done by railroad companies

Railroad cars: building, rebuilding, and repair done by railroad companies

Railroads, line-haul operating

Railroads, steam

Related classifications include No. 4013—Switching and Terminal Companies (operation of terminal facilities, movement of railroad cars between terminal yards, industrial sidings, etc. and No. 4021—Sleeping Car and Other Passenger Car Service.[6] The Interstate Commerce Commission (ICC) has further classified railroads by the level of their operating revenues. Class I line-haul carriers are those which have averaged $5,000,000 or more revenue during the previous three years; Class II, those with less revenue. In 1968 there were 75 Class I and 287 Class II line-haul companies. The Class I companies, however, operated 95.1 percent of the track mileage and employed 92.5 percent of

---

6. U. S. Bureau of the Budget, *Standard Industrial Classification Manual, 1967*, p. 202.

the railroad employees.[7] The analysis and conclusions presented here, although drawn largely from statistics of Class I companies, can be generalized to the total industry. This is especially true of the employment analysis because of the national scope of union agreements.

Although the ICC collects and publishes a plethora of data yearly, its major annual publication, *Transport Statistics in the United States,* does not consistently present data separately for Class I companies. Moreover, background census material aggregates data for all classes of line-haul and switching and terminal companies as well as for pullman car service and the Railway Express Agency (REA). When statistics presented represent more than Class I line-haul firms, the variation will be noted.

RESEARCH METHODOLOGY

Any study of this nature which relies solely on analysis of statistics must surely be superficial and possibly misleading. To be sure relevant employment statistics have been collected and carefully analyzed. This, however, has been secondary to personal interviews and correspondence with management, union, and government officials concerned with this problem. An understanding of the subjective elements may well be the key to eventual achievement of equal employment opportunity. Response to a lengthy questionnaire on company programs, personnel practices, and attitudes toward government policy has been obtained by personal interview for most of the larger companies and by mail for many smaller firms. Cooperating concerns employ over three-fourths of Class I railroad workers.

The Equal Employment Opportunity Commission (EEOC) and other agencies collecting racial employment data have agreed upon a standard reporting format for employers, EEO-1. This shows total employment by sex and by minority group (Negro, Oriental, American Indian, and Spanish surnamed Americans) in nine occupational categories. Railroads have chosen to employ a standard reporting procedure across all companies. The 128 occupations utilized in Interstate Commerce Commission reports have been categorized by skill level into the nine occupational categories of the EEO-1 form. This helps to eliminate the

---

7. Interstate Commerce Commission, *Transport Statistics in the United States,* 1968, Part 1, Tables 1 and 62.

practice too often found in other industries where, for example, jobs designated as operatives in one firm may well be classified as craftsmen in others. The industry has also chosen to file separate reports for each operating division, repair shop, terminal, and major office. Thus a more precise meaning can be attributed to each report, and comparability maintained across firms. The racial employment situation has fortunately generated considerable research interest over the past several decades. For the early history, *two* major studies were used extensively—Northrup, *Organized Labor and the Negro* and Spero and Harris, *The Black Worker.*[8] The postwar period, as the subject developed increased public interest and concern, has seen less information published by private researchers but more made available in government reports and court decisions. There remain, however, several time periods and subject areas which cannot be adequately analyzed because of a dearth of available material.

---

8. Herbert R. Northrup, *Organized Labor and the Negro* (New York: Harper & Brothers, 1944) and Sterling D. Spero and Abram L. Harris, *The Black Worker* (New York: Columbia University Press, 1931).

CHAPTER II

The Railroad Industry

Although the railroad industry remains essential to the nation's economy, its impact is now considerably less than it was at the turn of the century. The attempts by the industry to arrest a continuing decline have been well documented over several decades.[9] Although, as shown in Table 1, the industry did meet with some success in strengthening its operating position in the early 1960's, the results from 1967 and 1968 indicate that the crisis remains unresolved. Operating income fell in these two years to levels which were lower in constant dollars than that earned in 1932. Moreover, the eastern railroads earned less in actual income than they had in the same period of the Depression of the 1930's.[10] These years represent a distinct reversal of the trends in freight and passenger volume and operating revenue that had developed since the Korean War.

The slow growth during this period, however, was far below that needed to restore prosperity to the industry. Although freight traffic, which provides about 90 percent of the industry's revenue, had increased 30 percent in the decade from 1959 to 1968, real growth in Gross National Product (GNP) in the same period rose 49 percent.[11] Railroad carriers, rather than flourishing in this general period of prosperity, lost additional business to competing modes of transportation.

This problem has continually plagued the industry since the post-World War I period. Railroads unfortunately can deliver freight only to those points served by rail. A second method of

---

9. See, for example, Gilbert Burck, "The Railroads are Running Scared," *Fortune*, Vol. LXXIX (June 1969), pp. 122-125, 184, 188, 191.

10. *Ibid*, p. 122.

11. U.S. Bureau of Labor Statistics, *Handbook of Labor Statistics, 1970*, Table 173 and Association of American Railroads, *Statistics of Railroads of Class I in the United States, 1958 to 1968*, Statistical Summary No. 53, September 1969.

TABLE 1. *Class I Railroads*
Summary Operating Statistics
1959-1968

Year	Total Operating Revenues (Millions of Dollars)	Net Railway Operating Income	Percent Return on Revenue	Average Net Investment (Millions of Dollars)	Percent Return on Average Net Investment	Revenue Freight Ton-Miles (In Millions)	Revenue Passenger Miles (In Millions)
1959	9,825	748	7.6	27,484	2.7	575,529	22,047
1960	9,514	584	6.1	27,452	2.1	572,309	21,258
1961	9,189	538	5.9	27,320	2.0	563,361	20,283
1962	9,440	726	7.7	26,519	2.7	592,862	19,902
1963	9,560	806	8.4	25,802	3.1	621,737	18,494
1964	9,857	818	8.3	25,881	3.2	658,639	18,245
1965	10,208	962	9.4	26,041	3.7	697,878	17,378
1966	10,655	1,046	9.8	26,820	3.9	738,395	17,085
1967	10,366	676	6.5	27,545	2.5	719,498	15,193
1968	10,855	678	6.2	27,723	2.4	744,023	13,110

Source: Association of American Railroads, *Statistics of Railroads of Class I, 1959 to 1968*, Statistical Summary No. 53, September 1969.

conveyance must too often be provided to move the goods to their final destination. The infant trucking industry of the 1920's was, of course, the logical supplement. As trucking service spread, it soon became apparent that for certain types of freight, particularly highly profitable, bulky manufactured merchandise, trucks could provide cheaper, more convenient service. This competition, which was originally limited to shorthaul and local freight movement, has now spread to long distance hauling.

In the 1930's vast pipeline networks and coastal tankers were added to the transportation system to aid in the movement of petroleum. By 1939 railroad's share of intercity freight traffic had fallen from more than 90 percent in 1900 to only 62.4 percent and by 1968 to 41.2 percent. The annual volume today is virtually the same as that carried in 1944 while that of trucks, pipelines, and planes has at least doubled.[12]

TABLE 2. *Railroad Industry*
Percentage Distribution of Intercity Freight
Traffic by Type of Carrier
1939-1968

Year	Total Ton-Miles (In Millions)	Railroads	Motor Carrier	Great Lakes, Rivers and Canals	Oil Pipelines	Airlines
				(Percent)		
1939	534,534	62.4	9.7	17.7	10.2	*
1944	1,088,266	68.6	5.4	13.8	12.2	*
1950	1,062,637	56.2	16.3	15.4	12.1	*
1960	1,314,270	44.1	21.7	16.7	17.4	0.1
1968	1,834,300	41.2	21.6	15.7	21.3	0.2

Source: Association of American Railroads, *Yearbook of Railroad Facts, 1970 edition*, p. 42.

* Less than 0.05 percent.

The decline in passenger traffic has been even more dramatic. Railroads have all but abandoned attempts to compete for passengers in many regions and for many types of traffic. That passenger service which remains has more often been retained

12. Association of American Railroads, *Yearbook of Railroad Facts, 1970 Edition*, p. 42.

because of government edict than of its profitability. Many Class
I carriers have discontinued all passenger trains. By 1968 railroads carried passengers over only 1.2 percent of the total passenger miles. Automobiles, on the other hand, accounted for
86.7 percent of the passenger miles traveled.[13]

Two extraneous factors which have had an adverse effect on
the carrier's revenues have been the decreased demand for coal
and the dispersion of American industry. The former was previously a major source of income; the latter has reduced the potential for growth by eliminating many long-haul freight runs.

This general, unarrested decline in railroad business has been
the most important factor affecting the position of Negro employees in the industry. As traffic volume has fallen, so too has
employment. Total employment today is less than 30 percent of
the peak in the 1920's. Although skilled occupations have frequently declined as rapidly as unskilled, the jobs in which Negroes have traditionally been employed extensively have been
particularly hard hit. Notable among these occupations are those
in track maintenance and passenger service. While technological
change has similarly affected many occupations, the decline in
traffic volume has not only reduced manpower requirements; it
has also been responsible for the adverse financial position of
the industry, making it unwilling and unable to assume a non-
contractual burden to support or to train those laid off.

Attempts by the industry to regain its competitive position
have generally been unsuccessful. The Interstate Commerce Commission recently granted rate increases to the carriers stating
that "we have repeatedly characterized as substandard" rates of
return "in the range of 4 percent or less. . . ." [14] Even if we
disregard the great undervaluations of the industry's investment,
this figure is considerably higher than the average rate of return in recent years. Only the extraordinary business activity of
the World War II period, and to a lesser degree that of the Korean War years, has allowed the industry to approach an acceptable rate of return. In no other year since 1930 has the rate
of return gone above 4.0 percent. The annual rates of return
for the years 1931 to 1968 are summarized in Table 3.

---

13. *Ibid.*

14. Interstate Commerce Commission, *Ex Parte No. 259, Increased Freight
Rates*, decided November 25, 1968, at 16.

TABLE 3. *Railroad Industry*
Rate of Return on Net Investment
1931-1968

Period	Average Rate of Return (Percent)	Period	Average Rate of Return (Percent)
1931-1935	1.94	1951-1955	3.92
1936-1940	2.51	1956-1960	2.98
1941-1945	4.97	1961-1965	2.94
1946-1950	3.54	1966-1968	2.93

Source: Association of American Railroads, *Yearbook of Railroad Facts: 1970 edition*, p. 24; *1967 edition*, p. 22.

This in turn has made financing the needed improvements in property and equipment extremely difficult. Only rolling stock—locomotives and freight and passenger cars—can be financed externally. Since this equipment can be quickly repossessed, investments can be made relatively risk free. The industry has been able to invest an average of $900 million annually over the past decade in improved cars and locomotives.[15] On the other hand, yards and lines can be improved only if the necessary funds are available internally. The most important source of funds has been depreciation and amortization charges and retirements of equipment. Although expenditures to improve yard operations or to build new consolidated yards might well bring a greater return in increased efficiency than new rolling stock, the industry has been able to invest only $300 million a year in the same period.[16] Even with annual investment at this apparently high level, the total net investment in property and equipment is now no higher than at the start of this ten year period. (See Table 1.)

This is not to say that all the carriers are beset by similar financial problems. Moreover, there is little correlation between profitability and any single operating characteristic. The recent bankruptcy of the giant Penn Central shows that size alone will not produce operating efficiencies. In contrast, however, the Nor-

15. Burck, *op. cit.*, pp. 123-124.

16. *Ibid.*

folk and Western, which was the fourth largest railroad in 1968 and which competes with the Penn Central over much of its trackage, earned a 7.0 percent rate of return on net investment. The largest relative deficit in 1968 was shown by the New York, New Haven and Hartford, a relatively small carrier now part of the Penn Central system, which lost $22 million on revenues of $121 million.[17] Generally those companies with consistently high earnings typically specialize in certain classes of freight or are located in industrialized areas where industrial firms require frequent service for raw materials and finished products.

FIGURE 1. *Railroad Geographic Districts*

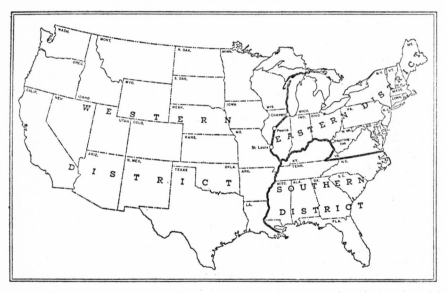

Source: Interstate Commerce Commission.

Note: The district groupings used throughout this study follow those used in Interstate Commerce Commission reporting. They were originally established during the World War I period of federal control. They do not conform totally to similarities in operating conditions or to similar freight-rate levels. The extensive interstate mileage of many carriers makes this system of geographic categorization as meaningful as any. This grouping will also be used in analyzing Negro employment data.

---

17. "The 50 largest U. S. Transportation Concerns," *Fortune*, Vol. LXXIX, (May 15, 1969), pp. 196-197.

The one characteristic which can have an important impact on operations and profitability is geographic location. The companies operating in the Western District, where the fewest Negroes reside, have the greatest potential for improvement because of the product mix (grain and other raw materials not easily shipped by truck), and distances and flat terrain between terminal points. In the South, where a substantial number of Negroes dwell, increasing industrialization and more aggressive competition with other carriers have augmented earnings and permitted investment and economies in operations that have paid off in further earnings improvements. In the East, short hauls, good highways, and considerable passenger service (soon to be assumed by government) keep earnings low except where the coal traffic in West Virginia, Virginia, and contiguous states has maintained high earnings.

Whatever the reason for the railroads' problems—ICC regulations, poor management, or simply problems inherent in current developments—the fact remains that their decline does not seem to have been halted, with continued layoffs of black and white workers seeming inevitable. Moreover, if the carriers had unlimited funds, there is the possibility of increased technological improvements which would have the immediate impact of reducing jobs further.

MANPOWER, TECHNOLOGY, AND DECLINING TRAFFIC

Since the war, in order to meet the growing competition from other forms of transportation, the railroads have embarked on a continually expanding program of dieselization and mechanization. Concurrent with the rapid introduction of the diesel have been important changes in roadway technology, equipment repair facilities, as well as in office procedures. Capital expenditures have risen from a low of one-half billion dollars annual average 1941 to 1945 to a level in excess of 1.5 billion since 1965.[18] The following discussion of manpower changes will point up the impact of technology and declining traffic on manpower and especially black employment.

The impact on carriers of lost business and of extensive developments in technology have caused the greatest postwar em-

---

18. *Yearbook of Railroad Facts: 1967 edition*, p. 70; *1970 edition*, p. 74.

ployment decline of any major industry.[19] The employment reduction since 1945 has been an acceleration of a long-run trend.
This attrition has received less attention than that received, for
example, by the cutbacks in coal mining employment perhaps
because its impact has not been concentrated on any one area of
the nation and because a significant proportion has occurred
through retirements and voluntary separations.

After reaching a peak of 2 million workers in 1920, railroad
employment declined nearly 50 percent prior to the increased
economic activity necessary to support our entrance into World
War II. From 1940 to 1945 the transportation demands of the
economy pushed employment of Class I Railroads to a new peak
of 1.4 million. The decline which followed the return to a peace
time economy has continued without interruption to the present.
By 1968 employment had fallen to 590,536, a decline of approximately 830,000 workers, or slightly less than 60 percent in two
decades.

The decline in employment has not occurred at the same rate
in all regions of the country. The Eastern District has felt the
impact of the attrition most sharply, declining by 57 percent
while that in the South and West have been reduced by less than
54 percent. This has caused the West to supplant the East as the
area of largest railroad employment. In 1968 the West employed
44 percent of the industry's workers, the East 42 percent, and
the South only 14 percent.[20] The Negro population is of course
concentrated in the latter two regions.

One consequence of the work force reductions and technological
change has been a significant increase in output per manhour.
From 1950 to 1968 productivity of Class I railroads increased
by 128.5 percent. Few other industries have experienced such
an accelerated increase in worker productivity. During this
period while freight traffic has remained relatively stable with
some cyclical fluctuation, the industry has been able to decrease
the number of manhours paid for (as opposed to actual hours
worked). Typically, during a period of business decline, produc-

19. The decrease in Class I railroad employment since 1945 is significantly
    more than either of the two industries with the next largest declines—
    textile manufacturing and bituminous coal mining. Textile employment
    has decreased nearly 154,100 since the end of the war while coal mining
    has experienced a drop of 243,000. See, U. S. Bureau of Labor Statistics,
    Employment and Earnings Statistics for the United States, 1909-68 and
    Employment and Earnings, March 1969, Table B-2.

20. *Yearbook of Railroad Facts, 1970 edition,* p. 78.

TABLE 4. *Class I Railroads*
Employment and Output per Man-hour
1940-1968

Year	Employment Total	Index	Output[a] Billions of Miles	Index	Man-hours[b] Millions of Hours	Index	Index of Output per Man-hour
1940	1,026,956	80.4	453	66.2	2,616	90.9	72.8
1945	1,420,266	111.2	911	133.2	3,980	138.3	96.3
1950	1,277,119	100.0	684	100.0	2,877	100.0	100.0
1955	1,058,216	82.9	701	102.5	2,503	87.0	117.8
1960	780,494	61.1	615	89.9	1,841	64.0	140.5
1962	700,146	54.8	633	92.5	1,672	58.1	159.2
1964	665,034	52.1	695	101.6	1,620	56.3	180.5
1966	630,895	49.4	773	113.0	1,541	53.6	210.8
1968	590,536	46.2	783	114.5	1,441	50.1	228.5

Source: Interstate Commerce Commission, *Transport Statistics of the United States* (Annual).

[a] Output is measured in terms of the number of revenue and non-revenue freight ton miles (billions) plus twice the number of passenger-miles (billions).

[b] Man-hours include all employee hours paid for.

tivity falls as reductions in employment lag behind changes in output. The volume of business handled by carriers may vary over a wide range before trains can be discontinued and crews reduced. Employment is dependent on the number of trains run rather than on the freight volume; the crew consist varies only slightly as train length increases or as the class of freight changes. Furthermore, the carriers have had intense opposition to proposed employment cutbacks from the industry's several labor organizations. The effect of these factors has been a restriction of productivity increases considerably below the potential developed through technological innovations.

Although employment has continued to decrease rapidly since World War II, the number of job opportunities has remained relatively high. Since 1963 the industry has hired over 70,000 new employees annually while also reemploying about 20,000 workers. The number of new hires today is less than in the immediate postwar period. Many of these new hires enter occupations which are heavily affected by seasonal fluctuation and budget cutbacks. Negro workers have always been afforded a disproportionately large number of positions in these less secure, often unskilled occupations. However, the gradual ageing of the work force which in some firms has cut employment in key occupations to critical levels, promises to make a significant number of more attractive job opportunities available well into the foreseeable future.[21] These openings should allow the industry to increase the number of Negro workers in those skilled occupations from which they have historically been excluded.

TABLE 5. *Railroad Industry*
Annual New Hires, Reemployment, and Separations
1940-1968

Year	New Hires	Reemployment (in thousands)	Total Hires	Separations
1940	253	40	293	272
1945	835	198	1,033	1,071
1950	256	137	393	367
1955	165	105	270	268
1960	63	33	96	161
1961	45	22	67	134
1962	57	28	85	123
1963	73	28	101	124
1964	80	23	103	122
1965	80	21	101	140
1966	103	23	126	149
1967	86	19	95	150
1968	81	21	102	150

Source: U.S. Railroad Retirement Board, *Annual Report, 1969* (Chicago, Railroad Retirement Board, 1970), Statistical Supplement, Table D-2.

Occupational Distribution

The postwar decrease in railroad employment has been felt by all occupational groups, although there have been important dif-

---

21. The proportion of workers over 40 years of age has risen from 50 percent of the work force in 1950 to 64 percent today. U.S. Railroad Retirement Board, *Annual Report, 1951* and *Statistical Supplement to the 1969 Annual Report.*

ferences in the rates of decline. Generally, in both blue collar and white collar occupations, employment has been cutback most rapidly in those jobs requiring the least skill or training. Although blue collar employees have declined as a percentage of railroad employment, they continue to be the dominant group in the industry, accounting in 1968 for 71.2 percent of total Class I line-haul employment. Only craftsmen among blue collar employees have increased proportionately, although suffering an actual decrease of over 150,000 workers since 1950. Those semi-skilled and unskilled occupations in which Negroes have historically been employed have undergone drastic reductions. Laborers, for example, are now only 11.4 percent of the work force and have declined by 77 percent since 1950. The statistics for Class I line-haul carriers are summarized in Table 6.

To provide a clearer understanding of the changes which have taken place in employment for the many diverse railroad occupations, the 128 standard ICC occupational divisions (classifications) have been grouped into broad categories based upon the nature of the service performed, and are summarized in Table 7.[22]

More than half of the decline in railroad employment between 1950 and 1968 occurred among maintenance personnel, who experienced a loss of 365,000 employees. In turn, more than half of these workers were engaged in the maintenance of equipment and stores, which includes the service and repair of locomotives, freight and passenger cars, and related equipment; and the warehousing of parts and supplies. The remaining employees were maintenance-of-way and structures employees who maintain roadways, bridges, buildings, and other structures and install and repair signal, communications and control systems.

The conversion from steam locomotives to diesels was the key factor affecting employment in the maintenance of equipment and stores category. As noted in the preceding section, the diesel not only requires less service but because of its greater availability, fewer units are required to handle traffic. In addition, several carriers have contracted out major diesel maintenance work. Part of the reduction in equipment maintenance employment has been induced by the reduction in the number of cars in service and by many small but cumulatively significant improvements in maintenance equipment, materials, and methods.

---

22. The categories used here are based upon those used in: U.S. Bureau of Labor Statistics, *Employment and Changing Occupational Patterns in the Railroad Industry*, Bulletin No. 1344, February 1963.

TABLE 6. *Class I Railroads*
Distribution of Employment by Occupational Group
1940-1968

Occupational Group	1940		1950		1960		1968		Percent Change		
	Employees	Percent	Employees	Percent	Employees	Percent	Employees	Percent	1940-50	1950-60	1960-68
Officials and managers	26,447	2.6	32,964	2.7	30,548	3.9	29,632	5.0	+24.6	− 7.3	− 3.0
Professionals	6,564	0.6	8,179	0.7	7,777	1.0	7,432	1.3	+24.6	− 4.9	− 4.4
Technicians	9,867	1.0	11,472	0.9	9,319	1.2	7,798	1.3	+16.3	−18.8	−16.3
Sales workers	11,207	1.1	11,925	1.0	10,535	1.4	8,125	1.4	+ 6.4	−11.7	−22.9
Office and clerical	168,425	16.4	202,991	16.6	154,920	19.8	117,215	19.8	+20.5	−23.7	−24.3
Total white collar	222,510	21.7	267,531	21.9	213,099	27.3	170,202	28.8	+20.2	−20.3	−20.1
Craftsmen (Skilled)	283,811	27.6	346,812	28.4	248,947	31.9	213,977	36.2	+22.2	−28.2	−14.0
Operatives (Semiskilled)	247,252	24.1	291,230	23.9	182,249	23.4	124,421	21.1	+17.8	−37.4	−31.7
Laborers (Unskilled)	238,235	23.2	275,561	22.6	112,461	14.4	67,302	11.4	+15.7	−59.2	−40.2
Service workers	35,148	3.4	39,650	3.2	23,738	3.0	14,634	2.5	+12.8	−40.1	−38.4
Total blue collar	804,446	78.3	953,253	78.1	567,395	72.7	420,334	71.2	+18.5	−40.5	−25.9
Total	1,026,956	100.0	1,220,784	100.0	780,494	100.0	590,536	100.0	+18.9	−36.1	−24.3

Source: Interstate Commerce Commission, *Wage Statistics of Class I Railroads in the United States,* Statement No. M-300, 1940, 1950, 1960, Statement No. A-300, 1968.

The 128 occupational divisions reported on Statement No. A-300 have been grouped by skill level by the Association of American Railroads to conform with the Equal Employment Opportunity Commission reporting format. (See Table A-1.)

TABLE 7. *Class I Railroads*
Employment Changes by Functional Group
1950-1968

Functional Group	Number of Employees		Percent Change
	1950	1968	
Maintenance of equipment and stores	348,181	132,114	−62.1
Maintenance of roadway	185,080	61,117	−67.0
Building and structure maintenance	32,773	14,129	−56.9
Signal installation and maintenance	20,034	13,670	−31.8
Train and engine service	145,556	84,910	−41.7
Passenger trains	37,246	12,925	−65.3
Freight trains	108,310	71,985	−33.5
Yard and terminal operations	122,242	90,170	−26.2
Freight terminals	70,615	22,028	−68.8
Passenger service	33,756	11,005	−67.4
Control of train movements	30,527	16,320	−46.5
Administrative and clerical operations	198,609	130,547	−34.3
Miscellaneous service inc. protective	33,411	14,526	−56.5
Total	1,220,784	590,536	−51.6

Source: Interstate Commerce Commission, *Wage Structure of Class I Railroads in the United States*, Statement No. M-300, 1950, No. A-300, 1968.

The smallest decline in employment within the equipment maintenance workers has been within the electrical workers, where few Negroes are employed. Employment in this occupation increased until 1958 as a direct result of the need for workers to maintain the extensive electric power and control equipment on the diesel locomotives. In recent years, the drop in the number of trains run and the decreased maintenance needs of later model locomotives has produced a decline in total employment.

The greatest declines in skilled employment have been among those occupations which were previously essential to the repair of steam locomotives—molders, blacksmiths, and boilermakers. With the introduction of the diesel, the use of replacement parts rather than the repair or reconstruction of original components became a common industry practice. The extent of the decline would have been greater had it not been for the increased use of track equipment necessitating additional maintenance activities.

Those workers in semiskilled and unskilled occupations had greater employment declines than those in the craftsmen and foremen categories. Significantly, among the less skilled groups, the apprentice and helper positions have experienced the greatest relative decrease. Although shortages of trained craftsmen are foreseen, the industry is reluctant to invest in extended training programs. Negroes have only recently been upgraded into crafts-men positions and the continuing trends in these occupations will not allow a significant alteration in the level of Negro employment.

A comparable decrease was felt among the maintenance of way and structures employees. During the eighteen year period from 1950 to 1968, employment in these maintenance occupations fell by 142,607 workers or 65.5 percent, with most of this decline in track maintenance employment.

Employment in track maintenance occupations decreased be-cause of increased mechanization, a reduction in track mileage, and the improvement in rails, ties, and other materials. Al-though single-purpose machines were introduced in track main-tenance early in the postwar period, it has been the more recent development of multipurpose equipment which has greatly affect-ed employment. When hand labor was used extensively to per-form maintenance operations, track crews of 100 and even as high as 300 were commonly required. Now, with the advances in portable equipment, track maintenance can be done with crews of fifteen to thirty men and several machines. Moreover, the decline in railroad business and the introduction of central-ized traffic control (CTC) systems has allowed the industry to use less track mileage more efficiently and to eliminate gradually many miles of track in branch lines, yards, and other locations. These changes combined with the previously discussed materials improvements produced drastic cutbacks in employment of track maintenance personnel.

In addition to the impact on the number of employees, the changes in track maintenance have changed the character of employment in these operations by motivating management to effect a reorganization and more efficient utilization of remaining manpower. Gang crews are now specialized, with separate crews replacing ties, relining rail and resurfacing track, while other crews may be laying welded track. Smaller "floating" mechanized gangs may be assigned to perform required maintenance between major roadbed renewals. Other small gangs may patrol the track inspecting rails, ties and roadbed for minor problems which need immediate repair.

All occupations, with the exception of portable equipment operators and roadmasters and general foremen have felt large declines in employment. At the same time, portable equipment operators nearly doubled in number. These changes represent drastic declines in Negro employment—some have been retained as portable equipment operators, but, of course, the number of opportunities have been relatively small.

Contraction of railroad plant and property largely accounted for the employment decline in structures maintenance. Uneconomical road structures were eliminated, many passenger stations were abandoned, freight stations were closed or consolidated and, with dieselization, fewer structures were needed for equipment repair. Furthermore, many smaller structures—control towers, steam locomotive fuel and water supply facilities, and others—were also eliminated as technological developments were installed.

Structures maintenance operations and employment were reduced also by the introduction of many of the changes common in the construction industry. Increased use was made of more durable materials such as brick, steel, and the various forms of reinforced concrete. Improved, longer lasting paints were developed. Mechanization was also increased with the addition of high capacity earth movers, jointed aerial booms in bridge maintenance, and the many portable construction tools powered by portable electric generators.

Masons, bricklayers, plasterers, and plumbers was the only employee group to show an increase during the period. The rise is attributed in part to the increased utilization of masonry rather than wood in railroad structures. In addition, the group of welders was included in this occupational classification. The largest decrease among the skilled crafts was experienced by painters, reflecting the reduction in wood structures.

The employees in signal and telegraph operations experienced the smallest decrease of the maintenance employees. Their employment probably rose over the first few years of the period as CTC systems were first installed by the major carriers. Their employment was also favorably affected by the increased use of automatic signaling devices along highways as well as in the major freight yards. On the other hand, the many miles of track eliminated and the development of equipment with fewer moving parts worked to decrease manpower requirements. Overall the decreases were relatively modest in relation to the other maintenance occupations. Negro workers have only been utilized in these occupations on a small number of railroads.

The decline in the number of operating employees was closely linked to the reduction in the number of freight and passenger trains, and to the technological changes which have allowed the remaining trains to travel faster with fewer delays. The elimination of many passenger trains resulted in the largest decline in employment among the operating employees. The decline in employment among those workers serving freight trains was caused not by a decrease in service but rather by the increased length of trains and higher average capacity of freight cars. These changes were made possible by the increased power of diesel locomotives. The use of diesels and the resultant increased length of trains has affected engineers and firemen more than it has affected conductors and brakemen. Furthermore, the generally higher seniority of passenger crews has allowed them to displace employees in freight service and thus maintain higher employment in freight service. Finally, the effect of the Presidential Railroad Commission's recommendations for the gradual elimination of locomotive firemen is clearly evident.[23]

Negro workers were employed historically only as locomotive firemen and that only in the South. The Brotherhood of Locomotive Firemen and Enginemen was, however, able to eliminate many of the Negroes from these positions by the end of World War II. This campaign by the Brotherhood will be discussed in detail in the following chapter. The occupations of locomotive engineer and conductor have been filled historically by white employees, although the industry has recently upgraded Negroes to these desirable positions.

More than one-half of the operating employees were engaged in yards and terminals. This work involves the transfer of cars from one railroad to another, movement of freight cars to and

---

23. This subject will be discussed in the concluding paragraphs of this section.

from industrial sidings, and "breaking-up" of incoming trains and "making-up" of new trains. The decline in employment among these operations was less severe than that in freight and passenger service.

Although the decline in the number of trains and technological change were responsible for general declines in terminal and yard employment, several factors worked to mitigate these declines. First, the forty-hour work week was not negotiated until 1952 and its general acceptance took several years. This helped to spread the work load over more employees. Second, the unpredictable nature of shipper demands and train arrival and departure times in many terminal facilities requires the carriers to keep a "stand-by" work force on hand to meet peak shipping periods.

The technological changes introduced in classification yards are gradually reducing the need for switchtenders to divert cars into appropriate tracks and for brakemen to ride and control the speed of "cut" freight cars as they are classified. The decreased need for firemen is also evident in these occupations. Negro workers have been employed in small numbers in these occupations as well as in hostler helper positions.

The number of employees at freight and passenger terminals, train control and communication centers, signal control towers and in passenger service aboard trains declined from 134,898 to 49,353, a 63.4 percent decrease. More than half of the reduction in this group occurred among railroad employees who load and unload freight cars, and weigh, check, and inspect freight at stations, and who operate the industry's remaining vessels.

Employment of small freight terminals fell and many terminals were eliminated as the trucking industry greatly reduced the volume of less-than-carload freight traffic (package freight), and mail shipments were shifted to planes and trucks. The decreased employment is attributed to the introduction of mechanized freight hauling equipment and mail sorting sysytems. These changes substantially reduced the number of truckers, loaders, checkers, and other freight handlers. Most of these occupations require little or no skill. Many small freight stations are located in rural communities with few Negro residents. The carriers have, however, employed a relatively large number of Negroes in these occupations in large towns and cities.

The rapid elimination of passenger trains has caused severe reductions among the personnel who sell tickets and handle reservations, serve and prepare food on trains, and provide other services to passengers. Other causes were the replacement of dining cars with snackbar food service and the introduction of electronic reservation service. Negroes, of course, have been employed extensively in many of these occupations, with the general exception of those involving supervisory responsibilities. The loss of job opportunities in passenger service occupations will continue to be heavy with a resultant disproportionate impact on Negro workers, depending, of course, on the extent to which the government takes over these operations.

The employees involved in the control of train movements and communications were another group who experienced a general decrease in manpower. The widespread introduction of automatically controlled and remote controlled switches and signals reduced the need for train control workers, especially at the numerous "on-site" control centers. The impact of these changes was generally on lower-level workers. The diesel locomotive further reduced manpower requirements among train control personnel because it required fewer stops for fuel or water, for setting and releasing retaining valves on steep slopes and because it allowed the carriers to reduce the number of trains run.

The decrease in train control requirements reduced the need for communications personnel. There were also extensive improvements in communication systems during the period, with many former telegraphers being completely eliminated or experiencing drastic changes in job content. These positions have historically been filled only by white employees.

The clerical group was the only major white collar group to decrease significantly. Total employment fell in the group by slightly over 40 percent from 1950 to 1968. However, the decline in the number of clerks, typists, stenographers, and other employees engaged in routine operations was much greater than that for the highly skilled clerical personnel.

Substantial numbers of clerical employees are in freight stations, passenger terminals, parts storerooms, and other small clerical operations. These employees were affected by the reductions in freight and passenger service along with the related manual workers. These clerical personnel were also affected by a trend toward centralization and consolidation of record keeping operations. Lower-grade clerks (B and C) may perform tasks which might elsewhere be classified as manual work. Negro workers have generally been limited to these positions.

The railroads have also adopted computers and other modern data processing equipment into office operations in major offices. The employment impact of these changes, however, was affected gradually as a result of collective bargaining agreements. Employment decreases on many railroads were allowed to occur through normal attrition.

The remaining occupational groups experienced varying degrees of employment change. As a general rule, low-skill occupations declined in importance significantly faster than high-skill occupations. For example, the various service occupations generally employed in office buildings as janitors and cleaners declined by at least 50 percent during this period. On the other hand, professionals and subprofessional assistants had an employment decrease of only 4 percent while executives, officials, and staff assistants experienced a slight increase, 4 percent. As a rule, Negro workers have never been employed in managerial, professional, or technical occupations, but have been heavily employed in the low-skill service areas.

The impact of these declines in employment has encouraged union "featherbedding," exacerbated union-management relations, and helped to induce unions to pursue virulently discriminatory racial policies, as will be discussed in ensuing chapters.

Unionization

Collective bargaining in the railroad industry has evolved into a complex, trilateral relationship with the carriers, labor organizations and the federal government as active participants. Over 90 percent of the industry's employees have been organized by thirty-nine national unions, several system associations, and a few remaining independent local unions. In 1968 these organizations held 4,961 contracts with firms operating in the railroad industry.[24] Many of these labor organizations have represented the employees of the major carriers since the turn of the century.

The importance of railroad service to the national economy and the ability of small work groups to cause a total cessation of railroad operations forced the federal government to intervene as early as 1888 in collective bargaining between the parties. Several statutes have been enacted since that date to assist in the

---

24. National Mediation Board, *Annual Report*, June 30, 1969, Table 8, p. 81.

adjustment of railroad labor disputes.[25] The present legislation, the Railway Labor Act of 1926, as amended, encompasses proposals advanced by representatives of both labor and management outlining comprehensive procedures and methods for the settlement of labor disputes founded upon the many years of experience under previous legislation, but by the 1934 amendments, generally modeled to union desires. During the past forty years, nearly every major labor agreement has been arrived at through government procedures, legal and extra-legal.

Union organization on the railroads has been characteristically along craft lines. The unions in train and engine service, the "operating unions," are among the oldest and strongest labor organizations in the country. They were already negotiating collective agreements in the 1880's, and since World War I have had virtually complete control of their respective crafts throughout the country.[26]

The shop crafts and other "nonoperating" groups were slower to form effective unions in the face of vigorous employer opposition. They were strengthened initially by government protection during World War I only to suffer a relapse when the protection was withdrawn after the war. The final consolidation of power for these unions did not come until the Railway Labor Act was amended in 1934 to outlaw "yellow dog" contracts, and the formation of company dominated or financed unions. These provisions, plus rising economic activity, sympathetic administration of the Railway Labor Act, and the general increase in union activity in other industries, contributed to the organization by national unions of nearly all nonoperating employees by the late thirties. Today, virtually all manual and clerical workers are covered by labor contract, making this one of the most highly unionized industries in the United States.[27]

The operating employees were organized originally into five brotherhoods: The Locomotive Engineers, the Firemen and En-

25. Early federal legislation controlling labor relations in the railroad industry includes: The Arbitration Act of 1888, The Erdman Act of 1898, The Newlands Act of 1913, The Adamson Act of 1916, The Period of Federal Control during World War I, and The Transportation Act of 1920.

26. For a discussion of the evolution of collective bargaining in the railroad industry, see Jacob J. Kaufman, "The Railroad Labor Dispute: A Marathon of Maneuver and Improvisation", North Western University, 1964, Mimeo.

27. *Ibid*, p. 45.

ginemen, the Trainmen, the Conductors, and the Switchmen. (See Table 8.) These unions have been the most powerful in the industry because of their virtually complete coverage of their respective crafts and because of the essential work performed by their members. As a rule, the five unions have bargained independently of the nonoperating unions, and often rather independently of each other or in one or two groups. After many years of intermittent cooperation and attempted mergers between different combinations of the five unions, the firemen, trainmen, conductors and switchmen were able to work out a merger agreement which became effective in January 1969.[28] The Brotherhood of Locomotive Engineers has chosen to continue acting independently. It remains to be seen how well the merged unions will overcome the "overlapping interests, jealousies, and . . . frequent conflicts" common to the previous relationships among these groups.[29]

The clerical, maintenance, shop crafts, train dispatching, and other nonoperating employees belong to some fifteen national unions. About half of these are confined to the railroad industry, while the remainder have a majority of their membership in other industries. There has been a minimum of interunion rivalry between these groups due to the generally sharp craft lines. In fact, the nonoperating labor organizations have cooperated closely in collective bargaining. Typically they have served joint demands on the carriers.

Although collective bargaining was initiated on a single carrier basis, and then developed into regional groupings, national negotiations was a development of the thirties. The carriers were, in part, responsible for this development when they demanded general wage reductions in 1931, 1932, 1933, and 1938. They apparently considered it advantageous to present a united front to the unions, and negotiations were on a national basis from the beginning. Also important at this time was the increasing use of government intervention to effect a contract settlement, and the use of regional settlements as "patterns" in other areas. This tendency toward national bargaining was strengthened further by the use of national contract settlements during World War II to ensure confronting with national wage

---

28. Correspondence with union officials.

29. Harry D. Wolf, "Railroads," in Harry A. Millis, ed., *How Collective Bargaining Works* (New York: Twentieth Century Fund, 1942), p. **324.**

TABLE 8.　*Railroad Industry*
Major Labor Unions

Union	Date of Founding	Total Membership	Local Unions	Railroad Membership
OPERATING UNIONS:				
Locomotive Engineers; Brotherhood of (Ind.)	1863	39,600	871	39,600
Transportation Union; United (AFL-CIO)	1969	254,500	2,733	255,000
Formed by merger in January 1969 of four operating unions:				
1. Brotherhood of Locomotive Firemen and Enginemen	1873	39,500	900	39,500
2. Brotherhood of Railroad Trainmen	1883	185,000	1,125	185,000
3. Order of Railway Conductors and Brakemen	1868	18,780	446	18,780
4. Switchmen's Union of North America	1894	11,306	262	11,306
NONOPERATING UNIONS:				
Boilermakers, Iron Shipbuilders, Blacksmiths, Forgers and Helpers; International Brotherhood of (AFL-CIO)	1881	140,000	425	5,000
Electrical Workers; International Brotherhood of (AFL-CIO)	1891	875,000	1,716	19,500
Hotel and Restaurant Employees and Bartenders International Union (AFL-CIO)	1890	450,000	505	3,600
Machinists and Aerospace Workers; International Association of (AFL-CIO)	1888	836,000	1,950	23,000

TABLE 8. (continued)

Union	Date of Founding	Total Membership	Local Unions	Railroad Membership
Maintenance of Way Employees; Brotherhood of (AFL-CIO)	1886	141,000	1,400	141,000
Railroad Signalmen; Brotherhood of (AFL-CIO)	1908	12,200	210	12,200
Firemen and Oilers; International Brotherhood of (AFL-CIO)	1898	45,000	600	14,000
Railroad Yardmasters of America (AFL-CIO)	1918	5,900	108	5,900
Railway Carmen of America; Brotherhood of (AFL-CIO)	1890	125,600	831	55,000
Railway, Airline and Steamship Clerks; Freight Handlers, Express and Station Employees; Brotherhood of (AFL-CIO)	1899	350,000	1,343	178,000
Merged in January 1969 with:				
1. Railway Patrolmen's International				
Merged in February 1969 with:				
1. Transportation-Communication Employees Union (Order of Railroad Telegraphers)				
Sheet Metal Workers' International Association (AFL-CIO)	1888	100,000	No Report	1,500
Sleeping Car Porters; Brotherhood of (AFL-CIO)	1925	2,000	54	2,000
Train Dispatchers Association; American (AFL-CIO)	1917	3,700	0	3,700
Transport Service Employees; United (AFL-CIO)	1937	3,000	77	3,000

Source: Correspondence by the author with the unions and U. S. Bureau of Labor Statistics, *Directory of National and International Labor Unions in the United States, 1967*, Bulletin No. 1596, 1968.

stabilization standards. The wage controls invoked during the Korean War had a similar effect.

National collective bargaining is now firmly established. As a matter of form, demands are still served on individual carriers throughout the country. Negotiation at the company level has become largely perfunctory, however, and the issues are speedily passed on to national negotiating teams. At meetings usually held in Washington the top officials of the unions involved meet with officials of the eastern, southern, and western carriers associations. If the dispute remains unsettled, the procedures of the Railway Labor Act are invoked and the negotiations are continued with the assistance of the National Mediation Board (NMB).[30]

The National Mediation Board was established by Congress in the 1934 amendments to the Railway Labor Act. It is responsible for mediation in "major" disputes. If these efforts fail, the Board is required to propose that the parties refer the dispute to private arbitration. This proposal is usually, though not invariably, refused by one or both parties. If, in the judgment of the Board, "the dispute threatens substantially to interrupt interstate commerce to a degree such as to deprive any section of the country of essential transportation service," the President is notified.[31] He may appoint an "emergency board" to study the dispute and make recommendations concerning it.

The Mediation Board has an additional duty to investigate representation disputes and to determine the representation desires of employees. The Board is authorized to hold a secret ballot of the employees involved or to utilize any other appropriate method of ascertaining the designated representative of the employees. The procedures for bargaining unit determination and representation elections are summarized in Chapter VII of this study. Board policy in these matters generally has not been beneficial to the interests of Negro employees.

The National Mediation Board does not have the responsibility, however, to resolve disputes arising out of the interpretation of agreements. The 1934 amendments established the National Railroad Adjustment Board as a bipartisan organization composed of an equal number of representatives of labor organiza-

---

30. The National Mediation Board and the effect it has had on Negro employment are discussed in Chapter VII.

31. National Mediation Board, *op. cit.*, p. 7.

tions "national in scope" and of carriers to handle these "minor" disputes. Under the amended law, grievances or claims that the existing agreement has been violated are first handled under the established procedure in the contract. If they are not resolved by the carrier and union, they may be submitted for a final decision to the adjustment board. The National Railroad Adjustment Board is divided into four divisions each of which hears cases submitted by specified groups of employees. Decisions of the Adjustment Board, which are also discussed in Chapter VII, have furthered the discrimination against Negroes.

Wages and Earnings

Railroad wage adjustments since 1937 have typically taken the form of a uniform cents-per-hour addition to the daily wage in each occupation. This produced a sharp compression of occupational differentials on a percentage basis. Manual workers rose relative to office workers; the non-ops rose relative to the operating crafts; and within the various departments, the low-skill, low-pay occupations gained steadily on the highly paid.

This trend was halted in 1964 when the six shopcraft unions departed from their practice of negotiating in cooperation with the other non-operating unions. The percentage of employees in the higher-rated shop occupations had increased considerably in relation to other shop occupations, and there was growing resentment among these employees over the progress of their wages relative to the wages of lower skilled workers. As a result, the shopcraft organizations broke away from the other non-operating unions and conducted separate wage negotiations with the carriers. This settlement and settlements in the industry since that time have reversed the long term narrowing of percentage differentials between wages.[32]

There has been great concern expressed by the unions since World War II that a wage inequity had developed between railroad wages and wages in other industries. Railroad wages have historically been comparatively high in our economy. Now, however, with railroad service declining and with the precarious financial positions of most carriers, it has become difficult to justify wage increases based on the traditional economic criteria, ability to pay and productivity increases. Emergency boards in

32. U. S. Department of Labor, *Railroad Shopcraft Factfinding Study*, 1968, Vol. I, pp. 113-114.

recent years have continued to discuss these criteria, but in order to develop acceptable wage proposals they have recommended wage adjustments based on cost-of-living increases and inter-industry wage comparisons. In fact, the completely external wage criteria, interindustry wage comparisons, has become the primary determinant of wages in the industry.[33]

Regardless of the validity of this reasoning, wage changes for the shopcrafts and assumedly for the other railroad occupations, because of the use of pattern settlements, have been similar to those in other industries for the period 1953 to 1968. Two distinct cycles are evident. First, shopcraft relative wages decreased from 1953 to 1955, "followed by substantial improvement by 1958; second, a more severe and prolonged deterioration in railroad pay relative to occupational pay in outside industry, beginning in 1959 and continuing until 1963-1964. Shopcraft relative pay began to show improvement in 1965, and by 1967, railroad journeymen and mechanics were generally in a better pay situation, relative to the selected nonrailroad occupations, than they had been at any time since the early 1960's, or in some cases, even earlier." [34]

Although wages remain relatively high in the industry, this general level is maintained in part by above average pay in many unionized clerical positions and in the low-skilled laboring and service occupations. The wage compression problem has been diminished, not eliminated.

Locomotive engineers and conductors, for instance, are still highly paid but are no longer among the elite of manual workers. Wages of bridge and building craftsmen remain high but are now not comparable with those recently negotiated by the construction trades. On the other hand, there are no low-paying jobs in the industry. Job opportunities in entry occupations must be considered attractive relative to those in other industries which require little or no prior training.

In summary, collective bargaining on the railroads takes place in a quasi-political context. The initial negotiations are carried on between powerful union and management organizations. The issues typically pass from their hands to an emergency board

---

33. Frederic Meyers, "Criteria in the Making of Wage Decisions by 'Neutrals': the Railroads as a Case Study," *Industrial and Labor Relations Review*, Vol. 4, (April 1951), p. 343.

34. Railroad Shopcraft Factfinding Study, *op. cit.*, pp. 174-175.

TABLE 9. *Class I Railroads
Hourly and Annual Earnings
by Reporting Division, 1968*

| Reporting Division | Straight Time Hourly Earnings | | Average Annual Earnings |
	Average	Range	
Executives, officials, and staff	$6.95	$5.76-8.63	$15,113
Professional, clerical, and general	3.54	2.81-5.51	7,873
Maintenance of way and structures	3.12	2.75-4.46	7,159
Maintenance of equipment and stores	3.39	2.72-4.47	7,689
Transportation, other than train, engine, and yard	3.30	2.71-5.27	7,809
Yardmasters, switchtenders, and hostlers	3.89	3.18-4.34	10,252
Train and engine service	4.34	3.54-7.69	10,380
Total	3.74	2.71-8.63	8,654

Source: Association of American Railroads, *Statistics of Railroads of Class I, 1957-1968*, Statistical Summary No. 53, September 1969.

or arbitration board, and since World War II have tended to be passed on to the White House for final adjudication. The reasons for this are inherent in the structure of the industry: the fact that it is a public utility, which means that its rates and finances are subject to close governmental control; the presence of strong unions which work through political as well as economic channels; and the essentiality of continuous operations, which ensures Presidential intervention when all else fails. These factors have produced a collective bargaining system which differs from that in any other industry.

The economic importance and political power of the parties also made them nearly immune to early government efforts to eliminate racial discrimination in the industry. In fact, there is evidence that the National Mediation Board and the National Railroad Adjustment Board worked with the unions and the carriers to prevent Negro employees from improving their employment opportunities in the industry. The factors which have had an effect on the attitudes of the railroad unions toward Negro employees are no less complex than those which have determined the collective bargaining relationships in the industry. During the first three decades of this century, Negro workers played crucial roles in industrial relations disputes throughout the industry. The following two chapters examine the historical events which have contributed to the present Negro employment picture in the railroad industry.

CHAPTER III

1718351

Negro Employment in the Era of the Steam Locomotive

The passage of the Civil Rights Act of 1964 marked the beginning of a third phase in the struggle for improved employment opportunities in the railroad industry. The initial phase included the growth and maturation of the industry, the decline of the 1930's, and the rapid expansion during the early years of World War II. Its climax came with the hearing held in 1943 before the newly instituted Fair Employment Practice Committee (FEPC) to investigate charges of racial discrimination in the industry. This was followed quickly by the Supreme Court's landmark decision in *Steele* v. *Louisville & Nashville Railroad Co.*[35] which imposed upon labor organizations the duty to represent fairly all workers in the bargaining unit.

Although the period prior to these two events was characterized by an intensive, publicly acknowledged campaign by the unions to limit or eliminate Negro employment in certain occupations, these initial signs of government concern over racial discrimination in employment compelled the unions to change not their objective but rather their tactics. Union constitutions retained the "all white" membership clauses but the more overt discriminatory practices were prudently modified to meet the tenor of the day. Negro employees, on the other hand, now with stronger government support, took the issue to the courts where a series of favorable decisions enjoining specific practices were set down in the next decade. Such temerity from Negro employees would have been met two decades earlier with threats of violence and physical injury. Traditional attitudes and practices, however, were too deeply ingrained to be altered quickly. Even today the impact of the industry's historical employment of Negroes is clearly evident in the carriers' racial employment poli-

---

35. 323 U. S. 192 (1944).

cies. This chapter is concerned with the early history of Negro employment in the industry, and the development of related attitudes and practices.[36]

THE OPERATING DEPARTMENT

Negro employment in those occupations responsible for the daily movement of trains for decades was confined almost entirely to the southern and border states. "Until World War I, it was usual for railroads in these areas to use Negro firemen and trainmen (brakemen, switchmen, or flagmen) on from 25 to 90 per cent of their runs."[37] Few Negroes employed in these occupations could hope to move up the normal seniority ladder to the positions of engineer and conductor. In fact, Negroes employed in all occupations in the operating department were forced by the "operating" unions to struggle endlessly to retain their jobs. The formerly five national unions[38] in the train and engine services, the Brotherhood of Locomotive Engineers, the Brotherhood of Locomotive Firemen and Enginemen, the Order of Railway Conductors, the Brotherhood of Railroad Trainmen, and the Switchmen's Union of North America, maintained the longest and probably the most virulent policies of racial discrimination of the many railroad unions.[39]

The efforts of the operating unions to limit the use of Negro employees in certain occupations originated from economic as well as social motives. Although the fraternal aspect of these organizations was important in their early history and unquestionably contributed to their exclusionary policies, they were motivated as well by the carriers' use of Negro employees to fight

---

36. The material presented in this chapter is based on the remarkable research efforts published in two early books on Negro employment, Sterling D. Spero and Abram L. Harris, *The Black Worker* (New York: Columbia University Press, 1931), pp. 284-315, and Herbert R. Northrup, *Organized Labor and the Negro* (New York: Harper & Bros., 1944), pp. 48-101.

37. Northrup, *ibid.*, p. 49.

38. The National Unions of the Locomotive Firemen, Conductors, Trainmen and Switchmen merged to form the United Transportation Union on January 1, 1969.

39. Each of these operating unions excluded Negroes from membership by constitutional provision, except in those states with FEP Legislation until 1960 or later. The last of the AFL-CIO unions to exclude Negroes formally were the Trainmen and the Firemen.

unions and depress wages. Negroes in the South were often employed as strikebreakers to replace white employees. Moreover, union wage demands had to remain restrained to avoid the replacement of white union members with Negroes who would accept lower wages. Negro firemen, for example, who worked for the Georgia Railroad in 1909 received "$1.75 for runs for which white men received $2.77, and $2.62 for runs for which white men received $3.62." [40]

"Since 1885," ran an article in the *Locomotive Firemens' Magazine*, "The Brotherhood of Locomotive Firemen has been victorious. The fireman of today knows nothing of what the firemen suffered before, through organization, they had thrown off the yoke of slavery. But why does not the Brotherhood accomplish similar results in the South? The answer is: 'The Negro'." [41]

The Brotherhoods had two possible methods for meeting the competition of unorganized Negro workers. They could take him into their organizations and "teach him and educate him," and fight management with a united front. They could also follow the second alternative, espoused by southern members, to eliminate Negro employees from train and engine service. The condition of the southern labor market made the second alternative impossible in the immediate future while the first method was made equally impossible by the attitudes of the white brotherhoods.[42]

In the period around 1910, both the Locomotive Firemen and the Railroad Trainmen succeeded in winning agreements through strikes or threats thereof which provided that Negro foremen or trainmen would not be utilized north of certain points; that "Negro firemen should not be assigned to more than one-half of the passenger runs or to more than one-half of the preferred freight runs"; [43] that the percentage of Negro yardmen or trainmen would be limited in any division or yard to that which existed on January 1, 1910; and that Negroes henceforth would not be employed as baggagemen, flagmen, or yard foremen.[44]

---

40. Spero and Harris, *op. cit.*, p. 289.

41. *Ibid.*, p. 287.

42. See Northrup, *op. cit.*, pp. 49-50.

43. Spero and Harris, *op. cit.*, p. 292.

44. Contract between the Brotherhood of Railroad Trainmen and the Southern Railroad Association, January 1910.

World War I Period

It was during World War I, however, that the most fundamental changes occurred. The high wages of the shipyards and other war industries induced Negroes to leave the railroad industry. The proportion of Negro employees on many lines fell rapidly. Tracks and cars fell into disrepair as a serious shortage of experienced labor developed.

Initially the carriers, both northern and southern, attempted to recruit new employees from among the large supply of Negro farm laborers in the South. Labor agents from many large employers were sent into rural areas. Railroads brought new employees into their regions by freight car. The Pennsylvania and Erie railroads, for example, brought 12,000 Negroes into Pennsylvania in the summer of 1916.[45] Many were housed in boxcars and tents. As an officer of the Illinois Central Railroad stated, "We took Negro labor out of the South until it hurt." [46]

Finally on May 25, 1918, after the federal government took over the railroads, William G. McAdoo, director-general of the railroads during the war, issued an order providing that "colored men employed as firemen, trainmen, and switchmen shall be paid the same rates as are paid white men in the same capacities." He referred to his order as "an act of simple justice." [47] The order stopped the Negro's drift away from the industry. Labor was scarce and the roads were glad to have steady employees regardless of their race.

The Post-World War I Period

Immediately after the war, the Brotherhoods renewed their efforts to eliminate Negro employees. The labor policy followed during the period of government control of the industry had greatly strengthened the railroad unions, and the pay equalization order had reduced the incentive to employ Negro workers. Furthermore, a decline in employment in the industry which began in 1921 made the white workers all the more anxious to displace Negroes. These factors worked very much to the benefit of the brotherhoods.

---

45. The American Academy of Political and Social Science, "Negro Migrant Families in Philadelphia," *The Annals*, Vol. XCVIII (November 1921), p. 174.

46. Spero and Harris, *op. cit.*, p. 162.

47. Northrup, *op. cit.*, p. 50.

The trainmen had forced the U. S. Railroad Administration in 1919 to agree to a new set of work rules. The revised rules stipulated that when new runs were created or vacancies occurred, the employee with the highest seniority would have "preference in choice of run or vacancy, either as flagman, baggageman, brakeman or switchman; except that Negroes are not to be used as conductors, flagmen, baggagemen or yard conductors." [48] Custom prior to this agreement had given the post of brakemen at the head of the train to Negroes, while the flagmen's job at the rear of the train was filled by white employees. Now white employees could exercise their seniority and "bump" junior Negro workers from brakemen positions, while younger white workers took their place as flagmen where they could not be bumped by Negro workers. This resulted in the displacement of many Negro workers.

The new rules also provided that white workers could not be used as porters and that "no porter (was) to have any trainman's rights except where he may have established same by three months continuously in freight service." [49] It had become customary for the carriers to employ porters as "porter-brakemen," handling brakemen's duties as well as their own, but at porter wages. The changes in work rules were intended to prevent porters from encroaching on occupations controlled by the trainmen. Since Negro porters had always been hired for passenger service, and never for freight service, they were prevented from ever serving three months in freight service.

The "full crew" movement arose in part as a consequence of using low-paid porters to perform the high-paid brakemen's duties. This legislation was generally promoted in the North as a necessary safety precaution but, in fact, it was demanded to guarantee the continuation of employment opportunities among the operating crafts. Legislation of this type usually provided that a train crew must consist of five persons: an engineer, a fireman, a conductor, a brakeman, and a flagman. Most of the full crew laws were enacted in the North and obviously not directed toward Negroes.

In the South, however, the Trainmen's union sponsored full crew legislation, not only as a makework measure, but also as a means of displacing Negro porters. As a rule, states with full

---

48. Spero and Harris, *op. cit.*, p. 300.

49. *Ibid.*

crew legislation disallowed the use of porters as brakemen, thus forcing the carrier to utilize highly paid brakemen.

The Locomotive Firemen also renewed its drive to eliminate Negroes from operating jobs after the war. Each new contract negotiated with the southern railroads reduced further both the percentage of Negro firemen and the type of service and the territory in which Negroes could be employed. On the Seaboard Air Line, Negro firemen were reduced from 90 percent of the firing force to 50 percent soon after the war. The Southern Railway, which had employed Negroes in 80 percent of its firing positions, employed Negro firemen in only 10 percent of its positions by 1929. The Atlantic Coast Line reduced its Negro firemen from 90 percent to 80 percent in this same period.[50]

In a number of instances, the two Brotherhoods were able to induce the carriers to stop hiring Negroes completely in occupations under union jurisdictions. Although most of these agreements were on smaller lines, the huge St. Louis-San Francisco system signed an agreement to fill all vacancies in train, yard, and shop service with white workers.

From the Great Depression to World War II

After remaining relatively stable at 1.6 million workers between 1921 and 1929, railroad employment began a further decline in 1930. By 1933 it had fallen below a million, and it continued to fluctuate at that level until World War II.[51] As jobs were abolished by technological innovations or declining business, Negro firemen and trainmen who had generally been hired before World War I were able to displace whites with less seniority.

This situation resulted in intense racial antagonism in the lower Mississippi Valley. A series of shootings took place over nearly thirty months, taking the lives of at least ten Negro firemen and trainmen, and wounding twenty-one others. The Illinois Central offered a reward of $5,000 but to no avail. The white union members were determined "to create vacancies . . . in the surest way possible, death, and, by stretching out the period of uncertainty and horror, to frighten away the others."[52]

50. *Ibid.*, p. 307.

51. Northrup, *op. cit.*, p. 54.

52. Malcom Ross, *All Manner of Men* (New York: Reynal and Hitchcock, 1948), p 120.

The Brotherhood of Locomotive Firemen in convention in 1931 planned a "concerted movement" to achieve finally the complete elimination of Negroes from their craft. It was subsequently reaffirmed by the 1937 convention, which passed a resolution authorizing such a campaign in the interest of "safety." [53]

The movement began with two separate agreements negotiated in 1937. The first agreement evolved out of a ruling by the Interstate Commerce Commission that all engines used in passenger or freight service would have to be equipped with mechanical stokers by July 1, 1943. Soon after the ICC made this ruling, the Firemen entered into a secret agreement with the Gulf, Mobile, & Ohio Railroad, in which the union waived its right to request higher wage scales in return for preference given members of its union on stokerized locomotives.[54] This was an obvious attempt to displace Negroes from the carrier's firing force.

The second agreement developed out of the introduction of the first diesel locomotives into train operations. The union was able to negotiate an agreement with the Association of American Railroads in February 1937 to place a fireman (helper) on all diesel locomotives. In order to restrict the assignments to white firemen, the union reached separate agreements over the next three years with the Seaboard Air Line, Atlantic Coast Line, and Gulf, Mobile and Ohio Railroads, which "specifically provide that the employment and assignment of Firemen under the terms of the Diesel-electric agreement shall be confined to those firemen duly qualified for service on such locomotives; and that only firemen in line for promotion (white firemen) shall be accepted as duly qualified for such service." [55]

The Firemen's objective, the elimination of Negroes from firing position, was almost accomplished by an agreement reached in February 1941. In negotiations beginning in 1940 the Locomotive Firemen attempted to induce nearly all the railroads employing Negro firemen into accepting a clause which would have allowed only promotable firemen (white firemen) to be employed on diesel locomotives, and would have further stipulated that all vacancies and new runs be staffed by promotable (white) men.[56]

---

53. Northrup, *op. cit.*, p. 62.

54. *Teague* v. *Brotherhood of Locomotive Firemen and Enginemen,* 127 F. 2d 53 (6th Cir. 1942).

55. Northrup, *op. cit.*, pp. 62-63.

56. *Ibid.*, p. 63.

The agreement finally signed in February by the union and twenty-one railroads, now known as the "Southeastern Carriers' Agreement," provided that nonpromotable firemen (Negroes) were not to be employed in excess of 50 percent of the diesel positions, and that in districts in which the percentage now exceeds 50 percent, only promotable firemen were to be hired. Finally it stated that all new runs and vacancies were to be filled by promotable firemen, and that "on any road having, in the opinion of BLF & E committee, more favorable rules or conditions may at the opinion of such committee be retained in lieu of the above provisions." The agreement was reached, witnessed, and cosigned by two members of the National Mediation Board, the federal agency with conciliation authority in the railroad industry.[57]

The agreement had been carefully written to allow the Brotherhood and the carriers to displace Negro firemen whenever they wished. Under the terms of the contract, all new runs must go to promotable firemen. New runs, however, were created if a terminal was changed, if the mileage was changed by at least twenty miles per day or if the number of trains in a "pool" was changed. "New runs," therefore, could be a rather common occurrence which would result in the displacement of many Negro workers. Furthermore, the contract stipulated that all vacancies must be filled by promotable firemen until the quota was reached. Senior white firemen began "bumping" junior Negroes wholesale, staying in the new position for only a short time and then moving to a better position, leaving behind a "vacancy" which could be filled only by a white fireman. Finally, of course, the 50 percent quota itself could be used to displace Negroes at management's discretion, since the Negroes could hardly prove what percentage were actually employed. This insidious contract stands as the peak of racial discrimination among American unions.[58]

While the Firemen were moving forward toward their stated goal, the Trainmen also continued their active opposition to Negro employees. At their 1931 convention they resolved to eliminate the porter-brakemen from further competition. They were to base their fight on the policy established by the National Railroad Adjustment Board, the agency created to decide grievance disputes in the industry, that all work in the operation of a

57. *Ibid.*
58. *Ibid.*, pp. 63-64.

railroad "belongs" to a particular class of employee. Any other class of employees is not entitled to perform work not specifically accorded to them.[59]

In a claim filed before the First Division of the Adjustment Board in 1939, the Trainmen argued that Negro porter-brakemen were performing tasks which rightfully should be performed by Brotherhood members. The union attached great importance to the case, contending "that the award covering this particular case shall also be applicable to all other instances of a like character." [60]

In Award 6640, the majority of the first division, consisting of the union members and a referee, upheld in full the claim of the trainmen in these words, "The use of porters or other employees, who do not hold seniority as brakemen, is in violation of claimants' seniority rights. . . . *Claim that like settlement shall be made in all instances of similar nature now on file is likewise sustained.*" [61]

Although this decision was later overturned in court on the grounds that the porters had not been given adequate notice before the Board's action, it was a serious threat to the earning power of many Negro workers throughout the 1940's.[62]

Negro Railway Unions in the Pre-World War II Period

While the Firemen and Trainmen Brotherhoods were carrying out their vicious attacks, Negro workers made several generally unsuccessful attempts to organize to protect their jobs. Initially Negro workers refused to organize for fear of offending their employers. Several groups appealed to railroad stockholders and executives, hoping that they could "rely upon the rich white man's sense of justice" as their best protection." [63] These efforts were to no avail.

One of the initial groups to gain recognition by employers was the Association of Colored Railway Trainmen and Locomotive

---

59. *Ibid.*, pp. 65-66.

60. *Ibid.*, p. 69.

61. *Ibid.*

62. *Hunter* v. *Atchison, Topeka and Sante Fe Ry.*, 188 F. 2d 294 (7th Cir. 1951). We shall discuss the role of these government boards below.

63. Spero and Harris, *op. cit.*, p. 315.

Firemen, Inc. Founded in 1912, the union reached a peak of 3,500 members in 1926, but by 1940 membership had fallen to only 1,000. Its success apparently was based on its willingness to accept wages below those of white employees performing similar work. For instance, an agreement with the Virginian Railway stipulated that "car riders" were to receive $6 per day. At the same time, on the nearby Norfolk & Western and the Chesapeake & Ohio, brakemen performing the same duties received $7.82 per day. The Association's other agreement covered Negro firemen and brakemen on the Louisiana & Arkansas Railway. Wages for Negro employees covered by this contract were from two to three dollars per day less than wages paid to white employees for similar work.[64]

Although several other Negro unions were formed between 1917 and 1934, none were really to become successful. They could exert almost no economic or political power. If they went out on strike, management simply threatened to replace them. Those wage concessions that were obtained could probably be attributed more to the carrier's generosity than to union bargaining power. All but the previously mentioned Association had become defunct by 1940.

The only Negro union which was successful in remaining active through the 1960's was the International Association of Railway Employees which won bargaining rights on the Florida East Coast Railway in 1946. These Negro workers were the last all Negro firing force. Until 1943 they had been represented by the Locomotive Engineers, the Grand Chief Engineer, and finally after his death, by his wife. It was only after the locomotive engineers employed by the carrier negotiated an agreement which gave the engineers seniority rights as firemen to protect them in case of layoffs, and further stipulated that white firemen were to be employed until 55 percent of the firing positions were filled by "promotable" men that the Negro firemen were willing to organize formally.[65] They were one of the few groups of Negro firemen who were able to fight off the attacks of the white brotherhoods in this period.

---

64. Northrup, *op. cit.*, pp. 73-74.

65. Letter from R. W. Wycoff, Vice-President of the Florida East Coast Line, July 18, 1969.

REPAIR SHOPS

Negroes have never occupied a position in the railroad repair shops comparable to that gained in train and engine service. Negro employment in shop occupations was limited to a large extent to southern railroads just as it was in the operating department. Employment opportunities prior to World War II were restricted to those of mechanics' helpers and laborers. A number of shops in the South employed only Negro helpers. In the northern shops, Negroes were typically employed only as laborers.[66]

The greatest gains by Negroes in the shops were made during strikes by shop craftsmen. The Illinois Central hired Negroes as strikebreakers during a system wide walkout in 1911. The shops were filled with Negro employees who were put to work under white foremen and instructors. The carrier's employment of Negroes as replacements finally forced the craft unions to submit to the firm's over three years after the initial shutdown.[67]

The nationwide strike by the shop unions in 1922 provided an even greater number of job opportunities for Negro workers. Negro helpers and laborers, who had been organized, went out with the white mechanics, and generally stayed out until an agreement was reached. Although the affected carriers tried to find Negro workers to fill the openings, there was not a sufficient supply of Negroes with experience in related fields to serve as strikebreakers. The railroads were forced to turn chiefly to white craftsmen to keep the rolling stock repaired. Yet, as a result of the strike, Negro mechanics were able to obtain permanent positions in several cities.

The use of Negro workers as strikebreakers did not arouse affection among the already antipathetic craft union members. Six of the seven unions with jurisdiction over shop workers either excluded Negroes from membership or relegated them to auxiliaries, controlled by white locals. The Machinists excluded Negroes by a provision in its ritual; the Electrical Workers did likewise by tacit consent. The Sheet Metal Workers refused to admit Negroes even though their rules would have permitted them to admit them to auxiliary locals. The Boilermakers barred Negroes from their union completely prior to 1937. After that year they were permitted to form auxiliaries with no voice in

---

66. Spero and Harris, *op. cit.*, p. 308.

67. Northrup, *op. cit.*, p. 78.

union affairs. The Blacksmiths followed this pattern after World War I, allowing Negroes to join auxiliaries, which were denied the right of representation in conventions, were forbidden to process the grievances of their own members, and were refused promotions in shops where white helpers were employed. The largest of the shop craft unions, the Carmen, excluded Negroes until 1921 when auxiliaries were established "on railroads where the employment of colored persons has become a permanent institution." [68]

The establishment of auxiliaries was designed to control the competition of Negro workers. In 1924, the Machinists, Boilermakers, Sheet Metal Workers and Electrical Workers, who still excluded Negroes from any form of membership, made an agreement with the Brotherhood of Firemen and Oilers to allow that union to organize the Negro workers who would normally come under the jurisdiction of these three crafts. The Negroes organized by the Firemen and Oilers continued to work under the rules of these respective crafts, and their grievances were handled by that craft's committee. The Negro workers were thus denied any voice in the determination of these working conditions. Needless to say, the craft unions did not always work to the benefit of the Negro workers. In fact, on some carriers, the craftsmen negotiated contracts providing that "none but white English-speaking helpers shall be employed when available." [69]

Even with these insidiously discriminatory efforts by the craft unions, Negro employees more than doubled their share of jobs in the railroad shops between 1910 and 1930. The occupational distribution of Negro workers had also improved during this period, with the percentage of unskilled Negro shop employees decreasing from 83 percent to 57 percent. Yet by 1930 Negro shop workers numbered only 16,000 out of a total shop employment of 226,000. The Census recorded only 600 Negro machinists in the industry, 180 blacksmiths, 231 boilermakers, and 63 electricians. [70]

Although comparable data are not available for 1940, Negro shopmen are believed to have lost many of their gains during

---

68. *Ibid.*, pp. 2-5, 78.

69. Agreement between the Missouri Pacific and the six shop craft unions, December 21, 1918, p. 14.

70. *U. S. Census of Population:* 1930: Vol. V, *General Report on Occupations*, Tables 2, p. 474. 1910: Vol. IV, *Occupational Statistics*, Table VI, p. 340.

layoffs incident to the depression.[71] Senior Negroes were laid off, while white employees with less seniority were retained. Jobs of Negro shopmen were abolished, recreated, and white workers employed to fill them. Even when the seniority system was followed without discrimination, senior white mechanics were able to displace junior Negro helpers during layoffs. The reverse, however, was not generally possible as helpers could not be promoted to mechanic positions.

MAINTENANCE OF WAY DEPARTMENT

Negro workers were generally employed in maintenance of way operations as track laborers only. They, however, were seldom considered for promotion to track gang foreman. These positions as well as those in bridge and building maintenance, and signal installation and maintenance were filled on most railroads with white workers. Southern railroads, following in the regional tradition of Negro craftsmen in the construction trades, have employed a few Negroes in these positions.

In 1910, 70,000 or 15.4 percent of the 453,925 "steam railroad laborer" positions were held by Negroes. In the South, 73.0 percent of the 77,882 such laborers were black. Twenty years later, reflecting the general increase in Negro employment during World War I, Negro employees in laboring positions represented 22.5 percent of the 435,058 employed. In the South, they remained 73 percent of the 82,972 laborers employed. The increased total laborer employment in the South in contrast to the overall industry decrease is attributed largely to the continued presence of many Negro workers . . . who were able to gain no better wages than the 15 to 25 cents per hour paid by the southern carriers.[72]

The depression evoked significant reduction in railroad maintenance operations and employment. Work force reductions were especially heavy in the South which suffered not only from busi-

---

71. This was true in six southern repair shops studied in 1934. The proportion of Negro workers in these shops ranged from 43 percent of a total work force of 725 to no Negro workers among a work force of 950. It is clear from the attitudes expressed by supervisory personnel in these shops that white workers received preference over Negro workers for all jobs during this period. Horace R. Cayton and George S. Mitchell, *Black Workers and the New Unions* (Chapel Hill: University of North Carolina, 1939), Chapter XV.

72. Northrup, *op. cit.*, pp. 92-93.

ness depression, but for the first time from mechanization and truck competition. The heavy reductions in this region, with its high Negro employment, accounted in part for a slight decline in the proportion of Negro laborers, from 22.5 percent in 1930 to 20.9 in 1940, in the industry as a whole.[73] The initial impact of minimum wage legislation, 40 cents per hour in the railroad industry, was causing an acceleration of mechanization, with a resultant displacement of laborers.

Unionism in maintenance of way employment was initiated by track foremen in the late 1890's. Later the organization assumed jurisdiction over all trackmen and changed its name to the Brotherhood of Maintenance of Way Employees. The Brotherhood restricted membership to white workers until 1917. In that year, the convention voted to allow Negro workers to join "allied lodges," which would be represented at conventions by delegates "selected from any white lodge." [74]

Although the Brotherhood ceased to be an organization composed only of foremen in the early part of this century, these lower management personnel retained the positions of power. This is to be expected since foremen were frequently the only permanent employees, most of the gang laborers being casually attached to the carrier and the industry and with little interest in the union. The foremen were also the controlling factor in the success of Brotherhood-called strikes since track laborers could easily be replaced. Finally, the strategic position of the foreman in his role as superior to the gang worker, provides a broader power base from which to control the union.

In the South, where frequently the foreman was white and the laborers were Negroes consigned to "allied lodges," the foreman was in a unique position to control the Negro track workers both as supervisors and as union representatives. In situations when other labor organizations have challenged the Brotherhood for control of Negro laborers, this dual position has given the Maintenance of Way Employees insuperable organizing power. For instance, in 1941 the United Transport Service Employees, the then independent Redcaps' union, and later a CIO affiliate, attempted to organize the Negro track workers on the Florida East Coast Railway. The Brotherhood had represented the white foremen and bridge and building workers since 1936, but had never

73. *Ibid.*, pp. 93, 94.

74. *Ibid.*, p. 94.

made a serious attempt to unionize the Negro laborers. Both organizations petitioned the Mediation Board for a representation election.[75]

The United Transport Service Employees urged that foremen and laborers be placed in separate classes on the grounds that the former were really the employers of the latter. The Board rejected this convention, however, as it had done in the past, on the grounds that both groups had bargained as one class in the past and that too many subdivisions of workers make collective bargaining difficult and thus tends to defeat the purpose of the Railway Labor Act.

The election among the carriers maintenance workers resulted in a 418 to 339 victory for the Brotherhood. The United Transport Service Employees filed a protest with the Board charging coercion by foremen-members of the Brotherhood, misconduct by the Board's mediator, and collusion among the mediator, foremen and county police which prevented the United Transport Service Employees' observers from being present. The Brotherhood's representative admitted that foremen had discharged several United Transport Service Employees members with long service records prior to the election, but stated that it was for "insubordination," not pre-election campaigning. The Mediation Board denied the protest and certified the Brotherhood as bargaining agent for all maintenance of way employees. This was later sustained in a federal district court.[76] It is doubtful, however, that coercion could have been prevented in any representation election held in the South under these Mediation Board policies. Clearly the interests of the Negro track laborers and the supervisory personnel within the Maintenance of Way Employees were frequently in conflict under the bargaining units established by the Mediation Board. As Negro workers were slowly promoted into positions as gang foremen and above, the interests of Negro workers were more frequently voiced at union meetings. The policies utilized by the Board in establishing bargaining units among maintenance of way employees were indicative of the emphasis placed on the interests of the established labor organizations, often to the detriment of the Negro workers. This theme is developed further in Chapter VII.

---

75. *Ibid.*, pp. 95-96. The bargaining unit election procedures of the National Mediation Board and their impact on Negro railroad workers is discussed in Chapter VII.

76. *Ibid.*, p. 96.

CLERICAL AND STATION EMPLOYEES

Negro workers were extensively employed in a number of service and laborer occupations in passenger service, freight handling, and building maintenance operations. The majority of the workers in these occupations come under the jurisdiction of the Brotherhood of Railway and Steamship Clerks, Express and Station Employees. It was founded in 1899 by clerks, a white collar group, and only white workers were made eligible for membership.[77]

Few Negroes had been employed as telegraphers, towermen, or agents. These occupations come under the jurisdiction of the Order of Railroad Telegraphers. This organization has limited membership to white workers since its inception in 1886. Even fewer Negro workers were ever used in the high-paying train dispatching positions. Most of the workers in this occupation were then organized into the Train Dispatchers' Association, which also excluded Negro workers.[78]

The Clerks' union did not have to deal with the problem posed by large numbers of Negroes under its jurisdiction until World War I. The union then enlarged its jurisdiction to include many of the occupation in freight and passenger stations. Negroes have been employed as freight handlers, janitors, redcaps, and attendants ever since railroads first hired workers to perform these tasks.

Negro freight handlers and station employees were first organized during the war into AFL Federal Locals, that is local unions affiliated directly with the AFL instead of with an international union. The AFL attempted to develop a plan which would have had the Clerks provide these Negro federal locals with representation assistance. The officials of the Clerks' union had no interest in strengthening the Negro locals, and by 1930 most of these federal locals had been disbanded.[79]

The Negro workers, however, acted as a wage depressant and this was soon realized by the Clerks' officials. The officers chose to reverse their former policy in 1934 and began to provide the necessary organizational assistance to build viable, effective federal locals. This policy was endorsed by the Brotherhood's 1935

---

77. *Ibid.*, p. 82.

78. *Ibid.*

79. *Ibid.*, pp. 82-83.

convention. In return for representation and grievance handling, members of the Negro federal locals paid a per capita tax to the local clerks' unions. The Negro employees made no contribution to the Clerks' national office, but instead paid it to the AFL directly. This arrangement was responsible for substantial wage increases and improved working conditions for many Negro union members.[80]

This arrangement satisfied neither the Negro workers who had no voice in union activities nor the Brotherhood which received too little financial support. A resolution passed at the 1939 national convention gave the Clerks' Executive Council the authority to establish "proper representation and a more immediate contact with colored employees."[81]

The plan adopted by the Executive Council called for the establishment of a Negro auxiliary, whose members would pay the same dues and receive the same insurance benefits as white members of the union, but who would be unable to handle their own grievances or to choose delegates to attend Brotherhood conventions. The auxiliary was launched in July 1940 over the vigorous protests of the Negro workers.[82]

Twenty one of the federal locals petitioned the AFL Executive Council to rescind the order transferring them to the Clerks auxiliary. The fight was carried to the 1940 AFL convention floor. They protested that they had not been consulted before they were told to transfer to the Clerks and that they were willing to join the Brotherhood, but were refused membership. The protests were to no avail, the AFL revoked the federal charters of those groups who did not accept membership in the Clerks' auxiliary by March 1, 1941.[83]

A large number of Negro freight handlers refused to follow the AFL Directive and instead chose to start their own organization, the National Council of Freight Handlers, Express and Station Employees. Their biggest struggle, however, lay not with the carriers with whom they hoped to negotiate agreements, but rather with the National Mediation Board. It had previously ruled that clerks, freight handlers, station and store employees should be included in the same bargaining unit because they had

---

80. *Ibid.*, p. 83.

81. *Ibid.*

82. *Ibid.*, pp. 83-84.

83. *Ibid.*

been grouped in this manner by previous custom, and that a proliferation of bargaining groups would make collective bargaining impossible. If the Mediation Board refused to separate
freight handlers and station employees from the customary bargaining unit, they would be outvoted by white workers in any
representation election. The Board ruled that there could be no
separation as it had done for several previous Negro groups and
the National Council gradually disintegrated.[84]

The reluctance of Negro workers to join the auxiliary also induced a significant proportion of the industry's redcaps or station porters to begin their own organizations. The custom of
employing porters to assist passengers with baggage was widespread by the turn of the century. As a general practice only
Negroes were employed as redcaps, although a few white employees worked as redcaps in midwestern cities. The first organizing
efforts by redcaps started as early as 1921, and by 1933 most
terminals had redcap locals handling grievances and other issues.
On most of the nation's carriers, however, the porter was re-
garded as an "independent contractor" who, while subject to discipline, worked exclusively for tips. This not only denied the
porters the opportunity to negotiate wage increases but it excluded them from the coverage of social and labor legislation.[85]

In an attempt to mitigate this management policy, several redcap unions met in Chicago in 1937 and founded the International Brotherhood of Redcaps. The name was changed in 1940
to the present name, United Transport Service Employees. Redcap unions in the East and Midwest were quickly induced to join,
and in 1941 those on the West coast joined the UTSE rather than
take out charters in the Clerks auxiliary.[86]

An intense rivalry developed between the UTSE and the Railway Clerks. On several occasions the Clerks were able to win
bargaining rights for redcaps merely by extending the "scope"
of an already existing agreement. The UTSE, however, was able
to obtain the majority of the industry's redcaps as members. It
had agreements covering the redcaps in most of the large terminals in eastern, midwestern, and far western cities. Only in the
South and Southwest, where Negro workers were most likely to

---

84. *Ibid.*, p. 85.

85. *Ibid.*, p. 86.

86. *Ibid.*, pp. 86-87.

accept without protest the status offered by the Railway Clerks, was the UTSE unsuccessful in their organizational drives.

Soon after the national union began in 1937, the UTSE petitioned the Interstate Commerce Commission to clarify their employment status with the carriers. In September 1938, one month before the Fair Labor Standards Act went into effect, the ICC ruled that redcaps were employees within the meaning of the Railway Labor Act.

The redcaps then attempted to clarify the status of tips under the Fair Labor Standards Act. If, in fact, tips were not wages, then the redcaps were entitled to the minimum wage plus tips. The railroads took the initiative and ordered the redcaps to report all tips to management. The redcaps were then compensated the difference between their tips and the minimum wage. In an effort to retain the formerly free redcap service, many carriers began discharging redcaps who reported less than the minimum for "dishonesty" or "inefficiency." Under these circumstances, a redcap who earned less than the minimum usually reported the minimum anyway to protect his job.[87]

It was not until March 1942 that the Supreme Court ruled in a case brought by the Railway Clerks that tips could be counted as wages under the Fair Labor Standards Act. Although this meant that the railroads could legally take title to tips, most of the companies had already abandoned the accounting and guarantee plan in favor of a flat charge of ten cents per bag. Checks attached to each bag permitted an accounting of the baggage handled. The redcaps were placed on the payroll at the minimum wage. They had thus won full recognition as employees but at the expense of many jobs and minimal financial gains. The disappearance of the redcap began with this legal "victory."

DINING CAR EMPLOYEES

Railroads have employed Negroes as dining car cooks and waiters since food service was added to rail transportation. Nearly 70 percent of the 5,124 "chefs and cooks" and of the 15,512 "waiters, camp cooks, kitchen helpers, etc.," working on Class I railroads in 1940 were Negroes.[88] On the other hand, very few Negroes were employed among the 1,639 "stewards and dining supervisors."

87. *Ibid.*, p. 87.

88. *Ibid.*, p. 96.

Unionization among dining car employees dates from World War I when several unions were formed. The most important of these was the Brotherhood of Dining Car Employees which won contracts with most of the carriers in the East and Southeast.

Most of the remaining cooks and waiters were organized by the Hotel and Restaurant Workers' Union. Although the AFL gave jurisdiction over dining car employees to the Hotel Workers in 1920, they were not successful in their organizational efforts until the mid-thirties.[89] The union set up a railroad department known as the Joint Council of Dining Car Employees. One national vice-president was allotted to the Joint Council.

The rules of the Hotel Workers' union restricted Negro members prior to 1936 to segregated locals or compelled them to join as members-at-large, with full privileges in both cases. Many locals, however, disregarded the national rules and admitted Negro members. Even these formal restrictions were removed in a convention in 1936. The 1938 convention went still further and amended the constitution to provide: "Any local law prohibiting the admission of any competent person, male or female, because of race, religion, or color is contrary to our laws and is, therefore, null and void." [90]

The Hotel Workers' successfully attacked the industry practice of putting waiters in charge of dining cars rather than stewards at a pay rate which was less than that normally paid to stewards. Thus, the Negro waiter was paid less for doing two jobs than the white steward was paid for performing one. The Pennsylvania Railroad agreed to pay the more equitable steward's pay rate rather than fight the issue before the National Railroad Adjustment Board.[91] The Negro waiters remained ineligible for promotion to steward, and thus were unable to acquire any seniority or claim to the position.

In the summer of 1941, the membership of the Dining Car Employees revolted against its president, and merged the Brotherhood with the United Transport Service Employees. At that time, the Dining Car Employees held contracts with the Atlantic Coast Line, the Southern, and the Boston & Maine. The UTSE soon lost their control over the employees of the Atlantic Coast Line to the Hotel Workers.[92]

---

89. *Ibid.*, p. 98.

90. *Ibid.*, p. 98.

91. *Ibid.*

92. *Ibid.*, p. 99.

The UTSE initialed an organizing drive among dining car employees shortly after its affiliation with the CIO in 1942. It soon won bargaining rights on the previously unorganized Colorado and Southern, and the Bangor and Aroostock. The rivalry between these two predominantly Negro labor organizations, the Joint Council and the UTSE, continued until after World War II.

PULLMAN PORTERS

The United Transport Service Workers and the Hotel Workers' Union were not the only predominantly Negro labor organizations in the railroad industry. The first successful union controlled by Negroes and unquestionably the dominant union among Negro organized labor groups was the Brotherhood of Sleeping Car Porters. Prior to 1925, the Pullman porters had made several unsuccessful attempts to organize. Then, in that year, the porters acquired the assistance of A. Philip Randolph, a rising young Negro writer and intellectual. Under his direction the fledgling Brotherhood gained a majority of the Pullman Porters as members within a year.[93]

The Sleeping Car Porters was established as an independent union, but in the early years of its history it received strong support from the AFL and, interestingly enough, the railway operating brotherhoods.[94] Randolph and his union first applied to the AFL Executive Council for an international charter in 1928. This application was blocked, however, by the claims of the Hotel Workers' Union which had previously been granted jurisdiction over the dining car employees and sleeping car porters. The Executive Council finally consented to charter the Brotherhood's locals as directly affiliated "federal" locals.

Initial union success was stalled in 1928 by strong company resistance to a Brotherhood strike threat. That Pullman Company, which at this time controlled all pullman car operations, had consistently refused to recognize the porters' organization. When the company called the union's bluff over the threatened strike, the strike was cancelled and the weakened union lost many members.

---

93. *Ibid.*, p. 75.

94. For additional information on the early history of the Brotherhood of Sleeping Car Porters, see Brailsford R. Brazeal, *The Brotherhood of Sleeping Car Porters* (New York: Harper & Brothers, 1946).

The Brotherhood was slowly able to regain its membership and in 1935 petitioned the Mediation Board to conduct a representation election among the porters, maids, and attendants of the Pullman Company. The victory in this election gave the union exclusive bargaining rights for these pullman employees. Two years later the Brotherhood signed its first contract with Pullman. The election victory also induced the AFL Executive Council to rescind its decision, and in August 1935 to grant the Porters an international charter.[95]

The Porters had to overcome opposition initially from an earlier Pullman union, the Order of Sleeping Car Conductors, an all white union. The Sleeping Car Conductors had held a contract with the Pullman Company since 1922. In 1934, for a brief period, the union was granted jurisdiction over the porters by the AFL. The Sleeping Car Conductors based their claim over the porters as necessary to protect the conductors from the industry practice of placing porters in charge of sleeping cars at a wage nearly $80 a month less than that paid to conductors. Strong propaganda attacks on this practice were carried out in the South, with several states passing laws forbidding the Pullman Company from operating sleeping cars in their states without conductors.[96] These changes, of course, limited the job opportunities and earnings of the Negro porters.

After winning their first contract with the Pullman Company, the Porters began to devote more effort to assisting other Negro railroad workers. Dining car and redcap employees were aided in forming local unions. The Brotherhood also attempted to alleviate the rapidly deteriorating position of Negro firemen. Although any Negro organizational efforts could not hope to win bargaining rights as a minority within the craft, the Sleeping Car Porters' union was successful in bringing together over 1,000 Negro firemen into a provisional committee to appeal to government and conduct campaigns to publicize their plight.[97]

Possibly more important than the organizing efforts of the Porters was the rapidly acquired position of Randolph and his union as the spokesman for Negro workers and their problems. Since the early 1930's, Randolph has been the dominant force agitating for change in the racial policies of the AFL and its

---

95. Northrup, *op cit.*, pp. 75-77.

96. *Ibid.*, p. 76.

97. *Ibid.*, pp. 77-78.

affiliates. As early as 1933 Randolph asked at the AFL convention that the Federation go on record as enlisting and employing Negro organizers to carry on the campaign for Negro organization.[98]

In 1934 Randolph's resolution demanding expulsion of excluding unions was changed to provide for the appointment of a five-man committee to investigate conditions of colored workmen and report to the next convention.[99] The committee appointed by the AFL held open hearings in Washington, produced evidence of widespread discrimination by unions, and formulated an educational and action program to harmonize union racial policies with AFL policy. AFL Vice-President George Harrison, of the Railway Clerks, wanted the committee to issue a statement which would have glossed over the problem. Randolph, however, was successful in obtaining a copy of the report and protested its handling at the next convention.[100]

Randolph and other Porter leaders introduced resolutions against discrimination at succeeding conventions.[101] This continuing agitation was to become one of the prime factors in the eventual mitigation of union racial policies among railroad unions affiliated with the AFL.

SUMMARY

Writing in the early 1940's, Professor Herbert R. Northrup found that fourteen unions excluded Negroes from membership by constitutional or ritual provision. Of these, ten were exclusively railroad unions and two others had some railway employee membership. Dr. Northrup further classified eight unions as excluding Negroes "by tacit consent." One of these was exclusively a railroad union and a second had some railway employee membership. Finally, Dr. Northrup listed nine unions "which afforded Negroes only segregated auxiliary status." Four of these were exclusively railroad unions and three others had rail-

98. Marc Karson and Ronald Radosh, "The American Federation of Labor and the Negro Worker, 1894-1949," in *The Negro and the American Labor Movement*, ed. Julius Jacobson (Garden City, N.Y.: Anchor Books, 1968), p. 162.

99. *Ibid.*, pp. 163-164.

100. *Ibid.*, pp. 164-171.

101. *Ibid.*, pp. 173-174.

way employee members.[102] With railway management employing
in a discriminatory fashion, with the industry's unions practicing
the most virulent discrimination, with government agencies aiding and abetting discrimination, and with employment declining
precipitously, the Negro railroad worker entered the decade of
the 1940's in his most precarious position to date. Only a reversal
of the policies of all parties to the discriminatory treatment of
Negroes and an improvement of economic conditions could seemingly alter the trend. Table 10 shows the status of Negroes in
the industry as of 1940.

TABLE 10. *Railroad Industry*
Employment by Color, Sex, and Occupational Group
Southern Region, 1940

Occupational Group	Male			Female		
	Total	Non-white	Percent Non-white	Total	Non-white	Percent Non-white
Officials and managers	19,866	21	0.1	85	1	1.2
Professional, semi-professional and kindred	2,064	2	0.1	42	1	2.4
Clerical, sales and kindred	49,626	738	1.5	6,775	8	0.1
Craftsmen	85,264	4,279	5.0	150	10	6.7
Operatives	48,383	8,254	17.1	187	55	29.4
Laborers	69,016	38,750	56.1	364	249	68.4
Service workers	16,109	10,127	62.9	598	310	51.8
Occupation not reported	914	186		19	6	
Total	291,242	62,357[a]	21.4	8,220	640[b]	7.8

Source: *U. S. Census of Population, 1940*, Vol. III, *The Labor Force*, Part I,
Table 82.

a Includes 90 men other than Negroes.

b Includes 1 female other than Negro.

---

102. Northrup, *op. cit.*, pp. 3-5.

CHAPTER IV

Racial Employment Policies and Traditions, 1940-1960

The period from 1940 to 1960 saw a continuation of the general decline in railroad employment which had begun after World War I. The economic buildups during the early years of World War II and again during the initial months of activity in Korea were responsible for temporary increased manpower needs in the industry. These rapid employment increases were quickly curtailed in each instance with the termination of hostilities. The relative increase in Negro employment in the railroad industry during the war periods exceeded the relative increases in total employment, but these gains were lost because of the disproportionately high separation rate of Negro employees in the late 1940's and again in the late 1950's. Although continued discrimination was in part responsible for these losses, the renewed layoff of newly hired railroad employees and increased movement of Negro workers into new geographic locations and industries were the fundamental causes of the decline in Negro employment. The position of Negro employees in the railroad industry by the end of the period, in both total employment and occupational distribution, was surprisingly similar to that in 1940.

Significant changes did occur, however, in the environmental factors affecting discrimination in the industry. The movement against racial injustice, led by A. Philip Randolph, President of the Brotherhood of Sleeping Car Porters, had its first impact on government policy. The President's Committee on Fair Employment Practices (FEPC), formed in 1941 by President Roosevelt, was first of its kind and the direct result of efforts by Randolph. Hearings held by this committee into the industry's discriminatory practices, and a number of subsequent Supreme Court decisions enjoining specific discriminatory practices were responsible for exposing and giving wide publicity to the practices of the industry, and for initiating subtle changes in the attitudes of unions and carriers. Moreover, state committees, similar to the federal FEPC, but with stronger legislative support, were able to eradicate some of the more invidious practices in their states. Most of the blatant practices of discrimination had been eliminated by the end of the period. Negro employees unfortunately were still not able to enjoy full equal employment opportunity because of the lack of job opportunities, the ingrained attitudes of management, the opposition of unions, and the other factors to be discussed later in this study.

HEARINGS OF THE FAIR EMPLOYMENT PRACTICE COMMITTEE

The opportunity for Negroes to make desired gains appeared with the outbreak of war in Europe and the beginning of the defense effort by the United States. The administration in Washington knew that to meet its military requirements, every available source of labor would have to be utilized. Discrimination against minority groups, as a factor preventing the efficient utilization of manpower, would have to be eliminated, or at least mitigated. However, at the beginning of 1940, the need for manpower had not yet become critical. There existed a reservoir of six million unemployed workers, many of whom were highly skilled. The administration, therefore, did not rush to confront the problem of discrimination. Initial attempts by Negro leaders to effectuate desired changes in government policy were very often rebuffed.

Meanwhile, a suggestion by Randolph, at the beginning of 1941, that the Negro people march on Washington, "to exact their rights in national defense employment and the armed forces of the country," gained recognition and support from Negro newspapers and leaders.[103] A March-on-Washington Committee was formed, consisting of many prominent Negro leaders. The march was officially scheduled for July 1. The number of marchers expected to participate grew from ten thousand to five times that number and then to one hundred thousand.

The administration in Washington obviously did not wish to be confronted by one hundred thousand Negro citizens protesting against discrimination. Pressure was put on the leaders to cancel the march. At last, President Roosevelt requested a meeting with the march committee. They accepted the President's invitation,

---

103. *Chicago Defender*, June 14, 1941, p. 3.

and on June 18, Randolph and three other Negro leaders met in the White House.[104] On June 25, 1941, however, President Roosevelt issued Executive Order 8802 reaffirming the policy of non-discrimination in government and defense industries. The strategy had worked, and the march was called off.

The Order established the Fair Employment Practice Committee whose members were to "receive and investigate complaints of discrimination," to redress valid grievances, and to recommend to government agencies and to the President measures required to implement the order.[105] One of the six appointed members, Milton Webster, was first international vice president of the Brotherhood of Sleeping Car Porters and chairman of its international executive board. The remaining five included a southern newspaper publisher, a Jewish industrialist, the leaders of the AFL and CIO, and a Negro lawyer.

The FEPC scheduled hearings on complaints against certain railroad companies and unions for January 25, 26, and 27, 1943. Pressure against the committee's activities built up and on January 11, 1943, Paul V. McNutt, War Manpower Administrator, under whose aegis FEPC was lodged, postponed indefinitely the railroad hearings. There was no prior consultation with the committee. The net impact was to cause the FEPC virtually to cease functioning. Pressure mounted to reestablish a committee independent of other agencies.[106]

On May 27, 1943, President Roosevelt issued Executive Order 9346,[107] creating a second FEPC as an independent agency, subject only to the authority of the President. The rights and duties of the new committee were similar to those of the first, but it was strengthened somewhat by the addition of several powers not included in the first order.

Discrimination on the railroads remained the most difficult and crucial problem facing the Committee. Hearings on the industry's practices had already been postponed three times. The Committee was at last successful, however, in opening hearings in

---

104. Louis Ruchames, *Race, Jobs, & Politics* (New York: Columbia University Press, 1953), p. 19.

105. Executive Order 8802, 6 *Fed. Reg.* 3109 (1941).

106. *New York Times*, January 12, 1943, p. 14. An unvalidated source cited a telephone call from the White House on January 9 as the cause for postponement.

107. Executive Order 9346, 8 *Fed. Reg.* 7183 (1943).

Washington on September 15, with twenty-two railroads and fourteen unions as defendants.[108] Bartley Crum, chief counsel for the Committee during the hearings, called the hearings "the most important ever held so far as minority groups are concerned either in this country or abroad." [109] Twenty-one railroads were represented by counsel. Only seven unions sent replies to the Committee, and none was represented at the hearings.

Discrimination against Negro railroad employees was particularly unacceptable in light of the shortage of experienced workers. As Mr. Crum stated, "Only two weeks ago, the Director of the Office of Defense Transportation, Mr. Joseph B. Eastman, announced in the most serious terms, a critical lack of railroad manpower. . . Among the points proposed by Mr. Eastman were a recruiting drive for railroad workers, the utilization of the services of women, the utilization of Mexican workers, and even the utilization of prisoners of war." [110]

Sydney S. Alderman, representing the Southern Railway Company, then replied on behalf of the carriers. Admitting the charges of discrimination and the validity of the evidence submitted by the Committee, he argued that the railroads had to abide by the customs, practices, and traditions of the areas in which they operated. These condoned discrimination and segregation, and could not be disregarded without harming railroad operations, endangering the safety and well-being of Negro workers, and disrupting the war effort. Explaining the labor agreements in question had been negotiated "by processes under the Railway Labor Act and earlier controlling United States labor laws, often with government assistance and approval," he asserted that the railroads were "not at liberty to disregard or violate those agreements." [111] Moreover, he denied that the efficiency of railroad operations had been impaired by discrimination or had in any way hindered the war effort.[112]

---

108. President's Committee on Fair Employment Practice, *A Hearing to Hear Evidence on Complaints of Racial Discrimination in Employment on Certain Railroads of the United States* (Washington: Alderson Reporting Co., 1943), pp. 5, 18.

109. *New York Times*, September 17, 1943, p. 4.

110. *Ibid.*, p. 15.

111. *Ibid.*, pp. 20-34.

112. *Ibid.*, p. 37.

At the conclusion of these statements, more than forty witnesses were called to testify. Prominent among these witnesses were Dr. Herbert R. Northrup, a staff member of the National War Labor Board and author of the soon to be published book, *Organized Labor and the Negro,* Dr. Clyde R. Miller, of the Institute for Propaganda Analysis, and Otto D. Tolischis, who had been a reporter for the *New York Times.* Dr. Northrup verified the continuing existence of discrimination on the railroads while Dr. Miller and Mr. Tolischis commented on the use of racial discrimination as part of the Japanese propaganda. The remainder of the testimony was supplied by railroad employees who had witnessed or suffered the consequences of discrimination in the industry.

On December 1, the FEPC made public directives that had been sent to twenty railroads and seven labor unions ordering them to cease their discriminatory practices and to advise the committee "within thirty days of the receipt of these directives, the steps taken or efforts made to comply therewith." [113] Ten of the carriers and one union were directed to set aside the Southeastern Carrier's Conference Agreement as a violation of the executive order. Both carriers and unions were advised that in the event they refused to comply with the directives, the matter would be referred to the President.

The reply of the railroads was not long in coming. Only two railroads, the Pennsylvania and the New York Central, indicated a willingness to comply. On December 14, the participants of the Southeastern Carrier's Conference Agreement sent a letter to the committee warning that any attempt to enforce the directives "would inevitably disrupt their present peaceful and cooperative relations with their employees, would antagonize the traveling and shipping public served by them. . . would result in stoppages of transportation, and would most gravely and irreparably impair the whole war effort of the country. These railroads cannot assume the responsibility for precipitating such disastrous results." The letter concluded with the contention that "your Committee was and is wholly without constitutional and legal jurisdiction and power to make and issue the directives which it made and issued, and for this reason the said directives are without legal effect." The reply was sent, simultaneously, to every member of Congress, along with a note requesting that the

---

113. *New York Times,* December 1, 1943, p. 15.

Committee's findings and directives, the carriers' original statement made at the hearings, and the answer to the directives be read into the *Congressional Record*.[114]

Two weeks later, the FEPC, by unanimous consent, sent the cases to President Roosevelt. Fourteen companies and seven unions were cited for their discriminatory practices. On January 3, 1944, President Roosevelt announced that he had appointed a committee of three leading citizens, led by Walter Stacy of the North Carolina Supreme Court, to mediate the dispute.[115] The Stacy Committee failed to achieve any results.

The railroad cases represented one of the few instances in which the FEPC was successfully defied by a group of employers and unions who admitted the discriminatory acts of which they were accused. Although the President might have ordered the industry to abandon its discriminatory practices, the strong political and economic forces supporting the carriers and unions, the exigencies of war, and the approaching presidential election prevented him from so doing.

THE STEELE DECISION

Even while the FEPC was exposing the practices of the railroad industry, a private suit brought by a Negro fireman, B. W. Steele, against the Louisville and Nashville Railroad Company was slowly proceeding through the courts. Steele had been one of the complainants in the FEPC's railroad hearings in September. He had been laid off as a direct result of the Southeastern Carriers' Agreement, even though he had seniority dating to 1910. Prior to April 1941, Steele was in the high-paying passenger pool of the L & N, with three other Negro firemen and one white fireman. The jobs of the Negro firemen were then declared vacant and subsequently filled by white employees, all of whom had less seniority than the Negro firemen they replaced. Steele was laid off for sixteen days and then assigned to a less desirable job than those in passenger service. On January 3, 1942, after suit was first filed in the Alabama state courts, he was reassigned to passenger service.

---

114. *Hearings on H. Res. 102 Before the House Special Committee to Investigate Executive Agencies*, 78th Cong., 1st and 2nd Sess., pt. 2, at 2129-2130 (1944).

115. *New York Times*, January 4, 1944, p. 4.

Furthermore, as Steele had testified during the committee hearings and again in court, nearly all the Negro firemen employed by the L & N had been similarly deprived of the jobs to which their seniority entitled them. When Steele was first hired, 98 percent of the firemen in his L & N district were Negroes. Prior to the Southeastern Carriers' Agreement, Negro workers still held 80 percent of the carrier's firing positions. By the time the FEPC hearings finally got underway, the proportion of Negro firemen had dropped to about 20 percent.

The case was first heard before the Alabama Supreme Court which found that as certified representative of the firemen, the Brotherhood had the authority either to create or to destroy the rights of members of the bargaining unit. On December 18, 1944, however, the United States Supreme Court unanimously reversed the state court and found that the union had violated the exclusive bargaining rights granted it by the Railway Labor Act. The Court took the view that the constitutionality of the Railway Labor Act would be open to question if it denied individuals the right to bargain for themselves without imposing a duty on unions to represent all members of the bargaining unit fairly.

The Court chose not to base its decision on the question of constitutionality. Instead, it ruled that "the Railway Labor Act . . . impose(s) on the bargaining representative of a craft or class of employees the duty to exercise fairly the power conferred upon it in behalf of all those for whom it acts, without hostile discrimination against them." [116]

This decision established the basic legal doctrine of union race relations, the duty of fair representation. Union members and nonunion members alike now had to be equally represented by the certified representative. Unions could no longer enter into agreements of the nature of the Southeastern Carriers' Agreement. Although the Court had specifically noted that it did not require unions to admit Negroes to membership, it had opened the legal doors to a wide spectrum of illegal union activities. The major Court decisions arising out of the railroad industry are examined in Chapter VII.

Although this decision was not widely publicized, railway labor leaders were most assuredly cognizant of its implications. Now Negro employees had the nation's court system to turn to for

---

116. *Steele* v. *Louisville & Nashville R. R.*, 323 U. S. 192, 202-203 (1944).

relief. The immediate effects of the *Steele* decision were not significant. In fact, the Brotherhood of Locomotive Firemen ignored the opinions and continued to enforce the now illegal Southeastern Carriers' Agreement until 1948, when damages were awarded against it for its policy on the Norfolk Southern Railway. Even then it continued to enforce it on other southeastern railroads and "separate suits . . . had to be filed on the Southern Railway, Atlantic Coast Line, and Seaboard Air Line Railroad to abrogate the agreement." [117] In the context of other events of this period, it represented a most significant change in public policy.

STATE FEP LEGISLATION

The hearings held by the President's Committee on Fair Employment Practice and the court ruling in *Steele* were directed primarily to the discriminatory practices of southern carriers and unions. Northern and western railroads were, however, also following racially discriminatory practices. The practices were less evident only because few Negro workers were employed in regions outside the South. Those Negro workers in the industry in the North and West were also limited to service and laborer occupations.

The experience of the former Pennsylvania Railroad is illustrative of the occupational distribution of Negroes on northern railroads during World War II. During September 1943 when the data in Table 11 were collected, the Pennsylvania employed more Negro workers than any other firm.[118] The Pennsylvania lines ran to New England, as far South as Washington, and as far West as St. Louis.

It is obvious that although the firm had hired a large number of Negroes, they had been hired into a limited number of occupations. The occupational distribution is indicative of the employment practices and union restrictions discussed in the preceding chapter. Few of the jobs in which Negroes were working provided any opportunity for advancement, regardless of union policy. Perhaps, more significant than the employment of Negroes

---

117. *Hearings on Federal Fair Employment Practice Act, Before a Special Subcommittee of the House Committee on Education and Labor,* 81st Cong. 1st Sess. 220 (1949).

118. "Occupational Status of Negro Railroad Employees," *Monthly Labor Review,* Vol. 56 (March 1943), p. 484.

TABLE 11. *Railroad Industry*
Negro Employees by Occupation
Pennsylvania Railroad, September 1942

Occupation	Number of Employees	
Shop Crafts		2,160
Boilermakers	18	
Carmen	40	
Electricians	5	
Helpers, all shop crafts	350	
Machinists	14	
Other shop craft occupations	75	
Maintenance of Way and Structures		6,257
Helpers	12	
Plumbers	2	
Track foremen and assistants	29	
Trackmen (laborers)	6,214	
Dining Car Service		3,147
Chefs and cooks	549	
Waiters, dishwashers, and kitchen help	2,598	
Station Service Employees		2,952
Baggagemen	317	
Freight truckers	2,012	
Porters	623	
Miscellaneous		1,639
General laborers inc. station	380	
Janitors and cleaners	437	
Watchmen	209	
Other occupations	613	
Total		16,155

Source: "Occupational Status of Negro Railroad Employees," *Monthly Labor Review*, Vol. 56 (March 1943), p. 485.

in the occupations listed is the complete lack of Negroes in train and engine service, clerical positions, and supervisory positions other than in track maintenance. There was not one Negro engineer, fireman, conductor, or trainman in the entire work force. Evidence indicates that this occupational distribution was common for Negro railroad workers in the North during the 1940's, and of course, prior thereto.

The existence of continuing employment discrimination in the North as well as the increasing public pressure to eliminate racial discrimination prompted several state legislatures to pass enforceable fair employment practice laws. The first state laws prohibiting employment discrimination were passed in 1945 by New York and New Jersey. They were followed by laws in Massachusetts in 1946, in Connecticut in 1947, and by twenty other states by 1964. In almost every state, unions were "prominent in the passage of these laws, and in states like California, Michigan, Pennsylvania, and New York the unions were probably the decisive forces causing the laws to be passed." [119]

The New York FEP law established the New York State Commission Against Discrimination (SCAD) as the earliest and strongest of the state committees. It should not be surprising that one of the first actions taken by the Commission was against the railroad unions which continued to restrict their membership to white workers. Largely as a result of the efforts of SCAD, the following railroad unions removed their color bars on the dates indicated: Maintenance of Way Employees, 1946; Railway Yardmasters of North America, 1946; Railway and Steamship Clerks, 1947; Switchmen's Union of North America, 1947; Blacksmiths and Boilermakers, 1947; and the International Association of Machinists, 1948.[120] The following organizations made their discriminatory clauses inoperative in New York state: the Brotherhood of Locomotive Engineers; the Brotherhood of Locomotive Firemen and Enginemen; Order of Railroad Telegraphers; Brotherhood of Railway Carmen; Order of Railroad Conductors; and the Railway Mail Association.[121]

The most obstinate of the unions was the Brotherhood of Locomotive Engineers. On October 10, 1947, one month before the

---

119. Ray Marshall, *The Negro and Organized Labor* (New York: John Wiley & Sons, Inc., 1965), p. 276.

120. *Ibid.*, p. 278. The Blacksmiths merged with the Boilermakers in 1952.

121. *Ibid.*

Grand Chief Engineer used his authority to waive the race bar in New York, a letter was sent to SCAD. In part the letter stated that:

We are of the opinion that your Commission does not understand that whether a person is admitted depends upon the will of the members in the respective subdivisions to which such a person makes application. And, it may interest you to know that included among members of the B. of L. E. are full blooded Indians, Mexicans, halfbreeds, etc.

Furthermore, the section of our laws to which your Commission objects has been in our Statutes for many, many years and we do not have any official record of any person having been denied membership because of race, religion, creed or color.[122]

Similar action was taken during this period by the recently established Massachusetts Fair Employment Practice Commission. In 1948, the first important cases involving employment discrimination were closed after joint action by the Massachusetts and New York commissions. These cases arose out of forty-eight complaints filed against a major eastern railroad alleging that Negro employees were denied equal promotion opportunities to the job of steward on dining cars. Furthermore, the railroad was then replacing dining cars with grill cars and staffing them with newly-hired white personnel. After investigation the allegations of these complaints were found to be substantially accurate. The complaints were eventually resolved through conciliation.[123]

Additional complaints were filed accusing the railroads of hiring only white track laborers and denying promotion opportunities to Negro redcaps. These cases were closed in 1949 with conciliated agreements to provide relief to the complainants.[124]

The simple elimination of formal race bars did not, of course, provide immediate access to improved job opportunities for Negro workers. In fact, the changes initiated in membership requirements were generally made more with a public relations motive than with an apparent concern for Negro rights. The actions of the Railway Clerks in the immediate post-war period are indicative of true union sentiment, and apparently illustrative of sentiment among the other unions which eliminated their formal membership restrictions.

---

122. *Ibid.*, p. 279.

123. Elwood S. McKenny, "Fair Employment in Massachusetts," Part II, *Phylon*, Vol. XIII, No. 2 (1952), p. 142-143.

124. *Ibid.*, p. 144.

The Clerks' Case

The New York State Commission Against Discrimination had notified the Clerks and other railroad unions in 1946 that unions which did not provide full membership rights to Negroes were in violation of state law. A committee including several prominent southern members was appointed by the then union president, George Harrison. This committee recommended to the 1947 convention that Brotherhood charters should be given to each of the auxiliary Negro lodges. In effect, auxiliary lodges were to become segregated lodges, differing from their prior status only in their now "equal" memberships within the union. Moreover, the convention delegates were assured by the Brotherhood's officers that the proposed changes would mean very little because each lodge maintained the right to determine its own membership qualifications and could refuse to accept traveling delegates.[125] Proponents of this change argued during heated debate that the Brotherhood was being denounced as un-American, it was at a disadvantage in representation elections, and that it was liable for prosecution under the new FEP laws. President Harrison revealed in his statement a factor of growing importance. He stated that he had become embarrassed at AFL conventions as delegates from other unions continually pointed to the Clerks as a union which discriminated, and that his embarrassment grew as the number of unions following restrictive practices diminished. After additional assurances from Harrison that the changes by the national union would not impose changes in local custom, the delegates voted to strike the word "white" from their constitution. Negro workers were then advised that they could join "white" locals and by 1950 the New York State Commission found only four Brotherhood auxiliaries in New York and New Jersey.[126]

Operating Brotherhoods and the Forced Promotion Rule

If the nonoperating unions were gradually eliminating the last vestiges of formal racial discrimination, at least at the national level, the operating Brotherhoods remained as intransigent as they had been at the end of World War I. Only the relatively small Switchmen's Union, the only AFL affiliate, had removed its formal color bar. The Brotherhood of Locomotive Engineers and

125. Marshall, *op. cit.*, pp. 92-93.

126. *Ibid.*, p. 93.

the Order of Railway Conductors, of course, did not have to expose their practices to close public scrutiny. There simply were no Negro workers in these occupations. This was a customary employment practice that was not to be changed until after the Civil Rights Act of 1964. On the other hand, the Brotherhood of Locomotive Firemen and the Brotherhood of Railroad Trainmen carried on a continuing battle against Negro encroachment on declining union job opportunities. Union efforts had become more discreet but their purpose remained the same.

The Brotherhood of Locomotive Firemen began what was apparently to be the last multiemployer campaign to eliminate Negro firemen in 1948. As indicated previously, the Brotherhood had continued in its efforts to enforce the Southeastern Carriers' Agreement until after World War II. By that time most Negro firemen had been eliminated from engine service on the major Southeastern carriers. At least one carrier, the Gulf, Mobile and Ohio Railroad, had not hired a Negro for a firing position since 1925.[127] This meant that most of the Negro firemen who had been laid off since the early 1940's had at least twenty years of seniority.

The Firemen's campaign began in 1947 when it negotiated an agreement which eliminated the previous contract clause which restricted the percentage of Negroes in diesel service to 50 percent. The new contract gained for the Brotherhood virtually the same provisions that it had been unable to gain in 1941. The new clause stipulated that only "promotable" firemen be employed on all passenger and freight runs. Nonpromotable firemen, Negroes, could be kept only in yard operations and on the "extraboard" or reserve work force.[128]

The Firemen, however, were still not satisfied. They devised a subtle plan for eliminating the few remaining Negroes from firing positions. On January 28, 1948, they proposed to the members of the Southeastern Carriers' Conference a plan to test all locomotive firemen to determine their eligibility for promotion to engineer positions. Each employee would be given three opportunities at ninety day intervals to pass the exams. Those who were still unsuccessful after three attempts were to be dismissed from service. On the surface, the plan was apparently equitable.

---

127. *Mitchell* v. *Gulf, Mobile & Ohio R.R.*, 91 F. Supp. 175, 177-179 (N.D. Ala. 1950).

128. *Id.*

In fact, the plan was manifestly unfair to the Negro firemen. With few exceptions, the remaining Negro firemen had been hired many years in the past. The only hiring qualifications necessary for these men had been the stamina to withstand the rigorous work of shoveling coal. Little attention had been paid to their educational background. They had been hired as firemen and were never expected to rise higher. The white firemen, on the other hand, had been placed in firing positions only to gain the requisite knowledge for promotion to engineer. Hiring criteria had been those used for engineers, not for firemen. Now to ask the Negro firemen to compete in examination with the white firemen would have meant immediate dismissal for all the last Negro firemen on these railroads. Fortunately, the plan was enjoined by the courts shortly after it was proposed.[129]

UNION SHOP AMENDMENT TO THE RAILWAY LABOR ACT

The final change prior to the 1960's in the legal environment pertaining to union discrimination was the passage of an amendment to the Railway Labor Act allowing the negotiation of union shop agreements. The debate in Congress over this issue closely followed related discussions during the passage of the Taft-Hartley Act. The Railway Labor Act as amended in 1934 outlawed the closed shop in an attempt to eliminate company dominated unions. Now that company unions had been eliminated, the standard unions desired to gain the union shop so that the employees must join the union within a stipulated time after hiring. If the employee refuses at the least to pay union dues and initiation fees, he is subject to discharge. Under the Taft-Hartley Act the employee may not be discharged for any reason other than payment of union financial obligations.

Spokesmen for Negro rights saw the coming Congressional action as an excellent opportunity to gain membership at last in the many railroad labor organizations. Certainly, if Congress was going to allow labor organizations to negotiate union shops, all employees under union jurisdiction should be entitled to full union membership. Until now, if the Negro employee so chose,

---

129. *Id.* See also, *Rolax* v. *Atlantic Coast Line R.R.,* 186 F.2d 473 (4th Cir. 1950); *Locomotive Firemen and Enginemen* v. *Palmer,* 178 F.2d 722 (D.C. Cir. 1950).

there were no provisions which obligated him to support the union. It was highly possible that this might now change.

During hearings before the House Committee on Intrastate and Foreign Commerce in May and June of 1950,[130] a long list of Negro labor leaders from the railroad industry appeared to propose amendments outlawing discrimination. Several long, documented descriptions of past union discrimination were submitted for the record. It was apparent, however, that regardless of personal sentiment Congress was not yet ready to proscribe the membership restrictions of the politically powerful railway unions.

The final amendment, Public Law No. 914, was clearly a compromise. Negro workers who were not permitted to join the union with full membership privileges were not obligated to support the union if a union shop agreement was agreed upon. There were no direct statements pertaining to union discrimination. As Congress stated, union shop provisions could be negotiated into labor agreements,

Provided, that no such agreement shall require such conditions of employment with respect to employees to whom membership is not available upon the same terms and conditions as are generally applicable to any other member or with respect to employees to whom membership was denied or terminated for any reason other than the failure of the employee to tender [financial obligations] . . .[131]

Although Congress had abstained from attacking directly the union racial policies, it did provide an important incentive for the unions to eliminate their restricted membership provisions. Membership rolls and union income had declined rapidly from the employment peak during the war. Congress had now provided the means to achieve needed income, the union shop. Yet the union could not gain the added financial support without altering their racial policies.

EMPLOYMENT TRENDS

Employment in the railroad industry rose to a peak in 1945 of over 1,460,000 workers. The employment decline that began in that year continued through 1960, with only a brief interrup-

130. *Hearings on Railway Labor Act Amendments Before the House Committee on Interstate and Foreign Commerce,* 81st Cong. 2nd Sess. (1950).

131. Public Law No. 914, ch. 1220, 64 U.S. Stat. 1238 (1951).

tion during the economic buildup of the first months of the
Korean War. Overall for the period 1940 to 1960 railroad employment fell by 17 percent, from 1,135,019 to 941,214. (See
Table 12.) Negro employment quite surprisingly fell only slightly more, by 20 percent, from 96,315 in 1940 to 77,194 in 1960.
Similarities in changing employment patterns for Negro and
white workers, however, go no further.

District Data

Although there are no data available for the growth in Negro
employment during World War II, it apparently was quite significant. Even as late as 1950 the number of Negro males working in the industry was 137,769, a 45 percent increase since 1940.
The growth in total male employment during the decade was
only 20 percent. This is quite surprising in light of the continued
hostility of the industry's labor movement. Moreover, these gains
made by Negro workers were not concentrated in any one area
of the country. Even in the Southern District, where Negro
workers were already extensively employed, the industry added
Negroes to its payrolls at a relative rate about equal to that of
white workers. While white employment rose 21 percent, Negro
employment rose 19 percent. In the Western District, which was
undergoing a vast postwar boom, total employment expanded by
29 percent while Negro employment grew by 59 percent. Similar
patterns developed in the Eastern District which had a growth
rate for total and Negro employment of 18 and 73 percent respectively. These growth rates reflect both the migratory patterns of the Negro population, and the expansion in railroad
services as economic development spread westward.

During this same period, female employment expanded even
more rapidly. War time labor shortages had forced the industry
to hire women not only for office work but also for maintenance
and operating duties. Even though returning service men rapidly displaced women, the number of women remaining in the industry in 1950 still stood at 72,753, a 104 percent increase since
1940. Negro women in this period had been hired as well but
generally only for manual positions. By 1950, the number of
Negro women working in the industry had grown by 358 percent
to 5,728. This growth had followed a geographic pattern similar
to that of Negro males.

TABLE 12. *Railroad Industry*
Employment by Race and Railroad Districts
United States, 1940-1960

District	1940			1950			1960		
	Total	Negro	Percent Negro	Total	Negro	Percent Negro	Total	Negro	Percent Negro
United States	1,135,019	96,315	8.5	1,386,961	143,497	10.3	941,214	77,194	8.2
Male	1,099,361	95,064	8.6	1,314,208	137,769	10.5	888,911	74,072	8.3
Female	35,658	1,251	3.5	72,753	5,728	7.9	52,303	3,122	6.0
Eastern District	613,241	35,027	5.7	724,213	60,563	8.4	480,758	35,398	7.4
Southern District	137,801	36,272	26.3	166,046	43,121	26.0	107,454	20,312	18.9
Western District	383,977	25,016	6.5	496,702	39,813	8.0	351,542	21,451	6.1

Source: *U.S. Census of Population:*

  1940: Vol. III, *The Labor Force*, Tables 76 and 18.

  1950: Vol. II, *Characteristics of the Population*, Tables 133 and 83.

  1960: Vol. II, *Characteristics of the Population*, Tables 213 and 129.

Note: The districts are not strictly comparable with those shown elsewhere. States of Michigan and Illinois were included in the Eastern District; Louisiana in the Western District. (See Figure 1, p. 12.)

The Decade of the 1950's

Industry employment in the following decade, from 1950 to 1960, showed a decline of 32 percent. Although this was only a continuation of a long term trend, it was the largest absolute decrease of any industry during the decade. Negro employees were hit particularly hard by payroll cutbacks. Forty-six percent of the Negro male workers were separated from the industry during the decade. Negro female employees lost a similar proportion of their jobs. In fact, Negro male workers had proportionately lost all the gains they had made during the previous decade. In 1940 Negro males accounted for 8.6 percent of the male work force; the 1960 statistics showed them as 8.3 percent.

The cutbacks in total employment for the decade were proportionately similar, reflecting the rather general industry decline and industry wide introduction of technological developments. The West experienced the smallest decline in total employment, 29 percent, reflecting the overall economic growth of the region. The Eastern District, on the other hand, had the slowest economic growth and a relative decline in railroad employment, 34 percent. Finally, the South, which was just beginning its economic growth and in which the railroad industry was traditionally more labor intensive, had a decline of 35 percent.

Negro employment totals by the end of the decade reflected the general decline in railroad activity. In each district except the East they had decreased more rapidly than total employment, which would be expected in light of the disproportionately large cutbacks in laborer and service occupations. Moreover, Negro employees would be expected to have had a differential in job tenure. They, as a group, would have had less job tenure because of their rapid hiring rate in the previous decade. In the Eastern District, 34 percent of the Negro employees were separated from the industry. The Western District experienced a 46 percent decline in Negro employment. The Southern District had the largest absolute and relative decrease in Negro employment, 53 percent. An additional factor in the South may well have been an increased retirement rate among Negro employees hired in the twenties and thirties.

Occupational Distribution

The occupational distribution for Negro employees did not change significantly during this twenty year period. Employment in all major occupations declined, with the largest cutbacks coming in the less skilled occupations. The skilled occupations declined rapidly through retirements and other attrition. Few employees were upgraded into these positions. The traditional industry employment practice of giving preference to relatives of present employees limited the movement of Negroes into these occupations. There were virtually no Negroes hired for white collar occupations.

In maintenance of equipment occupations, the shop craft unions had all eliminated formal racial bars by the early 1950's. A few Negro workers had been employed in these skilled occupations during the war years but they were employed largely in those shops which were not organized by the national unions. When Negroes in these occupations did come under the jurisdiction of the national unions, they were occasionally listed as American Indians or other circuitous means to allow them to join the local union. The Railway Carmen had the largest number of Negro members but they were generally employed as coach cleaners. The apprentice employee group experienced the largest cutback, with many large shops virtually eliminating training positions. A large number of Negroes were employed as helpers, an occupation differentiated from that of apprentice in many instances only by its lack of promotional opportunities. As one knowledgeable government employee stated, "Helpers only became craftsmen after everyone else had died." The prevalence of nepotism in initial hiring, the drastic cutbacks in employment, the strict adherence to established lines of progression and a typical location of shops outside major metropolitan areas limited employment gains by Negroes through the 1950's.

Negroes were able to gain new job opportunities in maintenance of way and structures occupations. Prior to 1940 and throughout most of the 1940's, Negro workers had been restricted to track laborer positions. By 1960 Negroes had moved into positions as section foremen in track maintenance, as portable equipment operators as new maintenance machines were introduced into track laying and repair and occasionally into positions as linemen and groundmen in signal maintenance. They were still not employed generally in structures maintenance, except in the South, as signalmen and signal maintainers. Even though laboring positions were cutback drastically during this period, Negro employment in these positions increased proportionately in all regions except the South.

In train and engine service, Negroes made few if any gains. Even as late as 1960 there were virtually no Negroes employed as locomotive engineers or train conductors. More important, however, were the job losses experienced by Negroes in locomotive firemen positions. Negroes filled 5.2 percent of these positions nationally in 1940, and 18.1 percent of the positions in the South. By 1960, only 2.3 percent of the nation's firemen and 7.3 percent of those in the South were Negro.[132] The continuing efforts of the Brotherhood of Locomotive Firemen which still maintained an all white clause in its constitution, was in part responsible for these losses, but an overriding factor was a differential in retirement rates among Negro and white firemen. Job tenure among Negro firemen began as a rule prior to World War II and generally much earlier, because few were employed thereafter. Likewise, few Negroes were employed in occupations coming under the jurisdiction of the Trainmen by the end of the period.

Those gains which Negroes did make in the operating occupations were generally made in yard positions. An increasing number of Negro workers were used as "car riders," or brakemen, and as switch tenders in "humping" operations. These positions are essentially unskilled positions but their acquisition represented a breakthrough for Negroes in the industry. Negroes continued to work as hostlers and hostlers helpers. Negroes were not employed, however, in supervisory positions in the yards.

In transportation occupations other than those in train, engine, or yard service, there was a great disparity in the proportion of Negroes working in the wide variety of jobs. Those occupations which provided services to passengers in terminals and in the few remaining dining cars, were staffed almost exclusively by Negroes. This was true to a lesser degree in the several freight handling occupations. On the other hand, few if any Negroes were employed in train control, communication, or station management. As a rule, those occupations which entailed decision making were staffed with white employees, while those which were routine, menial tasks were filled with Negro workers. This tradition has been invariant in the industry since the turn of the century and was still maintained by 1960.

---

132. *U. S. Census of Population: 1940:* Vol. III, *The Labor Force,* Part 1, Table 62; and *1960:* PC (1) 1D, *U. S. Summary, Detailed Characteristics,* Tables 205 and 257.

Among those occupations in railroad office buildings, a clear distinction can be made in the employment patterns in the traditional white collar occupations and in building maintenance and service occupations. Managerial, professional and clerical employees were white; Negroes were employed only as janitors, elevator operators, and building maintenance personnel. Even in large metropolitan areas few Negro workers, male or female, were hired into office positions. The only apparent exception to this otherwise clear occupational division was among lower level clerks which typically do not work in offices but rather perform such tasks as sorting mail in major postal distribution centers. The occupational division between Negro and white employees has been almost as distinct as that maintained in train and engine service.

A joint study by the New York and New Jersey state commissions against discrimination in June 1957 indicates the extent of continued pattern discrimination experienced by Negro workers at the end of the 1940-1960 period. The survey data, which included employment on nineteen railroads in New York and New Jersey, are summarized in Table 13. The employment patterns in other industries at this time support the assumption that Negro workers should have a "better" occupational distribution in this area than in any other large section of the nation. At the very least, the sample is representative of Negro employment in the railroad industry in an urban, industrialized region. It is striking how similar these statistics are to that of the Pennsylvania Railroad in 1942 presented in Table 11. An entirely new era of interest in civil rights had begun and yet Negro railroad employment had undergone little noticeable change.

In office and general jobs, 40 percent of the Negro workers were janitors and cleaners. Some degree of representation had been gained among clerks, secretaries, stenographers, typists, and office-machine operators. The report indicated that each of the seven largest carriers employed at least one Negro in these occupations. The carriers had hired 344 workers for office and general positions in the three month period from March 15 to June 14, 1957; only four of these were Negro. Two were hired as typists, one as a janitor, and one as a motor vehicle operator.

Negro employees were nearly excluded from operating positions. All but five of the 118 Negroes in these jobs were employed by one railroad, and even in this firm the work was mostly in yard occupations. There was one Negro brakeman and

TABLE 13.   *Railroad Industry*
Employment by Race and Occupation or Major Job Category
New York and New Jersey, 1957

Occupation or Major Job Category	All Employees	Negro	Percent Negro
Total	83,809	8,909	10.6
Office and general	16,836	627	3.7
Operating transportation	20,099	118	0.6
Transportation exclusive of operating	17,302	5,118	29.6
Chefs and cooks	353	345	97.7
Waiters, kitchen helpers, camp cooks	721	657	91.1
Train attendants	168	153	91.1
Baggage agents and assistants	86	33	38.4
Baggage, parcel and station attendants	2,342	1,248	53.3
Truckers	2,272	822	36.2
Callers, loaders, scalers, freight inspectors	2,142	929	43.4
Foremen, general	87	—	—
Foremen, assistant general	36	5	13.9
Foremen, gang	450	29	6.4
Laborers, common	1,135	622	54.8
Train dispatchers and directors	297	—	—
Station masters and agents, major stations	862	—	—
Station Agents, smaller stations	494	2	.04
Telegraphers and telephoners, chief	43	—	—
Telegraphers, telephoners, and towermen, other	1,438	2	0.1
Other transportation occupations	4,376	271	6.2

TABLE 13.   (continued)

Occupation or Major Job Category	All Employees	Negro	Percent Negro
Maintenance (equipment and way)	29,572	3,046	10.3
Foremen, general and department, and skilled labor	2,059	2	0.1
Foremen, other	1,196	34	2.8
Electrical workers	2,166	4	0.2
Machinists	2,094	17	0.8
Boilermakers and blacksmiths	493	1	0.2
Sheet metal workers	753	5	0.7
Carmen	5,175	238	4.6
Apprentices, regular (equipment & stores)	240	2	0.8
Skilled trades helpers (equipment)	1,885	128	6.8
Coach cleaners	1,640	700	42.7
Portable and pump equipment operators and helpers	530	33	6.2
Laborers, inc. extra gang and section men	7,585	1,813	23.9
Signal workers	1,360	—	—
Linesmen and groundsmen	381	2	0.5
Other maintenance occupations	2,015	67	3.3

Source: *Railroad Employment in New York and New Jersey,* A Joint Study by the New York State Commission Against Discrimination and the New Jersey Division Against Discrimination, 1957.

Note: 19 Companies.

one Negro road freight engineer. During the previous three month period, none of 291 new hires in operating transportation were Negro.

Nearly all the remaining Negro workers were employed in service and laborer positions in transportation, other than operating and maintenance. Among the shop crafts and skilled employees in structures maintenance (not listed), only the carmen and carpenters were more than 1.0 percent Negro. Hiring in the three month period for these groups included 1,587 employees, of which 442 were Negroes. Without exception, each new Negro employee was hired into positions in which substantial numbers of Negroes were already employed one dozen years after these states had enacted fair employment practice legislation.

SUMMARY

Throughout these two decades, A. Philip Randolph kept up his pressure on other union officials. His rallying cries against union discrimination were a feature of AFL and after the merger, AFL-CIO conventions. No little credit for the elimination of formal union bars against Negroes can be attributed to him. Moreover, since nearly all independent railroad unions except the engineers and the conductors joined the AFL-CIO after the merger, his continued pressure reached most unions.

The *Steele* and consequent court decisions also stopped some of the most virulent discrimination. Yet the net changes were few. Managerial hiring policy did not alter substantially and state fair employment practice legislation forced only gradual change. The occupational distribution for Negro (nonwhite) workers had remained stable since 1940. Although comparable Census data are not available for 1940 (nonwhite employment given only for the South) and 1960, it is clear that virtually no progress had been made in twenty years.

Nearly 80 percent of the nonwhite railroad workers in the South in 1940 held laboring or service positions; in 1960 70 percent were in such positions. The only significant change was the decrease in the percentage of nonwhite employees living in the South, 76.9 percent to 54.0 in 1960. Evidence indicates that the apparent decrease in Negro craftsmen may have been a fact with an aging work force and few upgradings.

The industry in 1960 held little promise for improved employment opportunities for Negroes. Business and employment had

TABLE 14.   Railroad Industry
Employment by Color, Sex, and Occupational Group
United States, 1960

	Male			Female		
Occupational Group	Total	Non-white	Percent Non-white	Total	Non-white	Percent Non-white
Managers and officials	79,847	372	0.5	627	—	—
Professional, technical, and kindred workers	16,629	62	0.4	1,100	61	5.5
Sales workers	1,906	20	1.0	20	—	—
Clerical and kindred workers	160,750	4,361	2.7	42,427	364	0.9
Craftsmen, foremen, and kindred workers	269,756	5,614	2.1	537	—	—
Operatives and kindred workers	198,252	10,680	5.4	944	121	12.8
Laborers	119,460	34,560	28.9	2,762	1,520	55.0
Service workers	35,142	18,958	53.9	2,574	995	38.7
Occupations not reported	11,020	1,865	16.9	675	40	5.9
Total	892,762	76,492	8.6	51,666	3,101	6.0

Source: U. S. Census of Population, 1960, PC(2) 7A Occupational Characteristics, Table 36.

Note: Negroes were 96.3 percent of the nonwhite employment.

declined precipitously since the end of World War II. The plight
of Negro employees was understandably a minor concern of
harassed industry officials. Moreover, the personnel function,
upon which successful minority employment programs must rest,
had only perfunctory responsibilities with little purpose other
than as a record keeping support function for collective bargaining. Hiring and recruitment programs were unnecessary;
employee referrals typically met employment needs. In general,

the carriers were unable and uninterested in supporting the necessary policy changes to afford Negroes improved employment opportunities. A strong stimulus was needed to reverse employment practices and traditions now proceeding for over a century.

The long history of discrimination had had an effect on the Negro community as well. While discrimination continued in the railroad industry, it was slowly being mitigated in many other industries. Whereas railroad employment, despite its obvious limitations, had once been among the most coveted work Negro workers could obtain, this was no longer true. Negroes now were beginning to apply for work in other industries which paid as well or better than the low skill railroad occupations open to them. The goodwill the carriers had always had with the Negro community had been allowed to dissolve.

CHAPTER V

Civil Rights in a Declining Industry, 1960-1969

The recessions of 1957-1958 and 1961 dealt the railroad industry a crippling blow. While the Gross National Product (in constant dollars) declined only in 1958, and in actual dollars continued to rise during the period 1957-1961 by an annual average of 4.2 percent, railroad operating revenues fell from $10.5 billion in 1957 to $9.2 billion in 1961, a 12.4 percent decline. Moreover, net operating income in the industry declined during the same period from $922 million to $538 million, a 42 percent decrease. It was not until 1966 that net income was to recover to the billion dollar level. The operating problems resulting from the financial crisis portended serious questions for the future of the generally low skilled Negro employees.

Among other consequences of the decline, the carriers began a protracted drive to effect labor cost reductions. Foremost among the several announced goals of the industry was the virtual elimination of firemen on diesel locomotives in freight and yard service. Other proposals included the revision of the 40-year-old mileage pay standards for engine and train crews to reflect the rapid increases in train speeds, elimination of the restrictions preventing the interchange of yard and road crews, and the abolishment of rules stipulating the size of train crews. The dispute over these proposed changes was not resolved until 1963 when a special compulsory arbitration panel established by Congress issued an award which in large part sustained the carriers' position.[133] As a result of the award, over 18,000 of the 35,000 firemen had been eliminated from service by 1966.[134] Although this lengthy dispute has been recently reopened, reem-

---

133. Public Law 88-108, 77 Stat. 132 (1963) and Railroad Arbitration Board Award No. 282.

134. *Wall Street Journal*, October 3, 1968, p. 3.

ployment of the firemen is most unlikely. Related work rule changes have become increasingly important as the *quid pro quo* for wage increases throughout the decade.

Concurrently a rapid mechanization and consequent reduction in employment in those occupations requiring little skill occurred. Employees in maintenance operations were particularly hard hit by these reductions. Track and structures maintenance employees generally were reduced by nearly 40 percent while employees in equipment maintenance operations declined by over 30 percent. Employees in laborer and helper positions, many of whom were Negro, experienced cutbacks which eliminated as much as 50 percent of the 1956 employment by the end of 1961. Although employment attrition was continued throughout the decade of the 1960's, the rapid initial reductions consequent to the financial crisis were an important factor exacerabating employee relations during the period. Attempts by predominantly white railroad labor organizations to preserve employment opportunities for their members meant increased resistance to Negro advancement, and at the same time reduced the number of openings available for such advancement.

STIRRINGS OF CHANGE, 1960-1968

Despite rapid attrition, the carriers continue to hire a large number of new employees annually. Since 1960 the industry has added an annual average of 75,625 workers with no previous railroad experience. In addition, an average of 23,125 workers were rehired. (See Table 5.) Although many of these men have been hired into transient positions related to annual maintenance programs, the high turnover affords the industry with an opportunity to improve gradually the Negro employment situation both qualitatively and quantitatively.

The 1962 New York Commission Study [135]

A study conducted by the New York State Commission for Human Rights in 1962 as a follow-up to the previously discussed analysis of railroad employment in New York and New Jersey in 1957, indicated that the assignment of black workers to menial tasks continued to be a fact. At the same time, however, the ap-

---

135. New York State Commission for Human Rights, "Railroad Employment In New York State, 1957 and 1962," mimeo. (1962).

pearance of black workers in occupations from which they had previously been excluded is evidence of the beginning of change. The 1962 study was limited to five carriers with a combined employment of 42,000 workers. Although total employment for these firms had decreased by 20.9 percent from the time of the earlier study, Negro employment had fallen by only 13.7 percent. Consequently, Negro workers increased as a percentage of all employees from 9.9 to 10.9 percent. Moreover, employment records for three-month periods immediately preceding each study showed that Negroes increased from 15.3 to 32.5 percent of the new hires. Over 90 percent of the Negro workers were still employed in maintenance positions or in transportation occupations other than those directly involved in the operation of trains.

The employees in passenger service occupations such as chef, cook, waiter, kitchen helper and train attendant were over 90 percent Negro; baggage, parcel and station attendants, callers, loaders, scalers, freight inspectors, truckers and laborers were together over 40 percent Negro. In contrast, among 700 train dispatchers, station masters and agents, only one was Negro; and among 689 telegraphers, telephoners and towermen, two were Negro. In maintenance operations, 1,093 of 1,399 Negro workers were in the unskilled jobs of laborer and coach cleaner. There was, however, a slight increase in Negro employment in the more skilled occupations of carmen, electricians and machinists. Significantly, Negro employees were hired into skilled maintenance positions for the first time on two railroads. Operating occupations in which 10,461 persons were employed remained closed in general to Negro workers; only 19 Negroes were so employed on the five railroads and all but three of these men were employed by one railroad. Finally, in office and general work, no Negroes were employed as executives, officials, staff assistants, professionals, chief clerks, traffic or claim agents, nor as ticket agents. The large group of clerks, secretaries, stenographers, typists and office machine operators were only about one percent Negro in 1962, a proportion similar to that in 1957. On the other hand, there were 151 Negro janitors and cleaners out of staffs totaling 247. Overall, of the five carriers included in the study, four reported Negro employees in job categories in 1962 where none had been reported in 1957. These occupations included certain clerical positions, ticket collector, skilled trademen, carmen, signalmen and motor vehicle operators—unimpressive changes but changes nevertheless.

Government Action and Discriminatory Unionism

Positive actions taken by the carriers were, of course, not initiated solely on their own volition. President Kennedy, in March 1961, had issued Executive Order 10925, which provided that contractors must take "affirmative action" to ensure that applicants and employees be treated without regard to their race, creed, color or national origin. Kennedy further established the President's Committee on Equal Employment Opportunity (PCEEO) which replaced a similar agency created by President Eisenhower. The Committee alone possessed the right, which it never exercised, to cancel government contracts as a result of noncompliance with the directives of the Committee. Consequent to the President's action, the General Counsel of the Post Office Department (POD) was assigned the responsibility of handling all complaints of discrimination by the railroad carriers. Later the authority to conduct compliance reviews was transferred from the General Counsel to the POD Office of Regional Administration. The director of the latter office became the Contract Compliance Officer for the industry, but the daily administrative problems were given to a deputy contracts compliance officer and a small staff of examiners. Although several exploratory discussions were held with major railroads in 1963, the POD did not initiate any intensive compliance programs until the last half of the decade had begun. As a result of Executive Order 11246, issued by President Johnson in September 1965, the PCEEO was replaced by the Office of Federal Contract Compliance (OFCC) to which the POD's compliance office presently reports.

By limiting the responsibility of the POD to the railroad and trucking industries, the compliance examiners investigating the employment practices of the carriers have been able to develop an expertise in the problems of the industry which has facilitated the development of relationships between the industry and the government. Although the EEOC and the OFCC have chosen not to focus their research efforts and limited monies on railroad employment practices as they have done for several other industries, ostensibly because the railroads have too few job opportunities, the POD compliance office has gained extensive cooperation from the industry.

Segregated Lodges and Fair Employment

Undoubtedly the most visible measures taken by government during the early 1960's continued to be those of the state agencies, particularly the New York Commission. That agency continued its vigorous interest in the discriminatory practices of the industry by taking action against the segregated locals maintained by the railroad brotherhoods. In attempting to integrate three lodges of the Brotherhood of Railway Clerks, the Commission was resisted by both white and Negro members, the latter fearing that their limited power would be negated as minority members of reformed lodges. After carrying on intermittent negotiations from 1957 to 1961, the Commission was able to gain compliance by threatening to prevent enforcement of union shop agreements in the case of Negro workers who did not have equal access to membership. Subsequently, thirty Negro workers were accepted by a previously all-white lodge.[136]

Similarly, in 1965 the Commission negotiated an agreement with the Brotherhood of Locomotive Engineers to allow a Negro employed as a motorswitchman to become a member.[137] This case was particularly significant in light of the continued exclusion of Negroes by constitutional provision. The provisions were finally deleted the following year, largely as a result of the efforts of the Commission.

The increasing national interest in racial discrimination was in part responsible for other changes during the early part of the decade, but the results were not always salutary. The Clerks' union, for example, began to eliminate many of its segregated locals. It frequently did so, however, by eliminating the jobs of Negro workers. Union agreements affecting segregated locals typically provided for job jurisdiction along racially separated lines, with the Negro locals having authority over only the menial positions. By reclassifying the traditional Negro job categories and declaring them to be within the jurisdiction of the white locals, the Brotherhoods were able to force the dis-

---

136. F. Ray Marshall, *The Negro and Organized Labor* (New York: John Wiley & Sons, Inc., 1965), pp. 279-280.

137. New York State Commission for Human Rights, Employment Division, "Report of Progress—1965." Mimeo. (1966). This agency was formerly known at the State Commission Against Discrimination. It now operates under a third name.

missal of Negro workers from long held jobs and further to replace them with less senior white employees.[138]

The concern of state and federal agencies with eliminating segregated locals is thus often a simplistic approach to the problem. The real issue is segregated seniority and discriminatory hiring and promotion policies. Studies of the tobacco and paper industries confirm what has been found here: that the segregated locals, although instituted as a blatantly discriminating device, have in fact served as a focal point for black protest and as pressure group for action within the international unions; and that their elimination has reduced, not enhanced, the ability of black workers to fight for their rights.[139]

In addition, the Brotherhood of Locomotive Firemen removed the provision in its constitution banning Negro members in 1964. Significantly, this change was not effected until "after the railroad 'work rules' arbitration had made it virtually certain that few, if any, additional firemen would ever be hired on American railroads." [140]

Evidence developed by the Department of Justice indicates that racially segregated locals and discriminatory lines of seniority still existed, at least on southern carriers, by the mid-1960's and perhaps later. Those Brotherhoods cited by the Justice Department as organizations which continued to maintain segregated locals were the Railway Clerks and Maintenance of Way Employees. In addition, the United Transportation Union was alleged to have excluded Negro workers from any form of membership.[141] Interviews conducted by the author have further found that at least the Railway Carmen among the other rail-

---

138. In 1965 the Equal Employment Opportunity Commission found "reasonable cause" in a Texas case against this union involving segregated locals and separate racial jobs classifications. (*Moses LeRoy* v. *Local 1534, Brotherhood of Railway Clerks*, Houston, Texas, Case No. 5-8-517, November 1, 1965.)

139. See Herbert R. Northrup and Richard L. Rowan, *Negro Employment in Southern Industry*, Studies of Negro Employment, Vol. IV (Philadelphia: Industrial Research Unit, Wharton School of Finance and Commerce, University of Pennsylvania, 1970), Part One, pp. 37-45, 55-58, 112-117 and Part Three, pp. 33-39, 84-87.

140. Arthur M. Ross, "The Negro in the American Economy," in Ross and Hill, eds., *Employment, Race and Poverty* (New York: Harcourt, Brace and World, 1967), p. 8.

141. Pre-trial brief for Plaintiff at 27, 28, *United States* v. *Jacksonville Terminal Co.*, Civil Action No. 68-239-Civil-J (1970).

road unions continue to maintain segregated locals in a few areas. Although it cannot be easily determined how prevalent such practices continue to be, the existence of discrimination by local lodges is evident. These problems are recognized by the national leaderships but action to correct the situation has been restricted and ineffective until very recently. Spokesmen for the labor organizations point out that the strong local autonomy of railroad brotherhoods makes it difficult to impose desired changes at the local level. Reversing a century of militant discrimination is not easily undertaken nor popular with a white membership concerned about declining job opportunities. A number of law suits have been filed and will probably be brought to trial in 1971 dealing with this issue.

NEGRO EMPLOYMENT, 1966-1969

In 1960, the Census reported that 8.6 percent of the male railroad employees were Negroes. The Equal Employment Opportunity Commission found (Table 24) that by 1966, as employment continued its rapid decline, Negro employees had decreased to 8.1 percent of the male work force. Similarly, female Negro workers had decreased as a proportion of the total female employees. Significantly, the proportion of Negroes working in craftsmen positions was found to have increased. The percentage changes for all occupational groups, however, are not of sufficient magnitude to allow conclusive argument that the changes did in fact occur. This is particularly true in light of the prominent differences in the data collection techniques. It is apparent, however, that Negro employees did not achieve gains in employment as they did in many other industries as a result of the building pressures of the civil rights movement during this period, but apparently they did not lose ground disproportionately either.

The 1966 data reported by the EEOC is inclusive of the total railroad industry as defined by the government industrial classification system discussed in Chapter I. As reported, Negro employees represented a negligible proportion of the industry's white collar labor force—0.8 percent. And within these occupations, 92 percent of the Negro workers were limited to office and clerical positions. In contrast the remaining Negro employees represented 10.6 percent of the 500,623 blue collar work force. Negro blue collar employees, in turn, were decidedly underrepresented in the skilled occupations. Only 2.2 percent of the craftsmen

TABLE 15. *Railroad Industry*
Employment by Race, Sex, and Occupational Group
788 Establishments
United States, 1966

Occupational Group	All Employees			Male			Female		
	Total	Negro	Percent Negro	Total	Negro	Percent Negro	Total	Negro	Percent Negro
Officials and managers	30,877	65	0.2	30,797	65	0.2	80	—	—
Professionals	7,110	9	0.1	7,018	9	0.1	92	—	—
Technicians	7,962	27	0.3	7,845	27	0.3	117	—	—
Sales workers	7,709	9	0.1	7,523	8	0.1	186	1	0.5
Office and clerical	128,847	1,276	1.0	98,364	1,115	1.1	30,483	161	0.5
Total white collar	182,505	1,386	0.8	151,547	1,224	0.8	30,958	162	0.5
Craftsmen	225,987	4,957	2.2	225,388	4,888	2.2	599	69	11.5
Operatives	156,561	8,004	5.1	156,189	7,948	5.1	372	56	15.1
Laborers	96,751	29,391	30.4	94,491	28,101	29.7	2,260	1,290	57.1
Service workers	21,324	10,512	49.3	20,521	10,317	50.3	803	195	24.3
Total blue collar	500,623	52,864	10.6	496,589	51,254	10.3	4,034	1,610	39.9
Total	683,128	54,250	7.9	648,136	52,478	8.1	34,992	1,772	5.1

Source: U.S. Equal Employment Opportunity Commission, *Job Patterns for Minorities and Women in Private Industry, 1966*, Report No. 1 (Washington: The Commission, 1968), Part II.

TABLE 16. Railroad Industry
Employment by Race, Sex, and Occupational Group
1169 Establishments
United States, 1967

Occupational Group	All Employees			Male			Female		
	Total	Negro	Percent Negro	Total	Negro	Percent Negro	Total	Negro	Percent Negro
Officials and managers	32,435	59	0.2	32,334	59	0.2	101	—	—
Professionals	7,590	17	0.2	7,462	16	0.2	128	1	0.8
Technicians	8,136	21	0.3	7,995	21	0.3	141	—	—
Sales workers	7,279	12	0.2	7,156	11	0.2	123	1	0.8
Office and clerical	135,792	1,977	1.5	101,928	1,557	1.5	33,864	420	1.2
Total white collar	191,232	2,086	1.1	156,875	1,664	1.1	34,357	422	1.2
Craftsmen	234,402	5,647	2.4	234,270	5,636	2.4	132	11	8.3
Operatives	158,515	8,893	5.6	158,035	8,734	5.5	480	159	33.1
Laborers	97,828	30,135	30.8	95,455	28,773	30.1	2,373	1,362	57.4
Service workers	21,453	10,832	50.5	20,469	10,533	51.5	984	299	30.4
Total blue collar	512,198	55,507	10.8	508,229	53,676	10.6	3,969	1,831	46.1
Total	703,430	57,593	8.2	665,104	55,340	8.3	38,326	2,253	5.9

Source: U.S. Equal Employment Opportunity Commission, Job Patterns for Minorities and Women in Private Industry, 1967, Report No. 2 (Washington: The Commission, 1970), Vol. 1.

TABLE 17. *Railroad Industry*
Employment by Race, Sex, and Occupational Group
984 Establishments
United States, 1969

Occupational Group	All Employees			Male			Female		
	Total	Negro	Percent Negro	Total	Negro	Percent Negro	Total	Negro	Percent Negro
Officials and managers	31,108	150	0.5	30,977	150	0.5	131	—	—
Professionals	7,079	38	0.5	6,931	36	0.5	148	2	1.4
Technicians	7,856	49	0.6	7,698	49	0.6	158	—	—
Sales workers	6,817	106	1.6	6,561	104	1.6	256	2	0.8
Office and clerical	118,229	3,021	2.6	88,197	2,241	2.5	30,032	780	2.6
Total white collar	171,089	3,364	2.0	140,364	2,580	1.8	30,725	784	2.6
Craftsmen	209,460	6,258	3.0	209,315	6,247	3.0	145	11	7.6
Operatives	142,296	8,135	5.7	141,875	8,068	5.7	421	67	15.9
Laborers	79,036	23,698	30.0	77,415	22,793	29.4	1,621	905	55.8
Service workers	14,453	6,910	47.8	13,673	6,671	48.8	780	239	30.6
Total blue collar	445,245	45,001	10.1	442,278	43,779	9.9	2,967	1,222	41.2
Total	616,334	48,365	7.8	582,642	46,359	8.0	33,692	2,006	6.0

Source: Preliminary Equal Employment Opportunity Commission Data, 1969.

TABLE 18. *Railroad Industry*

Percentage Distribution of Employment by Race and Occupational Group
United States, 1966-1969

Occupational Group	1966		1967		1968		1969	
	Total	Negro	Total	Negro	Total	Negro	Total	Negro
Officials and managers	4.5	0.1	4.6	0.1	4.7	0.1	5.0	0.3
Professionals	1.0	*	1.1	*	1.2	0.1	1.2	0.1
Technicians	1.2	*	1.2	0.1	1.3	0.1	1.3	0.1
Sales workers	1.1	*	1.0	*	1.2	*	1.1	0.2
Office and clerical	18.9	2.4	19.3	3.4	20.2	5.0	19.2	6.3
Total white collar	26.7	2.5	27.2	3.6	28.6	5.3	27.8	7.0
Craftsmen	33.1	9.1	33.3	9.8	35.4	12.0	34.0	12.9
Operatives	22.9	14.8	22.5	15.5	21.3	15.3	23.1	16.8
Laborers	14.2	54.2	13.9	52.3	12.1	51.1	12.8	49.0
Service workers	3.1	19.4	3.1	18.8	2.6	16.3	2.3	14.3
Total blue collar	73.3	97.5	72.8	96.4	71.4	94.7	72.2	93.0
Total	100.0	100.0	100.0	100.0	100.0	100.0	100.0	100.0

Source: Computed from Tables 15, 16, 17, and 19.

Note: 1968 is Field Sample and therefore is not strictly comparable with other years.

* Less than 0.05 percent.

were Negro. At the same time, over 70 percent of the Negro employees continued to be employed as laborers or service workers, where they represented 30.4 percent and 49.3 percent of the total work force respectively. Thus the historical pattern of Negro employment in the railroad industry was still very much in evidence in 1966.

In light of these patterns, the employment data compiled by the EEOC in subsequent years represent a distinct break with the past. Tables 16 and 17 provide summary statistics for 1967 and 1969 respectively. Although the EEOC has not released comparable data for 1968, a field sample of Class I carriers, which represents over 90 percent of the industry's employment, was collected by the author and is included as Table 19. Despite the fact that the 1968 data are therefore not strictly comparable with that reported by the EEOC, the sample carriers are broadly representative with regard to geographic location and company size among Class I railroads. The analysis of recent trends in Negro employment in subsequent sections of this chapter is based upon the 1968 sample data. The basic data for 1968 are shown in the Appendix.

Average employment in the industry fell from 909,000 in 1960 to 683,000 at the end of 1968.[142] (Class I employment declined from 780,000 to 591,000 during this same period.) The rate of decline was disproportionately greater among blue collar occupations, and especially high among those low-skill occupations in which Negroes have traditionally been employed. Nevertheless, the industry has been able to maintain high levels of Negro employment in low-skill occupations, and at the same time significantly increase the level of Negro employment in skilled blue collar and in white collar occupations generally. These trends evolved steadily throughout the period and appear to confirm the positive effect of the industry's developing concern with its personnel practices.

Preliminary data compiled by the Equal Employment Opportunity Commission for 1969 shows that Negro employment, both male and female, has at least doubled, both relatively and absolutely, across each of the white collar occupational groups. Whereas in 1966 Negroes represented only 0.8 percent of the white collar labor force, 2.0 percent of these employees were Negroes in 1969. The most striking increases during this period

---

142. Railroad Retirement Board, *Statistical Supplement to the 1969 Annual Report* (1970), Table D-1.

were experienced by male Negro managers and sales workers, and female Negro office and clerical employees—occupations from which Negroes were generally excluded prior to the last half of the 1960's. These trends represent a sharp break with the past. Still, however, Negro white collar employees represented only 7.0 percent of the Negro labor force in 1969.

In the blue collar occupational groups the industry has gradually upgraded Negroes into craftsmen and operative positions. Strict adherence to seniority systems imposes severe time restrictions on the upgrading of employees to the more highly skilled occupations. This is especially significant in light of the declining number of opportunities in these occupations. Moreover, Negro blue collar employees have historically been hired without regard to the qualifications desirable for promotion, which imposes an additional constraint on their rate of upgrading. The level of Negro employment in the laborer and service occupations has remained relatively constant throughout the 1966-1969 period—approximately 30 and 50 percent respectively. The percentage of the Negro labor force employed in these unskilled occupations has been reduced from 74 to 63 percent. Overall, during the period male Negro employees declined as a percentage of the total blue collar work force from 10.3 to 9.9 percent in 1969. This change is accounted for by the rapidly decreasing number of Negro service workers. The analysis of the occupational representation of Negroes in 1968 by the function of the reporting unit indicates more completely the recent employment patterns.

Officials and Managers [143]

The data in Tables 15 and 19 show that Negro managerial personnel have remained proportionately constant—0.2 percent of the total between 1966 and 1968. Most of the Negro managers are line supervisors, with authority over predominantly Negro work crews in maintenance or terminal operations. Those Negro employees who have assumed supervisory responsibilities have generally worked their way over many years through the seniority systems. The industry generally has not been successful in attracting recent Negro college graduates into managerial positions.

---

143. A list of the 128 railroad occupations classified by general occupational group and function is provided in Appendix A.

TABLE 19. Railroad Industry
Employment by Race, Sex, and Occupational Group
United States, 1968

Occupational Group	All Employees			Male			Female		
	Total	Negro	Percent Negro	Total	Negro	Percent Negro	Total	Negro	Percent Negro
Officials and managers	28,428	50	0.2	28,329	50	0.2	99	—	—
Professionals	7,126	24	0.3	6,987	24	0.3	139	—	—
Technicians	7,800	33	0.4	7,669	33	0.4	131	—	—
Sales workers	7,509	14	0.2	7,326	13	0.2	183	1	0.5
Office and clerical	123,379	2,198	1.8	92,964	1,645	1.8	30,415	553	1.8
Total white collar	174,242	2,319	1.3	143,275	1,765	1.2	30,967	554	1.8
Craftsmen	215,360	5,316	2.5	215,213	5,297	2.5	147	19	12.9
Operatives	129,401	6,743	5.2	129,119	6,684	5.2	282	59	20.9
Laborers	73,456	22,511	30.6	71,856	21,645	30.1	1,600	866	54.1
Service workers	16,066	7,178	44.7	15,254	6,977	45.7	812	201	24.8
Total blue collar	434,283	1,748	9.6	431,442	40,603	9.4	2,841	1,145	40.3
Total	608,525	44,067	7.2	574,717	42,368	7.4	33,808	1,699	5.0

Source: Appendix Tables B-1, B-2, B-3.

Note: Does not include Hawaii and Alaska.

The industry traditionally has utilized management personnel who have acquired extensive experience as blue collar workers in some function of the industry. The industry has, however, begun in recent years to increase their hiring of college graduates without prior industry experience. Negro employees who have the ability to gain supervisory positions have been prevented from rapidly acquiring broad managerial responsibilities, even when such promotions are demanded by federal agencies or top management, by the practice of strict departmental seniority and resulting narrow job knowledge. A few notable exceptions who have been recently promoted to positions with significant authority over the movement of trains, a heretofore unrealized opportunity for Negroes, have been cited by industry spokesmen, but, on the whole, Negro managers continue to be relegated to positions of limited responsibility.

The operating divisions include a diverse group of managers who are responsible for the movement of trains, freight, and passengers as well as for the maintenance of track, signals, and related properties. The managerial hierarchy is dominated by men who have gained their railroad experience in the operating divisions. Negroes had, of course, been excluded from train and engine service positions and consequently have never been employed as officers of the divisions. They had similarly been excluded from employment as train dispatchers, station agents, and as middle managers in signal, telegraph and electrical transmission. Employment in the positions directly below these managers is controlled by labor organizations which have been cited as practicing some form of discrimination in the past. The small number of Negro managers working in the operating divisions, as shown in Table 20, must therefore be employed, with few possible exceptions, as supervisors in track maintenance or in freight stations, warehouses, and marine operations. Negro employment in these positions is, however, significantly below the level of Negro employment in related blue collar occupations.

Managerial positions in the three remaining sectors—repair shops, terminals, and offices—are less heterogeneous and therefore less difficult to delimit. There, however, may be variations in company organizational structures which are responsible for discrepancies in the designation of individual reporting establishments. Thus, for instance, stations may be reported variously as separate terminals or as part of an operating division, or repair facilities may be operated as part of a larger switching

TABLE 20. Railroad Industry
Employment of Officials and Managers
by Industry Sector and Race, 1968

Industry Sector	Number of Establishments	Employees		
		Total	Negro	Percent Negro
Operating divisions	196	11,638	27	0.2
Repair shops	94	1,814	3	0.2
Terminals	40	1,048	3	0.3
Offices	45	6,656	9	0.1

Source: Data in author's possession.

Note: The data presented in this and the succeeding six tables are not strictly comparable with Table 19 since many small firms which file only consolidated reports have been omitted.

yard. Nevertheless, carrier locations designated as repair shops should be limited in their operations to the repair of locomotives, freight and passenger cars, and other mechanical equipment. Terminals are generally large, important locations for the reception and discharge of freight and passengers. They are frequently at the end points of heavily traveled routes. Office units should be separate and distinct from those related to operating divisions and terminals.

Negroes have never been employed in those equipment maintenance occupations from which repair shop supervisory personnel are selected. Likewise, they have been excluded from those occupations in terminals which may lead to supervisory positions. The low number of Negro managers in these two sectors in Table 26 reflect these discriminatory patterns. Historical employment data suggest that these few Negro managers may be found in positions with responsibility for movement of baggage and freight. The few Negro office managers are college graduates in staff positions.

Professionals and Technicians

Despite the apparent importance of technological change to railroad operations, the level of research and development activities has been maintained at an extremely low level. Those technical developments which have been significant were developed as a rule by the several railroad equipment manufacturers. In fact, only a few of the larger carriers employ technical research personnel. Most of technically trained professional personnel are employed in maintenance operations.

While annual employment information compiled by the Interstate Commerce Commission does not differentiate among the several professional occupations, statistics published in the census of 1960, although not strictly comparable, indicate that 17,729 professional, technical and kindred workers were employed in the industry.[144] Among the professional employees were 5,437 engineers, 5,811 accountants and auditors, 624 lawyers and 662 statisticians. These statistics are felt to be proportionately representative of the present occupational distribution.

Negro professionals in the industry comprised 0.1 percent of the total in 1966, and had risen to 0.3 percent in 1968. Thus far, Negro professionals have been assigned only to corporate staff positions. Further, they are employed, with few exceptions, by the largest carriers.

TABLE 21. *Railroad Industry Employment of Professionals and Technicians by Industry Sector and Race, 1968*

Industry Sector	Number of Establishments	Employees		
		Total	Negro	Percent Negro
Operating divisions	196	5,546	20	0.4
Repair shops	94	435	—	—
Terminals	40	259	1	0.4
Offices	45	4,910	29	0.6

Source: Data in author's possession.

Employees classified as technicians perform a great variety of functions. Included in the general occupational group are such diverse employees as storekeepers, sales agents, claim investigators, equipment inspectors, train directors, and chief telegraphers

144. *U.S. Census of Population, 1960*, PC(2)-7C, *Occupation by Industry*, Table 2.

and telephoners. The majority of these employees work in the operating divisions. Many of the technician positions have been unionized.

Negro technicians represented 0.3 and 0.4 of the total in 1966 and 1968 respectively. Although it is not known in what capacity these men were employed, historical employment patterns suggest that they were not employed in those positions which share responsibility for the movement of trains or for communications. Further, Table 21 indicates that they have been excluded as well from employment in repair shops.

Sales Workers

Industry generally has not employed Negroes in sales positions which require close contact with the public. The railroad industry has traditionally followed a similar policy. Only a small percentage of the sales workers serve in passenger service operations. The remainder are classified as traffic agents and investigators, with responsibility for industrial sales. The jobs of these employees differ significantly from the active solicitation of most sales positions.

The 1968 sample statistics in Table 19 show only 14 Negroes or 0.2 percent of the 7,509 sales workers. Most of these employees work as ticket agents or assistant ticket agents in major passenger terminals. The contrast in racial employment patterns between these and other passenger service occupations located in the same terminals is quite striking.

Office and Clerical

Office and clerical employees perform two general but rather distinct functions. The largest group are responsible for handling the huge volume of paper work necessary to keep an account of each piece of rolling stock and its contents, and to transact business with freight shippers and passengers. They work in railroad stations, yards, terminals, and company offices. The second group includes telegraphers, telephoners, and towermen who are concerned with controlling the movement of trains in accordance with instructions issued by train dispatchers. Included also are station agents in smaller stations where they may serve both as telegraphers and telephoners and as the representative to the public for the handling of freight and baggage.

The majority of railroad clerks do clerical work connected with business transactions such as collecting bills, investigating complaints, adjusting claims, tracing shipments, compiling statistics, and keeping books. In small offices and stations, one man may perform duties related to several of these tasks, but in large offices with many employees, each clerk usually handles a specialized job. A second group of more highly skilled employees consists of secretaries, stenographers, typists, and office machine operators who perform duties similar to those typical of clerical employees in other industries. Finally there is a large group of more responsible office employees who prepare technical reports for the government, deal with customers on uncollected freight bills, perform certain accounting tasks, or act in supervisory capacities for clerical activities. Significantly, the overwhelming majority of these employees are men. Further, nearly all are members of the Brotherhood of Railway Clerks.

Office and clerical employment generally has not been reduced as rapidly as that in other railroad occupations. To be sure, the introduction of the computer has produced a virtual revolution in the traditional methods of processing the voluminous records required for railroad operations. These changes have been the cause for several serious labor disputes in the last decade. These disputes have been resolved by the negotiation of job protection agreements for affected employees. The nature of the job content, however, has undergone significant change for many occupations.

In 1966, only 1.0 percent of 128,847 office and clerical workers were Negroes, while by 1968, the percentage had increased to 1.8 percent. Moreover, as Tables 15 and 19 indicate, female Negro employment has increased nearly four-fold. Most of the Negroes now working "office and clerical" positions have been hired in the last five years. As a result of the strict acceptance of seniority in promotions, most of these employees are still relegated to low-level positions. Moreover, since seniority affects the choice of work assignment and work location, the industry may have trouble recruiting additional Negro office workers in areas in which the labor market for these employees is tight. As Table 22 indicates, however, those Negro employees in office and clerical positions are distributed proportionately in all sectors of the industry.

TABLE 22. *Railroad Industry*
Employment of Office and Clerical Workers
by Industry Sector and Race, 1968

Industry Sector	Number of Establishments	Employees		
		Total	Negro	Percent Negro
Operating divisions	196	58,538	1,022	1.7
Repair shops	94	1,877	34	1.8
Terminals	40	4,643	203	4.4
Offices	45	30,297	609	2.0

Source: Data in author's possession.

The group of employees working as station agents in small stations and as telegraphers and telephoners include few, if any, Negro workers. These positions require employees either to assume complete responsibility for a station or communications tower or to work as a member of a small group. In general only white employees have been entrusted with these assignments.

Craftsmen

The railroad industry has never employed Negroes in craft positions or in apprentice positions leading to the skilled occupations. The history of the industry is replete with labor agreements, both verbal and written, which were intended to deny these opportunities to Negroes. Table 15 shows that only 2.2 percent of the craftsmen in the industry in 1966 were Negroes. The data for 1968 show a slight increase to 2.5 percent but the validity of this comparison is uncertain since the data are not strictly comparable. Nevertheless, it is apparent from our previous discussion of employment opportunities generally that rapid upgrading is impossible even without further union resistance.

The largest number of craftsmen, both white and Negro, are employed in the operating divisions. They, however, are employed in distinctly different occupational patterns. Today, over a century after the industry gained economic importance, the number of Negro engineers and conductors is strikingly low. In fact, Negro employment in these crafts has been so infrequent that it was not until December 1968 that a passenger train was placed under complete operational control of a Negro crew.[145] Negro workers have similarly been excluded from the related operating positions of yardmaster and assistant yardmaster.

Negro employees in operating divisions have generally been limited to track maintenance occupations. Both gang foremen and portable equipment operators, the two skilled positions in track maintenance, are filled by the promotion of track laborers. The carriers have not been hesitant to promote Negroes into these positions, particularly since they will still be working with predominantly Negro crews. In addition, a few Negroes have been employed in the South as masons, carpenters, and in other building trade positions. It has been recently, however, that Negroes were hired into signal maintenance and as linemen and groundsmen in communications maintenance. Table 23 indicates that Negro employment is proportionately lower in the operating divisions than in any other sector of the industry.

TABLE 23. *Railroad Industry*
Employment of Craftsmen by Industry Sector and Race
1968

Industry Sector	Number of Establishments	Employees		
		Total	Negro	Percent Negro
Operating divisions	196	123,325	2,711	2.2
Repair shops	94	37,311	1,322	3.5
Terminals	40	7,896	287	3.6
Offices	45	2,087	102	4.9

Source: Data in author's possession.

Although Negro craftsmen were employed during some of the early strikes in the railroad repair shops, they have never been afforded continuing opportunities in the shops except as craftsmen helpers. They have, however, performed functions as helpers which may be basically the same as those of the white crafts-

145. *The Albany Times,* January 8-15, 1969, p. 2.

men. Employment as helpers, in contrast to the similar but typically white apprentice positions, does not provide promotional opportunities to the skilled occupations. The experience that many Negroes gained as helpers now allows the industry to expand the size of the skilled Negro labor force more rapidly than would have otherwise been possible. The industry has been encouraged to do this not only by the government but in several instances by a shortage of skilled workers. Negro shop craftsmen have been most frequently employed as carmen and machinists.

The small group of stations masters and baggage agents have also been classified as craftsmen. Negroes have historically been utilized as baggage and parcel room attendants and a few of these workers may have been upgraded as pressure from the civil rights movement increased.

Operatives

The level of Negro employment in operative or semiskilled occupations varies greatly from location to location, and from occupation to occupation. Moreover, it has generally been in these occupations that white and Negro interests have most frequently conflicted. Negro operatives comprised 5.1 percent of the total in 1966 and 5.2 percent in 1968.

Negroes have long been employed in small numbers in train and engine service as brakemen and firemen, and more recently as ticket collectors on passenger runs. The bitter resistance to Negro employment by the Brotherhoods of Railroad Trainmen and Locomotive Firemen has been discussed previously. Although they were in general successful in their efforts to eliminate Negro workers from these jobs, Negroes continue to work in these occupations in varying numbers throughout the country. Frequently, Negro employment in yard operations is higher than that in freight and passenger service. This is particularly true in the occupations of switch tender and hostler.

There are very few operatives working in track maintenance. Inasmuch as the operative positions here are assistants or helpers to skilled employees, it is reasonable to assume that Negroes may frequently be employed.

Similarly, in maintenance of equipment semiskilled occupations, Negro employment has been historically high. Repair shops on several carriers have employed Negro helpers exclusively. In

TABLE 24. *Railroad Industry*
Employment of Operatives by Industry Sector and Race
1968

Industry Sector	Number of Establishments	Employees		
		Total	Negro	Percent Negro
Operating divisions	196	87,439	4,237	4.8
Repair shops	94	8,399	1,070	12.7
Terminals	40	4,706	566	12.0
Offices	45	529	86	16.3

Source: Data in author's possession.

addition, the Brotherhood of Firemen and Oilers which controls a diverse group of occupations in railroad powerhouses and other similar operations has not had a history of discrimination. It is assumed that Negro employment in the occupations under the jurisdiction of this union is proportionately higher than in repair shop occupations in general.

Laborers

Negroes have been utilized extensively in laboring positions throughout the industry. In the South, Negro laborers have frequently been employed exclusively. Tables 15 and 19 indicate that Negro employment in these occupations has remained relatively constant over the last few years—30.4 percent in 1966 and 30.6 percent in 1968—despite continuing reductions in the laboring work force. In general there is a very high turnover among laboring employees.

Laborers in the operating divisions perform two general functions. They are employed variously in positions related to freight and baggage handling in stations and terminals and in track maintenance. Table 25 shows that Negro employees comprise 50.4 percent of the total in the 1968 sample of terminals and 31.3 percent of the total in the operating divisions. There, however, is great geographic variation.

TABLE 25.   *Railroad Industry*
Employment of Laborers by Industry Sector and Race
1968

Industry Sector	Number of Establishments	Employees		
		Total	Negro	Percent Negro
Operating divisions	196	43,804	13,722	31.3
Repair shops	94	6,085	2,717	44.7
Terminals	40	3,580	1,805	50.4
Offices	45	1,265	648	51.2

Source: Data in author's possession.

Negroes have been similarly employed in railroad repair shops as coach cleaners and laborers. The 1968 sample data show that 44.7 percent of the shop laborers were Negro. The carriers have been providing an increasing number of promotional opportunities for coach cleaners to advance to the skilled carmen positions. Too often, however, the Negro workers in these occupations have such limited educational backgrounds that advancement is impossible.

Service Workers

It is in the service occupations that the image of the Negro railroad worker is most clearly engraved. Traditionally Negroes or other minority employees have worked as attendants and waiters on passenger trains. These typically were among the best positions Negroes could hope to gain in the early part of this century. The story of the struggle of the Brotherhood of Sleeping Car Porters, recounted briefly in this study, is one of the most interesting of modern labor history. Unfortunately the rapid decrease in passenger service has had a ruinous effect on this union and on employment opportunities generally in these occupations. In 1968, Negroes still comprised 44.7 percent of the service employees.

Negro workers have also been employed in offices as janitors and cleaners, and as elevator operators and other office attendants. Significantly, however, they have been excluded from employment in railroad police and guard occupations. As the his-

TABLE 26. *Railroad Industry*
Employment of Service Workers by Industry Sector and Race
1968

Industry Sector	Number of Establishments	Employees		
		Total	Negro	Percent Negro
Operating divisions	196	6,918	3,063	44.3
Repair shops	94	595	70	11.8
Terminals	40	1,282	264	20.6
Offices	45	2,005	880	43.9

Source: Data in author's possession.

tory of the industry so vividly illustrates, Negro employees have never been entrusted with positions of responsibility.

Female Employment

Women have historically been excluded from all but a limited number of railroad occupations. In 1968 the office and clerical positions accounted for 90 percent of the female railway employees. Even among these occupations, however, the proportion of female employees is decidedly less than that typically found in industry.

Several factors account for the distinct employment patterns of women in the industry. Initially, of course, the physical demands placed upon railroad employees preclude the use of women in most positions. Second, as a matter of routine, the employees in several occupations, most notably the operating crafts, spend time away from home, lodging in company facilities. Significantly, the frequent travel of management personnel, accompanied by necessary clerical assistants, established a tradition of male secretarial and office employees. Although railroad executives have altered their travel habits for the same reasons as have rail customers, male employees continue to work in these positions. Finally, among the office and clerical occupations, the occupational titles and classificatory schema obscure the undesirable nature of several "clerical and office" occupations.

Data compiled by the Railroad Retirement Board for 1968 show that only 13 of the 128 ICC occupations used for reporting employment had 500 or more women employees.[146] In fact, over 70 percent of the women worked in five occupational divisions: clerks, secretaries, stenographers and typists, mechanical-device operators, and telephone-switchboard operators and office assistants. Women comprised over 50 percent of the total employment in only four occupations, with the highest proportion occurring in the stenographers and typists group, 79.8 percent. Among the nonoffice related occupations, the only occupations in which 500 or more women were employed were coach cleaners and telegraphers, telephoners and towermen.

Women entered the industry as a result of the manpower shortages during World War II. They were hired not only for office work but also for maintenance and operating duties, which formerly had been considered unsuitable for them. In the years of peak wartime employment, women comprised more than 250,000 railroad employees, 9 percent of the work force. By 1948, female employment had fallen to less than 125,000. Table 19 shows that by 1968 the number of women employees had declined to 55,300. Although male employment in general has also declined rapidly since the war, in all occupations except office and clerical jobs, female employment has tended to decline more sharply.

The distribution of women by age and years of service still reflects the departures from the usual hiring practices which took place during the World War II period. The typical woman in the industry is now over 40 years old, and has at least 15 years of service. The largest concentration of women continues to be found among those age groups which would have been hired during the war emergency.

The 1968 sample data (Table 19) show that not a single Negro woman was employed by the industry in a supervisory, professional or technical capacity. In addition, only one Negro woman was employed in a sales position in the industry, in this case by a southern firm. The employment of white women in these occupations was, of course, inexplicably low as well. Finally, the small proportion of Negro women in office and clerical positions, 1.8 percent in 1968, is illustrative of the traditional position of these women in the industry. The largest number of office and clerical workers are employed as clerks, a position with a job content which may not be dissimilar to that of a production position, and it is in these low status positions that many Negro

---

146. U.S. Railroad Retirement Board, "Women in the Railroad Industry," *The RRB Quarterly Review*, April-June 1970, p. 23.

women are employed. Few Negro women have been upgraded or hired into the more attractive secretarial positions.

Since the railroad industry generally has not taken a leading role in the integration of minorities in white collar jobs, it is not surprising that Negro women have not been afforded better opportunities. Important also is the nature of office employment in the industry. Nearly all of the office and clerical positions are controlled by union contract. Although this may provide employees in these jobs with above average wages, it also forces new employees to endure the disadvantages of rigid seniority systems and similar work rules. This may mean that newly employed clerical employees may be required to work initially in small, isolated yard offices or other unattractive situations. Furthermore, the industry generally does not have the necessary image to compete successfully in the continuing tight labor market for female Negro office employees.

In the blue collar occupations, women employees account for less than one percent of the total work force, and this proportion is rapidly declining. The women in these positions with the exception of a few in service occupations were hired during World War II and age has now become an important factor. Negro women have fared better than their male counterparts in obtaining employment in these occupations. In 1968, 40.3 percent of the women in these occupations were Negroes. It is not clear how these Negro women were distributed among the many blue collar occupations. It is unfortunate, indeed, that the railroad industry has not developed an attractive employment opportunity similar to that of the airline stewardess.

THE IMPORTANCE OF COMPANY SIZE AND LOCATION

Both the size of a carrier and its location have an important impact on employment opportunities for Negroes. The surprisingly distinct patterns resulting from these two factors are summarized in Table 27.

As noted in Chapters III and IV, Negro workers have historically enjoyed significantly greater job opportunities in the South. The sample data show that in 1968 total Negro employment continued to be markedly higher in this area than either in the West or in the East. Negro employees in the South, however, are most heavily concentrated in laboring and service occupations. (See Appendix Tables B-1 to B-3.) Moreover, the proportion of Ne-

TABLE 27. Railroad Industry
Percent Negro Employment
by District and Company Size, 1968

Company Size	United States All Employees	Eastern District All Employees	Eastern District White Collar	Eastern District Blue Collar	Southern District All Employees	Southern District White Collar	Southern District Blue Collar	Western District All Employees	Western District White Collar	Western District Blue Collar
Small companies Less than 2,500 employees	5.8	2.8	0.5	3.8	18.0	0.5	26.2	1.4	0.3	1.9
Medium-size companies 2,500 to 9,999 employees	6.2	5.3	1.5	6.8	16.2	1.0	24.0	5.3	0.8	7.2
Large companies 10,000 employees and over	7.5	6.6	1.5	8.4	15.6	0.8	21.4	5.6	1.5	7.3
Total	7.2	6.1	1.5	7.9	15.7	0.8	21.9	5.5	1.4	7.2

Source: Table 19 and Appendix B.

Note: For geographic districts, see Figure 1, p. 12.

groes in white collar occupations is notably less in the South than in either of the other regions. In general, employment patterns in managerial, professional, technical, sales, and craftsmen occupations are similar across regions—Negro workers have simply not been employed in these occupations.

An equally significant locational factor in Negro employment is the urban/rural dichotomy. Needless to say, railroad employees are based variously across thousands of miles of track. The percentage of Negro employment is substantially higher in the urban areas where not only a large proportion of the Negro population dwells, but where white workers have access to a greater variety of comparable job opportunities. Many small rural communities are dominated by railroad yards or repair facilities, and employment there remains highly coveted by white residents. Moreover, the traditional Negro jobs in freight and passenger service are concentrated in the terminals of the major cities.

The factor of company size is significant. Not only do larger companies tend to employ more Negro blue collar employees, but as a group they employ proportionately more Negro white collar workers as well. Undoubtedly these variations are attributable in part to locational differences. Small railroads typically are based and operate in less populated areas, with fewer Negro residents. Moreover, these carriers frequently specialize in the transport of a limited variety of freight, such as coal or iron ore. In addition, the conduct of such firms has not come under close public scrutiny, nor has the government chosen to intervene strongly with firms which do little hiring. The limited future employment opportunities on small carriers should preclude any alteration in this pattern.

The exceptions to the general relationship between company size and Negro employment are found in the South. Here the smaller firms employ proportionately more Negro workers but they have frequently been limited to laborer or service occupations. It is assumed that the larger Negro population, particularly in rural areas, has been in part responsible for this variation. Further, the lack of public concern for the plight of Negro workers, an attitude which was not dissimilar from that generally accepted throughout the nation until recently, has allowed the southern carriers to continue their traditional policies without modification. These job opportunities have, after all, been among the best available to Negro workers in this region.

CHAPTER VI

Railroad Employment Policy: Shift to Affirmative Action

The preceding chapters have emphasized the economic and historical developments which are in part responsible for the current Negro employment picture in the railroad industry. Since, however, the total environment—social and economic—in which the employment process operates has been drastically altered, it is not possible to state that a company's record is acceptable solely because the proportion of Negro employment in a broad occupational category has risen, nor is it possible to state that an employment record is good because the proportion of Negro employees compares favorably with that of the Negro population in the related labor market. Too many variables affect the employment situation to allow the formulation of such generalized policies of evaluation.

To understand more fully the Negro employment situation in the industry and the problems confronting management and government officials who are responsible for implementing minority employment policy, the employment policies and practices of the carriers must be analyzed and evaluated as well as the results they produce. Employment remains a two-sided decision which must be entered into by both the employer and the applicant. If, after assuring all applicants and employees that the practices proscribed by legislation and government directive have been met in full, the firm is still unsuccessful in improving the Negro employment picture, then little criticism can be directed toward the employer. This chapter is intended to provide the limited analysis and evaluation that is possible in a comprehensive study of an entire industry. Policy formulation, recruitment and selection, training, and upgrading are examined in turn. The analysis is based upon interviews conducted by the author with management and government personnel.

114

EQUAL EMPLOYMENT POLICY

The first step in establishing an effective equal employment opportunity program must be a strong statement of policy. This step has proved to be particularly significant in the railroad industry. Traditionally the many operating divisions, terminals and stations, and repair yards have been run by local supervisory personnel as "little empires." To operate efficiently a company that may be spread over several thousand miles, top management must rely heavily on decentralized responsibility and authority. In the area of personnel administration, the local supervisory personnel have typically had complete freedom to hire, fire, and promote as long as they followed the procedures and limitations set forth in the many collective bargaining agreements and continued to maintain an efficient work force. Now, as directives in the sensitive areas of equal opportunity employment are formulated, local supervisors in many instances have resisted and effectively circumvented the requested changes. Racial prejudice is probably a factor in this resistance, but it may be attributed as well to the threatened diminution of authority that this must represent. The problem is so acute that one manager responsible for employment policy stated that he was looking forward to the settlement of a recent complaint filed with the EEOC as this would provide the necessary leverage to impose desired changes.[147]

The problem of strong policy implementation is intensified further by the corporate structure and traditional order of succession to top management positions. Power in the industry is concentrated among those men who are responsible for the daily movement of trains. This is easily discernible by only a cursory examination of the backgrounds of top management personnel and of comparative salaries by department. These men are, as expected, responsive first to daily transportation problems and not to the unprofitable problems of the Negro employment crisis. Moreover, many top managers first entered the industry as blue collar workers and have now worked their way through the managerial hierarchy. It is reasonable to assume that this experience, particularly as members of unions with long histories of racial discrimination, has not encouraged the development of sympathetic attitudes toward Negro problems. Regardless of

---

147. Interview, August 1968.

attitude, however, in an industry which is struggling to remain solvent, the concern of managerial personnel must be directed toward problems which economically appear more urgent.

Finally, the implementation of equitable employment policies has been made more onerous in the industry because of the lack of influence of the personnel function. To be sure several firms have professional staffs with high expertise. Too often, however, carriers in the industry maintain only minimal employee relations staffs, headed by men who have either been placed in the position to gain added experience before moving into other fields or by men who may be quietly ending their careers. The personnel practices employed generally in the industry have yet to be developed to the level of sophistication needed to resolve effectively the many issues intertwined in the area of equal employment opportunity. The impression one develops in studying these areas within the industry is that personnel is solely an adjunct of the union relations function, and that is to maintain the records necessary to support collective bargaining.

This harsh criticism may take on more relevance if the government's demands for "affirmative action" grow in intensity. Even now, after several years of working under the provisions of Executive Order 11246 and Title VII of the Civil Rights Act of 1964, Clarence H. Featherson, Contract Compliance Officer of the Post Office Department responsible for the railroad industry, has stated that affirmative action

requires the railroads to take the initiative in seeking minority employees and to upgrade minority employees already on the payrolls. *We have found very few railroads that are really doing this;* but perhaps there are others we don't know about.[148] (Italics supplied.)

Policy Statements

Policy pronouncements of the companies vary only slightly in their usual broad opening statements. Typically this statement ensures applicants and employees that they will be treated "without regard to race, color, religion, or national origin." This brief policy is then made available for wide distribution through company publications and press releases, employment advertisements, bulletin boards, and in collective bargaining agreements. No carrier has been contacted which does not have available an imposing policy statement ready for distribution.

---

148. Tom Shedd, "Where do Railroads Stand on EEO?" *Modern Railroads,* Vol. 24 (February 1969), p. 41.

Perhaps of more consequence than the initial, broadly stated policy is the set of plans established to implement this policy. These plans cover such points as internal and external communication of policy, responsibility for EEO policy, employment standards, training opportunities, and special projects to develop improved employment opportunities for minorities. It is in this declaration that an initial insight can be gained into the vigor of the firm's racial employment policies. The differences in company dedication can be quite striking. The following excerpt is taken from the guidelines of a major eastern carrier, which seemingly have gone beyond the level necessary to remain in compliance with government edicts:

> To ensure compliance with the company's equal employment opportunity policy, the following guidelines are established with respect to the functions of the company's Equal Employment Opportunity Officers and of the duties of all supervisory personnel of the company in relation to those functions:
>
> 1. All employing officers will prepare and keep current an inventory of all minority group employees, broken down by name, age, length of service, job location and job classification. These inventories will be submitted upon request to the appropriate Equal Employment Opportunity Officer.
>
> 2. *All vacancies in employment will be cleared with the appropriate Equal Employment Opportunity Officer before such vacancies are filled.* The Equal Employment Opportunity Officer will have *authority to require the employment of qualified minority group applicants and the promotion of qualified minority group employees.*
>
> 3. Qualified minority group employees should be promoted to white-collar and skilled jobs in preference to new hires if such employees are available to fill the vacancies.
>
> 4. There *will be* increased hiring of qualified minority group applicants. Where possible, consideration will be given *to minority group population ratios in particular areas.*
>
> 5. Employing officers will keep a record of the race of all persons who file with the company an employment application. Employing officers will submit to the President on or before the tenth day of each month a report of new hires

and of promotions made during the preceding month, categorized by race. Such reports will state the number of minority group employees who left the employment of the company during the preceding month *and the reasons for departure.* Equal Employment Opportunity Officers are authorized to contact employing Officers directly in order to request additional reports and information. These requests will be met promptly. (Italics supplied.)

Implementing Policy

The statement of policy, regardless of strength, is only the first step in a seemingly impossible task. To implement the directives the necessary personnel must next be employed. This task has proven difficult for industry generally, and decidedly so for the railroad industry which has employed few people who have had the necessary expertise to analyze the intricate problems in developing equitable personnel practices for minority applicants and employees. With few exceptions, those personnel techniques and tools utilized in the industry were developed many years ago. The first criteria used in selecting personnel practices then and today have been cost and simplicity rather than effectiveness. In addition, there has been little meaningful research conducted to aid in the validation of the industry's personnel practices. Even as basic and important a task as job evaluation has not been completed in over fifty years. Emergency boards have repeatedly requested that this be carried out to help eliminate wage inequities among railroad employees.[149] To be sure, the task of job evaluation has not been completed largely as a result of union opposition but, nevertheless, the absence of such basic information is indicative of the nature of the personnel function in the industry. Such an atmosphere is not conducive to the development of the competent personnel administrators needed for the necessary changes, nor is it conducive to easy recruitment of such personnel.

Compliance officers from the OFCC first established contact with the railroad industry in late 1963. This initial survey of the industry was focused on the major carriers, particularly those located in the northeastern states. While the OFCC attempted only to gain familiarity with the industry, its problems,

---

149. See, for example, *Report to the President by Emergency Board No. 145,* May 3, 1962, p. 8 and *No. 169,* March 10, 1967, pp. 9-10.

and its minority employment practices at this time, several key executives recognized the importance of the government's action and the changing tenor of the nation. Although no immediate action was taken by these men, preliminary discussion of mutual problems took place between officials from several major railroads.

These early meetings led in the spring of 1966 to the establishment of the Railroad Committee on Equal Employment Opportunity, under the auspices of the Association of American Railroads. This large committee is made up of one representative from each AAR member carrier. The group is believed to be the first industry-wide committee established exclusively to deal with racial employment issues. In fact, this committee has served as a model for committees set up by other industries. Formal meetings were held biannually from its inception. The focus of these meetings has been a number of speeches given by industry and government officials. Possibly, however, more value has been gained by carrier representatives during closed-door discussions of mutual problems. In an industry such as the railroad industry, with identical occupations and similar personnel problems, cooperation rather than rivalry and secrecy is far more rational in resolving nonprofit-related problems.

The AAR has also succeeded in setting up a joint committee with the Railway Labor Executives Association (RLEA). This committee deals exclusively with minority employment matters of common concern and exchanges information. By spring of 1969 two meetings had been held.

This provides the industry with an exceptionally good base from which to build an effective minority employment program. Each firm has access to the experience of other firms which have had similar problems arise. Resolution of the major technical problems in developing the desired programs appears within sight. The enduring obstacles will continue to be first and second level supervisors, and lack of influence in the personnel function. Counseling and advice from the personnel staff has proven to be ineffective; the final solution may well require a restructuring of the managerial hierarchy.

RECRUITMENT AND SELECTION

The railroad industry has not had to rely in the past on extensive recruiting efforts to maintain an efficient work force. For many railroad employees, work in the industry has been a family tradition. The unique working conditions, high pay, and the allure of railroading developed strong bonds between the industry, its employees, and their families. Union sentiment has demanded strict adherence to this nepotism; management has been only too willing to accept this source of dedicated employees. In general, nepotism has been most prevalent in the high-wage, high-status occupations. Such a system is obviously unacceptable in light of present demands for equal employment opportunity.

Well before government concern was directed toward practices of this type, the railroad industry had found that an adequate supply of employees was no longer forthcoming. Although employment as a locomotive engineer or shop craftsman might once have been a desirable employment goal of youth, it is not now necessarily true. Wages in certain railroad occupations are no longer as comparatively attractive; hours for entry-level jobs are irregular and undesirable; working conditions require constant exposure to weather extremes; and, of course, prospects for protracted job security are not certain. Sons of railroad workers, along with those of other high-pay, high-status blue collar occupations, are now choosing white collar occupations, often after college graduation. This is not to imply that there is a dearth of qualified applicants interested in the industry. The industry has, however, suffered from a decline in the enviable supply of workers it once enjoyed.

Unfortunately the changing status of railroad employment has been assessed by Negro youths as well as white. Those enviable railroad positions which were for so long held beyond the reach of Negro helpers and laborers are now often less acceptable than jobs opened recently to them in other industries. Moreover, the goodwill and image that railroads had developed over the years in the Negro community have been largely negated by changing attitudes. Those industries which formerly employed few, if any, Negroes can rapidly acquire a relatively good image by hiring a few Negro workers in "visible" occupations. The railroads, on the other hand, cannot quickly change the impression that Negroes are employed only in "red, white and blue" jobs—those with "red caps, white coats and blue denims." To be sure, carriers hiring in the South or in rural areas with little industry are able to offer comparatively high wage opportunities. In the cities, however, it has become very difficult in the current tight labor market to recruit young, qualified Negroes.

The industry has used a variety of ways to locate and hire needed hourly personnel. Although several firms presently do no formal recruiting, relying solely on referrals by present employees and walk-in applicants, peak hiring periods force the industry generally to seek actively additional workers. Newspaper employment advertisements and public employment agencies have been used most frequently. These routine channels are adequate to meet employment needs, but the percentage of applicants who are Negro is typically below that which must be screened to improve substantially the Negro employment picture. This has caused several employers to move outside the normal procedures in seeking Negro employees.

Special Programs

Special programs aimed directly at bringing Negroes into the firm have been utilized by most of the large carriers. To date, however, most of the efforts have been concentrated in major metropolitan areas, particularly those cities in which are located the firm's corporate headquarters and major terminals. In their attempts to attract Negro employees, railroads have placed advertisements in minority-oriented newspapers, contacted civil rights organizations, and spoken with high school students and counselors. In general, the results of these efforts have not justified the time and money invested. More recently, several carriers participated in the JOBS (Job Opportunities in the Business Sector) program of the National Alliance of Business (NAB). In fact, three railroad executives served as chairmen of this program in their respective headquarters cities. Each of the participating firms pledged to hire and train a stated number of disadvantaged people. Full participation by the industry in programs of this nature would be invaluable in helping to alleviate the overall Negro employment problem, and in renewing the (industry's) reservoir of goodwill in the Negro community.[150]

College recruiting presents an even more difficult problem for the industry. Most railroads as a general rule do not conduct formal college recruiting programs each year. Although the mammoth Penn Central recruited on nearly 100 campuses prior to its bankruptcy, most carriers recruit at no more than ten to thirty colleges. Among these lists of schools we can expect to

---

150. Tom Shedd, "Railroads & the Negro Renewing the Reservoir of Good Will," *Modern Railroads*, Vol. 24 (February 1969), pp. 44-45.

find at most four or five Negro schools. Large firms in other industries may well recruit at more than thirty Negro colleges! The reception given by graduates at all schools has been disappointing. The railroad industry has not been able to compete successfully for the type of student it desires; the image of a declining industry without the promise of rapid advancement is far below the expectations of current graduates. This is particularly true for the few recent Negro graduates with technical or business backgrounds who are able to command premium salaries. A personnel manager for a medium-sized company related his experience on the campus of a large midwestern university. During his visit he was placed in an interview cubicle next to a major aerospace contractor. He had three interviews with students spread over a full day while the aerospace representative was able to interest enough students in his firm to fill two company planes which were later flown in to transport applicants to the West Coast. Experience on Negro campuses has been even less profitable.

Selection Criteria

In general, firms in the industry have required proof of high school graduation (or its equivalent) and the successful completion of one or more tests for entering blue collar jobs. These requirements have been relaxed in recent years by several firms as a result of a recognized "systemic" discrimination, but the industry's common selection criteria remain a major cause for concern. Many jobs in the industry have traditionally been filled by casual laborers with very limited formal education. Recent technological change and resulting changes in manpower requirements, however, have forced the industry to initiate increasingly rigid criteria in applicant screening. There exists no evidence of validation for the use of current selection techniques, with the exception of tests for specific skills.

There is, to be sure, an obvious need for arithmetic and reading skills for most occupations in the industry. Rules and regulations must be understood thoroughly; reports must be filed; and crew orders must be read daily. The lack of direct supervision for train crews, maintenance-of-way crews, and certain other occupations makes this important for safety as well as efficiency. The high school diploma serves well as a quick and efficient technique for eliminating the poorly educated. Little proof has been developed, however, that any of the hourly occupations can be done only by men with a twelfth grade education, nor is there evidence that high school education insures the attainment of any specific skills level. The high school diploma may well be an effective measure of ability, initiative, and perseverance for middle class suburban youth, but for the ghetto resident it may represent a dull, unrewarding investment. It was not until the mid-1960's that any of the carriers began to eliminate this practice in favor of more valid selection standards.

Most of the firms also rely for selection on the applicant's score on one or more tests. Although several different tests are used by carriers to measure competence in specific mechanical and clerical skills, aptitude for acquiring these skills, and to measure general intelligence, there is one test which clearly has been more generally used than any other—the Wonderlic Personnel Test. This test was initially adopted by the industry before World War II to measure "general aptitudes," "potential," or "native intelligence." In form it is an abridgement and adaptation of the Otis Self-Administering Test of Mental Ability, with which its results are highly correlated.[151] Total testing time is a very quick and efficient twelve minutes. Today, after thirty years of use, the industry has yet to conduct the experimental studies to substantiate its efficiency as a predictor of job success. Furthermore, even the author of this test, upon direct question, has been unable to supply evidence of its validity in minority group testing.[152] On its face, the questions asked are culturally restricted and of little direct relevance to railroad operations. The railroad carriers have, however, recently downgraded the importance of this test or eliminated it completely from employee selection.

The inherent danger of discrimination in personnel testing has been recognized for many years. The "Intelligence" test, particularly, is generally recognized as a measure, not of native ability, but rather of "the present capability of demonstrating skill or knowledge from which, assuming the individual's *cultural opportunities to have been within the normal range,* one may infer . . . his likelihood of success in certain *academic endeavors.*" [153]

---

151. Anne Anastasi, *Psychological Testing* (New York: The Macmillan Co., 1961), p. 234.

152. Correspondence in author's possession.

153. Draft of statement by George K. Bennett, President, The Psychological Corporation, "Ability Testing and the Culturally Disadvantaged," October 6, 1966.

Even the widely used "aptitude" tests are known to be dependent upon past experience with the symbols or tools employed in the test. Very few tests in industry are not oriented to the background, education, and experiences of middle class child rearing practices.

Despite this knowledge, the government failed to recognize formally these weaknesses in personnel testing until 1966 when the EEOC issued its *Guidelines on Employment Testing Procedures*.[154] This statement was supplemented in September 1968 by a directive on testing issued by the then Secretary of Labor, Willard Wirtz. The latter statement is applicable only to those firms which are subject to Executive Order 11246, which established the Office of Federal Contract Compliance. Although the EEOC *Guidelines* are only suggestive of desirable testing procedures, the directive by Wirtz requires that each federal contractor have available for inspection, "within reasonable time, evidence that the tests are valid for their intended purposes. Such evidence shall be examined in compliance reviews for indications of possible discrimination, such as instances of higher rejection rates for minority candidates." The evidence of validity required by compliance examiners is to "consist of empirical data demonstrating that the test is predictive of or significantly correlated with important elements of work behavior comprising or relevant to the job(s) for which candidates are being evaluated." [155]

A decision by the U.S. Court of Appeals for the Fourth Circuit in the case of *Griggs* v. *Duke Power Co.*[156] has opened the entire question of employee selection, including the statements by the EEOC and the Secretary of Labor, to great uncertainty. The court ruled that selection criteria, including but not limited to test results, are valid if they met "a genuine business purpose" and the policy was not initiated to discriminate against minority employees. In effect, the ruling broadens the usual criteria for validity from correlation with job success to a general relation-

---

154. " 'Guidelines on Employment Testing Procedures' Adopted by Equal Employment Opportunity Commission," *White Collar Report* (No. 496), September 8, 1966, pp. C-1 to C-3.

155. *Federal Register*, "Validation of Employment Tests by Contractors and Subcontractors Subject to the Provisions of Executive Order 11246," Vol. 33 (September 24, 1968).

156. 420 F. 2d 1225 (4th Cir. 1970). The U. S. Supreme Court granted certiorari recently.

ship with an obvious business motive. This potentially far-reaching business needs test would seem to provide a wide umbrella of protection for all objective employment criteria not adopted for the intended purpose of discrimination. For example, an employer could attempt to justify given criteria with a defense as vague as "maintaining efficiency and morale."

Although the approach adopted by the EEOC and the OFCC has broad support among prominent psychologists,[157] it does pose many formidable problems. The elimination of objective employment criteria which make cultural differences significant in selection would require sweeping change. It is evident that such a requirement would necessitate the elimination of virtually all currently developed tests as well as the use of educational attainments and employment backgrounds. If it assumed that many present standards and criteria are forbidden by law because of their biased effect, the employer is left with mostly subjective techniques in making employment decisions. Past experience clearly indicates that this is not a desirable outcome. It remains, however, to the employers advantage to be able to select the best potential employees.

The railroad industry, through the Committee on Equal Employment Opportunities, began in October 1968 an extended testing program which may develop a satisfactory approach to the problem. Although individual firms could hardly be expected to screen an adequate number of applicants of the many culturally distinct groups, an entire industry can feasibly attempt such an effort, at little cost to the individual firms.

The project, as conceived, is to develop a validated testing program for eighteen jobs to which entrants into the industry will progress "within a reasonable period of time." It is being carried out in cooperation with Science Research Associates (SRA), who are supplying a lengthy battery of various types of tests. Each job is being analyzed, with a statement of general and specific duties and worker specifications prepared for each. Second, criteria are being selected to evaluate the performance of certain work elements. Plans call for the evaluation of 800 to 1,000 employees based upon these criteria. Employees will be selected from several cooperating firms. Finally, then, each se-

157. The *EEOC Guidelines* adopted the *Standards for Educational and Psychological Tests and Manuals*, prepared by a joint committee of the American Psychological Association, American Educational Research Association, and National Council on Measurement in Education.

lected employee will be tested and his scores will be correlated
with the evaluation of his performance. This is, of course, a
"concurrent" validation study which is considerably less valu-
able than a "predictive" study. The time saved in the current
study, in light of present hiring rates, would appear to make
this a minor compromise. The desired result then will be a series
of tests, validated for race, age, sex, and geographic location.
Although this project has not yet been completed, primarily because of the reluctance of several key companies to participate
fully, the latest results are very encouraging. Other industries
with similar problems would do well to examine this exciting pro-
totype. If projects of this nature are not successfully completed,
the future use of testing and other objective selection standards
will be seriously jeopardized since they will be readily open to
challenge in the courts.

TRAINING PROGRAMS

Most of the hourly jobs in the railroad industry are filled
through informal, on-the-job training. Formal apprenticeship
training has been utilized by most carriers in the skilled maintenance of equipment occupations, but the drastic decline in employment has reduced even these programs to minimal levels. As
a rule, training continues to be carried out in a manner similar
to that done half a century ago. Testing may be required to ascertain objectively the level of trainee skills and knowledge.

Classroom training has recently been initiated by several carriers for a limited number of occupations. Such an approach
is, however, limited by the small number of new hires entering
an occupation at any one time. In an industry in which many
jobs require a surprisingly large accumulation of diffuse knowledge, it is unfortunate that an employee's rate of acquisition
must to a degree be dependent on the cooperation of coworkers
and chance experience. On the other hand, the industry can ill
afford to have training personnel employed at each hiring point.

It was pointed out earlier in this study that Negroes have
been limited to certain jobs or lines of progression by contract
and by the use of certain testing procedures. These practices had
developed over several decades through formal and informal cooperation of previously noted unions and several carriers. A
series of court cases in the 1950's and the building civil rights
movement gradually eliminated these offensive practices, with the

possible exception of a few affecting single shops or terminals. Training and job opportunities are now restricted only as they are limited by the seniority system to be discussed in the next section.

Apprentice Training

Formal training then is largely confined to the maintenance of equipment occupations. Apprentice programs have been used to fill seven shop crafts—blacksmiths, boilermakers, carmen, electrical workers, machinists, molders, and sheet-metal workers. A survey conducted by the Department of Labor in early 1968 found that seventy-five of eighty-one firms responding have collective bargaining agreements which provide for the indenture of apprentices. Three other firms maintain apprentice programs although they are not covered in the labor-management contract. Each of these seventy-eight firms, however, does not provide apprentice training for each of the seven occupations. Only apprenticeships leading to machinists positions are provided by each of the carriers.[158]

The drastic reductions in employment among the shop crafts, particularly blacksmiths, boilermakers and molders, have virtually eliminated apprentice training on many railroads. Only seventy-one of the firms offering such programs have had apprentices enter into and/or complete training in one or more occupations in the five-year period, 1963-1967. Thirty-seven of those carriers have had less than ten apprenticeship completions in this span. The seventy-one firms using these apprentice arrangements had a total of approximately 11,800 new registrations compared to 3,400 apprenticeship completions. Thus, there were over three and one-half times as many registrations as there were completions.

Apprenticeship training is not the only route which can be followed to gain a journeyman position. In fact, of the 84,000 craftsmen covered in the survey, only 25 percent had completed a full four year apprenticeship. Over 55 percent had been upgraded to journeymen status either before completing an apprentice program or directly from other railroad occupations.

---

158. U.S. Department of Labor, Labor-Management Services Administration, *Railroad Shopcraft Factfinding Study* (Washington: U.S. Government Printing Office, 1968), pp. 35, 38, 39. Unless otherwise noted, all subsequent information pertaining to apprentice programs has been taken from this study.

The remaining journeymen were hired directly into these positions after being trained in other industries. Significantly, several railroads are now attempting to introduce greatly abbreviated training programs, which may provide easy access to better jobs.

Negroes historically have experienced a negligible rate of participation in apprentice programs. Previous discussion noted that they were barred from membership in most of the shopcraft unions until after World War II. Employment in shops was limited as a general rule to laborer or skilled trades helper occupations. It is through these occupations that a few Negroes have been upgraded recently to craftsmen positions. Nearly 33,000 workers were so upgraded during the 1963-1967 period from four unskilled shop occupations in which many Negroes have worked. This would seem to provide an excellent opportunity for carriers to quickly improve Negro representation in the seven basic skilled maintenance occupations. The small increase in job opportunities because of increased retirements in recent years may force several firms to quickly upgrade workers from this only source of experienced personnel.

The special training programs which are gradually being undertaken in other industries to raise the educational. level of present employees sufficiently to qualify them for upgrading have not proliferated among railroad concerns. Although there is very definite need for affirmative action programs of this nature, only one substantial program has thus far been initiated. A group of 166 Chicago area railroad employees recently completed an adult education program leading to the equivalent of a high school education. The program is run by the Board for Fundamental Education, a nonprofit organization chartered by Congress.[159] Courses are offered in reading and arithmetic skills and English for non-English speaking employees.

A few other companies have also established small training programs to retrain present employees who would otherwise have been furloughed or to provide special training to turn previous "hard-core" unemployed into productive employees. The low priority of such programs relative to the industry's critical problems has greatly diminished the possibility of many additional programs of this nature being instituted.

---

159. Association of American Railroads, "Information Letter," August 12, 1970.

SENIORITY AND PROMOTIONS

"Seniority is as inseparable a part of a railroad as wheels and whistles." [160] The railroad industry was the first to use seniority or job tenure as a mechanism for promotion and job security. Informal use of seniority in the industry was initiated well before the Civil War. When the first collective bargaining agreements were negotiated beginning in the 1870's, a lengthy segment of each was devoted to the rules that would govern promotions and work assignments. The use of seniority as a defense against the poor supervision too often prevalent on early railroads quickly spread throughout the industry. By the early 1900's each of the major unions had already standardized its seniority system in a form similar to that presently in use. The period of government control during World War I saw an extension of the several seniority systems to almost all railroad employees below the management level.

Today nearly 95 percent of the employees of each carrier come under the purview of a seniority system. This mechanism is the dominant criterion in promotions, layoffs, recalls, and work assignments. As a general rule, computed seniority is limited only to stated occupations in the labor contract. Seniority is further defined by geographic area, the "seniority district." Accumulated seniority is lost as the employee moves to an occupation which is not in the previous line of progression or as he moves to a different terminal or repair shop. The terms "plant seniority" or "department seniority" have little relevance in railroad negotiations.

The overall railroad seniority system is too complex to be described fully. Most railroad employees, however, rapidly develop an understanding of the system and its importance to them. The present attrition in most lines of progression and the wide variation in work assignments make the worker's place on the seniority roster of vital concern. Most lines of progression have only two or three occupational levels. For example, the applicant who is hired as a brakeman on a train has one step to progress to conductor. The same is true for the apprentice to journeyman line of progression and that of many other occupational lines. The seniority system, however, is most important in the choice of work assignment. In train and engine service, for instance,

---

160. Dan Mater, "The Development and Operation of the Railroad Seniority System," *Journal of Business*, Vol. 13 (October 1940), p. 388.

new employees are assigned to "extra board" or relief work, which will mean part time assignment to the position until he gains seniority. He then would move into the "pool," with assignments on unscheduled freight trains on a "first in, first out of terminal" basis. Finally, with increased seniority, they will gain permanent positions on regular, scheduled trains. Choices for assignment to one of the three "tricks" or shifts, to passenger or freight runs, and to numerous other variations in work assignments are based solely on seniority. Similar choices are made for each hourly occupation. The importance of the seniority systems to the industry is clearly evident.

Seniority systems have had a tragic impact on the opportunities for advancement by Negro employees. Negroes have either been ineligible for promotion, that is, from fireman to engineer, or have been forced to relinquish seniority to move to acceptable positions, i.e., from helper to journeyman. Several arrangements for limiting the advancement of Negro workers were discussed in Chapter III. Now that job barriers have generally been removed, few Negro workers are willing to give up accumulated seniority. They would rather retain the security of a relatively high-wage, low-skill job than become subject to the poor work assignments and possible layoff which follow with movement to more desirable positions.

The railroad seniority system has thus "frozen" Negro employees into historically, discriminatory employment patterns. This, as the court concluded in the precedent setting *Quarles* v. *Philip Morris, Inc.* case,[161] was not the intent of Congress. In *Quarles*, as in the railroad industry, interdepartmental transfers generally involved the loss of all seniority. The transfer policy was not limited to Negroes, but only Negroes had been limited in their job opportunities prior to the Civil Rights Act. The court held that, although the departmental structure "serves many legitimate functions," [162] job restrictions imposed on Negro workers were unlawfully perpetuated by the seniority system. The courts have directed the firm to implement a "mill seniority" system rather than the previous "job seniority" system to enable Negro employees to bid freely for all future job opportunities.

---

161. 279 F. Supp. 505 (E.D. Va. 1968).

162. *Id.*, at 513.

This theory has been accepted in general in subsequent decisions,[163] with the clarification that initial employment criteria which were applied equally to all applicants are acceptable and no relief is necessary.[164]

The decisions in these cases have critical importance for the railroads. The practices and consequent results that have been vigorously condemned are clearly similar to those promulgated by the railroad unions. A similar court order enjoining railroad companies and unions from following the traditional seniority systems would have a momentous impact on the industry. This, however, appears to be the underlying purpose in a civil suit filed by the Justice Department against the Jacksonville Terminal Company and sixteen railroad unions. In this suit the government has charged the parties with a "pattern and practice" of discrimination in initial job assignment, promotion, demotion, and layoff. Significantly, it is alleged that the craft seniority system perpetuates the effects of these acts and should be discontinued.

Although the District Court has initially ruled against the allegation of the Justice Department,[165] an appeal was filed in July 1970. The court in *Quarles* argued that "seniority rights . . . are not vested, indefeasible rights. They are expectancies derived from the collective bargaining agreement, and are subject to modification." [166] The modification sought by the plaintiff in the *Jacksonville Terminal* case would allow employees to transfer to any occupation if their tenure *since initial hiring* and ability warrant promotion. If the precedent previously established in *Crown-Zellerbach* were to be adopted, employees would have to

---

163. See, for example, *Local 189, United Papermakers* v. *United States*, 416 F. 2d 980 (5th Cir. 1969), aff'g 282 F. Supp. 39 (E. D. La. 1968), cert. denied, 397 U.S. 919 (1970). For further discussion of the *Quarles* and *Papermakers* cases, see Herbert R. Northrup and Richard L. Rowan, *Negro Employment in Southern Industry*, Studies of Negro Employment, Vol. IV (Philadelphia: Industrial Research Unit, Wharton School of Finance and Commerce, University of Pennsylvania, 1970), Parts One and Three.

164. *Griggs, supra,* note 156 at 1229.

165. *United States* v. *Jacksonville Terminal*, Civil No. 68-239 (M.D. Fla., May 5, 1970).

166. *Quarles, supra* note 161 at 520.

be qualified. However, the company would have to provide reasonable training to enable some employees to transfer.[167]

This would allow all employees, regardless of previous occupational experience or union affiliation, to transfer to any desired occupation provided that they had sufficient "plant" seniority, and met reasonable qualifications. If a Negro employee of long tenure wished to become, for example, a locomotive engineer, he could bid for an opening as fireman, obtain the requisite training, and not only obtain a position but after becoming qualified, could move ahead of present engineers in desirable work assignments provided his "plant" seniority exceeded theirs.

If the required changes set forth in *Crown-Zellerbach* would be implemented in full in the railroad industry, the results could also be chaotic and burdensome. It would enable Negro employees to gain their "rightful place" after years of discrimination, but the costs to the industry in possible labor strife, temporary decline in efficiency due to work force instability and in the development of training programs may be detrimental to the precarious position of the industry. The final decision in the *Jacksonville Terminal* case should be of interest both for its impact on the railroad industry and on the use of seniority generally. Moreover, the EEOC and the Department of Justice are planning a number of other cases involving railroads and railroad unions which together should devise a body of law that determines the nature of relief to be given to Negro railroad employees.[168]

---

167. *Daily Labor Report*, "Memorandum Opinion and Decree of U. S. District Court, Eastern District of Louisiana, in Case of U.S. v. United Papermakers and Crown-Zellerbach Corporation," July 2, 1969 (No. 127), Section D. See also, Northrup and Rowan, *op. cit.*

168. Interviews with EEOC legal staff, November 1970.

CHAPTER VII

Government Policy: A Study in Contrasts

The various branches of the federal government concerned with the problems of railroad labor have not consistently instituted policies designed to expedite equal employment opportunity. As early as World War I, it was noted, the government attempted to eliminate pay differentials for Negro employees. Then, in 1941, Franklin Roosevelt issued the first of several executive orders requiring private concerns holding contracts with the federal government to agree not to discriminate against Negroes in employment. The influence exerted by these orders, albeit weak in the railroad industry, marked a significant shift in national policy. In addition, the courts beginning with the previously cited *Steele* v. *Louisville & Nashville Railroad* case set down a number of decisions enjoining specific discriminatory practices. Although these events provided some relief to Negro railroad employees, the policies of both the National Mediation Board and the National Railroad Adjustment Board continued often to be injurious to the interests of Negro employees. The pertinent actions of each of these government branches and agencies are examined in detail in this chapter.

PRESIDENTIAL EXECUTIVE ORDERS

We have already discussed the impact of the Executive Orders of Presidents Roosevelt and Kennedy on Negro job opportunities in the industry. In addition, the impact of the state fair employment practice laws, particularly of New York, has been noted. Between the Roosevelt and Kennedy periods, each President issued executive orders pertaining to fair employment by government contractors, but although the railroads have been cited as one of three industries responsible for the largest number of complaints, prior to 1960, no action was ever taken on these cases on the grounds of jurisdictional problems with other federal agencies.[169]

Actually, meaningful government compliance activity for railroads did not begin until after President Kennedy issued his second executive order in 1963. In an effort to avoid duplication of investigative effort, the Post Office Department was designated as the Predominant Interest Agency (PIA) for investigating complaints and otherwise securing compliance with the Order in the railroad and trucking industries. The authority to conduct compliance reviews was assigned to an office of the POD Office of Regional Administration, headed by Paul Nagle as Deputy Contracts Compliance Officer.

Compliance activity in the railroad industry has since been moderate but seemingly as effective as that in most other industries. As a result of the relative lack of job opportunities in the industry, Nagle and his successor, Clarence Featherson, have chosen to concentrate their limited resources on the trucking industry which has problems with more ready solutions. Although the Post Office Compliance staff was expanded during 1968, reliance has been heavily left to the "pattern of discrimination" suits filed by the Department of Justice because of their wide impact and clearly legal basis.

CONGRESSIONAL ACTION

Congressional action relating to railroad civil rights issue has taken several roadways involving most directly the Equal Employment Opportunity Commission and other activities arising from Title VII of the Civil Rights Act of 1964, but indirectly and very pertinently, the Railway Labor Act and its administrative agencies, the National Mediation Board and the National Railroad Adjustment Board. We have already discussed the key *Jacksonville Terminal* case arising out of "patterns of discrimination" suits filed pursuant to Title VII, and noted that this case and similar suits now being filed may well be the most pertinent

169. Paul H. Norgren and Samuel E. Hill, *Toward Fair Employment* (New York: Columbia University Press, 1964), p. 173. The other industries cited were petroleum refining and construction. The latter still rates high as a source of complaints and discrimination. See also, Herbert R. Northrup and Richard L. Rowan, *Negro Employment in Basic Industry*, Studies of Negro Employment, Vol. I (Philadelphia: Industrial Research Unit, Wharton School of Finance and Commerce, University of Pennsylvania, 1970), Part Five.

actions of government to date. We shall refer again to the court suits below. Suffice here to note that we have not discerned any particularly favorable results from EEOC conciliation activity except as a means of developing data for further legislation. The reason may well be that nearly all cases require a change of union contracts for relief, and the unions have been unwilling, and probably because of membership pressure, unable to alter their practices without court imposed rulings.

The National Mediation Board

The National Mediation Board, a three man agency created by the 1934 amendments to the Railway Labor Act of 1926, is charged with using its good offices to mediate labor disputes arising on the railroads, and since 1936, the airlines also. In addition, Section 2, Ninth, of the Amended Act requires the NMB "to investigate such dispute(s) and to certify to both parties . . . the name or names of the individuals or organizations that have been designated and authorized to represent the employees involved in the dispute, and certify the same to the carrier." [170] A certification of the Board is final and not subject to court review.[171] Upon receipt of a certification from the Board, the carrier is obligated to "treat with the representative so certified as the representative of the craft or class for the purposes of this Act." [172]

The Railway Labor Act provides the Board with wide discretion in determining who shall participate in the choice of the representative, and in deciding on the method for choosing the bargaining agent. The NMB is authorized "to take a secret ballot of the employees involved, or to utilize any other appropriate method of ascertaining the names" of the representative preferred by the majority of the employees. "In the conduct of any election for the purposes herein indicated, the Board shall designate who may participate in the election and establish the rules to govern the election . . ." [173]

---

170. National Mediation Board, *Administration of the Railroad Labor Act by the National Mediation Board, 1934-1957*, (Washington: Government Printing Office, 1958), p. 56.

171. *Switchmen's Union of North America* v. *National Mediation Board*, 320 U.S. 297 (1943); *General Committee of Adjustment* v. *Missouri-Kansas-Texas R.R.*, 320 U.S. 323 (1943).

172. National Mediation Board, *loc. cit.*

173. *Ibid.*, pp. 56-57.

This legislation then does not clearly specify how the appropriate bargaining unit is to be determined. Congress required only that the bargaining unit be a craft or class, but it did not clearly define these terms. It stated further that a majority of the designated bargaining unit may determine the representative, but the implementation of this decree was subject to the interpretation of the NMB. The policies and the procedures of the Board with regard to unit determination and the selection of the bargaining representative are then solely within the discretion of the National Mediation Board.

The Mediation Board chose early to maintain an informal, unstructured approach to these problems. This function of the NMB in deciding both who can participate in the selection of representation and how he is to be chosen is, of course, adjudicatory, and it was decided that the adoption of a formal role similar to that of the National Labor Relations Board would conflict with the primary purpose of the Mediation Board, conciliation in the settlement of threatened work stoppages. Since the NMB deals constantly with the same unions, they were undoubtedly correct in this assumption. The lack of structure, however, made it very difficult for small groups of Negro workers to protect their rights. It was not until the Administrative Procedures Act [174] was passed in 1946 that the National Mediation Board was forced to establish permanent, well defined rules and procedures. Prior to that time no written statement of the policies of the Board had ever been prepared for the use of interested parties.

The definition of "craft or class" proved to be the most significant policy decision to be made. At first, the Mediation Board attempted "to avoid any general ruling, but to decide each case on the basis of the facts developed by the investigation of the case." The Board found, however, that pressure was building "to split classes of employees hitherto considered a unit into more and smaller groups." After some decisions had been made yielding to this pressure, "demands were made that the Board follow the same rulings in subsequent cases, and other groups of employees within a class or craft insisted they, too, were entitled to separation as distinct crafts." [175]

---

174. 60 Stat. 237.

175. National Mediation Board, *op. cit.*, p. 21.

The Mediation Board contended, however, that continued subdivision of "recognized crafts or classes of employees has already gone too far," and that the main purposes of the Act, the making and maintenance of contracts, and the avoidance of labor disputes, may be accomplished only with increased difficulty. For this reason it declared that henceforth it would be "inclined . . . to avoid unnecessary multiplication of subcrafts or subclasses, and to maintain, so far as possible, the customary groupings of employees into crafts or classes as they have been established by accepted practice over a period of years in the making of wage and rule agreements." [176] This policy has been closely followed by the Board since 1935.

In general, collective bargaining under the Railway Labor Act has been facilitated by this policy. The proliferation of bargaining units tends needlessly to increase competition among unions bargaining with the same carriers and to make union-management relationships excessively complex. In fact, the number of separate bargaining units which have been designated in the railroad industry may well be one of the major problems affecting railroad labor relations. This policy also amounts to a complete victory for the "standard" railway labor organizations; these unions are the ones which have "established . . . accepted practice." In effect, *"the Mediation Board defines the bargaining unit to suit the jurisdictional claims of the standard railway unions."* [177]

This policy has been applied to all minority interest groups. Since Negroes were not accepted for membership or had been relegated to inferior status in auxiliary locals in most of the standard unions, they have quite naturally attempted, from time to time, to form their own organizations. These attempts, however, were effectively thwarted by the Mediation Board policy. Statements of policy by the Board indicate that it has long been aware of the existence of discrimination in the industry. The Board, nevertheless, has strictly adhered to a policy of apparent neutrality to the race issue:

The Board has definitely ruled that a craft or class of employees may not be divided into two or more on the basis of race or color for the purpose

176. *Ibid.*, p. 21.

177. Herbert R. Northrup, "The Appropriate Bargaining Unit Question Under the Railway Labor Act," *Quarterly Journal of Economics;* Vol. 60 (February 1946), p. 254.

of choosing representatives. All those employed in the craft or class regardless of race, creed, or color, must be given the opportunity to vote for the representatives of the whole craft or class.[178]

The effect of this policy is graphically illustrated in the case of *Brotherhood of Railway and Steamship Clerks* v. *United Transport Service Employees of America*.[179] This case involved the conflicting claims of the two rival labor organizations concerning the right to represent forty-five Negro redcaps (porters) employed at the Union Depot in St. Paul, Minnesota. Although these workers were then ineligible for full membership in the Clerks union because of their race, and had unanimously designated the UTSEA as their bargaining agent, the Mediation Board dismissed the representation application of the UTSEA on the grounds that station porters are part of the clerical, freight handling, station and store employee class and not a separate class or craft for the purposes of the Act and that no dispute over representation has been found to exist among the craft or class of such employees in the service of the Company.[180]

In an action brought by the UTSEA to review this ruling a federal district court declared the dismissal order void; it found that the porters were a separate and distinct class or craft, and directed the Mediation Board to certify the UTSEA as the bargaining representative of the porters.[181] The Court of Appeals affirmed [182] with a scathing criticism of the Board's ruling by then Chief Judge Groner. He first pointed out that "the effect of the action of the Board is to force this particular group of employees to accept representation by an organization in which it has no right to membership, nor right to speak or be heard in its own behalf." This result he termed "so inadmissible, so palpably unjust and so opposed to the primary principles of the Act as to make the Board's decision upholding it wholly untenable and arbitrary." The victory gained by the UTSEA was short-lived, however, for the Supreme Court reversed the deci-

178. National Mediation Board, *op. cit.*, p. 22.

179. 137 F. 2d 817 (D.C. Cir. 1943); reversed on procedural grounds, 320 U.S. 715 (1943).

180. In the Matter of Representation of Employees of the St. Paul Union Depot Co., Car No. R-635, Nov. 26, 1940.

181. Herbert R. Northrup, *Organized Labor and the Negro* (New York: Harper & Bro., 1944), p. 89.

182. *Brotherhood of Railway and Steamship Clerks, supra* note 179.

sion, on the basis of the then recently established rule that Mediation Board certifications are not subject to judicial review.[183]

Similar cases have arisen affecting other Negro "clerical" employees, Negro firemen, Negro maintenance of way laborers and other Negro employees. They have been placed, almost without exception, into locals where they were denied any effective voice in union affairs. The Board's policy has been to refuse to certify a bargaining unit smaller in scope than an entire carrier. Consequently, even in those instances in which Negro employees have been the majority of the craft or class at one location, they seldom control enough votes to carry a system-wide election. In light of the racial policies of the "standard" unions, the Mediation Board insured results unfavorable to Negro interests, regardless of the extent of participation in the election. Although Negro employees have only gained majority status in carrier-wide bargaining units on a few small carriers, evidence indicates that even in these instances white employees and their unions, with the possible cooperation of the staff of the Mediation Board, have been able to deny effectively the statutory rights of the Negro workers to select a representative. For example, in an election conducted on the Atlanta, Birmingham and Coast Railroad in April 1940, the Mediation Board certified the Brotherhood of Locomotive Firemen and Enginemen as the exclusive bargaining agent of both the engineers, firemen, hostlers, and hostler helpers. At the time of the election, however, the A.B. & C. employed ninety-four firemen, hostlers, and outside hostler helpers, of whom only twenty-five were white. The engineers and the few white firemen were represented by a local organization, the Railway Employe's Co-operative Association; the Negro firemen and hostlers by their own local union, the Colored Hostler Helpers and Locomotive Firemen, Inc.

Both the white organization and the Negro organization were denied a place on the ballot. During the election no Negro observers were allowed into the polling areas, and the ballots were counted in a hotel room to which no Negro workers were admitted. According to the Board's records, the BLF&E defeated "other organizations or individuals" in the election, 43 to 2 in the engineers class, and 47 to 41 in the firemen and hostler class. The Negro union protested the results to the Board, claiming that the Negro voters had overwhelmingly voted for their

183. 320 U.S. 715 (1943).

union as a write-in choice, but the protest was disallowed. Protests involving questionable election outcomes also have been raised by the trainmen on the A.B. & C., trackmen on the Florida East Coast, firemen on the Central of Georgia, and the redcaps in the St. Paul terminal.[184]

Furthermore, even in those instances in which white unions have not been interested in organizing Negro employees, the Negro group has found it difficult to have their choice for representation certified by the Board. The Florida East Coast Railway employed only Negroes as locomotive firemen prior to World War II. Before the passage of the Railway Labor Act and continuing until the latter part of 1928, the Negro firemen were represented by the all-white Brotherhood of Locomotive Engineers (BLE). Then in 1929, the Board of Mediation certified Jessie Helm, former General Chairman of the BLE, as an individual, as the bargaining agent for the firemen. Upon his death in 1936, his widow was named as representative and served in that capacity until 1943. Despite this "representation" the carrier entered into an agreement in 1942 which restricted opportunities for Negroes in these positions.

Consequently, the Negro firemen took the initiative and gained recognition in 1943 for the Florida East Coast Association of Colored Locomotive Firemen, Inc. This organization was replaced in 1946 by another Negro union, the International Association of Railway Employees, which was established in the 1940's to attempt to unite the few local Negro unions.[185] (Although this organization remains the designated representative, under a 1962 agreement between the company, the union, and a subsidiary trucking company, all firemen with less than ten years seniority were transfered to employment with the trucking concern. Locomotive firemen with greater seniority continued in employment until separated through normal attrition. This, of course, is the period during which the industry was engaged in a bitter struggle to eliminate locomotive firemen from employment on diesels.)

The already noted decision in *Steele*,[186] and that in a subsequent 1946 case before the Supreme Court of Kansas, *Betts* v.

---

184. Northrup, *Organized Labor and the Negro, op. cit.*, p. 60.

185. Letter from R. W. Wyckoff, Vice President, Florida East Coast Railway, July 18, 1969, and Northrup, *ibid.*, pp. 23-78.

186. *Steele* v. *Louisville & Nashville R.R.*, 323 U.S. at 203 (1944).

Easley,[187] should presumably have had some impact on the unit determination policies of the National Mediation Board. The bargaining agent, as the Court in *Steele* stated, has the imposed duty to represent fairly all members of the bargaining unit. The judicial remedies of injunction and damages are available when a breach of that duty has occurred. The Supreme Court did, however, specifically note that "the statute does not deny to . . . a bargaining labor organization the right to determine eligibility to its membership." [188] The inherent injustice in the continuation of segregated locals or other form of unequal membership was further delineated by the Kansas Court when it declared that the actions associated with the Carmen's control of a Negro local was in violation of the Fifth Amendment. The implications arising from these two early cases have unfortunately never been recognized in NMB policy. This is in contrast to the policies adopted by the National Labor Relations Board shortly after *Steele.*[189]

The National Mediation Board further reduced the opportunity for Negroes to gain just representation or to reject undesired representation by its balloting procedures in cetrification elections. The effect of two NMB policy decisions employed in concert greatly enhances the possibility of domination by a minority of white workers. First, the Board has chosen to certify a union on the basis of a majority of the votes cast, as opposed to a majority of employees eligible to vote (provided that a majority of those eligible to vote did so). This policy was sanctioned by the Supreme Court in *Virginia Railroad Co.* v. *System Federation No. 40,*[190] wherein the railroad questioned the exact meaning of the word "majority." This, as the Court of Appeals noted, is all that is required in governmental elections in which the public participates. Second, the Board has continually refused to include a provision on the ballot for voting for "No Union." Employees not desiring to be represented are able to

187. 161 Kan. 459 (1946).

188. 323 U.S. at 204.

189. See, for example, *Bethlehem-Almeda Shipyard, Inc.,* 53 NLRB 999; *Larus & Brother Co.,* 16 LRR 717; *Atlanta Oak Flooring,* 16 LRR 689; *Carter Manufacturing Co.,* 59 NLRB 804. Later the NLRB found such discrimination an unfair labor practice by unions. See Herbert R. Northrup and Richard L. Rowan, *Negro Employment in Basic Industry,* Studies of Negro Employment, Vol. I, pp. 473-476.

190. 84 F. 2d 641 (4th Cir. 1936), aff'd 300 U.S. 515 (1937).

indicate their choice only by not voting. Thus, if less than a majority of the eligible votes are cast, no representative is certified.

Even before the *Virginia R.R.* case was heard by the Supreme Court, the National Labor Relations Board discontinued its requirement of a majority of the entire bargaining unit and, in addition, changed its ballot to allow employees to reject representation. The thrust of the *Virginia R.R.* decision, as the NLRB interpreted it, was that those employees who do not vote are presumed to acquiesce in the choice made by those voting. The NLRB stated that this was a contradiction to apply this presumption without allowing an employee to vote "No Union." In *Interlake Iron Corp.*, a case decided soon after the change, the NLRB stated:

(I)f the opportunity of voting against the organizations named on the ballot were denied, a majority might be forced against its will to accept representations by one or the other of the nominees. The policy adopted by the Board is designed merely to make sure that the votes recorded for a particular representative express a free choice rather than a choice in default of the possibility of expressing disapproval of both or all proposed representatives.[191]

The National Mediation Board, on the other hand, has refused to recognize this contention. It has continued to use the same form of ballot as that originally adopted for representation elections—one which makes no provision for voting against representation. In fact, the only form of valid ballot is one cast *for* a representative. A ballot marked "No representation" is considered invalid and considered as not having been cast.[192]

By not allowing a vote for "No Union" under the Supreme Court definition of "majority," the Mediation Board greatly diminished the opportunity for Negro employees to gain desirable representation. Indeed, in most elections Negroes will be a small minority and must assuredly lose. A Negro majority, however, may be allowed to choose between several white unions. Such a choice is, of course, fatuous, and any votes cast can only be by default. Thus, if Negro employees submit to fate and choose not to vote, a white minority can carry the election. Under the earlier definition of "majority" this would have been impossible. For example, if a craft or class of thirteen employees has a

---

191. 4 NLRB 55 (1937).

192. *Allegheny Airlines, Inc.*, NMB Case No. R-3470 (1962).

choice of two unions, A and B, and six desire neither organization, four favor union A, and three want Union B, the six who want other representation can express their sentiment only by not voting. Under Mediation Board policy, the election results would be determined by the seven ballots cast, and Union A would be certified. On the other hand, under NLRB policy a runoff election would be held between Union A and "No Union." Equity decrees that the Mediation Board should either provide a space for voting against representation or should return to the policy of requiring a majority of the bargaining unit, not a majority of the votes cast.

The intent of Congress in passing the Railway Labor Act as amended was manifest, "to see that the men have absolute liberty to join or not join any union or to remain unorganized." [193] The choice between the least of the "evils," discriminatory representation or no representation, is repugnant to the tradition of industry. To assume that those who refrain from voting "assent to the expressed will of the majority" is an untenable argument under the election procedure of the National Mediation Board.

The Supreme Court, however, has continuously argued that election procedures are prerogatives solely of the National Mediation Board and are not subject to court review.[194] Section 2, Ninth, empowers the Board to establish the rules governing elections. It leaves the details to the discretion of the Board with only the caveat that it insure freedom from carrier interference. Thus, the Court has allowed the Board to continue stubbornly to deny employees the full right of participation.

That the Mediation Board would choose to favor the interests of the "standard" railroad unions should have been foreseen by the authors of the Railway Labor Act. The primary function of the Board is to aid in the resolution of disputes over wages, work rules, and other issues. This is clear both from the law and from the pronouncements of the Board. The Board not only regards the determination of representation disputes as a secondary function, but it has repeatedly called attention to the disturbing effect of the latter duty on mediation work. Nor should this be surprising. The Mediation Board must maintain har-

---

193. *Hearing on S. 3266, Before the Senate,* 73d Cong., 2d Sess. (1934).

194. *Brotherhood of Railway Clerks* v. *Ass'n for Benefit of Non-Contract Employees,* 380 U.S. 650 (1965).

monious relationships with the parties with whom it deals. Any attempt by the Board to permit bargaining units which do not coincide with the preferred jurisdictional claims of the "standard" unions would have been detrimental to these relationships, and arguably would have been contrary to the Congressional purpose of avoiding labor-management disputes.[195]

National Railroad Adjustment Board

Unsettled controversies "between an employee or group of employees and a carrier or carriers growing out of grievances or out of the interpretation or application of agreements concerning rates of pay, rules, or working conditions," are referred under Section 3, First of the Act to the National Railroad Adjustment Board. This unique agency is composed of thirty-six members, half of whom are selected by the carriers and half by unions "national in scope." It is divided into four divisions, each with jurisdiction over different groups of employees, and is actually four separate Boards rather than a single agency.[196] A deadlock within any division is broken by the decision of a neutral referee chosen by the division members; if they cannot agree, the referee is chosen by the Mediation Board.

The NRAB has exclusive jurisdiction to settle all disputes arising under the terms of existing collective bargaining agreements. In two cases decided separately but on the same day, *Slocum* v. *Delaware, L & W R. Co.*[197] and *Conductors* v. *Southern Railway Co.*[198] the Supreme Court supported "a denial of power in any court—state as well as federal—to invade the jurisdiction conferred on the Adjustment Board by the [RLA].[199]

---

195. This point was repeatedly made clear by Professor Northrup's writings. See *Organized Labor and the Negro, op. cit.;* and "The Railway Labor Act and Railway Labor Disputes During Wartime," *American Economic Review*, Vol. XXXVI (June 1944), pp. 324-343.

196. The First Division hears cases involving train, engine and yard employees; the Second covers shop employees; the Third, station, station tower and telegraph personnel, dispatchers, maintenance of way employees, signal men, freight handling express, station and stores employees, clerical, and dining and sleeping car employees. The remaining employees are assigned to the Fourth Division.

197. *Slocum* v. *Delaware, Lackawanna and Western R.R.*, 339 U.S. 239 (1950).

198. *Order of Railway Conductors* v. *Southern Ry.*, 339 U.S. 255 (1950).

199. *Slocum, supra* note 197 at 244.

Until amended in 1966, only carriers could contest awards in court, and then only by refusing to comply. Now, either party may have an award reviewed by the court under Section 3, first (q).[200] The court, however, cannot shape a new order; it must "affirm" or "set it aside, in whole or in part." It may deny the award on the following grounds:

1) failure of the board to comply with the requirements of the RLA

2) failure of the order to conform or confine itself to matters within the scope of the board's jurisdiction

3) fraud or corruption by a member of the board.

The Supreme Court's preference for the administrative remedy does not deprive the courts of primary jurisdiction for disputes which are not within the scope of the NRAB's authority. As the statute indicates, it is authorized to consider only those disputes arising between employees and a carrier or carriers. Those disputes which involve an employee and his bargaining representative, as in *Steele*,[201] between two employees,[202] or between an employee and a carrier other than his employer [203] may be adjudicated in court.

Negro employees have received perhaps even less equitable treatment in the several divisions of the NRAB than they have from the Mediation Board. The Railway Labor Act provides for the selection of union representatives by the national labor organizations already represented, with the minor proscriptions that no union (or carrier) should have more than one representative on any division of the Board, and that only those unions which are "national in scope" are eligible to participate. The standard railway unions were certified as eligible to participate by the Secretary of Labor shortly after the amended Act became effective. These unions have handled appointments largely through the Railway Labor Executives Association (RLEA).

As a result, only two unions with large Negro memberships, the Hotel and Restaurant Workers and the Sleeping Car Porters, have been certified to participate in the selection of labor repre-

200. Public Law 89-456, 80 Stat. 208-210.

201. 323 U.S. 192 (1944).

202. *Long* v. *Van Osdale*, 218 Ind. 483 (1940).

203. *Stephenson* v. *New Orleans and N.E. R.R.*, 180 Miss. 147 (1937).

sentatives. Both groups have joined the RLEA since 1934. With only eighteen labor representatives seated on the four divisions of the Adjustment Board, the chances of having a representative chosen from either union has been small. Thus, as the Supreme Court noted in *Steele,*

> the Negro firemen would be required to appear before a group which is in large part chosen by the respondents against whom their real complaint is made. In addition § 3, Second provides that a carrier and a class or craft of employees, "all acting through their representatives, selected in accordance with the provisions of this Act," may agree to the establishment of a regional board of adjustment for the purpose of adjusting disputes of the type which may be brought before the Adjustment Board. In this way the carrier and the representative against whom the Negro firemen have complained have power to supersede entirely the Adjustment Board's procedure and to create a tribunal of their own selection to interpret and apply the agreements now complained of to which they are the only parties. We cannot say that a hearing, if available, before either of these tribunals would constitute an adequate administrative remedy.[204]

This argument, of course, would have been applicable to all Negro employees.

The procedures of the Adjustment Board in general were frequently the subject of strong, early criticism as a result of their inconsistencies and inequities.[205] Although Congress attempted to provide the minimum requirements of fair administrative procedure in all federal agencies when it enacted the Administrative Procedures Act in 1946, the railway labor unions were able to obtain the inclusion in this law of Section 2(a)(1), which excepts from its coverage "agencies composed of representatives of the parties or of representatives of organizations of the parties to the disputes determined by them. . . ." Since the NRAB obviously falls within this definition, it was able to avoid the direly needed changes. The parties thus were free to develop procedural policies which were advantageous to their interests. Although it is true that the practices of the Adjustment Board were gradually improved over time, the NRAB was not con-

---

204. 323 U.S. 192, 206.

205. See Harry E. Jones, ed., *Inquiry of Attorney General's Committee on Administrative Procedure Relating to the National Railroad Adjustment Board* (New York: 1941); Lloyd K. Garrison, "The National Railroad Adjustment Board: A Unique Administrative Agency," *Yale Law Journal,* Vol. 46 (1937), p. 567; Herbert R. Northrup and Mark L. Kahn, "Railroad Grievance Machinery: A Critical Aanalysis," *Industrial and Labor Relations Review,* Vol. 5 (April 1952), pp. 365-382, and (July 1952), pp. 540-559.

ceived as, nor is it expected to be, a disinterested body working to protect the rights of aggrieved employees. Indeed, the labor representatives to the National Railroad Adjustment Board continually worked against the interests of Negro employees unless the claim presented was clearly beneficial to the unions as well. There is no alternative forum for those employees whose claims conflict with the interests to the parties to the Board.

Although the Supreme Court has recognized the inherent inequity in the structure of the Adjustment Board, it has continued to disallow Negro employees the opportunity to seek relief in court. This is in light of the early procedure of the labor members to refuse to hear or to submit grievance claims of employees who were not union members, or who were members of unions other than those represented on the NRAB. By refusing to represent the aggrieved employee, the labor representatives could prevent consideration of these employee's claims.[206]

This issue was most acute for Negro employees. For example, Steele initially took his complaint to the Brotherhood of Locomotive Firemen but its officials refused to submit the case to the Adjustment Board. The Supreme Court in *Steele* found that 400 cases submitted by individuals had been rejected by the labor members.[207] This policy was eventually eliminated by court decisions and by changing labor personnel. Still, less than 700 of the 69,100 cases docketed with the NRAB between 1934 and 1969 were submitted by individuals.[208]

A related controversy existed for some time over the right of third parties to be notified when a decision in a pending case might affect them adversely. Once again, it was the labor organizations which were responsible for this denial of individual rights. This practice was repeatedly criticized by the courts until the procedure was changed.[209]

---

206. See Garth L. Mangum, "Grievance Procedures for Railroad Operating Employees," *Industrial and Labor Relations Review,* Vol. 15 (July 1962), p. 482.

207. 323 U.S. 192, 201.

208. Compiled from annual reports of the National Mediation Board, 1935-1969.

209. *Missouri-Kansas-Texas R.R.* v. *Brotherhood of Railway and Steamship Clerks,* 188 F. 2d 302 (7th Cir. 1951); *Hunter* v. *Atchison, Topeka & Sante Fe Ry.,* 188 F. 2d 294 (7th Cir. 1951); *Estes* v. *Union Terminal,* 89 F. 2d 768 (5th Cir. 1937); *Brotherhood of Railway Trainmen* v. *Templeton,* 181 F. 2d 527 (8th Cir. 1950); *Griffin* v. *Chicago Union Station,* 13 F. Supp. 722 (N.D. Ill. 1936).

Typical of the damage possible under this procedure is that incurred by the Negro porter-brakemen on the Atchison, Topeka and Santa Fe Railway in 1942. The Brotherhood of Railroad Trainmen was able to annex jobs performed by Negro employees since 1899 by filing a complaint with the First Division of the NRAB, charging that the carrier was violating the seniority rights of its brakemen by assigning part of "their" work to Negro porter-brakemen. The porter-brakemen had no notice of this action and were given no opportunity to be heard. In April 1942 the First Division handed down Award No. 6640, holding that the disputed work was the exclusive property of the Trainmen.[210] The aggrieved Negro employees turned to the courts for relief but it was not until 1951 that a final decree was issued.[211] The court, however, did not provide the desired relief; it simply stated that all parties adversely affected by an Adjustment Board order are entitled to notice of the hearing of that order. The result of this lengthy litigation then is that porter-brakemen are insured of the right to notice and hearing in any future proceeding on this issue. In any such case, the BRT would be represented on the Adjustment Board, while the porter-brakemen would not.

The previously limited relief available to employees thus discriminated against is illustrated further in the case of *Randolph* v. *Missouri-Kansas-Texas Railroad*.[212] This case also evolved out of a blatant attempt by the BRT to acquire Negro porter-brakemen jobs. In this instance, however, the Negro workers were represented by the Brotherhood of Sleeping Car Porters, which had a contract with the carrier. The BRT was eventually successful in obtaining the desired positions, this time by economic pressure. The Porters secured an injunction in the District Court, only to have the Circuit Court of Appeals dissolve the injunction on the grounds that the jurisdiction to determine rights under a labor agreement was vested in the NRAB. To the contention by the Porters that it could not secure fair treatment before either the Adjustment Board or the National Mediation Board, the court replied, with complete disregard for the realities of the situation, that "there is nothing in the record to indi-

---

210. See Northrup, *Organized Labor and the Negro, op. cit.*, pp. 69-71.

211. Hunter, 188 F. 2d 294 (7th Cir. 1951); cert. denied, 342 U.S. 819.

212. 68 F. Supp. 1007 (N.D. Mo. 1946); remanded, 164 F. 2d 4 (8th Cir. 1947); cert. denied, 334 U.S. 818 (1948).

cate that racial consideration has anything to do with this labor dispute." [213]

The case was returned to the District Court, where a motion of the Porters to file a supplemental motion was denied and the case dismissed.[214]

The plight of the Negro porter-brakemen has been nearly as unfortunate as that of the Negro firemen. After the wage differentials were eliminated, the carriers lost interest in using Negroes to perform brakemen's tasks. At the same time, the Brotherhood of Railroad Trainmen were only too willing to utilize every forum possible to secure these positions for white union members. The results of the cases cited are illustrative of the situation on many carriers during and immediately after World War II. It is indeed unfortunate that as the cases discussed briefly in the final section of this chapter indicate the Negro porter-brakemen are still struggling to protect their employment rights.

COURT DECISIONS

Negro railroad workers have initiated court proceedings on several occasions to protect their employment rights from the insidious assaults by the railroad unions. Indeed, as a result of the policies of the National Mediation Board and the National Railroad Adjustment Board, the federal court system represented the last recourse for these employees. It is not surprising therefore that the first case questioning the legality of racial discrimination in employment, *Steele*, involved a railway union. Moreover, precedent setting cases on specific aspects of employment discrimination have arisen more often than not from complaints by Negro railroad employees. The effectiveness of the courts in eliminating discrimination, however, was limited, prior to the Civil Rights Act, because of the high cost of litigation and the uncertainty of the legal questions.

The Court, in rendering its decision in the Steele case, established the basic legal doctrine of union race relations. In the words of the court,

So long as a labor union assumes to act as the statutory representative of a craft, it cannot rightly refuse to perform the duty, which is inseparable from the power of representation conferred upon it, to repre-

213. 164 F. 2d 4 (8th Cir. 1947).

214. 78 F. Supp. 727 (W.D. Mo. 1948).

sent the entire membership of the craft. While the statute does not deny
to such a bargaining labor organization the right to determine eligibility
to its membership, it does require the union, in collective bargaining and
in making contracts with the carrier, *to represent non-union or minority
union members of the craft without hostile discrimination, fairly, im-
partially, and in good faith.* (Emphasis supplied)[215]

The courts gradually included a wide range of discriminatory
union practices under the duty of fair representation. The *Steele*
decision held that unions could not seek the removal of Negroes
from their jobs. In *Rolax* v. *Atlantic Coast Line Railroads*,[216]
the court ruled that unions could not seek the removal of Negroes indirectly by seeking to institute a testing program to determine the promotability of all employees, Negro as well as
white. This case arose from the 1948 "Forced Promotion" contract which required all firemen in line for promotion to be
tested, with those failing to qualify dismissed. Overturning a
lower court,[217] the Court of Appeals, stated:

To say that the forced promotion order put all firemen on an equal basis
is to shut one's eyes to the real situation which existed and to allow the
Brotherhood to make cruel use of its bargaining power to get rid of the
helpless minority whose rights the courts have been attempting to
protect.[218]

The court saw through the insidious attempt by the union to
impose meaningless promotional criteria upon a generally old,
poorly educated Negro firing force. The white firemen who were
to be tested had been hired with the qualifications needed to become locomotive engineers. On the other hand, the Negro firemen
had been hired only as firemen, with no expectation of future
promotion. The proposed testing program, therefore, would have
had a devastating effect on the Negro firing force. Two other
cases also decided in 1950, *Salvant* v. *Louisville & Nashville Railroads*[219] and *Brotherhood of Locomotive Firemen and Enginemen*
v. *Palmer*,[220] supported this decision.

---

215. 323 U.S. 192, 204

216. 186 F. 2d 473 (4th Cir. 1950).

217. 91 F. Supp. 585, 592 (E.D. Vir. 1950).

218. *Rolax, supra,* note 216 at 479.

219. 83 F. Supp. 391 (W.D. Ky. 1950).

220. 178 F. 2d 722 (D.C. Cir. 1950).

The courts not only ruled against the discriminatory layoff or dismissal of Negro employees but they have imposed as well the obligation to provide equal promotional opportunities to Negro workers. Negro "machinist helpers" in *Dillard* v. *Chesapeake & Ohio Railroad Co.*[221] were passed over in promotion to machinists position by white employees with less seniority. Similarly, in *Clark* v. *Norfolk & Western Railroads,*[222] Negro yardmen were not given the opportunity to become "car retarder operators." The first protest against this denial of opportunity was filed by the Negro employees in 1942, but the plaintiffs were not able to gain final relief until 1958. Although the term "nonpromotable" was then removed from the labor agreement, Negro employers were still not given the opportunity to operate car retarders. The Court, in rendering its decision, was fully cognizant of the complete breach of the "fair representation" doctrine by the defendants:

There is no question that the defendants have been fully acquainted with the effect of the decisions cited. (*Steele,* etc.) Let over a period of ten or twelve years they persistently and flagrantly disregarded them and deliberately persisted in their discrimination against the Negro employees. They paid no attention to the protests which the plaintiffs and other Negroes made as to the discrimination practiced against them, and it was only after this action was brought that the discriminatory contract was amended.[223]

Grievance handling for Negro employees was also included under the duty of fair representation. The Supreme Court held that handling of grievances by the Brotherhood of Railway Clerks in *Conley* v. *Gibson* [224] was discriminatory and that plaintiffs were entitled to relief. In this case forty-five Negro employees were not protected from demotions and discharges which were allegedly in violation of a collective agreement. Almost all of the Negro employees who had their jobs abolished were replaced by white employees. The Court noted that the union's duty of fair representation does not come to an abrupt end upon the execution of the collective bargaining agreement. It extends to the day-to-day administration of the agreement after its execution.

---

221. 136 F. Supp. 689 (S.D. W.Va. 1955).

222. *Race Relations Reporter,* Vol. 3 (October 1958), p. 988 (W.D. Vir. 1958).

223. *Ibid.,* pp. 991-992.

224. 355 U.S. 41 (1957).

Even though an agreement is nondiscriminatory on its face, it may be administered in such a way as to be flagrantly discriminatory.

The duty of fair representation apparently imposed a parallel obligation on the union to use its bargaining power to remove discrimination by the employee in violation of the contract. The facts of *Conley* v. *Gibson* called only for affirmation of a representative's duty to vindicate everyone's rights under a contract already in existence. The Court implied, however, that the union cannot accept benefits which would be preferential to whites only. In the Court's words, "we are clear that once it *undertook to bargain* or present grievances for some of the employees it represented it could not refuse to take similar action in good faith for other employees just because they were Negroes." [225] In other words, Negroes are entitled to the same representation as whites in the negotiation of agreements as well as in the processing of grievances.

Only one Court of Appeals, the Fifth Circuit, has had occasion to contribute anything with more direct bearing on the issue. In *Central of Georgia Railway* v. *Jones*,[226] even though the discriminatory practices complained of had been in effect and included in agreements for more than thirty years, the court approved an injunction barring enforcement of the contract and requiring both railroad and union to grant the same opportunities to the jobs in question to Negro and white employees alike. The view of the majority of the court was that "The Brotherhood had . . . the profound obligation fully and earnestly to bargain to prevent, and, where necessary, remove, discriminations." [227]

The court in this case noted that the employer may be held jointly for participating knowingly in a union's violation of its duty to fair representation. The court reasoned that the company knew, or should have known, that the union had violated its legal obligation; therefore, the discriminatory provision was illegal and the contract should have been read as if it did not exist.

The following year, 1957, in the case of *Richardson* v. *Texas and New Orleans Railroad Co.*, a federal district court held that the Texas and New Orleans Railroad was jointly liable for damages on the same basis as the Central of Georgia:

---

225. *Id.* at 47.

226. 229 F. 2d 648 (5th Cir. 1956) ; cert. denied, 353 U.S. 848 (1956).

227. 229 F. 2d 648, 650.

It takes two parties to reach an agreement, and both have a legal obligation not to make or enforce an agreement or discriminatory employment practice which they either know, or should know, is unlawful. Unless financial responsibility for a joint breach of such duty is required from both sides of the bargaining table, the statutory policy implied under *Steele* will be impracticable of enforcement. . . .[228]

The final issue relevant to the railroad industry that has been examined by the courts is the denial of union membership to Negro employees. Union arguments on this problem have revolved around the voluntary nature of union association. This theory was recognized in *Steele* where the court ruled that the Railway Labor Act "does not deny to such bargaining labor organization the right to determine eligibility to its membership. . . ."[229]

The assumption of the court in *Steele*, of course, was that unions can be expected to represent a worker fairly even though it excludes him from membership. This assumption was the object of frequent criticism until it was invalidated by the Civil Rights Act. As one observer has argued, "No collective bargaining agent can possibly accord equal treatment to nonmembers in the day-to-day activities of the union. . . . The elected officials of a union . . . can hardly be expected to devote themselves as wholeheartedly to the interests of those who cannot vote as they do to the interests of those who can."[230] This argument was recognized by the Supreme Court of Kansas in *Betts* v. *Easley*[231] when it ruled that segregated lodges in the Carmen (who provided membership for Negroes only in segregated, subordinate locals) were unlawful to the extent that they carry with them inequality of participation in union affairs.

On the other hand, an argument presented by a group of Negro firemen that it was impossible for them to get the fair representation to which they were entitled as long as the BLFE refused to admit them to full membership was denied by the Ohio federal district court.[232] The court ruled that the real question

228. 242 F. 2d 230, 236 (5th Cir. 1957).

229. 323 U.S. at 204.

230. Joseph L. Rauh, Jr., "Civil Rights and Liberties and Labor Unions," *Labor Law Journal*, Vol. 7 (December 1957), p. 875.

231. *Supra* note 187.

232. *Oliphant* v. *Brotherhood of Locomotive Firemen and Enginemen*, 156 F. Supp. 89 (N.D. Ohio 1957).

was not whether the Negro firemen had been discriminated
against by the specific acts complained of, but whether the
plaintiffs' ineligibility for membership in the union was responsible for the discrimination that they alleged and was, therefore,
federal action that violated the Fifth Amendment. The court
ignored the realities of the situation, and argued that "[t]here
can be no real assurance that membership in the defendant
would prevent discrimination, since it is my opinion under the
evidence here that the effective discrimination is by the railroad
employer, rather than by the Brotherhood, and the railroad employers are not parties to the action." [233]

With the exception, then, of the right to union membership, the
courts established a legal framework which theoretically guaranteed to Negro employees many of the same rights included in
Title VII of the Civil Rights Act. Still, the unions, and often
the carriers, continued freely to abrogate these rights until the
passage of the Act in 1964. The inherent weakness of the judicial system in institutionalizing its decisions in the powerful
railroad industry was recognized as early as 1947 in the *Final
Report* of the President's Committee on Fair Employment Practices:

> Although the Court's opinions left no doubt as to the illegality of the
> discriminatory agreements, the agreements are so numerous and apply
> to so many railroads that to invalidate them by litigation would require
> a multiplicity of suits and the expenditure of much time and money.[234]

Moreover, the committee, fully realizing its impotence, noted that
"only an administrative agency with the necessary authority can
deal successfully with the problems presented by such . . . agreements." This statement was made nearly twenty years before
Title VII of the Civil Rights Act of 1964 provided "the necessary
authority." [235]

Cases Under the Civil Rights Act

During the past four years the federal courts have struggled
to interpret the procedural issues surrounding enforcement of
the Civil Rights Act's substantive guarantees. In the process

233. *Id.* at 91.

234. Fair Employment Practice Committee, *Final Report* (Washington:
Government Printing Office, 1947), p. 13.

235. *Ibid.*, p. 14.

many Negro railroad employees involved in early suits pursuant to Title VII suffered initial setbacks as their complaints were dismissed by the courts as a result of technical errors. However, following continuing litigation by these and other Negro employees similarly affected, many of the technical requirements have now been removed. Consequently, several railroad cases have been remanded for trial on the substantive issues of the allegations.

Typical of the legal difficulties encountered by Negro employees is that which has delayed settlement of a complaint filed in September 1965 by James Dent, a former employee of the St. Louis-San Francisco Railway and member of the Brotherhood of Railway Carmen. The substance of his complaint was that the company had, on account of race, terminated his employment and that of other Negroes, eliminated the job classification in which they were employed and excluded them from employment in and training programs for other job classifications. Further, he alleged that the company maintained racially segregated facilities and that the Brotherhood maintained segregated local unions. The District Court, however, in reviewing the legislative history of the machinery established in Title VII, concluded that the EEOC must attempt conciliation before an individual can bring suit in the federal courts. As a result of the unexpectedly large number of complaints that were filed with the EEOC and the extremely small staff available, no conciliation had been attempted. Therefore, the court chose to dismiss the suit.[236]

In deciding the case the court rejected the argument that a strict reading of the requirement of prior EEOC effort is unfair to the employee, suggesting that the ruling did not deprive the plaintiff of his day in court. The employee would still be entitled to proceed with a civil action once conciliation was attempted.

On appeal, however, this decision (as well as several others similarly decided) was reversed.[237] The Court of Appeals argued, in overruling the lower courts, that the Act sets forth only two requirements for an aggrieved party before he can initiate legal action: (1) he must file a charge with the EEOC and (2) he must receive the statutory notice from the Commission that voluntary compliance was not obtained. The Civil Rights Act, the

---

236. *Dent v. St. Louis-San Francisco Ry.*, 265 F. Supp. 56 (N.D. Ala. 1967).

237. *Dent*, 406 F. 2d 399 (5th Cir. 1969).

court noted, reflects an "unequivocal intent on the part of Congress to create a right of action in the aggrieved employee." [238] The cases were, therefore, remanded to the district courts for trial.

Similarly, a complaint filed by another member of the Carmen working for the St. Louis-San Francisco Railway, James Glover, was dismissed by the lower courts because the affected employees in this instance had not exhausted the administrative remedies provided for them in the grievance machinery.[239] The plaintiffs contended that the carrier had denied them the opportunity for promotion from Carmen Helper to Carman because of their race. This practice was contrary to the collective bargaining agreement which provided for upgrading Carmen Helpers. The lower courts argued that discriminatory performance of a labor agreement is a grievance properly adjusted by the National Railroad Adjustment Board. As the Supreme Court stated in a different recent non-railroad case, "[I]t is settled that the employee must at least attempt to exhaust exclusive grievance and arbitration procedures established in the bargaining agreement." [240]

The Supreme Court in the instant case, however, in reversing the lower courts,[241] contended that with the present circumstances an exception is necessary as the effort to proceed with contractual remedies "would be wholly futile." Attempts by the plaintiffs to process grievances even though they were refused by the union representatives, satisfied the requirement to exhaust contractual remedies. Moreover, the suit in this case was brought against the employees' own union as well as against the carrier and thus is arguably not within the jurisdiction of the NRAB. The Court, therefore, returned the case for trial on the substantive issues of the complaint.

In a more recent and more significant case [242] the long harassed Negro porter-brakeman attempted again to preserve their positions against the declining passenger traffic and predatory raids

---

238. *Id.* at 403.

239. *Glover* v. *St. Louis-San Francisco Ry.*, 386 F. 2d 452 (5th Cir. 1967).

240. *Vaca* v. *Sipes*, 386 U.S. 171 (1967).

241. *Glover* v. *St. Louis-San Francisco Ry.*, Decision of United States No. 38, October Term 1968, as reported in *Daily Labor Report*, No. 9 (January 14, 1969), p. E-1.

242. *Norman* v. *Missouri Pacific R.R.*, 414 F. 2d 73 (8th Cir. 1969).

by the Brotherhood of Railroad Trainmen. The plaintiffs in this case are employees of the Missouri Pacific Railroad.

The Negro employees allege that they were classified as train porters because of race and that by reason of such classification they are denied equal employment opportunities with white brakemen. Further, they contend that they perform the same functions as white brakemen, and that the "class or craft" of train porters was established historically to discriminate against Negro employees.

These are basically the same allegations which have been frequently set forth in litigation between the Negro porters and the carriers and unions commencing in 1946.[243] The trial court in the instant dispute relied on these decisions and held that only the National Mediation Board has jurisdiction over the matters alleged in the complaint. The court pointed out that the carrier was obligated to deal with the certified representative of the "craft or class", and that the porter-brakemen cannot be reclassified without the concurrence of the NMB and both the Brotherhoods of Sleeping Car Porters and Railroad Trainmen. It viewed the difference in employment conditions as resulting from the different bargaining representatives. The court, therefore, sustained a motion to dismiss the complaint for lack of jurisdiction.

The Court of Appeals stated that although the plaintiffs were foreclosed from judicial relief with regard to possible reclassification of their craft by the Mediation Board, they did have certain protections under the Civil Rights Act. The court argued that there is a cause of action under Title VII unless there is something in the Railway Labor Act that gives either the Mediation Board or the Adjustment Board exclusive jurisdiction. The court then found that there was no representational dispute so as to give the NMB jurisdiction nor question of contract interpretation or denial of contractual rights so as to constitute a dispute cognizable by the NRAB. In the words of the court, "[t]he gravemen of the complaint here is that the racially oriented classification of train porters with its inherent discrimina-

---

243. Related cases include *Howard* v. *Thompson*, 72 F. Supp. 695 (E.D. Mo. 1947); *Howard* v. *St. Louis-San Francisco Ry.*, 191 F. 2d 442 (8th Cir. 1951); *Brotherhood of Railroad Trainmen* v. *Howard*, 343 U.S. 768 (1952); *Howard* v. *St. Louis-San Francisco Ry.*, 215 F. 2d 690 (8th Cir. 1954); *Howard* v. *St. Louis-San Francisco Ry.*, 361 F. 2d 905 (8th Cir. 1966), cert. denied, 385 U.S. 986 (1966), and *Nunn* v. *Missouri Pacific R.R.*, 248 F. Supp. 304 (E.D. Mo. 1966). All these cases grew out of attempts of the Brotherhood of Railroad Trainmen to eliminate the Negroes and the support therefor by the NRAB.

tion in employment opportunities for advancement and compensation is now proscribed . . . by Title VII." Therefore, the court reinstated the case for trial on the merits of the complaint.

Similarly, in a suit brought against the Illinois Central by Negro porters, the court denied a carrier motion for summary judgment, holding that the legality of the company's method of selecting conductors under Title VII is a question that can only be determined at trial.[244] A "genuine dispute" exists between the parties on such material facts as the presence or absence of racial discrimination as a factor motivating the promotion system and the possible overlap of functions between the Negro porters and the brakemen. These questions will now be resolved at trial.

The most recent railroad case to be tried under the Civil Rights Act is the aforementioned *U.S.* v. *Jacksonville Terminal Co.*[245] The Justice Department contends that the company, an important terminal through which much of the freight and mail for southern Florida must pass, has discriminated against Negro employees in initial job assignment, promotion, demotion, and layoff. Moreover, it is alleged that the system of craft seniority in effect at the terminal has perpetuated the effects of the discriminatory acts. The relief requested by the Department of Justice would require the company to discontinue its discriminatory hiring and initial job assignment practices and, in addition, would require the company to discontinue use of the craft seniority system, and to substitute in its place a system based on total company seniority.

The terminal employs workers in 102 job categories. As of August 6, 1969, all but nine of 257 Negro employees were assigned to one of only seventeen job categories which have traditionally been held by Negroes. Five of these nine Negroes working in traditionally white jobs were promoted to these positions after the complaint was filed. On the other hand, only two of 275 white employees were working in these same seventeen Negro job categories. With a single exception, the highest paying Negro job pays less than the lowest paying job currently held by white employees. A similar pattern of employment, it is alleged, has existed as far back as company personnel records have been maintained—some 40 or 50 years.

---

244. *Int'l Association of Railway Employees* v. *Illinois Central R.R.* (N.D. Ill. 1969), *Daily Labor Report*, No. 197 (October 10, 1969), p. A-6.

245. *U.S.* v. *Jacksonville Terminal Co.*, Civil No. 68-239 (M.D. Fla. May 5, 1970), appeal pending.

With regard to initial job assignment, only sixteen of the 275 white employees were assigned at the time of hiring to work in Negro jobs and all but one of them has since been promoted to a traditional white job. In contrast none of the Negroes was initially assigned to work in a white job.

The employees in the accounting and purchasing department and in the baggage and mail department are represented by the Brotherhood of Railway Clerks. Under the labor agreement covering these workers, jobs are classified as either "Group 1" or "Group 3." Group 1 jobs include such clerical and minor supervisory jobs as chief clerk, ticket-baggage clerk, cashier chief account and general foreman while Group 3 jobs include the more menial tasks of porter, loader, tractor driver, and separator. Negro workers have historically been assigned to Group 3 positions as they have generally throughout the industry. Moreover, it was not until November 1962 that a contractual right to promotion to Group 1 positions was obtained. Since that date only three Negro employees at the terminal have been promoted permanently to Group 1 jobs. Each of these three workers had worked from fourteen to sixteen years in Group 3 positions. However, white employees have traditionally been hired directly into Group 1 jobs.

In the transportation department Negroes are currently being hired only as station Redcaps or porters. The jobs of switchman, fireman, and hostler helper were at one time performed primarily by Negroes but have gradually been taken over by white employees. A Negro hired as a switchman in 1963 and another as a hostler helper in 1967 were the first hired in nearly forty years. Moreover, those Negro workers in these positions were ineligible for the promotions afforded routinely to white employees. These allegations were substantiated by the Justice Department both from letters between union and management officials and from the company's employment records.

The maintenance of way department is subdivided into three sub-departments, the roadway department, the bridge and building department, and the signal department. Until December 1968 Negroes were confined to the jobs of laborer in the roadway and bridge and building sub-departments. At that time the first Negro ever to receive a promotion in either of these departments was elevated to the position of welder helper. Negroes have never been employed in the signal sub-department. Evidence developed by the Department of Justice indicates that Negro laborers were not considered for promotion, nor were notices of vacancies posted so that laborers could see them until company policy was changed in March 1969 to provide for this possibility.

Finally, in the mechanical department, Negroes historically have been relegated to the job of laborer and craftsmen helper. According to the Justice Department, from at least 1943 to April 1969 when three Negro machinist helpers were promoted to the job of machinist, no Negro employee was promoted above the job of helper. It was not until December 1969 that the company and the Carmen and Machinists effectuated an agreement permitting the upgrading of Negro helpers. White employees, on the other hand, have been assigned initially to apprentice positions and then are routinely upgraded to craftsmen. Notably, the practices applicable to the occupation of electrician differ from this general pattern. Electrician helpers are eligible for promotion while only apprentices in the other crafts are eligible for promotion except in unusual circumstances. Not surprisingly, only white employees have ever worked as electrician helpers.

Thus, the employment patterns at the Jacksonville Terminal Co. conform closely to the general pattern that had been institutionalized throughout the industry by World War II. When Negroes have been employed in the industry, they have almost invariably been relegated to an occupational status similar to that at Jacksonville. The limited evidence presented in this study strongly supports this conclusion.[246] Although a few small but significant changes in railroad racial employment practices have been instituted in the period subsequent to the passage of the Civil Rights Act, the railroad seniority system continues to perpetuate the effects of the past discriminatory practices.

The trial court, however, found that, in contrast to the documented history of discrimination in the industry generally, the Jacksonville Terminal Company's employment and practices "have at all material times been applied equally and without regard to race as to each and every employee." Further, the court found that the company sought, "with respect to each and every person hired or promoted since the effective date of the [Civil Rights] Act, to obtain the best qualified person then available for the job . . . and that the Government failed to prove that any Negro

246. The patterns of Negro employment described by the Justice Department agree materially with the well documented analysis presented in Northrup, *Organized Labor and the Negro, op. cit.*, Chapter III.

not hired or promoted possessed qualifications equal to or greater than those possessed by persons hired or promoted." [247]

Significantly, as the court carefully noted, the deputy contracts compliance officer of the U. S. Post Office Department advised the company in July 1965 that the company's actions to provide equal employment opportunity to all applicants and workers had resolved all outstanding complaints. In addition, the company has formulated and filed with the Post Office Department, the required affirmative action compliance program. These events "make it plain that the Company does not have an intention to violate the Civil Rights Act nor to establish or maintain any patterns, practices or acts of racial discrimination."

This decision then is contrary to the evolving legal definition of discrimination. The statistical evidence of discrimination which was here denied by the court has been accepted in at least two leading cases. "The Act . . . permits the use of evidence of statistical probability to infer the existence of a pattern or practice of discrimination." [248] The historical record of Negro employment at the Jacksonville Terminal is not an "historical accident" as argued by the company and should not be ignored. The Negro and white populations from which the company drew its work force cannot be so dissimilar as to make possible such disparate results.

The contention of the court that the tacit approval of the company's policies and practices with regard to Negro employees by the Post Office compliance officer are proof on nondiscrimination is significant only as it may necessitate an examination of the role of the agencies working under Executive Order 11246. A reversal of the situation was cited in previously discussed case, *Local 189 Papermakers and Paperworkers* [249] v. *United States* (generally known as the Crown-Zellerbach case), wherein the OFCC and the Department of Justice attacked company practices tentatively approved by the EEOC. The court in this case easily

247. *U.S.* v. *Jacksonville Terminal Co., supra* note 245.

248. *United States* v. *Sheet Metal Workers Int'l Local 36*, 416 F. 2d 123, 127 n. 7 (8th Cir. 1969). See also, *United States* v. *Bethlehem Steel Corp.*, (W.D.N.Y. 1970), as reported in *Daily Labor Report*, No. 80 (April 24, 1970), p. D-1.

249. 416 F. 2d 980 (5th Cir. 1969). For further discussion of this case, see Northrup and Rowan, *Negro Employment in Southern Industry*, Studies of Negro Employment, Vol. IV, Part One.

brushed aside the defendant's contention that the approval by the EEOC precluded action by the Department of Justice. Although the legal questions differ, it is apparent that the generally informal, conciliatory approach of the Post Office Department should in no way affect detrimentally the right of employees or the government to seek redress.

The inherent difficulty in this case is the development of an adequate remedy. Although there are undoubtedly Negro employees at Jacksonville who were hired many years ago, without the requisite qualifications to perform satisfactorily in jobs now held exclusively by white workers, those Negroes who continue to be deprived of promotional opportunities to which their skills entitle them as a result of discrimination in initial placement should be provided with equitable relief. There are many railroads which have hired greater numbers of Negroes in recent years who are similarly affected and who would derive important economic benefits from an appropriate remedy.

The government would require the company to abandon the traditional craft seniority system and to award jobs to the senior qualified bidder, with seniority based on length of service with the company rather than length of service in the craft. Under the present system each of the Negro jobs is on a different seniority roster from any of the white jobs. Negroes desiring to move to a white job are forced to start at the bottom of the seniority roster for the white job, receiving no credit for tenure in the Negro job. As a practical matter, then, incumbent Negro workers are no better off than non-employees in respect to the filling of vacancies in white jobs. The relief requested by the Justice Department would allow Negroes access to all jobs provided only that the company retain the right to determine employee qualifications.

The trial court, however, has rejected this proposal. James E. Wolfe, former chairman of the National Railway Labor Conference (NLRC), the organization which represents the railroads in national negotiations, testified at length during the trial to the uniformity of the seniority system throughout the railroad industry, regardless of the presence or absence of Negro employees.

The court noted that national acceptance of the system dates to the period of federal control of the railroads during World War I and to subsequent decisions of the Railroad Labor Board. Although the system was imposed upon all railroads at this time, the court could have established an earlier history for the development of the basic framework of seniority system on individual railroads. Racial discrimination was not, in fact, an important determining factor in this development and with the possible exception of a few specific occupations under the jurisdiction of the Brotherhood of Railway Clerks, negotiations with regard to the establishment of the system were not motivated by the desire to affect Negro job opportunities. The system is, therefore, "bona fide" as required by the Civil Rights Act and arguably meets the "business necessity" criteria cited in recent cases.[250]

Although the seniority system has played a crucial role in railroad labor relations, continued strict adherence is not necessary and has been so argued by the railroads in bargaining with the unions. Furthermore, it is not necessary to abolish the entire system to effect the desired relief.

Provided that an employee has certain basic personal qualifications, it is possible to acquire the requisite job skills for most railroad occupations in considerably less time than necessary to progress through the seniority system. The court in *Crown-Zellerbach* established minimum time limits for affected Negro workers before they could progress to succeeding jobs in the seniority ladders.[251] It should be possible to negotiate similar agreements in the railroad industry which will allow qualified Negro workers to advance and yet compel them to obtain adequate experience to perform desired jobs. Negroes able to progress under such a system could retain company seniority but have that seniority confined to the occupational ladder initially selected. They would thus assume a "rightful place" similar to that of the white employees hired during the same time periods. There are some dangers inherent in the proposed changes, particularly in the reaction of the white employees who have long awaited promotions claimed by Negroes who are new to the crafts, but these problems must be overcome. It is hard to conceive of a decision affording less protection being found consistent with previous decisions by the Fifth Circuit Court of Appeals. This case may well become a landmark in the quest by Negroes to obtain equal employment opportunities in the railroad industry.

---

250. See, for example, *United States* v. *H. K. Porter*, 296 F. Supp. 40 (N.D. Ala. 1968), appeal pending.

251. *United States* v. *Local 189 Papermakers and Paperworkers*, 301 F. Supp. 906, Appendix A (E.D. La. 1969). See also Northrup and Rowan, *op. cit.*

CHAPTER VIII

The Determinants of Industry Policy

At various points throughout this study several factors were discussed which have contributed to the racial employment patterns in the railroad industry. To conclude this study, the major factors will be briefly summarized.

THE JOB STRUCTURE

The job structure in the railroad industry during the early years of this century was very favorable for the employment of disadvantaged, unskilled workers. In fact, progression system and later railroad seniority agreements covering most occupations required workers to enter and remain in generally unskilled positions for time periods far exceeding those which would be necessary to develop the requisite job knowledge. Few, if any, employees entered directly into the various skilled occupations. In addition, a significant number of the occupations required the performance of unskilled, personal services for the then important railroad passengers.

Negroes, as well as the expanding labor force of immigrants, were widely utilized by the industry in the lower level positions. For many of these workers no comparable employment opportunities were available. The manufacturing industries were still in the early stages of their development and railroad employment meant both high pay and high status. Advancement was slow but the relative job security provided by the early maturation of the industry and by the strong union movement made railroading an attractive career choice.

Negro workers who may otherwise have been limited to agricultural or personal service occupations sought railroad employment. The railroads, particularly those in the South, were willing to accept this ready source of labor but only, it seems, when a reduction in the prevailing wage could be secured. This forced white workers into direct competition with Negroes. Further, the carriers purposely exacerbated the sentiment of white workers by hiring Negroes as strikebreakers during several early work stoppages. Rather than attempt to fight such practices by organizing the Negro workers, the white employees and their unions chose to resist Negro encroachment into the desirable occupations through a concerted series of discriminatory actions. Their success during this period was all too complete. A system of well-defined "Negro jobs" evolved which has existed until the present. Moreover, as jobs improved in working conditions and pay, the white unions exerted pressure to eliminate Negroes—and again achieved substantial success.

Now the rapid decline of passenger service and changing technology have reduced employment in "Negro jobs" to minimal levels. Moreover, the rigid seniority system necessitates the hiring of employees who have the capacity to learn the top jobs in the several lines of progression. In the past the industry attracted the best qualified Negro applicants. Most of these workers might easily have acquired the necessary skills if they had been given the opportunity. The carriers are no longer able to attract similar applicants. Too many other industries with more attractive images in the Negro communities are able and willing to provide jobs with comparable pay and greater job security.

THE DEMAND FOR LABOR

Employment reductions have, of course, not been limited to those jobs in which Negroes have been traditionally employed. The overall decrease in the railroad labor force since World War II has been larger than that in any other industry. Traditionally in our economy Negro employees have experienced disproportionately heavy losses of job opportunities during such periods. Although this was apparently true in the railroad industry after World War II and during the 1950's, the last decade has seen an equalization in the rate of decline for white and Negro employees. The level of Negro employment today is comparable with that which prevailed in the early 1960's and at the same time Negro employees have been shifted gradually away from the laborer and service occupations to the more skilled occupations.

Although Negroes made significant gains in the industry during World War II and in other early periods of labor shortages, the recent period of tight labor markets has not had impact on

the level of Negro employment. This is true despite the annual
employment of new hires and re-entrants into the industry which
exceeds 10 percent of the industry's labor force. To be sure,
seasonal employment fluctuations account for a significant proportion of the industry's hiring, but excessive employee separations because of retirement, quits, or discharges and shifts in the
focus of railroad operations periodically open job opportunities
on all carriers. In fact, the ageing labor force in certain skilled
occupations has forced the industry to become concerned about
the available labor supply.

Nevertheless, the limited evidence indicates that the industry
has found it difficult to recruit an adequate number of Negro
workers to expand and upgrade the Negro labor force. This is
undoubtedly attributable in part to the rapid expansion of comparable job opportunities for Negroes in other industries which
do not suffer from the unattractive railroad image.

The stress on civil rights and on employment of disadvantaged
job seekers has required that railroad management re-examine
their employment standards in order to distinguish those criteria which are essential for proper job performance. The industry failed to take full advantage of the resource of Negro talent
available to it early in this century. Neither the industry nor
the nation can afford to allow these talents to be wasted once
again. Few industries have as many employment opportunities
which can provide economic assistance to unskilled and, perhaps,
otherwise unemployable people, but the opportunities must be
utilized.

LOCATIONAL AND REGIONAL FACTORS

Locational and regional factors have had an important effect
on Negro employment levels in the industry. Although the pattern of Negro employment does not differ significantly by geographic area, the level of Negro employment has historically been
decidedly higher in the South. Furthermore, Negro employment
has been much higher in urban areas where large Negro labor
supplies are available. It is in the urban areas too that passenger
service operations and the attendant "Negro jobs" have been
concentrated. In contrast, however, the large railroad switching
yards and repair shops have been located in suburban areas and
small towns which lack Negro workers.

The nature of railroad operations necessitates a highly dispersed work force. Consequently, hiring has been traditionally controlled at the many yards and stations by local supervisors rather than by a centrally controlled personnel staff. Even now, as the industry attempts to improve the Negro employment record, the continuing power of these supervisors, with their understandable reluctance to alter traditional hiring practices, remains one of the foremost obstacles to be circumvented.

UNIONISM AND SENIORITY

The long history of manifest discrimination by railroad labor organizations has been paralleled only by the recently publicized practices of the building trades unions. Several of the unions, of course, are active in both industries. The resistance to Negro employment and upgrading extended into each of the brotherhoods, with the single exception of the black-led Brotherhood of Sleeping Car Porters, and continued unabated until at least World War II. The policies and practices of the unions have varied greatly in both nature and intensity, with gradual improvement evolving over an extended period commencing shortly after World War I. Even today, there is a continuing reluctance to improve the position of Negro members in each of the national railroad brotherhoods.

Given the historical experience of labor organizations, however, it is improbable that disparate attitudes could have been developed. The impetus for organization began among all the major brotherhoods shortly after the Civil War. Moreover, several of the unions were started in areas in which slave trading had been practiced. In fact, slaves frequently were utilized in the building of the early railroads. In addition, insurance firms during this period refused to provide coverage for railroad employees. Consequently, the workers organized in part to develop the necessary insurance protection. Negroes were unfortunately considered poorer insurance risks and the brotherhoods were reluctant to extend coverage to them. Finally, the unique working conditions and long hours away from home developed an important and continuing meaning in the term "brotherhood" among railroad workers. The position of Negroes in society during this period, therefore, precluded any part for these workers in all but a few radical labor organizations. The carriers then proceeded to aggravate union sentiment toward Negro workers by using them to defeat union movements. As concern for job security developed in the late 1920's, it is little wonder that the elimination of Negro workers frequently became a union objective.

The unions were able to continue discriminating against Negroes despite increasing civil rights pressures. Although the public attention directed toward the union racial policies during the 1943 hearings of the President's Committee on Fair Employment Practice and by the succeeding, key court decisions was sufficient to force the organizations to eliminate the overt discriminatory acts, there is little doubt that equally effective subtle pressures on the power of the brotherhoods was and remains too great to allow the federal and state agencies responsible for administering civil rights legislation to take the necessary decisive action in the industry. The 1943 debacle ended official government concern with the situation in the industry until the Post Office Department was able to develop sufficient support to renew pressure on the industry. The freedom of the industry to continue its former practices has been enhanced by the almost complete isolation of the industry's labor relations practices under the Railway Labor Act.

Regardless of outside pressure or even concern on the part of union leaders, it would have been difficult to force local lodges to correct the situation. The brotherhoods have historically been highly decentralized and structurally democratic. This tradition may undoubtedly be traced back to the autonomy and dispersion within the industry, particularly during its growth years. Mergers and consolidations may bring carriers together but this does not necessarily mean that affected lodges will develop closer ties. Local lodges must still be concerned with the variations in working conditions which affect their men. It was after all the carriers who produced the national bargaining which is now so characteristic of the industry when they requested general wage reductions in the 1930's.

Undoubtedly significant as well in understanding the absence of change in union policies is the very nature of union composition. Few national unions until very recently have had more members in significant numbers from the South or rural areas. In addition, the railroad work force and union membership has been older than that common to industry. This is particularly true of the union leaders, most of whom have been firmly entrenched in the hierarchies of the brotherhoods for many years. The importance of the status quo in the railroad industrial relations system cannot be overemphasized, and it has remained similarly important in the area of Negro rights.

White and Negro local lodges both continue to resist any attempts either by their leaders or the government to merge and integrate them. In many instances the Negroes as a numerical minority would lose what little power they may possess. Further, the Negro leaders know that they personally will never be able to regain positions of comparable stature. Although the federal government continues to press such integration, it may well be that the Negro members would be affected to their detriment by complete integration, as indeed they have been in many cases.

The railroad seniority system, however, was not developed as a heinous plan to perpetuate the effect of racial discrimination. Rather it is the codification of a generally logical training and upgrading system which was necessary for the complex manpower utilization problems inherent in any heterogeneous industrial system. The great diversity of occupations in the industry requires close adherence to a craft system of promotion. The foundation for the system evolved long before Negroes were able to compete for jobs in the industry. Undoubtedly, there have been racial overtones affecting policy decisions during those periods such as the years of government control during World War I when the system was formalized and extended. Nevertheless, the system remains inviolate nationally regardless of the race of the workers in the lines of progression.

The system has, of course, been perverted by race discrimination in the initial assignment of employees. Court litigation to give the "affected class" its opportunity to achieve its "rightful place" is therefore justified. It will, unfortunately, be very difficult to implement a system similar to that which seems to be evolving in recent court decisions. Employees affected by changes in the seniority rosters must be concerned more with the avoidance of layoff than with the freedom to progress. Moreover, for operating employees the position on the roster is of such critical importance in determining income and working conditions that any displacement of present employees may portend violent consequences. At the same time, however, Negroes cannot be expected to accept positions at the bottom of the roster which would allow infrequent work as extra men were needed. If equitable measures can be resolved, there is no reason to try to effect basic changes in the seniority system provided it is administered without discrimination in employee job placement.

Assuming that the basic system of training, promotion, and seniority is continued, it will be several years before marked changes in the occupational status of Negroes will occur. Once Negroes are within the promotional systems leading to the top jobs, there is little question that they will eventually achieve their "rightful place." The bars to Negro advancement are being torn down, but there is no more time consuming seniority system than that in the railroad industry.

GOVERNMENT PRESSURE

It is tragic that the federal government has had such an over-all detrimental effect on Negro railroad workers, although recent efforts by the EEOC and the POD promise greatly to improve employment opportunities for those Negroes presently employed. To be sure, many actions taken by the agencies responsible for the railroad industry were directed toward issues which argu-ably override the problem of Negro employment. There have, however, been too many instances in which government officials have chosen to ignore or even to collude in practices which were to have disastrous effects on groups of Negro employees. The courts too often provided relief, if they chose to provide relief at all, long after the damage was complete. Similarly, the pro-tection intended in legislation and executive mandates has never been fully instituted with respect to the railroads.

Given the importance of the mediatory function of the Na-tional Mediation Board, it is little wonder that this agency has placed such great emphasis on its relationship with the parties as opposed to the protection of Negro employee rights. This is in direct contrast to the position adopted by the National Labor Relations Board which chose to attack union racial discrimina-tion on a limited basis. It was a serious legislative error to ex-pect a single agency such as the NMB to undertake successfully the conflicting tasks of adjudication and mediation. Similarly, the composition of the National Railroad Adjustment Board places it in direct opposition to the interests of unrepresented unions and minority groups such as the Negro workers. That these defects have gone unchanged is an important comment on the political power of the railroad brotherhoods.

Notwithstanding the actions taken by these two unique agencies, the federal government was responsible for the initiation in 1943 through the wartime FEPC of a critical change in the political environment related to employment discrimination. Although the political power of the railroad brotherhoods and the carriers prevented the government from taking meaningful action at that time the industry did seemingly realize that the continuation of overt discrimination would no longer be ignored. Unfortunately, the task of inducing the necessary corrections had to be left to the few states who were able to develop political support for such a policy. The effect of this change in the government's stand on this question was to cause a shift to more subtle and covert forms of discrimination. Many local lodges have yet to eliminate the final traces of discrimination.

The progress toward equal employment opportunity in the industry has not been assisted by the jurisdictional overlap of the OFCC and the Post Office Department with the EEOC. The absence of coordination between these agencies as well as with the several state agencies has caused frustration which can only be injurious to the achievement of their objectives. Generally, the industry prefers to deal with the compliance examiners of the Post Office Department whose approach has been less aggressive but more understanding of the problems inherent to the industry. Despite these bureaucratic problems, these agencies have been responsible for initiating an important reconsideration of related personnel practices.

MANAGERIAL POLICY

Despite apparently significant statistical differences in the level of Negro employment by geographic location, and by company size, the carriers have approached the problem with similar attitudes. Employment patterns and practices in the industry were unfortunately institutionalized prior to the first expressions of public concern for the plight of Negro workers. Most other industries were still establishing employment relationships during the evolutionary period of government racial employment policy, but on the railroads the "place" of Negro workers was already firmly established. Moreover, the continuing low levels of new hires into the industry never produced the critical periods of labor shortages which may necessitate rapid advancement of Negro workers into heretofore "white" jobs. There is currently, however, a developing shortage of skilled craftsmen which may be profitably used to increase Negro employment in these occupations.

The industry further maintains a reluctance to adopt new approaches to personnel administration. The policies and practices of both the industrial relations and personnel functions vary little today from those which had been developed prior to the growing concern over racial discrimination. This is attributable in part to the nature of the industry's operations which have remained basically unaltered in this century. Technological and operating changes have, of course, been critical in the survival of the industry, but employee job content, with the exception of a few occupations, has remained strikingly similar over a long period of time. In addition, the Railway Labor Act and its administrative agencies provide the necessary structure for preserving the status quo. As civil rights pressures have increased in the 1960's, the carriers have recognized the inequities which affect Negro workers within the industry, but management officials were willing until recently to undertake the difficult and drastic changes necessary to provide relief.

The difficulty in developing and implementing the necessary changes is increased by the isolated position of the industry within the economy. Few railroad management personnel have worked for extended periods in their careers in other industries. Moreover, both the railroad labor unions and controlling government agencies are in general unique to the industry. Consequently, the industry does not have access to, nor is it motivated to learn from the experience in other industries. Railroad officials develop totally within the industry, with an indoctrination only to the practices and traditions therein. The inherent dangers in such a system can be seen in many of the industry's problems aside from that of Negro employment.

Railroad racial employment policies historically were determined not by the initiative of management but rather by the source and level of external pressures. Prior to the commencement of government concern with the problem, the industry was only too willing to acquiesce to the expressed desires of the white employees and their unions. As government's stand on the problem was gradually strengthened by legislation and other official statements of policy, the industry was induced to gradually alter its policies. Unfortunately, the government has been unable to develop the political support necessary for a concerted movement against the remaining employment discrimination within the industry. The industry further is not consumer oriented and therefore does not have to concern itself with the public pressures which may develop therefrom. The previously discussed case involving the Jacksonville Terminal Company and of the related cases represent the first general condemnation of the industry's racial employment record, and their outcome thus will have an important effect on the future of many Negro employees within the industry.

The changes in the governmental stance during the past few years have provided concerned industry officials with the opportunity for implementing changes which would otherwise have been impossible. Many officials are deeply committed to correcting past inequities, but too often these men have been thwarted in their efforts to initiate meaningful changes. The personnel function has little power within the railroad corporate hierarchy. Consequently it will be difficult for the industry to establish the solidly supported programs necessary without insistent pressure from the government. In a recent speech, William Brown, chairman of the EEOC, noted that while the industry has made a clear commitment to the concept of equal opportunity, they are not living up to their commitment.[252] If the cases now before the courts follow the trend of decisions in other industries, there should no longer be any question about fulfilling that commitment.

---

252. See *Daily Labor Report*, No. 238 (December 9, 1970), p. A-7.

Appendix A

TABLE A-1. *Railroad Industry*
Occupational Group by Function and Skill Level

Occupational Group	ICC Division No.	Description of Position
OFFICIALS AND MANAGERS:		
		Executives, Officials, and Staff Assistants
	1	Executives, general officers, and assistants
	2	Division officers, assistants, and staff assistants
		Maintenance of Way and Structures
	27	Roadmasters, general foremen, and assistants
	44	General and assistant general foremen and inspectors (signal, telegraph and electrical transmission)
		Maintenance of Equipment and Stores
	50	General, assistant general, and department foremen
	51	General and assistant general foremen (stores)
		Transportation (Other than train, engine and yard)
	75	Chief train dispatchers
	78	Station agents (supervisory—major stations)
	88	General foremen (freight stations, warehouses, grain elevators, and docks)
	89	Assistant general foremen (freight stations, warehouses, grain elevators, and docks)

PROFESSIONALS:

3   Professionals and subprofessional assistants

TECHNICIANS:

Professional, Clerical, and General

11   Storekeepers, sales agents, and buyers
13   Traveling auditors and accountants
20   Claim agents or investigators
21   Freight claim agents or investigators
22   Chief claim agents or investigators

Maintenance of Equipment and Stores

52   Equipment, shop, electrical, material, and supplies inspectors

Transportation (Other than train, engine, and yard)

76   Train dispatchers
77   Train directors
81   Chief telegraphers and telephoners or wire chiefs

SALES WORKERS:

Professional, Clerical, and General

12   Ticket agents and assistant ticket agents
19   Traffic and various other agents, inspectors, and investigators

OFFICE AND CLERICAL:

Professional, Clerical, and General

4   Supervisory or chief clerks (major departments)
5   Chief clerks (minor departments) and assistant chief clerks, and supervising cashiers
6   Clerks and clerical assistants (A)
7   Clerks (B and C)
8   Mechanical device operators (office)
9   Stenographers and secretaries (A)
10   Stenographers and typists (B)

TABLE A-1. (continued)

Occupational Group	Division No.	Description of Position
OFFICE AND CLERICAL (cont'd):		
	14	Telephone switchboard operators and office assistants
	15	Messengers and office boys
		Transportation (Other than train, engine, and yard)
	79	Station agents (smaller stations)
	80	Station agents (telegraphers and telephoners)
	82	Clerk-telegraphers and clerk-telephoners
	83	Telegraphers, telephoners, and towermen
CRAFTSMEN:		Maintenance of Way and Structures
	28	Maintenance of way and scale inspectors
	29	Bridge and building gang foremen (skilled labor)
	30	Bridge and building carpenters
	31	Bridge and building ironworkers
	32	Bridge and building painters
	33	Masons, bricklayers, plasterers, and plumbers
	35	Portable equipment operators
	38	Gang foremen (extra gang and worktrain laborers)
	39	Gang foremen (bridge, building, signal, and telegraph laborers)
	40	Gang or section foremen
	45	Gang foremen (signal and telegraph skilled trades labor)
	46	Signalmen and signal maintainers
	47	Linemen and groundmen

Maintenance of Equipment and Stores

53	Gang foremen and gang leaders (skilled labor)
54	Blacksmiths
55	Boilermakers
56	Carmen (A and B)
57	Carmen (C and D)
58	Electrical workers (A)
59	Electrical workers (B)
61	Machinists
62	Molders
63	Sheet metal workers
68	Gang foremen (shops, enginehouses, and power plants)
69	Gang foremen (stores, ice, reclamation, timber treating plants)
73	Stationary engineers (steam)

Transportation (Other than train, engine, and yard)

84	Station masters and assistants
85	Supervisory baggage agents
86	Baggage agents and assistants
90	Gang foremen (freight station, warehouse, grain elevator, and dock labor)
99	Transportation and dining service inspectors

Transportation (Yardmasters, switch tenders, and hostlers)

105	Yardmasters
106	Assistant yardmasters

Transportation (Train and engine)

111	Road passenger conductors
113	Road freight conductors (through freight)
114	Road freight conductors (local and way freight)
119	Yard conductors and yard foremen

TABLE A-1.   (continued)

Occupational Group	Division No.	Description of Position
CRAFTSMEN: (cont'd) :	121	Road passenger engineers and motormen
	122	Road freight engineers and motormen (through freight)
	123	Road freight engineers and motormen (local and way freight)
	124	Yard engineers and motormen
OPERATIVES:		*Professional, Clerical, and General*
	23	Miscellaneous trades workers (other than plumbers)
	24	Motor vehicle and motor car operators
		Maintenance of Way and Structures
	34	Maintenance of way and structures helpers and apprentices
	36	Portable equipment operator helpers
	37	Pumping equipment operators
	48	Assistant signalmen and assistant signal maintainers
	49	Signalmen and signal maintainer helpers
		Maintenance of Equipment and Stores
	60	Electrical workers (C)
	64	Skilled trades helpers (M. of E. and stores)
	65	Helper apprentices (M. of E. and stores)
	66	Regular apprentices (M. of E. and stores)
	74	Stationary firemen, oilers, coal passers, and water tenders
		Transportation (Other than train, engine, and yard)
	91	Callers, loaders, scalers, sealers, and perishable freight inspectors
	100	Parlor and sleeping car conductors
	102	Bridge operators and helpers

Transportation (Yardmasters, switch tenders, and hostlers)

107 Switch tenders
108 Outside hostlers
109 Inside hostlers

Transportation (train and engine)

112 Assistant road passenger conductors and ticket collectors
115 Road passenger baggagemen
116 Road passenger brakemen and flagmen
117 Road freight brakemen and flagmen (through freight)
118 Road freight brakemen and flagmen (local and way freight)
120 Yard brakemen and yard helpers
125 Road passenger firemen and helpers
126 Road freight firemen and helpers (through freight)
127 Road freight firemen and helpers (local and way freight)
128 Yard firemen and helpers

Professional, Clerical, and General

25 Teamsters and stablemen

Maintenance of Way and Structures

41 Extra gangmen
42 Section men
43 Maintenance of way laborers (other than track and roadway) and gardners and farmers

Maintenance of Equipment and Stores

67 Coach cleaners
70 Classified laborers (shops, enginehouses, and power plants)
71 General laborers (stores and ice, reclamation, and timber-treating plants)

LABORERS:

TABLE A-1.   (continued)

Occupational Group	ICC Division No.	Description of Position
LABORERS (cont'd):		Transportation (Other than train, engine, and yard)
	87	Baggage, parcel room and station attendants
	92	Truckers (station, warehouses, and platforms)
	93	Laborers (coal and ore docks and grain elevators)
	94	Common laborers (stations, warehouses, platforms, grain elevators)
	103	Crossing and bridge flagmen and gatemen
		Transportation (Yardmasters, switch tenders, and hostlers)
	110	Outside hostler helpers
SERVICE WORKERS:		Professional, Clerical, and General
	16	Elevator operators and other office attendants
	17	Lieutenants and sergeants of police
	18	Patrolmen and watchmen
	26	Janitors and cleaners
		Transportation (Other than train, engine, and yard)
	95	Stewards, restaurant and lodginghouse managers, and dining car supervisors
	96	Chefs and cooks (restaurant or dining cars)
	97	Waiters, camp cooks, kitchen helpers, etc.
	98	Officers, workers, and attendants on barges, launches, ferry boats, towing vessels and steamers, and shore workers
	101	Train attendants

Source: Letter from Albert R. Beatty, Association of American Railroads, to member railroads, February 23, 1966.

Appendix B

BASIC STATISTICAL DATA ON NEGRO EMPLOYMENT, 1968

TABLE B-1. *Railroad Industry*

Employment by Race, Sex, and Occupational Group
30 Companies, Eastern District, 1968

Occupational Group	All Employees			Male			Female		
	Total	Negro	Percent Negro	Total	Negro	Percent Negro	Total	Negro	Percent Negro
Officials and managers	10,822	28	0.3	10,798	28	0.3	24	—	—
Professionals	2,482	10	0.4	2,421	10	0.4	61	—	—
Technicians	3,191	8	0.3	3,139	8	0.3	52	—	—
Sales workers	2,492	8	0.3	2,473	8	0.3	19	—	—
Office and clerical	49,801	961	1.9	37,620	675	1.8	12,181	286	2.3
Total white collar	68,788	1,015	1.5	56,451	729	1.3	12,337	286	2.3
Craftsmen	92,349	2,424	2.6	92,280	2,411	2.6	69	13	18.8
Operatives	55,616	2,133	3.8	55,536	2,115	3.8	80	18	22.5
Laborers	28,085	7,639	27.2	27,395	7,281	26.6	690	358	51.9
Service workers	7,733	2,308	29.8	7,426	2,207	29.7	307	101	32.9
Total blue collar	183,783	14,504	7.9	182,637	14,014	7.7	1,146	490	42.8
Total	252,571	15,519	6.1	239,088	14,743	6.2	13,483	776	5.8

Source: Data in author's possession.

TABLE B-2. Railroad Industry
Employment by Race, Sex, and Occupational Group
14 Companies, Southern District, 1968

Occupational Group	All Employees			Male			Female		
	Total	Negro	Percent Negro	Total	Negro	Percent Negro	Total	Negro	Percent Negro
Officials and managers	5,493	5	0.1	5,472	5	0.1	21	—	—
Professionals	1,086	2	0.2	1,057	2	0.2	29	—	—
Technicians	1,051	7	0.7	1,039	7	0.7	12	—	—
Sales workers	1,414	4	0.3	1,276	3	0.2	138	1	0.7
Office and clerical	16,813	199	1.2	12,840	161	1.3	3,973	38	1.0
Total white collar	25,857	217	0.8	21,684	178	0.8	4,173	39	0.9
Craftsmen	30,892	1,238	4.0	30,886	1,238	4.0	6	—	—
Operatives	17,841	2,506	14.0	17,820	2,502	14.0	21	4	19.0
Laborers	11,591	8,348	72.0	11,415	8,207	71.9	176	141	80.1
Service workers	2,511	1,656	65.9	2,380	1,618	68.0	131	38	29.0
Total blue collar	62,835	13,748	21.9	62,501	13,565	21.7	334	183	54.8
Total	88,692	13,965	15.7	84,185	13,743	16.3	4,507	222	4.9

Source: Data in author's possession.

TABLE B-3. *Railroad Industry*
Employment by Race, Sex, and Occupational Group
25 Companies, Western District, 1968

Occupational Group	All Employees			Male			Female		
	Total	Negro	Percent Negro	Total	Negro	Percent Negro	Total	Negro	Percent Negro
Officials and managers	12,113	17	0.1	12,059	17	0.1	54	—	—
Professionals	3,558	12	0.3	3,509	12	0.3	49	—	—
Technicians	3,558	18	0.5	3,491	18	0.5	67	—	—
Sales workers	3,603	2	0.1	3,577	2	0.1	26	—	—
Office and clerical	56,765	1,038	1.8	42,504	809	1.9	14,261	229	1.6
Total white collar	79,597	1,087	1.4	65,140	858	1.3	14,457	229	1.6
Craftsmen	92,119	1,654	1.8	92,047	1,648	1.8	72	6	8.3
Operatives	55,944	2,104	3.8	55,763	2,067	3.7	181	37	20.4
Laborers	33,780	6,524	19.3	33,046	6,157	18.6	734	367	50.0
Service workers	5,822	3,214	55.2	5,448	3,152	57.9	374	62	16.6
Total blue collar	187,665	13,496	7.2	186,304	13,024	7.0	1,361	472	34.7
Total	267,262	14,583	5.5	251,444	13,882	5.5	15,818	701	4.4

Source: Data in author's possession.

TABLE B-4. *Railroad Industry*
Employment by Race, Sex, and Occupational Group
19 Large Companies, 1968

Occupational Group	All Employees			Male			Female		
	Total	Negro	Percent Negro	Total	Negro	Percent Negro	Total	Negro	Percent Negro
Officials and managers	22,013	45	0.2	21,928	45	0.2	85	—	—
Professionals	5,776	17	0.3	5,679	17	0.3	97	—	—
Technicians	6,376	32	0.5	6,275	32	0.5	101	—	—
Sales workers	5,975	12	0.2	5,805	11	0.2	170	1	0.6
Office and clerical	99,878	1,853	1.9	75,183	1,372	1.8	24,695	481	1.9
Total white collar	140,018	1,959	1.4	114,870	1,477	1.3	25,148	482	1.9
Craftsmen	177,453	4,593	2.6	177,329	4,577	2.6	124	16	12.9
Operatives	105,645	5,806	5.5	105,392	5,755	5.5	253	51	20.2
Laborers	58,035	18,509	31.9	56,661	17,730	31.3	1,374	779	56.7
Service workers	13,328	6,250	46.9	12,677	6,074	47.9	651	176	27.0
Total blue collar	354,461	35,158	9.9	352,059	34,136	9.7	2,402	1,022	42.5
Total	494,479	37,117	7.5	466,929	35,613	7.6	27,550	1,504	5.5

Source: Data in author's possession.

Note: Companies with 10,000 or more employees.

TABLE B-5. *Railroad Industry*
Employment by Race, Sex, and Occupational Group
22 Medium-Size Companies, 1968

Occupational Group	All Employees			Male			Female		
	Total	Negro	Percent Negro	Total	Negro	Percent Negro	Total	Negro	Percent Negro
Officials and managers	4,794	3	0.1	4,788	3	0.1	6	—	—
Professionals	1,071	6	0.6	1,032	6	0.6	39	—	—
Technicians	1,183	1	0.1	1,155	1	0.1	28	—	—
Sales workers	1,243	1	0.1	1,233	1	0.1	10	—	—
Office and clerical	19,419	321	1.7	14,681	250	1.7	4,738	71	1.5
Total white collar	27,710	332	1.2	22,889	261	1.1	4,821	71	1.5
Craftsmen	30,720	568	1.8	30,698	565	1.8	22	3	13.6
Operatives	19,770	731	3.7	19,743	724	3.7	27	7	25.9
Laborers	12,544	3,316	26.4	12,323	3,231	26.2	221	85	38.5
Service workers	2,202	789	35.8	2,067	772	37.3	135	17	12.6
Total blue collar	65,236	5,404	8.3	64,831	5,292	8.2	405	112	27.7
Total	92,946	5,736	6.2	87,720	5,553	6.3	5,226	183	3.5

Source: Data in author's possession.

Note: Companies with 2,500 to 9,999 employees.

TABLE B-6. Railroad Industry

Employment by Race, Sex, and Occupational Group
28 Small Companies, 1968

Occupational Group	All Employees			Male			Female		
	Total	Negro	Percent Negro	Total	Negro	Percent Negro	Total	Negro	Percent Negro
Officials and managers	1,621	2	0.1	1,613	2	0.1	8	—	—
Professionals	279	1	0.4	276	1	0.4	3	—	—
Technicians	241	—	—	239	—	—	2	—	—
Sales workers	291	1	0.3	288	1	0.3	3	—	—
Office and clerical	4,082	24	0.6	3,100	23	0.7	982	1	0.1
Total white collar	6,514	28	0.4	5,516	27	0.5	998	1	0.1
Craftsmen	7,187	155	2.2	7,186	155	2.2	1	—	—
Operatives	3,986	206	5.2	3,984	205	5.1	2	1	50.0
Laborers	2,877	686	23.8	2,872	684	23.8	5	2	40.0
Service workers	536	139	25.9	510	131	25.7	26	8	30.8
Total blue collar	14,586	1,186	8.1	14,552	1,175	8.1	34	11	32.4
Total	21,100	1,214	5.8	20,068	1,202	6.0	1,032	12	1.2

Source: Data in author's possession.

Note: Companies with less than 2,500 employees.

TABLE B-7. *Railroad Industry*

Employment by Race, Sex, and Occupational Group

5 Large Companies, Eastern District, 1968

Occupational Group	All Employees			Male			Female		
	Total	Negro	Percent Negro	Total	Negro	Percent Negro	Total	Negro	Percent Negro
Officials and managers	7,686	23	0.3	7,669	23	0.3	17	—	—
Professionals	1,725	3	0.2	1,699	3	0.2	26	—	—
Technicians	2,392	7	0.3	2,358	7	0.3	34	—	—
Sales workers	1,809	6	0.3	1,796	6	0.3	13	—	—
Office and clerical	36,840	738	2.0	28,072	514	1.8	8,768	224	2.6
Total white collar	50,452	777	1.5	41,594	553	1.3	8,858	224	2.5
Craftsmen	70,628	1,963	2.8	70,573	1,953	2.8	55	10	18.2
Operatives	43,107	1,719	4.0	43,041	1,706	4.0	66	13	19.7
Laborers	19,824	6,153	31.0	19,309	5,864	30.4	515	289	56.1
Service workers	5,907	1,887	31.9	5,723	1,804	31.5	184	83	45.1
Total blue collar	139,466	11,722	8.4	138,646	11,327	8.2	820	395	48.2
Total	189,918	12,499	6.6	180,240	11,880	6.6	9,678	619	6.4

Source: Data in author's possession.

Note: Companies with 10,000 or more employees.

TABLE B-8.   *Railroad Industry*
Employment by Race, Sex, and Occupational Group
4 Large Companies, Southern District, 1968

Occupational Group	All Employees			Male			Female		
	Total	Negro	Percent Negro	Total	Negro	Percent Negro	Total	Negro	Percent Negro
Officials and managers	4,505	5	0.1	4,488	5	0.1	17	—	—
Professionals	934	2	0.2	908	2	0.2	26	—	—
Technicians	961	7	0.7	949	7	0.7	12	—	—
Sales workers	1,237	4	0.3	1,103	3	0.3	134	1	0.7
Office and clerical	14,222	167	1.2	10,805	131	1.2	3,417	36	1.1
Total white collar	21,859	185	0.8	18,253	148	0.8	3,606	37	1.0
Craftsmen	27,601	1,076	3.9	27,595	1,076	3.9	6	—	—
Operatives	15,238	2,140	14.0	15,219	2,137	14.0	19	3	15.8
Laborers	9,704	7,120	73.4	9,533	6,983	73.3	171	137	80.1
Service workers	2,134	1,388	65.0	2,009	1,356	67.5	125	32	25.6
Total blue collar	54,677	11,724	21.4	54,356	11,552	21.3	321	172	53.6
Total	76,536	11,909	15.6	72,609	11,700	16.1	3,927	209	5.3

Source: Data in author's possession.

Note: Companies with 10,000 or more employees.

TABLE B-9. Railroad Industry
Employment by Race, Sex, and Occupational Group
10 Large Companies, Western District, 1968

Occupational Group	All Employees			Male			Female		
	Total	Negro	Percent Negro	Total	Negro	Percent Negro	Total	Negro	Percent Negro
Officials and managers	9,822	17	0.2	9,771	17	0.2	51	—	—
Professionals	3,117	12	0.4	3,072	12	0.4	45	—	—
Technicians	3,023	18	0.6	2,968	18	0.6	55	—	—
Sales workers	2,929	2	0.1	2,906	2	0.1	23	—	—
Office and clerical	48,816	948	1.9	36,306	727	2.0	12,510	221	1.8
Total white collar	67,707	997	1.5	55,023	776	1.4	12,684	221	1.7
Craftsmen	79,224	1,554	2.0	79,161	1,548	2.0	63	6	9.5
Operatives	47,300	1,947	4.1	47,132	1,912	4.1	168	35	20.8
Laborers	28,507	5,236	18.4	27,819	4,883	17.6	688	353	51.3
Service workers	5,287	2,975	56.3	4,945	2,914	58.9	342	61	17.8
Total blue collar	160,318	11,712	7.3	159,057	11,257	7.1	1,261	455	36.1
Total	228,025	12,709	5.6	214,080	12,033	5.6	13,945	676	4.8

Source: Data in author's possession.

Note: Companies with 10,000 or more employees.

TABLE B-10. Railroad Industry
Employment by Race, Sex, and Occupational Group
12 Medium-Size Companies, Eastern District, 1968

Occupational Group	All Employees			Male			Female		
	Total	Negro	Percent Negro	Total	Negro	Percent Negro	Total	Negro	Percent Negro
Officials and managers	2,268	3	0.1	2,265	3	0.1	3	—	—
Professionals	634	6	0.9	601	6	1.0	33	—	—
Technicians	675	1	0.1	658	1	0.2	17	—	—
Sales workers	576	1	0.2	570	1	0.2	6	—	—
Office and clerical	10,608	210	2.0	7,777	149	1.9	2,831	61	2.2
Total white collar	14,761	221	1.5	11,871	160	1.3	2,890	61	2.1
Craftsmen	17,641	411	2.3	17,627	408	2.3	14	3	21.4
Operatives	10,461	399	3.8	10,447	394	3.8	14	5	35.7
Laborers	6,755	1,274	18.9	6,581	1,205	18.3	174	69	39.7
Service workers	1,500	397	26.5	1,398	385	27.5	102	12	11.8
Total blue collar	36,357	2,481	6.8	36,053	2,392	6.6	304	89	29.3
Total	51,118	2,702	5.3	47,924	2,552	5.3	3,194	150	4.7

Source: Data in author's possession.

Note: Companies with 2,500 to 9,999 employees.

TABLE B-11. *Railroad Industry*

Employment by Race, Sex, and Occupational Group

2 Medium-Size Companies, Southern District, 1968

Occupational Group	All Employees			Male			Female		
	Total	Negro	Percent Negro	Total	Negro	Percent Negro	Total	Negro	Percent Negro
Officials and managers	559	—	—	558	—	—	1	—	—
Professionals	90	—	—	88	—	—	2	—	—
Technicians	32	—	—	32	—	—	—	—	—
Sales workers	44	—	—	43	—	—	1	—	—
Office and clerical	1,814	25	1.4	1,459	23	1.6	355	2	0.6
Total white collar	2,539	25	1.0	2,180	23	1.1	359	2	0.6
Craftsmen	1,858	64	3.4	1,858	64	3.4	—	—	—
Operatives	1,750	177	10.1	1,749	177	10.1	1	—	—
Laborers	1,204	803	66.7	1,200	800	66.7	4	3	75.0
Service workers	215	160	74.4	211	156	73.9	4	4	100.0
Total blue collar	5,027	1,204	24.0	5,018	1,197	23.9	9	7	77.8
Total	7,566	1,229	16.2	7,198	1,220	16.9	368	9	2.4

Source: Data in author's possession.

Note: Companies with 2,500 to 9,999 employees.

TABLE B-12. *Railroad Industry*

Employment by Race, Sex, and Occupational Group
8 Medium-Size Companies, Western District, 1968

Occupational Group	All Employees			Male			Female		
	Total	Negro	Percent Negro	Total	Negro	Percent Negro	Total	Negro	Percent Negro
Officials and managers	1,967	—	—	1,965	—	—	2	—	—
Professionals	347	—	—	343	—	—	4	—	—
Technicians	476	—	—	465	—	—	11	—	—
Sales workers	623	—	—	620	—	—	3	—	—
Office and clerical	6,997	86	1.2	5,445	78	1.4	1,552	8	0.5
Total white collar	10,410	86	0.8	8,838	78	0.9	1,572	8	0.5
Craftsmen	11,221	93	0.8	11,213	93	0.8	8	—	—
Operatives	7,559	155	2.1	7,547	153	2.0	12	2	16.7
Laborers	4,585	1,239	27.0	4,542	1,226	27.0	43	13	30.2
Service workers	487	232	47.6	458	231	50.4	29	1	3.4
Total blue collar	23,852	1,719	7.2	23,760	1,703	7.2	92	16	17.4
Total	34,262	1,805	5.3	32,598	1,781	5.5	1,664	24	1.4

Source: Data in author's possession.

Note: Companies with 2,500 to 9,999 employees.

TABLE B-13. *Railroad Industry*
Employment by Race, Sex, and Occupational Group
13 Small Companies, Eastern District, 1968

Occupational Group	All Employees			Male			Female		
	Total	Negro	Percent Negro	Total	Negro	Percent Negro	Total	Negro	Percent Negro
Officials and managers	868	2	0.2	864	2	0.2	4	—	—
Professionals	123	1	0.8	121	1	0.8	2	—	—
Technicians	124	—	—	123	—	—	1	—	—
Sales workers	107	1	0.9	107	1	0.9	—	—	—
Office and clerical	2,353	13	0.6	1,771	12	0.7	582	1	0.2
Total white collar	3,575	17	0.5	2,986	16	0.5	589	1	0.2
Craftsmen	4,080	50	1.2	4,080	50	1.2	—	—	—
Operatives	2,048	15	0.7	2,048	15	0.7	—	—	—
Laborers	1,506	212	14.1	1,505	212	14.1	1	—	—
Service workers	326	24	7.4	305	18	5.9	21	6	28.6
Total blue collar	7,960	301	3.8	7,938	295	3.7	22	6	27.3
Total	11,535	318	2.8	10,924	311	2.8	611	7	1.1

Source: Data in author's possession.

Note: Companies with under 2,500 employees.

TABLE B-14. Railroad Industry
Employment by Race, Sex, and Occupational Group
8 Small Companies, Southern District, 1968

Occupational Group	All Employees			Male			Female		
	Total	Negro	Percent Negro	Total	Negro	Percent Negro	Total	Negro	Percent Negro
Officials and managers	429	—	—	426	—	—	3	—	—
Professionals	62	—	—	61	—	—	1	—	—
Technicians	58	—	—	58	—	—	—	—	—
Sales workers	133	—	—	130	—	—	3	—	—
Office and clerical	777	7	0.9	576	7	1.2	201	—	—
Total white collar	1,459	7	0.5	1,251	7	0.6	208	—	—
Craftsmen	1,433	98	6.8	1,433	98	6.8	—	—	—
Operatives	853	189	22.2	852	188	22.1	1	1	100.0
Laborers	683	425	62.2	682	424	62.2	1	1	100.0
Service workers	162	108	66.7	160	106	66.2	2	2	100.0
Total blue collar	3,131	820	26.2	3,127	816	26.1	4	4	100.0
Total	4,590	827	18.0	4,378	823	18.8	212	4	1.9

Source: Data in author's possession.

Note: Companies with less than 2,500 employees.

TABLE B-15. *Railroad Industry*
Employment by Race, Sex, and Occupational Group
7 Small Companies, Western District, 1968

Occupational Group	All Employees			Male			Female		
	Total	Negro	Percent Negro	Total	Negro	Percent Negro	Total	Negro	Percent Negro
Officials and managers	324	—	—	323	—	—	1	—	—
Professionals	94	—	—	94	—	—	—	—	—
Technicians	59	—	—	58	—	—	1	—	—
Sales workers	51	—	—	51	—	—	—	—	—
Office and clerical	952	4	0.4	753	4	0.5	199	—	—
Total white collar	1,480	4	0.3	1,279	4	0.3	201	—	—
Craftsmen	1,674	7	0.4	1,673	7	0.4	1	—	—
Operatives	1,085	2	0.2	1,084	2	0.2	1	—	—
Laborers	688	49	7.1	685	48	7.0	3	1	33.3
Service workers	48	7	14.6	45	7	15.6	3	—	—
Total blue collar	3,495	65	1.9	3,487	64	1.8	8	1	12.5
Total	4,975	69	1.4	4,766	68	1.4	209	1	0.5

Source: Data in author's possession.

Note: Companies with less than 2,500 employees.

Index

PART TWO

THE NEGRO
IN THE AIR TRANSPORT INDUSTRY

by

HERBERT R. NORTHRUP
ARMAND J. THIEBLOT, JR.
and
WILLIAM N. CHERNISH

TABLE OF CONTENTS

LIST OF TABLES

viii

CHAPTER I

Introduction

Air transport is the elite of the transportation services. Its equipment is the most sophisticated and technologically advanced. Its employees require the most detailed training and have the most awesome safety responsibilities. Operating employees are classified as "professionals," not "operatives" or even "craftsmen," and are compensated accordingly. Within a very short period, air transportation has wrested the intercity passenger business from railroads and has passed buses in that traffic while at the same time so dominating transoceanic passenger routes that most ocean liners have been retired. Moreover, in recent years air cargo has steadily risen.

The elitist character of the airline originally contributed to its position as the most exclusionist of transportation industries. The original flyers were a tight knit group among whom Negroes were not welcome. The failure of the armed forces to admit Negroes to flying opportunities contributed substantially to this attitude and to the continuing pattern of discrimination in the industry. In the late 1950's, however, the prodding of state human relations commissions resulted in the beginning of change, and the civil rights programs of the 1960's saw substantial improvement. Nevertheless, Negroes continue to be disadvantaged by lack of training opportunities and inferior educational backgrounds.

This study examines the air transport industry's current racial policies after describing the nature of the industry and the extent of Negro participation therein before 1960. The basic data utilized in the study were developed in the 1967-1969 period, and include field visits to eleven trunk airlines and two smaller carriers. The analysis will pertain particularly to the twelve major carriers which together employ more than 90 percent of all airline personnel.

CHAPTER II

The Air Transport Industry

Air transportation is the product of the technology of this century and is therefore the most recently developed of the fully formed transportation systems. Although airline growth seems to have been slowing in the most recent years, commercial and public acceptance of the service advantages offered by the industry has generally outstripped the most optimistic projections. Airlines hold undisputed first place among commercial common carriers of domestic intercity passenger traffic, having passed buses, the closest competition, in 1957. The airlines' share of domestic intercity traffic continued to increase rapidly, and by 1967, only ten years later, airlines served approximately 70 percent of this market, compared with 20 percent for buses, and 10 percent for railroads.[1]

DEVELOPMENT AND GROWTH OF THE INDUSTRY

Commercialization of aviation was a natural outgrowth of the increasing sophistication of the airplane, fired by continued aeronautical experimentation and government assistance during the 1920's and fueled by growing public and investor interest and confidence in the new field. The first of what subsequently came to be known as the "trunk" airlines (with which we shall be dealing here) was established in 1925. More than forty operators were in business by 1930, flying almost 550 aircraft over approximately 30,000 route miles. Although the industry at that time was dominated by three large combination manufacturing-transportation companies,[2] most of the operators were small independent carriers whose motivation for establishment lay in the airmail contracts being awarded by the Post Office Department.

---

1. Air Transport Association, *1968 Air Transport Facts and Figures* (Washington: The Association, 1968), p. 41.

2. They were the Aviation Corporation of Delaware (American), General Motors-North American Aviation Group (Eastern, TWA, Western), and United Aircraft and Transport Corporation (United).

Interest in passengers was secondary to the more important and profitable business of flying the mails. Almost two and one-half times the 85,000,000 passenger miles flown during the entire year of 1930 are now flown each day by our domestic trunk airline system.

The first major reorganization of the airlines' competitive structure came about as a result of a cancellation of airmail contracts in February 1934. At that time, the Postmaster General, suspecting collusion in the setting of airmail rates, annulled commercial airmail contracts and turned over the mails to the army, which flew them for about three months. Before reopening mail contracts for bids from the experienced commercial carriers, the government insisted on major internal reorganizations among the competing lines. One of the requirements involved separation of the aviation manufacturing industry from that of air transport. Holding companies which had formerly combined the functions of manufacture and operation of aircraft were split, and from that separation grew what has now become two strong independent industries: aerospace and air transport.

The second area of major change was brought about by the passage of the Air Mail Act of 1934, which made provisions for airmail regulation, including one that the Interstate Commerce Commission was to set "fair and reasonable" rates of mail pay, and a second that the Bureau of Air Commerce of the Department of Commerce was to regulate the airline industry and be responsible for airport maintenance and development. Although the federal government was not to be in the business of transporting airmail, it was nevertheless to be involved intimately with the conditions of transport. From this act grew the extensive government regulation under which the industry now operates, and pursuant to which the federal government can and does affect employment policies including civil rights.

Perhaps more significant to the developing structure of the industry, the 1934 activities relating to airmail alerted the carriers to the importance of the passenger. At the time of the mail contract cancellation, even the most passenger-oriented lines in the industry derived almost 50 percent of their income from airmail revenues. The airlines began looking toward the passenger markets to insure themselves against a repetition of the chaotic conditions of 1934. (Racial policies have, of course, been profoundly affected by this passenger orientation.) This created severe competitive pressures among the lines which, combined with intensified governmental and operational problems, produced insecure financial conditions and an unsure future for the lines during the later 1930's. These conditions motivated the carriers themselves, among others, to sponsor comprehensive federal regulations to save the industry through effective control of it. This was accomplished with the passage of the Civil Aeronautics Act of 1938.

The Civil Aeronautics Act of 1938

The Act of 1938 was a comprehensive document which, as a minimum, brought far-reaching changes to both the conduct and the composition of the airline industry, and essentially established the air carrier system which we know today. It set forth a statement of policy in accordance with which the Civil Aeronautics Board was authorized to regulate air transportation in the public interest, and control the economic conditions within it. Under the powers granted to it, the CAB restricted entry into the field by requiring that a "certificate of public convenience and necessity," issued by the board, be held by any airline engaging in common carriage. It restricted exit by the certificated lines from routes already held and barred entry into new markets; it required thirty days' notification and approval by the Board of rate changes and prohibited rebates or deviations from the published tariffs; it continued control over the award of airmail contracts, and maintained jurisdiction over consolidation of control, mergers, interlocking directorates, pooling arrangements, and other communities of interest. And, as noted below, it evidenced government interest in employee relations through minimum pilot salaries and adherence to federal labor legislation. Civil rights, however, was not a factor in CAB regulation before 1960.

With the Act of 1938, the CAB institutionalized the status quo by establishing what has come to be known as the "grandfather clause." This rendered automatic the certification of existing airlines for routes over which they had provided continuous service for the preceding six months. The group of carriers to whom this clause applied are known as "trunk" lines. Originally nineteen in number, and with one addition in 1938 and one in 1940, the trunks have declined through attrition and merger and now comprise only eleven lines: the "big four" and the seven "regionals." Pan American World Airways, which operates only as an international carrier, is the twelfth key airline.

STRUCTURE OF THE INDUSTRY

There are many more carriers in operation in the United States than the eleven surviving trunk lines plus Pan American. In fact, there are over fifty carriers certificated by the Civil Aeronautics Board for operations of various types. The classification of certificated carriers is as follows:

1. Domestic Trunk Carriers include those carriers which presently have permanent operating rights to serve cities within the continental United States. There are currently eleven trunk lines, most of which operate high density routes between the principal traffic centers of the United States. Within the trunk carrier group is a generally recognized subdivision known as the "big four" carriers: American Airlines, Eastern Air Lines, Trans World Airlines (TWA), and United Air Lines. The others in the trunk carrier group are the "regionals": Braniff International, Continental Airlines, Delta Air Lines, National Airlines, Northeast Airlines, Northwest Airlines, and Western Air Lines.

2. International and Territorial Carriers include all of the U.S.-flag air carriers operating between the United States and foreign countries other than Canada, and over international waters. There are fourteen such carriers, some of which conduct operations between foreign countries, and some of which act as extensions of domestic trunk lines into Mexico and the Caribbean and to Alaska and Hawaii. By far the most important of the international carriers (in international operation) are Pan American World Airways and Trans World Airlines. All of the domestic trunk lines hold certificates in this category. Pan American, however, is not certificated to fly passengers and cargo between points within the continental United States.

3. Domestic Local Service Carriers have, with one exception, all been certificated since 1945. These nine carriers operate routes of lesser traffic density between smaller traffic centers, and between these and major metropolitan centers where they connect with the trunk carrier operations. The local service carriers are sometimes referred to as "feeder airlines." The number of local service carriers has been diminishing rapidly in recent years as individual lines merge with one another in attempts to improve operating revenues and gain the economies of scale associated with more extensive route structures. The current operators of this class are: Air West, Allegheny, Frontier, Mohawk,

North Central, Ozark, Piedmont, Southern, and Texas International.

4. Territorial Carriers operate solely between the various islands which constitute the state of Hawaii, and within the state of Alaska.

5. Helicopter Carriers presently operate between airports, central post offices, and suburbs of New York, Chicago, Washington, Los Angeles, and San Francisco. These carriers were originally certified to serve as mail carriers only, but now fly passengers, air freight, express, and mail.

6. All-Cargo Carriers operate scheduled flights carrying freight, express, and mail between designated areas in the United States, and in one case to the Caribbean, and in another case, to Europe. There are five such lines. The trunk and feeder lines also carry cargo.

7. Supplemental Air Carriers hold certificates issued by the Civil Aeronautics Board authorizing them to operate passenger and cargo charter services supplementing the scheduled service of the certificated route air carriers. There are about fifteen carriers which hold supplemental certificates.[3]

In addition to the above carriers, there are a number of smaller air carriers in operation which do not hold certificates of public convenience and necessity. These consist of air taxi operations, charter services, intrastate carriers, irregular carriers, freight forwarders, and the like.

In terms of total revenue, the eleven-carrier trunk group, when added to the international operations of Pan American and TWA, represents nearly 90 percent of the entire certificated passenger industry.[4] It is for this reason that the primary emphasis of this study is placed upon these carriers. Although the smaller carriers do operate a significant number of aircraft, and do serve a large number of locations, from the standpoint of share of the market—and as we shall see of employment—it is evident that the emphasis of this study must fall upon the domestic trunk carriers plus Pan American.

The basic statistics relating to these lines are set forth in Table 1. United, the largest, operates more than 500 airplanes on nearly 13 million annual route miles. In contrast, Northeast, the

3. Air Transport Association, *op. cit.*, p. 43.

4. *Aviation Week and Space Technology*, Vol. 90 (March 10, 1969), pp. 185-220.

smallest of the trunk carriers, has less than 40 airplanes operating on about 2.5 million annual route miles.

In terms of employment, the twelve airlines listed in Table 1 employ more than 90 percent of all personnel associated with the air transport industry. Moreover, the five largest lines, in turn, employ almost 70 percent of the total employees of the twelve carriers. These five airlines thus employ a majority of the industry's employees. By virtue of their dominating size, they set the standards for the industry, including those pertaining to civil rights posture and policies, and will therefore be given special attention in this study.

INDUSTRY CHARACTERISTICS

Success in the airlines industry has depended primarily on how well an individual line was placed in the competitive structure of 1938, on its aggressiveness in securing route modifications or rate changes from the Civil Aeronautics Board, and on its choice of primary equipment. To a greater extent than in most industries, however, factors affecting competition are beyond the control of individual firms. Weather (and therefore the location of the firm's route structure in relation to weather) has always been significant. Fare changes for flights between given cities may be requested by the lines, but the Civil Aeronautics Board has the power to accept, reject, or modify such requests according to how it interprets the public interest, and once established, the tariffs for any market segment are the same for all carriers serving it. In addition, the technology of the industry has imposed its own natural restraints.

In general, the constraints under which the industry operates and which form the basis of the competition within it are the following: [5]

1. Intensive government regulation controls the manner, place, time, and price at which air transportation may be produced and sold, and of course impacts on all airline policies including racial postures.

2. Services must be provided round-the-clock, seven days per week. This is partially due to the public service basis of the industry. Additionally, fixed costs are such that all lines must

5. See Charles M. Mason, "Collective Bargaining Structure: The Airlines Experience," in Arnold R. Weber (ed.), *The Structure of Collective Bargaining* (New York: Free Press of Glencoe, 1961).

TABLE 1. *The Twelve Major Airlines* *Basic Statistics, 1969*

Carrier and 1969 Rank among Transportation Companies	Headquarters	Operating Revenues	Assets	Net Income	Invested Capital	Number of Employees	Net Income as a Percent of	
		(Thousands	of	Dollars)			Operating Revenue	Invested Capital
United Air Lines (2)	Chicago	$1,477,546	$1,945,703	$44,693	$588,115	52,207	3.0	7.6
Tran World Airlines (4)	New York	1,098,440	1,421,896	19,894	361,829	63,898	1.8	5.5
Pan American World Airways (5)	New York	1,045,047	1,626,282	(25,888)[a]	462,811	39,376	—	—
American Airlines (6)	New York	1,032,960	1,490,798	38,468	403,300	37,073	3.7	9.5
Eastern Air Lines (10)	New York	869,563	1,030,348	(2,323)[a]	224,925	31,900	—	—
Delta Air Lines (15)	Atlanta	516,113	634,265	39,191	226,515	18,985	7.6	17.3
Northwest Airlines (18)	St. Paul	467,938	742,732	51,466	426,797	12,695	11.0	12.1
Braniff International (21)	Dallas	325,648	376,154	6,215	87,577	10,920	1.9	7.1
National Airlines (24)	Miami	260,399	320,645	18,936	128,030	7,256	7.3	14.8
Continental Airlines (26)	Los Angeles	255,660	399,144	3,207	96,291	8,163	1.3	3.3
Western Air Lines (27)	Los Angeles	240,352	367,588	(12,199)[a]	79,309	9,225	—	—
Northeast Airlines (35)	Boston	122,089	69,781	(28,843)[a]	(21,957)[a]	4,317	—	—

Source: *Fortune*, Vol. LXXXI (May 1970), pp. 210-211.

Note: By 1971, Northeast was attempting to merge with Northwest, and Western with American.

[a] Deficit.

strive for maximum utilization of equipment. Much freight transportation or routine servicing of aircraft is scheduled for night or other passenger-slack times. Nighttime work force requirements are varied and extensive.

3. Over many route segments, competition is essentially the same with respect to equipment, schedules, and handling procedures. This forces competitive efforts to be focused on details of services to the passengers, and on advertising to attempt to differentiate the product of a given line. On the other hand, costs must be held to a minimum in order to generate sufficient profit margins.

4. The product of the airlines industry, as in all types of passenger transportation, is extremely perishable. A seat mile which is not flown on one day cannot be made up at a later time; there is no inventory, and business lost due to work stoppage cannot be regained. On the other hand, if there is insufficient capacity for a particular flight, the overflow passengers may be permanently lost to competitors. Since business once lost is lost forever, airlines strive to avoid work stoppages or any potential service interruption.

5. The operations of a carrier are spread over a wide geographic area—on a regional basis for the smaller carriers, across the nation for the large trunk carriers, and throughout the world in the case of the international airlines. Moreover, the operations of a carrier must be integrated and coordinated over its entire operating system, and its procedures and projected image must be consistent.

6. The industry is characterized by tremendous capital investment in aircraft and facilities which become obsolete within relatively short periods of time and which require constant and very expensive maintenance, and a high quality of maintenance mechanics—an occupational group in which Negroes have been traditionally underrepresented.

7. The work force of the airline industry consists of a large percentage of highly skilled employees, many of whom are licensed by the federal government and are directly responsible for the safe operation of aircraft. These include the pilots, technical employees, mechanics, and numerous others. Given their disadvantaged educational status, Negroes have found it difficult to obtain these jobs.

8. The industry has been subject to rapid and frequent technological change which has had a direct effect upon employees

and employment as well as upon the basic ability of lines to remain competitive. The most obvious example of technological change in the industry concerns the evolution of the primary flight equipment which the lines operate. Although minor variations in speed or comfort factors seem to mean little to the average passenger, significant changes, such as those which accompanied the introduction of the turboprop and turbojet, have had significant impact; at least one airline failed as a direct result of choosing the wrong primary equipment; [6] and qualifications of employees have had to keep pace with the changing technology.

REVENUES AND COSTS

Table 2 shows airline revenues for the domestic trunk lines averaging approximately $3.3 billion per year between 1963 and 1967. Operating expenses for this same period averaged slightly under $3 billion, leaving average annual operating income for the trunk lines of $341,280,000. After deduction of interest, taxes, and other adjustments, net profits averaged only $170,495,000 per year for the aggregate of all eleven lines, barely 5 percent of sales. Since 1969, most airlines have incurred heavy losses.

Operating expense breakdowns in Table 2 are those required by the Civil Aeronautics Board, and used by the airlines as standard expense accounting. To a large degree, they disguise the importance of personnel to the operating cost structure. Table 3 presents a percentage distribution of operating expenses (flow of funds) which makes clear that personnel costs are vitally important to the airlines, accounting for more than 38 cents of every dollar spent. Training new employees or upgrading disadvantaged persons can thus be a major corporate cost.

REGULATION

It has been previously noted that the Civil Aeronautics Board, established by the Civil Aeronautics Act of 1938, vitally affects the revenue and competitive status of the carriers. In addition to controlling tariff structures and other factors already mentioned, the board also has regulatory power over the types of

---

6. Capital Airlines, which merged with United in 1961, was on the verge of bankruptcy in large part because of overinvestment in the Viscount, a British-made turboprop which lacked the capability for Capital's needs.

TABLE 2.   *Air Transport Industry*
Domestic Trunk Airlines
Operating Revenues and Expenses
1963-1967 Averages

	1963-1967 average ($000)
Operating revenues	
Passenger	2,951,192
U.S. mail	75,090
Public service revenue	2,567
Express	28,910
Freight	173,728
Other[a]	85,850
Total revenue	3,317,337
Operating expenses	
Flying operations	808,598
Maintenance	575,496
Passenger service	273,634
Aircraft and traffic service	513,837
Promotion and sales	364,362
Administrative	121,827
Depreciation and amortization	318,303
Total expenses	2,976,057
Net operating income	341,280
Interest, taxes, and income adjustments	170,785
Net profits	170,495
Margin on sales	5.1

Source: Computed from Air Transport Association, *1968 Air Transport Facts and Figures* (Washington: The Association, 1968), pp. 28-32.

[a] Includes revenues from excess baggage, foreign mail, charter operations, and incidental revenues.

TABLE 3. *Air Transport Industry*
Domestic Trunk Airlines
Percentage Distribution of Representative Funds
1967

Operating Expenses	Percent of Total
Employees	38.4
Materials, supplies, and services	21.7
Fuel and oil	11.2
Passenger food	3.3
Promotion and advertising	2.7
Depreciation and amortization	8.5
Taxes (except payroll)	4.9
Interest	2.3
Other expenses	0.4
Total operating expenses	93.4
Income	6.6
Total usage of funds	100.0

Source: Air Transport Association, *1968 Air Transport Facts and Figures* (Washington: The Association, 1968), p. 18.

Note: For year ending September 30, 1967.

service offered to the flying public, such as the one- two- or three-classes of passenger service.

Further regulation of the industry comes in the form of licensing imposed by the Federal Aviation Agency. This administration has had the duty to certify every new aircraft introduced into commercial service, and to provide maintenance standards for the safe operation of such aircraft. Additionally, the Federal Aviation Agency imposes and enforces license requirements for all personnel charged with the maintenance of the aircraft. This means that all pilots must hold licenses of the appropriate type before they are permitted to engage in flying, and the same is true for flight engineers, radio operators, mechanics, and others. This regulation serves to promote the safe operation of the airline industry, but it also has the effect of making it more difficult for minority group members to qualify for certain positions because of the educational and other requirements necessary to obtain and hold an appropriate license.

In addition, the Civil Aeronautics Act of 1938 provides that pilots must be paid no less than that required by a complicated formula evolved in the early 1930's—they are paid much more in actual practice. Finally, the act requires that carriers conduct their labor relations in accordance with the Railway Labor Act, which was extended to air transportation in 1936.

Railway Labor Act Coverage

The extension of the Railway Labor Act to air transport in 1936 shaped labor relations in that industry in a number of ways, for at that time only the pilots were unionized. The act provides for government mediation and fact finding, and thus emphasized governmental intervention at the expense of collective bargaining.[7] More significantly for Negro employment, it restricted collective bargaining units to a "craft or class," thus discouraging intraplant mobility and the upgrading of employees. With Negroes concentrated in lower bracket jobs, this has been an added barrier to advancement. And by its policies, the National Mediation Board, which administers this phase of the law, has tended to define the bargaining units to suit the jurisdictional claims of certain railway unions who since the 1930's, with some success, have endeavored to organize airline employees. Since these unions traditionally excluded Negroes, and even today generally give little support to changes in the social-occupational status quo, their effect on Negro aspirations has been largely negative. We shall examine in detail the impact of the Railway Labor Act and of union policies on Negro employment in Chapter IV.

Civil Rights Regulation

The air transport industry is also subject to civil rights legislation. Because it is engaged in interstate commerce and is also a contractor to the federal government, it is subject both to the policies of the Equal Employment Opportunities Commission, which administers Title VII of the Civil Rights Act of 1964, and

---

7. For a discussion of the Railway Labor Act, see Herbert R. Northrup and Gordon F. Bloom, *Government and Labor* (Homewood, Illinois: Richard D. Irwin, 1963), Chapter 12.

of the Office of Federal Contract Complance, which administet
the equal employment provisions of various executive orders, suc
as Executive Order 11246, relating to the regulation of the minot
ity employment patterns of contractors to the government. Th
airlines have also been subject to the civil rights regulations c
the Department of Defense, as the key agency purchasing thei
services, and more recently this regulatory effort has been trans
ferred to the Federal Aviation Agency of the Department c
Transportation. Finally, airlines are subject to the regulatio
and policies of state and local human relations commissions an
other civil rights agencies in the localities in which they operat
These are numerous because of the wide geographical extent c
airline operations. On the whole, the air transport industry :
perhaps the most regulated of all American industries.

MANPOWER

The competitive, regulatory, and structural characteristics c
the airline industry combine to make personnel vitally importat
to it. Extremely well trained and well qualified personnel are re
quired for safety's sake in flight operations, and the same cor
siderations apply to maintenance and repair facilities. Traine
and courteous personnel in the reservations, passenger boardin¡
and other visible passenger-contact areas can have considerabl
effect on traffic and revenues. In addition, personnel costs are
very large percentage of total revenue expenditures.

Despite occasional layoffs, such as occurred in the late 1950'
or more recently in 1969-1970, airline employment has rise
steadily since the 1930's. The great boom of the 1960's, follow
ing the introduction of the jets, added over 155,000 employees t
the industry, as shown in Table 4. Long range projections ca
for continued employment expansion in all job categories an
classifications. Despite the current declines, if such expansio
does occur the outlook for an increase in Negro participation i
the industry will be enhanced because Negroes have historicall
gained most in times of employment expansion. Also, the ex
pansion is likely to continue the domination of the five larges
carriers who employ well over one-half of the employees in th
industry and, as we shall point out, an even greater percentag
of the industry's black personnel.

TABLE 4.   *Air Transport Industry*
Employment
1947-1969

Year	Employees (000)	Year	Employees (000)
1947	81.7	1959	160.9
1948	77.9	1960	171.6
1949	76.7	1961	175.4
1950	75.9	1962	175.9
1951	85.5	1963	180.5
1952	97.1	1964	190.7
1953	104.9	1965	205.9
1954	105.2	1966	223.2
1955	114.3	1967	270.1
1956	131.0	1968	302.4
1957	148.4	1969	316.7
1958	148.8		

Source: U.S. Bureau of Labor Statistics, *Employment and Earnings Statistics for the United States, 1909-68*, p. 126; and *Employment and Earnings*, Vol. 15, No. 9 (March 1969), Vol. 16, No. 9 (March 1970), Table B-2.

Note: Data include certificated and uncertificated air carriers (SIC 451, 2).

Occupational Distribution

In terms of numbers, the airline industry is at best a medium size employer. It employs less than one-half as many employees as the railroad industry, despite the sharp decline in employment which the latter has experienced. Steel, automobiles, aerospace, and many other manufacturing industries employ far more persons. In terms of the nature of the jobs, however, the airline industry, like its manufacturing counterpart the aerospace industry,[8] has significance beyond its numbers if only because of the high visibility of the work and the glamour and skill attached to flight operations.

Table 5 shows the percentage distribution of scheduled airline employment by occupational group as it was estimated for 1970. The largest occupational group is that of aircraft and traffic

TABLE 5. *Air Transport Industry*
Scheduled Airlines
Percentage Distribution of Employment by Occupation
1970 Estimate

Occupation	Percent of Total
Aircraft and traffic servicing workers	31.8
Office workers	19.8
Maintenance workers	17.5
Flight attendants	7.3
Pilots and copilots	6.7
Other flight personnel	1.9
Communications workers	2.0
Other workers	13.0
Total	100.0

Source: U.S. Bureau of Labor Statistics, *Employment Requirements and Changing Occupational Structure in Civil Aviation*, Bulletin No. 1367 (Washington: Government Printing Office, June 1964), Table 15.

8. The aerospace industry, despite heavy cutbacks in defense and space exploration expenditures, retains a very large personnel force. See Herbert R. Northrup, Richard L. Rowan, *et al.*, *Negro Employment in Basic Industry*, Studies of Negro Employment, Vol. I (Philadelphia: Industrial Research Unit, Wharton School of Finance and Commerce, University of Pennsylvania, 1970), Part Three.

servicing workers. This group is about equally split between those engaged in cargo and baggage handling and those parking, fueling, doing routine inspections, and aircraft cleaning. In general, these employees are semiskilled, some doing very routine or hard labor, but all required to exercise care and reasonable concern for accuracy and safety. This group includes the largest percentage of Negroes in the industry.

Within the office worker category, the largest group is the "counter personnel" who write tickets, make space reservations, or do promotional sales work. Also included are those who do the record keeping, secretarial work, and routine statistical and compilation work in connection with ticket sales, as well as general management personnel, lawyers, traffic solicitors, purchasing agents, engineers, meteorologists, and others. More and more Negroes are being hired in the reservations group.

Those classified as maintenance workers are machinists, airplane mechanics, carpenters, electricians, and other skilled craftsmen and their assistants. Many of these personnel must hold appropriate licenses from the Federal Aviation Agency. As in most industry, it has been difficult for Negroes to break into the skilled mechanic classifications.

Among flight personnel are the flight attendants, who make up the largest segment of this grouping. These are almost entirely stewardesses, although roughly 10 percent of the flight attendants are either stewards or pursers, who are the chief attendants on intercontinental flights. Negro girls are now being recruited in sizeable numbers as stewardesses.

Pilots and copilots, the prime human resource of the airlines, make up less than 7 percent of the total airline employment, and together with the other flight personnel—flight engineers and navigators—are diminishing in proportion to total airline employment. This is a result of the increase in size and lifting capacity of modern aircraft. Few Negroes are so employed.

The proportion of communications workers—ground radio operators, teletypists, telegraphers, etc.—is also diminishing as computers and automation decrease the requirements for human operators. Few, if any, Negroes are among this group.

Finally, there are those classified as "other workers." These are involved with all of the ancillary services necessary to operate the airline and cater to its passengers. These include, among others, hotel, restaurant, and food service workers, trainers and instructors, watchmen, porters, and guards. For many years, such service employment was the only type open to Negroes in the airline industry.

The prestige jobs on the airlines are very definitely those connected with flight itself. Rarely have these jobs been subject to periodic shortages of applicants. Even when they were, however, airlines have quite properly been extremely hesitant to modify or to lower employment standards for them because of their close association with safety of operations. In fact, the majority of airline jobs fall into one of two sensitive areas: they are either concerned directly with the safety of operations of the aircraft or they are public contact jobs whose holders must project an image of the airline compatable with the ideals of the traveling public. In both of these areas, the airlines have been cautious about engaging in sociological experimentation. This fact has contributed, until very recently, to the failure of the airlines to hire minority group personnel in any other than the "traditional" cleaner, porter, or food service jobs.

The EEO Classifications

In nearly all the studies in the Racial Policies of American Industry series, racial data have been reported and analyzed in the only available form—the report forms which companies must file annually with the Equal Employment Opportunity Commission and which some companies filed prior to 1966 either with Plans for Progress or the President's Committee on Equal Employment Opportunity (now the Office of Federal Contract Compliance). The occupational breakdowns utilized in this form are appropriate for manufacturing, but considerably less useful in other types of industries. Nevertheless, data in this form are available, and are useful for our study purposes as long as they are properly used and clearly understood.

Table 6 shows the occupational distribution for the twelve major airlines within the EEOC form context (known as EEO Form No. 1). The first thing of significance is the clear domination of the white collar group—57.3 percent of all workers so classified. Actually, confusion and/or disagreement as to how to classify stewardesses results in underestimating the white collar percentage. Some airlines classify these charming flight attendants as sales workers, but others, including United, the largest place them in the service worker group. If all stewardesses were added to the white collar categories, the blue collar groups would probably include only about one-third of all employees.

TABLE 6. *Air Transport Industry*
Employment by Occupational Group
12 Companies, 1968

Occupational Group	Number of Employees	Percent of Total
Officials and managers	16,298	7.4
Professionals	33,244	15.0
Technicians	4,931	2.2
Sales workers	39,901	18.1
Office and clerical	32,282	14.6
Total white collar	126,656	57.3
Craftsmen	42,223	19.1
Operatives	20,326	9.2
Laborers	7,068	3.2
Service workers	24,815	11.2
Total blue collar	94,432	42.7
Total	221,088	100.0

Source: Appendix Table A-3.

Note: See discussion in text in regard to inclusion of stewardesses in "service worker" classification.

Pilots and associated flight crew employees are classified as professionals. Reservation agents, ticket agents, and related personnel, along with stewardesses and other flight attendants in most airlines, are considered sales personnel. The office and clerical group is the traditional secretarial and clerical body as in industry generally, and officials and managers include, also as in industry generally, all management personnel from chief executive to line supervisors.

The craftsman group is a larger percentage in the EEO form than estimated by the Bureau of Labor Statistics study (Table 5), indicating that some of those classified as aircraft and traffic service have been listed as craftsmen. As a result, craftsmen include the largest percentage found in any of the EEO-1 categories, slightly exceeding that for sales workers and professionals, the next two largest. In fact, craftsmen comprise almost one-half of all blue collar workers and probably would in fact, if stewardesses were eliminated from the service worker classification.

Operatives include most of those in aircraft or traffic service below the craftsmen category, such as baggage handlers, ramp service personnel, and those few classified as laborers. Service workers include porters, meal service preparation workers, etc. The few in these last two categories again emphasize the high caliber of the skill or personal service required by airline work and the resultant difficulty which the disadvantaged will inevitably encounter in seeking employment in the industry.

Female Employment

The airline industry has always offered females interesting positions as stewardesses and reservation agents, in addition to the usual office and clerical jobs. Today more than one-quarter of the industry's employees are women, and the trend is upward, as Table 7 shows. There is every indication that this trend will continue since the jobs in which females are concentrated will tend to increase as the industry expands. Since the airlines have been quite successful in recruiting Negro women, this trend is likely to result in more jobs for black women in the future.

TABLE 7. *Air Transport Industry*
Employment by Sex
1960-1969

Year	All Employees (000)	Female Employees (000)	Percent Female
1960	171.6	40.0	23.3
1961	175.4	40.8	23.3
1962	175.9	41.2	23.4
1963	180.5	43.5	24.1
1964	190.7	46.8	24.5
1965	205.9	51.6	25.1
1966	223.2	56.6	25.4
1967	270.1	69.4	25.7
1968	302.4	79.3	26.2
1969	316.7	85.8	27.1

Source: U.S. Bureau of Labor Statistics, *Employment and Earnings Statistics for the United States, 1909-68;* and *Employment and Earnings*, Vol. 15 (March 1969), Vol. 16 (March 1970), Tables B-2 and B-3.

Note: Data include certificated and uncertificated air carriers.

Compensation and Hours

In view of the diversity of employees, overall earnings data are not too meaningful. Pilots are paid on a complicated formula that takes into consideration plane size, speed, weight, and hours, while their hours aloft have been limited to 85 per month in domestic flying since the early 1930's.[9] Today second officers start at $600 per month and captains earn annually as much as $57,000 depending upon the equipment flown. Average pilot compensation in 1969 was about $23,000 per year. Stewardesses also fly a maximum of 85 hours per month. Their compensation averaged about $7,100 per year in 1969.[10]

Reservation and ticket agents work a standard forty hour week and are paid in accordance with their responsibility, seniority, etc. Typical compensation for nonmanagerial personnel in such positions was $735 per month in 1969. Airline office personnel receive wages competitive with those paid in similar offices in the area. Whether unionized or not, their pay reflects prevailing local standards.

Aircraft mechanics hold extremely responsible positions and receive compensation that befits their status. Thus the most recent union agreement covering United Air Lines personnel provides for a top rate of $6.48 per hour by 1971 for mechanics. Lower-rated personnel covered by the same or similar agreements at United include ramp servicemen, an entry job, who will earn $4.54 to start by 1971.

In addition to good pay, airline employees have available generous fringe benefits such as pensions, health and welfare plans, and sick leave. Moreover, all airlines have "pass" programs which permit employees a specified number of free or reduced fare trips per year for themselves and their families, depending upon seniority. Working conditions are good, although work is required for many occupations on a shift basis since positions must be manned around the clock, on weekends and holidays, and in emergencies because of the essential service performed.

---

9. The pilots' pay formula was worked out by the National Labor Board of the National Industrial Recovery Act in 1933 and since expanded by collective bargaining and emergency boards appointed pursuant to the Railway Labor Act. For the historical background, see Herbert R. Nrothrup, "Collective Bargaining by Air Line Pilots," *Quarterly Journal of Economics*, Vol. LXI (August 1947), pp. 533-576. Collective bargaining has reduced the maximum flying hours even further.

10. Data based on collective bargaining agreements.

Unionization

The air transport industry is a highly unionized one. The dominant organization in terms of prestige and bargaining power is the Air Line Pilots Association, which represents pilots on all airlines save American. There a schism developed and the American pilots seceded from ALPA to form their own union, the Allied Pilots Association. ALPA affiliated with the American Federation of Labor one year after its founding in 1930.

Besides organizing pilots, ALPA has established a number of subsidiary organizations. One has bargaining rights for stewardesses on a number of carriers; another, the Air Line Employees Association, represents the clerical and reservations group on National and on a number of feeder lines.

Originally many airlines employed mechanics as flight engineers. Now most utilize pilots for the third seat in the cockpit. When the engineer's function is performed by a pilot "second officer," he is represented by ALPA; in the few cases where nonpilots are still used, the Flight Engineers International Association holds bargaining rights. Controversies over this position between ALPA and FEIA have caused several serious strikes and much controversy, but the practical and economic situation will surely result in the gradual elimination of nonpilot flight engineers.

The dominant ground force union is the International Association of Machinists and Aerospace Workers, a longtime AFL affiliate and now one of the largest in the AFL-CIO. The IAM represents mechanics and miscellaneous aircraft and ground service employees on eight of the twelve major carriers, on several feeders, and (on some airlines) other employees as well. Its two main rivals for these employees are the Transport Workers Union and the Teamsters. The former, a onetime CIO affiliate, holds bargaining rights for American and Pan American ground forces and for the few navigators on overseas carriers. In addition, a stewardess organization broke with ALPA and affiliated with TWU, which now represents the attendants on several carriers.

The Teamsters has succeeded in gaining a substantial foothold in air transport in recent years. It has displaced the IAM as bargaining agent for mechanics and ground service employees at Western and likewise displaced the Brotherhood of Railway, Airline and Steamship Clerks, Freight Handlers, Express and Station Employees (BRC) for the right to represent clerical and reservations personnel at Pan American and Braniff. The BRC was once dominant among clerical and reservation groups, but today is bargaining agent only for Northwest and Western.

Table 8 summarizes union representation in the airlines as of June 30, 1970. It will be noted that a number of smaller groups are represented by various unions. Delta is the only major airline that is largely nonunion, but clerical and passenger services of most of the Big Four domestic airlines are also unorganized. The multitude of unions and the representation fragmentation are direct results of the already noted "class or craft" restrictions written into the Railway Labor Act. The illogical grouping into one bargaining group of office personnel, reservation agents, and passenger service groups is the result of the insistence of the National Mediation Board on defining bargaining units on the basis of railroad, not airline experience and moreover, on experience designed to favor existing unions.

We shall return to a discussion of union policies in Chapter IV. Suffice it to note here that two of the major unions, the Brotherhood of Railway and Airline Clerks and the International Association of Machinists, either barred Negroes entirely from membership or confined them to inferior status until the post-World War II period, as did the small Air Line Dispatchers' Association. Likewise the Air Line Pilots Association had a "white only" membership clause till the early 1940's. Our analysis of union policies in the industry will show that it has varied, with few exceptions, from antagonistic to indifferent, and that it has not been a significant help nor hindrance to the advancement of Negroes in the industry in recent years.

INDUSTRIAL LOCATION

By the very nature of their business, airline operations are geographically dispersed, and cover the entire country. Nevertheless, concentrations of employment occur at the headquarters locations for office and clerical personnel, and at the maintenance and overhaul bases for maintenance personnel, technicians, and engineers. Although some headquarters have been moved to New York City, most remain in the area in which the regional line first operated. The extremely congested New York City and Chicago areas are avoided as overhaul bases which are even more widely scattered than headquarters. Table 9 shows the headquarters location, overhaul base location, and other major em-

TABLE 8. Air Transport Industry
Union Representation on Selected Air Carriers
June 30, 1970

Airline	Pilots	Flight Engineers	Flight Navigators	Flight Dispatchers	Stewardesses and Pursers	Radio and Teletype Operators	Mechanics	Clerical, Office, Stores, Fleet and Passenger Service[a]	Stock and Stores
Airlift, International	ALPA	—	TWU	—	—	—	AMFA	ALEA	IBT
Air West	ALPA	—	—	ALDA	ALPA	—	IAM&AW	ALEA	IAM&AW
Allegheny Airlines	ALPA	—	—	LU	ALPA	—	IAM&AW	—	IAM&AW
American Airlines	APA	FEIA	—	ALDA	TWU	TWU	TWU	TWU	TWU
Braniff International	ALPA	—	—	ADA	ALPA	CWA	IAM&AW	IBT	IBT
Continental Airlines	ALPA	—	—	ALDA	ALPA	—	IAM&AW	—	IAM&AW
Delta Air Lines	ALPA	—	—	ALDA	—	—	—	—	—
Eastern Air Lines	ALPA	ALPA	—	ALDA	TWU	CWA	IAM&AW	IAM&AW	IAM&AW
Flying Tiger Lines	ALPA	IBT	TWU	ALDA	IBT	—	IAM&AW	—	IAM&AW
Frontier Airlines	ALPA	—	—	ALDA	ALPA	—	IAM&AW	ALEA	IAM&AW
Los Angeles Airways	ALPA	—	—	ALDA	ALPA	—	IAM&AW	IAM&AW	IBT
Mohawk Airlines	ALPA	—	—	ALDA	ALPA	—	IAM&AW	—	IAM&AW
National Airlines	ALPA	FEIA	—	ALDA	ALPA	CWA	IAM&AW	ALEA	IAM&AW
North Central Airlines	ALPA	—	—	ALDA	ALPA	—	IAM&AW	ALEA	IAM&AW
Northeast Airlines	ALPA	—	—	ALDA	TWU	TWU	IAM&AW	TWU	—

Airline	ALPA	IAM&AW	TWU	ALDA	TWU	TWU	IAM&AW	BRAC	IAM&AW
Northwest Airlines	ALPA	—	—	ALDA	ALPA	IBT	AMFA	IAM&AW	IBT
Ozark Air Lines	ALPA	FEIA	—	ALDA	TWU	—	TWU	IBT	IBT
Pan American World Airways	ALPA	—	TWU	ALDA	ALPA	—	—	—	—
Piedmont Airlines	ALPA	IBT	—	ALDA	IUFA	—	TWU	—	TWU
Seaboard World Airlines	ALPA	—	TWU	—	TWU	—	TWU	ALEA	—
Southern Airways	ALPA	—	—	ALDA	IBT	—	—	ALEA	IAM&AW
Texas International	IBT	IBT	IBT	ALDA	TWU	ALEA	IAM&AW	ALEA	—
Trans World Airlines	ALPA	ALPA	TWU	TWU	ALPA	CWA	IAM&AW	—	IAM&AW
United Air Lines	ALPA	—	TWU	ALDA	ALPA	CWA	IAM&AW	BRAC	IBT
Western Airlines	ALPA	—	—	ALDA	ALPA	CWA	IBT	BRAC	IBT

Source: National Mediation Board, *Thirty-sixth Annual Report*, prepublication data.

[a] On most airlines, the unions listed actually represent only a small portion of the group, generally non-white collar workers. In fact, the clerical staffs of American, Delta, Eastern, Trans World, and United are nonunion.

Abbreviations:

ADA	Air Transport Dispatchers Association	CWA	Communications Workers of America
ALEA	Air Line Employees Association	FEIA	Flight Engineers' International Association
ALDA	Air Line Dispatchers Association	IAM&AW	International Association of Machinists and Aerospace Workers
ALPA	Air Line Pilots Association	IBT	International Brotherhood of Teamsters, Chauffeurs, Warehousemen & Helpers of America
AMFA	Aircraft Mechanics Fraternal Association		
APA	Allied Pilots Association	OPEIU	Office & Professional Employees International Union
BRAC	Brotherhood of Railway, Airline & Steamship Clerks, Freight Handlers, Express and Station Employees	TWU	Transport Workers Union of America

TABLE 9. *Air Transport Industry*
Location of Major Employment Centers
12 Companies, 1968

Carrier	Headquarters	Overhaul Base	Other Major Employment Centers
American	New York City	Tulsa	Chicago, Los Angeles, Detroit, Boston, Dallas
Braniff	Dallas	Dallas	Chicago
Continental	Los Angeles	Los Angeles	Chicago, Denver, Dallas, Kansas City, Mo.
Delta	Atlanta	Atlanta	New Orleans, Houston, Chicago, New York
Eastern	New York City	Miami	Atlanta, Boston, Houston, Chicago, New Orleans, Washington, D.C.
National	Miami	Miami	New York, Washington, D.C.
Northeast	Boston	Boston	New York
Northwest	St. Paul	St. Paul	Minneapolis, New York, Seattle, Anchorage
Pan American	New York City	New York City	Miami, San Francisco, Honolulu, Chicago
Trans World	New York City	Kansas City, Mo.	Chicago, San Francisco, Phoenix, Los Angeles, St. Louis
United	Chicago	San Francisco	Los Angeles, New York City, Denver, Washington, D.C., Cleveland, Pittsburgh, Honolulu
Western	Los Angeles	Seattle	San Diego, San Francisco

Source: Moody's Transportation Manual, 1968; company annual reports.

Note: In all cases, airlines have other centers of employment in cities in which they have headquarters and/or overhaul bases. New York City includes the three major airports, one of which is Newark, New Jersey.

ployment centers for the major lines. Overall, there is wide geographical dispersion.

Location of the major employment centers of the major lines does give some insights into the minority employment pattern of the lines. Although the majority of the headquarters locations are in the large metropolitan city areas which typically have large Negro populations, many overhaul bases are located in areas identified with large numbers of other minority group members. In Dallas, Los Angeles, and Miami, it is important to consider the role of Spanish-speaking Americans in the minority group structure in employment; in San Francisco and Seattle, Oriental minorities figure heavily; and in Tulsa, Oklahoma, it is important to look at the role of the American Indian. In this study, however, we shall be dealing only with the role of Negroes in the air transport industry.

Location has another, and unfavorable, aspect. Overhaul and modification centers, as well as much of the reservation function are located at airports which are in turn on the outskirts of cities. With Negroes concentrated in center cities, and with public transit facilities poor, this often means that Negroes have difficulty in finding or accepting work in the industry. We shall return to this problem after reviewing the history of Negro employment to 1960 in Chapter III, and discussing the present status in Chapter IV.

CHAPTER III

Negro Employment to 1960

Negro employment in the air transport industry until at least the late 1950's was confined largely to blue collar ground service jobs, and even there the number so employed was not large. By the end of the 1950's, however, the pressures were building up for a change. This chapter analyzes developments in the years before the 1960's.

THE AIRLINE MORES

The traditional mores of the transportation industries kept the Negro "in his place," and that place was not in responsible employment. Air transportation as the elite branch of an elite group emphasized these practices. Negroes were historically not employed as railroad engineers or conductors; ship captains, mates, or engineers; urban transit platform men; over-the-road bus drivers, or even, to any appreciable extent, as long distance truck drivers.[11] Some of these jobs were certainly not skilled, but all involved prestigious positions in the labor market and responsibility for the safety and comfort of the passengers and public. Public attitudes, employer hiring policies, and union membership standards and desires to limit competition all combined to bar Negroes from key jobs in the transportation industries.

The newest transportation industry—airlines—was originally the most racially restrictive. The early fliers were trained in World War I, or in that era, when most Negroes lived in the rural South. Few Negroes had the opportunity to be pilots or mechanics or, in the rare case that they did, found mechanical jobs closed to them because of lack of training, employment discrimination, or union restrictions. Aviation training in the armed forces was also closed to Negroes. Those who manufactured the early planes, or established aviation companies, or flew or serviced them, were a close-knit group into whose "brotherhood" the black man could not be received as an equal. Even the airplane manufacturers before World War II had what *Fortune* magazine

---

11. See the trucking, railroad, and urban transit studies in this series.

termed "an almost universal prejudice against Negroes . . . you almost never see Negroes in aircraft factories. . . ." [12] The same could have been said for the air transport industry but for the Negroes employed as "sky caps" in terminals, and as cleaners and janitors in airplane servicing.

FROM WORLD WAR II TO 1950

Just prior to World War II the famous Douglas DC-3, first of the modern planes in the piston era, was introduced, greatly improving the comfort and economy of flight. World War II delayed the introduction of four engine craft, but greatly simulated air travel as thousands of people were flown for the first time. After the war, the industry began its rise to domination of the passenger traffic market. Employment, as reported by the U.S. Census of Population, quadrupled between 1940 and 1950 and then doubled during the following decade, despite traffic declines in recession periods.

Table 10 shows that Negroes increased their representation in the industry over the decades between 1940 and 1960. The five-fold increase between 1940 and 1950 was followed by a slightly slower gain in the next decade, although Negro employment continued to increase at a more rapid rate than did employment in the industry as a whole.

TABLE 10. *Air Transport Industry Employment by Race and Sex United States, 1940, 1950, and 1960*

	All Employees			Male			Female		
	Total	Negro	Percent Negro	Total	Negro	Percent Negro	Total	Negro	Percent Negro
1940	23,175	760	3.3	20,878	729	3.5	2,297	31	1.3
1950	98,241	3,993	4.1	78,977	3,576	4.5	19,264	417	2.2
1960	198,139	9,096	4.6	154,863	8,201	5.3	43,276	895	2.1

Source: *U.S. Census of Population:*

1940: Vol. III, *The Labor Force,* Part 1, Table 76.
1950: Vol. II, *Characteristics of the Population,* Table 133.
1960: PC(1) 1D, *U.S. Summary,* Table 213.

12. "Half a Million Workers," *Fortune,* Vol. XXIII (March 1943), pp. 98, 163. See also, Northrup, Rowan, *et al., The Negro in Basic Industry,* Part Three, pp. 145-147.

Table 11 shows the same data on a regional basis. Of particular interest is the fact that the South had the highest percentage of Negroes for each of the three census years. The reason for the higher figure in the South is clear. The industry increased its employment of Negroes throughout the country during and after World War II, but did not alter its racial-occupational employment pattern. The clerical forces, the flight crews, the top mechanics jobs, and of course, the executive, managerial, and technical positions remained all white. The higher percentages of Negroes found in the South in 1940, 1950, and 1960 resulted from the greater use of blacks in unskilled jobs there.

The greater use of Negroes by the southern sector of the industry in this period is also illustrated by Table 12, which shows the employment of male mechanics and repairmen by regions, as reported by the census for 1950 and 1960. Again the highest percentage of blacks is found in the South. Our study of the industry indicates that the great majority of the Negroes in these classifications were service employees or helpers. Few held government licenses required for the mechanics' status. Educational disabilities, employment discrimination, and union opposition all contributed to keeping the top layer of jobs in this group white.

The 1950 and 1960 censuses included small occupational samples of pilots and navigators (Table 13). In 1950, some 60 Negro pilots were included in this sample, 0.4 percent of the total. The armed forces began admitting Negroes to pilot training during World War II, first on a segregated basis, and then in the 1950's on an integrated basis. But by 1950 no Negro pilot was employed by a scheduled airline. Indeed not even a Negro stewardess was then so employed. The flight crews remained all white.

THE 1950's: THE IMPACT OF STATE LEGISLATION

The 1950's saw the first tentative breakthroughs in opening up better jobs for Negroes. Considerable, and probably prime, credit for this improvement is due to the antidiscrimination legislation and agencies of the states of Massachusetts, New Jersey, and above all, New York. Under the leadership of the New York State Commission for Human Rights,[13] systematic efforts were

---

13. Like many state organizations in this field, this agency has had several names. Originally the New York State Commission Against Discrimination, it is now the New York State Division of Human Rights.

TABLE 11. *Air Transport Industry Employment by Race and Sex Four Regions, 1940, 1950, and 1960*

Region	All Employees			Male			Female		
	Total	Negro	Percent Negro	Total	Negro	Percent Negro	Total	Negro	Percent Negro
Northeast									
1940	6,484	152	2.3	5,793	137	2.4	691	15	2.2
1950	23,738	697	2.9	18,977	633	3.3	4,761	64	1.3
1960	48,090	2,123	4.4	36,582	1,834	5.0	11,508	289	2.5
North Central									
1940	5,751	144	2.5	4,947	140	2.8	804	4	0.5
1950	22,531	695	3.1	17,617	592	3.4	4,914	103	2.1
1960	38,202	1,612	4.2	28,443	1,426	5.0	9,759	186	1.9
South									
1940	6,214	393	6.3	5,788	381	6.6	426	12	2.8
1950	31,976	2,133	6.7	26,367	1,922	7.3	5,609	211	3.8
1960	64,160	3,915	6.1	52,519	3,593	6.8	11,641	322	2.8
West									
1940	4,726	71	1.5	4,350	71	1.6	376	—	—
1950	19,996	468	2.3	16,016	429	2.7	3,980	39	1.0
1960	47,687	1,446	3.0	37,319	1,348	3.6	10,368	98	0.9

Source: *U.S. Census of Population:*

    1940: Vol. III, *The Labor Force*, Part 1, Table 77.
    1950: Vol. II, *Characteristics of the Population*, Part 1, Table 161.
    1960: PC(1) 1D, *U.S. Summary*, Table 260.

Regions are defined as follows:

Northeast

  New England: Connecticut, Maine, Massachusetts, New Hampshire, Rhode Island, Vermont.
  Middle Atlantic: New Jersey, New York, Pennsylvania.

Midwest (North Central)

  East North Central: Illinois, Indiana, Michigan, Ohio, Wisconsin.
  West North Central: Iowa, Kansas, Minnesota, Missouri, Nebraska, North Dakota, South Dakota.

South

  South Atlantic: Delaware, District of Columbia, Florida, Georgia, Maryland, North Carolina, South Carolina, Virginia, West Virginia.
  East South Central: Alabama, Kentucky, Mississippi, Tennessee.
  West South Central: Arkansas, Oklahoma, Louisiana, Texas.

West

  Mountain: Arizona, Colorado, Idaho, Montana, Nevada, New Mexico, Utah, Wyoming.
  West Coast (Pacific): California, Oregon, Washington.

TABLE 12. *Air Transport Industry*
Employment of Male Airplane Mechanics and Repairmen by Race
Four Regions, 1950 and 1960

Region	Male Mechanics and Repairmen		
	Total	Negro	Percent Negro
Northeast			
1950	13,331	167	1.3
1960	19,854	584	2.9
North Central			
1950	8,917	75	0.8
1960	16,835	286	1.7
South			
1950	24,054	475	2.0
1960	39,670	1,336	3.4
West			
1950	23,265	349	1.5
1960	36,154	1,088	3.0

Source: *U.S. Census of Population:*

    1950: Vol. II, *Characteristics of the Population,* Part 1, Table 159.

    1960: PC(1), 1D, *U.S. Summary,* Detailed Characteristics, Table 257.

Note: See Table 11 for regional definitions.

TABLE 13. *Air Transport Industry*
Employment of Pilots and Navigators by Race
Sample Survey, United States, 1950 and 1960

	Sample as a Percent of Total	Pilots and Navigators		
		Total	Negro	Percent Negro
1950	3.3	13,650	60	0.4
1960	5.0	26,859	81	0.3

Source: *U.S. Census of Population:*

    1950: Vol. IV, *Special Reports,* Occupational Characteristics, Table 3.

    1960: PC(2) 7A, *Occupational Characteristics,* Table 3.

made to alter the position of the airlines in excluding Negroes from clerical, skilled mechanic, flight crew, and other high rated positions. All of these commissions received numerous complaints of discrimination, particularly from young Negroes desirous of breaking into an expanding industry that had caught the imagination of youth everywhere, and yet was so closed to their race.

The New York Record

A study by the New York antidiscrimination commission covering the 1945 to 1962 period found progress slow.[14] The first breakthroughs came with reservation clerks. Colonial Airlines (merged with Eastern later in the 1950's), had a Negro ticket seller in a Manhattan office in 1951, and American Airlines had a Negro girl reservation clerk in Buffalo in 1952. Gradually other airlines followed suit so that by 1960, in New York and contiguous areas, the Negro reservation clerk was no longer a rarity. Nevertheless, the percentage of blacks in these jobs remained small at that date, and some airlines, notably National, had few if any Negroes in office or clerical work.

The New York study is not clear as to Negro progress in mechanical jobs. It appears from the data provided that some Negroes held skilled ground crew positions, but that most continued to be employed as airplane cleaners, janitors, fuelers, ramp servicemen, or flight kitchen personnel.

In 1957, Mohawk Airlines, a Northeast regional carrier, employed the first Negro stewardess in the industry. By 1960, Trans World and Capital (later merged with United) had followed suit, the former after a complaint was made to the New York agency, the latter after being ordered to do so following a hearing by the same agency.

Negro pilot employment proceeded even more slowly. The first Negro pilot in regularly scheduled service was apparently employed by Seaboard and Western, a cargo carrier, in 1955. Previously this pilot was employed by an unscheduled carrier. In 1956, New York Airways (New York City's helicopter airline) also employed a Negro pilot. Thus by 1960, the New York agency could report only these two pilots, none employed by a

14. Much of the information for this period comes from a report in the files of the New York agency, *The Airlines Industry: A Report on Verified Complaints and Informal Investigations, July 1, 1945-June 30, 1962,* mimeo, New York State Commission for Human Rights, 1962.

major airline, and three stewardesses among the flight crews of airlines coming within its survey purview.[15]

Other State Findings and Developments

Like its New York counterpart, the Pennsylvania Commission also made a study of racial patterns in airlines. The 1961 report of this agency painted an even more dismal picture of the situation than was true in New York. In Pittsburgh and Philadelphia, for example, it counted 823 airline sales department employees (including reservation clerks) not one of whom was black. Moreover, 62 of the 69 Negroes among the 1,026 airline operations department employees in these two cities were members of two all-Negro porter units. No Negro flight crew employees were reported in Pennsylvania in 1961.[16]

In Massachusetts, the situation was similar. Complaints for refusal to employ Negroes were pushed by the Massachusetts Commission Against Discrimination, but little actual progress made.[17] As in New York and Pennsylvania, studies six years later would show a changed picture.[18]

In Colorado, an attempt of a qualified Negro to enter the pilot training school of Continental Airlines was resisted all the way to the United States Supreme Court on the grounds that state agencies had no jurisdiction. The Supreme Court ruled in the plaintiff's favor in 1963, thus establishing the state agencies' jurisdiction beyond question.[19] Shortly thereafter, of course, Congress enacted the Civil Rights Act of 1964, which expressly granted concurrent jurisdiction to such laws.

In such cities as Chicago, San Francisco, Detroit, and Los Angeles, a few Negroes won employment as reservation clerks or were upgraded to mechanics. American Airlines broke the barriers in Dallas-Ft. Worth in 1958 by hiring the first black reser-

---

15. It is, of course, possible that some of the major airlines employed Negroes in other areas of the country, but it is doubtful that there were many other blacks represented among flight crews at this time. Certainly there does not seem to have been any more pilots.

16. Pennsylvania Human Relations Commission, *Sixth Annual Report*, 1961, p. 8.

17. Leon H. Mayhew, *Law and Equal Opportunity, A Study of the Massachusetts Commission Against Discrimination* (Cambridge: Harvard University Press, 1968), p. 205.

18. See Chapter V, below.

19. *Green v. Continental Air Lines, Inc.*, 372 U.S. 714 (1963).

vation clerk there, but the Southeast largely remained lily white
in both categories. Negro pilots trained by the armed forces
could not break into the major airlines. A black colonel, now a
friend of the senior author, flew four engine aircraft for the
Military Air Transport Service all over the world, but was turned
down by major carriers despite his clearly evident qualifications,
demonstrated leadership, and long experience. That government
was not doing its part in the 1950's is demonstrated by the fact
that the Civil Aeronautics Authority also declined to employ him
to check pilot performance although he topped candidates in a
civil service examination.[20]

As jet planes were being introduced and a new era promised,
the 1950's ended with a slowdown in airline expansion and layoffs affecting major carriers. Progress and breakthroughs in
Negro employment would await the upsurge in civil rights activity in the 1960's, which happily coincided with the greatest
boom in air traffic.

20. Interviews, March 1970.

CHAPTER IV

Civil Rights in the Jet Age

The air transport industry began the 1960's on an uncertain note. Traffic profits and employment were adversely affected by recession; vast expenditures loomed ahead for the expensive jets. Yet public acceptance for the jets seemed most promising. And in the civil rights area, tentative moves, such as the introduction of a very few Negro stewardesses and even fewer pilots seemed to involve no adverse consumer reaction. As prosperity returned and then air traffic expanded far beyond previous highs, and as government pressure for an improved civil rights posture increased, the airlines moved to change historic practices in regard to Negro employment. This chapter analyzes the developments of this historic decade.

FEDERAL INTERVENTION AND POLICY CHANGES

Soon after his inauguration, President Kennedy established the strongest federal policy up to that time of governmental support of equal employment opportunity. Executive Order 10925 of March 6, 1961 introduced the concept of affirmative action into the field of equal employment opportunity and in addition expanded its coverage into areas where government procurement had not hitherto been considered a strong basis for action. The carrying of mails by airlines and their contracts for military cargo and passengers were among the areas marked for supervision of racial employment policies under the new administration.

In addition, the new program involved for the first time federal encouragement of minority employment action by a commitment registered and signed between companies and government. These "Plans for Progress" were pushed among large industry by the then Vice-President, Lyndon B. Johnson. The airlines committed to affirmative action under this aegis included the major trunk carriers—American, Eastern, Trans World, and United—plus Pan American and Northwest. With affirmative action the number and percentage of Negroes in these major carriers rose. Active recruitment of black stewardesses commenced beyond the token stage, and the first steps were taken toward employing Negro pilots. Such airlines as Braniff, Continental, Delta, National, Northeast, and Western did not substantially alter their policies during this period.

Despite greater attempts to employ Negroes, the percentage of black employees did not increase substantially in the first four years of the 1960's. Those airlines which were attempting affirmatively to increase their minority representation were expanding rapidly, employing large numbers of whites as well as blacks. Hence the percentage of Negroes rose only slowly at most. In addition, prior to the passage of the Civil Rights Act of 1964, some airlines, as noted, felt no need to alter their policies.

THE 1966 EEOC DATA

In 1960, the United States Census reported that 4.6 percent of the air transport industry's employees were black. In 1966, the Equal Employment Opportunity Commission placed that ratio at 4.3 percent (Table 14). Of course, Census and EEOC data are not strictly comparable. The former are based on replies of individuals to enumerators; the latter on forms filled out by companies from payroll records. In addition, the 1966 EEOC data included only concerns with 100 or more employees. Nevertheless, the almost identical percentages for 1960 and 1966 indicate quite clearly that the somewhat improved position of Negroes in some carriers was not sufficient by early 1966 [21] to change substantially, if at all, the overall racial employment picture in the industry.

Table 14 also shows a discouraging occupational picture indicative of overall improvement during the first half of the 1960 decade. Only 1.1 percent of the white collar employees in the industry were black, and more than 50 percent so classified were in the office category with an additional one-third in sales—mostly reservation clerks. (Some airlines include stewardesses in the sales category, while others classify them as service workers.) [22]

21. These data are actually from payrolls pertaining to late 1965 or early 1966.

22. The EEO form on which such data are presented is obviously designed primarily for manufacturing enterprise and does not provide pertinent occupational breakdowns for other industrial groups as might be desired.

TABLE 14. Air Transport Industry
Employment by Race, Sex, and Occupational Group
United States, 1966

Occupational Group	All Employees			Male			Female		
	Total	Negro	Percent Negro	Total	Negro	Percent Negro	Total	Negro	Percent Negro
Officials and managers	18,275	75	0.4	17,312	73	0.4	963	2	0.2
Professionals	31,073	62	0.2	30,464	60	0.2	609	2	0.3
Technicians	4,609	42	0.9	4,104	39	1.0	505	3	0.6
Sales workers	32,605	460	1.4	15,954	183	1.1	16,651	277	1.7
Office and clerical	38,991	763	2.0	18,002	478	2.7	20,989	285	1.4
Total white collar	125,553	1,402	1.1	85,836	833	1.0	39,717	569	1.4
Craftsmen	54,003	1,178	2.2	53,246	1,175	2.2	757	3	0.4
Operatives	23,934	2,217	9.3	23,648	2,178	9.2	286	39	13.6
Laborers	6,648	1,998	30.1	6,426	1,883	29.3	222	115	51.8
Service workers[a]	21,405	3,070	14.3	9,130	2,765	30.3	12,275	305	2.5
Total blue collar	105,990	8,463	8.0	92,450	8,001	8.7	13,540	462	3.4
Total	231,543	9,865	4.3	178,286	8,834	5.0	53,257	1,031	1.9

Source: U.S. Equal Employment Opportunity Commission, *Job Patterns for Minorities and Women in Private Industry, 1966*, Report No. 1 (Washington: The Commission, 1968), Part II.

Note: Excludes Alaska and Hawaii. Totaling the employees for the different regions shown in Tables 19, 21, 23, and 25 results in slightly smaller figures than are shown on this table for the United States because EEOC did not publish data for those states with less than 10 reporting establishments unless the state had at least 5 establishments and a total of at least 2,000 employees.

[a] Some airlines report stewardesses as service workers and thus include key white collar employees in our blue collar categories.

Pilots are included in professionals, of whom 62, or 0.2 percent, were black. In 1966, it is doubtful that the scheduled airlines employed 20 Negro pilots, judging from the records obtained for this study.[23]

In the blue collar jobs, Negroes continued to be concentrated in the lowest occupational group. Only 2.2 percent of the mechanics were black, but 30.1 percent of the laborers and 14.3 percent of the service employees were Negroes. (Classifying stewardesses as service workers further complicates comparative analysis.) Laborers and service workers combined in 1966 comprised approximately 12 percent of the total work force and 26 percent of all blue collar employees. Negro laborers and service workers combined, on the other hand, made up 51 percent of the total black labor force and almost 60 percent of all black blue collar workers.

The 1966 EEOC data show also that, overall, Negro females continued to be even more underrepresented in the air transport industry than were males, with less than 2 percent of all females being black. Negro females did fare slightly better than males in the white collar area because of increased employment of black reservation clerks and stewardesses (sales), but still their ratio to total females—1.4 percent—was meager indeed.

THE 1964-1968 FIELD SAMPLE

Because the 1966 EEOC data apply to a period just prior to July 1965 when the Title VII of the Civil Rights Act of 1964 became effective, and because at least through mid-1968, airline employment was expanding, they do not reflect changes induced by events of the latter half of the 1960's. Fortunately, we were able to develop samples of the major airlines for 1964, 1966, and 1968. The 1964 data are less inclusive than those of the latter two years, but they do include eight of the largest airlines. For 1966 and 1968, the same twelve airlines were included in the data. These twelve companies employ about 80 percent of the industry's work force.

For all three years, and especially for 1964, the data were expected to have a slight upward bias since they cover the largest airlines, and in general, the ones which have been most active since 1965 in attempting to expand their Negro employment.

23. Based on interviews by the authors, 1966-1970.

This would be especially true where the key classifications of pilots and stewardesses are concerned. A comparison of the 1966 EEOC data in Table 14 with those of our 1966 sample in the Statistical Appendix, Table A-2 (or the summary thereof in Table 15) indicates, however, that the largest twelve airlines had in 1966 exactly the same percentage of Negroes as did the industry as a whole,[24] and that the blue collar ratios of the two groups were virtually identical. In the white collar area, the proportion of professionals, presumably pilots, was also identical for our sample and for the more complete EEOC coverage. The twelve large airlines employed a higher proportion of Negroes as stewardesses, reservation clerks, and in other office, clerical, and sales positions, thus resulting in a 1.5 percent black ratio for our field sample as compared with 1.1 percent for the EEOC data in the total white collar area. It is clear, however, that our sample is genuinely representative of the scheduled airlines, all the ones except the smallest regional or feeder lines being included for 1966 and 1968.

Racial Employment Trends, 1964-1968

Table 15, summarizing Appendix Tables A-1 to A-3, compares the percentage of Negroes in our 1964, 1966, and 1968 sample by sex and by occupational group. Overall, the data show slow but steady improvement in the proportion of Negroes during the four-year period. In addition, improvement occurred in all classifications except the bottom three—operatives, laborers, and service workers. Even in these three categories the data reveal improvement, because the decline in the proportion of Negro laborers and service workers is the result of upgrading those in these positions and of employing black persons for the other jobs instead of shunting them into the lowest categories. Despite the evident progress, the number of Negroes in our sample remained at less than 5 percent of the total by 1968, with only 2.2 percent in the white collar categories.

OCCUPATIONAL ANALYSIS

Table 16 shows the percentage of all employees and of Negroes in each occupational category for 1964, 1966, and 1968.

---

24. The EEOC data are, of course, not completely industry wide if any company failed to report data or had less than 100 employees in 1965 and therefore no obligation to report data.

TABLE 15. *Air Transport Industry*
Percent Negro Employment by Sex and Occupational Group
United States, 1964, 1966, and 1968

Occupational Group	All Employees			Male			Female		
	1964	1966	1968	1964	1966	1968	1964	1966	1968
Officials and managers	0.2	0.3	0.6	0.2	0.3	0.6	0.3	0.3	0.6
Professionals	0.1	0.2	0.3	0.1	0.2	0.3	0.6	0.3	0.8
Technicians	0.2	0.5	0.5	0.2	0.5	0.5	—	0.7	1.1
Sales workers	1.3	2.3	3.3	1.1	1.8	2.6	1.5	2.7	3.8
Office and clerical	1.9	2.4	3.7	2.5	3.3	4.5	1.4	1.7	3.2
Total white collar	1.0	1.5	2.2	0.8	1.1	1.5	1.4	2.2	3.4
Craftsmen	1.3	1.7	2.3	1.3	1.7	2.3	—	—	2.1
Operatives	11.0	10.2	10.6	10.8	10.1	10.5	32.4[a]	28.8[a]	20.9[a]
Laborers	27.1	33.7	25.9	27.6	33.4	25.2	12.6[a]	39.7[a]	45.7[a]
Service workers	15.5	12.7	11.7	33.6	32.2	32.8	2.6	2.6	2.8
Total blue collar	7.8	8.1	8.3	8.5	9.0	9.5	3.1	3.4	3.5
Total	3.9	4.3	4.8	4.6	4.9	5.3	1.8	2.5	3.4

Source: Appendix Tables A-1, A-2, A-3.

Note: See note regarding stewardesses on Table 14. Data for 1964 cover
8 companies; data for 1966 and 1968 cover 12 companies.

[a] Very small numbers involved.

TABLE 16. *Air Transport Industry*

Percentage Distribution of Employees by Race and Occupational Group
United States, 1964, 1966, and 1968

Occupational Group	1964		1966		1968	
	Total Employees	Negro Employees	Total Employees	Negro Employees	Total Employees	Negro Employees
Officials and managers	8.1	0.5	7.8	0.6	7.4	0.9
Professionals	13.8	0.4	14.8	0.6	15.0	0.9
Technicians	2.0	0.1	1.9	0.2	2.2	0.3
Sales workers	16.0	5.4	17.2	9.3	18.1	12.4
Officer and clerical	17.6	8.7	15.8	9.0	14.6	11.3
Total white collar	57.5	15.1	57.5	19.7	57.3	25.8
Craftsmen	22.2	7.6	19.7	7.8	19.1	9.3
Operatives	8.6	24.3	10.0	23.9	9.2	20.2
Laborers	2.2	15.0	2.2	17.0	3.2	17.2
Service workers	9.5	38.0	10.6	31.6	11.2	27.5
Total blue collar	42.5	84.9	42.5	80.3	42.7	74.2
Total	100.0	100.0	100.0	100.0	100.0	100.0

Source: Appendix Tables A-1, A-2, A-3.

Note: See note regarding stewardesses on Table 14. Data for 1964 cover 8 companies; data for 1966 and 1968 cover 12 companies.

Nearly 60 percent of all employees in the industry are salaried—a situation, as noted in Chapter II, which is unique in transportation and which stems in part from classifying pilots as professionals and stewardesses as sales personnel, and in part because of the heavy agent (sales) and clerical force. Yet in 1964, almost 85 percent of the industry's Negro employees were blue collar workers—twice the percentage of total employees, and only 15 percent were white collar workers, about one-fourth of the total employees so classified.

In the four-year period covered by our data, the occupational distribution of overall employment did not change significantly, but that of the black employees did, altering by 10 percentage points, which was an increase in the salaried portion of about 66 percent. All white collar classifications showed higher Negro representations, but the most significant were in sales (reservation clerks and stewardesses) and in office and clerical. Negro representation in the top blue collar category—craftsmen—also increased, while in the lower rated classifications, it declined. Upgrading obviously occurred.

Despite these significant gains, about 75 percent of the Negroes employed by the twelve airlines in our sample continued to be found in blue collar categories in 1968, as compared with 42.7 percent for the employees as a whole (again subject to stewardesses misplaced as service workers complicating the analysis). Moreover, in 1968, one-half of all Negro employees of these airlines—44.7 percent—were laborers or service workers as compared with 14.4 percent of all employees. In the salaried classifications little progress was being made in the top three classifications, in contrast to the bottom two. Obviously, despite considerable progress, the industry's data reveal that there is considerable room for progress. Why this is so and what problems are associated with attempts to expand minority employment in air transport can best be understood by examining the situation in each occupational group.

Officials and Managers

The air transport industry is no different from most others in its paucity of Negro officials and managers. In 1968, the twelve airlines in our sample reported only 94 Negroes in this category —0.6 percent of the total—and yet more than twice the number so reported in 1966. (See Appendix Tables A-2 and A-3.) It is unlikely, moreover, that any of these 94 black managers had any substantial operating authority. A few held staff personnel jobs, usually involving civil rights or minority employment work, but most were relatively subordinate officials and many were newly recruited or promoted.

As in most industry, officials and managers are recruited from within the organization or industry. Long exclusion of Negroes from this industry inevitably means that they have not been in a position to bid for top jobs even in the rare situations when they would have been considered.

Another source of management talent in air transport has been the pilot group. Many managers and executives were once fliers, especially in earlier years. Here again, exclusion at the entry level has meant exclusion at the top.

Today the major airlines are competing with other industry for the short supply of Negro college graduates. Few Negroes are studying aeronautical engineering or are enrolled in business schools, although the number in the latter are increasing. Those who are available find that opportunities for promotion and managerial responsibility are not likely to occur as quickly in public utilities or transportation concerns as in manufacturing enterprise, and the pay is generally higher in the latter as well. Hence recruitment of Negroes has gone more slowly than some of the more aggressive equal employment minded airline management would prefer. All in all, increases in Negro airline managers and officials must be expected to occur slowly.

There is, however, one area where advancement to managerial positions may come more rapidly. That is in the station and reservation agent group. Here, as we shall discuss below, the airlines are employing large numbers of Negroes. With the turnover relatively high in such jobs, and with advanced education not a prerequisite for many supervisory positions, a steady increase in the number of black officials may be expected.

Professionals—Pilots

Professionals include, first of all, pilots. Today less than 100 of the 33,000 pilots of the nation's commercial airlines are black. Table 17 shows the estimated distribution of Negro pilots among the nation's principal air carriers for May 1969. (Pilots include captains, co-pilots or first officers, and second officers.)

TABLE 17. *Air Transport Industry
Employment of Pilots by Race
Six Carriers, May 1969*

Carrier	Total Pilots	Negro Pilots	Percent Negro
American	3,300	10	0.3
Eastern	3,300	6	0.2
Delta	1,596	2	0.1
Pan American	3,600	6	0.2
Trans World	4,099	16	0.4
United	5,800	11[a]	0.2
Total industry	33,000	85[b]	0.3

Source: Company interviews and *Chicago Tribune*, May 18, 1969.

[a] Includes three flight instructors.

[b] Authors' estimate.

Since our records indicate that none of the major airlines not listed in Table 17 employed Negro pilots as of mid-1969, about one-third of black commercial pilots work for feeder, nonscheduled or other smaller lines, and two-thirds for the large carriers listed in Table 17.

Airlines do not train their pilots to fly. Rather they recruit about 90 percent from the military, the balance from civilian flying schools. Overwhelmingly they prefer air force and navy training. As one personnel executive explained: "The armed forces teach men not only to fly but also to stay alive. Civilian schools do not have the facilities, the equipment or the know-how. Rarely do we employ anyone not air force or navy trained." [25]

During 1964 and 1965, pilot retirements, predictions of air traffic growth, and a paucity of applicants led a number of airlines, including United, the largest, to be concerned about a possible pilot shortage. United therefore offered to guarantee employment to any person with a federal commercial license and to provide necessary training for a position as a pilot second officer The response was overwhelming and the ultimate consequence was a realization that there was really no lack of qualified people Although some jobs were guaranteed to people on this training

25. Interview, November 1968.

program, the number of qualified pilots who came to United and other airlines established the fact that a very large number of pilots were not seeking flying jobs because of a false belief that no jobs were available in the industry.

Thus the airlines still can be (and given safety considerations, should be) very selective. They employ well qualified personnel as pilots who have all the necessary mental and physical prerequisites, several years experience flying multi-engine aircraft, with perhaps 2,000 hours aloft, with instrument ratings and other advanced qualifications in addition to the Federal Aviation Authority license. Generally, military helicopter or single engine fighter pilots have a more difficult time meeting the select qualifications of the large commercial carriers.

The commercial carriers usually also limit employment to those 30 years or under primarily as an economic matter. During the course of a pilot's career, the airline may expect to spend one million dollars in the training, retaining, and checking of a pilot. The most qualified military trained multi-engine pilot is still put through a rigorous training schedule in order to qualify him for the third seat (if any) on a plane. Moreover, each pilot must be "checked out" for each type of plane that the airline flies and for each airport to which he is scheduled to land; and then continuously rechecked and retrained throughout his career.

The safety record of airlines in the United States would seem to support their approach to pilot employment and training. If a new method of pilot recruitment could be devised to improve Negro representation among pilots, it would first have to be demonstrated that it contributed to safe practice. It is unrealistic to suppose that this will be done. Therefore an increase in Negro representation among pilots can be accomplished only by increasing the number of Negro air force and navy pilots. Here again the obstacles are formidable.

As we noted in Chapter III, those who fly in the armed services have always considered themselves an elite group. These branches of the military continue to attract highly qualified recruits and are able to set high standards for acceptance. Most military aviation cadets have a college degree and all must have at least two years of college. This, of course, adversely affects Negroes, given their disadvantaged educational status. Intelligence tests and physical examinations add to the rigorous entrance requirements, but even so, a high proportion of the cadets are "washed out," and do not obtain their wings. Again in such a situation, those with disadvantaged backgrounds are likely to have a disproportionately difficult time in succeeding. Yet so much is at stake that a less rigorous training could only cause harm and possible loss of life and property.

An Associated Press study appearing in the *Chicago Tribune* in May 1969 reported that only 252 of the 52,650 navy and air force flight personnel were black (Table 18). As low as is this percentage, it is still almost twice that in commercial aviation. Unfortunately, all military pilots are not available for the airlines. According to a Negro pilot for American Airlines, "Once a Negro does make it as a military pilot, he's often reluctant to chance a civilian career." [26] Given the fact that real opportunities have been available for less than a decade, one can readily understand the reluctance to leave the hard-won security of the military for the more risky, if potentially more lucrative, opportunities in commercial aviation. In addition, to the extent that the Negro military pilots are flying helicopters or single engine fighters, they are not considered top prospects for commercial airline employment.

There is thus little likelihood of a substantial increase in the number of black pilots in the immediate future. Both the airlines and the Negro pilots are therefore hoping to change this in the more distant future. Not only have the airlines been making an effort to find eligible Negroes, but they have joined with the organization of Negro pilots, Negro Airmen International, to induce young black people to obtain the requisite training. This is, of course, a long process, but there do not seem to be any shortcuts to overcome the deficiencies and discrimination of

TABLE 18. *Air Force and Navy*
Employment of Pilots by Race
May 1969

Service	Total Pilots	Negro Pilots	Percent Negro
Air Force	37,000	236	0.6
Navy	15,650	16	0.1
Total	52,650	252	0.5

Source: *Chicago Tribune*, May 18, 1969.

26. "Air Lines Seek More Negroes," *Chicago Tribune*, May 18, 1969.

the past. With many airlines having over one thousand applicants waiting for pilot positions to open, with air force and naval air arm recruiting still short of black candidates, and with several hundred pilots on layoff in early 1971, it is difficult to believe that the percentage of black pilots will increase substantially in the 1970's. On the other hand, a recent study by the U.S. Bureau of Labor Statistics projects pilot employment on United States certificated, supplemental, and commercial air carriers to reach 51,100 by 1977, a gain of 18,000 over 1967.[27] If this projection proves accurate (and it now seems optimistic), opportunities for Negro pilots should be greater in a few years than they are now.

Nonpilot Professionals and Technicians

Besides pilots, airlines employ a variety of professionals—meterologists, engineers, economists, lawyers, accountants, etc. Like industry generally, they employed few, if any, Negroes in these categories until recently, and now find that they must compete with industry generally for the very few Negroes who are trained and available in these professions. Despite most earnest attempts by several airlines, these staffs remain overwhelmingly white. This is likely to be the situation for many years.

For overseas flights, airlines include navigators in flight crews. The authors know of no Negroes among the small number of navigators.

Flight engineers, as such, are rapidly disappearing from flight crews. Originally conceived as a flying technician and mechanic, the concept has changed so that the duties have been largely assumed by a pilot-trained person, who is the second officer and works up the progression to first officer and then captain. Hence persons in this category are mostly included in the pilot data. A few Negroes (two or three) are known to be among the nonpilot engineers still flying.

Technicians in the industry include draftsmen, statisticians, analysts, etc., much as in many other industries. The category is not large. Few Negroes are found in this group, as is the case in industry generally.

---

27. U. S. Bureau of Labor Statistics, *Pilots and Mechanics in Civil Aviation, 1967-1977: A Study of Manpower Requirements*, Bulletin No. 1655 (Washington: Government Printing Office, 1970), Part II, Long-Range Manpower Requirements, p. 8.

Sales and Service—Stewardesses and Flight Attendants

The stroke of genius of United Air Lines in sending a charming flight attendant aloft with passengers in the 1930's rapidly became industry practice around the world. Like so many improvements in service and technology, however, it had its unfortunate aspects. For as the airlines took over long distance passenger hauling from the railroads, it meant that the white female flight attendant replaced the Negro male pullman and train porter.

The early stewardesses were nurses, but this qualification was discarded during World War II. Now the airlines look for attractive girls, usually in their early twenties, who meet the required physical standards of height, weight, visual and hearing perception, etc. The job is a glamorous one despite mundane work (waitresses aloft), with opportunities for exciting travel, meeting new people, and earnings in the neighborhood of $600 per month. The turnover is high, the stay on the job averaging about 2.5 years, with marriage the leading cause of termination.[28]

As of January 1, 1969, United States airlines employed 31,573 stewardesses,[29] with United, the largest airline, employing more than 5,000. The number of stewardesses employed, unlike the situation with pilots, increases as planes are made larger. Hence there has been a rapid expansion of stewardesses as air traffic has risen. Between 1965 and 1969, for example, the number of stewardesses in service doubled.

As was noted in the previous chapter, the airlines were slow to employ Negroes as stewardesses and only did so in the late 1950's after considerable prodding by state fair employment practice commissions. Airline management feared that the traveling public would not accept black stewardesses, a fear which has proved totally unwarranted. There are an estimated 900 Negro girls flying as stewardesses for the commercial carriers today. Their acceptance has been extremely good, with few or no ra-

---

28. Now that the Equal Employment Opportunity Commission has determined that termination of stewardesses at marriage violates Title VII of the Civil Rights Act of 1964, tenure of stewardesses may be longer. Airline executives question whether enthusiasm for the mundane work aloft will not wane and service decline as a result. As frequent travelers, we believe government intervention into such a trivial matter is already beginning to have deleterious effects.

29. "Hostess Corps Up to 33,804," *International Stewardess News*, February 1969.

cially directed complaints from passengers. The experience of the airlines has been that these young ladies do as good a job as the average white girl hired from the normal sources.[30]

At first, the airlines tended to employ relatively light skinned Negro girls and carefully assigned them to areas where their acceptance would be assured. For example, on one airline, if a Negro stewardess bid on a southern run, the airline management talked her into changing to another. Soon, however, these policies proved unnecessary so that today there is little concern by airline management whether a girl is jet black or on what run she may decide to bid.

Because of the large numbers of girls employed as stewardesses and the relatively high turnover of this position, the airlines have made special efforts to recruit Negroes into these positions. Normally, a carrier has to interview between 20 and 30 girls for each one hired as a stewardess. The airlines have made special efforts to go to predominantly Negro schools and to cooperate with Negro organizations in order to attract and to seek out qualified Negro applicants. The requirements for the job are such that a girl must have a pleasing personality, must be well groomed and attractive, and must be able to get along with and communicate with people with facility. A high school education is usually required as evidence of maturity and capability to handle the paper work and communication skills involved in the job. In addition, airlines have minimum and maximum weight and height requirements based upon the physical needs of the job.

Once the stewardess is employed, she reports to a training school conducted by the airline, or for a few airlines, by an independent contractor. There she is taught not only the rudiments of her job, but also given a "finishing school" course in charm, dress, makeup, etc. The result is usually a delight for passengers and the airlines' best public relations contact with passengers.

Although the proportion of Negro girls employed as stewardesses is still quite low—about 3 percent—Negroes are being recruited at a faster rate and their proportion is likely to expand considerably in the 1970's. In a few cases, airlines may have relaxed their demanding entrance requirements in order to attract Negro girls. But most carriers have reported that this has

---

30. The fact that some airlines include stewardesses as sales workers, others as service workers, confuses our statistics, as already noted.

not been necessary. The airlines are finding that they can attract Negro girls, as they have always attracted whites, because of the glamorous nature of the work. Negro stewardesses, like their white counterparts, are a select group, who respond well to training, and perform equally satisfactorily on the job.

Besides stewardesses, international flights usually carry a "purser," or chief attendant, who has historically been male. The number of these employees is probably not 5 percent of the total airline stewardess employment, with at most one or two Negroes. In many cases, airlines require bilingual proficiency. This has attracted a number of Puerto Ricans, who are the principal minority so employed.

Sales—Reservation Personnel

Reservation agents and clerks selling tickets or providing information comprise about 25 percent of the airlines' labor force. Because of the large number of females involved and because of the tendency of men so employed to be promoted to better jobs or to engage in such work only temporarily (while attending college, or until better opportunities elsewhere present themselves), there is considerable turnover among such personnel. In addition, as air transport reached new highs in the 1960's, the airlines considerably expanded this portion of the labor force.

Reservation agents and clerks must deal with the public courteously and often under trying circumstances; they must understand the significance of care and accuracy, be competent to handle the reservation equipment, be able to respond to and/or to execute complicated reservation requests involving multiple destinations, several airlines, and a variety of fares; and those that sell tickets must be able to handle cash and to execute credit card forms as well. A high school education or its equivalent and reasonably high intelligence are required for such jobs.

Again because of the public contact aspects of the job, the airlines were slow to employ Negroes, but since 1963, most of them have energetically recruited blacks, both men and women, for these jobs. Today, Negro reservation clerks, ticket agents, and associated personnel can be seen at ticket offices in most large city airports, including those in the South, as well as in branch ticket offices located in other parts of the cities. Moreover, as already noted, these positions have the earliest potential for movement into the supervisory and managerial ranks, and thus afford Negroes good potential for such promotion.

Ticket offices located within large cities are readily accessible to concentrations of Negro population, but those at airports— the most important in terms of employment—are generally a considerable distance from where most Negroes dwell. In addition, computerized reservation headquarters tend to be built in the suburbs or otherwise away from large cities. Urban crime waves accelerate this trend. Eastern Air Lines, for example, moved its New York City central reservations communication headquarters to a New Jersey suburb, partially because of the threat of crime and violence involving its clerical staff, including many women who must be on the job around the clock. The net effect, given current housing problems and inadequate public urban transportation, could put Negroes at a disadvantage in seeking such employment. At Eastern, however, this did not occur because of the careful preparations which Eastern made to handle the problem. Thus an Eastern official wrote the senior author:

Approximately two years prior to the relocation of this office from mid-town Manhattan to Woodbridge, a concentrated recruitment program was conducted in the New Jersey area by Eastern, utilizing to a great degree various organizations that specialize in minority referrals. As a result, the ratio of minorities and Blacks to the total work force in the Woodbrige office has been maintained at a slightly higher level than when the office was located in mid-town Manhattan. Specifically, in December of 1969, 20.8 percent of the officials and managers were minorities, 11.3 percent of the officials and managers were Blacks; 20.1 percent in the sales workers (reservations agent) classification were minorities and 16.7 percent of the sales workers were Black. Since this office was opened, slightly better than 25 percent of all new hires have been Black.[31]

Another negative factor in encouraging Negro ticket agent employment in several airlines is a seniority clause which requires some employees to start as baggage handlers or in other essentially laboring jobs before assignment to ticket selling or related work. This has tended to turn away black applicants desirous of white collar employment.

Negro employment is considerably less in smaller airports and stations than in those in the larger cities. In most cases this can be attributed to the smaller proportion of Negroes in the population of small cities than in larger ones. Moreover, the turnover and personnel expansion of the smaller locations have not been

---

31. Letter from R. C. Coleman, Manager, Corporate Equal Opportunity Programs, July 14, 1970.

proportionately as great as in larger ones, so that the ratio of job openings has been lower. In addition, however, the authors sense a lesser enthusiasm of management to commit such jobs to blacks, probably because of local pressures, and a concomitantly greater hesitation of Negroes to apply for them. This is especially noticeable in the South, where the agent force at the smaller airports remains overwhelmingly white.

In spite of these handicaps, most airlines have seen in their ticket agent forces an opportunity for affirmative action. They have tried not to reduce standards because of the sensitive customer relationships involved, but to recruit and to train qualified Negroes. In this regard, Trans World Airlines adapted to the American scene a program originally designed in the 1950's to spur employment at its facilities in Rome. This is a special training program designed to bring up to its employment standards disadvantaged urban males who aspire to ticket or reservation agent positions. TWA reports a number of successes in employing such youths after intensive training.

The increase in the number of Negroes employed in the ticketing and reservation function is apparent to the air traveler. Given the relatively high turnover among such employees and the fact that the major airlines report minority hiring well in excess of current employment ratios, one can safely predict a continuing increase in the black ratio of the sales group over this decade.

Office and Clerical

The office and clerical group in the airline industry is comprised of the usual jobs—secretaries, stenographers, office clerks, key punch operators, and so forth. Ticket and reservation processing and governmental relationships insure the need for a major clerical force—almost 15 percent of the total industry labor force.

Like most industry, the airlines have been making a major effort since 1963 to expand the number and percentage of their Negro force. They have had some success, raising the rates to almost 4 percent by 1968. In addition to the fact that fewer Negroes are trained for such employment than the number of jobs available, a situation that affects all industry, but one which is improving, airlines face the already noted locational problem This is particularly important insofar as female employment is concerned.

The headquarters of American, Eastern, Pan American, and Trans World are in Manhattan, and therefore quite accessible to a Negro population concentration. Most other airlines are head-quartered at or near airports—United, near Chicago's O'Hare; Braniff, adjacent to Dallas's Love Field; and so forth. These are considerable distances from local centers of Negro population and particularly at United's facility, require a long, arduous, and expensive commute. The demand for clerical help is such that Negro girls who are qualified can find perfectly satisfactory jobs in center city offices much more convenient to their dwelling places. Married women, in particular, find that long commuting interferes with homemaking obligations. Unless housing patterns alter, the airlines will continue to find it difficult to attract a sizable number of black clerical personnel to those offices located convenient to airports instead of in center cities.

Craftsmen

The airlines require skilled mechanics to overhaul, modify, and maintain their aircraft. All major airlines have large overhaul and modification centers where aircraft are periodically examined, rechecked, and engines, wiring, and aircraft bodies stripped down and rebuilt. In addition, they employ forces at the major points of call for emergency maintenance and minor corrections.

Nearly 20 percent of all airline employees are classified as craftsmen. A much smaller percentage are top rated mechanics who are licensed by the Federal Aviation Agency either as A & P (airframe and power plant) or radio mechanics. These are the elite blue collar employees. Few Negroes are found among them. The situation here is somewhat analogous to that of a pilot in that many of the licensed mechanics who are employed by the airlines were previously employed in similar positions by various branches of the military. Despite great progress toward integration in the armed services, the mechanical complement therein apparently remains heavily white.

The military, however, is not the sole supply of this type of airline employee. There are several private schools which specialize in training individuals who seek to become licensed aircraft mechanics, and the airlines themselves have long been engaged in training activities to qualify their employees for licensed jobs and to fill employment needs. The problem of the lack of Negroes in these jobs, then, is probably attributable to the unwillingness in previous times to encourage Negroes to apply for and to en-

gage in this sort of training, to trade union discrimination, which
will be discussed below, to the general historical (and essentially
correct) belief among Negroes that craft jobs in most industries,
including airlines, were not open to them, and to the national
failure to insist that craft training be stressed more in schools
and that it be open to all.

That segregated and discriminatory patterns of the past are
difficult to overcome long after they have been discarded has been
noted in many of the studies in this series. The airlines are no
exception to this. At a time when most carriers are consciously
making an effort to encourage Negroes to obtain necessary training for upgrading, or to provide that training, that job is rendered more difficult by past practice. Many Negroes were hired
in past years for menial service or laboring work with qualifications fitting only such jobs and with little or no consideration
for future upgrading. Such employees need much more than
ordinary training to qualify for advancement, particularly in
mechanical jobs, where shop mathematics, blueprint reading, and
other basic educational tools are essential. Moreover, the airlines
have found, as have other industries, that the qualified Negro is
more attuned to college than to apprentice or similar type training.

The job of increasing the ratio of black mechanics (only 2.3
percent in 1968) is complicated, as in the aerospace industry, by
the simple fact that safety allows no diminution of skill requirements or training. Thus it is not easy to overcome years of disadvantage. Expensive, intensive training is the only way to
achieve results, and progress is and will inevitably be slow, although some improvement can be noted since 1966.

U.S. Bureau of Labor Statistics projections foresee a demand
for 70,000 mechanics for United States air carriers by 1977 as
compared with 52,000 which were employed ten years earlier, a
gain of 18,000.[32] If these jobs actually materialize, and if blacks
could obtain a sizeable portion of them, the racial makeup of the
industry would be substantially moved toward fair employment.

Operatives

Operatives include a multitude of semiskilled functions most of
which involve ground crews working on plane maintenance and
service at airports and airline modification centers. Some of this

32. U.S. Bureau of Labor Statistics, *op. cit.*, Part II, p. 9.

work places the individual in the progression line for potential qualification and upgrading as a mechanic (craftsman); other types are essentially deadend—baggage and freight handling, for example, but even those employees can qualify themselves for upgrading under most seniority arrangements.

The number of persons so employed is only about one-half that of craftsmen, illustrating again the high skill content of blue collar jobs in the industry. In 1968, 10.6 percent of these jobs were held by Negroes, and the proportion has probably increased since then. The jobs require little formal education, and several airlines, including American, Braniff, Pan American, United, and Eastern, have developed special hardcore training programs which have graduated employees into these jobs.

Again locational problems are an inhibiting factor. Airports are located by necessity in outlying areas and aircraft modification centers are equally by necessity located at or adjacent to airports. Hence both on-line and major maintenance usually require considerable and often expensive commuting from the centers of Negro population. The effect has been a heavy turnover of new recruits for such jobs and a difficulty in recruiting.

Nevertheless, the industry has continued to attract a sizeable percentage of Negroes—10.6 in 1968—for such work. It is important that it do so because upgrading from some of the operative classifications offers the best avenue for Negroes to advance to craftsmen. The major airlines provide considerable training in order to maintain the necessary complement of skilled and licensed mechanics. Given the difficulties of recruiting apprentices and the failure of public schools, particularly in center cities and in the rural South where most Negroes dwell, to provide a high caliber of vocational education, it is obvious that in-service training offers the best potential to expand the ratio of black craftsmen.

Unfortunately, several airlines have found that their Negro operatives seem reluctant to seek advancement. Perhaps many do not really believe that the opportunity exists, or lack confidence in their ability to "make the grade." Others may find the paucity of black craftsmen already on the job an indication of trouble ahead if they aspire too high. This, of course, has been found true in other industries studied in this series. Yet the large numbers of Negroes being attracted to the semiskilled ground crew and maintenance jobs is encouraging because the doors are now open for advancement, and the major airlines are committed to seeking out and encouraging Negroes to take advantage of opportunities to advance. A slow but steady upward progression of black crewmen may therefore be expected.

Laborers and Service Workers

Only 3 percent of the airlines' total work force is classified as laborers, but of these about one-fourth are Negroes. Most such employees are janitors or cleaners, doing menial work around airplanes, airports, or company facilities. The overconcentration of Negroes in such jobs is typical of American industry generally and a relic of past discrimination and continuing disadvantage.

As already stressed, the service employee classification is a confused one, including United's 5,000 stewardesses, as well as those of some smaller airlines, plus considerable unskilled work, such as flight kitchen employees where inflight meals are prepared and many unskilled service jobs. If the stewardesses could be removed from these data, the ratio of Negroes would be considerably higher. For such unskilled jobs again, the situation in the airline industry is similar to industry generally.

The results of civil rights pressures and affirmative action since the mid-1960's can be seen in the decline of the Negro's share of the lowest two occupational categories, particularly with regard to laborers, since the stewardess data confuses the service worker classification. In 1966, the twelve airlines in our sample employed 3,941 laborers of whom 33.7 percent were black; the number of laborers rose to 7,068 by 1968, but only 25.9 percent were Negroes. Obviously they were upgrading Negroes and not employing Negroes just as laborers as the decade progressed.

Skycaps—A Special Situation

As airports were developed, they followed the railroad station tradition of employing Negro porters. Whereas the railroad porters were termed "redcaps" as a result of their head gear style, those at airports were designated "skycaps." Some have been employed by airlines, others by airport management authorities.

In the early 1960's, the airlines thought that the skycaps would provide an internal labor source for upgrading and affirmative action. This has proved to be a quite erroneous belief. Most skycaps have politely declined to be promoted or given jobs such s in reservations or ground maintenance. The reasons are clear. With gratuities, their income has far exceeded starting wages in the jobs offered, or often even wages considerably higher in the progression. Moreover, as air traffic has increased, so has the income of the skycaps.

Most skycap crews remain all black. Whites decline to accept such jobs, and so do most young Negroes. With surprisingly high earnings (in some cases allegedly up to $15,000 per year) and curbside check in of passengers, the number of skycaps is increasing. Airline passengers may be spared the task of lugging their own baggage or pushing carts despite the seemingly low prestige and social standing of the skycap's work.

Negro Female Employment

The high proportion of females in the airline industry affords interesting opportunities for Negro women in jobs other than the typical office and clerical routine which most industries assign to women. Stewardesses and reservation personnel comprise most of these jobs, and, as we have noted, the airlines have pushed hard to increase their recruiting of Negroes for such work. The steady upward trend noted in Table 15 indicates both what improvement has been made and the extent to which progress remains to be obtained.

Of special interest is the fact that in the salaried group, the proportion of black women exceeds that of black men. This is the result of the nearly 4 percent Negro female sales (reservation) representation, as well as recruitment of stewardesses and clerical personnel. Given the turnover of such personnel, one may expect continued improvement. Of course, airlines are also employing an increasing number of black men in the reservation functions, but given the difficulties of improving pilot and mechanic ratios, as compared with stewardess and clericals, one can predict a faster improvement among salaried black women than men in the immediate future.

In the blue collar area, the proportion of females is low. If the stewardesses were separated from our service data, there would probably not be more than 8,000 to 10,000 females so classified. Janitorial type jobs predominate among these women, and Negroes comprise a disproportionate number so employed, as is the case in all industry.

LOCATIONAL FACTORS

The influence of locational factors in determining airline em
ployment has already been noted in the discussion of various oc
cupational groups, but except for flight crews, it is sufficientl,
significant to be stressed once more. Insofar as flight crews ar
concerned, it is, to be sure, largely immaterial. Potential pilot
and stewardesses are not deterred by location. They are hig.
flying nomads who are based where sent until they have sufficien
seniority to select a favored domicile. The distance of airport
from center city locations is irrelevant because flight crew job
are out of the reach of the disadvantaged who have neither th
knowledge nor funds to reach outlying work.

The fact that airlines maintain numerous central city ticke
offices is a plus factor in seeking black reservation and sale
personnel. Particularly for women this aids recruiting and jo
finding. Likewise, the location of American, Eastern, Pan Amer
ican, and Trans World executive offices in Manhattan facilitate
the employment of Negro office and clerical personnel.

Unfortunately, the disadvantages of location far exceed th
advantages. Like the aerospace industry,[33] air transport head
quarters, maintenance facilities, and general work operations are
by their very nature, or because of obvious economics or conven
ience, mostly incompatible with center city locations. The airpor
is more and more located long distances from the city, and ofte
in newer areas that, as in the case of Chicago, Detroit, St. Louis
or Washington's Dulles airport are on the opposite sides of tow
from concentrations of Negro population.

In a few cases, like Philadelphia or Boston, airports are rea
sonably close to the city; in Cleveland, a new urban transit fa
cility runs from center city to the airport. In addition, the met
ropolitan New York airports are either reasonably close to, o
have transportation from, sizeable black housing areas. But thes
arrangements are exceptional. Usually only private cars or ex
pensive airport buses connect the downtowns to the airport an
the buses run to the downtown hotel, not to disadvantaged dwell
ing areas.

Airport and airline employment includes a substantial numbe
of low skill, easy to learn operative, laborer, and service jobs t
which those poorly educated or prepared can aspire and obtai

---

33. See Northrup, Rowan, *et al.*, *Negro Employment in Basic Industry*, Pa
   Three, pp. 185-188.

relatively secure employment. Yet these are the very people who are unlikely to know where the jobs are or how to get to them or to be able to afford the necessary commuting costs. This transit problem is likely to remain a negative factor in black airline employment for years to come, except to the extent that institutionalized housing patterns, inadequate transit facilities, and poor labor market knowledge can be overcome by government or individual company affirmative action, as discussed in the following chapter.

UNIONISM, THE RAILWAY LABOR ACT, AND INTRAPLANT MOBILITY

When unions were organized in the air transport industry, they quite naturally looked to the most successful transportation unions of the period as models for their constitutions and policies, and these were then the railroad brotherhoods. Thus the Air Line Pilots Association, founded in 1930, initially restricted its membership to white persons as did all the major railroad unions. This provision was deleted from the union's constitution in 1942 before Negroes were hired as pilots,[34] but for some time the ALPA retained the restrictive and exclusionist outlook and policies typical for so long of the fraternal craft unions on the railroads. For example, investigations by the senior author and by the New York State Commission for Human Rights in the immediate post-World War II period revealed allegations of anti-Jewish bias in ALPA membership policies.[35] Such discrimination can be potent, for the first and second officers' careers as pilots can be hindered or even ended if captains refuse to fly with them or give them derogatory ratings. Since these events occurred many years ago, and since we have no evidence that ALPA has restricted membership or opposed integration in recent years, it seems very unlikely that its policies have materially affected Negro employment on flight crews.

In addition to ALPA, two smaller unions, the Air Line Dispatchers Association and the Air Line Mechanics Association originally restricted membership to white persons. The former

---

34. For an early history and analysis of ALPA's government and policies, see Herbert R. Northrup, "Collective Bargaining by Air Line Pilots," *Quarterly Journal of Economics*, Vol. LXI (August 1947), pp. 533-576.

35. See Herbert R. Northrup, "Race Discrimination in Trade Unions," *Commentary*, Vol. 2 (August, 1946), p. 126; New York State Commission for Human Rights, *The Airlines Industry*, p. 12.

altered its policies following the enactment of the pioneer New York antidiscrimination law,[36] and the latter went out of existence after World War II, as will be noted below.

Of much more significance than these restrictive clauses in their long range impact was the Air Line Pilots Association's decision to emulate the railroad unions by placing the air transport industry under the law governing railroad labor relations— the Railway Labor Act. The ALPA, with American Federation of Labor support, accomplished this by congressional enactment in 1936, as a divided industry took no position. At this time, only the pilots were unionized and no one could envision the future size, scope, and potential of the industry and its aircraft. What this law did, therefore, was to restrict labor relations in a new, expanding industry to the mold established by an older and already declining one. In retrospect, it is likely that few public policy decisions pertaining to industrial relations have been more unfortunate. This is so for industrial relations generally;[37] it is even more the case insofar as Negro air transport employment is concerned. For the extension of the Railway Labor Act to the airlines in effect invited into that industry certain railway unions, which had a long history of invidious racial discrimination; it also restricted the structure of bargaining to the craft and class concept with consequent impediments on intraplant mobility; and it placed the industry under an administrative body, the National Mediation Board, which has rigidly adhered to railroad concepts in applying the Railway Labor Act to airlines and which has in addition a long record of dealing with Negro problems varying from insensitivity to outright furtherance of discrimination.[38]

Craft or Class Concept

Prior to the 1960's the impact of national policy on Negro employment in the air transport industry was clearly not positive. Although all presidents since Franklin D. Roosevelt issued execu-

---

36. From the senior author's field notes of the post-World War II period. See also New York State Commission, *loc. cit.*

37. On this see, Northrup and Bloom, *Government and Labor*, Chapter 12, especially pp. 340-345; and "Symposium on Air Transport Labor Relations," *Journal of Air Law and Commerce*, Vol. XXXV (Summer 1969), pp. 313-530.

38. For this sordid story, see Herbert R. Northrup, *Organized Labor and the Negro* (New York: Harper and Brothers, 1944), Chapter III; and the railroad study in this series.

tive orders banning racial discrimination in employment,[39] the administrators of these orders quite understandably concentrated their efforts in industries where jobs seemed more likely to be obtained by the black population. In view of the relative absence of Negroes in all key transportation jobs except those in urban transit, where the barriers had been broken down during World War II,[40] upgrading Negroes to key jobs in the elite transportation industry seemed a Utopian dream at least up to the late 1950's. Consequently, federal intervention in airline employment policies was left largely to the procedures of the Railway Labor Act.

The Railway Labor Act's major dispute procedures are the product of railroad labor relations history and agreement between railroad unions and carriers which produced the Railway Labor Act of 1926. The other aspects of the act—representation, grievance arbitration, and unfair labor practice penalties—are all part of the 1934 and subsequent amendments to the act which were adopted primarily at the behest of the railway unions and usually over carrier opposition. The three-man National Mediation Board, which administers the major dispute and representation procedures, was created by the 1934 amendments to replace a previous agency whose members had lost the confidence of the leaders of railroad labor unions. A key criterion for appointment to the National Mediation Board has always been approval by the leaders of the key railroad unions.[41]

Given its history and its practical relationships, it is understandable that the National Mediation Board members have always been solicitous of the desires and aspirations of the major railroad unions. Moreover, in order to be successful in administering what they regard as the key feature of the Railway Labor Act—the procedures to settle labor disputes between carriers and unions—good relationships with the major unions have been essential. Therefore, it should be no surprise that the National Mediation Board has tended to determine issues in a manner

---

39. Executive Order Nos. 8802, June 25, 1946 and 9346, May 27, 1943, by President Roosevelt; No. 10308, December 3, 1951, by President Truman; No. 10479, August 13, 1953, by President Eisenhower; Nos. 10925, March 6, 1961 and 11114, June 22, 1963, by President Kennedy; and No. 11246, September 24, 1965, by President Johnson. President Nixon has retained the Johnson Order, format, and administrative procedure.

40. See the various transportation studies in this series.

41. See Northrup and Bloom, *op. cit.*, Chapter 12.

that has been generally pleasing to the railway unions, or in cases involving disagreements among the unions, to the largest and most powerful union.[42]

The most direct impact of the Railway Labor Act and the National Mediation Board administration thereof upon Negro airline employees occurred as a result of its bargaining unit determinations. The act restricts the bargaining unit to "craft or class." Thus employees are, in effect, required to unionize on this basis and denied the opportunity to choose industrial unionism. In practice this has meant that a carrier inevitably deals with a large number of unions. Such fragmentation encourages union rivalries and interunion disputes, and complicates the obtaining of industrial peace. Insofar as Negro employment opportunity is concerned, craft organization adds barriers to intraplant movement because seniority generally does not extend beyond union jurisdiction.

Assume, for example, that a semiskilled person in ramp or aircraft service has aspirations and capacity for a mechanic's job, and desires transfer to a learner or helper position that would eventually qualify him for such a position. The rules governing such transfer would vary according to terms of union contracts, but the likelihood that transfer could be accomplished at all would be much greater if such transfer did not require change from one union jurisdiction to another; and the likelihood that an employee could transfer and still retain seniority in his old job in case of layoffs or cutbacks would be high if one union were involved, but very unlikely if two unions were in the picture.

Thus the Railway Labor Act's limitation of bargaining units to craft or class can be a restrictive factor in the upward movement of those at the bottom of the occupational hierarchy. Given the fact that Negroes are concentrated in these jobs, it requires no belaboring to see that any barriers imposed by law would add to the other difficulties encountered by black employees desiring to improve their occupational status.

National Mediation Board Administration

To the barriers erected by law the National Mediation Board added more. This was not with the intent of discriminating

---

42. It is perhaps unnecessary to note that the NMB's policies have not succeeded in achieving the labor peace for which has been sacrificed what we believe would have been a more balanced administration of the act.

against Negroes; rather it evolved first from the NMB's apparent desire to force upon the airline industry the bargaining unit mold which grew up in the railroad industry around the jurisdictional claims of railroad unions; and second from the rules adopted by the NMB to govern representation matters.

For example, the NMB has generally insisted on placing in one conglomerate "craft or class" ramp service personnel, ticket agents, and office personnel. The reason appears to be that similar groupings have been made in the railroad industry; and the reason why they were made in the railroad industry was indisputably because this suited the jurisdictional claims of the Brotherhood of Railway and Steamship Clerks, Freight Handlers, Express and Station Employees, long a large and powerful railroad union. The clerks were assisted in gaining a major foothold in the airline industry ("airline" has been added to its long name) by the decision which was made in a case long after the ramp servicemen had unionized in groups with mechanical and service groups, not with clerical groups. In addition, the clerks were handed jurisdiction over "sky caps" at a time when they denied Negroes equal membership—a factor which the NMB refused to consider pertinent.[43]

In determining its bargaining unit policies, the National Mediation Board has attempted to give a generally broad interpretation to the definition of craft or class. This has suited the jurisdictional claims of the standard railway unions and would seem to offset some of the above objections raised to the craft or class limitation. Actually, however, because the NMB groupings have been based more on railroad than airline practice, conglomerate and disparate, not continuous and natural groupings have resulted. Thus blue collar service personnel are combined with white collar reservation agents, and both with the central office and clerical groups, placing an additional barrier between some blue collar personnel who work with mechanics and might have aspirations to work into the mechanical jobs. At the same time, on some airlines, employees who desire to become reservation agents must start in blue collar jobs. In the former situation, many black employees are effectively barred advancement; in the latter case, potential black employees look elsewhere because they

---

43. See *Determinations of Craft or Class of the National Mediation Board, July 1, 1934 to June 30, 1948* (Washington: Government Printing Office, 1948), Vol. I, pp. 181, 423-443, and 445-447; and Glen Harlan, "Developments: Past and Future in the NMB's Determination of 'Craft or Class' ", *Journal of Air Law and Commerce*, Vol. XXV (Summer 1969), pp. 394-407.

do not desire to doff their hard-won white collar backgrounds for blue collar service before they can become part of the reservation force.

There are other ways in which the Railway Labor Act and its administration by the National Mediation Board raise questions of public policy, but most of these appear to affect all employees rather than only Negroes and hence need not be discussed here.[44]

Union Policy

Union policy in the airline industry has varied from hostile to passive insofar as Negro employment is concerned. The Air Line Pilots Association, as already noted, is not now attempting to block the black pilots' opportunities. The few Negro pilots have organized a group known as the Negro Airmen International, which is open to all black flyers, whether employed as such or not. It is not competitive to ALPA, but rather acts to encourage Negroes to train as pilots and airlines to employ them. In any case, union policy has not been a factor of significance in determining the number of employed Negro pilots.

Stewardesses were unionized largely by pilots, but a split between their leadership and ALPA's led about one-half of them to affiliate instead with the Transport Workers Union, which is strong in the New York City area, as discussed below. TWU has also organized navigators. The few flight engineers left are members of their own organization, the Flight Engineers International Association. None of these groups have actively opposed Negro employment, and only TWU has actively supported it.

In the mechanics' group, union policies have been more important but not more constructive. The dominant union is the International Association of Machinists and Aerospace Workers. (The "aerospace" was added recently.) Founded in the railroad shops of Atlanta, and later expanded into a variety of industries, it is now the dominant union in airline maintenance, having agreements with eight of the twelve major airlines. The IAM

---

44. These include lack of decertification procedures, failure to list "no union" on representation election ballots, refusal to define a bargaining unit of less than all carrier scope, and generally loose administrative procedures. On the railroads these matters were a definite instrument of racial discrimination. (See Northrup, *Organized Labor and the Negro, op. cit.,* Chapter III.) On the airlines, they have not been, partially because of the paucity of blacks employed. For a discussion of these problems, see *Journal of Air Law and Commerce,* Vol. XXXV (Summer 1969), pp. 323-531.

originally restricted its membership to "competent white mechanics" by a provision in its ritual, but this provision was deleted in 1948. By then, many of its far-flung locals had already admitted Negroes and other nonwhites.

The IAM gradually dislodged a one-time independent, the Air Line Mechanics Association, in the 1930's and 1940's. In the post-World War II years, the latter affiliated with the United Automobile Workers, but had by then, or soon thereafter, lost bargaining rights at all airlines except Braniff. When the Dallas local at Braniff refused to admit Negroes on an equal basis, the UAW expelled it in 1952.[45] The local promptly affiliated with the IAM and the UAW lost its last foothold in the airline industry.

The national offices of the IAM exert little authority over the racial policies of the locals (or in many cases over other local policies). As a result where a dominant white membership is discriminating, no strong moderating force is likely. Our field study indicated that by the late 1960's, most locals were relatively passive. None was found which actively supported affirmative action, and at least two in the South opposed it. In all cases, however, employer policy was decisive. If the employer was actively seeking to expand Negro employment, the IAM proved to be no bar.

In two large airlines, American and Pan American, the Transport Workers Union is the bargaining agent for ground crews, including mechanics. It is a former CIO affiliate, with principal strength among transit employees in New York and a few other large cities. The fact that Pan American still has, and American formerly had, the main overhaul base in the New York area accounts for the TWU's strength in these airlines.

TWU has always championed the Negro's cause as a matter of union policy, and its locals have cooperated with management in affirmative action programs. Again, however, management policy has been decisive and there is little to indicate that the TWU has been other than a cooperative junior partner.

Of the two remaining airlines, Delta has no union among its ground crews, and Western deals with the Teamsters, which a few years ago wrested bargaining rights for mechanics and related personnel from the IAM. The Teamsters, despite espousing liberal policies in general after forming the Alliance for Labor

---

45. Ray Marshall, *The Negro and Organized Labor* (New York: John Wiley & Sons, 1965), pp. 178-179, 203-204.

Action with the United Automobile Workers, has a poor to non-committal record within its union insofar as Negro employment is concerned.[46] At Western, its local has made no discernible impact on the racial policies of the company.

In recent years, the Teamsters has been making other gains in the airlines, particularly at the expense of the Brotherhood of Railway and Airline Clerks (BRC), displacing the latter at Braniff and Pan American. The Teamsters' policies are best described as *laissez-faire*. It operates basically a "business" union, neither pushing nor opposing integration.

The BRC, which was once the dominant clerical union, represents only Northwest and Western today. Originally a railroad union which barred nonwhites, the BRC amended its constitution in the 1930's to admit Negroes to "auxiliary locals." Under that setup, the black "members" had the right to pay dues but little else. After World War II, under prodding by the New York State antidiscrimination agency, the restrictive clauses were finally removed. Since then the BRC has admitted Negroes, but like the IAM, takes no affirmative position.

The final clerical and reservation group union of note is the Air Line Employees Association, a catchall "subsidiary" of the Air Line Pilots Association, which has won bargaining rights for clerical groups at National and at several feeder lines. Again there is no evidence that the union is a significant factor in racial policy determination. American, Delta, Eastern, Trans World, United, and several smaller airlines do not have unions among their clerical or station agent employees.

Union and NMB Policy—Final Comment

Union policy in the airlines thus has been somewhat of a deterrent to Negro employment, but not as significant as National Mediation Board policies. Both union and NMB policies, however, have been considerably less significant in airlines than in the railway industry. Generally discriminatory managerial employment policies preempted racial issues for the unions prior to the late 1950's. In the 1960's, expanding employment and strong civil rights policies of government have reduced union opposition where formerly extant and generally contributed to a *laissez-faire* approach by unions, with management initiative the key factor.

---

46. See the study of trucking in this series for details of Teamster policy.

DEVELOPMENTS SINCE 1968

Just prior to the publication of this study, the Equal Employment Opportunity Commission issued its 1967 data and made available those for 1969. Table 19 summarizes those data and compares them with the 1966 EEOC figures and with our 1968 field sample. (The EEOC has not published 1968 data).

These data show a continued upward trend of Negro employment, but given the low base from which progress began, still much improvement is needed. Thus the EEOC data reveal a more than doubling of the white collar ratio between 1966 and 1969, but still only a 2.4 percent black ratio. The greatest improvement has occurred for the reasons already noted in the sales and office and clerical percentages among salaried personnel and among operatives in the blue collar group. In 1969, as in the previous year, the gains in the top three salaried groups and in the craftsman category are quite modest.

Since 1969, whatever improvement has occurred could only have taken place in the high turnover occupations, such as reservation clerks and stewardesses. Most airlines suffered severe losses in 1970 as a result of increasing costs and declining business, and laid off a substantial number of employees. The immediate prospects for improvement are therefore not bright, although a return to expansion for the industry is considered likely within the next three years.

TABLE 19. Air Transport Industry
Percentage Negro Employment by Sex and Occupational Group
United States, 1966-1969

Occupational Group	All Employees				Male				Female			
	1966	1967	1968	1969	1966	1967	1968	1969	1966	1967	1968	1969
Officials and managers	0.4	0.4	0.6	0.8	0.4	0.4	0.6	0.8	0.2	0.3	0.6	0.8
Professionals	0.2	0.2	0.3	0.4	0.2	0.2	0.3	0.3	0.3	0.5	0.8	1.4
Technicians	0.9	0.9	0.5	1.3	1.0	0.9	0.5	1.2	0.6	0.8	1.1	1.4
Sales workers	1.4	2.2	3.3	3.9	1.1	1.6	2.6	2.9	1.7	2.7	3.8	4.6
Office and clerical	2.0	2.5	3.7	3.7	2.7	3.3	4.5	4.7	1.4	1.9	3.2	2.9
Total white collar	1.1	1.5	2.2	2.4	1.0	1.1	1.5	1.7	1.4	2.2	3.4	3.7
Craftsmen	2.2	2.5	2.3	2.6	2.2	2.5	2.3	2.6	0.4	2.2	2.1	4.4
Operatives	9.3	9.3	10.6	12.1	9.2	9.2	10.5	12.0	13.6[a]	13.0[a]	20.9[a]	20.2[a]
Laborers	30.1	24.8	25.9	34.2	29.3	24.2	25.2	31.9	51.8[a]	40.3[a]	45.7[a]	68.6[a]
Service workers	14.3	13.5	11.7	11.2	30.3	29.7	32.8	27.2	2.5	2.6	2.8	2.8
Total blue collar	8.0	8.5	8.3	9.2	8.7	9.3	9.5	10.2	3.4	3.5	3.5	4.8
Total	4.3	4.6	4.8	5.4	5.0	5.3	5.3	6.0	1.9	2.5	3.4	4.0

Source: Table 14 and Appendix Tables A-3, A-31 and A-32.

[a] Very small members involved.

CHAPTER V

Impact of Region, Carrier, and Government

Thus far we have discussed the overall racial policies of the air transport industry. Such policies, however, are subject to regional and individual carrier variations. This chapter first discusses the regional characteristics of these policies, and then examines the different policies, approaches, and affirmative action programs of the individual carriers. A final section assesses the role of government in affecting airline racial policies.

REGIONAL VARIATIONS

Regional variations are not too significant for flight crews of nationwide airlines because the crew members tend to gravitate to the favorite locations of the individuals concerned. Each airline has "domiciles"—key major airport locations—from which it originates and commences daily flights. Flight crew members stationed there do not receive "off domicile" compensation or expenses. As crew members rise in the seniority list, they tend to choose runs from the domicile in which they desire to settle.

Although the regional data do not necessarily signify area variations in flight crew employment patterns, they do reflect such patterns for other employees. Moreover, regional data are also affected by the racial policies of regional carriers and thus provide a background for discussion of individual carrier differences discussed later in this chapter. (Regional definitions are in Table 11, Chapter III.)

The Northeast

As in our analysis of the overall data in Chapter IV, we have a three-year field sample by region, the basic tables for which are presented in Appendix A and summarized in this chapter. In addition, this chapter utilizes the data published by the Equal Employment Opportunity Commission for 1966 to compare with and to validate our sample. Table 19 presents the EEOC data for the Northeast and Table 20 the summary of our sample for the three years, 1964, 1966, and 1968.

Table 20, based on data supplied to the Equal Employment Opportunity Commission, shows that in 1966, 4.2 percent of all employees in the Northeast region were black. Our field sample of twelve major carriers for that year (Table 21) shows a 4.4 ratio. In white collar areas, our sample is 2.3 percent for 1966; the EEOC data only 1.8; for blue collar jobs, the percentages are almost identical—8.1 percent for our sample, 8.0 percent for the EEOC data. Thus as in the national data analysis, our Northeast sample is very representative, but reflects what appears to be the slightly higher employment of Negroes in white collar jobs by the major carriers as compared with others in the industry who employed 100 or more persons in 1966. In view of the more current data available in our sample and its availability in three years, we shall utilize it for our regional analysis also.

The first notable aspect of the data summarized in Table 21 is the general improvement in the position of the Negro between 1964 and 1968. This occurred in both the share of the jobs held and in the character of those jobs. Overall in the Northeast, Negroes enjoyed a higher share both of total available jobs, and total white collar jobs than they averaged for the country generally. For example, in 1968, 2.2 percent of the white collar employees and 4.8 percent of all employees in the industry were black (Table 15), whereas the comparable figures in the Northeast were 3.0 and 5.1 percent. The lead of the Northeast over the national ratios was maintained in all classifications except operatives, laborers, and service workers, where the Northeast had smaller concentrations of blacks in these bottom jobs. Moreover, the Northeast ratio of mechanics was 4.8 percent as compared with 2.3 percent nationally, more than twice as advantageous to Negroes.

Within the Northeast region, there are considerable differences. The largest concentrations of airline employees are found in the New York City-Newark, New Jersey area. Here also are the largest concentrations of Negroes in the region, and probably in the country. In this area the most progress toward equal employment has been made in a number of occupations. There are several reasons for this, including the early impact of state fair employment practice legislation. Also important is that New York City is the headquarters of four of the five largest airlines

TABLE 20. *Air Transport Industry*
Employment by Race, Sex, and Occupational Group
Northeast Region, 1966

Occupational Group	All Employees			Male			Female		
	Total	Negro	Percent Negro	Total	Negro	Percent Negro	Total	Negro	Percent Negro
Officials and managers	4,932	44	0.9	4,617	44	1.0	315	—	—
Professionals	7,452	32	0.4	7,239	31	0.4	213	1	0.5
Technicians	1,242	22	1.8	1,112	20	1.8	130	2	1.5
Sales workers	8,875	181	2.0	4,155	74	1.8	4,720	107	2.3
Office and clerical	13,677	382	2.8	6,743	217	3.2	6,934	165	2.4
Total white collar	36,178	661	1.8	23,866	386	1.6	12,312	275	2.2
Craftsmen	9,844	397	4.0	9,759	397	4.1	85	—	—
Operatives	5,641	404	7.2	5,581	388	7.0	60	16	26.7
Laborers	1,182	187	15.8	1,170	187	16.0	12	—	—
Service workers	6,359	843	13.3	2,915	727	24.9	3,444	116	3.4
Total blue collar	23,026	1,831	8.0	19,425	1,699	8.7	3,601	132	3.7
Total	59,204	2,492	4.2	43,291	2,085	4.8	15,913	407	2.6

Source: U.S. Equal Employment Opportunity Commission, *Job Patterns for Minorities and Women in Private Industry, 1966* (Washington: The Commission, 1968), Part II.

TABLE 21. Air Transport Industry
Percent Negro Employment by Occupational Group
Northeast, New England, and Middle Atlantic Regions
1964, 1966, and 1968

Occupational Group	Northeast			New England			Middle Atlantic		
	1964	1966	1968	1964	1966	1968	1964	1966	1968
Officials and managers	0.4	0.6	0.8	—	0.3	—	0.5	0.6	1.0
Professionals	0.2	0.3	0.5	—	0.3	0.1	0.3	0.3	0.5
Technicians	0.6	1.1	1.0	—	3.2	0.7	0.6	0.9	1.0
Sales workers	3.0	3.9	4.6	0.6	1.7	2.1	3.4	4.3	5.2
Office and clerical	3.1	3.2	4.7	0.6	0.8	1.0	3.2	3.6	5.0
Total white collar	1.9	2.3	3.0	0.4	1.1	1.2	2.0	2.5	3.3
Craftsmen	3.5	3.7	4.8	0.7	1.5	1.3	3.7	4.1	5.4
Operatives	8.6	8.3	9.1	1.8	1.9	2.5	9.8	9.6	10.2
Laborers	20.9	22.5	14.7	5.7	19.6	7.9	22.2	23.2	18.1
Service workers	12.8	10.8	11.1	29.7	24.6	10.1	12.1	10.2	11.2
Total blue collar	8.3	8.1	8.7	5.8	5.8	5.0	8.5	8.4	9.4
Total	4.3	4.4	5.1	2.6	2.8	2.8	4.4	4.6	5.5

Source: Appendix Tables A-4 to A-12.

Note: For regional definitions, see Table 11.

d has heavy employee concentrations of all five. We shall find
at the major airlines are much more advanced in equal em-
oyment practice than are their smaller competitors.

Table 21 also summarizes the occupational data for the two
bregions of the Northeast—New England and Middle Atlantic.
esides the New York-Newark area, the latter includes Phila-
lphia, Pittsburgh, and Buffalo. Nevertheless, it does heavily
flect the concentrations in the New York-Newark area, which
ntains a high percentage of Negroes and an improved distri-
ition thereof over the total Northeast region. The percentages
' sales workers, office and clerical, total white collar, and crafts-
en are substantially above the national average. We shall also
id that the Middle Atlantic region is the only area where of-
ials and managers and technicians were one percent black in
*68, and the overall white collar ratio is the highest of any
gion.

The Middle Atlantic region also leads in the number and per-
ntage of Negro craftsmen. Again credit must be given to the
rly antidiscrimination legislation in these states, to the re-
uiting and upgrading policies of the major airlines, and to the
ct that the Transport Workers Union, unlike its larger rival
e International Association of Machinists and Aerospace Work-
s, has not had a long history of opposition to black worker
lvancement. Qualitatively, the Middle Atlantic region affords
egro airline workers equal or better opportunities than any-
here else.

he Midwest

The situation for Negro airline workers in the Midwest (North
entral) region is somewhat different. Overall, this area is both
ialitatively and quantitatively behind the Northeast in Negro
:ilization. Its areas in which Negroes are concentrated, how-
ver, utilized Negroes more heavily than in any other region in
)68, although Negro employment in the better jobs lagged.

Table 22 shows the occupational breakdown by race and sex
or 1966 as supplied to the Equal Employment Opportunity Com-
ission. Table 23 summarizes our 1964, 1966, and 1968 field
imples. The EEOC data show a 4.6 percent complement of
acks in the region for 1966, as compared with 4.0 percent for
ir sample. Our underestimation is confined to blue collar per-
innel since both 1966 compilations produce a 1.4 percent white
llar Negro ratio.

TABLE 22. Air Transport Industry
Employment by Race, Sex, and Occupational Group
North Central Region, 1966

Occupational Group	All Employees			Male			Female		
	Total	Negro	Percent Negro	Total	Negro	Percent Negro	Total	Negro	Percent Negro
Officials and managers	2,981	7	0.2	2,798	5	0.2	183	2	1.1
Professionals	4,417	6	0.1	4,297	6	0.1	120	—	—
Technicians	443	2	0.5	369	2	0.5	74	—	—
Sales workers	5,664	172	3.0	2,405	53	2.2	3,259	119	3.7
Office and clerical	7,256	113	1.6	2,955	54	1.8	4,301	59	1.4
Total white collar	20,761	300	1.4	12,824	120	0.9	7,937	180	2.3
Craftsmen	6,148	52	0.8	6,100	52	0.9	48	—	—
Operatives	3,815	356	9.3	3,788	346	9.1	27	10	37.0
Laborers	1,058	246	23.3	1,033	237	22.9	25	9	36.0
Service workers	3,425	662	19.3	1,865	581	31.2	1,560	81	5.2
Total blue collar	14,446	1,316	9.1	12,786	1,216	9.5	1,660	100	6.0
Total	35,207	1,616	4.6	25,610	1,336	5.2	9,597	280	2.9

Source: U.S. Equal Employment Opportunity Commission, Job Patterns for Minorities and Women in Private Industry, 1966 (Washington: The Commission, 1968), Part II.

TABLE 23. *Air Transport Industry*
Percent Negro Employment by Occupational Group
North Central and East North Central Regions
1964, 1966, and 1968

Occupational Group	North Central			East North Central		
	1964	1966	1968	1964	1966	1968
Officials and managers	0.1	0.2	0.4	0.2	0.3	0.6
Professionals	—	0.2	0.2	—	0.3	0.2
Technicians	0.3	0.2	0.3	0.7	0.3	0.2
Sales workers	1.4	2.8	4.6	1.6	3.2	5.4
Office and clerical	1.1	1.6	2.5	1.2	1.9	2.6
Total white collar	0.8	1.4	2.3	1.0	1.8	2.9
Craftsmen	0.7	0.7	1.1	1.1	1.0	1.2
Operatives	10.1	10.8	10.9	11.5	11.8	12.4
Laborers	14.4	17.9	17.1	23.0	28.3	28.1
Service workers	16.4	14.4	14.2	23.3	22.1	21.2
Total blue collar	7.2	7.7	7.7	12.7	12.9	13.3
Total	3.6	4.0	4.6	5.1	5.6	6.5

Source: Appendix Tables A-13 to A-18.

The trend was upward over the period from 1964 to 1968, as was the case in the overall industry. The North Central area, however, lagged behind the Northeast in all white collar classifications except sales workers where the percentages of Negroes were identical in 1968. The low utilization of Negroes in office and clerical jobs in the North Central area may be attributable to the great distance of airports and offices from black population concentrations. This is emphasized by the fact that the East North Central area, which includes the heavily Negro populated areas of Cleveland, Detroit, and Chicago, shows about the same utilization of Negro office and clerical workers as does the total region. The airports of all these cities are located far from the centers of Negro population, as is the national headquarters of United Air Lines, which is near Chicago's O'Hare field.

In terms of the overall percentage of Negroes employed, the East North Central ranks first among regions in the country with a 6.5 black percentage. Heavy employment of Negroes in blue

collar jobs *below* the rank of craftsmen is the principal reason
for this area's primacy in this regard. This spotty record is
further emphasized by a 1.2 percent Negro craftsmen figure, the
lowest of any northern area, contrasted with a 5.4 percent black
sales worker force, the highest anywhere. Judging by the increase in the latter figure over the four-year period, it would
appear that in the Midwest, the airlines have been unable or
unwilling to overcome barriers to increasing the number of Negro
craftsmen, but instead have concentrated their efforts on improving Negro employment among reservation agents and similar
sales jobs. Since the same major airlines (plus various regional
ones) operate in all regions, we have been unable to determine
precisely why the situation varies so in the Midwest. One key
reason may well be that in the Midwest states, fair employment
or equal opportunity laws were not adopted until a decade or
more after they became effective in the Northeast. Management
and union concern with upgrading blue collar workers lacked the
urgency found in the Northeast. The higher turnover in sales
jobs and the greater availability of Negroes for such jobs have
permitted considerable progress since 1960, but for craftsmen,
greater time and effort is needed and progress is slower.

The West

The West, and particularly the West Coast area, follow the
eastern pattern. The Rocky Mountain region has, of course, the
fewest Negroes of any of the nation's regions. Moreover, relatively few airline employees are domiciled there, except at Denver. Hence the most significant for our purposes are the Pacific
Coast states.

In contrast to the Midwest area, our field sample for 1966
shows a higher percentage of Negroes than does the EEOC data
(Tables 24 and 25). In each case, however, the difference is not
large or probably not significant.

The West Coast area sample shows a slightly smaller overall
but relatively similar dispersion of Negroes by occupation. A
larger utilization of Negro office and clerical personnel but smaller
one in sales are indicated. Given the smaller percentage of Negroes living in the Pacific Coast states, their percentage is, in
many ways, the most impressive anywhere in the industry. It is
noteworthy that our previous studies of the aerospace industry
found that the West Coast, and particularly Southern California,
also had a high utilization of Negroes as compared with other

TABLE 24. Air Transport Industry
Employment by Race, Sex, and Occupational Group
West Region, 1966

Occupational Group	All Employees			Male			Female		
	Total	Negro	Percent Negro	Total	Negro	Percent Negro	Total	Negro	Percent Negro
Officials and managers	3,518	15	0.4	3,332	15	0.5	186	—	—
Professionals	7,608	13	0.2	7,494	13	0.2	114	—	—
Technicians	1,194	10	0.8	1,046	9	0.9	148	1	0.7
Sales workers	4,534	63	1.4	2,317	38	1.6	2,217	25	1.1
Office and clerical	6,880	184	2.7	3,291	138	4.2	3,589	46	1.3
Total white collar	23,734	285	1.2	17,480	213	1.2	6,254	72	1.2
Craftsmen	12,051	257	2.1	11,625	254	2.2	426	3	0.7
Operatives	3,691	463	12.5	3,614	462	12.8	77	1	1.3
Laborers	1,567	385	24.6	1,507	378	25.1	60	7	11.7
Service workers	5,429	340	6.3	1,761	286	16.2	3,668	54	1.5
Total blue collar	22,738	1,445	6.4	18,507	1,380	7.5	4,231	65	1.5
Total	46,472	1,730	3.7	35,987	1,593	4.4	10,485	137	1.3

Source: U.S. Equal Employment Opportunity Commission, *Job Patterns for Minorities and Women in Private Industry, 1966* (Washington: The Commission, 1968), Part II.

TABLE 25. *Air Transport Industry*
Percent Negro Employment by Occupational Group
West and West Coast Regions
1964, 1966, and 1968

Occupational Group	West			West Coast		
	1964	1966	1968	1964	1966	1968
Officials and managers	0.4	0.4	0.6	0.5	0.4	0.7
Professionals	0.1	0.2	0.3	0.1	0.2	0.3
Technicians	—	0.7	0.6	—	0.5	0.6
Sales workers	1.2	1.9	2.8	1.3	2.1	3.0
Office and clerical	2.8	4.0	6.0	3.3	4.6	6.6
Total white collar	1.2	1.6	2.4	1.3	1.9	2.6
Craftsmen	1.6	2.7	3.7	1.7	2.9	3.8
Operatives	13.0	12.4	12.0	14.6	14.3	14.0
Laborers	30.7	30.2	25.1	35.1	33.7	28.6
Service workers	9.1	7.1	7.5	8.8	7.0	7.2
Total blue collar	7.0	7.1	7.7	7.2	7.5	7.9
Total	4.1	4.4	5.0	4.3	4.7	5.3

Source: Appendix Tables A-19 to A-24.

regions, particularly in the better jobs.[47] Undoubtedly this has contributed both to the propensity of airline management to employ blacks and to the latter's qualifications and interest in airline jobs.

The South

In the South, the air transport industry, like most others, displays a racial-occupational employment pattern very different from that of other regions of the country. Table 26 shows the southern data for 1966 as reported to the EEOC. Table 27 summarizes the data from our field sample for the South and for the border states for 1964, 1966, and 1968. It will be seen that our field sample data for 1966 show a very slight upward bias for white collar employees. Differences, however, are so slight as to

47. Northrup, Rowan, *et al.*, *Negro Employment in Basic Industry*, Part Three, pp. 199-204.

TABLE 26. *Air Transport Industry*
Employment by Race, Sex, and Occupational Group
South Region, 1966

Occupational Group	All Employees			Male			Female		
	Total	Negro	Percent Negro	Total	Negro	Percent Negro	Total	Negro	Percent Negro
Officials and managers	5,973	8	0.1	5,714	8	0.1	259	—	—
Professionals	10,357	11	0.1	10,204	10	0.1	153	1	0.7
Technicians	1,505	7	0.5	1,378	7	0.5	127	—	—
Sales workers	10,762	41	0.4	5,067	17	0.3	5,695	24	0.4
Office and clerical	9,228	79	0.9	4,149	65	1.6	5,079	14	0.3
Total white collar	37,825	146	0.4	26,512	107	0.4	11,313	39	0.3
Craftsmen	22,378	441	2.0	22,254	441	2.0	124	—	—
Operatives	9,393	943	10.0	9,275	931	10.0	118	12	10.2
Laborers	2,470	1,094	44.3	2,359	995	42.2	111	99	89.2
Service workers	4,646	1,054	22.7	2,004	1,007	50.2	2,642	47	1.8
Total blue collar	38,887	3,532	9.1	35,892	3,374	9.4	2,995	158	5.3
Total	76,712	3,678	4.8	62,404	3,481	5.6	14,308	197	1.4

Source: U.S. Equal Employment Opportunity Commission, *Job Patterns for Minorities and Women in Private Industry, 1966* (Washington: The Commission, 1968), Part II.

TABLE 27. *Air Transport Industry*
Percent Negro Employment by Occupational Group
South Region and South Atlantic Border States
1964, 1966, and 1968

Occupational Group	South			South Atlantic Border States[a]		
	1964	1966	1968	1964	1966	1968
Officials and managers	*	0.1	0.5	—	—	0.8
Professionals	*	—	0.1	—	—	0.3
Technicians	—	0.1	0.3	—	—	—
Sales workers	0.3	1.2	1.8	1.3	2.4	3.8
Office and clerical	0.2	0.8	1.5	0.3	1.4	3.0
Total white collar	0.2	0.6	1.1	0.5	1.3	2.4
Craftsmen	0.3	0.5	0.7	0.1	1.0	1.0
Operatives	13.0	9.9	10.6	10.1	11.3	12.0
Laborers	51.3	64.5	57.8	62.1	63.8	52.0
Service workers	32.9	25.1	20.6	20.0	20.3	17.1
Total blue collar	8.4	9.1	9.1	10.4	13.4	13.5
Total	3.6	4.3	4.5	4.4	5.5	6.2

Source: Appendix Tables A-25 to A-30.

* Less than 0.05 percent.

[a] Area includes Delaware, Washington, D.C., Maryland, and northern Virginia.

indicate that our sample is representative and indeed very accurate.

The history of southern Negro airline employment, as set forth in Chapter III, has featured a larger percentage of Negroes employed than has been the case nationally, but this has been attributable to a greater utilization of Negroes in the low skilled jobs—indeed sufficient to offset a considerably smaller utilization of Negroes as craftsmen and white collar employees.

The southern syndrome continued through 1968 insofar as meager employment of Negroes in white collar or craftsmen jobs was concerned. By 1968, the overall figures for the region found a less than 2 percent representation in all white collar categories and less than one percent black craftsmen as well.

Negro white collar employment even as reservation agents or clerical workers has not made much progress in the South except in the border areas and in the large cities such as Atlanta, New Orleans, Miami, and Dallas. In the smaller locations, not only is the number of jobs available proportionately less, but turnover is lower too. Given past practice of employing only whites, this greatly reduces opportunities for Negroes. Moreover, in smaller southern locations concepts of equal employment opportunity have been accepted more slowly than elsewhere. Finally, the largest airlines have pushed fair employment, as we shall note, more than their smaller counterparts. Several southern regional carriers did little until prodded in the late 1960's by the federal government. Since the largest carriers generally have fewer employees and flights in small locations, their influence is not felt there to a substantial degree.

The southern craftsmen ratio reflects southern mores and the failure of the airlines having substantial craft employment there to overcome traditional employment practices. It is worthy of note that the airlines have done a substantially poorer job in recruiting Negro craftsmen in the South than has the aerospace industry, which in 1968 had a 3.2 percent black ratio in this key category, as compared with the airline industry's 0.7 percent.[48] The same training, care, and responsibility for life rests with craftsmen in both industries. One must conclude that the airline industry in the South has not made the same efforts at integration as has its manufacturing counterpart.

The failure of the industry in the South to improve its white collar and craftsman employment picture for blacks is the more serious because this area has also failed to increase the proportion of blacks in the lower rated jobs. Thus the Negro blue collar ratio in the South remained static between 1966 and 1968, while it expanded elsewhere. By 1968, the other regions were approaching the South's blue collar ratio and two subregions— Middle Atlantic and East North Central—exceeded it. The net effect of the southern area's failure to progress, qualitatively or quantitatively, proportionately with the rest of the country, left it by 1968 with the lowest overall percentage of Negro employment of any region whereas historically it boasted the highest.

Within the South, the northern border area of Delaware, Maryland, the District of Columbia, and the sections of Virginia

---

48. *Ibid.*, pp. 204-214.

where Washington airports are located shows the highest overall
and blue collar black ratios of anywhere in the nation. Yet even
in this segment of the South, little progress has been made by
the industry in employing Negro craftsmen. Somewhat greater
progress in white collar areas is evident in the border areas,
but not nearly as much as one might hope for, considering the
high percentage of Negro population there.

Female Employment by Region

In general, female employment follows the same regional pattern as total employment. Between 1964 and 1968, Negro females increased their percentage of total employment and of
total white collar employment in all regions. Nearly all of these
gains were concentrated in the sales (reservation agents and
stewardesses) and office and clerical groups. Some of the gains
in stewardess employment are also reflected in changes in the
service worker category. (See tables in Appendix A for detailed data.)

Table 28 compares the percent Negro employment by occupational group and region. It is quite apparent from these data
that much of the increase in Negro employment in recent years
is attributable to increased Negro female employment in the
categories noted. The high percentages shown in some of the
lower rated blue collar jobs involve only a few people and, read
without the data in the appendix tables, could be misleading. It
is in the two key white collar groups of sales and office and
clerical where the large numbers and the real gains are involved. Few females and even fewer Negro females are found in
the top three white collar categories.

Comparing the various regions with the United States percentage, we find, as was the situation in total employment, that
the Middle Atlantic, East North Central, and West Coast areas
all show a higher percentage of Negro females than does the
country as a whole. The South, and even the southern border
states lag, although the population percentage of Negroes therein
is higher than in other regions. Obviously, the heritage of discrimination and unequal employment opportunity must be the
reason for this situation. Moreover, the heritage of discrimination takes its toll. As one airlines personnel director noted, "The
factor of economic and educational handicaps of the Negro in
the South has often left them unprepared for competitive posi-

TABLE 28. Air Transport Industry

Percent Negro Female Employment by Occupational Group

12 Companies

United States and Regions, 1968

Occupational Group	Total United States	North-east	New England	Middle Atlantic	North Central	East North Central	West	West Coast	South	Southern Border
Officials and managers	0.6	0.7	—	0.8	1.1	1.4	0.9	1.0	—	—
Professionals	0.8	1.4	—	1.5	—	—	1.3	1.4	—	—
Technicians	1.1	1.5	—	1.6	—	—	4.3	5.4	—	—
Sales workers	3.8	5.2	2.5	5.9	5.8	6.7	2.8	2.9	2.0	4.2
Office and clerical	3.2	4.5	1.1	4.8	2.6	2.0	4.2	4.4	0.7	2.5
Total white collar	3.4	4.7	2.0	5.1	4.1	4.6	3.3	3.5	1.5	3.7
Craftsmen	2.1	—	—	—	—	—	5.6[a]	6.2[b]	—	—
Operatives	20.9	37.8	—	37.8	18.6	50.0	12.9	14.3	16.7	—
Laborers	45.7	9.1[c]	—	10.0[d]	40.8	48.8	6.7	6.7	90.3	—
Service workers	2.8	3.7	1.4	4.1	3.5	5.8	2.2	2.3	1.9	3.1
Total blue collar	3.5	4.1	1.4	4.5	4.3	7.4	2.3	2.4	4.9	3.1
Total	3.4	4.5	1.9	4.9	4.1	5.1	2.8	3.0	2.2	3.6

Source: Appendix tables of 1968 data.

Note: For regional definitions, see Table 11. Southern Border includes Delaware, Washington, D.C., Maryland, and northern Virginia.

[a] Three of 54.
[b] Three of 48.
[c] One of 11.
[d] One of 10.

tions. Example—a Negro hostess applicant who has been brought up and educated in a segregated society often makes a very poor impression in an employment interview, where her ability to project her personality and to communicate is so vitally important. This situation is changing, but [one] . . . should recognize this factor." [49]

The highest percentages of black women are found in the East North Central and West Coast areas. The former area leads because of what has already been noted—an effective recruiting job in the sales category, and an overconcentration of black women in the lowest skilled jobs. Noteworthy is the fact that the office and clerical percentage in the East North Central region is less than one-half that in the Middle Atlantic and West Coast areas and even below the total for the North Central and Southern Border areas. As previously discussed, airport and airline office location in the principal midwestern cities apparently lead black women to look for clerical jobs much closer to their homes in order to avoid long and expensive travel to work. This factor is more likely to affect the lowest rated white collar females than it does either blue collar or higher rated white collar groups—a fact noted in many of our previous studies.[50]

On the West Coast, the reverse seems to be true. The sales ratio for black females is low, the office and clerical ratio high. The reasons for this are not clear, other than that the airlines located on the West Coast must be doing a better job recruiting clerical help than reservation personnel.

The Middle Atlantic region has the most consistent pattern— 5.9 percent black female sales workers and 4.8 percent black female office and clerical. The overall percentage is lower than in two other regions but the cause is a lower concentration of Negro females in the lowest job classifications. The reasons are again clear: the early impact of state nondiscrimination legislation, the favorable location patterns near the concentration of Negro population, and the impact of the headquarters of four major carriers.

The picture in the South remains dismal, qualitatively and quantitatively. The only bright spot is a percentage of Negro female sales workers in the border states nearly equal to the

49. Letter dated June 12, 1970.

50. See, e.g., Northrup, Rowan, *et al.*, *op. cit.*, Part Two, pp. 89-96, Part Three, pp. 185-188, and Part Five, p. 450.

national average, albeit far below the population of the area. Certainly, the airline industry's employment in the South in 1968 was far below what one could term any reasonable standard, nor had it exhibited the progress that one could reasonably hope to expect. Our discussion below of individual airline policies will return to this subject.

CARRIER DIFFERENCES

We have noted on a number of occasions that the major carriers—United, Pan American, American, Trans World, and Eastern—are more advanced in their equal employment position than are the seven regional ones. Tables 29 and 30 compare the occupational data for these two groups for 1968.

Overall, the data do not reveal significant percentage differences. Thus 4.5 percent of the employees of the seven regional carriers were black in 1969 as were 4.9 percent of those of the five majors. Looking at Tables 29 and 30 more closely, however, we find the Negro employees of the seven regionals much more disproportionately concentrated in laboring jobs and much less represented in white collar jobs than was the case with the majors. Thus 40.4 percent of the laborers of the seven regionals were black, as compared with 19.9 percent of those of the majors. On the other hand, only 1.4 percent of the regionals' white collar employees and 1.9 percent of their craftsmen were Negroes as compared with 2.4 percent and 2.5 percent, respectively, for the majors.

Within the white collar group, significant differences are found in the sales worker and office and clerical categories, and in female white collar employment. An even greater disparity between the majors and the regionals would be shown if United classified its stewardesses as sales instead of service. The higher percentage of Negro "service workers" for the majors reflects this unfortunate classification system.

Table 31, which compares the percentage distribution by occupational group for the five majors and seven regionals, clearly shows the different racial employment patterns of the two groups. In both, the white collar/blue collar distributions of Negroes are substantially less favorable than are those for whites, as shown by the fact that whereas a majority of all employees are white collar employees, an overwhelming majority of Negroes are found in blue collar jobs.

TABLE 29. *Air Transport Industry*
Employment by Race, Sex, and Occupational Group
Five Major Carriers, 1968

Occupational Group	All Employees			Male			Female		
	Total	Negro	Percent Negro	Total	Negro	Percent Negro	Total	Negro	Percent Negro
Officials and managers	12,425	79	0.6	11,648	73	0.6	777	6	0.8
Professionals	25,958	83	0.3	25,156	76	0.3	802	7	0.9
Technicians	4,180	22	0.5	3,896	20	0.5	284	2	0.7
Sales workers	29,250	1,118	3.8	11,653	345	3.0	17,597	773	4.4
Office and clerical	27,188	1,054	3.9	12,232	540	4.4	14,956	514	3.4
Total white collar	99,001	2,356	2.4	64,585	1,054	1.6	34,416	1,302	3.8
Craftsmen	32,508	798	2.5	32,399	795	2.5	109	3	2.8
Operatives	14,527	1,900	13.1	14,414	1,862	12.9	113	38	33.6
Laborers	5,025	1,002	19.9	4,876	969	19.9	149	33	22.1
Service workers	16,178	2,123	13.1	4,580	1,751	38.2	11,598	372	3.2
Total blue collar	68,238	5,823	8.5	56,269	5,377	9.6	11,969	446	3.7
Total	167,239	8,179	4.9	120,854	6,431	5.3	46,385	1,748	3.8

Source:　Data in authors' possession.

Note:　Carriers are American, Eastern, Pan American, Trans World, and United.

TABLE 30. *Air Transport Industry*
Employment by Race, Sex, and Occupational Group
Seven Regional Carriers, 1968

Occupational Group	All Employees			Male			Female		
	Total	Negro	Percent Negro	Total	Negro	Percent Negro	Total	Negro	Percent Negro
Officials and managers	3,873	15	0.4	3,641	15	0.4	232	—	—
Professionals	7,286	11	0.2	7,155	11	0.2	131	—	—
Technicians	751	5	0.7	684	3	0.4	67	2	3.0
Sales workers	10,651	201	1.9	4,331	64	1.5	6,320	137	2.2
Office and clerical	5,094	146	2.9	1,496	74	4.9	3,598	72	2.0
Total white collar	27,655	378	1.4	17,307	167	1.0	10,348	211	2.0
Craftsmen	9,715	187	1.9	9,681	187	1.9	34	—	—
Operatives	5,799	247	4.3	5,725	246	4.3	74	1	1.4
Laborers	2,043	826	40.4	1,949	748	38.4	94	78	83.0
Service workers	8,637	791	9.2	2,857	685	24.0	5,780	106	1.8
Total blue collar	26,194	2,051	7.8	20,212	1,866	9.2	5,982	185	3.1
Total	53,849	2,429	4.5	37,519	2,033	5.4	16,330	396	2.4

Source: Data in authors' possession.

Note: Carriers are Braniff, Continental, Delta, National, Northeast, Northwest, Western.

TABLE 31.   *Air Transport Industry*
Percent Distribution by Race and Occupational Group
Five Major and Seven Regional Carriers, 1968

Occupational Group	Five Major Carriers		Seven Regional Carriers	
	Total	Negro	Total	Negr
Officials and managers	7.4	0.9	7.2	0.(
Professionals	15.5	1.0	13.5	0.!
Technicians	2.5	0.3	1.4	0.:
Salesworkers	17.5	13.7	19.8	8.:
Office and clerical	16.3	12.9	9.5	6.(
Total white collar	59.2	28.8	51.4	15.(
Craftsmen	19.4	9.8	18.0	7.'
Operatives	8.7	23.2	10.8	10.:
Laborers	3.0	12.2	3.8	34.
Service workers	9.7	26.0	16.0	32.
Total blue collar	40.8	71.2	48.6	84.
Total	100.0	100.0	100.0	100.(

Source: Tables 29 and 30.

Comparing black employment occupational distribution, how
ever, Table 31 shows that almost twice the percentage of Negro
employed by the majors are white collar personnel than is tl
case with the regionals. Indeed, if United's stewardesses we
included in sales, there probably would be more than a doul
ratio in favor of the majors. Noteworthy is the fact that
each of the white collar classifications as well as in the craft
man category, the black ratio for the majors exceeds that
the regionals, but in the three lowest blue collar groups the r
verse is true. There can be no doubt that the major airlines a
far ahead of their regional competitors in fair employme
practice.

Southern Regional Carrier Patterns

Some of the differences between the majors and the region:
are part of the already noted southern syndrome. Thus the thr
airlines with headquarters in the South—Braniff, Delta, and N

>nal—were quite slow to alter traditional employment prac-
:es. American Airlines, for example, began employing Negro
servation clerks in the Southwest in the late 1950's, and con-
1ued to do so despite individual pressures of some of its em-
oyees and customers, but Dallas-based Braniff did not move
reward until a decade later, and then only after a change in
vnership. Likewise Eastern moved far ahead of its southeast
vals, Delta and National, in integrating offices in cities in that
gion. Braniff now has a few black stewardesses and some reser-
.tion agents, but most of its Negro employees are in the bottom
bs.

One can, however, overdo blaming southern customs in these
atters. When Braniff took over a northern Midwest-based car-
ər in the World War II period, it was pressured by local of-
ials of the International Association of Machinists not to alter
e lily-white character of that carrier's maintenance force.
:aniff, however, continued to employ Negroes in the lower rated
bs as before. (At Braniff, it will be recalled, the United Auto-
obile Workers revoked the mechanics' charter because of dis-
imination and the local then affiliated with the IAM.)

Braniff has participated in the JOBS program of the National
.liance of Businessmen and has employed and trained the hard-
re unemployed for starting ground jobs. It has also offered a
ecial grooming, fashion, and makeup course for disadvantaged
rls, and it has been active in summer employment and school
otivation programs in Dallas. It has not yet succeeded in em-
oying Negro pilots although offers have been made; the men
ve accepted jobs with other airlines. Like other southern car-
ərs, Braniff feels that Negroes confined to segregated schools
e poorly trained and poorly equipped to deal with the pre-
minantly white public. To overcome these problems, Braniff
ployed a Negro stewardess supervisor and later made her as-
stant manager of the Dallas stewardess base. With another
egro hostess, she recruited at Negro colleges (Braniff ordi-
rily does not recruit hostesses at colleges) and helped to in-
ease Braniff's black hostess complement from 3 in 1969 to 22
1970.

Because of its location, Braniff's work force includes about as
any Mexican-Americans as Negroes. Its substantial efforts for
l minorities began in earnest in 1967. By 1970, its total minor-
* employment had risen 94 percent, its Negro employment, 54
rcent. During this period, its total employment increased

only 11 percent. Substantial qualitative improvements acco
panied this increased minority employment, and placed Bran
substantially ahead of the other southern based and most otl
regional carriers in this regard.

The South's largest and most profitable carrier, Delta *A*
Lines, is headquartered in Atlanta. Its policies were southe
and paternalistic. Segregation was followed in facilities and
Negroes were employed above the porter or "cleaner" classifi
tions before 1963. Then facility integration began under t
pressure of President Kennedy's President's Committee on Eq
Employment Opportunity. Some upgrading followed in 1965. *A*
firmative action to recruit Negroes began in 1967, again becaι
of government pressure, this time from PCEEO's successor, t
Office of Federal Contract Compliance.

In September 1970, the Southern Christian Leadership Cι
ference announced a boycott of Delta. At that time, Delta spok
men stated that the carrier employed 1,734 Negroes, who co
prised 8.3 percent of its work force. The bulk of these were ι
skilled, including a large number hired under the JOBS pι
gram of the National Alliance of Businessmen. Included al
however, were these Negro personnel:

2 pilots and 2 more in training
52 stewardesses
89 reservation agents
22 mechanics
8 traffic agents
3 station agents
one lead reservations agent
182 service agents [51]

National is one of the three airlines with heavy employme
in the Miami, Florida area. Its headquarters are there, alo
with Eastern's overhaul base and a major headquarters, a
Pan American's regional headquarters for South American ope
tions. Both Pan American and Eastern were active in the JOβ
program in the Miami area by September 1968, with prograι
and government contracts to train and to employ hardcore ι

---

51. "SCLC Plans Boycott of Delta Air Lines," *Washington Post*, Septemβ
    3, 1970. Boycotts of this type by SCLC have been unsuccessful agaiι
    major industries. Only if an easily picketed store or transit service
    involved, can such a boycott inflict real damage.

employed blacks. National was not involved in this or previous affirmative action activities. Indeed National lagged in all civil rights activities until forced into action by the OFCC. It was the last of the twelve carriers studied to employ a Negro stewardess, it has no Negro pilots, its Negroes are heavily concentrated in the bottom occupations, and its percentage of Negroes remains low.

Northern and Western Regional Carriers

Northeast is the smallest and least profitable of the twelve carriers. Until it won routes to Washington and the South, it served primarily the New England area where the Negro population is small but also served New York City. In 1966, the Massachusetts Commission Against Discrimination made a study of employment discrimination in the transportation industry. The report was highly critical of one airline while praising the others serving Boston.[52] The airline which is found "not interested in doing its share" we have identified as Northeast. Despite its New England location, it followed until very recently a hiring pattern similar to the southern airlines. It now has employed Negro stewardesses, reservation agents, and others and this has somewhat altered its racial profile.

The federal government has given approval to Northeast to merge with Northwest, headquartered in the Minneapolis-St. Paul area. Northwest flies the northern route across the country and to Alaska, Hawaii, and Japan, and also connects some of its key cities to Florida. An early Plans for Progress company, it employs the largest percentage of its workers in a location where few Negroes dwell. Nevertheless, by energetic recruiting in such areas as Chicago, where a large percentage of blacks are available, by participation in NAB-JOBS programs, and by other means, Northwest has been able to raise its share of Negroes above some carriers which serve more heavily black populated areas. Nevertheless, its minority representation remains very low.

Western Air Lines operates primarily on the West Coast, although it also serves a few other areas. Its main employment areas are Los Angeles, San Francisco, and Seattle, where its overhaul base is located. Western's attitude toward equal em-

---

52. Unpublished report of the Commonwealth of Massachusetts Commission Against Discrimination, pp. 14, 24.

ployment opportunity may best be termed "conservative." Like most other regional carriers, it was slow to initiate any affirmative action, nor did it take advantage of expansion periods in the mid-1960's to increase substantially its minority employment. It has no Negro pilots, but it does employ a few black stewardesses and some black reservation agents, with a distribution of Negro employment within the system similar to the other regional carriers. It has, however, employed a much higher percentage of Mexican-Americans in recent years. Western will merge with American if the CAB approves.

Continental Air Lines, the last of the seven regional carriers in our sample, operates from Chicago west, with most of its flights west of the Mississippi, and its headquarters in Los Angeles. Known for imaginative leadership, Continental adopted a program in 1967 of seeking employees through minority and community agencies. These groups are furnished detailed job descriptions and a weekly list of job openings. To further its integration program, Continental eliminated all tests that did not pertain directly to job qualifications, lowered educational requirements on entry jobs, and took an aggressive and active part in the NAB-JOBS program to train and to retrain hardcore minorities. The result has been a substantial increase in Continental's black employment. Continental also employs Negro stewardesses, reservation agents, and blacks in similar capacities. It does not, however, employ any Negro pilots.

THE MAJOR CARRIERS

It is the major carriers, as we have noted, who have led the way toward integration. All five, plus Northwest, joined Plans for Progress at an early date. They have participated in the NAB-JOBS program, instituted center city hiring, made special efforts to recruit Negroes, and otherwise reacted to the demands of the civil rights era much more fully than most of their regional rivals. Being larger and more visible, they reacted to avoid problems with civil rights groups or with government. National in scope and not southern based, they were not constricted by ideology or locational bias. Expanding rapidly in the 1960's—a situation no longer true—they had opportunities for Negroes and a need for their services. As a group, they led the industry in integration. Individually, each followed policies designed to increase the numbers of Negro employees and to improve their occupational standings.

United Air Lines

United acquired a dying Capital Airlines in 1961 and thereby became the nation's largest carrier. Under the leadership of the late Charles M. Mason, one of industry's outstanding personnel executives, United pioneered a hardcore training program before the National Alliance of Businessmen was created. In recent years, it has expanded this training and concentrated on re-cruiting and upgrading Negroes and other minorities for the better jobs.

Prior to the early 1960's, however, United's black employees, like those of other carriers, were concentrated in the bottom jobs. Affirmative action began in 1964 "to help convince the Negro community that any qualified applicant has an opportunity with United." [53] This included a survey of Negroes on the payroll to determine their upgrading potential (which produced some de-served promotions, but the usual refusal of sky caps to accept new jobs because of their high earnings); recruiting at Negro institutions and through Negro agencies; and special programs to make Negroes eligible for airline jobs.

One special program began at Chicago's O'Hare field in 1966 when United persuaded the U.S. Department of Labor to under-write a training program for potential ramp servicemen recruited "with less than the usual qualifications." This in turn led to United taking a large role in the NAB-JOBS program, training 420 hardcore and disadvantaged persons in various cities as of February 1970 not only for ramp service jobs, but for a variety of other entry positions, clerical as well as blue collar. During 1970, some 500 additional workers are expected to be trained and hired through these programs. [54]

Meanwhile United's recruiting has greatly added to its black complement among stewardesses, reservation and sales personnel, and others. In August 1969, former President George E. Keck reported that United employed eight Negro pilots, three Negro flight instructors, and 99 Negro stewardesses; 211 "minority

---

53. Statement of W. A. Patterson, former (and long) President of United Air Lines, quoted by Stephen Habbes, *Company Experiences with Negro Employment*, Personnel Policy Study No. 201 (New York: National Industrial Conference Board, 1966), Vol. II, p. 79. This study contains an account of United's program to that date.

54. "Black Employment at United Doubles in 5 Years," *Pittsburgh Courier*, February 7, 1970; "Air Line to Train 500 Jobless," *Chicago Tribune*, August 27, 1969.

members of management" (other than Negroes are included as
minorities) ; and 640 minority sales employees.[55] The number of
Negro stewardesses at United was close to 150 by mid-1970, and
substantial increases have also occurred in Negro reservation
and ticket agents and other sales employees.

United uses its black employees and successful graduates of
training programs to recruit and to sell the fact that opportunities do indeed exist for black citizens at United. Equal employment coordinators are responsible for monitoring the affirmative
action programs at all major locations, and a careful check is
maintained at United's central office by the personnel section to
see that company policies are followed. Data showing United's
progress toward fair employment through December 1969, as
released by the company are set forth in Table 32. Layoffs in
1970 could have hurt the new black workers.

Trans World Airlines

TWA, a major factor both in domestic and international air
transportation, passed Pan American in 1969 to become the
country's second largest air carrier. TWA's progress in equal
employment opportunity has also increased substantially in re
cent years. Although it employed one of the first three Negro
stewardesses, TWA was slow to push affirmative action. As a
result, its racial posture compared unfavorably to its major com
petitors as late as 1966.

Today, however, that is no longer the case. By energetic action
TWA has increased the number and proportion of Negroes in its
employ and upgraded their status so that it has few peers, if
any, within the industry. TWA has 16 Negro pilots, the largest
number of any carrier; it employs about 150 stewardesses—approximately the same number as United; its Negro representation in sales and reservations is steadily increasing; and it has
made progress in placing Negroes in positions of managerial
responsibility.

TWA has made this progress because of its new, innovative programs. For example, in San Francisco, TWA took the
leading part in a series of special six-week programs held in the
evening with TWA instructors on how to act in an employment
interview, how to react to testing, what is a work environment,
what employers expect, and how to groom. Of the original 16

---

55. *United Air Lines Shield*, Vol. XXXVIII (August 1969), p. 20.

TABLE 32. *Air Transport Industry*
Employment by Race and Occupational Group
United Air Lines, 1965-1969

Employment	1965	1966	1967	1968	December 1969
Total Work Force					
Total employees	36,383	41,516	45,249	49,120	52,207
Total minority employees	2,926	3,862	4,454	5,353	6,222
Total Negro employees	1,789	2,235	2,600	3,113	3,634
Percent minority employees	8.0	9.3	9.8	10.9	11.9
Percent Negro employees	4.9	5.4	5.7	6.3	7.0
Minority Work Force					
Management, professional, and technical		122	165	203	237
Office and clerical		393	477	591	715
Skilled		639	693	757	857
Sales		311	465	589	790
Semiskilled, unskilled, and service		2,388	2,656	3,213	3,623
Negro Work Force					
Management, professional, and technical		33	45	66	82
Office and clerical		186	236	284	371
Skilled		170	304	232	278
Sales		208	323	426	590
Semiskilled, unskilled, and service		1,659	1,792	2,105	2,313

Source: *Pittsburgh Courier*, February 7, 1970, based on data from United Air Lines, Inc.

who took the course, TWA hired 7 as reservation agents and other companies most of the rest.

In New York, TWA participates in the Urban League course for black secretaries and has employed several graduates. It has established employment offices in Harlem, the Jamaica section of Brooklyn, and the Watts area of Los Angeles in order to employ persons there. And it has participated in major cities in the NAB-JOBS and summer employment programs.

TWA's international experience contributed to its capacity to advance in minority employment and to train the hardcore. Already by necessity a multinational and multiracial company, it developed a cadet program to train disadvantaged Italian youths in Rome in 1950. Using this experience, TWA developed a similar program in San Francisco for minorities and then adopted it at other major locations.

Perhaps most significantly, TWA's top officers have made a practice in recent years of setting hiring goals and seeing that they are met. Thus in 1969, employment of at least 100 Negro stewardesses was decided as a policy, and that policy more than met. Severe losses, however, caused layoffs in 1970.

Partially as a result of a charge brought to the Equal Employment Opportunity Commission, TWA has altered or abolished tests for a number of its lower rated occupations.[56] Previously, the company vice-president for industrial relations anticipated these changes by stating:

The personnel requirements to meet our own growth represent one of our most pressing problems. They will become increasingly acute in the years immediately ahead as our passenger traffic triples and cargo service jumps at least six-fold. Therefore, we are taking a whole new approach to our employment procedures. This approach includes a re-look at such policies and procedures in terms of the job seeking problems of minority people—including those seriously disadvantaged—the so-called hard core group. Our pre-employment requirements are being reviewed. We are re-evaluating and considering modification of the usual tests of education, character and police record.

We already have instituted pilot programs in these areas at some locations. We are considering bringing into our organization on a controlled basis small numbers of Negroes without high school diplomas and even with police records. We will consider hiring them

56. *Trans World Airlines, Inc.* v. *Equal Employment Opportunity Commission*, U.S. District Court, W.D., Mo., Civil Action No. 17663-3, January 20, 1970.

with scores below the usual test minima but high enough to fulfill certain duties and hopefully to progress to higher positions.

We are doing so, again, not only because it is right, but because, like other companies, and as practical people, we feel we can no longer afford not to program the Negro and other minorities into the very fiber of our organizational setup and into the mainstream of our national economy.[57]

Pan American World Airways

Pan American, America's pioneer and largest international airline, connects major American cities with foreign countries all around the world, but unlike TWA, does not carry passengers between cities within the continental United States. Because of greater competition on its routes from both other national and foreign flag carriers, among other reasons, Pan American dropped from the second to the third position among American carriers in 1969.

Pan American has large concentrations of employees at the gateway cities of New York, Miami, and San Francisco, and smaller numbers at numerous other cities. Pan American's Negro employment, as its general employment, is concentrated in these three cities. Like the other major airlines, Pan American's black labor force was heavily concentrated in the unskilled laboring and service jobs prior to 1960. In the early 1960's, Pan American, the first airline to join Plans for Progress, began efforts to expand Negro employment, with most accretions at first again in the lower skill jobs. Then in the latter half of the decade, great emphasis was put on upgrading and employment of Negroes in the higher skilled jobs. By the beginning of 1969, it employed three Negro pilots, two Negro flight engineers, one Negro flight instructor, and about thirty Negro stewardesses. The last group has since been substantially expanded.

On many of its international flights, Pan American requires stewardesses and cabin attendants to be bilingual. It has a large force of Spanish-Americans since it serves Puerto Rico, South America, and Spain, but the language requirements limit opportunities for Negro Americans, who are as unlikely to have acquired good language skills in high school as their white counterparts.

---

57. David J. Crombie, "A Flight Plan for Job Opportunities," remarks before the Annual Meeting of the Urban League of Kansas City, May 8, 1968, pp. 5-6.

In 1968, Pan American employed 250 hardcore at its three largest locations and trained them for jobs as fleet and aircraft servicemen, keypunch and duplicating machine operators, and supply clerks. Pan American also participated in the 1968 summer employment program for disadvantaged youths. To employ these disadvantaged personnel, Pan American waived the high school education requirement which it otherwise maintains for employment.

Since mid-1969, Pan American has been suffering financial losses and laying off personnel—200 pilots and flight engineers and 300 ground personnel were discharged in an economy drive reported in October 1969.[58] By March 1970, employment had been reduced by 2,000.[59] Except in high turnover areas such as the stewardess function, it is not likely that Pan American's Negro labor force can expand until its economic climate improves. Because of its sizable proportion of Spanish-Americans, as well as its Negro employees, Pan American employs a higher proportion of minorities than any other airline.

American Airlines

American Airlines is the second largest domestic and fourth largest air carrier of the United States. Its main routes connect the major cities of the country on East-West flights and in the Southwest; its overhaul base is in Tulsa, Oklahoma. American's black employees were originally concentrated in the lower classifications, but the company has done some imaginative work to alter this.

American, for example, was the first to employ Negroes in white collar jobs in the Southwest. Like the other major airlines, it has participated in the NAB-JOBS program and employed the graduates in a wide variety of semiskilled and white collar jobs in New York, Tulsa, Chicago, Detroit, Los Angeles, and other key cities on its routes. About 350 hardcore were trained in 1968-1969. Three of American's programs, however, deserve special mention.

In order to increase its black stewardess complement, American in 1968 began a program of joint recruitment with the Urban League of Greater New York. The American and Urban League

---

58. *Wall Street Journal*, October 20, 1969. Further layoffs were announced in 1971.

59. Stephen M. Aug, "Pan Am's Holders Told Airline Faces 3 Difficult Years," *Washington Evening Star*, March 26, 1970.

representatives agreed on standards for accepting Negro candidates. The League then prescreened candidates and referred good prospects for interviews by American personnel at the League's offices. Fourteen of the first 32 were accepted for training. The program has been expanded to Boston, Chicago, Los Angeles, San Francisco, and Washington.

To further its recruitment potential in center city areas, American sponsored the "American Youth Beauty Workshop," a group of black and white stewardesses trained to help girls in impoverished neighborhoods prepare for better jobs. The workshop toured major cities along American's routes giving young girls instructions in posture, diction, care of clothing, and grooming. With the help of cosmetic firms, American supplied each teenager with lipstick, skin cleansers, make-up, hair preparations, and other beauty aids. The stewardesses then instructed the participants in the use of cosmetics. Classes were held in store fronts, apartment house basements, schoolrooms, and office buildings in hardcore neighborhoods.

Perhaps the most significant action of American is its cooperative program with Negro Airmen International, Inc., which claims a membership of 175 to 200 Negro pilots from 13 states, the Bahamas, and the Caribbean. Its members also include Negro flyers in the armed services, some of whom are on active duty in Vietnam. Negro Airmen International has aided American in the recruitment of Negro pilots, of whom it now has ten. Cooperating with its own Negro pilots and with NAI, American has followed a long range program to induce black youngsters to pursue a pilot career. Contacts are now made by American whenever Negro pilot training is a possibility, including private schools and the five predominantly black schools where Air Force ROTC units exist.

In Philadelphia, the Urban Coalition established an "Academy of Aerospace and Aviation" at a high school in an effort to satisfy the interest of Negro youngsters in aviation. Electronics for aviation is taught at a General Electric space facility while TWA and United provide passenger service training. David Harris, one of the country's few black captains—an American pilot—visited the school to explain his job.[60] Pilot training, however, is beyond such enterprises. American's support and encouragement of Negro Air Force ROTC units and its encourage-

60. Paul C. Heintz, "Aviation Hakes Move for Black Education," *Philadelphia Sunday Bulletin*, April 12, 1970.

ment of existing Negro pilots to upgrade their skills and to qual
ify for airline pilot training remains a more hopeful but equally
long range route to a greater share of pilot jobs for Negroes.

Eastern Air Lines

Although Eastern operates in many parts of the country, it.
major routes are along the East Coast and its two largest areas
of employment are in the New York City area, where its execu
tive offices are located, and in Miami, where its overhaul base is
situated. Eastern, the smallest of the Big Five, has had difficulty
for many years in operating profitably. This has, of course
affected its capacity to expand employment or to offer better
opportunities for minorities. As late as the mid-1960's Eastern
like the other airlines, had most of its black employees in the
lowest rated jobs. (Having a number of South American and
Caribbean routes, Eastern has had a much higher percentage of
Spanish-Americans in its salaried groups for many years.)

Until recently, Eastern also lacked a well-developed personnel
department for staff assistance and policy formulation. Never
theless, it has pursued significant policies. Eastern was the first
carrier to employ Negroes in such Southeast city ticket counters
as Atlanta, Birmingham, Charlotte, Columbia, Mobile, and New
Orleans. It was also the first carrier to establish a special section
in its personnel department devoted entirely to developing and
administering corporate equal employment policies and to employ
qualified Negroes in its key regional personnel offices with not
only equal employment but a total personnel function.

Traveling Eastern's routes, one notices a substantially higher
percentage of black reservation and stewardess personnel than
heretofore existed. In 1969, Eastern employed six Negro pilots

Eastern and Pan American have cooperated in National Al
liance of Businessmen activity in Miami, and Eastern employed
disadvantaged youths in 13 cities in 1968. Eastern also has par
ticipated in the NAB-JOBS program in 17 cities and pledged 250
jobs for its hardcore in 1968 and 370 in 1969. Moreover, East
ern has successfully recruited, trained, and employed the dis
advantaged as reservation agents, ticket office agents, and cus
tomer service agents, as well as in the lower rated blue collar
jobs.

Comment on Airline Differences

The review of the individual airline experiences indicates some of the problems remaining as well as the progress made toward equal employment in the airline industry. In some cases, managements have dragged their feet; in others, they have accepted the challenges with enthusiasm. In all cases, problems remain.

There is, first of all, the extant educational gap between blacks and whites, and with it the economic gap. Despite great progress, Negro educational and economic attainments remain substantially below those of whites. Given the high requirements for key airline positions and their close relationship to performance and safety, it follows inexorably that any group disadvantaged educationally and economically will have a difficult time qualifying for jobs in air transportation. It also follows, however, that special efforts must be made—in short, affirmative action—if the disadvantaged groups are to have any reasonable number of jobs. Our survey of the individual airlines shows clearly that those carriers which, for whatever reason, made an effort to expand Negro employment in a realistic, well considered, and organized manner, had by far the greatest success in accomplishing these goals. Our analysis also demonstrates the significance of the role of government.

THE GOVERNMENT IMPACT

From its inception, the airlines have had, by necessity, a close relationship to the government. Federal funds support pilot and mechanic training, airplane design, airport construction and expansion, and air safety and navigational aids. Many airlines owe their incubation and survival to government subsidies and payments for carrying the mail. And in time of crisis, the airlines' equipment is at governmental disposal.

Historically, government aid to airlines was given without regard to racial employment policies. In transportation, employment mores which confined Negroes to menial jobs and especially proscribed their use in positions of prestige and public safety were adopted by the airlines without serious thought or challenge. A government which did not train Negroes to fly in the armed services could hardly fault an airline for having an all-white pilot crew. Government policy prior to and during most of World War II supported the then exclusionist and discriminatory racial

policies of the airlines. And government policy further hinder
improvement by placing the air transport industry under t
Railway Labor Act, which has been historically administered
further the aims of some of the most discriminatory unions th
have existed in America.

The first note of change came during and after World War
The armed forces commenced training Negro pilots, and th
state commissions against discrimination, particularly the pione
New York one, opened a legal attack on airline employment d
crimination. Slowly the bastions began to fall: the late 195(
brought the first Negro reservation personnel and stewardess
and the early 1960's affirmed the legal right of state comm
sions to jurisdiction over airline employment.

The stage was thus set for the 1960's and affirmative actic
Unquestionably, government action was necessary. For tho
airlines whose managements desired to progress, a governme
role assured that they would not be subject to reprisal, boyco
or other injury by opponents of civil rights cases. For two, a
possibly four others, a threat of contract rejection was requir
to alter existing patterns of operation. It is likely that continu
government surveillance is essential if progress is to contin(
although it is difficult to believe that committed managemen(
like those of United, TWA, and American, would backtrack
this stage.

CHAPTER VI

Policy Determinants, Problems, and the Future

By way of conclusion, we shall review the determining factors of airline racial policies previously discussed, pointing up the problems and problem areas. Finally, we shall estimate the immediate and long range future of Negro employment in the industry.

THE RACIAL EMPLOYMENT MORES

We have written of the racial employment mores of the transportation industries and their deleterious impact on Negro employment in airlines—the elite transportation industry. At least until the early 1950's these were, in fact, the community mores. Airlines are above all subject to consumer pressures. As one airline executive noted:

We are a truly customer-oriented service industry. Our contact with the travelling public is regular, constant and frequently in circumstances requiring the best in tact, personality, intelligence, flexibility of response and good judgment. We do not have large assembly lines involving the repetitive performance of routine tasks.

There is also in our industry the constant and overriding preoccupation with safety.[61]

One would expect an industry in such circumstances to be in tune with the community. The airlines were so when they were employing Negroes only in menial jobs; they were also conforming when they commenced altering their policies, and later when affirmative action policies were developed and put into practice.

It is likewise not surprising that the major airlines as a group have gone substantially beyond their regional counterparts in

---

61. David J. Crombie, "A Flight Plan for Job Opportunities," remarks before the Annual Meeting of the Urban League of Kansas City, May 8, 1968, p. 6.

equal employment activity. They are more visible, less suscep
tible to regional pressures yet more likely to be pressured b
government, and more attuned to the realities of employmen
needs in large metropolitan areas. They also have greater re
sources to expend both on special employment policies and o
special sales policies which can reap the rewards of affirmativ
action. One would expect that the majors will continue to lea
the way in civil rights matters in the years ahead.

THE GOVERNMENTAL ROLE

Little needs to be repeated here about the governmental rol
over what was stated in the previous chapter. The armed force
are the prime source of pilots and a major source of mechanics
Negro progress in these two key groups will depend almost a
much on the recruitment and training by the armed forces a
by the airlines. But progress generally in some carriers require
continuous monitoring by government. Since there is no evidenc
of slackening in this regard, continued progress is likely.

THE DEMAND FOR LABOR

No matter what policies exist, progress except in rare circum
stances in fair employment is at best hesitant and slight unles
employment is expanding and jobs are being created. Durin
the 1960's, when the airlines (and most industries) made th
greatest progress in employing Negroes, total airline jobs in
creased by one-third. Since mid-1969, however, traffic has slowe
and most airlines have cut back on their number of employees
Layoffs have affected all job classifications.

As long as this situation lasts, increased Negro employmen
can occur only in those jobs where turnover is high, particularl
the female positions such as stewardess, some reservation an
ticket agent work, and in entry jobs. The industry is very senior
ity oriented, and no new persons are employed if anyone is lai
off. Moreover, promotions are governed largely by seniority also
so that in times of declining employment, advancement up th
occupational ladder is drastically slowed.

There is, however, no reason to suppose that the industry i
at its peak. Continued long term growth is forecast, and wit
that growth is likely to come continued improvement in the par
ticipation of black workers. The demand for labor, therefore

must be viewed as a positive factor despite temporary negative impacts.

THE JOB STRUCTURE

In general, we have found that the greater skill content which an industry requires, the smaller, other things being equal, is likely to be the proportion of Negroes found in that industry. This is the unfortunate corollary of the fact that Negroes as a group are less well educated, trained, and experienced in industry than whites. Certainly the airline industry requires higher skill, intelligence, and good judgment from its employees than does the average industry. Moreover, much of that skill and preparation cannot be compromised because of the necessary constant and overriding preoccupation with safety.

Given the needs of the industry and the history of racial discrimination, underemployment, and lack of opportunities for Negroes, it is obvious that the qualifications of Negroes for airline jobs will continue to be a problem for years to come. Pilot training affords the classic example of an occupation where progress will be slow for that reason, but many other positions involving skills and customer contacts cannot absorb the black worker faster than educational equality is attained.

On the other hand, there remain scores of jobs at the lower end of the scale where such exalted education and training are not required. The success of the major airlines in training the so-called hardcore for these jobs attests to the fact that the airlines do not need high educational attainments for all positions. This fact indicates that all airlines might well reexamine the qualifications of such positions, as many already have, and possibly lower them without deterioration of service or safety.

INTRAPLANT MOBILITY

The airlines as an industry place much stress on loyalty and seniority. Long service is typical in the industry and long service is well rewarded. Promotion from within is a religion sanctified by management and solidified by unions. Thus new employees must start at the bottom of the line. Since Negroes in the better jobs are largely new, they are today clustered in the lower ranks of categories in which they are found.

Job movement follows narrow rather than broad lines. The nature of the industry is such that widely different functions are necessary but experience or competence in one function does not fit a person for advancement in another. The most experienced mechanic is not qualified by seniority to be a pilot, or even a reservations agent or cabin attendant. Intraplant mobility is thus along occupational lines or groups and likely to be vertical rather than horizontal. Organization of unions along craft lines pursuant to the Railway Labor Act institutionalized these limitations to movement.

In such a situation the person who has hired in, or in hiring been directed to, a particular job category has in effect made a decision which is compounded over time. If his choice or assignment leads to an excellent job at the end of a seniority hierarchy, all is well. But the job category may result in a deadend job. Negroes in the past have been largely directed to deadends. Since by now their rates are good and their seniority high in these jobs, even where change to a different seniority line is possible it would not be financially rewarding for many years.

Seniority is not the sole criterion of advancement in the industry's occupational structures. Competence must be proved and earned where safety is a factor; seniority alone does not make a mechanic. But here again, education and training pay off and Negroes disproportionately lack both.

Training is significant too, but not initial training. With the possible exception of the aerospace industry, the airlines probably spend more money on formal training than does any other industry. More than $125 million was spent on training in 1968 exclusive of training equipment, plant, or other nonpersonnel items. Table 33 shows the breakdown of these training costs. Almost two-thirds was for pilot and stewardess training and about 15 percent for maintenance personnel training. Huge training costs are expended despite the fact that pilots and mechanics are qualified in their crafts prior to being employed.

If the airlines were forced to train pilots and all mechanics prior to their acquisition of their basic skills, such training costs would be substantially increased. Obviously, they prefer to select the already trained and to improve their competence with further training. Thus the emphasis is on the latter training except for recent activities with hardcore and others hired for lower skilled jobs.

All this reinforces the belief that Negroes will progress very slowly in the pilot and mechanic positions. The greater fluidity of stewardesses and reservation clerks and agents make these

TABLE 33. *Air Transport Industry
Training Costs by Department
1968*

Department	Payroll Costs	Percent of Total
Flight training	$ 82,079,000	65.3
Maintenance	18,584,000	14.8
Aircraft and traffic servicing	19,373,000	15.4
Promotion, reservation, and sales	3,269,000	2.6
General administrative	882,000	0.7
Servicing administration	1,577,000	1.2
Total	$125,764,000	100.0

Source: William J. Grinker *et al., Climbing the Job Ladder: A Study of
Employee Advancement in Eleven Industries* (New York: E. F.
Shelly and Company, 1970), p. 148.

the areas where progress is likely to be much greater. But a
disproportionate number of blacks, educationally disadvantaged,
are likely to be found in the lower rated jobs throughout the
1970's.

LOCATIONAL AND REGIONAL PATTERNS

Locational patterns of the airline industry are favorable for
Negro employment in some ways, but probably predominantly
unfavorable. The existence of center city headquarters and ticket
offices are favorable, but airports and overhaul centers, as well
as many central offices, are by necessity located away from the
centers of Negro population. Given the typical lack of public
transit facilities in most cities, this inhibits employment of clerical personnel, especially women, and of lower rated personnel
generally. It has little or no effect on those such as pilots and
stewardesses who fly anywhere, anytime.

The South has had a significantly different historical pattern,
and one that is now much less advantageous, than is the case
in other regions. Negroes were once both more heavily concentrated in the lowest rated jobs but more numerously employed
in the South than elsewhere. Now only the former is the case.
The southern syndrome is exacerbated by the failure of regional

airlines there to move as rapidly as the majors toward fair employment, as well as by regional patterns, prejudices, and educational deficiencies.

UNION IMPACT

The dominant unions in the industry have not been, with the possible exception of the Transport Workers Union, very helpful to Negro employment; the International Association of Machinists and the Brotherhood of Railway and Airline Clerks, among others, have been obstructionistic. The latter two brought with them to the air transport industry the biases which have been so typical and virulent among railroad unions. Although they now admit Negroes, their policies are certainly more negative than positive. Whether unions are positive or negative, however, their policies have not had major significance in the industry's racial policies. The dynamics of action rest with the carriers. It is their racial policies which are the most significant and in fact determinative. Unions may help, or pull or haul or balk; or they may solidify opposition, or work to overcome that opposition. The employment function, however, rests with the carriers. How well they carry out that function, develop affirmative programs, or resist efforts to reduce affirmative action, remain the crucial determinants of what action will occur.

PROBLEMS OF THE CIVIL RIGHTS ERA

The problems of introducing Negroes into the better airline jobs have been surprisingly few. When United brought Negro stewardesses into its training school, one white girl left. That was apparently the high point of protest from fellow employees or customers. In another incident, however, an exstewardess sued United after being discharged for refusing to change her so-called African hairdo. United settled the case for $5,000 alleged lost wages after a hearing before the Illinois Fair Employment Practice Commission, but the complainant declined United's offer of reinstatement.[62]

---

62. "Natural Hairdo Stewardess in Fight for Her Job," *Chicago Sun-Times,* August 13, 1970; David Gilbert, "$5,000 to Stewardess Fired for Afro Hairdo," *Chicago Tribune,* September 3, 1970. One may question whether state and federal civil rights legislation was intended to deny an airline the right to establish grooming regulations.

Negro reservation personnel have had few problems or slights. Negro pilots report that they are received on the basis of professional competence. Passengers in our experience accept Negro stewardesses as a matter of course and usually have no idea of the pilots' color.

As in most industries, employment of the hardcore has meant problems. Many have to be taught the mores of industrial society. Many others seize the opportunity for what it is and make the most of it. Turnover is usually slightly better than for those employed off the streets in a tight labor market.

The employment of the hardcore often causes severe tensions in the labor force and this has occurred in the airlines too. Negroes already employed fear, often correctly, that all blacks will be considered "hardcore." Both whites and Negroes who "made it" without special attention resent the double standard that is often necessary in the first few weeks to maintain the once disadvantaged on the payroll and to teach them the prerequisites of job behavior. Yet these problems have been relatively minor. United overcame the opposition by offering refresher and upgrading courses to those already employed. Other carriers utilized counseling, special meetings, and other communication media to maintain calm and encourage cooperation. All in all, the problems were slight.

CONCLUDING REMARKS

From an overwhelmingly white industry, the airlines have moved toward meaningful integration. Progress in jobs with high turnover is likely to continue to move forward at a good pace. In the pilot position, especially, but also in the mechanic craft, progress will be slow, filtered by rigorous selection and training by the industry after that of the armed forces. Government policy might well concentrate on necessary recruiting and utilization of Negroes in these capacities in the armed forces as a significant long range step toward greater civilian integration in the air transport industry.

As the 1970's commenced, the airlines were in a slump, laying off personnel and reducing service. Forecasts, however, remain optimistic. The potential for increased participation in the industry will depend heavily on the accuracy of forecasts which predict another expansionist decade for the industry.

Appendix

BASIC STATISTICAL TABLES

TABLE A-1. *Air Transport Industry*

Employment by Race, Sex, and Occupational Group
8 Companies, United States, 1964

Occupational Group	All Employees			Male			Female		
	Total	Negro	Percent Negro	Total	Negro	Percent Negro	Total	Negro	Percent Negro
Officials and managers	10,659	26	0.2	10,045	24	0.2	614	2	0.3
Professionals	18,237	21	0.1	17,722	18	0.1	515	3	0.6
Technicians	2,717	6	0.2	2,446	6	0.2	271	—	—
Sales workers	21,087	278	1.3	10,227	114	1.1	10,860	164	1.5
Office and clerical	23,287	445	1.9	10,665	270	2.5	12,622	175	1.4
Total white collar	75,987	776	1.0	51,105	432	0.8	24,882	344	1.4
Craftsmen	29,384	389	1.3	29,293	389	1.3	91	—	—
Operatives	11,303	1,247	11.0	11,201	1,214	10.8	102	33	32.4
Laborers	2,846	772	27.1	2,751	760	27.6	95	12	12.6
Service workers	12,541	1,948	15.5	5,221	1,756	33.6	7,320	192	2.6
Total blue collar	56,074	4,356	7.8	48,466	4,119	8.5	7,608	237	3.1
Total	132,061	5,132	3.9	99,571	4,551	4.6	32,490	581	1.8

Source: Data in authors' possession.

TABLE A-2. *Air Transport Industry*
Employment by Race, Sex, and Occupational Group
12 Companies, United States, 1966

Occupational Group	All Employees			Male			Female		
	Total	Negro	Percent Negro	Total	Negro	Percent Negro	Total	Negro	Percent Negro
Officials and managers	14,412	45	0.3	13,433	42	0.3	979	3	0.3
Professionals	27,288	43	0.2	26,711	41	0.2	577	2	0.3
Technicians	3,525	18	0.5	3,123	15	0.5	402	3	0.7
Sales workers	31,587	732	2.3	13,484	238	1.8	18,103	494	2.7
Office and clerical	28,977	707	2.4	12,968	432	3.3	16,009	275	1.7
Total white collar	105,789	1,545	1.5	69,719	768	1.1	36,070	777	2.2
Craftsmen	36,224	609	1.7	36,118	609	1.7	106	—	—
Operatives	18,356	1,871	10.2	18,238	1,837	10.1	118	34	28.8
Laborers	3,941	1,329	33.7	3,732	1,246	33.4	209	83	39.7
Service workers	19,534	2,479	12.7	6,639	2,140	32.2	12,895	339	2.6
Total blue collar	78,055	6,288	8.1	64,727	5,832	9.0	13,328	456	3.4
Total	183,844	7,833	4.3	134,446	6,600	4.9	49,398	1,233	2.5

Source: Data in authors' possession.

TABLE A-3. *Air Transport Industry*

Employment by Race, Sex, and Occupational Group

12 Companies, United States, 1968

Occupational Group	All Employees			Male			Female		
	Total	Negro	Percent Negro	Total	Negro	Percent Negro	Total	Negro	Percent Negro
Officials and managers	16,298	94	0.6	15,289	88	0.6	1,009	6	0.6
Professionals	33,244	94	0.3	32,311	87	0.3	933	7	0.8
Technicians	4,931	27	0.5	4,580	23	0.5	351	4	1.1
Sales workers	39,901	1,319	3.3	15,984	409	2.6	23,917	910	3.8
Office and clerical	32,282	1,200	3.7	13,728	614	4.5	18,554	586	3.2
Total white collar	126,656	2,734	2.2	81,892	1,221	1.5	44,764	1,513	3.4
Craftsmen	42,223	985	2.3	42,080	982	2.3	143	3	2.1
Operatives	20,326	2,147	10.6	20,139	2,108	10.5	187	39	20.9
Laborers	7,068	1,828	25.9	6,825	1,717	25.2	243	111	45.7
Service workers	24,815	2,914	11.7	7,437	2,436	32.8	17,378	478	2.8
Total blue collar	94,432	7,874	8.3	76,481	7,243	9.5	17,951	631	3.5
Total	221,088	10,608	4.8	158,373	8,464	5.3	62,715	2,144	3.4

Source: Data in authors' possession.

TABLE A-4. Air Transport Industry
Employment by Race, Sex, and Occupational Group
7 Companies, Northeast Region, 1964

Occupational Group	All Employees			Male			Female		
	Total	Negro	Percent Negro	Total	Negro	Percent Negro	Total	Negro	Percent Negro
Officials and managers	3,259	14	0.4	3,037	12	0.4	222	2	0.9
Professionals	5,617	14	0.2	5,301	12	0.2	316	2	0.6
Technicians	876	5	0.6	794	5	0.6	82	—	—
Sales workers	5,241	157	3.0	2,354	59	2.5	2,887	98	3.4
Office and clerical	8,069	249	3.1	3,572	132	3.7	4,497	117	2.6
Total white collar	23,062	439	1.9	15,058	220	1.5	8,004	219	2.7
Craftsmen	5,739	200	3.5	5,734	200	3.5	5	—	—
Operatives	3,296	285	8.6	3,275	271	8.3	21	14	66.7
Laborers	661	138	20.9	658	138	21.0	3	—	—
Service workers	4,083	522	12.8	1,717	453	26.4	2,366	69	2.9
Total blue collar	13,779	1,145	8.3	11,384	1,062	9.3	2,395	83	3.5
Total	36,841	1,584	4.3	26,442	1,282	4.8	10,399	302	2.9

Source: Data in authors' possession.

Note: For regional definitions, see Table 11.

TABLE A-5. Air Transport Industry
Employment by Race, Sex, and Occupational Group
10 Companies, Northeast Region, 1966

Occupational Group	All Employees			Male			Female		
	Total	Negro	Percent Negro	Total	Negro	Percent Negro	Total	Negro	Percent Negro
Officials and managers	3,926	24	0.6	3,639	22	0.6	287	2	0.7
Professionals	6,783	17	0.3	6,564	16	0.2	219	1	0.5
Technicians	1,039	11	1.1	899	10	1.1	140	1	0.7
Sales workers	8,456	329	3.9	3,414	96	2.8	5,042	233	4.6
Office and clerical	9,559	309	3.2	4,383	163	3.7	5,176	146	2.8
Total white collar	29,763	690	2.3	18,899	307	1.6	10,864	383	3.5
Craftsmen	6,375	238	3.7	6,370	238	3.7	5	—	—
Operatives	4,259	355	8.3	4,234	343	8.1	25	12	48.0
Laborers	876	197	22.5	871	197	22.6	5	—	—
Service workers	4,955	537	10.8	1,974	429	21.7	2,981	108	3.6
Total blue collar	16,465	1,327	8.1	13,449	1,207	9.0	3,016	120	4.0
Total	46,228	2,017	4.4	32,348	1,514	4.7	13,880	503	3.6

Source: Data in authors' possession.

TABLE A-6. *Air Transport Industry*
Employment by Race, Sex, and Occupational Group
10 Companies, Northeast Region, 1968

Occupational Group	All Employees			Male			Female		
	Total	Negro	Percent Negro	Total	Negro	Percent Negro	Total	Negro	Percent Negro
Officials and managers	4,354	37	0.8	4,063	35	0.9	291	2	0.7
Professionals	8,724	42	0.5	8,360	37	0.4	364	5	1.4
Technicians	1,455	14	1.0	1,322	12	0.9	133	2	1.5
Sales workers	10,569	485	4.6	4,028	144	3.6	6,541	341	5.2
Office and clerical	10,530	491	4.7	4,401	215	4.9	6,129	276	4.5
Total white collar	35,632	1,069	3.0	22,174	443	2.0	13,458	626	4.7
Craftsmen	7,661	366	4.8	7,654	366	4.8	7	—	—
Operatives	4,571	415	9.1	4,534	401	8.8	37	14	37.8
Laborers	2,300	337	14.7	2,289	336	14.7	11	1	9.1
Service workers	6,170	682	11.1	2,106	530	25.2	4,064	152	3.7
Total blue collar	20,702	1,800	8.7	16,583	1,633	9.8	4,119	167	4.1
Total	56,334	2,869	5.1	38,757	2,076	5.4	17,577	793	4.5

Source: Data in authors' possession.

TABLE A-7. Air Transport Industry
Employment by Race, Sex, and Occupational Group
5 Companies, New England Region, 1964

Occupational Group	All Employees			Male			Female		
	Total	Negro	Percent Negro	Total	Negro	Percent Negro	Total	Negro	Percent Negro
Officials and managers	222	—	—	205	—	—	17	—	—
Professionals	308	—	—	306	—	—	2	—	—
Technicians	2	—	—	2	—	—	—	—	—
Sales workers	708	4	0.6	343	1	0.3	365	3	0.8
Office and clerical	312	2	0.6	168	1	0.6	144	1	0.7
Total white collar	1,552	6	0.4	1,024	2	0.2	528	4	0.8
Craftsmen	402	3	0.7	401	3	0.7	1	—	—
Operatives	457	8	1.8	457	8	1.8	—	—	—
Laborers	53	3	5.7	53	3	5.7	—	—	—
Service workers	165	49	29.7	78	49	62.8	87	—	—
Total blue collar	1,077	63	5.8	989	63	6.4	88	—	—
Total	2,629	69	2.6	2,013	65	3.2	616	4	0.6

Source: Data in authors' possession.

Note: For regional definitions, see Table 11.

TABLE A-8. *Air Transport Industry*
Employment by Race, Sex, and Occupational Group
8 Companies, New England Region, 1966

Occupational Group	All Employees			Male			Female		
	Total	Negro	Percent Negro	Total	Negro	Percent Negro	Total	Negro	Percent Negro
Officials and managers	381	1	0.3	339	1	0.3	42	—	—
Professionals	391	1	0.3	391	1	0.3	—	—	—
Technicians	62	2	3.2	58	2	3.4	4	—	—
Sales workers	1,441	24	1.7	555	7	1.3	886	17	1.9
Office and clerical	1,200	10	0.8	848	7	0.8	352	3	0.9
Total white collar	3,475	38	1.1	2,191	18	0.8	1,284	20	1.6
Craftsmen	924	14	1.5	924	14	1.5	—	—	—
Operatives	690	13	1.9	690	13	1.9	—	—	—
Laborers	168	33	19.6	168	33	19.6	—	—	—
Service workers	232	57	24.6	115	57	49.6	117	—	—
Total blue collar	2,014	117	5.8	1,897	117	6.2	117	—	—
Total	5,489	155	2.8	4,088	135	3.3	1,401	20	1.4

Source: Data in authors' possession.

TABLE A-9. Air Transport Industry
Employment by Race, Sex, and Occupational Group
9 Companies, New England Region, 1968

Occupational Group	All Employees			Male			Female		
	Total	Negro	Percent Negro	Total	Negro	Percent Negro	Total	Negro	Percent Negro
Officials and managers	493	—	—	467	—	—	26	—	—
Professionals	969	1	0.1	928	1	0.1	41	—	—
Technicians	139	1	0.7	130	1	0.8	9	—	—
Sales workers	2,109	45	2.1	808	13	1.6	1,301	32	2.5
Office and clerical	822	8	1.0	361	3	0.8	461	5	1.1
Total white collar	4,532	55	1.2	2,694	18	0.7	1,838	37	2.0
Craftsmen	1,132	15	1.3	1,132	15	1.3	—	—	—
Operatives	653	16	2.5	653	16	2.5	—	—	—
Laborers	772	61	7.9	771	61	7.9	1	—	—
Service workers	670	68	10.1	115	60	52.2	555	8	1.4
Total blue collar	3,227	160	5.0	2,671	152	5.7	556	8	1.4
Total	7,759	215	2.8	5,365	170	3.2	2,394	45	1.9

Source: Data in authors' possession.

TABLE A-10. *Air Transport Industry*
Employment by Race, Sex, and Occupational Group
7 Companies, Middle Atlantic Region, 1964

Occupational Group	All Employees			Male			Female		
	Total	Negro	Percent Negro	Total	Negro	Percent Negro	Total	Negro	Percent Negro
Officials and managers	3,037	14	0.5	2,832	12	0.4	205	2	1.0
Professionals	5,309	14	0.3	4,995	12	0.2	314	2	0.6
Technicians	874	5	0.6	792	5	0.6	82	—	—
Sales workers	4,533	153	3.4	2,011	58	2.9	2,522	95	3.8
Office and clerical	7,757	247	3.2	3,404	131	3.8	4,353	116	2.7
Total white collar	21,510	433	2.0	14,034	218	1.6	7,476	215	2.9
Craftsmen	5,337	197	3.7	5,333	197	3.7	4	—	—
Operatives	2,839	277	9.8	2,818	263	9.3	21	14	66.7
Laborers	608	135	22.2	605	135	22.3	3	—	—
Service workers	3,918	473	12.1	1,639	404	24.6	2,279	69	3.0
Total blue collar	12,702	1,082	8.5	10,395	999	9.6	2,307	83	3.6
Total	34,212	1,515	4.4	24,429	1,217	5.0	9,783	298	3.0

Source: Data in authors' possession.

Note: For regional definitions, see Table 11.

TABLE A-11. *Air Transport Industry*
Employment by Race, Sex, and Occupational Group
9 Companies, Middle Atlantic Region, 1966

Occupational Group	All Employees			Male			Female		
	Total	Negro	Percent Negro	Total	Negro	Percent Negro	Total	Negro	Percent Negro
Officials and managers	3,545	23	0.6	3,300	21	0.6	245	2	0.8
Professionals	6,392	16	0.3	6,173	15	0.2	219	1	0.5
Technicians	977	9	0.9	841	8	1.0	136	1	0.7
Sales workers	7,015	305	4.3	2,859	89	3.1	4,156	216	5.2
Office and clerical	8,359	299	3.6	3,535	156	4.4	4,824	143	3.0
Total white collar	26,288	652	2.5	16,708	289	1.7	9,580	363	3.8
Craftsmen	5,451	224	4.1	5,446	224	4.1	5	—	—
Operatives	3,569	342	9.6	3,544	330	9.3	25	12	48.0
Laborers	708	164	23.2	703	164	23.3	5	—	—
Service workers	4,723	480	10.2	1,859	372	20.0	2,864	108	3.8
Total blue collar	14,451	1,210	8.4	11,552	1,090	9.4	2,899	120	4.1
Total	40,739	1,862	4.6	28,260	1,379	4.9	12,479	483	3.9

Source: Data in authors' possession.

TABLE A-12. *Air Transport Industry*
Employment by Race, Sex, and Occupational Group 9 Companies, Middle Atlantic Region, 1968

Occupational Group	All Employees			Male			Female		
	Total	Negro	Percent Negro	Total	Negro	Percent Negro	Total	Negro	Percent Negro
Officials and managers	3,861	37	1.0	3,596	35	1.0	265	2	0.8
Professionals	7,755	41	0.5	7,432	36	0.5	323	5	1.5
Technicians	1,316	13	1.0	1,192	11	0.9	124	2	1.6
Sales workers	8,460	440	5.2	3,220	131	4.1	5,240	309	5.9
Office and clerical	9,708	483	5.0	4,040	212	5.2	5,668	271	4.8
Total white collar	31,100	1,014	3.3	19,480	425	2.2	11,620	589	5.1
Craftsmen	6,529	351	5.4	6,522	351	5.4	7	—	—
Operatives	3,918	399	10.2	3,881	385	9.9	37	14	37.8
Laborers	1,528	276	18.1	1,518	275	18.1	10	1	10.0
Service workers	5,500	614	11.2	1,991	470	23.6	3,509	144	4.1
Total blue collar	17,475	1,640	9.4	13,912	1,481	10.6	3,563	159	4.5
Total	48,575	2,654	5.5	33,392	1,906	5.7	15,183	748	4.9

Source: Data in authors' possession.

TABLE A-13. *Air Transport Industry*
Employment by Race, Sex, and Occupational Group
7 Companies, North Central Region, 1964

Occupational Group	All Employees			Male			Female		
	Total	Negro	Percent Negro	Total	Negro	Percent Negro	Total	Negro	Percent Negro
Officials and managers	2,207	3	0.1	2,086	3	0.1	121	—	—
Professionals	3,412	—	—	3,329	—	—	83	—	—
Technicians	382	1	0.3	353	1	0.3	29	—	—
Sales workers	4,027	57	1.4	2,084	21	1.0	1,943	36	1.9
Office and clerical	6,555	69	1.1	2,826	34	1.2	3,729	35	0.9
Total white collar	16,583	130	0.8	10,678	59	0.6	5,905	71	1.2
Craftsmen	6,175	42	0.7	6,157	42	0.7	18	—	—
Operatives	2,670	269	10.1	2,656	261	9.8	14	8	57.1
Laborers	881	127	14.4	853	127	14.9	28	—	—
Service workers	2,882	473	16.4	1,041	423	40.6	1,841	50	2.7
Total blue collar	12,608	911	7.2	10,707	853	8.0	1,901	58	3.1
Total	29,191	1,041	3.6	21,385	912	4.3	7,806	129	1.7

Source: Data in authors' possession.

Note: For regional definitions, see Table 11.

TABLE A-14. *Air Transport Industry*
Employment by Race, Sex, and Occupational Group
10 Companies, North Central Region, 1966

Occupational Group	All Employees			Male			Female		
	Total	Negro	Percent Negro	Total	Negro	Percent Negro	Total	Negro	Percent Negro
Officials and managers	2,787	5	0.2	2,578	4	0.2	209	1	0.5
Professionals	4,908	9	0.2	4,787	9	0.2	121	—	—
Technicians	591	1	0.2	514	—	—	77	1	1.3
Sales workers	5,973	167	2.8	2,663	45	1.7	3,310	122	3.7
Office and clerical	7,504	119	1.6	3,045	58	1.9	4,459	61	1.4
Total white collar	21,763	301	1.4	13,587	116	0.9	8,176	185	2.3
Craftsmen	6,866	50	0.7	6,846	50	0.7	20	—	—
Operatives	4,077	442	10.8	4,051	433	10.7	26	9	34.6
Laborers	974	174	17.9	923	158	17.1	51	16	31.4
Service workers	3,759	542	14.4	1,083	431	39.8	2,676	111	4.1
Total blue collar	15,676	1,208	7.7	12,903	1,072	8.3	2,773	136	4.9
Total	37,439	1,509	4.0	26,490	1,188	4.5	10,949	321	2.9

Source: Data in authors' possession.

TABLE A-15. *Air Transport Industry*
Employment by Race, Sex, and Occupational Group
10 Companies, North Central Region, 1968

Occupational Group	All Employees			Male			Female		
	Total	Negro	Percent Negro	Total	Negro	Percent Negro	Total	Negro	Percent Negro
Officials and managers	3,148	12	0.4	2,964	10	0.3	184	2	1.1
Professionals	5,620	10	0.2	5,430	10	0.2	190	—	—
Technicians	762	2	0.3	714	2	0.3	48	—	—
Sales workers	8,134	377	4.6	3,279	93	2.8	4,855	284	5.8
Office and clerical	8,145	200	2.5	3,094	67	2.2	5,051	133	2.6
Total white collar	25,809	601	2.3	15,481	182	1.2	10,328	419	4.1
Craftsmen	8,294	88	1.1	8,269	88	1.1	25	—	—
Operatives	4,452	484	10.9	4,393	473	10.8	59	11	18.6
Laborers	1,541	263	17.1	1,492	243	16.3	49	20	40.8
Service workers	4,246	601	14.2	1,059	490	46.3	3,187	111	3.5
Total blue collar	18,533	1,436	7.7	15,213	1,294	8.5	3,320	142	4.3
Total	44,342	2,037	4.6	30,694	1,476	4.8	13,648	561	4.1

Source: Data in authors' possession.

TABLE A-16. Air Transport Industry
Employment by Race, Sex, and Occupational Group
7 Companies, East North Central Region, 1964

Occupational Group	All Employees			Male			Female		
	Total	Negro	Percent Negro	Total	Negro	Percent Negro	Total	Negro	Percent Negro
Officials and managers	1,305	3	0.2	1,207	3	0.2	98	—	—
Professionals	2,047	—	—	1,974	—	—	73	—	—
Technicians	137	1	0.7	121	1	0.8	16	—	—
Sales workers	3,421	55	1.6	1,702	21	1.2	1,719	34	2.0
Office and clerical	3,495	41	1.2	1,386	26	1.9	2,109	15	0.7
Total white collar	10,405	100	1.0	6,390	51	0.8	4,015	49	1.2
Craftsmen	1,610	18	1.1	1,610	18	1.1	—	—	—
Operatives	2,140	247	11.5	2,127	239	11.2	13	8	61.5
Laborers	483	111	23.0	466	111	23.8	17	—	—
Service workers	1,512	353	23.3	688	309	44.9	824	44	5.3
Total blue collar	5,745	729	12.7	4,891	677	13.8	854	52	6.1
Total	16,150	829	5.1	11,281	728	6.5	4,869	101	2.1

Source: Data in authors' possession.

Note: For regional definitions, see Table 11.

TABLE A-17. *Air Transport Industry*
Employment by Race, Sex, and Occupational Group
9 Companies, East North Central Region, 1966

Occupational Group	All Employees			Male			Female		
	Total	Negro	Percent Negro	Total	Negro	Percent Negro	Total	Negro	Percent Negro
Officials and managers	1,770	5	0.3	1,596	4	0.3	174	1	0.6
Professionals	3,262	9	0.3	3,162	9	0.3	100	—	—
Technicians	307	1	0.3	252	—	—	55	1	1.8
Sales workers	4,987	160	3.2	2,111	42	2.0	2,876	118	4.1
Office and clerical	4,090	78	1.9	1,491	45	3.0	2,599	33	1.3
Total white collar	14,416	253	1.8	8,612	100	1.2	5,804	153	2.6
Craftsmen	1,886	19	1.0	1,886	19	1.0	—	—	—
Operatives	3,184	375	11.8	3,166	366	11.6	18	9	50.0
Laborers	541	153	28.3	505	137	27.1	36	16	44.4
Service workers	1,945	430	22.1	635	331	52.1	1,310	99	7.6
Total blue collar	7,556	977	12.9	6,192	853	13.8	1,364	124	9.1
Total	21,972	1,230	5.6	14,804	953	6.4	7,168	277	3.9

Source: Data in authors' possession.

TABLE A-18. *Air Transport Industry*
Employment by Race, Sex, and Occupational Group
9 Companies, East North Central Region, 1968

Occupational Group	All Employees			Male			Female		
	Total	Negro	Percent Negro	Total	Negro	Percent Negro	Total	Negro	Percent Negro
Officials and managers	2,009	12	0.6	1,861	10	0.5	148	2	1.4
Professionals	3,414	6	0.2	3,276	6	0.2	138	—	—
Technicians	411	1	0.2	385	1	0.3	26	—	—
Sales workers	6,747	363	5.4	2,575	85	3.3	4,172	278	6.7
Office and clerical	4,264	111	2.6	1,477	56	3.8	2,787	55	2.0
Total white collar	16,845	493	2.9	9,574	158	1.7	7,271	335	4.6
Craftsmen	2,071	25	1.2	2,068	25	1.2	3	—	—
Operatives	3,635	450	12.4	3,617	441	12.2	18	9	50.0
Laborers	737	207	28.1	696	187	26.9	41	20	48.8
Service workers	2,228	473	21.2	676	383	56.7	1,552	90	5.8
Total blue collar	8,671	1,155	13.3	7,057	1,036	14.7	1,614	119	7.4
Total	25,516	1,648	6.5	16,631	1,194	7.2	8,885	454	5.1

Source: Data in authors' possession.

TABLE A-19. *Air Transport Industry*
Employment by Race, Sex, and Occupational Group
7 Companies, West Region, 1964

Occupational Group	All Employees			Male			Female		
	Total	Negro	Percent Negro	Total	Negro	Percent Negro	Total	Negro	Percent Negro
Officials and managers	1,788	8	0.4	1,671	8	0.5	117	—	—
Professionals	4,576	5	0.1	4,534	5	0.1	42	—	—
Technicians	497	—	—	462	—	—	35	—	—
Sales workers	3,085	36	1.2	1,609	23	1.4	1,476	13	0.9
Office and clerical	4,157	117	2.8	2,213	97	4.4	1,944	20	1.0
Total white collar	14,103	166	1.2	10,489	133	1.3	3,614	33	0.9
Craftsmen	7,083	113	1.6	7,077	113	1.6	6	—	—
Operatives	2,046	265	13.0	2,008	263	13.1	38	2	5.3
Laborers	785	241	30.7	737	236	32.0	48	5	10.4
Service workers	3,711	339	9.1	1,111	296	26.6	2,600	43	1.7
Total blue collar	13,625	958	7.0	10,933	908	8.3	2,692	50	1.9
Total	27,728	1,124	4.1	21,422	1,041	4.9	6,306	83	1.3

Source: Data in authors' possession.

Note: For regional definitions, see Table 11.

TABLE A-20. *Air Transport Industry*
Employment by Race, Sex, and Occupational Group
11 Companies, West Region, 1966

Occupational Group	All Employees			Male			Female		
	Total	Negro	Percent Negro	Total	Negro	Percent Negro	Total	Negro	Percent Negro
Officials and managers	2,750	10	0.4	2,532	10	0.4	218	—	—
Professionals	7,436	17	0.2	7,345	16	0.2	91	1	1.1
Technicians	743	5	0.7	679	4	0.6	64	1	1.6
Sales workers	5,154	96	1.9	2,339	49	2.1	2,815	47	1.7
Office and clerical	5,607	226	4.0	2,777	169	6.1	2,830	57	2.0
Total white collar	21,690	354	1.6	15,672	248	1.6	6,018	106	1.8
Craftsmen	9,710	259	2.7	9,682	259	2.7	28	—	—
Operatives	3,183	394	12.4	3,166	391	12.3	17	3	17.6
Laborers	1,141	345	30.2	1,060	339	32.0	81	6	7.4
Service workers	7,324	523	7.1	2,241	439	19.6	5,083	84	1.7
Total blue collar	21,358	1,521	7.1	16,149	1,428	8.8	5,209	93	1.8
Total	43,048	1,875	4.4	31,821	1,676	5.3	11,227	199	1.8

Source: Data in authors' possession.

TABLE A-21. Air Transport Industry
Employment by Race, Sex, and Occupational Group
11 Companies, West Region, 1968

Occupational Group	All Employees			Male			Female		
	Total	Negro	Percent Negro	Total	Negro	Percent Negro	Total	Negro	Percent Negro
Officials and managers	3,265	20	0.6	3,030	18	0.6	235	2	0.9
Professionals	9,925	34	0.3	9,770	32	0.3	155	2	1.3
Technicians	1,187	7	0.6	1,141	5	0.4	46	2	4.3
Sales workers	7,293	202	2.8	3,057	85	2.8	4,236	117	2.8
Office and clerical	6,794	409	6.0	3,213	260	8.1	3,581	149	4.2
Total white collar	28,464	672	2.4	20,211	400	2.0	8,253	272	3.3
Craftsmen	11,541	422	3.7	11,487	419	3.6	54	3	5.6
Operatives	3,544	427	12.0	3,513	423	12.0	31	4	12.9
Laborers	1,949	489	25.1	1,859	483	26.0	90	6	6.7
Service workers	10,208	769	7.5	2,821	606	21.5	7,387	163	2.2
Total blue collar	27,242	2,107	7.7	19,680	1,931	9.8	7,562	176	2.3
Total	55,706	2,779	5.0	39,891	2,331	5.8	15,815	448	2.8

Source: Data in authors' possession.

TABLE A-22. Air Transport Industry
Employment by Race, Sex, and Occupational Group
6 Companies, West Coast Region, 1964

Occupational Group	All Employees			Male			Female		
	Total	Negro	Percent Negro	Total	Negro	Percent Negro	Total	Negro	Percent Negro
Officials and managers	1,521	8	0.5	1,413	8	0.6	108	—	—
Professionals	3,857	3	0.1	3,821	3	0.1	36	—	—
Technicians	444	—	—	420	—	—	24	—	—
Sales workers	2,498	33	1.3	1,252	22	1.8	1,246	11	0.9
Office and clerical	3,527	115	3.3	1,879	96	5.1	1,648	19	1.2
Total white collar	11,847	159	1.3	8,785	129	1.5	3,062	30	1.0
Craftsmen	6,656	111	1.7	6,650	111	1.7	6	—	—
Operatives	1,749	255	14.6	1,712	253	14.8	37	2	5.4
Laborers	670	235	35.1	622	230	37.0	48	5	10.4
Service workers	3,358	296	8.8	963	255	26.5	2,395	41	1.7
Total blue collar	12,433	897	7.2	9,947	849	8.5	2,486	48	1.9
Total	24,280	1,056	4.3	18,732	978	5.2	5,548	78	1.4

Source: Data in authors' possession.

Note: For regional definitions, see Table 11.

TABLE A-23. Air Transport Industry
Employment by Race, Sex, and Occupational Group
10 Companies, West Coast Region, 1966

Occupational Group	All Employees			Male			Female		
	Total	Negro	Percent Negro	Total	Negro	Percent Negro	Total	Negro	Percent Negro
Officials and managers	2,366	10	0.4	2,182	10	0.5	184	—	—
Professionals	6,279	13	0.2	6,196	12	0.2	83	1	1.2
Technicians	588	3	0.5	537	2	0.4	51	1	2.0
Sales workers	4,215	90	2.1	1,843	45	2.4	2,372	45	1.9
Office and clerical	4,869	223	4.6	2,394	168	7.0	2,475	55	2.2
Total white collar	18,317	339	1.9	13,152	237	1.8	5,165	102	2.0
Craftsmen	8,993	259	2.9	8,965	259	2.9	28	—	—
Operatives	2,616	373	14.3	2,599	370	14.2	17	3	17.6
Laborers	996	336	33.7	916	330	36.0	80	6	7.5
Service workers	6,370	448	7.0	1,876	367	19.6	4,494	81	1.8
Total blue collar	18,975	1,416	7.5	14,356	1,326	9.2	4,619	90	1.9
Total	37,292	1,755	4.7	27,508	1,563	5.7	9,784	192	2.0

Source: Data in authors' possession.

TABLE A-24. *Air Transport Industry*
Employment by Race, Sex, and Occupational Group
10 Companies, West Coast Region, 1968

Occupational Group	All Employees			Male			Female		
	Total	Negro	Percent Negro	Total	Negro	Percent Negro	Total	Negro	Percent Negro
Officials and managers	2,763	19	0.7	2,557	17	0.7	206	2	1.0
Professionals	8,825	30	0.3	8,681	28	0.3	144	2	1.4
Technicians	1,028	6	0.6	991	4	0.4	37	2	5.4
Sales workers	5,979	180	3.0	2,425	78	3.2	3,554	102	2.9
Office and clerical	5,972	397	6.6	2,826	258	9.1	3,146	139	4.4
Total white collar	24,567	632	2.6	17,480	385	2.2	7,087	247	3.5
Craftsmen	10,944	420	3.8	10,896	417	3.8	48	3	6.2
Operatives	2,924	409	14.0	2,896	405	14.0	28	4	14.3
Laborers	1,641	469	28.6	1,552	463	29.8	89	6	6.7
Service workers	8,914	642	7.2	2,287	489	21.4	6,627	153	2.3
Total blue collar	24,423	1,940	7.9	17,631	1,774	10.1	6,792	166	2.4
Total	48,990	2,572	5.3	35,111	2,159	6.1	13,879	413	3.0

Source: Data in authors' possession.

TABLE A-25. Air Transport Industry
Employment by Race, Sex, and Occupational Group
8 Companies, South Region, 1964

Occupational Group	All Employees			Male			Female		
	Total	Negro	Percent Negro	Total	Negro	Percent Negro	Total	Negro	Percent Negro
Officials and managers	3,405	1	*	3,251	1	*	154	—	—
Professionals	4,632	2	*	4,558	1	*	74	1	1.4
Technicians	962	—	—	837	—	—	125	—	—
Sales workers	8,734	28	0.3	4,180	11	0.3	4,554	17	0.4
Office and clerical	4,506	10	0.2	2,054	7	0.3	2,452	3	0.1
Total white collar	22,239	41	0.2	14,880	20	0.1	7,359	21	0.3
Craftsmen	10,387	34	0.3	10,325	34	0.3	62	—	—
Operatives	3,291	428	13.0	3,262	419	12.8	29	9	31.0
Laborers	519	266	51.3	503	259	51.5	16	7	43.8
Service workers	1,865	614	32.9	1,352	584	43.2	513	30	5.8
Total blue collar	16,062	1,342	8.4	15,442	1,296	8.4	620	46	7.4
Total	38,301	1,383	3.6	30,322	1,316	4.3	7,979	67	0.8

Source: Data in authors' possession.

Note: For regional definitions, see Table 11.

* Less than 0.05 percent.

TABLE A-26. *Air Transport Industry*
Employment by Race, Sex, and Occupational Group
10 Companies, South Region, 1966

Occupational Group	All Employees			Male			Female		
	Total	Negro	Percent Negro	Total	Negro	Percent Negro	Total	Negro	Percent Negro
Officials and managers	4,949	6	0.1	4,684	6	0.1	265	—	—
Professionals	8,161	—	—	8,015	—	—	146	—	—
Technicians	1,152	1	0.1	1,031	1	0.1	121	—	—
Sales workers	12,004	140	1.2	5,068	48	0.9	6,936	92	1.3
Office and clerical	6,307	53	0.8	2,763	42	1.5	3,544	11	0.3
Total white collar	32,573	200	0.6	21,561	97	0.4	11,012	103	0.9
Craftsmen	13,273	62	0.5	13,220	62	0.5	53	—	—
Operatives	6,837	680	9.9	6,787	670	9.9	50	10	20.0
Laborers	950	613	64.5	878	552	62.9	72	61	84.7
Service workers	3,496	877	25.1	1,341	841	62.7	2,155	36	1.7
Total blue collar	24,556	2,232	9.1	22,226	2,125	9.6	2,330	107	4.6
Total	57,129	2,432	4.3	43,787	2,222	5.1	13,342	210	1.6

Source: **Data** in authors' possession.

TABLE A-27. Air Transport Industry

Employment by Race, Sex, and Occupational Group

10 Companies, South Region, 1968

Occupational Group	All Employees			Male			Female		
	Total	Negro	Percent Negro	Total	Negro	Percent Negro	Total	Negro	Percent Negro
Officials and managers	5,531	25	0.5	5,232	25	0.5	299	—	—
Professionals	8,975	8	0.1	8,751	8	0.1	224	—	—
Technicians	1,527	4	0.3	1,403	4	0.3	124	—	—
Sales workers	13,905	255	1.8	5,620	87	1.5	8,285	168	2.0
Office and clerical	6,813	100	1.5	3,020	72	2.4	3,793	28	0.7
Total white collar	36,751	392	1.1	24,026	196	0.8	12,725	196	1.5
Craftsmen	14,727	109	0.7	14,670	109	0.7	57	—	—
Operatives	7,759	821	10.6	7,699	811	10.5	60	10	16.7
Laborers	1,278	739	57.8	1,185	655	55.3	93	84	90.3
Service workers	4,191	862	20.6	1,451	810	55.8	2,740	52	1.9
Total blue collar	27,955	2,531	9.1	25,005	2,385	9.5	2,950	146	4.9
Total	64,706	2,923	4.5	49,031	2,581	5.3	15,675	342	2.2

Source: Data in authors' possession.

TABLE A-28. Air Transport Industry
Employment by Race, Sex, and Occupational Group
7 Companies, South Atlantic Border States, 1964

Occupational Group	All Employees			Male			Female		
	Total	Negro	Percent Negro	Total	Negro	Percent Negro	Total	Negro	Percent Negro
Officials and managers	401	—	—	377	—	—	24	—	—
Professionals	748	—	—	741	—	—	7	—	—
Technicians	50	—	—	43	—	—	7	—	—
Sales workers	912	12	1.3	439	7	1.6	473	5	1.1
Office and clerical	667	2	0.3	365	2	0.5	302	—	—
Total white collar	2,778	14	0.5	1,965	9	0.5	813	5	0.6
Craftsmen	918	1	0.1	917	1	0.1	1	—	—
Operatives	464	47	10.1	454	47	10.4	10	—	—
Laborers	132	82	62.1	131	81	61.8	1	1	100.0
Service workers	295	59	20.0	89	56	62.9	206	3	1.5
Total blue collar	1,809	189	10.4	1,591	185	11.6	218	4	1.8
Total	4,587	203	4.4	3,556	194	5.5	1,031	9	0.9

Source: Data in authors' possession.

Note: Area includes Delaware, District of Columbia, Maryland, and northern Virginia.

TABLE A-29. *Air Transport Industry*
Employment by Race, Sex, and Occupational Group
9 Companies, South Atlantic Border States, 1966

Occupational Group	All Employees			Male			Female		
	Total	Negro	Percent Negro	Total	Negro	Percent Negro	Total	Negro	Percent Negro
Officials and managers	454	—	—	420	—	—	34	—	—
Professionals	1,049	—	—	1,043	—	—	6	—	—
Technicians	22	—	—	12	—	—	10	—	—
Sales workers	1,644	40	2.4	706	16	2.3	938	24	2.6
Office and clerical	656	9	1.4	337	7	2.1	319	2	0.6
Total white collar	3,825	49	1.3	2,518	23	0.9	1,307	26	2.0
Craftsmen	806	8	1.0	805	8	1.0	1	—	—
Operatives	618	70	11.3	617	70	11.3	1	—	—
Laborers	160	102	63.8	160	102	63.8	—	—	—
Service workers	467	95	20.3	142	89	62.7	325	6	1.8
Total blue collar	2,051	275	13.4	1,724	269	15.6	327	6	1.8
Total	5,876	324	5.5	4,242	292	6.9	1,634	32	2.0

Source: Data in authors' possession.

Note: Area includes Delaware, District of Columbia, Maryland, and northern Virginia.

TABLE A-30. *Air Transport Industry*
Employment by Race, Sex, and Occupational Group
9 Companies, South Atlantic Border States, 1968

Occupational Group	All Employees			Male			Female		
	Total	Negro	Percent Negro	Total	Negro	Percent Negro	Total	Negro	Percent Negro
Officials and managers	473	4	0.8	433	4	0.9	40	—	—
Professionals	1,191	3	0.3	1,171	3	0.3	20	—	—
Technicians	15	—	—	11	—	—	4	—	—
Sales workers	2,102	80	3.8	803	25	3.1	1,299	55	4.2
Office and clerical	667	20	3.0	343	12	3.5	324	8	2.5
Total white collar	4,448	107	2.4	2,761	44	1.6	1,687	63	3.7
Craftsmen	730	7	1.0	729	7	1.0	1	—	—
Operatives	722	87	12.0	720	87	12.1	2	—	—
Laborers	198	103	52.0	198	103	52.0	—	—	—
Service workers	696	119	17.1	155	102	65.8	541	17	3.1
Total blue collar	2,346	316	13.5	1,802	299	16.6	544	17	3.1
Total	6,794	423	6.2	4,563	343	7.5	2,231	80	3.6

Source: Data in authors' possession.

Note: Area includes Delaware, District of Columbia, Maryland, and northern Virginia.

TABLE A-31. Air Transport Industry
Employment by Race, Sex, and Occupational Group
921 Establishments, United States, 1967

Occupational Group	All Employees			Male			Female		
	Total	Negro	Percent Negro	Total	Negro	Percent Negro	Total	Negro	Percent Negro
Officials and managers	22,098	97	0.4	20,765	93	0.4	1,333	4	0.3
Professionals	38,364	63	0.2	37,302	58	0.2	1,062	5	0.5
Technicians	5,477	48	0.9	4,871	43	0.9	606	5	0.8
Sales workers	41,593	918	2.2	18,494	296	1.6	23,099	622	2.7
Office and clerical	41,716	1,048	2.5	18,414	601	3.3	23,302	447	1.9
Total white collar	149,248	2,174	1.5	99,846	1,091	1.1	49,402	1,083	2.2
Craftsmen	56,214	1,397	2.5	55,937	1,391	2.5	277	6	2.2
Operatives	26,990	2,506	9.3	26,697	2,468	9.2	293	38	13.0
Laborers	10,396	2,581	24.8	10,021	2,430	24.2	375	151	40.3
Service workers	28,756	3,895	13.5	11,627	3,458	29.7	17,129	437	2.6
Total blue collar	122,356	10,379	8.5	104,282	9,747	9.3	18,074	632	3.5
Total	271,604	12,553	4.6	204,128	10,888	5.3	67,476	1,715	2.5

Source: U.S. Equal Employment Opportunity Commission, Job Patterns for Minorities and Women in Private Industry, 1967, Report No. 2 (Washington: The Commission, 1970), Vol. 1.

TABLE A-32. Air Transport Industry
Employment by Race, Sex, and Occupational Group
1,169 Establishments, United States, 1969

Occupational Group	All Employees			Male			Female		
	Total	Negro	Percent Negro	Total	Negro	Percent Negro	Total	Negro	Percent Negro
Officials and managers	24,608	200	0.8	23,176	188	0.8	1,432	12	0.8
Professionals	46,474	179	0.4	44,637	153	0.3	1,837	26	1.4
Technicians	8,946	112	1.3	7,845	97	1.2	1,101	15	1.4
Sales workers	55,885	2,202	3.9	22,061	642	2.9	33,824	1,560	4.6
Office and clerical	46,180	1,708	3.7	21,397	996	4.7	24,783	712	2.9
Total white collar	182,093	4,401	2.4	119,116	2,076	1.7	62,977	2,325	3.7
Craftsmen	64,887	1,670	2.6	64,593	1,657	2.6	294	13	4.4
Operatives	32,168	3,890	12.1	31,837	3,823	12.0	331	67	20.2
Laborers	10,768	3,688	34.2	10,065	3,206	31.9	703	482	68.6
Service workers	36,601	4,082	11.2	12,541	3,414	27.2	24,060	668	2.8
Total blue collar	144,424	13,330	9.2	119,036	12,100	10.2	25,388	1,230	4.8
Total	326,517	17,731	5.4	238,152	14,176	6.0	88,365	3,555	4.0

Source: Preliminary Equal Employment Opportunity Commission Data, 1969.

Index

144

PART THREE

PART THREE

THE NEGRO
IN THE TRUCKING INDUSTRY

by

Richard D. Leone

TABLE OF CONTENTS

LIST OF TABLES

LIST OF FIGURES

CHAPTER I

Introduction

One hot summer day in 1967, a Negro youth noticed that there were relatively few black truck drivers on the streets of Cincinnati.

> In the 90 degree temperature of Monday, June 12, as throughout the summer, Negro youngsters roamed the streets. . . . Negro youths watched white workers going to work at white-owned stores and businesses. One Negro began to count the number of delivery trucks being driven by Negroes. During the course of the afternoon, of the 52 trucks he counted, only one had a Negro driver. His sampling was remarkably accurate. According to a study conducted by the Equal Employment Opportunity Commission less than 2 percent of the truck drivers in the Cincinnati area are Negro.[1]

Unlike many other industries where factory walls can hide the number of Negroes employed, the trucking industry's racial composition, for the most part, is subject to public scrutiny. An awareness of the extremely low number of Negro truck drivers contributed to the Negro youths of Cincinnati interfering with deliveries made by white drivers. This event precipitated a racial confrontation. By the time the National Guard had left Cincinnati, there were sixty-three persons injured—twelve of them requiring hospitalization. If the number of lives lost and the amount of property destroyed are valid criteria to judge the seriousness of civil disorders, then this was a minor incident, but it easily could have escalated into a major one.

Like the young Cincinnati Negro, this study is concerned with the employment of blacks working in the for-hire segment [2] of the motor trucking industry. It is concerned not only with Cincinnati but with the nation as a whole, not only with the driver

---

1. *Report of the National Advisory Commission on Civil Disorders,* March 1968 (Washington: U.S. Government Printing Office), p. 26.

2. For-hire motor carriers are those providing transportation of freight that belongs to someone else, in contradistinction to private carriers who use their own vehicles or leased trucks under their direct control for moving their own goods in furtherance of a principal business activity other than transportation.

1

job category but also with other job classifications in the industry. It attempts to show why Negroes are employed in some jobs and by some firms and not in other jobs or by other firms. A major part of the study will be concerned with governmental efforts at promoting equal employment opportunities among public carriers, the effects of law in this field, and current industrial response to this governmental action.

The Teamsters' Union [3] exerts a powerful influence upon the trucking industry. We shall therefore examine the organizational structure of this union and the political and economic factors bearing upon it in order to examine at what level union decisions are made which influence the employment and promotion of Negroes. Likewise, union-management agreements will be studied to ascertain whether they inhibit Negro employment.

THE SCOPE OF THE STUDY

In 1968, there were an estimated 15,900,000 trucks [4] registered in the United States, exclusive of those owned by the government. All of these vehicles are owned and operated by what is referred to generically as the motor carrier industry, which consists of two broad subdivisions: "private carriers" and "for-hire carriers."

The private carriers, which are divided into farm and nonfarm operators, comprise that heterogeneous group of firms which use their vehicles or leased trucks to move their own goods in furtherance of a principal business activity other than transportation. For example, although many oil refineries maintain large fleets of trucks, their primary business interest is not the sale of transportation services, but the sale of petroleum products. The following companies (none of which are included in this study) are in this category: Coca Cola, Sears Roebuck, Anheuser Busch, and American Telephone and Telegraph, owners of more trucks than any other private carrier.

For-hire or public carriers are those firms providing transportation for freight belonging to others. Depending on whether

---

3. The full title of the union is the International Brotherhood of Teamsters, Chauffeurs, Warehousemen and Helpers of America. This union subsequently will be referred to as the IBT or the Teamsters.

4. American Trucking Associations, *American Trucking Trends, 1968* (Washington: American Trucking Associations, 1969), p. 3.

they obtained their operating rights from a state regulatory agency or from the Interstate Commerce Commission, for-hire carriers are referred to respectively as intrastate or interstate operators. Interstate carriers are divided into common carriers and contract carriers.

Common carriers are those available to the general public to transport, at published rates, specific types of freight between points which the Interstate Commerce Commission, or a state or local authority, has authorized them to serve. Contract carriers operate under continuing contracts with one or a limited number of shippers. They assign vehicles to the customer, with or without drivers, to meet the specific trucking needs of individual shippers.

This study is limited to the racial employment practices of interstate common and contract carriers. Thus, the 3,397 Class I and Class II carriers,[5] regulated by the Interstate Commerce Commission as to rates and types of commodities transported constitute the industrial scope of this study. The entire industry is diagrammed in Figure 1.

The public interstate carriers have grown considerably since 1935, when they came under government regulation, and they comprise a relatively homogeneous unit in the field of transportation. In 1966 the 3,973 Class I and Class II carriers, including about 700 local cartage firms under the jurisdiction of the Interstate Commerce Commission, employed approximately 573,400 people.[6]

METHODOLOGY

Much of the information and data for this study were obtained through personal interviews, conducted throughout the country with representatives of the trucking industry, govern-

---

5. Regulated carriers with gross annual revenues averaging more than one million dollars over a three-year period are designated as Class I carriers and those with gross revenues averaging between $300,000 and one million dollars are considered Class II carriers. Class III carriers are those with annual revenues below $300,000. Data used in this study were obtained from *Trinc's Blue Book of the Trucking Industry* (1966 edition), published annually by Trinc Associations, Ltd., Washington, D.C.

6. American Trucking Associations, *op. cit.*, p. 23.

FIGURE I

The Motor Carrier Industry

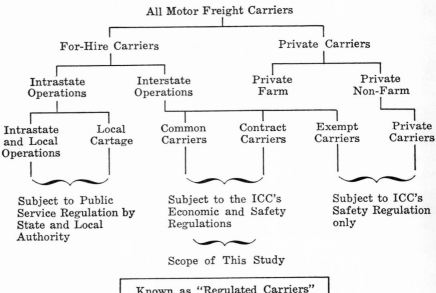

All Motor Freight Carriers

For-Hire Carriers

Private Carriers

Intrastate Operations

Interstate Operations

Private Farm

Private Non-Farm

Intrastate and Local Operations

Local Cartage

Common Carriers

Contract Carriers

Exempt Carriers

Private Carriers

Subject to Public Service Regulation by State and Local Authority

Subject to the ICC's Economic and Safety Regulations

Subject to ICC's Safety Regulation only

Scope of This Study

Known as "Regulated Carriers" (Class I, II) or as the "Trucking Industry" ment, and the union. This methodology necessitated establishing a representative sample of the carriers covered by this study. When officials of the selected companies were contacted, a pre-formulated questionnaire was used.[7]

Nonstructured interviews were used to obtain additional information from officials of the Teamsters' Union, from members of human relations and fair employment practice commissions, and from those in charge of public and private truckdriver training programs. Necessary background data were gleaned from publications of the U.S. Bureau of the Census, the Equal Employment Opportunity Commission, and other government and private sources.

Obtaining information about employment in the trucking industry presented a number of serious problems. For one thing, government data frequently lump together all types of trucking. In addition, the two-digit Standard Industrial Classification (SIC) No. 42, Motor Freight Transportation and Warehousing includes, as the name indicates, more than trucking. Since warehouse manpower policies involve less prestigious, and probably less skilled work, and a somewhat different employment environment, data included under SIC 42 must be evaluated carefully if they are to be at all meaningful for our purposes. In 1968, companies included under SIC 42 employed 1,056,100 people.[8] Figure 2 shows the trucking industry as delineated by SIC four-digit classifications. Our study covers a part of SIC 4213, for within this classification we find the 3,397 Class I and Class II interstate carriers which are of primary interest.

Moreover, information about the trucking industry's manpower is somewhat sketchy. As one comprehensive study noted, manpower data for the for-hire segment of the motor carrier industry "leaves us a great distance from the hard data which has

---

7. A copy of the questionnaire can be found in Richard D. Leone, O.S.F.S., "Negro Employment in the Trucking Industry: An Analysis of the Efforts of the Office of Federal Contract Compliance", unpublished Ph.D. dissertation, Philadelphia, University of Pennsylvania, 1969, Appendix III. See Appendix A for details of sample selection and Appendix B for statistical methods used.

8. *Employment and Earnings*, Vol. 15, No. 9 (March 1969). Table B-2, p. 61.

FIGURE 2

Standard Industrial Classification

SIC 42   MOTOR FREIGHT TRANSPORTATION AND WAREHOUSING

This major group includes establishments furnishing local or long distance trucking, transfer, and draying services, or engaged in the storage of farm products, furniture and other household goods, or commercial goods of any nature. The operation of terminal facilities for handling freight, with or without maintenance facilities, is also included. This group does not include delivery departments or warehouses operated by business concerns for their own use. Companies primarily engaged in the storage of natural gas are classified in SIC 4922.

SIC 421   TRUCKING, LOCAL AND LONG DISTANCE

SIC 4212   *Local Trucking and Draying, without Storage*

Companies primarily engaged in furnishing trucking, transfer, and draying services without storage, in a single municipality, contiguous municipalities, or a municipality and its suburban areas. Companies primarily engaged in collecting and transporting refuse by processing or destruction of materials are classified in SIC 4453.

SIC 4213   *Trucking, Except Local Companies*

Companies primarily engaged in furnishing "over-the-road" trucking service either as common carriers or under special and individual contracts or agreements.

SIC 4214   *Local Trucking and Storage, Including Household Goods*

Companies primarily engaged in furnishing trucking and storage services in a single municipality, contiguous municipalities, or a municipality and its suburban areas. Warehousing and storage of household goods when not combined with trucking is classified in SIC 4224.

Source: *Standard Industrial Classification* (Washington: U.S. Government Printing Office, 1967), p. 206.

proven so useful in other areas of transportation." [9] The discussion concerning the structure and growth of the industry, set forth in Chapter II, notes industry characteristics which make data collection difficult, and these characteristics also determine, to a considerable extent, the racial practices of the industry.

9. George Delehanty and D.K. Patton, *Manpower Profiles, Manpower Allocation and Labor Relations in Transportation, with Special Reference to the Trucking Industry* (Evanston, Ill.: Northwestern University Press, 1965), p. 42.

CHAPTER II

The Trucking Industry

Prior to World War I, trucks presented no real competitive threat to the railroads because (1) the trucks with their solid tires were equipped with low horsepower engines and thus could not travel at speeds in excess of fifteen to twenty miles an hour; (2) the trucks were so prone to breakdowns that distance, in the absence of garages and filling stations, was too great a risk; and (3) the century-old problem of adequate and dependable highways had not as yet been resolved. In spite of these shortcomings, however, the number of registered trucks increased dramatically from 2,200 in 1906 to 158,506 by 1915.

Because the war overburdened the railroads, the motor carrier industry was called upon to contribute to the transportation needs of a nation at war. This afforded the industry an opportunity to exhibit its value and usefulness as a swift, convenient, and economic medium in distributing goods. Truck registration increased from 158,506 in 1915 to 605,496 in 1918.[10]

In the 1920's and the early 1930's, trucking firms were usually small and family-owned, and nepotism in hiring prevailed. An enterprising risk-taker, after saving several hundred dollars or less for a down payment, procured a truck and found himself the president of a new trucking firm. Such firms, purchasing one truck at a time, were often financed by truck manufacturers who knew in advance that many of these men lacked the basic managerial skills needed to survive in a highly competitive market. Easy credit permitted almost unlimited entry into the industry and many searched in vain for fortunes acquired by relatively few. If successful, the owner augmented his fleet of trucks and, to keep costs down, hired his sons, cousins, in-laws, and friends, and, of course, few Negroes.

The small, family-owned and operated firms that were typical of the industry in its formative years were not likely to have Negroes in any but menial jobs. An exception must be made for the South, where driving had been considered a "Negro job" un-

---

10. American Trucking Associations, *American Trucking Trends, 1968* (Washington: American Trucking Associations, 1969), p. 3.

til the economic decline of the 1930's encouraged whites to accept such work. The southern carriers, however, often kept Negroes in an effort to keep the Teamsters' Union out. But once these firms were organized, wage rates and working conditions improved, and white employees sought employment with these companies. This is, of course, similar to the experience of Negroes in unionized construction in the South.

During the Great Depression, merchants neither had, nor could they borrow, the capital necessary to support large inventories. To minimize customer loss because of inadequate stocks, merchants turned more and more to the trucking industry, which met the needs of the times in two important respects: (1) trucks could transport small quantities of commodities swiftly; and (2) in the absence of federal regulations, trucks were willing to cut their rates in an effort to survive.

GOVERNMENTAL REGULATION

In the early 1930's, the federal government began to weigh the necessity of including trucking within the ambit of its transportation regulatory authority.[11] Federal intervention was prompted partially by pressure from the railroads, who were feeling the motor carrier industry's competitive presence, and also by the failure of the industry to practice uniform rules of road safety.

Against this background, Congress enacted the Motor Carrier Act (MCA) of 1935, which was amended as Part II of the Interstate Commerce Act of 1940, and amended several times since. Under the original and the amended Act, the Interstate Commerce Commission, assigned to administer the Act, does not regulate local cartage, that is, truckers who transport commodities within a radius of twenty miles. Also expressly excluded are all private carriers and haulers of agricultural commodities, but carriers hauling products manufactured from agricultural commodities are included.

The MCA provides regulation in the area of economics and safety requirements. The ICC has jurisdiction over the economic regulations, but its former authority to establish safety regulations, of which more will be said later, was transferred to the Department of Transportation in 1967. The economic regulations

---

11. William T. Ashby (ed.), *Motor Truck Redbook* (New York: Traffic Publishing Co., Inc., 1943), p. 94.

include: (1) the regulation of rates to stabilize rate competitio through bureaus established for this purpose; (2) the mandator certification of carriers in an effort to end unlimited and destruc tive entry; (3) the need for ICC approval of all consolidation if the number of vehicles exceed twenty; (4) the requiremer that motor carriers file uniform reports with the ICC; and (5 the establishment of uniform insurance requirements.

In keeping with the underlying spirit of the Act, the ICC wa supposed to restrict competition and this philosophy influence interpretation of the law, especially the provisions concernin entry.[12] The MCA recognized that existing motor carriers ha unilaterally staked out routes for themselves which the ICC coul not radically alter. Consequently, the Commission had to grar certificates of public "convenience and necessity" to existing car riers under what came to be known as the "grandfather clause. The carriers had to prove that they had shipped substantia amounts of cargo, over specific routes, with a sufficient degree c regularity. The objective of discouraging entry by first recogniz ing existing routes was effective, and those wishing to start trucking company had to demonstrate to the ICC's satisfactio that they were able and willing to perform the proposed servic As a result of the Motor Carrier Act, there began the trend tc ward a smaller number of larger carriers, which has continue to this day. This eliminated the smaller, possibly nonunio trucker who might have utilized Negro employees to a greate degree.

INDUSTRIAL STRUCTURE

The exact number of firms comprising the entire motor car rier industry is not known. Privately owned carriers are dif fused throughout the entire economy and are difficult to identify The ICC, nevertheless, estimates that there are between 55,00 and 60,000 private fleets throughout the country operated by variety of shippers that are not transportation companies a such.[13] Unlike the private carriers, the for-hire carriers are com

---

12. John B. Lansing, *Transportation and Economic Policy* (New York The Free Press, 1966), p. 254.

13. Automobile Manufacturers Association, *Motor Truck Facts 1966*, pp. 42 43. Here can be found a list of the larger private carriers accordin to a broad industrial classification. Further editions of this publicatio do not contain a listing similar to the one noted above.

pelled to file comprehensive annual reports with the ICC.[14] As a result, from 1940 to the present, there has been made available a fairly consistent body of data relevant to the scope of this study.

The number of Class I, II, and III carriers has declined since 1945, but the industry as a whole has grown tremendously. The total ton-mileage has increased from 81,992,000 in 1946 to 388,500,000 in 1967, while the number of registered trucks has increased from 245,060 in 1945 to 690,097 in 1963.[15] Table 1 illustrates the carriers' decline in absolute terms, and indicates changes in criteria used to determine carrier classifications. For example, in 1945 a trucking firm was classified as a Class I carrier if its gross revenue was only $100,000 or more; since 1957 the break point has been raised to $1,000,000. Although the absolute number of Class II and Class III carriers has declined annually since 1951, except for 1959 and 1965, the number of Class I carriers has increased every year since 1940, except 1950 and 1967 when revenue requirements for the category were redefined upward.

For-Hire Carriers' Share of the Transportation Market

The trucking industry has grown primarily at the expense of the railroads. In 1940, for-hire motor carriers accounted for 10.0 percent of the total ton-miles shipped throughout the nation. Among other modes of transportation, the public carriers were third in the number of ton-miles hauled, because the railroads controlled 61.3 percent of this business and the waterways hauled 19 percent of all ton-miles moved in intercity transport. By 1966, the private carriers had doubled their share of all the transportation services rendered, accounting for 22 percent of the ton-miles hauled. From 1940 to 1967, the railroads' share declined from 61.3 percent to 43 percent, and the waterways' share fell from 19 percent to 15 percent.[16]

---

14. These reporting requirements are constantly revised. The *1966 Annual Report* for all Class I motor carriers was a comprehensive fifty-page document (Budget Bureau No. 60-R052.21). The *1966 Class II Annual Report* (Budget Bureau No. 60-R336.7), and the *Class III Annual Report* for the same year (Budget Bureau No. 60-R266.13) were forty-three pages and four pages, respectively. Class III carriers do not report their number of employees.

15. American Trucking Associations, *op. cit.*, p. 8.

16. *Ibid.*

TABLE 1. *Trucking Industry*
Number of For-Hire Carriers by Class
1945-1967

Year	Class I	Class II[a]		Class III[a]	Total
	$100,000 or More	$25,000 to $100,000		Under $25,000	
1945	2,001		18,871		20,872
1946	2,099		19,019		21,118
1947	2,211		18,787		20,998
1948	2,507		18,337		20,884
1949	2,728		17,334		20,062
	$200,000 or More	$50,000 to $200,000		Under $50,000	
1950	2,053		17,544		19,597
1951	2,178		17,542		19,720
1952	2,361		17,001		19,362
1953	2,576		16,338		18,914
1954	2,640		15,694		18,334
1955	2,843		15,298		18,141
1956	2,939		14,957		17,896
	$1,000,000 or More	$200,000 to $1,000,000		Under $200,000	
1957	933	2,055		14,779	17,767
1958	988	2,167		14,105	17,260
1959	1,009	2,256		14,383	17,648
1960	1,053	2,276		12,947	16,276
1961	1,106	2,336		12,556	15,998
1962	1,148	2,495		12,340	15,983
1963	1,175	2,533		11,910	15,618
1964	1,195	2,536		11,748	15,479
1965	1,250	2,615		11,700	15,565
1966	1,298	2,675		11,453	15,426
1967	1,384	2,769		11,238	15,396

Source: *American Trucking Trends, 1968* (Washington: American Trucking Associations, 1969), p. 13.

[a] Separate figures on Class II and Class III carriers are not available prior to 1957. As of November 1968, Class II carriers must have revenues of $300,000 to $1,000,000, while Class III carriers are those having revenues below $300,000.

The awesome growth of the trucking industry and its relative share of the transportation market is demonstrated by an investigation of the revenue distribution among all the federally regulated carriers. Table 2 shows that in 1940 the trucking industry received 17.7 percent of the shippers' dollar. For the same year, the railroads received 75.4 percent of the dollars paid by the shippers. As shippers turned more and more to the motor carrier industry, the railroads' share of revenue dollars declined to 42.5 and the trucking industry increased its share to 49.3 percent. The loss of jobs by Negroes in railroad transportation was not, unfortunately, compensated for by an expansion of jobs in trucking.

Thus, despite the trend favoring bigger concerns, the trucking industry remains fragmented and, by comparison, one of small entrepreneurs. Highly competitive, the efforts of trucking companies have been narrowly directed toward immediate marketing and operating problems. The industry's personnel problems have not been given a high priority other than the need to get along with the Teamsters. Civil rights, as we shall note, falls in the somewhat neglected area of personnel.

By 1968, Class I, II, and III regulated public motor carriers accounted for 49.4 percent of the revenue received by all of the regulated freight carriers. In that year, however, only eight public motor carriers were found in the *Fortune* list of the top fifty transportation companies. In 1968, the Penn Central railroad ranked first among U.S. transportation companies, with slightly over two billion dollars in operating revenues. The largest trucking company, Consolidated Freightways, was nineteenth among all transportation companies, with operating revenues of $387,999,000. To further place trucking company size in perspective, it should be noted that ten railroads, seven airlines, and the Greyhound Corporation, among transportation concerns, had revenues in 1968 exceeding that of the largest trucking company, and that in terms of assets, the trucking companies are even more outdistanced by their air and rail competitors. Table 3 sets forth pertinent data for the eight trucking companies which are listed among the fifty largest transportation carriers.

Industrial Concentration

As the larger firms have grown, ease of entry has declined. General commodity haulers have decreased from 6,602 in 1957 to 5,566 in 1965. The increased dominance of larger firms be-

TABLE 2. Trucking Industry
Revenue Distribution among Regulated Freight Carriers 1940-1967

	Railroads Class I and II		Motor Carriers Class I, II, III		Water Carriers Class A, B, C and Maritime		Pipelines (oil)		Airways	
	Thousands of Dollars	Percent of Total	Thousands of Dollars	Percent of Total	Thousands of Dollars	Percent of Total	Thousands of Dollars	Percent of Total	Thousands of Dollars	Percent of Total
1940	3,686,375	75.4	867,000	17.7	85,394	1.7	225,760	4.6	22,719	0.5
1944	7,228,979	80.2	1,351,900	15.0	77,835	0.9	310,194	3.4	43,654	0.5
1948	8,271,158	71.1	2,698,100	23.2	190,396	1.6	377,034	3.2	89,765	0.8
1952	9,142,896	62.9	4,417,478	30.4	275,570	1.9	562,268	3.9	130,723	0.9
1956	9,320,230	56.8	5,828,877	35.5	335,351	2.0	737,386	4.5	180,508	1.1
1960	8,390,026	49.4	7,213,911	42.5	335,257	1.9	770,417	4.5	278,118	1.6
1963a	8,507,630	45.8	8,548,257	46.0	301,092	1.6	840,260	4.5	371,384	2.0
1965a	9,286,628	44.1	10,068,243	47.9	314,070	1.5	903,817	4.3	463,327	2.2
1966b	9,750,959	43.6	10,853,300	48.5	328,200	1.5	941,100	4.2	502,616	2.3
1967b	9,606,418	42.5	11,165,000	49.3	313,200	1.4	993,300	4.4	550,517	2.4

Source: *American Trucking Trends 1969* (Washington: American Trucking Associations), p. 9.

Note: Included are revenues of federally regulated carriers only; a major portion of the traffic handled by motor and water carriers is not subject to this regulation—for example, not reflected are the revenues or value of service generated by intrastate, local and exempt for-hire and private motor carriers. The total value of all motor carrier services would approximately triple the 10.9 billion shown in 1966; consequently, this table does not compare the economic significance of different modes of transportation.

a Revised figures for 1963 and 1965.

b Estimated figures for 1966 and 1967.

TABLE 3. *The Eight Largest Public Carriers, 1968*

Company and 1968 Rank among Transportation Companies	Headquarters	Operating Revenues	Assets	Net Income	Invested Capital	Number of Employees	Net Income as Percent of	
		Thousands		of	Dollars		Operating Revenue	Invested Capital
Consolidated Freightways	(19) San Francisco	387,999	192,851	13,963	70,993	16,523	3.6	19.7
Leaseway Transportation	(30) Cleveland	222,535	189,824	7,144	36,671	11,000	3.2	19.5
Roadway Express	(35) Akron	183,832	81,725	7,505	45,245	10,448	4.1	16.6
Pacific Inter-Mountain Express	(39) Oakland	135,003	65,904	3,862	24,052	6,375	2.9	16.1
Yellow Freight System	(40) Kansas City	132,658	72,416	7,031	32,683	5,000	5.3	21.5
McLean Trucking	(44) Winston-Salem	113,861	64,263	5,217	26,520	6,194	4.6	19.7
Associated Transport	(47) New York	109,227	66,597	1,006	21,312	8,000	0.9	4.7
Spector Industries	(50) Chicago	97,691	51,955	186	11,986	4,887	n.a.	n.a.

Source: *Fortune*, Vol. LXXIX (May 15, 1969), pp. 196-197.

comes more apparent through an analysis of the distribution of
revenue over a period of time. For example, in 1957 only one
percent of the firms reporting had revenues over $10 million.
These few firms, nevertheless, received 32.8 percent of all the
revenues received by all the firms constituting the total population. By 1965, 2.5 percent of the reporting firms had revenues
of $10 million or more and received 58.5 percent of all reve-
nues.[17]

Industrial Location

The trucking industry covers the entire country, with corporate headquarters located primarily in urban centers, where most
Negroes are concentrated. Table 4 is an array of the twenty-
five largest SMSA's, showing Class I, II, and III carriers with
corporate offices headquartered in these same twenty-five distinct
geographical areas.

The most recent Negro population data on the basis of an
SMSA are the statistics found in the 1960 census. Estimates have
been made of the number of Negroes residing in the nation's
larger cities (the heart of the SMSA's) rather than the SMSA
proper. Projections for 1970 indicate that in the twenty-five
cities included in Table 4, we should expect to find a total population of 31,671,000 people, of which 8,485,000 or 26.8 percent
are Negroes.[18]

Included in the twenty-five SMSA's are 1,238 Class I and
Class II carriers, or 36.5 percent of the total 3,397 such carriers
found throughout the country in 1965. This then does not indicate where the industry is concentrated according to the gross
revenue received from the particular markets it serves, nor does
it reflect the number of employees found in each of these SMSA's.
It does offer the opportunity to compare the industry geographically, and it also raises some questions as to why the firms' concentration pattern differs from area to area.

The concentration of large versus small companies in particu-
lar SMSA's is due to the geographical location of a particular
SMSA in relationship to other markets and the density of each
SMSA's population. For example, there are proportionately more

---

17. Interstate Commerce Commission, *81st Annual Report* (Washington:
    U.S. Government Printing Office, 1967), p. 152.

18. Cf. *The Negro Population: 1956 Estimates and 1970 Projections* (Peek-
    skill: The Center of Research in Marketing, Incorporated).

TABLE 4. *For-Hire Carriers*
Location of Headquarters in Selected SMSA's
1966

SMSA by Size	Number of Carriers		
	Total	Class I and II Carriers	Class III Carriers
New York	397	119	278
Los Angeles	211	145	66
Chicago	307	153	154
Philadelphia	240	94	146
Detroit	74	54	20
San Francisco	96	61	35
Boston	172	65	107
Pittsburgh	127	61	66
St. Louis	116	59	57
Washington	33	15	18
Cleveland	79	43	36
Baltimore	63	26	37
Newark	110	36	74
Minneapolis-St. Paul	64	40	24
Buffalo	49	23	26
Houston	49	25	24
Milwaukee	57	33	24
Seattle	66	35	31
Dallas	41	26	15
Cincinnati	41	23	18
Kansas City	53	33	20
San Diego	10	6	4
Atlanta	29	20	9
Miami	19	8	11
Denver	67	35	32
Total	2,570	1,238	1,332

Source: *Trinc's Blue Book of the Trucking Industry* (1966 Edition), published annually by Trinc Associates, Ltd., Washington, D.C.

small carriers with headquarters in New York because of its position of centrality to many nearby markets. Conversely, there are more large carriers than small ones headquartered in Atlanta and Denver. Atlanta, the South's transportation hub, is a breaking point for shipments traveling the eastern coast and to the Midwest. In any case, the trucking industry has few locational problems relative to the Negro labor force.

MANPOWER

Table 5 shows that in 1966 the Class I and II carriers employed 573,304 people. Within the short span of nine years (1957-1966), the trucking industry increased its employment by 149,307, while the number of Class I and II carriers increased by 1,170. Although employment increased in absolute terms, the average number of employees per firm remained relatively constant.

TABLE 5. *For-Hire Carriers*
Employment by Class
1957-1966

Year	Number of Class I and II Carriers[a]	Number of Employees	Average Number of Employees
1957	2,988	423,997	141.9
1958	3,155	415,859	131.8
1959	3,265	458,080	140.3
1960	3,329	466,726	140.2
1961	3,442	468,456	136.1
1962	3,643	509,656	140.0
1963	3,708	519,490	140.1
1964	3,731	534,279	143.2
1965	3,865	556,560	144.0
1966	4,158	573,304	137.9

Source: *American Trucking Trends, 1968* (Washington: American Trucking Associates, 1968), pp. 13 and 23.

[a] Included among these carriers are approximately 700 interstate carriers under ICC regulation with sufficient revenue to include them as Class I or II carriers.

Occupational Distribution

In sharp contrast to the relatively high ratio of white collar workers found in such industries as aerospace, only 25.6 percent of the trucking industry's employees, as Table 7 shows, are found in the white collar job category. The ratio of white collar workers in the trucking industry approximates what we find in such industries as paper and rubber tire. In the latter two, however, we find a smaller percentage of office and clerical employees. Only 10 percent of all trucking employees are found in occupations demanding more than a high school education. Consequently, we might assume that even with their disadvantaged educational status Negroes should find it relatively easy to secure employment in the majority of jobs available in the trucking industry. This is not the case, however, and why it is not so will be discussed in future chapters.

TABLE 6. *Trucking Industry*
Employment by Occupation, 395 Class I Motor Carriers
1967

Occupational Group	Number of Employees	Percent of Total
Officials and Managers	21,004	7.7
Professionals	783	0.3
Technicians	975	0.4
Sales workers	6,298	2.3
Office and clerical	40,306	14.9
Total white collar	69,366	25.6
Craftsmen	20,553	7.6
Operatives	145,250	53.6
Laborers	32,066	11.8
Service workers	3,862	1.4
Total blue collar	201,731	74.4
Total	271,097	100.0

Source: Table 10, p. 37.

Under the heading of blue collar workers, we find that onl 7.6 percent of all employees are craftsmen or skilled employee Operatives, mostly the drivers, account for more than one-half o all employees. Although technically considered semiskilled, the frequently earn wages comparable to skilled workers in othe industries. Although road drivers do not receive their trainin through formal apprenticeship programs, they have a tendenc to view their occupation as a craft. They reserve these jobs fo their friends and relatives, just as craft unions practice nepotisr in accepting apprentices into their training programs. We shoulc therefore, expect to find that Negroes, in their effort to be em ployed as road drivers, must face some of the problems associate with being accepted in construction crafts.

Unionization

Since the mid-1930's, unionized long-haul motor carriers hav had to contend with the International Brotherhood of Teamster at present the nation's largest union, and generally considere the most powerful one. In 1899, the American Federation o Labor granted a charter to the union, then known as the Team Drivers International, permitting it to organize those drivin horse-drawn carts. Over the years, the IBT expanded its juri diction and consequently its present membership [19] of approxi mately 1.6 million includes workers from such diverse industrie as foundries, bakeries, airlines, undertaking establishments, an steel plants, as well as warehousing and trucking. An estimate 350,000 of the IBT's total membership are employed by truckin firms and these members belong to one of the union's sixtee trade divisions.

From 1900 to 1935, the vast majority of the IBT's member were employed as bread, laundry, milk, and ice and coal truc drivers. It is impossible to obtain precise data on the number o Negroes among the IBT's membership for this period. A Team ster representative stated that "probably" very few Negroes wer members during these earlier years, unless they were originall

---

19. The Teamsters periodically issue official data on the number of dues paying members. The "official" data are highly inflated. For exampl the *International Teamster*, April 1968, maintained that the Februar membership was 1,911,212. The discrepancy between the 1.6 millio figure used in this study and the "official" figure arises because dues paying members are allowed to pay their dues on a quarterly basi Therefore, if a man pays his dues for three months in January (for th first quarter of the year) he is counted as three members.

employed as helpers in the livery stables before the horse-drawn carts were replaced with trucks. There are several reasons why Negroes would not be found within the ranks of the Teamsters once the trucks replaced the horse-drawn carts.

First, although trucking was initially considered a Negro job in the South, Teamsters locals were concentrated in urban areas outside the South prior to 1935. Second, the bread, laundry, and milk drivers comprising the majority of the IBT's membership came in direct contact with the consumer as driver-salesmen, and anti-Negro sentiment often precluded their gaining admission to these jobs. Third, many IBT locals were dominated by distinct national and religious blocs which reserved these jobs for their own members. Fourth, although white strikebreakers outnumbered Negroes by more than seven to one, during the celebrated Teamsters strike of 1905 in Chicago, Negroes, because of their visibility, were blamed for taking the places of white men.[20] As a consequence, Negroes were prototyped as strikebreakers and much of this anti-Negro sentiment continued to exist over the years.

Most of the over-the-road drivers were brought into the Teamsters' Union in the 1930's. Prior to then, Daniel Tobin, longtime president of IBT, resisted organizing such "trash," [21] but he was persuaded to change his views by the Troskyite Socialist, Farrell Dobbs, then head of the Minneapolis Teamsters. Dobbs, the organizational tutor of James Hoffa, used secondary boycotts and other leverage techniques to bring the bulk of the nation's over-the-road drivers into the union.[22] With the combination of over-the-road, local cartage, and warehouse workers into a single organization, the IBT is, as Mr. Hoffa has commented, very powerful.

Without the city cartage and the road organized in a territory . . . you cannot organize the rest of the city. Any employer who wants to fight you in any other branch of our business can whip the strongest local union unless you have the support of the road and city cartage. But once you organize the road, the city, the warehouses, nobody can whip the Teamsters union, nobody.[23]

20. Sterling D. Spero and Abram L. Harris, *The Black Worker* (New York: Atheneum, 1968), p. 132.

21. Ralph C. James and Estelle Dinerstein James, *Hoffa and the Teamsters* (New York: D. Van Nostrand Co., Inc., 1965), p. 91.

22. *Ibid.*, Chapters 5 and 6.

23. *Ibid.*, p. 57.

The over-the-road drivers did not alter the prevailing attitude of the IBT toward Negroes. As craft conscious as the local salesmen-drivers, they also saw their members displace lower-paid blacks after southern firms were organized. Because of the significance of the Teamsters in the industry, we shall deal with its policies in depth in succeeding chapters.

Future Employment Needs

There are no indications that recent increases in productivity, and new adaptations, such as containerization,[24] will compel the trucking industry to decrease its demand for labor. If anything, the trucking industry is one of the nation's growth industries and should continue to offer jobs requiring a minimal amount of formal education and/or training; jobs that disadvantaged persons, many of whom are Negroes, should be able to fill.

Between 1961 and 1965, line drivers increased the tons hauled per man-hour by 2.6 percent, while the miles per man-hour increased by 1.1 percent. Moreover, pickup and delivery drivers increased the tons per mile they hauled by 1.5 percent. Platform employees increased the tons per man-hour they handled by 1.1 percent.[25] These increases in tons and miles per man-hour are indicative of the industry's ability to adapt to new technologies and to use more efficiently their manpower resources.

As a percentage of GNP, the nation's total freight bill has decreased, while the percentage of revenues received by the trucking industry has increased. That is, as the total freight bill as a percentage of GNP decreased from 9.2 percent in 1958 to 8.9 percent in 1964, the trucking freight bill, for the same period, increased from 5.9 to 6.3 percent. Of greater significance is the fact that in 1964 all trucking accounted for 71.2 percent of total freight service, while the projected 1980 figure is 78.6 percent.[26] Therefore, productivity increases in trucking should be more than offset by the industry's growth, and demand for labor in absolute terms should increase.

Motor freight transportation and warehousing industries are expected to increase their manpower requirements by one-fifth,

---

24. For details about some of the limitations in containerization, see *Wall Street Journal*, May 28, 1968, p. 34.

25. Unpublished data made available by the American Trucking Associations, Inc.

26. Edward V. Kiley, "Looking Ahead," *Trucking and the Economy* (Washington: American Trucking Associations, Inc., 1966), pp. 26-28.

rising to approximately 1.2 million, between 1966 and 1975.[27] Although we can expect 129,000 truck driver openings annually through 1975,[28] intercity motor carriers are not expected to expand in the future as rapidly as they did in the past. Local driver openings should increase annually at the rate of 74,000, while over-the-road drivers should increase at the annual rate of 55,000 through 1975. The demand for local drivers should increase more rapidly than that of over-the-road drivers because of an increase in the number of suburban shopping centers, and as a result of industry relocating away from the center city areas.

The greatest employment growth is expected to occur among larger firms which, compared to smaller companies, have a higher proportion of professional workers, clerical workers, mechanics and repairmen, and foremen. In the past, the ratio of sales workers to all other workers has been relatively low. Demand for salesmen, however, is expected to rise appreciably over the next decade as competition from other modes of transportation, in particular air carriers, increases. Computer usage might well tend to moderate the growth rates of clerical positions that should increase as the industry expands.

Of basic importance to the employment of the Negro is the fact that the demand for blue collar workers is increasing within the trucking industry. From 1961 to 1966, all blue collar jobs throughout the nation increased at an annual rate of 700,000, but in 1967 the increase was only 300,000.[29] Therefore, unlike the steel industry [30] where job opportunities are being phased out by new technologies, and unlike the aerospace industry [31] where

---

27. U.S. Bureau of Labor Statistics, *Tomorrow's Manpower Needs*, Vol. II, Bulletin No. 1606 (Washington: U.S. Government Printing Office, 1969), pp. 83-85.

28. U.S. Bureau of Labor Statistics, *Occupational Outlook Quarterly*, Vol. 12, No. 2, May 1968 (Washington: U.S. Government Printing Office), p. 6. Annual average openings are those jobs arising because of growth, death and retirement losses. It does not include transfers out of the occupation. A shortage of dependable drivers exists in New York City. For details, see *Wall Street Journal*, November 11, 1969, p. 1.

29. *Wall Street Journal*, June 4, 1968, p. 1.

30. Herbert R. Northrup *et al.*, *Negro Employment in Basic Industry*, Negro Employment Studies, Vol. I (Philadelphia: Industrial Research Unit, Wharton School of Finance and Commerce, University of Pennsylvania, 1970), Part Four.

31. *Ibid.*, Part Three.

many jobs are highly skilled, the motor freight industry is increasing its demand for blue collar workers. Although road drivers view their occupation as a craft, there are no formal procedures a man must follow to learn how to drive. When truck manufacturers incorporate new improvements into the trucks, most drivers can learn how to operate these vehicles without a great deal of formal training. Consequently, Negroes who may suffer from such handicaps as poor education should in the future find this a relatively easy industry in which to find employment. But this possibility must be viewed in light of some of the obstacles Negroes have found in the past, which we will discuss in subsequent chapters.

CHAPTER III

Negro Employment Prior to 1960

Prior to 1960, Negroes employed in over-the-road trucking were found mostly in the South. Particularly before World War II, and in the postwar years as well, as noted in Chapter II, many of the trucking firms were small, family-owned and managed concerns. Consequently, their hiring procedures were very informal. The smaller firms relied on friends and relatives to meet their needs. The larger firms, with terminals located throughout the country, usually relied on recommendations from their present employees in hiring new ones. Negroes employed in the South were hired largely by nonunion firms whose wages were low and hours and working conditions substandard.

Table 7 shows the number of Negroes employed from 1940 to 1960 by the trucking and warehousing industries and the percentage of the work force they represented, with breakdowns for males and females and four geographical regions. A word of caution is called for, however, because these census statistics represent racial employment patterns not only for trucking, but also for warehousing. Compared to the range of jobs available in the trucking industry, warehousing offers jobs of less status and relatively poorer pay. If the statistics shown on Table 7 were for trucking alone, rather than warehousing and trucking, it is safe to assume that the number of Negroes employed would be somewhat lower. Furthermore, the methodology used in collecting census data (personal interview) suggests that private carrier employers are included in the statistics as reported.

From 1940 to 1960, the proportion of Negro employment in trucking and warehousing increased only by five-tenths of a percentage point. Although male Negro employment increased from 7.6 percent in 1940 to 8.3 percent in 1960, female Negro employment, during the same period, remained relatively constant. The South accounted for the largest percentage of Negroes, but the ratio of Negroes decreased there, while the percentage of Negroes increased in the Northeast and West and remained relatively stable in the Midwest. It is likely that, in fact, Negroes lost jobs in trucking in the South and gained warehousing jobs in other areas.

TABLE 7. *Trucking and Warehousing Industry*
Employment by Race and Sex
United States and Regions, 1940-1960

Region	Year	All Employees			Male			Female		
		Total	Negro	Percent Negro	Total	Negro	Percent Negro	Total	Negro	Percent Negro
United States	1940	488,816	36,210	7.4	470,023	35,698	7.6	18,793	512	2.7
	1950	696,165	50,373	7.2	649,247	48,709	7.5	46,918	1,664	3.5
	1960	841,418	66,243	7.9	774,621	64,477	8.3	66,797	1,766	2.6
Northeast	1940	137,221	5,858	4.3	131,739	5,756	4.4	5,482	102	1.9
	1950	183,835	9,593	5.2	171,915	9,279	5.4	11,920	314	2.6
	1960	205,536	14,327	6.9	191,206	13,879	7.3	14,330	448	3.1
Midwest	1940	174,159	4,042	2.3	167,065	3,980	2.4	7,094	62	0.9
	1950	251,088	8,019	3.2	234,042	7,605	3.2	17,046	414	2.4
	1960	298,288	8,764	2.9	273,561	8,405	3.1	24,727	359	1.5
South	1940	122,763	25,712	20.9	119,206	25,372	21.3	3,557	340	9.6
	1950	171,325	30,903	18.0	161,116	30,071	18.7	10,209	832	8.1
	1960	206,826	40,113	19.4	190,898	39,245	20.6	15,928	868	5.4
West	1940	54,673	598	1.1	52,013	589	1.1	2,660	8	0.3
	1950	89,917	1,858	2.1	82,174	1,754	2.1	7,743	104	1.3
	1960	130,768	3,039	2.3	118,956	2,948	2.5	11,812	91	0.8

Source: *U.S. Census of Population:*

  1940: Vol. III, *The Labor Force*, Part I, Table 77.

  1950: Vol. II, *Characteristics of the Population*, Table 161.

  1960: PC (1) 1D, *Detailed Characteristics*, Table 260.

Note: Regions are defined as follows:

Northeast: Connecticut, Maine, Massachusetts, New Hampshire, New Jersey, New York, Pennsylvania, Rhode Island, Vermont.

Midwest: Illinois, Indiana, Iowa, Kansas, Michigan, Minnesota, Missouri, Nebraska, North Dakota, Ohio, South Dakota, Wisconsin.

South: Alabama, Arkansas, Delaware, Florida, Georgia, Kentucky, Louisiana, Maryland, Mississippi, North Carolina, Oklahoma, South Carolina, Tennessee, Texas, Virginia, West Virginia.

West: Arizona, California, Colorado, Idaho, Montana, Nevada, New Mexico, Oregon, Utah, Washington, Wyoming (Hawaii and Alaska included 1960).

SOCIAL INFLUENCES

Prior to the passage of the Civil Rights Act of 1964, Negroes were often refused admission to places offering public lodging. Employers, especially those with terminals in the South, contend that this was the primary reason why they did not hire Negro road drivers. Since the amount and nature of freight crossing terminal thresholds varies from day to day, truckers must have the freedom to assign drivers. To have as road drivers Negroes who would be unable to accept certain trips because they could not find public accommodations, would have deprived the employers of the flexibility they needed in assigning drivers to different runs.

On long trips, more than one driver is assigned to the job, with one driver sleeping in a cab-bunk, or the drivers sharing rooms en route. Custom and belief made white drivers extremely adverse to having a black "buddy"—a factor still militating against Negro employment today.

Many of the black road drivers found today working for trucking companies were hired during World War II, when the union and employers were compelled by the tight labor markets to admit some Negroes into these high-paying jobs. Even so, tight labor markets did not operate as favorably for Negroes in trucking as they did in some other industries from which they had been excluded prior to World War II. According to Leiter:

> More Negroes were employed, especially in the South, but even greater absorption of this group would have been possible if company and union discrimination had not been practiced. The labor needs of the trucking industry were mostly for replacements. Labor shortages experienced by the industry in each community corresponded with the inadequacy of the general labor supply in that geographical area.[32]

Thus, during World War II and the years thereafter, Negro gains in trucking remained quite limited. Like railroad firemen, they were used in the South as a source of cheap labor, but such usage declined as southern wages rose. In other parts of the country, the trucking industry's stance on Negro employment was similar to that of other industrial segments in transportation—railroad, airlines, and shipping companies. The most prestigious jobs of airline flight officer and maritime vessel officer, or rail-

---

32. Robert D. Leiter, *The Teamsters Union* (New York: Bookman Associates, 1957), p. 145.

road engineer and conductor remained virtually all white. The highly paid, but less prestigious, over-the-road truck operators had only a few Negroes in their ranks. And particularly like the railroad situation, the decision to maintain Negro employment at a minimum was, over the years, strongly influenced by union policy and structure representing the institutionalized prejudices of the white employees.[33]

TEAMSTER INFLUENCE

Prior to the election of James Hoffa as Teamster president in the late 1950's, the union was operated as a confederation of highly independent locals and conferences.[34] Daniel Tobin, president from 1908 to 1952, was content to permit maximum local autonomy. If a local, therefore, wished to confine its members to whites, Tobin did not make it the concern of the national office. As a matter of fact, if Tobin's own preference had been influential, the results would not have been salutary for Negroes. One of the current union officials stated, in a confidential interview: "Tobin did not like Italians, Jews, or Negroes; as a matter of fact, the only people he did like were Irish Catholics." [35] Tobin's attitude, and those of many of the officers of local unions, exemplified the craft conscious, work scarcity feelings found in the building trades unions.[36] The milk, bread, and other salesmen-driver locals were traditionally white and their customer contact jobs increased their white collar, as well as craft, orientation. Over-the-road drivers added their club-like feelings to the group, all of whom felt that Negroes had little or no place in their midst.

---

33. Howard W. Risher, Jr., *The Negro in the Railroad Industry*, The Racial Policies of American Industry, Report No. 16 (Philadelphia: Industrial Research Unit, Wharton School of Finance and Commerce, University of Pennsylvania, 1970).

34. The area conferences, four in number, came upon the scene as area agreements expanded to include several states under the contracts. The Western Conference includes eleven western states. The Eastern Conference is confined to the states along the Atlantic coast as far South, and including, the Carolinas. The Central and Southern Conferences include those states indicated by their very titles.

35. Interview, 1965.

36. See, for example, Herbert R. Northrup, *Organized Labor and the Negro* (New York: Harper and Brothers, 1944), Chapter II.

Given these feelings, it is likely that Tobin clearly reflected the feelings of his membership toward Negroes. Even if he did not, however, local autonomy in the union was so pronounced that it is doubtful if Tobin could have done much to insure Negro employment even if he had so desired.

Under David Beck, president of the Teamsters from 1952 through 1958, the union's structure and posture toward Negroes encountered little change. Local autonomy prevailed, and action toward improved Negro employment opportunity was largely nonexistent. Beck, on a number of occasions, did place locals under national trusteeship (indeed, his propensity to do this was a factor in regulating such activity when Congress enacted the Landrum-Griffin Act of 1959), suspending local officers, and instructing his trustees to admit to membership all applicants into those locals. Allegedly this was done because he viewed it as a means of weakening the political machine controlling the local, not because he was an egalitarian reformer. If, through custom, some employment opportunities were considered "Negro jobs," such as taxicab drivers in the South who provided services for Negroes only, segregated locals provided union services for these members.[37]

When James R. Hoffa succeeded to the Teamsters presidency, he had acquired a reputation of being more interested in Negro support and Negro rights. His prime goals, however, appeared to be the consolidation of power to the national presidency at the expense of the locals and conferences, and, as part of this program, the signing of a national trucking agreement. He therefore seemed to view the enlargement of Negro membership in the union only in relation to its effects upon his prime goals. Hoffa's objectives and the internal political climate of the union, therefore, tended to relegate Negro rights approximately the same low status that they occupied during previous Teamster presidents' administrations.[38]

We may sum up this brief review by noting that there was little or no pressure from the top of the Teamsters' Union for

---

37. A discussion of Beck's attitudes and philosophy is found in Donald Garnel, "Teamsters and Highway Truckers in the West—The Evaluation of Multiemployer Bargaining in the Western Trucking Industry," unpublished Ph.D. dissertation, University of California, Berkeley, 1966; and Sam Romer, *The International Brotherhood of Teamsters: Its Government and Structure* (New York: John Wiley and Sons, Inc., 1962).

38. See Romer, *op. cit.*, and James, *op. cit.*, *passim*.

nondiscriminatory practices during the period covered. On the contrary, the pressures in favor of discrimination in the locals were largely uninhibited. Even the union's constitution was, during this period, and remains today, equivocal. It provides:

Any person shall be eligible to membership in this organization, provided that hereafter no person shall be eligible for membership in the International Union who has willfully refused to become a citizen of either the United States or Canada or the country in which his Local Union is chartered, at his option.[39]

Union constitutions prohibiting the exclusion of members because of race, color, or creed are certainly no guarantee that a union is truly fair in admitting members. Even so, the Teamsters' constitution, which states that any person shall be eligible, does not allude to race, color, or creed. During Beck's regime, Teamster officials discussed whether specific mention should be made about the union's willingness to accept everyone regardless of race, color, or creed. This change was never made, on the assumption that if it were changed, it might be interpreted to mean that the union had been guilty of discrimination over the years. Therefore, to the degree that such explicit nondiscriminatory eligibility clauses found in other union constitutions are of any value, it is well to note that the Teamsters constitution was —and is—silent on this point.

During the latter part of Tobin's regime, and in more recent years, the Teamsters' Union has aggressively organized employees—first in warehouses, then in a variety of industries wherever it could obtain members. Many of the nontrucking firms organized by the Teamsters (including those in the South where the union is apparently growing the fastest) employ considerably more Negroes than do the motor carriers. In such cases the union has often adopted a pro-black stance, utilizing Negro organizers where it deems them effective. Yet in the key industry—public interstate trucking—the union has few Negro members and has demonstrated little zeal in altering this situation. Moreover, it is the over-the-road truckers on which the Teamsters union relies to assist in organizing other industries. Within the union, therefore, this group is the most powerful, politically and economically. Union officials have been reluctant to advocate positive programs for equal employment because they

---

39. International Brotherhood of Teamsters, Chauffeurs, Warehousemen and Helpers of America, *Constitution*, 1966, Article II, Section 2(a).

could affect this internal balance of power. In turn, the indus
try has been compelled to negotiate collective bargaining agree
ments with a formidable foe and is not anxious to make change
in work rules, seniority rights, and changes in their operation
that might in any way grant the union a competitive advantag
at the bargaining table. To what extent this status quo has bee
affected by developments of the 1960's, including especially th
Civil Rights legislation and activity of that period and the ne
leadership of the Teamsters' Union, will be discussed in the fo
lowing chapters.

CHAPTER IV

Negro Employment in the 1960's

The trucking industry entered the decade of the 1960's with few Negro over-the-road drivers. The data developed for this chapter show that this pattern had not changed significantly by 1968. Why the institutional factors limiting Negro employment proved too difficult to overcome is discussed in this and subsequent chapters after a review of the data.

THE OVERALL PICTURE

Employment in motor freight transportation and warehousing by race, sex, and broad occupational group was reported on by the Equal Employment Opportunity Commission in 1966 (Table 8). Like the 1960 census data, the EEOC compilation includes warehouse employees as well as truckers. Unfortunately the EEOC and census data are not strictly comparable. The former is based upon reports from employers of 100 or more, whereas the latter is the result of responses of individuals to interviewers. Thus, the census includes drivers of companies with less than 100 employees and undoubtedly drivers working for private carriers, plus any discrepancies resulting from differences in how individuals view themselves as compared with how they are viewed by their employers.

Nevertheless, the significant fact is the closeness of the results. In 1960, the census found (Table 7 above) that 7.9 percent of those in trucking and warehouses were Negroes, with a male ratio of 8.3 percent and a female one of 2.6 percent. Table 8 lists EEOC results as 6.3 percent Negro overall, 6.6 male and 2.3 percent female. Allowing for differences resulting from the different statistical and sampling methods, it would appear that Negroes made no progress, or were actually set back, in the first half of the 1960's.

A comparison of the employment data reported to the EEOC in 1966 by the motor carrier and warehousing industries with the data submitted by all industries or manufacturing industries

TABLE 8. *Motor Freight Transportation and Warehousing (SIC 42) Employment by Race, Sex, and Occupational Group United States, 1966*

Occupational Group	All Employees			Male			Female		
	Total	Negro	Percent Negro	Total	Negro	Percent Negro	Total	Negro	Percent Negro
Officials and managers	30,728	127	0.4	30,060	121	0.4	668	6	0.9
Professionals	2,353	17	0.7	2,272	17	0.7	81	—	—
Technicians	921	25	2.7	867	23	2.7	54	2	3.7
Sales workers	8,245	56	0.7	8,016	50	0.6	229	6	2.6
Office and clerical	55,026	582	1.1	25,394	315	1.2	29,632	267	0.9
Total white collar	97,273	807	0.8	66,609	526	0.8	30,664	281	0.9
Craftsmen	34,424	1,736	5.0	34,331	1,733	5.0	93	3	3.2
Operatives	198,228	11,313	5.7	197,798	11,265	5.7	430	48	11.2
Laborers	53,044	8,929	16.8	51,835	8,635	16.7	1,209	294	24.3
Service workers	7,394	1,632	22.1	7,115	1,493	21.0	279	139	49.8
Total blue collar	293,090	23,610	8.1	291,079	23,126	7.9	2,011	484	24.1
Total	390,363	24,417	6.3	357,688	23,652	6.6	32,675	765	2.3

Source: Equal Employment Opportunity Commission, *Job Patterns for Minorities and Women in Private Industry, 1966,* Report No. 1 (Washington: The Commission, 1968), Part II.

Note: For a definition of SIC 42, see Figure 2, p. 6.

alone, reveals that the former's white-Negro employment ratio is lower than that reported by either all industries or manufacturing industries (Table 9). For example, only 0.8 percent of all white collar workers employed by the trucking and warehousing industries were Negroes, while all industries reported that 2.6 percent of their white collar workers were Negroes, and manufacturing industries reported that 1.2 percent of their white collar workers were Negroes. A similar differential arises when we assess the employment statistics compiled under the blue collar classification. Also, the ratio of the Negroes employed as service workers is high for the three industrial groups listed in Table 9. Thus, the trucking and warehousing industries in 1966 employed more Negroes as service workers than did manufacturing industries, but they employed slightly less percentagewise than that reported by all industries. The varied circumstances and factors which have caused these divergent racial employment profiles to arise will be discussed in subsequent chapters.

The 1967 Sample

We have already noted that if statistics were available for trucking alone, the proportion of Negroes would be less than that for trucking and warehousing combined. Data set forth in Table 10, covering 395 Class I motor carriers for 1967, substantiate this. Only 4.5 percent in this sample are black, as compared with 6.3 percent in Table 9. This table also points up the concentration of Negroes in the lower job classifications. Less than one percent of the salaried workers were black, as were only 3.7 percent of the craftsmen and 4.6 of the operatives. On the other hand, 10.7 percent of the laborers and 23 percent of the service workers were Negroes. Although Table 8 shows the same wide representation of Negroes in white collar employment, it does show a better representation of Negroes in the top two blue collar classifications, although an even greater concentration of Negroes as laborers. Overall, it would appear that Negroes are not only better represented in warehousing than trucking, but have had better opportunities in the top blue collar jobs in the former as well.

The data in Table 10 are, of course, from the larger Class I carriers only and it is possible that the smaller firms employ a larger percentage of Negroes. In addition, the occupational groups in Table 9 are more suitable to manufacturing than to transportation employment. In an unpublished study made avail-

TABLE 9. *Motor Freight Transportation and Warehousing (SIC 42)*
Compared with All Industries and Manufacturing Industries
Employment by Race, Sex, and Occupational Group
Total United States, 1966

Occupational Group	All Industries			Manufacturing Industries			Motor Freight Transportation and Warehousing		
	Total	Negro	Percent Negro	Total	Negro	Percent Negro	Total	Negro	Percent Negro
Officials and managers	2,077,663	18,106	0.9	878,497	4,991	0.6	30,728	127	0.4
Professionals	1,689,886	22,333	1.3	670,818	3,732	0.6	2,353	17	0.7
Technicians	1,137,952	46,503	4.1	448,217	6,563	1.5	921	25	2.7
Sales workers	1,796,574	42,417	2.4	346,136	4,160	1.2	8,245	56	0.7
Office and clerical	4,264,770	151,105	3.5	1,307,982	26,193	2.0	55,026	582	1.1
Total white collar	10,966,845	280,464	2.6	3,651,650	45,639	1.2	97,273	807	0.8
Craftsmen	3,626,470	130,543	3.6	2,199,536	82,343	3.7	34,424	1,736	5.0
Operatives	6,499,351	702,234	10.8	5,020,500	531,586	10.6	198,228	11,313	5.7
Laborers	2,465,901	523,970	21.2	1,623,100	297,509	18.3	53,044	8,929	16.8
Service workers	1,952,135	452,036	23.2	247,082	53,521	21.7	7,394	1,632	22.1
Total blue collar	14,543,857	1,808,783	12.4	9,090,218	964,959	10.6	293,090	23,610	8.1
Total	25,510,702	2,089,247	8.2	13,741,868	1,010,598	7.4	390,363	24,417	6.3

Source: Equal Employment Opportunity Commission, *Job Patterns for Minorities and Women in Private Industry, 1966,* Report No. 1 (Washington: The Commission, 1968), Part II.

Note: For a definition of SIC 42, see Figure 2, p. 6. Table does not include Alaska and Hawaii.

TABLE 10. *Trucking Industry*
Employment by Race, Sex, and Occupational Group
395 Class I Motor Carriers
1967

Occupational Group	All Employees			Male			Female		
	Total	Negro	Percent Negro	Total	Negro	Percent Negro	Total	Negro	Percent Negro
Officials and managers	21,004	54	0.3	20,616	53	0.3	388	1	0.3
Professionals	783	1	0.1	742	1	0.1	41	—	—
Technicians	975	2	0.2	955	2	0.2	20	—	—
Sales workers	6,298	3	0.1	6,229	3	0.1	69	—	—
Office and clerical	40,306	348	0.8	17,945	144	0.8	22,361	204	0.9
Total white collar	69,366	408	0.6	46,487	203	0.4	22,879	205	0.9
Craftsmen	20,553	762	3.7	20,547	762	3.7	6	—	—
Operatives	145,290	6,709	4.6	145,241	6,707	4.6	9	2	22.2
Laborers	32,006	3,537	10.7	32,040	3,534	10.7	26	3	11.5
Service workers	3,862	889	23.0	3,695	829	22.4	167	60	35.9
Total blue collar	201,731	11,897	5.9	201,523	11,832	5.9	208	65	31.2
Total	271,097	12,305	4.5	248,010	12,035	4.9	23,087	270	1.2

Source: Data in author's possession.

able to the author for 1967, seventeen carriers were found to employ 10,639 road drivers, of whom only 71, or 0.7 percent were black.[40] This would seem to corroborate both the lack of representation of Negroes as drivers and their concentration in lower-paid jobs.

The 1968 Field Sample

In order to examine the Negro employment situation more thoroughly, a careful field study was made in 1968 of a selected sample of large and small carriers in forty-eight metropolitan areas.[41] These data are set forth in Table 11 by occupations found in the trucking industry.

Negroes comprise 7.6 percent of the labor force of these firms, as compared with the 4.5 percent of the ratio for 395 Class I carriers in 1967 (Table 10). Allowing for some increase in the employment of Negroes between 1967 and 1968, the difference is both substantial and easily explained. The data in Table 10 are comparable to those for large firms in Table 11. The latter has a Negro proportion of 5.7 percent, higher than the figure for the 395 Class I carriers, but possibly attributable to the stringencies of the labor market in 1968 over 1967 for lower-rated jobs.

On the other hand, in the smaller firms included in this sample, 11.3 percent of the employees and 5.3 percent of the road drivers were black. Only 0.9 percent of the large company drivers were Negroes. Because the work is distasteful and difficult in some of these smaller companies, Negroes find it easier to find employment with them, for example, as brick movers and household movers. Also, small nonunion firms, particularly in the South, traditionally employ a larger number of Negroes.

For both large and small firms, the data in Table 10 corroborate those in previous tables in so far as occupational distribution is concerned. Except for the local drivers, 50 percent of the Negroes in the sample are employed in the lower pay and lower status jobs, such as docksmen, oilers, washers, service workers, and helpers. The more prestigious occupation of driver, seemingly unattainable to large numbers of Negro workers, demands a more detailed examination.

---

40. Data in author's possession.

41. Small firms consist of Class I and II carriers employing 100 or less hourly employees. See Appendix A and B for methodology.

TABLE 11. *Trucking Industry*
Employment by Race, Occupation, and Company Size
United States, 1968

Job Classifications	All Firms			Small Firms[a]			Large Firms[b]		
	Total	Negro	Percent Negro	Total	Negro	Percent Negro	Total	Negro	Percent Negro
Management	14,337	13	0.1	4,753	—	—	9,584	13	0.1
Road drivers	59,887	1,417	2.4	19,669	1,037	5.3	40,218	380	0.9
Local drivers	53,920	5,865	10.9	25,602	3,977	15.5	28,318	1,888	6.7
Dockmen	31,336	3,968	12.7	5,914	1,702	28.8	28,318	2,266	8.9
Mechanics	13,051	775	5.9	3,376	179	5.3	9,675	596	6.2
Oilers	354	231	65.3	22	22	100.0	332	209	63.0
Washers	849	786	92.6	206	206	100.0	643	580	90.2
Service workers	2,564	1,115	43.5	451	301	66.7	2,113	814	38.5
Dispatchers	4,270	8	0.2	1,575	—	—	2,695	8	0.3
Warehousemen	706	100	14.2	412	43	10.4	294	57	19.4
Helpers	6,559	1,239	18.9	4,062	619	15.2	2,497	620	24.8
Clerical workers	23,406	538	2.3	5,473	—	—	17,933	538	3.0
Total	211,239	16,055	7.6	71,515	8,086	11.3	139,724	7,969	5.7

Source: Data in author's possession.

Note: See Appendix A for details of sample selection and Appendix B for the methodology used to adjust the original data for this and subsequent tables.

[a] Small firms are those having 100 or less employees.

[b] Large firms are those having 101 or more employees.

THE ROAD DRIVERS

The Motor Carrier Act of 1935 established safety regulations which forced employers to be more exacting in the employment of interstate drivers. These regulations, and their subsequent modifications over the years, not only compel a potential driver to meet specific health requirements, but to be familiar with the rules and regulations associated with safe driving.[42] In addition, each state has rules governing licenses for commercial drivers which very from state to state.

Driver Qualifications

Although the Department of Transportation's regulations stipulate that a long-haul driver must be at least twenty-one years old, most employers insist that they be older. This age requirement varies from firm to firm, but the average minimal age among the firms interviewed was twenty-six. Regardless of a firm's size, nature, or locale, the companies argue that a man below this minimal age is not mature enough to assume the responsibility for a piece of equipment valued at $35,000, containing commodities sometimes worth well over $100,000.

The over-the-road driver must be able to drive safely a gasoline or today's more popular diesel-powered tractor, which with the loaded trailers are difficult to handle. In addition to meeting the age requirement, the Department of Transportation compels a potential over-the-road driver to pass a physical examination and, in the larger firms, to take a written examination to demonstrate his knowledge of safety rules and regulations. The applicant must also be able to speak and write English because a driver must keep a daily log of his road activities, and, in case of an accident, must file a detailed report. Besides being capable of handling the various types of vehicles operated by the hiring firm, the applicant must have a satisfactory driving record and he should have no criminal record. These latter two requirements often are used by employers as reasons for not hiring Negroes as road drivers. Yet, some firms use a very narrow

---

42. For more details, see U.S. Department of Transportation, Federal Highway Administration, Bureau of Motor Carrier Safety, *Motor Carrier Safety Regulations* (Washington: U.S. Government Printing Office, 1968). For a discussion of proposed revision of the safety regulations and the Teamsters objection to same, see "Federal Highway Commission Revising Driver Qualifications," *The International Teamster,* Vol. 60, No. 9 (September 1969), pp. 15-16.

definition of what constitutes a criminal record, while others will refuse to hire the man only if the criminal charge has been serious and recent.

Over and above the health and safety regulations spelled out by the Department of Transportation, there are also standards established by the industry, primarily by custom. Virtually all firms, regardless of size or geographical location, will not hire a driver for an over-the-road opening unless he has had approximately three years' experience driving a tractor trailer, including some experience under conditions comparable to those he should encounter in his new job. As subsequent analyses will demonstrate, one of the real obstacles faced by Negroes in being employed as line-haul drivers is the employers' contention that they lack sufficient experience as drivers.

With prior experience a necessary condition of employment, some of the larger firms sponsor and finance their own training programs, and pay the trainee according to a graduated pay schedule. One firm, sponsoring what is considered by many employers at the best training program in the country, prefers that the trainee not have driven a truck for any other motor carrier firm. Second, there are private truck driver training schools throughout the country, some costing as much as $800. As a rule, employers are not satisfied with the graduates of these schools, and are reluctant to hire them. In practice, most over-the-road drivers enter the occupation by first driving a small truck as a local driver for private or public carriers; then after gaining experience, they move to the larger and more complicated vehicles. Some gain entrance into the driving occupation by working as helpers with local truck drivers.

Drivers employed by public carriers frequently start on the "extra board," bidding for regular runs on the basis of seniority as vacancies occur. The extra board consists of a rotating list of drivers who substitute for regular drivers when they are on vacation, or who make extra trips when the demand for truck transportation increases. The seasonal variations in truck transportation are caused by holiday buying patterns and by peak periods of stocking merchandise. As a general rule, Monday and Friday are the carriers' busiest days of the week because neither they nor the shippers want merchandise tied up on platforms over the weekend. The extra board and the use of casual drivers enable the employer to use his labor force more flexibly as the demand for truck services changes.

The seemingly objective requirements stated above must be viewed in conjunction with personal demands made on over-the-road drivers.[43] They must be willing to spend time away from home. Senior drivers, who are able to bid on the better-paying runs, have been known to spend as many as 250 nights per year sleeping in the cab of a tractor trailer or in dormitory facilities provided by the employer at distant terminals.

On extremely long runs, a two-man sleeper team is operative; one man drives while the other sleeps in the bunk behind the cab. Normally, a driver on such a team may choose his driving partner. Most IBT contracts grant over-the-road drivers the right to choose new driving partners annually. The duration of these "marriages," as they are referred to, depends on the ability of the men to work together in such close quarters and the existence of this arrangement adds to the reluctance of employers to hire Negro road drivers.

When sleeper teams are used, they travel nonstop to a terminal location where the freight is delivered to receivers in the area by local drivers using smaller trucks, and the driver has a layover before the return trip. During the actual trip, moreover, the driver has two four-hour periods of sleep or rest in the berth of the truck. This meets the Department of Transportation's regulation which calls for eight hours off duty following ten hours of driving. Even so, under these conditions a team of drivers may remain away from the base terminal for seventy hours during an eight-day period, often making two or three such round trips a week.

Over-the-road driving is well paid. Wages range from $10,000 to $20,000 per year, with the average annual wage in the neighborhood of $11,500 per year. Given the lack of formal education required, the jobs do attract capable people. Negroes desiring such work find considerable white worker competition for the jobs.

Negro Availability

Approximately 90 percent of the companies interviewed suggested that they were more than willing to hire Negroes as over-the-road drivers as long as qualified Negroes applied. They emphatically stated that if the federal government or any of the

43. See Ross A. McFarland and Alfred L. Moseley, *Human Factors in Highway Transport Safety* (Boston: Harvard School of Public Health, 1955).

several city and state agencies would just produce one qualified Negro road driver, they would hire him tomorrow. At the same time they argued that morality cannot be legislated, and as a group they seemed insensitive to that nebulous idealization labeled "corporate responsibility." Thus, the companies generally fear hiring marginal employees because of the cost involved, and they refuse to lower their hiring standards. In practice, however, only the giant firms in the industry employ hiring procedures that are somewhat consistent and seemingly equitable. Most of the others seemed to assume that all Negroes are marginal and unqualified.

The real test of the companies' contention that they cannot find qualified Negro road drivers is in determining whether or not the nation's labor markets do in fact contain Negroes who would meet the government's requirements and the companies' standards. The record demonstrates that the Post Office Department does find qualified Negroes to fill openings arising among their road drivers who perform the same tasks as do drivers of trucking companies.

Table 13 shows the total number and percentage of Negroes employed as tractor trailer and motor vehicle operators by the Post Office within the SMSA's that comprise this study's sample labor markets. Although representatives from the private carriers argue that competent Negro road drivers cannot be found, the statistics indicate that, of the tractor trailer drivers employed by the Post Office Department, 553 or 62.3 percent are Negroes. When other motor vehicle operators, who substitute when necessary for tractor trailer operators, are included, the percentage of Negroes is 60.5. The type of equipment used, the work setting, and the basic occupational requirements existing at these various Post Office locations are identical to that found in the private sector of the economy. It would appear that the inadequate supply argument used by the trucking industry is not supported by the evidence.

Supervisory personnel working for the POD who were interviewed by the author report that the Negroes' absenteeism, lateness, and turnover rates are no higher than those prevailing among white employees. On the other hand, public carriers without any Negro road drivers suggested in interviews that Negroes are in short supply and, as a group, are not dependable. This all-pervading attitude is difficult to evaluate in quantifiable terms, but these biases are apparently harbored by many em-

TABLE 12. *Tractor Trailer and Motor Vehicle Operators*
Post Office Department Employment by Race
Selected SMSA's, 1968

SMSA[a]	Tractor Trailer and Motor Vehicle Operators[b]			Tractor Trailer Operators[b]			Motor Vehicle Operators[b]		
	Total	Negro	Percent Negro	Total	Negro	Percent Negro	Total	Negro	Percent Negro
Atlanta	27	18	66.7	27	18	66.7	—	—	—
Boston	89	12	13.5	38	5	13.2	51	7	13.7
Chicago	296	200	67.6	197	120	60.9	99	80	80.8
Detroit	49	43	87.8	16	14	87.5	33	29	87.9
Dallas	11	6	54.5	11	6	54.5	—	—	—
Denver[c]	1	—	—	1	—	—	—	—	—
New York	377	210	55.7	367	204	55.6	10	6	60.0
Philadelphia	87	73	83.9	31	27	87.1	56	46	82.1
St. Louis	144	58	40.3	35	25	71.4	109	33	30.3
San Francisco	71	63	88.7	71	63	88.7	—	—	—
Los Angeles	80	66	82.5	80	66	82.5	—	—	—
Birmingham	15	6	40.0	14	5	35.7	1	1	100.0
Total	1,247	755	60.5	888	553	62.3	359	202	56.3

Source: U.S. Post Office Department.

[a] Winston-Salem and Charlotte SMSA's, that were included in the sample used elsewhere in this study, have been excluded from this analysis because the Post Office Department does not employ tractor trailer or motor vehicle operators in these two SMSA's.

[b] The figures under this heading also include substitute employees.

[c] Denver fills these positions as necessary.

ployers. At the same time, however, 87 percent of the companies interviewed who did employ Negroes maintained that they were excellent workers, or that as a group their dependability was no worse than that of the average white employee performing the same task.

It might be argued that the federal government is fostering racial job equality at any price, or that the lack of urgency prevailing throughout the bureaucratic structure of the Post Office Department is the type of work setting in which poorly motivated Negroes can perform best. These objections could, of course, be true to a degree, but the difference in the percentage of Negroes employed by the Department and the ratio found in private industry is just too great—63.7 percent versus 2.7 percent—to justify such objections. Several Department supervisors even informed the author that white drivers from private carriers often cannot maneuver their equipment in and around Department platforms without assistance from their own drivers, including the Negro ones. In brief, there is no substantial evidence whatsoever in support of the contention that Negro drivers employed by this federal agency are incompetent.

Tractor trailer drivers employed by the POD are included in the Post Office Field Service Classification No. 7. Depending upon their seniority, these drivers earn from $6,044 to $8,266 per year. Although on a national basis in 1967 18.9 percent of all postal employees were Negroes,[44] only 8.1 percent of all employees in PFS level No. 7 were Negroes. The percentage of Negroes employed as road drivers (63.7) is thus far above both the percentage of Negro employees for the Post Office Department as a whole and PFS No. 7 in particular. The differences found in the data above are sufficient to counter the employers' suggestion that Negroes are employed for social and political reasons rather than for their qualifications.

Three Negro drivers questioned at the Philadelphia Post Office recounted how, in 1962, they tried to obtain road jobs with a private carrier, whose name they mentioned. They stated that they were denied employment because the Teamsters and the employer gave them the "run around." This consisted of their continually being told that they lacked the proper training. As of 1966, this same firm had no Negroes in any of its job classifications. It is interesting to note that the Post Office Department

---

44. These data come from an in-house survey conducted by the Post Office Department in 1967.

supervisors claim that a person who can drive smaller trucks ca
be trained (in an 80-hour course which they sponsor) to handl
the more cumbersome tractor trailers.

The "Loss of Customers" Argument

Employers are sometimes apprehensive about hiring Negroe
for the first time because they fear this would occasion the los
of customers. In recent years it has become less of a probler
because white consumers are becoming used to seeing Negroes i
a greater variety of jobs.[45]

With the exception of two contract carriers, none of the othe
111 firms interviewed thought customer reaction had any bear
ing on why they employed so few Negroes. Even the two firm
that expressed a fear of losing business if they hired Negroe
were somewhat vague as to why shippers would turn to othe
carriers, but they implied that some people believe that a firr
that employs a disproportionate number of Negroes is second
rate. Contract carriers are different from the common carrier
in that they serve a few select customers; thus, the firm's racia
employment profile is easy for the customers to detect. Ironicall
contract carriers who worry about customer reaction employ pr
portionately more Negroes than the common carriers who mair
tain that the possible loss of customers does not influence thei
hiring of Negroes.

The consensus among most companies was that their driver
seldom come in direct contact with the shippers but rather wit
other drivers, platform men, and helpers. Consequently, it is un
likely that the apprehension over a general customer revolt con
tributes to the industry's reaction to equal employment programs
It might be well to note that among private carriers wher
drivers are often salesmen, the reaction of the consumer was
factor in establishing hiring policies.[46]

---

45. Georges F. Doriot (supervisor), *The Management of Racial Integratio
    in Business*, Special Report to Management, Harvard Graduat
    School of Business Administration (New York: McGraw-Hill, 1964)
    p. 82; see also, Edward C. Koziara and Karen S. Koziara, *The Negr
    in the Hotel Industry*, The Racial Policies of American Industry, Repor
    No. 4 (Philadelphia: Industrial Research Unit, The Wharton School o
    Finance and Commerce, University of Pennsylvania, 1968), p. 35.

46. New York State Commission Against Discrimination, *The Employmen
    of Negroes as Driver Salesmen in the Baking Industry* (New York
    The Commission, 1960).

The Reaction of White Employees

Presumably, many industries would label a white rank and file revolt caused by the employment of Negroes as a sociological and psychological difficulty rather than as an economic issue. Through coercion and persuasion, supervisors in some self-contained work settings have been able to discipline white employees reacting adversely to the hiring of Negroes. Because of the special nature of the trucking industry, however, there can be some unusual economic consequences if fleetmen insist upon hiring Negroes against the will of the white majority. Once the vehicle leaves the terminal, supervisory personnel have no direct control over the activities of the driver. Private studies have been conducted for the industry to determine the approximate amount of time various long haul and even city runs should take. Spotters often are hired by the larger companies to check on their road drivers, and drivers are notified if they exceed the posted speed limits or if they are guilty of other safety violations. In this loosely disciplined work setting, companies hiring Negroes might face a rebellious rank and file which would give vent to their displeasure not by *violating* speed and safety regulations, but rather by *observing* them. This is particularly true in local or city operations. For should a driver choose to observe all the motor vehicle regulations in any given city, the movement of goods could well slow down to such a degree that shippers would start turning to another motor carrier, or purchase their own fleet of trucks and become one among the many private carriers.

Although employers are aware of their responsibility to have their drivers observe safety regulations, they sometimes take the risk of dispatching trailers whose weights exceed the maximum prescribed by law. They are not unaware that drivers double park in congested downtown city streets, carry excess weight loads over bridges, and violate the posted speed limits. The subtle sabotage on the part of white drivers of following all the rules would leave the employer with no recourse before the law or the Teamsters. Of all the economic consequences arising because an employer hired Negroes, this could be the most costly and the most difficult to control.

Teamster members realize that legal slowdowns of this nature may cost a carrier customers, and ultimately may force it out of business. Generally, however, the attitude of the rank and file is that the demand for motor carrier service is unlimited, and they are willing to follow the freight as it goes from one carrier

to another. Since drivers work alone for a greater part of th
day, they have a tendency to identify more with the union an
job opportunities at large than with a particular firm. Employer
and union personnel alike acknowledge that this is a formidabl
obstacle to the creation of effective fair employment practices.

One employer aptly stated:

> I might hire a few Negro road drivers if I could find some that I wa
> convinced would be reliable and handle my equipment safely and courte
> ously. But I'm not ready to risk absenteeism, damaged equipment, fights
> slowdowns, or other problems with my present drivers. Besides, I'v
> got a good crew here; we get along, you know what I mean, and wh
> bust all that up? Anyhow no damn government can tell me how to ru
> my business.[47]

Approaches to Recruitment

Because the private carriers have grown in such a topsy-turv
fashion, and since their hiring procedures have been subjected t
extraordinary pressures exerted by the Teamsters, their screen
ing and hiring procedures are riddled with fetishes and contra
dictions. Needless to say, the industry is of the opinion that thei
hiring techniques are reasonable and uniformly administered. It
sole justification for this claim seems to be that it obtains em
ployees when needed. Some firms in hiring road drivers, fo
example, will not hire anyone with too high an I.Q., claiming
that intelligent people daydream as they drive and that they hav
a tendency to be trouble makers, often meaning potential unio
leaders. Simultaneously, other companies welcome intelligent ap
plicants for road driving postitions because they believe that the
make better drivers. It is not unusual to find two nearly identica
firms bidding for long haul drivers in the same labor market
but setting different age and experience standards for new ap
plicants. For example, while one firm insists on having its new
road drivers undergo its own formal driver training programs
and will not permit local drivers to become road drivers and vice
versa, another firm possessing identical corporate characteristics
will insist that all road drivers must have worked with them
as local drivers. Last, but not least, the total person must be
judged before allowing him full responsibility over the com
pany's equipment. Obviously, where unproven, nebulous, and in
consistent hiring procedures prevail, it is easy to judge Negroes

---

47. "Trucking Comes Under the Civil Rights Gun," *Commercial Car Journa*
    (June 1966), p. 108.

as totally different persons who are not to be trusted on their own. Moreover, when the government puts pressure on the companies to hire Negro road drivers, they immediately point to their highest standards for admission, when it is evident that these standards are relaxed when whites apply for employment.

There is some merit in the position that personnel directors should establish policies compelling terminal managers to hire the best applicants. Industry leaders report, however, that except for those of five or six of the larger carriers, personnel staffs are not necessarily qualified to select the best. Many personnel people have been taken out of drivers' ranks and few have had formal training in personnel relations; often they attend seminars in highway safety, and, in some instances, the safety directors serve as personnel directors. Part of the problem causing diverse hiring standards to prevail is the lack of qualified leadership. This leadership vacuum is of even greater significance as the government prods the industry to view Negro employment in terms of affirmative action programs. Better managed firms, which are usually the larger ones, issue employment manuals to their terminal managers. These manuals spell out the Department of Transportation's and the firm's qualifications for each job specification and the procedures to be followed in interviewing, screening, and testing applicants. Terminal or operations managers make the initial hiring decision at the local level. Because of the geographical distribution of the terminals, headquarters screens the hiring of road drivers by checking out the veracity of the information submitted by the new employee.

Smaller firms frequently bypass the screening process in the hiring of drivers. Representatives of the union find themselves confronted with cases during grievance hearings in which they are compelled to represent the interests of a man whom the firm never should have hired in the first place. Employers concede that in such cases the union usually is extremely fair. Should a local union be going through the throes of an internal political feud, however, this same driver may become a *cause celebre* for one of the feuding factions. In this case, the floating incompetent driver can be extremely costly to the company.

One of the most difficult procedures to police in the hiring of drivers is the road test, in which the applicant actually drives a truck in the company of one of the senior drivers. It is common in smaller firms for a driving applicant to find that the screening process consists of nothing but a road test. The one responsible for hiring will simply say to one of the senior drivers, "See if this guy can drive." The applicant is then taken to whatever place the senior driver selects for a road test. If the applicant is a Negro, there is no way for the company to evaluate the degree to which a senior driver's possible anti-Negro biases may influence his evaluation of the man.

Some Teamster locals are more powerful than others. It is not unusual, moreover, to find that companies party to the same contract are treated differently by a local. The unevenness of local union strength and the special privileges enjoyed by some companies permit certain employers to bypass contract provisions. Where local unions are aggressive and constantly questioning any change in the companies' operations, the latter have a tendency to abide scrupulously by terms specified in the contract. Besides providing for a union shop, the National Freight Agreement also states:

When the employer needs additional men he shall give the Local Union equal opportunity with all other sources to provide suitable applicants, but the Employer shall not be required to hire those referred by the Local Union.[48]

Here, the company clearly has the final say over hiring employees, yet some employers point to this clause in explaining the absence of Negroes. It is probably true, however, that some employers, having been harrassed and unrelentingly badgered by the IBT, usually ask the shop steward or business agent if any union member is looking for employment. Of greater significance than the terms of the contract, in regard to Negro employment, is the fact that employers rely mainly on an informal referral method in the hiring of dockmen, helpers, and mechanics, as well as drivers.

Companies constituting the sample of this study were questioned as to what sources they found best in recruiting hourly employees (Table 13). They were asked to rank these choices according to the order of their importance. At first glance it is easy to see that employers as a rule do not rely on either newspaper ads or employment agencies. Manpower needs are essentially met by employers first asking present employees if they know of anyone seeking employment, and second, by going to the IBT. The other source noted by employers consists of

---

48. National Master Freight Agreement, Article 3, Section I(c).

TABLE 13. *Trucking Industry
Employers' Preference as to Sources of
Recruitment of Hourly Employees*

Sources	1st Choice	2nd Choice	3rd Choice	4th Choice	5th Choice
Newspaper ads	—	2	1	—	3
The union	32	41	13	7	—
Referrals	62	43	30	12	—
Employment agencies	—	—	3	—	1
Others	2	10	47	53	13

Source: Personal interviews.

Note: Some employers were so vague about the sources they used to obtain new hires that they were not included; nevertheless, over 90 percent of all respondents are included.

pirating employees from other trucking companies or absorbing the employees of a company which has moved its terminal facilities or merged with another carrier. United Parcel Service in Philadelphia, for example, was involved in a protracted labor dispute in 1967, resulting in the facility being permanently closed down. It is estimated that 800 competent drivers, dockmen, and mechanics (only a few of whom were Negroes) were thrown into the Philadelphia labor market. Both informal referrals and union contracts expose the companies to a very narrow slice of all labor markets. This fact must be weighed against the companies' contention that experienced Negro employees are not available.

Indeed, where firms employ only one or two Negroes or none at all, there is little likelihood that Negro applicants will be forthcoming. As job openings arise, terminal managers will ask their employees if they know anyone looking for a job and within a racially segregated society white employees will rarely refer Negroes. Clusters of friends, relatives, neighbors, or schoolmates dominate in some terminals. Like other blue collar workers, employees view job opportunities as conquered small kingdoms over which they have the right to divide the spoils.

Responses to a question as to how long Negroes have bee
employed corroborated the results obtained regarding sources c
employment. The longer that firms had employed Negroes, th
higher the percentage of Negro employees.

The Teamsters' Union as a source for new hires can functio
in two ways: (1) terminal supervisory personnel can ask th
steward or business agent if any of "his boys" are interested i
permanent work, or (2) employers can call the IBT's hiring ha
for casual drivers. Union officials constitute an informal info
mation system on the availability of drivers, platform men, an
mechanics. Disgruntled union members keep the business agent
informed of their wanting to change jobs. Business agents als
are aware of changes in companies' operations and of merger
Anti-Negro sentiment and the political constraints within a loc
militate against union officials recommending Negro union men
bers for the more desirable jobs. Some terminals, labeled "N
gro barns" by union members, are sent only Negro washers, oi
ers, helpers, and dockmen. In an industry where there are rel
tively few Negroes in the first place, it is highly unlikely tha
many Negroes will be found in the ever-fluid and more desirab
driver pool.

Except in the South, the Teamsters maintain hiring halls i
the larger cities having a concentration of terminals. Should a
employer need a temporary driver (referred to as a casual dri
er), he will telephone the hall and make his needs known. Th
employers constantly complain about these floaters, who, the
contend, are poor drivers, more interested in playing checker
and enjoying companionship at the hall than they are in workin
Despite such complaints, the industry objected vehemently whe
the IBT tried to close some of its halls, and they were reopene
Carriers often need extra local drivers before Christmas, whe
merchandisers are stocking their shelves, and on Mondays an
Fridays during the year because neither they nor the shippe
want the shipments standing still over the weekends. Halls, ther
fore, provide the employers with a necessary and flexible mar
power pool. If the relationship between the company and th
union has been somewhat amiable, the employer is given th
opportunity to choose from the available drivers. Companie
however, often maintain a list of the better floating drivers, s
that if a permanent opening occurs, they will specify a particula
man.

When Negro drivers "bat out of the hall," they are often sent out on dirty and difficult jobs. If Negroes are sent out to the better paying and easier jobs, they mysteriously do not seem to remain with one of these employers long enough to gain seniority rights. Some employers insist that they have been calling the hall for years, and they have never been sent a single Negro. Inasmuch as Negro casuals without seniority rights save the employer money—and because local union leaders do not want a white rebellion on their hands—it is advantageous to both parties surreptitiously to exclude Negroes from permanent employment.

Seniority Provisions

Although the National Master Freight Agreement embodies guidelines relating to seniority provisions, the numerous regional and local supplemental agreements contain certain exceptions and amendments. In the event that two companies merge or consolidate, the National Agreement provides that the IBT and the acquiring firm must mutually agree on how the once separate seniority lists are to be blended. Besides this broad statement of mutual agreement the contract also contains specific rules and regulations that are to be followed.

In an industry where mergers, acquisitions, and consolidations are common, these rules governing seniority are necessary. Mergers usually are followed by a total revamping of the carriers' operations and the shutdown of certain terminals. No doubt some employees are affected adversely in these corporate and operational changes, but there is no evidence that the Teamsters or the companies purposely agree to changes in seniority rosters to lay off Negroes. Other seniority provisions, however, may militate against hiring Negroes, and also may inhibit the Negroes' mobility in the job hierarchy.

The National Master Freight Agreement states, "The extent to which seniority shall be applied as well as the methods and procedures of such application shall be set forth in each of the Supplemental Agreements." [49] This broad mandate gives rise to an infinite variety of seniority provisions throughout the country.

---

49. National Master Freight Agreement, Article 5, Section I.

The general rule is that drivers can bid [50] on various runs and those at the top of the list bid first. To familiarize the drivers with the options open to them, the employer must post the runs in a conspicuous place. Since some hauls pay more, and because some necessitate that drivers remain away from home for longer durations of time, senior drivers are given the first choice at what they subjectively consider to be the best run.

Open bidding could adversely affect Negro employment in two ways. First, as a general rule white drivers resent Negroes who have more seniority than they do and open bidding constantly reminds the white driver that a Negro is earning more than he is for the same kind of work. Second, as the bidding progresses down the seniority list, some runs are bypassed and the employer must make the assignment himself. He may be compelled, for reasons of economy, to assign a white and Negro together in a sleeper-cab operation. For obvious reasons, companies are apprehensive about such an arrangement and argue that they lose a needed flexibility in assigning drivers by having Negroes among them.

Any employer who compels a white driver to ride with a Negro in a sleeper cab must be willing to face the clandestine sabotage that the white rank and file can shower upon him. Feigned grievances, which will be discussed later, may start cropping up all over. Nevertheless, in one case in which an employer categorically told a white driver that if he refused to ride with an assigned Negro driver, he would be discharged, the white driver reluctantly accepted the assignment, and the employer was faced with neither grievances nor slowdowns. This exceptional case is no doubt explained by the fact that the company was one of the giants of the industry, and had taken a firm stand against discrimination. By way of contrast, another large carrier allegedly promised its white employees that regardless of what the government says or does, it will never hire Negro road drivers.

---

50. The Supplemental Agreement for Local 85 in San Francisco reads: "Job seniority will be used in bidding for assignments to equipment. . . ." Section 7. The Supplemental Agreement covering seven IBT locals in Philadelphia and vicinity states: "All regular runs (except those 'House Concerns' with original drivers), positions, starting time, classification and shifts are subject to seniority and shall be posted for bids. Posting shall be at a conspicuous place so that all eligible employees will receive notice of the vacancy, run or position open for bid, and such posting of bids shall be made not more than once each calendar year; vacancies, new runs, new positions shall be posted for bid immediately, unless otherwise mutually agreed upon. Peddle runs shall be subject to bidding provided driver is qualified." Section 4(a).

Carriers with road drivers, local drivers, and dockmen working out of the same terminal may have a single seniority list or several of them. If an employee switches from the local drivers' list to the road seniority roster, he must go to the bottom of the latter. If an employer has an opening among his road drivers, he usually will give the men at the top of the local list the opportunity to fill this job opening. Purely subjective reasons influence the local drivers' decision to accept or reject this offer. Although there are no reliable data on the subject, it is estimated that once a man has ten or more years seniority on the local roster, he is reluctant to risk his seniority rights by switching to long haul driving. With a greater percentage of Negroes employed as local drivers, it would seem that many of them could gain entry into the firm through this door, and then be promoted to the better-paying, long haul work, but such is not the case. Carriers maintaining both local and road seniority lists contend that Negroes themselves refuse these better jobs. Yet, the same carriers agree that white drivers are willing to accept the risk and move from the top of a local seniority roster to the bottom of a road list. Since the employer must determine competency for road work, he is not forced to use seniority alone in making these promotions. At the same time, the Negro is starkly aware of the economic pressures exerted upon the employer and the sociological adjustments he must make within the various work groups. Although seniority is not a bottleneck to whites on the promotional ladder, it often is an obstacle for Negroes because of the personal risks involved.

Grievance Procedures

In most industries unions and management alike run the risk of having discrimination charges lodged against them in the event an arbitration decision is handed down against a Negro employee, even if the Negro is deserving of an adverse decision. When a Negro is party to a case submitted to arbitration, those responsible for deciding the case take the possible charge of discrimination into account. In most grievance procedures the onus of proving nondiscrimination is shared by an impartial arbitrator. The Teamsters, however, have fashioned what is known as an open-end grievance procedure which seldom permits the use of an impartial arbitrator and gives the union a leverage technique which most employers fear. This "major control mechanism" [51] allows for the union to call a strike if both sides fail to reach agreement in a given case. According to James:

> . . . in a collective bargaining structure which stresses uniformity, the open-end grievance procedure, operating without precedent, enables the union to behave, to a degree at least, like a discriminating monopolist. The contract may be enforced more stringently against employers who can afford to provide better conditions while it retains the advantages derived from apparent equality.[52]

Inasmuch as neither side in a dispute in the trucking industry is hampered by precedent, there is a tendency to trade grievances off. The trucking industry cannot stockpile the services it sells, and "in the absence of fixed rules and standards, the union invariably wields the upper hand at grievance meetings, for strikes are dreaded by most trucking operators." [53] This does not imply that the Teamsters always hold trump cards over every employer. A decision in a given grievance case, however, may well become the basis of a union demand at the next collective bargaining session. So employers must weigh a single case in terms of future costs.

In an arbitrary grievance setting, where grievances are more readily traded off at lower levels, no employer wants unnecessary complaints to arise simply because he insisted upon the hiring of Negroes. The shop steward or the business agent, depending on who handles grievances, could insist upon a literal interpretation of the contract and thus constrain the employer in his day-to-day operations. If the employer fails to comply precisely with specific terms of the contract, grievances might well be cropping up every time he made a decision. To the degree an employer has won special concessions from the IBT, either in grievance cases or in changes of his operations, to the same degree he owes something to the union officials who granted the favors. One of the concessions the employer might make in return is his guarantee not to employ Negroes—especially if pressure from the rank and file is being put on the union official himself. In brief, employers view the hiring of Negroes against the will of the rank and file as "muddying the water" in a situation where their problems with, and the reaction of, the Teamsters is unpredictable and potentially costly.

---

51. James, *op. cit.*, p. 168.

52. *Ibid.*, p. 172.

53. *Ibid.*, p. 171.

The Availability of Public Accommodations

Another variable, noted in Chapter III, which militated against the hiring of Negro road drivers in the South was their inability to find eating and sleeping facilities prior to the enactment of federal legislation outlawing discrimination in public accommodations. Fearing that the hiring of Negroes would lead to a certain inflexibility in assigning drivers, the employers singled out the public accommodations problem as a reason for not hiring Negro road drivers. In turn, this facilitated the creation of all-white, tightly-knit work groups, characterized by considerable cohesiveness. Although the enactment of federal legislation now outlaws such discrimination, Negroes are still excluded from the white fraternity.

Larger carriers maintain their own dormitories located in or near the strategic breaking-point terminals. Although this enables the company to operate more sleeper cab vehicles, the Teamsters contend it also has a tendency to keep men away from home too long. Interestingly enough in several instances where companies have hired Negro road drivers and white drivers have been compelled to accept them in the dormitories there have been no problems. One southern firm commented on the fact that in one of their dormitories which previously had been all white, the Negro drivers had been seen playing checkers with white employees. Most carriers, however, remain reluctant to assign runs to Negroes if the run requires them to sleep in company dormitories.

A carrier domiciled in the South hired two Negro road drivers for a sleeper cab run. Both of these drivers proved to be relatively competent, but after about six months one of them quit. Ostensibly, he left this carrier because his wife was against his being away from home several nights a week. But, in fact, the attitude of the white drivers also influenced his decision to seek employment as a local driver elsewhere.[54]

Nearness to Negro Labor Markets

The final variable helping to explain Negro employment patterns in the various labor markets is that most terminals are not located near the sections of cities where Negroes are concentrated. The author can attest to this because, as he visited

---

54. Personal interview, 1968.

the many and varied cities throughout the country, he discovered that the wharves of San Francisco, narrow streets under the Brooklyn Bridge, and unpaved cinder roads in the South were not accessible to public transportation. The older terminals, once located in what are now urban ghetto neighborhoods, have been moved closer to the industrial parks orbiting the nation's cities. Some carriers moved from the hub cities to avoid congested traffic patterns. Also, as the inner city neighborhoods started to disintegrate, carriers moved to avoid pilferage and damage to their properties and equipment. Although the majority of firms moved prior to the beginning of the racial unrest that has recently plagued our cities, the effect is that the trucking industry is no longer within easy access for Negro labor.

As an interesting illustration of this factor in Negro employment a company representative in Philadelphia noted that his company had several Negro local drivers who had been working for the carrier for over twenty years and were now at the top of the seniority list. Yet there was a long gap between those found at the top of the seniority list and three new Negro employees found at the bottom of the seniority list. A tight wartime labor market situation may have accounted for the firm hiring these few Negroes over twenty years ago, but the employer attributed these hirings to the fact that the terminal had been located near a Negro neighborhood, but moved away eighteen years ago. He also said that the older Negro drivers "having arrived" were reluctant to recommend either friends or relatives when job openings were available. The new Negro employees had come in off of the street when drivers were in short supply. The employer believed that they had applied because lately Negroes have acquired enough courage to seek employment outside of their "known world." Therefore, to the degree that distance in the absence of adequate public transportation constitutes a barrier to the mobility of Negroes in the nation's labor markets, it is valid to assume that this factor partially explains the relatively low ratio of Negroes found in the industry.

LOCAL DRIVERS AND HELPERS

Hiring standards for local drivers are not quite as stringent as those for road drivers. The nature of these two different driving jobs has influenced the employer's use of a different set of criteria to determine competency. Unlike the long-haul driver, who spends practically all of his time driving a large tractor trailer, the local driver spends considerable time in loading and unloading freight transported in smaller vehicles. Sometimes these "peddle" drivers,[55] as they are called, have a helper who does not drive, but helps the driver load and unload the freight. The Teamsters, over the years, have permitted employers to use fewer helpers if they passed some of the savings in wages on to the local drivers; helpers are consequently disappearing from the scene. Because the local cartage agreements are supplemental agreements appended to the national freight agreement, the wage rates and provisions permitting the use of helpers vary from area to area.

Since most of the local operations take place in urban or suburban areas where freight is moved from terminals, warehouses, and factories to wholesalers and retailers, local drivers are more likely to come in contact with consumers than are road drivers, and terminal managers take this into account in hiring. Those wishing to become local drivers must be familiar with the layout of a city, the location of specific streets, and local parking regulations. Such requirements work against many urban Negroes who, even if they are not new arrivals in a city, may not have had the necessary experience to meet these requirements.

Our 1968 sample found that 10.9 percent of all local drivers were Negroes. It would seem that the normal line of progression from local to road driver should afford Negroes the opportunity to gain admission to the better-paying road jobs, but for reasons discussed in a previous section of this chapter, this is not the case. Some of the employers generally interested in promoting equal employment have indicated that in the last few years they have made a concerted effort to hire Negroes as local drivers in those terminals employing the least number of Negroes. Hopefully, the Negroes' presence could dilute the deep anti-Negro prejudices held by predominantly white work crews,

---

55. The Ohio Rider to the Central States area over-the-road Motor Freight Supplemental Agreement states:

> A Local or Peddle-Run Driver shall be one who originates and terminates at his Domicile Terminal daily and whose duties are pick-up and delivery service only from or to consignee or shipper. However, a Peddle or Local Run that is now established as such by the Employer shall not be disturbed unless proven to the satisfaction of the Committee representing the Union and the Employer's Group, that the same is subterfuge to defeat the purpose of this Agreement.

and induce more Negroes to apply and more employers to accept them for long haul driving jobs.

NONDRIVER MANUAL WORKERS

Trucks usually are loaded during the evening by dockmen or, as they are sometimes called, platform men. These jobs can be filled by any male able to read bills of lading and physically capable of handling the freight passing through the firm's terminal location. Most dockmen earn less than the local drivers but more than the helpers. If they work on the dock as fork-lift operators—and not as platform men per se—their hourly rate of pay is often the same as that paid to local drivers.

The percentage of platform men and fork-lift operators employed at any given terminal location, in relationship to the total number of employees, depends on whether or not the type of freight handled permits palletization. Unlike those applying for driver jobs, applicants for dock positions do not find safety and health regulations a hurdle to entry. In these less prestigious jobs Negroes have found employment much easier to obtain. In 1968, our sample showed that 12.7 percent of all dockmen were Negroes.

Transportation equipment is the one single item for which trucking firms must allocate most of their capital. If they are to protect their investment in moving stock, and if they intend to keep the shipping public satisfied by avoiding breakdowns on the road, they must sponsor comprehensive preventive maintenance programs. Mechanics, tiremen, greasers, and washers are responsible for keeping the company's equipment in excellent operating condition. The titles indicate the job content, but it is not unusual to find an employee with the title of mechanic greasing the trucks and changing tires.

The type of work performed, in conjunction with seniority, determines whether or not a mechanic should be considered a journeyman mechanic, the highest formal classification a mechanic can achieve, which pays the highest union wage rate.[56] In turn, it is not unusual for the top mechanic of a particular shop to receive wages in excess of what is specified in the contract.

---

56. Most shop personnel belong to the International Association of Machinists AFL-CIO. In some areas the Teamsters include these employees in their local unions.

The nonspecialist employed at the terminal level may be hired as a "jack of all trades" and classified as a helper. With truck manufacturers extending the warranty period, the firms are hiring more of what they call "part replacers." Employees engaged as full-time washers, tire changers, and lubricators, or who perform a combination of these jobs, are at the bottom of the job scale and classified as miscellaneous garage employees. There are so many intra- and inter-firm variations regarding the classification and pay differentials of garage personnel that pay scales spelled out in contracts are not necessarily indicative of the hourly rate. Nevertheless, journeymen mechanics make in the area of $4.00 per hour, and in union shops those at the bottom of the pay scale usually make a dollar or more less. Negroes are commonly employed as helpers.

MANAGEMENT PERSONNEL

Except for top executives, management in the trucking industry is relatively low paid.[57] It is conceded generally by personnel directors that low starting salaries, coupled with an apparently unchallenging future, deter college graduates from entering the industry. As a general rule, the degree to which management positions are competently filled is in direct proportion to the size of the firm. The smaller firms usually rely on family members to fill decision-making positions, and it is not unusual to find management personnel who started out as truck drivers or terminal managers. Yet this tradition of coming up through the ranks is slowly dying out as the number of smaller firms declines.

Successful, highly profitable firms have grown so fast that in many cases they have not given enough attention to the recruitment of management personnel. Some have attempted to compensate for these shortcomings by inaugurating their own management training programs. College graduates are being recruit-

---

57. For a more detailed account of some of the problems discussed in this chapter, see the Proceedings of the Annual National Forum on Trucking Industrial Relations. These publications are as follows: 11th Annual National Forum, *Organizing Trucking Management* (1959); 12th Annual National Forum, *Personnel Practices in the Trucking Industry* (1961); 13th Annual National Forum, *Motivating Middle Management in Trucking* (1962); 15th Forum, *Profit Sharing and Incentives for Trucking Employees* (1965) (Washington: American Trucking Associations, Inc.).

ed as salesmen, maintenance engineers, terminal managers, ac
countants, personnel specialists, and safety directors. Althougl
the above list is not exhaustive, it is representative of the var
ious job opportunities available to a college graduate with a de
gree in transportation, marketing, or general business.

The number of Negroes in these training programs is smal
but growing. Competition for trained black graduates is great
however, and trucking companies are not bidding heavily in thi:
market. With only 0.1 percent of its management personnel Ne
gro in 1968, the trucking industry must undertake a concertec
program if more Negroes are to be employed as managers. Th•
problem of equal employment opportunities at this level of th•
job hierarchy is somewhat reflective of the industry's inabilit)
to establish comprehensive management training programs fo»
blacks and whites alike. Since Negroes have not been able tc
bring economic pressure to bear upon the industry, and since
further, the great majority of firms are family controlled, the
idea of having Negroes as managers is something that trucking
management did not seriously consider prior to 1965.

Middle Management

Each terminal employing approximately 200 persons requires a
variety of administrative positions. The terminal manager is
responsible to the home office for the total operations of the
terminal, including the hiring and dismissal of employees. Tc
assist him there also may be an operations manager who directs
the work on the platform, and an office manager who is in
charge of the clerical force. Most of the present terminal, operations, and office managers have come up through the ranks.
Inasmuch as there were few Negro drivers hired over the years,
there are now even fewer in these managerial positions today.

Large firms have regional supervisors who serve as interme-
diaries between headquarters and the numerous terminal managers. They may have as many as twenty terminals under their
jurisdiction. Again, the larger and better-managed firms are replacing supervisory personnel who came up through the ranks
with younger men from their management training programs.

The salary of the terminal manager, which is much higher
than that of an operations or office manager, may range from
$10,000 to $14,000 per year. Most firms determine terminal
managers' salaries by the terminal's revenue and annual profits.
Nevertheless, many terminal managers make less than the senior

drivers. In any case, employers are still reluctant to have Negroes coordinate the work of predominantly all-white work crews.

Dispatchers

The dispatcher's primary function is to coordinate and plan the movement of freight between terminals. He telephones the drivers to let them knew when they are needed, assigns loads, and works closely with the garage to obtain various types of equipment. The dispatcher must be familiar with the geographical area covered by the system, labor contracts and the most recent interpretations of these contracts, and Interstate Commerce Commission regulations. He must be able to provide the drivers with directions in the event of a breakdown, accident, or any other unforeseen delay while out on the road. In brief, it is the dispatcher's duty to see that the company's equipment and manpower are used in the most economical and profitable manner, consonant with efficient service for the customer.

Like other supervisory personnel employed by the majority of firms at the terminal level, most dispatchers have previously been drivers. After spending years behind the wheel of a large tractor trailer or fighting city traffic on local runs, drivers sometimes welcome the responsibility and prestige associated with the dispatcher's job. Some drivers, however, refuse dispatching responsibilities because they often can earn more driving a truck. Again, the method of selecting dispatchers and the fact that the crews supervised are almost all white militates against Negroes occupying these jobs. In 1968, only 0.2 percent of all dispatchers employed by the sample firms were Negroes.

CLERICAL WORKERS

In addition to female typists and file clerks, other clerical jobs in trucking, sometimes staffed by men, include rate clerks, manifest clerks, cashiers, tracing clerks, and O.S.D. (over freight, short, and damage) clerks. At small terminal locations, women secretaries usually perform a variety of clerical jobs. The larger terminals will have a number of clerks, depending on the volume of traffic handled.

The most demanding job is that of the rate clerk, who must be thoroughly familiar with a host of prevailing rates for a vast number of commodities hauled. Billing clerks, the most nu-

merous of all the clerical workers, transfer information from th
bill of lading to the freight bill which is subsequently sent t
the shipper. They must be fast and accurate typists, and earne
approximately $2.75 per hour in 1968. Billing clerks are a class
all to themselves and have a tendency to float from firm to firm
apparently feeling that the job will somehow become more cha:
lenging if they do not remain at any one terminal for too long
Many of the billing clerks employed by the industry started ou
as file clerks with a pay scale ranging from $1.60 to $1.85 a
hour.

   In 1968, 3.0 percent of the male clerical workers and 2.3 per
cent of the female clerical help were Negroes. In the small firm
there were no Negro clerical employees. Smaller firms have s
few employees doing clerical work that a "sorority" type of at
titude prevails and Negroes are not welcome. Although th
larger carriers admit that this is relatively an easier area i:
which to pursue equal employment, they must bid against othe
industries, whose offices are more accessible to public transpor
tation and who can often offer female Negro applicants highe
salaries and better working conditions.

   Of all the jobs available in the trucking industry, sample
firms found the various clerical jobs usually performed by mei
(rate clerks, billing clerks, manifest clerks, and O.S.D. clerks'
usually the most difficult to fill. In some areas of the country
special training programs have been established to meet the nee
for an adequate supply of competent clerks. Employers seen
more willing to hire Negro male clerks than they have been t
employ Negroes as road drivers and in management positions
This willingness is probably attributable to the tight labor mar
ket conditions.

THE IBT AND CIVIL RIGHTS

   We have already noted in the previous chapter that civil rights
was not high on the Teamsters agenda under President James R
Hoffa, or under his predecessors. The IBT attitude is illustrated
further by action to a resolution introduced at the 1966 IBT
National Convention by a Negro delegate from a Los Angeles
freight drivers' union. It read in part:

   NOW THEREFORE BE IT RESOLVED, that this International Union
expresses its endorsement and extends its united support in furtherance
of removing each and every barrier and injustice which is inherent
within the deadly seeds of racial discrimination and prejudice.

BE IT FURTHER RESOLVED, that the facilities of this International Union shall be available in support of any and every program which may be determined by the General President of this Union, designed to give meaning and intent to the carrying out of this resolution.[58]

Vice President Harold Gibbons, who had been executive assistant to Hoffa until December 1963, commented that the Teamsters adhered to a policy of nondiscrimination stressed by Hoffa when he assumed office in 1958. Consequently, the Teamsters eliminated those "few examples of Jim Crow local unions which existed around the country." [59] Gibbons also mentioned that the General Executive Board had passed a resolution in support of the whole Negro community.

More significant than Gibbons' broad observations about the Teamsters' nondiscrimination policy was his admission that two local unions rebelled when the International gave $25,000 to the late Dr. Martin Luther King, Jr.[60] The anti-Negro sentiment in these locals was so strong that Hoffa had to speak personally to the membership of one of the locals, while Gibbons spoke to the other.

The only applause during Gibbons' speech came when he tied the plight of the Negro with the necessity of voting antiunion Congressmen out of office. One attendant told the author that the applause at the end of the speech was cordial, but certainly not enthusiastic.[61]

With the conviction and jailing of Hoffa, the acting president, Frank Fitzsimmons, restored considerable local and regional autonomy. Given the background already described, there is no reason to suppose that this move will promote a more progressive Teamster attitude toward the employment of Negro long haul drivers.

The formation of the Alliance for Labor Action (ALA) by the Teamsters and the United Automobile, Aerospace and Agricultural Workers (UAW) in 1968 with a program stressing community action, drives to organize the unorganized, and civil rights is also not likely to alter the Teamster approach to Negro

---

58. International Brotherhood of Teamsters, Chauffeurs, Warehousemen and Helpers of America, *Proceedings—Nineteenth Convention* (Miami, Florida, July 4-7, 1966), p. 165.

59. *Ibid.*, p. 166.

60. *Ibid.*, p. 167.

61. Personal interview, 1968.

employment. In a number of areas, especially on the West Coast, Teamster locals and joint councils [62] have made grants to local poverty or community action groups, and otherwise acted "socially minded." [63] This, however, has not opened driver jobs to Negroes any more than Teamster organization on a nondiscriminatory basis in areas outside of motor transportation—which has occurred for many years—has altered its exclusivist approach to trucking. As we shall note in a later chapter, discrimination in the trucking industry has resulted in a number of law suits pursuant of Title VII of the Civil Rights Act, including charges of patterns of discrimination filed by the U.S. Department of Justice, which include both companies and the IBT as defendants. The facts alleged in these suits seem to indicate a continuation of past practices that do not seem to be affected by any new "socially-minded" approaches or goals.

The Alliance for Labor Action selected Atlanta as the location for its initial concerted campaign to organize an estimated 50,000 workers employed by companies located in the area of this southern industrial hub. Although Negroes are employed by these concerns, the ALA faces a real dilemma. It must project the image of being truly impartial toward the hiring of Negroes by all industries, including trucking, in order to attract those unorganized companies where Negroes constitute a majority. And, at the same time, it must not seem too pro-Negro, as employers having a predominantly white work force might try to use this to dissuade their employees from voting for unionization. For example, a company in Selma, Alabama [64] conveyed the notion to its white employees that the IBT's contribution to Dr. King, noted above, was indicative of the Teamsters' pro-Negro stance. In this case, the National Labor Relations Board sup-

---

62. Within the structure of the Teamsters there are joint councils: fifty-five in the United States and six in Canada. As early as 1904 joint councils were established to give the specialized locals in a metropolitan area strength in their bargaining activities, and to assist in settling any jurisdictional disputes which might arise between the locals. The joint councils are found in the major cities or they may include a whole state where the IBT is relatively weak, such as Arkansas. Inasmuch as these bodies of affiliated locals are not that important regarding civil rights, further elaboration is unnecessary.

63. See, for example, *The International Teamster*, Vol. 66, No. 9 (September 1969), p. 13 and Vol. 66, No. 11 (November 1969), p. 11.

64. For details, see Bush Hog, Inc., 161 NLRB No. 1136 (1966), as reported in *Race Relations Law Review* 505 (1967).

ported the trial examiner's contention that this reference, in conjunction with threats to integrate the plant if the union won, constituted a violation of Section 8(a)(1) of the National Labor Relations Act. This company blatantly exploited the Negro problem in an effort to persuade its employees to reject overtures of the IBT, but others are learning to be more surreptitious in reference to the Negro issue, and thus avoid the censure of the NLRB.

There are, to be sure, significant personal consequences that might befall a local Teamster leader, especially in the South, should he take the lead or cooperate with trucking employers in the hiring or promoting of Negroes as over-the-road drivers. Unlike their national counterparts, local union officials must be more responsive to the aspirations and wishes of the rank and file. Thus, local union officials might be voted out of office should they fail to take into account that their constituents often harbor deep-seated anti-Negro sentiments.

CHAPTER V

Regional and City Differences, 1968

In this chapter we will use 1968 employment data to describe the patterns of Negro employment within four broad geographical regions and thirteen distinct Standard Metropolitan Statistical Areas. We shall find that the differences in Negro employment among regions and SMSA's are differences of degree, corroborating the findings in the previous chapter. The subsequent racial employment statistics reported on the basis of four distinct geographical areas, the Northeast, South, Midwest, and West, were derived by expanding the original data obtained through research in the field. (See Appendixes A and B for details.)

NEGRO EMPLOYMENT IN THE NORTHEAST

Data representative of ten SMSA's located in the Northeast region [65] of the country were derived from the three following sample SMSA's: Philadelphia, New York, and Boston. Company representatives from thirty-four firms with corporate headquarters in these three SMSA's were interviewed. Of this total, eleven were large firms, employing 101 or more, and twenty-three were small firms employing one hundred or less.

The percentage of Negroes employed in all job classifications for firms with corporate headquarters in forty-eight SMSA's throughout the country was 7.6, while the Northeast, as Table 14 shows, has a 9.8 percent Negro work force. When the three sample SMSA's in the Northeast are viewed independently, the percentage of Negroes employed in each is as follows: Philadelphia, 10.5 percent; New York, 15.8 percent; and Boston, 1.4 percent. The percentage of Negroes employed in all job classifications and found in the labor markets comprising these three SMSA's are shown on Tables 15, 16, and 17, respectively.

---

65. The Northeast includes firms with corporate headquarters in the following SMSA's only: New York, Philadelphia, Boston, Pittsburgh, Washington, D.C., Baltimore, Newark, Buffalo, Jersey City, and Rochester.

TABLE 14. Trucking Industry
Employment by Race, Occupation, and Firm Size Northeast Region, 1968

Job Classifications	All Firms			Small Firms[a]			Large Firms[b]		
	Total	Negro	Percent Negro	Total	Negro	Percent Negro	Total	Negro	Percent Negro
Management	3,295	5	0.1	1,379	—	—	1,916	5	0.3
Road drivers	7,394	353	4.8	2,255	283	12.5	5,139	70	1.4
Local drivers	16,692	1,749	10.5	9,721	1,077	11.1	6,971	672	9.6
Dockmen	5,205	830	15.9	1,745	387	22.2	3,460	443	12.8
Mechanics	2,323	122	5.3	855	42	4.9	1,468	80	5.5
Oilers	234	111	47.4	22	22	100.0	212	89	42.0
Washers	138	109	79.0	22	22	100.0	116	87	75.0
Service workers	19	19	100.0	—	—	—	19	19	100.0
Dispatchers	1,182	—	—	539	—	—	643	—	—
Warehousemen	320	11	3.4	224	11	4.9	96	—	—
Helpers	2,423	792	32.7	1,803	395	21.9	620	397	64.0
Clerical workers	6,008	346	5.8	1,619	—	—	4,389	346	7.9
Male	747	31	4.1	143	—	—	604	31	5.1
Female	5,261	315	6.0	1,476	—	—	3,785	315	8.3
Total	45,233	4,447	9.8	20,184	2,239[c]	11.1	25,049	2,208[d]	8.8

Source: Data in author's possession.

Note: Data are based on Philadelphia, New York, and Boston SMSA's. See Appendixes A and B.

[a] Small firms are those having 100 or less employees.
[b] Large firms are those having 101 or more employees.
[c] Estimated Negroes—2,277 (± 28.9 percent).
[d] Estimated Negroes—2,319 (± 34.9 percent).

TABLE 15. *Trucking Industry*
Employment by Race, Occupation, and Firm Size
Philadelphia SMSA, 1968

Job Classifications	All Firms			Small Firms[a]			Large Firms[b]		
	Total	Negro	Percent Negro	Total	Negro	Percent Negro	Total	Negro	Percent Negro
Management	520	—	—	264	—	—	256	—	—
Road drivers	2,795	179	6.4	824	127	15.4	1,971	52	2.6
Local drivers	2,785	415	14.9	2,357	349	14.8	428	66	15.4
Dockmen	683	168	24.6	465	116	24.9	218	52	23.9
Mechanics	602	21	3.5	232	21	9.1	370	—	—
Oilers	59	59	100.0	11	11	100.0	48	48	100.0
Washers	120	54	45.0	11	11	100.0	109	43	39.4
Service workers	—	—	—	—	—	—	—	—	—
Dispatchers	125	—	—	106	—	—	19	—	—
Warehousemen	32	—	—	32	—	—	—	—	—
Helpers	35	—	—	21	—	—	14	—	—
Clerical workers	1,101	33	3.0	465	—	—	636	33	5.2
Male	195	23	11.8	53	—	—	142	23	16.2
Female	906	10	1.1	412	—	—	494	10	2.0
Total	8,857	929	10.5	4,788	635	13.3	4,069	294	7.2

Source: Data in author's possession.

[a] Small firms are those having 100 or less employees.

[b] Large firms are those having 101 or more employees.

TABLE 16. *Trucking Industry*
Employment by Race, Occupation, and Firm Size
New York SMSA, 1968

Job Classifications	All Firms			Small Firms[a]			Large Firms[b]		
	Total	Negro	Percent Negro	Total	Negro	Percent Negro	Total	Negro	Percent Negro
Management	1,239	5	0.4	454	—	—	785	5	0.6
Road drivers	600	—	—	—	—	—	600	—	—
Local drivers	6,700	874	13.0	2,820	279	9.9	3,880	595	15.3
Dockmen	2,359	509	21.6	444	134	30.2	1,915	375	19.6
Mechanics	666	70	10.5	196	—	—	470	70	14.9
Oilers	50	25	50.0	—	—	—	50	25	50.0
Washers	30	30	100.0	—	—	—	30	30	100.0
Service workers	20	20	100.0	—	—	—	20	20	100.0
Dispatchers	555	—	—	165	—	—	390	—	—
Warehousemen	121	10	8.3	21	10	47.6	100	—	—
Helpers	1,565	735	47.0	940	320	34.0	625	415	66.4
Clerical workers	2,212	270	12.2	382	—	—	1,830	270	14.7
Male	326	—	—	31	—	—	295	—	—
Female	1,886	270	14.3	351	—	—	1,535	270	17.6
Total	16,117	2,548	15.8	5,422	743	13.7	10,695	1,805	16.9

Source: Data in author's possession.

[a] Small firms are those having 100 or less employees.

[b] Large firms are those having 101 or more employees.

TABLE 17. Trucking Industry
Employment by Race, Occupation, and Firm Size
Boston SMSA, 1968

Job Classifications	All Firms			Small Firms[a]			Large Firms[b]		
	Total	Negro	Percent Negro	Total	Negro	Percent Negro	Total	Negro	Percent Negro
Management	424	—	—	120	—	—	304	—	—
Road drivers	924	10	1.1	220	10	4.5	704	—	—
Local drivers	1,637	25	1.5	640	20	3.1	997	5	0.5
Dockmen	606	5	0.8	110	—	—	496	5	1.0
Mechanics	252	5	2.0	60	—	—	192	5	2.6
Oilers	37	—	—	—	—	—	37	—	—
Washers	27	—	—	—	—	—	27	—	—
Service workers	—	—	—	—	—	—	—	—	—
Dispatchers	141	—	—	50	—	—	91	—	—
Warehousemen	50	—	—	50	—	—	—	—	—
Helpers	250	10	4.0	250	10	4.0	—	—	—
Clerical workers	751	16	2.3	90	—	—	661	16	2.4
Male	48	—	—	—	—	—	48	—	—
Female	703	16	2.3	90	—	—	613	16	2.6
Total	5,099	71	1.4	1,590	40	2.5	3,509	31	0.9

Source: Data in author's possession.

[a] Small firms are those having 100 or less employees.

[b] Large firms are those having 101 or more employees.

New York, with its polyglot population of nationalities, accounted for a larger proportion of Negro employees than the other two sample SMSA's used in this area. Even though the New York trucking firms' manpower is 15.8 percent Negro, a disproportionate number of Negroes were employed in the low-paying jobs or worked for special commodity haulers where the work is dirty and back breaking. Also, the numerous carriers hauling for New York's garment industry often employ teenage Negroes as sorters and checkers, but they pay them minimum wage rates for working after school and at night.

Boston accounted for the smallest percentage of Negro employees, not only among the three SMSA's in the Northeast, but among all thirteen SMSA's constituting the national sample. The one most significant factor explaining the poor showing in the Boston SMSA is that the Irish, as a group, have captured the industry and they also control the local Teamster unions. Boston had only 1.4 percent Negro employees in the trucking industry, but the nonwhite population for 1960 was only 3.4 percent. To understand Boston's poor posture, it is necessary to compare it with the difference found between the percentage of nonwhites in all sample SMSA's and the percentage of Negroes employed by the industry in these same SMSA's. This will be done later.

With the exceptions noted above, the Northeast is typical of the nation with reference to the occupational distribution of Negro employment. None of the participating firms were located in the heart of Negro neighborhoods. With the exception of those firms located outside the cities proper, companies interviewed in the Philadelphia, Boston, and New York SMSA's were more dependent upon the union as a source for employees than those in other areas of the country.

A larger percentage of female Negro clerical help was found in New York. Most of the clerical personnel employed in the other two SMSA's were white. Smaller firms have a tendency to employ more Negroes as dockmen, helpers, and local drivers than do the larger firms, but these small firms employed no female Negroes in clerical positions. Apparently the larger firms have at least one white employee willing to help a Negro secretary during the period of adjustment. In addition, the secretarial help in the smaller firms are a tightly-knit group often consisting of two or three secretaries who are friends or relatives.

Interestingly enough, when asked about Negro employment at terminal locations in cities other than the ones visited, all firms having such facilities in Baltimore and Washington pointed then out as cities where they employed more Negroes. They sug gested this was due not only to the fact that proportionatel more Negroes live in these cities but also because the makeup o the Teamster locals is different. Historically, no single ethni group has dominated the locals in Baltimore or Washington D.C., as they do in northern New Jersey, for example, wher Italians have a grip on the local unions, or in Boston where th Irish are in control.

As might be expected, all of the sample firms were unio companies. Several of the company representatives agreed tha the industry as a whole is weak at the level of middle manage ment, and this partially accounts for their inertia regarding th employment of more Negroes. They suggested, however, tha the Teamsters share some of the responsibility for the smal percentage of Negroes employed in the better-paying jobs an in particular as road drivers. They were extremely vague as t the degree union leaders could or would be willing to do some thing about removing or modifying hiring procedures which hav worked against Negroes.

The smaller, poorly-managed firms, whether they had a hig percentage of Negroes on their payrolls or not, immediately wen on the defensive and told the author: "We never discriminate against anyone." "Why, even some of our best friends ar Negroes." "The Irish, Italians, and Poles made it on their own Why can't the Negroes?"

Representatives from the larger firms were somewhat more can did about equal employment problems. At the same time, n doubt fearing recrimination from the Teamsters, the representa tives from the larger firms were unwilling to state categoricall the degree to which the Teamsters are responsible for the variou racial patterns of employment. They were willing to tell "horro stories" about the union, its leaders, and its unreasonable de mands, but when it came to the topic of interest they talked i vaguer terms.

NEGRO EMPLOYMENT IN THE SOUTH

The four SMSA's comprising the sample areas for the souther region [66] of the country are: Birmingham, Charlotte, Atlanta

---

66. The Southern firms with corporate headquarters in the following SMSA' only: Atlanta, Miami, New Orleans, Tampa, Louisville, Birmingham Memphis, Charlotte, Norfolk, Winston-Salem Greensboro, Houston, Dal las, San Antonio, Fort Worth, and El Paso.

ıd the combined cities of Winston-Salem and Greensboro. Seven
ıall firms and eight large firms made up the sample selected
ır the four combined SMSA's.

Prior to the Civil War, slaves in the South welcomed the op-
ırtunity to drive a wagon rather than labor with a hoe gang in
ıe fields. Negro slaves hired out by owners to work in the
ıwns were trained in many kinds of manual labor, including
ıe driving of horse-drawn carts. During the Civil War, Negroes
. the Union Forces were sometimes found to be more competent
ıivers than whites.[67] The dependence upon Negroes as draymen
. the late nineteenth-century South laid the foundation upon
hich driving was viewed as a "Negro job." As motor vehicles
ıplaced the horse-drawn carts and the work became less burden-
ıme and dirty, whites moved into the driving occupations. This
ansition was gradual and imperceptible.

'hen tractors and motor trucks are introduced, new "white men's jobs"
'e created out of old "Negro jobs" on the farm and in transportation.
. . Progress itself seems to work against the Negroes. When work
ıcomes less heavy, less dirty, or less risky, Negroes are displaced.
ld-fashioned, low-paying, inefficient enterprises, continually being driven
ıt of competition, are often the only ones that employ much Negro
bor.[68]

At present, there are no jobs in the trucking industry which
'e defined as "Negro jobs" by either the Teamsters or the in-
ıstry. Two causes seem to have occasioned the fact that in the
ıuth "Negro jobs" have disappeared. The large unionized firms
ıy such high wage rates that these jobs are coveted by whites.
ıcond, small nonunion firms, usually family owned, have a pre-
ıminantly Negro work force with which whites as a rule re-
ıse to work. Therefore, racial patterns of employment vary
ıtween union and nonunion firms.

Technological changes on the platform, which made the tasks
ıce performed by Negro dockmen less heavy, pushed some Ne-
ıoes out of these jobs. Prior to the 1950's, for example, many
ırminals hired Negroes as dockmen, but the checkers were ex-

---

i7. Bell Irvin Wiley, *Southern Negroes 1861-1865* (New Haven: Yale University Press, 1938), p. 111.

i8. Arnold Rose, *The Negro in America* (Boston: The Beacon Press, 1956),
   p. 69. This work is a condensation of Gunnar Myrdal's classic work,
   The American Dilemma.

clusively white. The introduction of front-end fork lifts an other mechanical devices reduced dependence on strong backs t move and separate freight on the platform. The Teamsters ge a substantial increase for their checkers, which led employers t change the work assignments on the platforms. The white checl ers were given jobs on the new equipment and the Negro docl men were discharged. The employers said illiterate Negroe might have been able to learn how to handle the new equipmen but they were not able to read and record the bills of ladin; There is no evidence that the Teamsters had sought the wag increases primarily to displace the Negroes, for it is in keepin with the IBT's objectives to gain for its members higher wage with improved working conditions. In any event, the results wer much the same as in the past: Negroes were displaced wit the advent of new technologies.

As Table 18 shows, there is a higher percentage of Negroe employed by the southern domiciled truckers than there is b firms in the Northeast section of the country. When the fou SMSA's in the South are viewed independently, the percentage c Negroes in each is as follows: Winston-Salem Greensboro, 7. percent (Table 19); Birmingham, 25.2 percent (Table 20); Chai lotte, 16.2 percent (Table 21); Atlanta, 10.8 percent (Table 22) In the Northeast, 9.8 percent of all employees are Negroes, whil in the South, 15.0 percent of the employees are Negroes. I isolation, these data seem to indicate that the South is less dis criminatory than other areas of the country, but this is not th case. In the South the small firms employ 3,557 or 59.8 percen of the total 5,942 Negroes working there. It is estimated tha over one-half of the firms in Birmingham are nonunion. The pa scale for drivers is approximately $2.50 an hour for a fifty-hou week in these nonunion firms. Therefore, the presence of a hig percentage of Negroes in the South is caused not by the souther employer's desire for equal employment, but rather by the fac that Negro labor is cheaper and that sometimes Negroes ar employed to keep the unions out.

The trucking industry arrived on the southern scene later thai it did in other parts of the country, and the South was the las part of the country to be unionized by the Teamsters. Whei trucking started to garner the long haul work, the IBT was abl to organize the South by means of secondary boycotts and late

TABLE 18. Trucking Industry
Employment by Race, Occupation, and Firm Size South Region, 1968

Job Classifications	All Firms			Small Firms[a]			Large Firms[b]		
	Total	Negro	Percent Negro	Total	Negro	Percent Negro	Total	Negro	Percent Negro
Management	2,791	—	—	504	—	—	2,287	—	—
Road drivers	16,411	702	4.3	3,386	566	16.7	13,025	136	1.0
Local drivers	6,183	2,501	40.4	3,195	2,197	68.8	2,988	304	10.2
Dockmen	3,640	1,360	37.4	305	283	92.8	3,335	1,077	32.3
Mechanics	3,112	404	13.0	465	137	29.5	2,647	267	10.1
Oilers	120	120	100.0	—	—	—	120	120	100.0
Washers	220	220	100.0	61	61	100.0	159	159	100.0
Service workers	496	367	74.0	178	89	50.0	318	278	87.4
Dispatchers	640	—	—	192	—	—	448	—	—
Warehousemen		—	—		—	—		—	—
Helpers	474	224	47.3	474	224	47.3	—	—	—
Clerical workers	5,609	44	0.8	829	—	—	4,780	44	0.9
Male	78	10	12.8	61	—	—	17	10	58.8
Female	5,531	34	0.6	768	—	—	4,763	34	0.7
Total	39,696	5,942	15.0	9,589	3,557[c]	37.1	30,107	2,385[d]	7.9

Source: Data in author's possession.

Note: Data are based on Burmingham, Charlotte, Atlanta, and Winston-Salem Greensboro SMSA's. See Appendixes A and B.

[a] Small firms are those with 100 or less employees.
[b] Large firms are those with 101 or more employees.
[c] Estimated Negroes—3,938 (27.1 percent).
[d] Estimated Negroes—3,008 (16.5 percent).

TABLE 19. Trucking Industry
Employment by Race, Occupation, and Firm Size
Winston-Salem Greensboro SMSA, 1968

Job Classifications	All Firms			Small Firms[a]			Large Firms[b]		
	Total	Negro	Percent Negro	Total	Negro	Percent Negro	Total	Negro	Percent Negro
Management	386	—	—	18	—	—	368	—	—
Road drivers	2,546	19	0.7	96	9	9.4	2,450	10	0.4
Local drivers	328	19	5.8	48	12	25.0	280	7	2.5
Dockmen	593	181	30.5	15	6	40.0	578	175	30.3
Mechanics	928	35	3.8	18	—	—	910	35	3.9
Oilers	105	105	100.0	—	—	—	105	105	100.0
Washers	—	—	—	—	—	—	—	—	—
Service workers	61	61	100.0	9	9	100.0	52	52	100.0
Dispatchers	95	—	—	15	—	—	80	—	—
Warehousemen	—	—	—	—	—	—	—	—	—
Helpers	—	—	—	—	—	—	—	—	—
Clerical workers	1,125	14	1.2	15	—	—	1,110	14	1.3
Male	4	4	100.0	—	—	—	4	4	100.0
Female	1,121	10	0.9	15	—	—	1,106	10	0.9
Total	6,167	434	7.0	234	36	15.4	5,933	398	6.7

Source: Data in author's possession.

[a] Small firms are those having 100 or less employees.

[b] Large firms are those having 101 or more employees.

TABLE 20. *Trucking Industry*
Employment by Race, Occupation, and Firm Size
Birmingham SMSA, 1968

Job Classifications	All Firms			Small Firms[a]			Large Firms[b]		
	Total	Negro	Percent Negro	Total	Negro	Percent Negro	Total	Negro	Percent Negro
Management	311	—	—	55	—	—	256	—	—
Road drivers	1,507	136	9.0	187	132	70.6	1,320	4	0.3
Local drivers	955	625	65.4	715	605	84.6	240	20	8.3
Dockmen	—	—	—	—	—	—	—	—	—
Mechanics	153	35	22.9	33	11	33.3	120	24	20.0
Oilers	—	—	—	—	—	—	—	—	—
Washers	62	62	100.0	22	22	100.0	40	40	100.0
Service workers	48	40	83.3	—	—	—	48	40	83.3
Dispatchers	55	—	—	11	—	—	44	—	—
Warehousemen	—	—	—	—	—	—	—	—	—
Helpers	—	—	—	—	—	—	—	—	—
Clerical workers	466	—	—	66	—	—	400	—	—
Male	22	—	—	22	—	—	—	—	—
Female	444	—	—	44	—	—	400	—	—
Total	3,557	898	25.2	1,089	770	70.7	2,468	128	5.2

Source: Data in author's possession.

[a] Small firms are those having 100 or less employees.

[b] Large firms are those having 101 or more employees.

TABLE 21. Trucking Industry
Employment by Race, Occupation, and Firm Size
Charlotte SMSA, 1968

Job Classifications	All Firms			Small Firms[a]			Large Firms[b]		
	Total	Negro	Percent Negro	Total	Negro	Percent Negro	Total	Negro	Percent Negro
Management	330	—	—	90	—	—	240	—	—
Road drivers	2,092	80	3.8	680	40	5.9	1,412	40	2.8
Local drivers	684	190	27.8	160	150	93.8	524	40	7.6
Dockmen	856	412	48.1	120	120	100.0	736	292	39.7
Mechanics	512	64	12.5	100	—	—	412	64	15.5
Oilers	—	—	—	—	—	—	—	—	—
Washers	94	54	57.4	70	30	42.9	24	24	100.0
Service workers	100	—	—	40	—	—	60	—	—
Dispatchers	—	—	—	—	—	—	—	—	—
Warehousemen	—	—	—	—	—	—	—	—	—
Helpers	180	100	55.6	180	100	55.6	—	—	—
Clerical workers	770	8	1.0	130	—	—	640	8	1.3
Male	—	—	—	—	—	—	—	—	—
Female	770	8	1.0	130	—	—	640	8	1.3
Total	5,618	908	16.2	1,570	440	28.0	4,048	468	11.6

Source: Data in author's possession.

[a] Small firms are those having 100 or less employees.

[b] Large firms are those having 101 or more employees.

TABLE 22. *Trucking Industry*
Employment by Race, Occupation, and Firm Size
Atlanta SMSA, 1968

Job Classifications	All Firms			Small Firms[a]			Large Firms[b]		
	Total	Negro	Percent Negro	Total	Negro	Percent Negro	Total	Negro	Percent Negro
Management	195	—	—	45	—	—	150	—	—
Road drivers	1,325	50	3.8	450	38	8.4	875	12	1.4
Local drivers	587	123	21.0	315	68	21.6	272	55	20.2
Dockmen	488	120	24.6	—	—	—	488	120	24.6
Mechanics	170	47	27.6	45	45	100.0	125	2	1.6
Oilers	—	—	—	—	—	—	—	—	—
Washers	—	—	—	—	—	—	—	—	—
Service workers	8	5	62.5	—	—	—	8	5	62.5
Dispatchers	40	—	—	15	—	—	25	—	—
Warehousemen	—	—	—	—	—	—	—	—	—
Helpers	30	—	—	30	—	—	—	—	—
Clerical workers	397	5	1.3	135	—	—	262	5	1.9
Male	5	2	40.0	—	—	—	5	2	40.0
Female	392	3	0.8	135	—	—	257	3	1.2
Total	3,240	350	10.8	1,035	151	14.6	2,205	199	9.0

Source: Data in author's possession.

[a] Small firms are those having 100 or less employees.
[b] Large firms are those having 101 or more employees.

by "hot cargo clauses" [69] in the contracts. Unlike other urban areas in the country, there are no hiring halls found in southern cities. In theory, the southern employers thus are freer to hire whomover they desire—including Negro road drivers. In practice, the Teamsters in the South can still exercise enough indirect control through other devices to keep Negroes out. Most likely, any union official in the South who would side with the employer in the hiring of Negroes would be voted out of office by the white majority. Ironically, the Southern Conference of Teamsters, the smallest of the Conferences, is growing faster than any of the other three conferences. Yet, the Southern Conference's increased membership is coming from small manufacturing firms where many of the employees are Negroes. The dilemma facing the Teamsters is that as they try to organize Negroes working for nontrucking firms in the South, they must project a nondiscriminatory image, but at the same time they cannot afford to incur the wrath of the white members employed by the trucking industry.

NEGRO EMPLOYMENT IN THE MIDWEST

Detroit, Chicago, and St. Louis are the three SMSA's comprising the sample areas for the Midwest.[70] Of the thirty-four companies constituting the sample firms in these three SMSA's, seventeen were large firms, while the remaining seventeen were small.

In the Midwest all firms interviewed were union companies. This is not only the very heartland of the trucking industry, but the very area in which Farrell Dobbs first organized the road drivers. It was from this geographical base that the union reached out and subsequently organized the road drivers throughout the country. The union enjoys a long history of strength in

---

69. Basically, where "hot cargo clauses" are included in the contracts it means union members will not handle goods hauled by a nonunion carrier. If a nonunion firm does not serve the point of destination because his operating rights do not permit it, he must interchange the freight with another carrier. Therefore, southern firms must depend on companies throughout the country with whom they interchange freight. This technique enabled Hoffa to bludgeon the southern firms into capitulating and accepting a union shop.

70. The Midwest includes those firms with corporate headquarters in the following SMSA's only: Chicago, Detroit, St. Louis, Cleveland, Minneapolis and St. Paul, Milwaukee, Cincinnati, Indianapolis, Dayton, Columbus, Akron, and Toledo.

this area, which is reflected in the employers blaming the union for the industry's refusal to hire more Negroes. It seems that those earlier and much more turbulent years of the Teamsters in Detroit and Chicago have scared the industry more in this area than some other areas.

Ethnic blocs in Detroit and Chicago, while not as easily distinguishable as the Irish in Boston, dominate many of the better-paying jobs. This phenomenon, in conjunction with the indifference and inability of union leaders to control the rank and file, partially accounts for the relatively few Negroes employed in this area. Table 23 shows that in the twelve SMSA's included in this study located in the Midwest, only 4.6 percent of all employees are Negroes. In the South, smaller nonunion firms accounted for a larger percentage of Negroes, whereas in the Midwest the difference between the percentage of Negroes employed by large and small firms is insignificant. The attitude that other minority groups were able to pull themselves up by their boot-straps is a recurring theme. Yet employers concede that, historically, Negroes have never found it easy to get the better-paying jobs available in the industry. Formerly located behind the stockyards of Chicago, companies were able to find an ample supply of labor among the Polish and other ethnic groups living "behind the yards." As the companies moved their terminal locations to such places as Cicero and its environs, Negroes were afraid to look for employment in these all-white enclaves. In addition, employers still relied on informal referrals and union officials as a means of making job vacancies known. The clerical help in this area is also predominantly white. Tables 24, 25, and 26 show this job classification and others for the three SMSA's used in this area separately.

NEGRO EMPLOYMENT IN THE WEST

Denver, San Francisco, and Los Angeles are the three sample areas of the West.[71] Company representatives from thirty firms having corporate headquarters in these three SMSA's were interviewed—twelve were large firms; eighteen were small. The percentage of Negroes employed in all job classifications for firms having corporate headquarters in forty-eight SMSA's throughout

---

71. The West includes those firms with corporate headquarters in the following SMSA's only: Denver, Seattle and Portland, Phoenix, Los Angeles, San Diego, Oklahoma City, Kansas City, and Omaha.

TABLE 23. *Trucking Industry*
Employment by Race, Occupation, and Firm Size
Midwest Region, 1968

Job Classifications	All Firms			Small Firms[a]			Large Firms[b]		
	Total	Negro	Percent Negro	Total	Negro	Percent Negro	Total	Negro	Percent Negro
Management	3,829	—	—	1,437	—	—	2,392	—	—
Road drivers	19,115	214	1.1	6,520	93	1.4	12,595	121	1.0
Local drivers	20,936	1,146	5.5	7,277	483	6.6	13,659	663	4.9
Dockmen	16,456	947	5.8	2,125	538	25.3	14,331	409	2.9
Mechanics	3,390	249	7.3	1,102	—	—	2,288	249	10.9
Oilers	—	—	—	—	—	—	—	—	—
Washers	287	263	91.6	29	29	100.0	258	234	90.7
Service workers	626	331	52.9	91	91	100.0	535	240	44.9
Dispatchers	1,499	—	—	414	—	—	1,085	—	—
Warehousemen	386	89	23.1	188	32	17.0	198	57	28.8
Helpers	3,536	186	5.3	1,754	—	—	1,782	186	10.4
Clerical workers	6,523	63	1.0	1,701	—	—	4,822	63	1.3
Male	577	—	—	85	—	—	492	—	—
Female	5,946	63	1.1	1,616	—	—	4,330	63	1.5
Total	76,583	3,488	4.6	22,638	1,266[c]	5.6	53,945	2,222[d]	4.1

Source: Data in author's possession.

Note: Data are based on Chicago, St. Louis, and Detroit SMSA's. See Appendixes A and B.

[a] Small firms are those having 100 or less employees.

[b] Large firms are those having 101 or more employees.

[c] Estimated Negroes—1,482 (±28.5 percent).

[d] Estimated Negroes—2,215 (±13.6 percent).

TABLE 24. *Trucking Industry*
Employment by Race, Occupation, and Firm Size
Chicago SMSA, 1968

Job Classifications	All Firms			Small Firms[a]			Large Firms[b]		
	Total	Negro	Percent Negro	Total	Negro	Percent Negro	Total	Negro	Percent Negro
Management	796	—	—	396	—	—	400	—	—
Road drivers	1,571	26	1.7	1,327	21	1.6	244	5	2.0
Local drivers	8,727	571	6.5	2,568	25	8.8	6,159	346	5.6
Dockmen	1,215	181	14.9	610	118	19.3	605	63	10.4
Mechanics	1,165	210	18.0	257	—	—	908	210	23.1
Oilers	—	—	—	—	—	—	—	—	—
Washers	52	52	100.0	32	32	100.0	20	20	100.0
Service workers	215	112	52.1	—	—	—	215	112	52.1
Dispatchers	442	—	—	139	—	—	303	—	—
Warehousemen	—	—	—	—	—	—	—	—	—
Helpers	1,559	107	6.9	107	—	—	1,452	107	7.4
Clerical workers	2,206	15	0.7	449	—	—	1,757	15	0.8
Male	59	—	—	—	—	—	59	—	—
Female	2,147	15	0.7	449	—	—	1,698	15	0.9
Total	17,948	1,274	7.1	5,885	396	6.7	12,063	878	7.3

Source: Data in author's possession.

[a] Small firms are those having 100 or less employees.

[b] Large firms are those having 101 or more employees.

TABLE 25. *Trucking Industry*
Employment by Race, Occupation, and Firm Size
St. Louis SMSA, 1968

Job Classifications	All Firms			Small Firms[a]			Large Firms[b]		
	Total	Negro	Percent Negro	Total	Negro	Percent Negro	Total	Negro	Percent Negro
Management	397	—	—	105	—	—	292	—	—
Road drivers	1,689	32	1.9	578	21	3.6	1,111	11	1.0
Local drivers	1,204	123	10.2	368	79	21.5	836	44	5.3
Dockmen	3,349	194	5.8	280	122	43.6	3,069	72	2.3
Mechanics	240	—	—	70	—	—	170	—	—
Oilers	—	—	—	—	—	—	—	—	—
Washers	—	—	—	—	—	—	—	—	—
Service workers	42	26	61.9	26	26	100.0	16	—	—
Dispatchers	139	—	—	35	—	—	104	—	—
Warehousemen	29	20	69.0	18	9	50.0	11	11	100.0
Helpers	—	—	—	—	—	—	—	—	—
Clerical workers	527	11	2.1	131	—	—	396	11	2.8
Male	—	—	—	—	—	—	—	—	—
Female	527	11	2.1	131	—	—	396	11	2.8
Total	7,616	406	5.3	1,611	257	16.0	6,005	149	2.5

Source: Data in author's possession.

[a] Small firms are those having 100 or less employees.

[b] Large firms are those having 101 or more employees.

TABLE 26. *Trucking Industry*
Employment by Race, Occupation, and Firm Size *Detroit SMSA, 1968*

Job Classifications	All Firms			Small Firms[a]			Large Firms[b]		
	Total	Negro	Percent Negro	Total	Negro	Percent Negro	Total	Negro	Percent Negro
Management	466	—	—	142	—	—	324	—	—
Road drivers	4,195	32	0.8	658	—	—	3,537	32	0.9
Local drivers	2,056	32	1.6	733	—	—	1,323	32	2.4
Dockmen	511	16	3.1	117	—	—	394	16	4.1
Mechanics	357	—	—	125	—	—	232	—	—
Oilers	—	—	—	—	—	—	—	—	—
Washers	108	97	89.8	—	—	—	108	97	89.8
Service workers	98	49	50.0	—	—	—	98	49	50.0
Dispatchers	168	—	—	33	—	—	135	—	—
Warehousemen	95	5	5.3	25	—	—	70	5	7.1
Helpers	360	27	7.5	333	—	—	27	27	100.0
Clerical workers	669	—	—	167	—	—	502	—	—
Male	211	—	—	17	—	—	194	—	—
Female	458	—	—	150	—	—	308	—	—
Total	9,083	258	2.8	2,333	—	—	6,750	258	3.8

Source: Data in author's possession.

[a] Small firms are those having 100 or less employees.

[b] Large firms are those having 101 or more employees.

the country is 7.6 percent, while the West, as Table 27 shows, has a 4.4 percent Negro work force. When the three sample SMSA's in the West are viewed independently, the percentage of Negroes employed in each is as follows: Denver, 3.1 percent; San Francisco, 5.3 percent; and Los Angeles, 4.9 percent. The percentage of Negroes found in the various job classifications within the labor markets comprising these three SMSA's are shown in Tables 28, 29, and 30.

Although all participating firms were signatories to collective bargaining agreements negotiated by the Teamsters, the degree of union control over the hiring of employees differed from firm to firm. In other parts of the country, a strong local union usually does not exercise the same degree of power over all companies; some firms, because of past practices, or because of the nature of their operations, are not compelled to do all their hiring through union sources. In the West, all the smaller firms seemed to be more dependent upon the union for new drivers than were companies of similar size in other parts of the country. This partially explains why the smaller firms do not employ substantially more Negroes than the larger firms.

Many firms in the West blamed the Teamsters for discriminatory practices. For example, Teamster Local 85 in San Francisco, according to employers, has only a few Negro members. Employers attribute the absence of Negroes in this local to racial attitudes harbored by the rank and file, and not to biases or policies fostered by the union leaders. The industry representatives explicitly stated that unless Teamster officials convince the business agents and shop stewards that the union welcomes all—regardless of race—integration in the trucking industry is nothing more than a wishful hope. Indeed, these employer sentiments were expressed in other areas of the country, but they were stated in stronger terms in the West, and in the San Francisco area in particular.

On a regional basis, 4.4 percent of employees in the western SMSA's were Negro. Employers conceded that their terminals outside this area do not employ proportionately more Negroes. One employer stated that the most difficult jobs in which to place Negroes are clerical positions in their southern terminals. As was true of firms throughout the nation, those with corporate headquarters in the West demand different standards for similar jobs, and use diverse hiring and screening procedures. One company preferred that road drivers be over forty years old, in contrast to the 25-35 year age range preferred by most employers.

TABLE 21. Trucking Industry

Employment by Race, Occupation, and Firm Size
West Region, 1968

Job Classifications	All Firms			Small Firms[a]			Large Firms[b]		
	Total	Negro	Percent Negro	Total	Negro	Percent Negro	Total	Negro	Percent Negro
Management	4,422	8	0.2	1,433	—	—	2,989	8	0.3
Road drivers	16,967	148	0.9	7,508	95	1.3	9,459	53	0.6
Local drivers	10,109	469	4.6	5,409	220	4.1	4,700	249	5.3
Dockmen	6,035	831	13.8	1,739	494	28.4	4,296	337	7.8
Mechanics	4,226	—	—	954	—	—	3,272	—	—
Oilers	—	—	—	—	—	—	—	—	—
Washers	204	194	95.1	94	94	100.0	110	100	90.9
Service workers	1,423	397	27.9	182	120	65.9	1,241	277	22.3
Dispatchers	949	8	0.8	430	—	—	519	8	1.5
Warehousemen	—	—	—	—	—	—	—	—	—
Helpers	126	37	29.4	31	—	—	95	37	38.9
Clerical workers	5,266	85	1.6	1,324	—	—	3,942	85	2.2
Male	369	12	3.3	51	—	—	318	12	3.8
Female	4,896	73	1.5	1,273	—	—	3,623	73	2.0
Total	49,727	2,177	4.4	19,104	1,023[c]	5.4	30,623	1,154[d]	3.8

Source: Data in author's possession.

Note: Data are based on Denver, San Francisco, and Los Angeles SMSA's. See Appendixes A and B.

[a] Small firms are those having 100 or less employees.

[b] Large firms are those having 101 or more employees.

[c] Estimated Negroes—984 (±19.6 percent).

[d] Estimated Negroes—1,112 (±17.5 percent).

TABLE 28. Trucking Industry
Employment by Race, Occupation, and Firm Size
Denver SMSA, 1968

Job Classifications	All Firms			Small Firms[a]			Large Firms[b]		
	Total	Negro	Percent Negro	Total	Negro	Percent Negro	Total	Negro	Percent Negro
Management	888	4	0.5	72	—	—	816	4	0.5
Road drivers	3,008	4	0.1	816	—	—	2,192	4	0.2
Local drivers	964	20	2.1	360	16	4.4	604	4	0.7
Dockmen	960	64	6.7	96	32	33.3	864	32	3.7
Mechanics	800	—	—	96	—	—	704	—	—
Oilers	—	—	—	—	—	—	—	—	—
Washers	16	16	100.0	16	16	100.0	—	—	—
Service workers	288	132	45.8	—	—	—	288	132	45.8
Dispatchers	92	4	4.3	32	—	—	60	4	6.7
Warehousemen	—	—	—	—	—	—	—	—	—
Helpers	—	—	—	—	—	—	—	—	—
Clerical workers	1,292	12	0.9	88	—	—	1,204	12	1.0
Male	116	—	—	—	—	—	116	—	—
Female	1,176	12	1.0	88	—	—	1,088	12	1.1
Total	8,308	256	3.1	1,576	64	4.1	6,732	192	2.9

Source: Data in author's possession.

[a] Small firms are those having 100 or less employees.

[b] Large firms are those having 101 or more employees.

TABLE 29. Trucking Industry
Employment by Race, Occupation, and Firm Size
San Francisco SMSA, 1968

Job Classifications	All Firms			Small Firms[a]			Large Firms[b]		
	Total	Negro	Percent Negro	Total	Negro	Percent Negro	Total	Negro	Percent Negro
Management	682	—	—	244	—	—	438	—	—
Road drivers	2,372	28	1.2	1,128	19	1.7	1,244	9	0.7
Local drivers	2,711	65	2.4	1,015	28	2.8	1,696	37	2.2
Dockmen	2,058	365	17.7	310	122	39.4	1,748	243	13.9
Mechanics	850	—	—	132	—	—	718	—	—
Oilers	—	—	—	—	—	—	—	—	—
Washers	89	38	42.7	56	38	67.9	33	—	—
Service workers	145	—	—	47	—	—	98	—	—
Dispatchers	—	—	—	—	—	—	—	—	—
Warehousemen	—	—	—	—	—	—	—	—	—
Helpers	—	—	—	—	—	—	—	—	—
Clerical workers	658	9	1.4	197	—	—	461	9	2.0
Male	33	5	15.2	—	—	—	33	5	15.2
Female	625	4	0.6	197	—	—	428	4	0.9
Total	9,565	505	5.3	3,129	207	6.6	6,436	298	4.6

Source: Data in author's possession.

[a] Small firms are those having 100 or less employees.

[b] Large firms are those having 101 or more employees.

TABLE 30. *Trucking Industry*
Employment by Race, Occupation, and Firm Size
Los Angeles SMSA, 1968

Job Classifications	All Firms			Small Firms[a]			Large Firms[b]		
	Total	Negro	Percent Negro	Total	Negro	Percent Negro	Total	Negro	Percent Negro
Management	1,116	—	—	546	—	—	570	—	—
Road drivers	3,580	76	2.1	1,155	52	4.5	2,425	24	1.0
Local drivers	2,635	219	8.3	1,418	84	5.9	1,217	135	11.1
Dockmen	1,153	92	8.0	588	63	10.7	565	29	5.1
Mechanics	949	—	—	210	—	—	739	—	—
Oilers	—	—	—	—	—	—	—	—	—
Washers	93	93	100.0	21	21	100.0	72	72	100.0
Service workers	448	32	7.1	52	32	61.5	396	—	—
Dispatchers	376	—	—	178	—	—	198	—	—
Warehousemen	—	—	—	—	—	—	—	—	—
Helpers	94	24	25.5	32	—	—	62	24	38.7
Clerical workers	1,119	34	3.0	472	—	—	647	34	5.3
Male	81	5	6.2	52	—	—	29	5	17.2
Female	1,038	29	2.8	420	—	—	618	29	4.7
Total	11,563	570	4.9	4,672	252	5.4	6,891	318	4.6

Source: Data in author's possession.

[a] Small firms are those having 100 or less employees.

[b] Large firms are those having 101 or more employees.

A representative from one of the larger carriers in the West ∶knowledged that separate seniority lists have a tendency to ∶ck Negroes into the poorer-paying jobs because Negroes are less ∶ely to transfer from the local driver's seniority list to the bot- ∙m of the over-the-road list. But this company representative ∶dicated that separate seniority lists afforded terminal managers well-defined specialized work group which the industry pre- ∶rred. Yet, he believed the industry eventually will have to re- ∕aluate the use of separate seniority lists if Negroes are to gain ∶mission into the higher paying jobs.

Prior to 1965, the federal government had done virtually ∶thing to persuade either the trucking industry or the Team- ∶ers to grant Negroes equal employment opportunities. Yet, ∶ual employment was a public policy as early as 1941. Recent ∶gal, social, and political changes have enabled the federal gov- ∶nment to inquire into the trucking industry's racial employment ∶licies and practices. We now turn to these inquiries and the ∶dustry's response.

CHAPTER VI

Government Equal Opportunity Action and Industry Response

Beginning with Franklin D. Roosevelt in 1941, each succeedir president has issued executive orders intended to encourage go ernment contractors to grant Negroes equal employment oppo tunities.[72] All of these presidential proclamations demand, as minimal requirement, the inclusion of a nondiscrimination clau in federal contracts. The first Kennedy Order, No. 10925, Mar 6, 1961, also stipulated that contractors must "take affirmativ action to ensure the applicants are employed and that employe are treated during employment without regard to their rac creed, color or national origin." [73] This was the first use of t "affirmative action" doctrine—the implication that complaint pr ceedings for alleged claims of discrimination were secondary to company's obligation to reach out into the nation's labor marke to find qualified Negroes.

As a consequence of Executive Order 10925, the General Cou sel of the Post Office Department was assigned the responsibili of handling all complaints arising where companies had contrac with the Post Office Department. The Department did have n merous contracts with truckers who hauled mail, but the m jority of these were with small contract carriers employing rel tively few people. In practice, postal inspectors incurred the r sponsibility of investigating complaints of alleged discriminatio in hiring and upgrading. Although postal inspectors handle these complaints in a rather cursory manner, they performed th function until April 1964. Insofar as the trucking industry i

---

72. President Roosevelt's Executive Order No. 8802, June 25, 1941, covere only defense contractors, while his second Order No. 9346, May 29, 194 covered all government contractors. In subsequent years the followin orders were promulgated: President Truman's No. 10308, December 1951; President Eisenhower's No. 10499, August 13, 1953; Presiden Kennedy's Orders Nos. 10925, March 6, 1961 and 11114, June 22, 1963 and President Johnson's No. 11246, September 24, 1965.

73. Executive Order No. 10925, Section 301.

oncerned, however, there was little actual government compli-
nce activity prior to the second Executive Order of President
Kennedy in 1963.

On June 22, 1963, President Kennedy modified his former or-
er when he issued Executive Order 11114.[74] The chief difference
between the second order and the first regarding the trucking industry was that the latter specified that a bill of lading bound the
carrier to the terms of the Executive Order. Although a normal
ontract had to be in an amount of at least $10,000 before the
overnment could inquire about a company's employment prac-
ices, no minimum applied to a bill of lading. This brought the
rucking industry under the executive orders in a comprehensive
manner for the first time.

In the event a company had contracts with more than one
ederal agency, each federal agency could conduct an investiga-
ion and the business community pointed out that this resulted
n duplication of effort and cost. In an effort to minimize the
bureaucratic red tape, the government assigned different indus-
ries to specific agencies. In April 1964, the Post Office Department, which had more business contacts with the railroads and
motor carriers than did any other agency, was designated the
Predominant Interest Agency (PIA) for investigating the minor-
ty employment practices in the transportation industry. At this
ime, Paul Nagle, a former administrative vice president of the
United Federation of Postal Clerks, was named Deputy Con-
racts Compliance Officer. The authority to conduct compliance
eviews was transferred from the Office of the General Counsel
f the Post Office Department to the Office of Regional Adminis-
ration, and compliance investigations began in earnest in the
rucking industry.

INVESTIGATION AND RESPONSE

Nagle hired a staff and began a pilot study of the firms headquartered in the Charlotte, North Carolina area. The examiners
discovered that, with rare exception, Negroes were not employed
n clerical positions or as road drivers. They were, however, employed as warehousemen, dock workers, and in some instances as

---

74. The Order entitled, "Extending the Authority of the President's Committee on Equal Employment" did not substantially change the substance of Executive Order 10925, but it extended the government's
jurisdiction to include federally assisted construction programs.

city drivers. Although approximately one-half of the compan᷄
had sleeper cab operations, no Negroes were employed in this ȷ
classification. One nonunion firm had thirty Negro road drive᷄
but it did not operate sleeper cab vans. As the Department's cc
tract compliance examiners expanded their efforts geographical
they discovered that the Charlotte area was representative
other areas of the country.

Another consistent phenomenon was that no company appear᷄
ready to alter its hiring and upgrading procedures. The co᷄
panies domiciled in the Charlotte area requested that they be ε
cused from undertaking individual and independent action
integrating their sleeper cab operations. The Post Office Depa᷄
ment believed that the issuance of sleeping bags by each compa᷄
might minimize the opposition for white drivers. This has ᷄
been tried, partly because of the cost to the companies, and it
extremely doubtful that it would work. The Department also f
vored the hiring of Negro employees in teams, which would ha
eliminated, for the present, having Negro and white drive᷄
working together in close quarters for extended periods of tin᷄
Most employers, however, fearing the reaction of the IBT a᷄
not wanting to establish a precedent that might hinder the
freedom in assigning drivers, rejected this means of integrati᷄
sleeper cab operations.

The IBT immediately opposed all Post Office Department re
ommendations to overcome some of the human problems th᷄
might arise should companies hire Negro road drivers. Wh᷄
aroused the ire of the rank and file was a rumor that the D
partment would "blackball" any driver leaving a firm because
integrated its sleeper cabs. In vain, the Department tried to i
form Teamster officials that this rumor, which began in t᷄
Charlotte area, had absolutely no basis in fact. Ultimately, b
cause southern locals allegedly objected to the hiring of "so man᷄
Negroes, Hoffa communicated with Paul Nagle to object to t᷄
government's attempt at integrating sleeper cab operations.[75]

Hoffa made two points: (1) he defended the industry a᷄
maintained that no employer ever denied Negroes employmen᷄
and (2) he stated categorically that he would never allow a᷄
firm to hire drivers under any arrangement other than what w᷄
stipulated in the National Master Freight Agreement. Hoff᷄
warned Nagle that if a single company hired a Negro driver b᷄

75. This section is based upon interviews conducted with Post Office a᷄
company officials.

cause of government pressure, he would call a strike. "Not a wheel would turn," said Hoffa, and "the government could give its business to a wheelbarrow." He suggested that the Post Office Department would do better to investigate its own practice of giving business to every farmer and "hay shaker" who can afford a "broken down truck."

The Post Office Department at first relied primarily on conciliation and persuasion in an attempt to have the industry hire Negro over-the-road drivers. Neither the IBT nor the industry, however, was willing to alter the status quo even slightly. On March 9, 1965, Paul Nagle addressed the American Trucking Associations' Industrial Relations Committee.[76] The tone and content of this speech, and the questions raised by industry representatives afford an excellent insight into the stance of government and industry on equal employment objectives.

Nagle explained to the company representatives the distinction between the intent of the Civil Rights Act of 1964 and the objectives of contract compliance programs, hoping that a mutually agreeable program could be worked out. Although he believed that all individual complaints should and could be handled by the Equal Employment Opportunity Commission, Nagle interpreted complaints as a sign that his office and the industry had failed in a mutual undertaking. Ironically, as the Post Office Department tried to integrate the sleeper cab operations—perhaps the most difficult hiring and upgrading practice to change—Nagle idealistically assumed that the industry intended to cooperate fully. For example, he told the meeting:

Assuming that you as corporate officer were to learn that action is being taken against you under Title VII, we would if we knew of it attempt to help you with the Equal Employment Opportunity Commission in Washington and to have the issue resolved.[77]

The implication was that if the Department's report to the President's Committee was favorable, then it would be impossible for EEOC to sustain adverse action under Title VII. Nagle contended that the Department believed it was responsible for seeing that the Teamsters' Union did not discriminate where informal referral and hiring hall systems prevailed, although by the terms of the order the Department had no authority over the

---

76. Remarks of Paul A. Nagle before the ATA's Industrial Relations Com-
77. *Ibid.*
mittee, March 9, 1965, Miami Beach, Florida.

unions. Companies were reminded that Form 38, a notice sent to
labor unions to notify them of a company's nondiscrimination
policy, was still mandatory. Nagle suggested that companies ask
the union to respond by mail indicating the union's understanding of the significance of Form 38. Should the IBT call a strike
because of integration efforts on the part of the companies, firm
representatives were guaranteed that the Department would go
directly to the top union leaders.

The industry was assured that the Post Office Department
would respect all reasonable tests used to screen employees.
"Reasonable" was interpreted to mean that the tests would be
acceptable to the government, as long as they were not structured
primarily to exclude minorities. Company policies against nepotism likewise were to be respected by the government. In the
event an impasse arose between the Department and the industry
over hiring practices or possible sanctions, the President's Committee, then responsible for administering the executive order,
had the power to make the final judgment.

Impact on Industry

Mr. Nagle's conciliatory approach made no clearly visible
change in the industry's or union's attitudes toward opening up
more long haul trucking jobs to Negroes. The white-Negro employment patterns existing in 1965 did not radically change. Some
personnel directors, safety directors, and industrial relations
people since then have gained the support of top management at
the highest echelons and have honestly tried to employ more
Negroes, but this is the exception and certainly not the rule.
The fear of union reprisals, the economic consequences of a rebellious white rank and file, and deep antigovernment sentiments
caused most employers to treat equal employment simply as a
nuisance and not as something they were obligated to promote.
Attempts by the Post Office to obtain more detailed and supplementary reports in addition to the forms required under Title
VII of the Civil Rights Act ran into considerable industry opposition.

The Johnson Executive Order (No. 11246, September 24, 1965),
which created a new agency, the Office of Federal Contract Compliance (OFCC) in place of the Kennedy President's Committee
on Equal Employment Opportunity and placed OFCC within the
Department of Labor, nevertheless continued most of the provisions of the second Kennedy order and the Post Office re-

mained in charge of compliance in the trucking industry. Both the Post Office and the OFCC found that truckers were reluctant to alter their hiring practices and particularly feared making a change in the sleeper cab situation. It became very obvious that only government compulsion could effectuate a change. Fear of union opposition, of white worker resentment, and of being ostracized by management peers all contributed to the reluctance to change.

While the companies want to fall in line, an official says, they also want someone to blame for hiring Negroes. [A Post Office Department official said:] "We're willing to take the blame." "This way they can go to the country club and blame the damn government and escape any personal reaction by their friends. We've even had midnight conferences with employers at their request so other business men won't see what's going on." [78]

Top echelon Teamster officials were not making any public statements about government efforts to integrate the industry. It is not difficult to substantiate the employer's contention that local union leaders were antagonistic about hiring Negroes. The president of Teamsters' Local 100 in Cincinnati made public his sentiments when he said, "Would you like to climb into a bunk bed that a nigger just got out of?" [79] The president of Teamster Local 24, located in Akron, Ohio, declared, "To my knowledge, no law has been written yet that says a white has to bed down with Negroes." [80]

Admittedly, there were differences among employers and among local union officials as to the extent to which they would assist in promoting equal employment in the trucking industry. But the firms that realized they would eventually have to hire Negroes for the better-paying jobs were rare exceptions.

In 1967, one firm in the South hired two Negro road drivers to drive together in a sleeper cab operation. When one of the Negro drivers voluntarily quit, the company decided to place the remaining Negro road driver on what is referred to as the extra board. Normally, the men on this board are assigned on a first-in, first-out basis—depending, of course, on the volume and type of trucking services demanded on any particular day. When the Negro road driver reached the top of the list, the company, con-

---

78. "Bias Behind the Wheel," *Commercial Car Journal*, June 1966, p. 114.

79. *Wall Street Journal*, March 31, 1966.

80. *Ibid.*

trary to terms of the contract, simply bypassed him. As top man on the list, the Negro driver could have bid on a sleeper cab operation and chosen his partner. The company argued that it bypassed the Negro driver so as to avoid dismissing a white driver who might refuse to ride with him.

Although the company took the above action to avoid a direct confrontation with the local union, union officials attempted to solicit complaints from the white road drivers because the company had bypassed the Negro, and a grievance was filed and later withdrawn. The IBT's impetus was not that of protecting the Negro's rights, but actually was an attempt to make things so difficult for the company that it would discharge the Negro driver. Company spokesmen contend that the grievance was withdrawn because of pressure exerted by top echelon union officials who were pressured by some top government leaders.

While some companies apparently made some efforts to comply, others fought the government head on. One southern firm refused to desegregate its facilities. Other firms would agree to meet with the compliance examiner, but then would claim that the official the examiner was to talk with was sick or out of town when the government's representative arrived for the meeting. In many cases, local union leaders were less willing to meet with compliance examiners than were company officials.

In July 1967, Nagle was named by Postmaster General O'Brien to head the Equal Employment Opportunity Office within and for the Post Office Department. Nagle was committed to equal employment goals and communicated this spirit to his men in the field. The general impression was that Congressmen had started to receive complaints from white drivers and that Nagle was transferred to supervise a less sensitive activity.

Although Nagle resigned as Deputy Contract Compliance Officer in July 1967, a replacement was not named until February 1968. In the interim, the Department's contract compliance examiners continued to review the equal employment posture of new companies, or conducted follow-up reviews to determine the degree to which companies were implementing affirmative action programs. In addition, the examiners investigated cases of alleged discrimination arising because of individual complaints. Between July 1, 1967 and July 1, 1968 the Post Office Department processed approximately sixty such complaints. Should a firm refuse to make the necessary adjustments where discrimination was evident, the Department would hold informal hearings.

Hearings were also held when particular companies refused to demonstrate any intention of abiding by the provisions of Executive Order 11246. The Department conducted these informal hearings in Washington or if the companies refused to send representatives to Washington, at the companies' corporate headquarters. The industry soon discovered that it was better to send spokesmen to Washington because when examiners scheduled an informal hearing at a particular corporate location, they used this occasion to visit all the firms in the area. Much of the governments' activity was an exercise in futility, however. As one Department staff member put it, "During these informal hearings [the companies] said they were going to do something, but in fact they did nothing." [81]

In retrospect, the problem plaguing the Office of Federal Contract Compliance and the Post Office Department has remained the same over the years: the questionable nature of their authority to place companies found in violation on a proscribed list. The Department continued to threaten individual firms and the industry as a whole with debarment, but the industry was well aware that in the absence of legal precedents, the government was groping in the dark. No company in any industry has ever been debarred from contracts, perhaps because the penalty is so severe and the authority of the government to act remains uncertain.

THE POST OFFICE, THE OFCC, AND AFFIRMATIVE ACTION

Affirmative action is a nebulous term that means different things to different people. Government officials have never defined it precisely or legally, but Paul Nagle came close with his remarks on what was necessary to comply with the Presidential Executive Orders:

1. A company should have a declaration of policy.

2. The company should also have a person designated to administer that policy.

3. That person should also be designated to receive reports about how the various echelons of management are doing. The company should evaluate its operation to determine where it might be discriminating. For example, I've encountered some companies who had segregated

---

81. Personal interview, 1968.

washrooms without having been aware that they did have these
washrooms at some terminals. We've also had the problem where the
Negro local drivers had not been able to get into over-the-road
positions.

A broader aspect which I consider useful is. . .

4. Present employees should be evaluated from the standpoint of their
   potential to see whether they have been employed at a lower level
   than what they might be capable of doing. This should apply to applicants of any race to see whether they might have skills which
   are going untouched for some reason.

5. To provide training for persons who had previously been denied
   training opportunities granted to the majority of employees.

6. To advance a person who has been given this type of training if it's
   possible.

7. To make sure that the normal suppliers of personnel are aware that
   the company is not only stating a freedom from discrimination
   policy, but is actively pursuing it.

8. To make sure that seniority is used to aid rather than to hinder
   equal opportunity.

9. To have a fixed program of going out to determine what the community thinks of the particular company's pattern of behavior.

10. To go to schools in the vicinity to make sure the schools are aware
    of the affirmative action plan.

This is a comprehensive program and any combination of ten points is
a limited category of affirmative action but taken together those points
constitute a very forthright approach.[82]

Edward C. Sylvester, former director of the Office of Federal Contract Compliance, made it quite clear to the motor carriers that the government had no intention of defining affirmative action. Sylvester asserted that even if employers were to
follow all the suggested steps issued by the POD, they still might
not be operating in accordance with the Executive Order's intent. The very rationale of the order was to place the responsibility of affirmative action upon the employers' shoulders. Individual employers were expected to evaluate their potential hiring

---

82. Remarks of Paul A. Nagle, Deputy Contracts Compliance Officer, before
American Trucking Associations' Industrial Relations Committee, San
Francisco, California, November 15, 1965. A more detailed assessment
of the Post Office Department's understanding of affirmative action is
found in Appendix C.

needs and were to take any action they believed would augment the number of minorities on their payrolls. Once the employer did this, it was the government's task to determine whether the actions taken were "adequate and sufficient." [83]

Sylvester's contention that affirmative action will vary from one contractor to another, from one area to another, and even "from one day to the next," [84] reflects the breadth of the concept, but it left the industry in somewhat of a quandry. There virtually were as many opinions as to what constituted affirmative action as there were trucking firms contacted by the POD. While one employer maintained that the government was demanding that his firm hire Negroes in proportion to the number of Negroes living in a given area (quotas), another company representative believed the government was going to evaluate intent and not results per se.

One employer noted that at corporate headquarters his firm had approximately 100 people on the payroll. He claimed that the contract compliance examiner assigned to his company told him that there were 5.2 percent Negroes residing in the city, and that in ninety days the government expected to find the same percentage of Negroes employed by his company. It was, in the words of the employer, "just cut and dried." [85] The examiner even suggested that the company sponsor an open house of the company's facilities for Negroes. The firm refused to go this far, but it did put ads in the paper and it contacted a private employment agency in quest of Negro applicants. Yet no Negroes applied.

The second employer said that what the Post Office Department wanted the companies to do was "to go out and beat the bushes." [86] The government did not expect employers to hire unqualified people. What it did want the industry to do was to contact new employment sources which might be closer to the Negro labor supply. In fact, the Post Office Department had supplied his firm with Negro labor sources for twelve distinct terminal facilities.

A southern-domiciled firm questioned its obligation to contact minority groups. The firm's representative reported that their

---

83. *Applying Equal Employment in Trucking, Proceedings of the 16th Annual National Forum on Trucking Industrial Relations*, p. 18.

84. *Ibid.*

85. *Ibid.*, p. 188.

86. *Ibid.*, p. 189.

legal counsel even advised against it.[87] The rationale was that
it had no idea of the leadership of these Negro groups; the implication was that they did not want to deal with any "radical"
Negro groups.

Looming behind the scene of this discussion of affirmative action was the industry's concern about where they were to obtain
Negro drivers and whether the latters' accident rate was greater
than that among white drivers. We have already demonstrated
that the Post Office Department has no trouble in obtaining
qualified drivers for its own trucks. In addition, a representative
from Greyhound Lines said that his company had no difficulty in
finding qualified Negroes to drive buses. During their training
period they had a higher dropout record, but upon completing
the training program Negro bus drivers performed as well as
white drivers.[88] As for the Negroes' accident experiences, the
Greyhound representative said, ". . . I have yet to hear of one
of them being involved in a serious accident." [89]

The motor carriers were told that taking affirmative action did
not place them in a "Utopia Area." [90] The employer making this
observation recounted how his firm had two Negro drivers—one
with twenty-five years' experience and another with sixteen—
who drove as a team. Pressure exerted by the Post Office Department caused the company to split these two drivers up and
hire two more Negroes, but "still the pressure is being applied." [91]

One employer insisted that the government via its affirmative
action doctrine was asking the industry to show the Negro preferential treatment. He objected to advertising in Negro papers
because, "Then I'm going to have to advertise in a Jewish
neighborhood newspaper, and an Irish, and a Polish" one.[92] Although this particular employer's criticism of affirmative action
can be interpreted as somewhat extreme, the industry, in the
summer of 1966, seemed more concerned with the technicalities
of what to do to avoid government sanctions leveled against it
than with the positive steps it should take to hire more Negroes.

---

87. *Ibid.*, p. 177.

88. *Ibid.*, p. 102.

89. *Ibid.*, p. 110.

90. *Ibid.*, p. 184.

91. *Ibid.*

92. *Ibid.*, p. 183.

Affirmative Action in Practice

Our own observation that the larger companies refused to change their hiring practices was supported by information obtained by another method from that employed in this study. In June 1968, the Post Office Department asked its compliance examiners to submit special reports detailing the breakthroughs that had been made by the companies for which they were responsible. In these reports the examiners enumerated the variables which they believed influenced the companies in their less-than-enthusiastic response to equal employment opportunities hiring procedures and goals. Below is a brief summary from the reports submitted by seventeen of the Department's examiners.

The examiners acknowledged that without meaningful affirmative action programs employers would be virtually unable to increase the number of Negroes on their payrolls. First, the present hiring procedures—pirating from other firms, informal referral systems, and reliance upon union hiring halls—were employment streams in which Negroes were unlikely to be found. Second, Negroes are reluctant (even when aware of openings and qualified) to seek employment in hostile environments. Finally, most of the companies found in the motor carrier industry lacked the administrative talent necessary for the implementation of successful equal employment opportunities programs.

Against this background, not a single firm, according to the contract compliance examiners, had made any breakthroughs.[93] Employers were simply complacent. Although some companies did make slight advances in employing Negroes, the net result was mere tokenism. In general, the examiner discovered that a few companies were hiring more Negroes, even as road drivers, but only at one or two terminal facilities. Discrimination prevailed throughout the industry, according to the examiners, because management did not realize fully what compliance meant, or because of duplicity and insincerity in their dealing with the government, or a combination of these. It was estimated that less than 15 percent of all Class I motor carriers had taken the minimal first step—writing an affirmative action program. Companies have been reluctant, furthermore, to view training programs as a means of enhancing an affirmative action program, even when drivers were in short supply.

---

93. Information based on interviews, 1968.

Later Developments and Progress

In February 1968, Clarence H. Featherson, former EEOC field investigator, was named Deputy Contract Compliance Officer, the position vacated by Nagle in June 1967. The Post Office compliance staff was expanded, and the Post Office Department inaugurated a special review program designed to gather more precise information about the equal employment practices of a representative group of nineteen of the nation's larger carriers. Such information could provide the basis for "pattern of discrimination" cases filed by the U.S. Department of Justice pursuant to Title VII of the Civil Rights Act, as will be discussed later in this chapter. The decision of the courts in the cases involving discriminatory seniority systems in the tobacco [94] and paper [95] industries provided possible clues to action in other industries, such as trucking, where management and union policies were adversely affecting Negro job opportunities.

With this objective in mind, examiners assigned to these nineteen trucking companies were instructed to: (1) take an inventory of all employees by job category, indicating race and national origin; (2) identify persons on the seniority rosters by race; (3) list new hires for the preceding six months by race and job categories; (4) obtain a copy of the company's equal employment policy statement; (5) obtain copies of letters sent to referral sources stating the company's equal employment opportunity commitment; (6) obtain copies of current collective bargaining agreements; (7) obtain a current list of qualifications for job categories; and (8) obtain samples of tests administered to job applicants.

The examiners were also requested to: (1) interview minority employees to determine what is actually occurring with regard to hiring, promotion, transfer, training, etc., and (2) interview community organizations to determine the extent to which the contractor has communicated with minority referral sources, specifically: (a) the nature of such contact—whether oral or written; (b) the content of such contact, i.e., whether actual job referrals have been solicited or whether contact has consisted only of statements of philosophy; and (c) the consequences of

---

94. *Quarles* v. *Philip Morris, Inc.*, 279 F Supp. 505 (E.D. Va. 1968).

95. *United States* v. *Local 189, United Papermakers and Paperworkers, et al.*, 282 F Supp. 39 (E.D. La., 1968); affirmed, —— F. 2d —— (5th Cir., 1969).

such contact: whether referrals have been made to the company and what the results of such referrals may have been.

Table 31 shows the number of Negroes these nineteen companies had on their payrolls prior to January 1968, and the number of Negroes employed during the first six months of 1968. During this period the total number of Negroes employed by the nineteen companies increased slightly from 2,171 to 2,509. The proportion of Negroes among the total number of people employed increased from 4.0 percent to 4.3 percent.

Since 1965, the Post Office Department has concentrated its affirmative action drive on the over-the-road driver job classification. The nineteen companies increased the number of Negro road drivers from 62 out of a total of 9,168 to 98 out of a total of 9,845. Although this is admittedly a nearly 60 percent increase in the number of Negro drivers, from January to June 1968, it represents only a miniscule percentage increase from 0.7 to 1.0 percent of the drivers employed.

Negroes made their greatest advance in the operatives category as city drivers. Of the 227 city drivers hired in the six-month period, 42 or 18.5 percent were Negroes. Should this trend continue, it is possible that more Negroes, having gained acceptance as city drivers, will eventually be employed as road drivers.

The first half 1968 new hire data, as shown in Table 31, are indicative of Negro manpower utilization for the nation at large and do not reflect the degree to which particular labor markets have supplied blacks to the trucking industry. A government spokesman maintained, however, "that the most encouraging minority utilization did not come from the Northern or Western cities, but instead from two Southern-domiciled corporations." [96] In turn, these two southern firms employed 90 percent of the Negro drivers and 25 percent of the minority office and clerical employees.

The continued absence of Negroes in white collar jobs, and why relatively few companies responded to the government's request to establish effective affirmative action programs is explained, according to a government spokesman, by two factors. First, although most companies have established what they con-

---

96. Remarks made by Clarence H. Featherson, the Post Office Department's deputy contract compliance officer. These comments appeared in *Trucking Labor Relations Information*, Vol. 23, Sec. 4, No. 33, November 15, 1968 (Washington: American Trucking Associations), p. 2.

TABLE 31. *Trucking Industry*
Total Employees and New Hires by Race
19 Class I Carriers, January 1 to June 30, 1968

Job Categories	Prior and New Hires			Prior Employment			New Hires			Difference—Present and Former Per cent Negro
	Total	Total Negro	Percent Negro	Total	Total Negro	Percent Negro	Total	Total Negro	Percent Negro	
Officials-Managers	4,748	20	0.4	4,475	11	0.2	273	9	3.3	+0.2
Professionals	250	5	2.0	239	4	1.7	11	1	9.1	+0.3
Technicians	113	4	3.5	90	2	2.2	23	2	8.7	+1.3
Sales workers	1,313	1	0.1	1,223	—	—	90	1	1.1	+0.1
Office-clerical	8,684	219	2.5	7,641	130	1.7	1,043	89	8.5	+0.8
Craftsmen	3,797	126	3.3	3,523	98	2.8	274	28	10.2	+0.5
Operatives										
Road drivers	9,845	98	1.0	9,168	62	0.7	677	36	5.3	+0.3
City drivers	4,850	328	6.8	4,623	286	6.2	227	42	18.5	+0.5
Dockmen	3,974	332	8.4	3,574	275	7.7	400	57	14.3	+0.7
Others	16,690	1,006	6.0	16,133	997	6.2	557	9	1.6	−0.2
Laborers (Unskilled)	3,349	257	7.7	3,110	210	6.8	239	47	19.7	+0.9
Service workers	465	113	24.3	424	96	22.6	41	17	41.5	+1.7
Total	58,078	2,509	4.3	54,223	2,171	4.0	3,855	338	8.8	+0.3

Source: U.S. Post Office.

sider to be worthwhile affirmative action programs, these corporate endeavors had effectuated little change in practice. Second, comprehensive minority employment plans were often formulated at the corporate level, but there was a communication breakdown between headquarters and the companies' many terminals.[97]

Throughout 1969 the Post Office Department not only continued to conduct compliance reviews at the corporate and terminal levels, but it also started to stress the necessity of companies cooperating in the development of training programs. These governmental efforts at promoting training and the industry's response to this will be discussed in some detail later in this chapter. Table 32, however, shows how many Negroes were new hires during the first six months of 1969 and also the jobs in which they were hired. These recent new-hire trends are a consequence of the federal government's continued prodding of the industry and not primarily a result of training programs.

TABLE 32. *Trucking Industry*
New Hires by Race and Occupational Group
358 Trucking Companies, January 1 to June 30, 1969

Occupational Groups	New Hires		
	Total	Negro	Percent Negro
Officials and managers	1,186	15	1.3
Professionals	15	—	—
Technicians	429	6	1.4
Sales workers	410	4	1.0
Office and clerical	5,804	251	4.3
Total white collar	7,844	276	3.5
Craftsmen	1,270	128	10.1
Operatives			
Road drivers	5,589	567	10.1
City drivers	5,711	573	10.0
Dockmen	5,348	1,078	20.1
Others	40	7	17.5
Laborers	789	195	24.7
Service workers	451	125	27.7
Total blue collar	19,198	2,673	13.9
Total	27,042	2,949	10.9

Source: U.S. Post Office Department.

97. *Ibid.*

The 358 firms from which the first-half 1969 statistics wer
obtained, employed in 1968 a total of 231,325 people, of whicl
17,794 [98] or 7.7 percent were minority employees. Although thi
minority classification included American Indians and Spanish
speaking workers in addition to Negroes, it should be noted tha
during the first six months of 1969 2,949 or 10.9 percent of th
27,042 new hires were Negroes. Because the 1968 new hire sta
tistics, as shown in Table 31, represent the employment result
of nineteen Class I motor carriers, while the 1969 data are rep
resentative of the hiring activities of 358 trucking companies, i
is difficult to infer the precise significance of these yearly differ
ences. Yet, it does seem that Negroes are making some gains i
some of the better-paying job classifications included under th
blue collar category. For example, 10.1 percent of all road driv
ers hired in 1969 were Negroes. Even when we allow for th
different sources of statistics for 1968 and 1969, the trend is
upward when we consider the fact that only 5.3 percent of th
road drivers hired by the nineteen Class I carriers in 1968 wer
Negroes.

Training as Affirmative Action

In recent years the larger carriers have debated openly the
necessity of the industry's promoting coordinated driver training
programs. Although some state trucking associations have sponsored intermittent driver training schools and the American
Trucking Associations [99] has investigated the feasibility of such
programs, the net effect of these efforts has been rather insignificant. Funding, control, and screening are several of the basic
fundamentals over which disagreement within the industry
abounds. Because various types of carriers necessarily insist
upon diverse skill requirements for their drivers, it is difficult
to develop a comprehensive program capable of satisfying the divergent needs of all. Consequently, the industry has been reluctant to promote or sponsor training programs, even in a tight
labor situation when competent drivers are hard to find. The
subsequent presentation pertaining to the employers' attitudes
toward training programs must be viewed against this background of past inertia and failures in respect to such programs.

---

98. Data in author's possession.

99. For a discussion of some of the obstacles presented in establishing and
   implementing training programs, see *Training in the Trucking Industry*
   (Washington: American Trucking Associations, 1963).

The possibilities of affirmative action would seem to be great. Of the 111 firms interviewed, 88, or 79 percent, acknowledged that they were unable to find sufficient skilled drivers. Of these 88 firms, 34 percent said that this shortage of drivers was confined to the over-the-road job classification. Another 9 percent of the firms maintained that their difficulty was in finding local drivers, and 57 percent contended that they were short of both local and over-the-road drivers. In turn, of the 88 firms, 84 percent reported that the shortage of drivers was system-wide, while the remaining 16 percent said it was confined to specific labor markets. (The variation in the labor markets noted was so great that it was not possible to discern any pattern of labor shortage in specific areas of the nation.)

Private truck driver training schools are located throughout the nation, usually near the large urban centers where a great number of terminals are located. The tuition, which is usually paid by the trainee, can range from $500 to $800. Sixty-six, or 59 percent of the companies interviewed, knew of existing private schools in the areas where they maintained terminals, but only 23 companies, or 21 percent, had ever hired drivers who had graduated from these schools. Companies that did hire these drivers were not satisfied with their driving ability and, consequently, the company had to give further on-the-job training. Driving hazards and conditions are nearly impossible to simulate and the schools do not enable their trainees to cope with the psychological pressures associated with driving a truck day in and day out. Some employers contended that these private schools often accepted candidates who lacked even the basic qualifications, and engaged in misleading advertising campaigns. It would be well beyond the scope of this study to evaluate driver training programs, but note should be taken that some advances have been made in programs under federal auspices.

For the most part, larger carriers also are reluctant to establish their own training programs because of the expense entailed and because pirating employees is a common practice among firms in the industry. Seven of the 111 firms interviewed underwrite their own driver training schools, but only three of these are conducted on a permanent basis and they can serve only a few labor markets.

In raising questions related to training, the author was not interested in training as such, but rather sought to determine whether the employers, without prompting, would admit to a direct correlation between formal training and the affirmative action mandate embodied in Executive Order 11246. Only three representatives of the companies interviewed took the lead and implied that this should be the route followed by the industry if it seriously desired to meet the government's mandate. This indicates that the industry as a whole does not intend to provide training as an important and constructive avenue of affirmative action.

In early 1969, the Post Office Department shifted its emphasis from conducting compliance reviews to developing comprehensive manpower training programs. The government probably concluded that compliance reviews, usually conducted every ninety days, were no longer having a significant impact upon the hiring of Negroes in the better-paying jobs. Therefore, in an effort to encourage a fuller utilization of Negro manpower, and in particular, black over-the-road drivers, the Post Office Department began stressing the importance of training programs as an integral ingredient of the Executive Order's affirmative action provision. Coupled with this emphasis on training was the government's insistence that employers validate screening procedures used in hiring.

Rather than develop a comprehensive national model for these training programs, the Post Office Department directed its compliance examiners in the field to try to obtain the cooperation of the Teamsters, state trucking associations, individual employers, and community groups in twenty distinct labor markets. The responses of the industry and the Teamsters have been mixed. Some companies have released instructors and supervisory personnel to help develop these training programs, but this is the exception and certainly not reflective of the industry in general. Most companies, moreover, are unwilling to guarantee that they will hire any of those completing these proposed training programs.

Early in 1969 the government expressed an intention to establish training centers in twenty major labor markets, but as of the early months of 1970, only six programs had begun. Of these six embryonic programs, only the one proposed in Cleveland had a reasonable degree of employer support, and even this one is not likely to be in operation until mid-1970.

The employer's less-than-enthusiastic response to the government's overtures requesting their cooperation in the area of training must be viewed against a background of the industry's historic attitude toward training programs. Before equal employ-ment was even a factor in employment practices, trucking com-panies were reluctant to participate in multiemployer training programs. Even though the majority of employers contend that they cannot find qualified applicants, they know that as wages increase among public carriers they will be able to continue to pirate—especially drivers—from the private carriers.

Sanctions under the Executive Order

The only sanction under the Executive Order is debarment from doing business with the government. This has never been used against the trucking or any other industry, probably for two reasons. First, it is too strong a penalty, involving as it does for most industries loss of business not only with the gov-ernment, but with all concerns doing business with the govern-ment as well. The net effect is most likely forced cessation of business and unemployment for those employed—an action not likely to be without broad political, as well as economic, repercus-sions.

Second, there is a very real legal question of the propriety of what is, without doubt, executive law making which must re-strain even the most activist among the federal officials in the civil rights field. For example, in early 1967, the Post Office Department forwarded the case histories of four of the more recalcitrant trucking companies to the OFCC, and requested that this latter agency apply sanctions against these companies. The OFCC returned these cases to the Department, claiming that the information was inadequate. The Department resubmitted these cases in mid-1967, but at the time of this writing action is still pending. One can well imagine the hesitation of the government to open the Pandora's box involved with court perusal of the legality (and meaning) of affirmative action, for example, or even of the right of the Executive to issue orders going beyond the terms of what Congress has already legislated. It is perhaps for this reason that enforcement proceedings pursuant to the Civil Rights Act of 1964 have been preferred by the Department of Justice and other government officials, rather than hazarding action pursuant to an Executive Order.[100] The following section discusses such cases.

---

100. The Executive Order has been included in some legal proceedings, but the key thrust has been pursuant to Title VII of the 1964 law.

COURT PROCEEDINGS

The lack of progress in equal employment in the trucking industry led to a number of court cases, filed both by individual
complainants after the Equal Employment Opportunity Commission had failed to resolve the issue by conciliation, and by the
Department of Justice, pursuant to Section 707 of the Civil
Rights Act of 1964. Under this law, the Attorney General has
the authority to sue whenever he

. . . has reasonable cause to believe that any person or group of persons
is engaged in a pattern or practice of resistance to the full enjoyment
of any of the rights secured by this title, and that the pattern or practice
is of such a nature and is intended to deny the full exercise of the rights
herein described.[101]

A brief review of the key court cases, and their status as of
December 1969, points up further the civil rights problems in
the industry. The precise sequence of events are enumerated in
the first case only, but the basic procedure for cases filed by
individuals in the remaining cases are similar.

Richard Johnson, Jr. v. Georgia Highway Express [102]

Georgia Highway Express is a general freight carrier headquartered in Atlanta, maintaining approximately thirty terminal
facilities throughout Georgia, Alabama, and Tennessee. The complainant contended that he was discharged from the terminal in
Atlanta because of his civil rights activities.

In February 1966, the man allegedly discriminated against
attended a meeting at the Atlanta facility attended by some of
his Negro coworkers. Acting as spokesman for the group, he
asked the company representatives present at the meeting what
the firm intended to do about equal employment. In particular,
the Negro spokesman noted the equal employment posters and
asked when Negroes would be permitted to apply for jobs other
than that of dockmen—especially road driver positions. Although
the complainant had worked for the company since August 1961,
he was discharged on March 22, 1966.

---

101. The Civil Rights Act of 1964, Section 707(a).

102. *Richard Johnson, Jr.* v. *Georgia Highway Express*, C.A. No. 11.598 (N.D.
Ga.) 59 L.C. 9193 (October 8, 1968).

All the Negroes employed at this particular terminal are dockmen. As a result of the meeting, three Negroes were promoted to supervisory positions on the docks, but none were given jobs as drivers. During the past fifteen years, the company continually promoted white dockmen to the position of city driver, but this line of progression was not open to Negroes. This practice persisted even though over 90 percent of the dock workers were Negroes.

On March 31, 1966, within ninety days of his discharge (this ninety-day period was stipulated in Title VII at that time) the complainant filed his case with the EEOC. Sixteen months later, in July 1967, the Commission notified the aggrieved party that within the meaning of Title VII, it had reasonable cause to believe that the company had committed an unlawful practice. The Commission, after failing to eliminate said practice by conciliation, notified the complainant on January 29, 1968 that he was entitled to seek relief through civil action before the federal district court.

Seeking adequate relief, the lawyers for the plaintiff requested the court to issue a private and permanent injunction against Georgia Highway Express, and to compel the company to give the plaintiff back pay to compensate for the loss of income he suffered as a result of the discharge. In addition, the plaintiff also sought to protect all people of his class by forcing the company to hire Negroes as local and road drivers.

The company argued that the court lacked jurisdiction because as a discharged employee the plaintiff no longer represented the interest of the firm's employees. The company also contended that the aggrieved party was discharged because of his high rate of tardiness and absenteeism. The defendant, in turn, argued that the Attorney General can prosecute a company whenever he "has reasonable cause to believe that any person or group of persons is engaged in a pattern and practice of resistance." [103] Inasmuch as the Attorney General failed to take such action, the defendant argued that it was not in fact engaged in a "pattern and practice" of discrimination as the lawyers for the plaintiff implied. Georgia Highway Express requested, moreover, that there should be trial by jury.

The U.S. District Court ruled in June 1968 that the injunction would be denied because the plaintiff could not process this case as a class action. The lawyers for the plaintiff filed a motion to

---

103. *Ibid.*

permit an interlocutary appeal because the status of class actions in a civil rights case was a controlling question of law about which there is substantial ground for a difference of opinion. The judge in the case conceded that a true question of law existed and granted the plaintiff the right of appeal.

The case was appealed, and on October 30, 1969 the United States Court of Appeals (Fifth Circuit) handed down a decision in favor of the plaintiff. The District Court had restricted the scope of the class the plaintiff could represent to those persons who had been discharged because of their race. Upon appeal, however, the higher court acknowledged that the appellant's suit was an " 'across the board' attack on unequal employment practices alleged to have been committed by the appellee pursuant to its policy of racial discrimination," [104] and that he could represent applicants, as well as Negroes who may have been discharged. In upholding the plaintiff's right to sue for all Negroes in a class action, the court referred to a former school desegregation case which stated:

> The peculiar rights of specific individuals were not in controversy. It [the suit] was directed at the system wide policy of racial discrimination. It sought obliteration of that policy of system wide racial discrimination. In various ways this was sought through suitable declaratory orders and injunctions against any rule, regulation, custom or practice having any such consequence. *Potts* v. *Flax*, 5 Cir. 1963, 313 F.2d 284, 289.[105]

As for the trial by jury which was requested by the company, this likewise was denied the defendant. In arguing that the only issue was a claim for back pay, the company contended that this should be decided by a trial jury. The circuit court, in denying the defendant his request for trial by jury, held that only after the case had been heard on a class action could the court decide if the plaintiff had de facto been discriminated against. In turn, if the fact of discrimination is established in future litigation, it will be the court's obligation to decide the back pay issue.

As of January 1970, the lawyers for the plaintiff were still engaged in pretrial discovery procedures. In some of these racial employment discovery procedures employers are often requested to supply answers and evidence to as many as 250 posed ques-

---

104. *Richard Johnson, Jr.* v. *Georgia Highway Express, Inc.*, C.A. No. 11.598 (N.D. Ga. 1968) 59 L.C. 9193; reversed and remanded —— F. 2d —— (5th Cir., 1969).

105. *Idem.*

tions. It is estimated that a case of this nature can take any-where from three months to a year before it is scheduled and the class action allegation is ultimately decided by the court. It is well to recall that the plaintiff's initial complaint to the Equal Employment Opportunity Commission was submitted in March 1966.

Lee v. Observer Transportation [106]

This case involves a nonunion trucker located in Charlotte, North Carolina. Eighteen Negroes filed a charge against this firm because of alleged lower wages paid Negroes. They alleged that Negro drivers received $1.50 per hour, while white drivers were being paid $1.79 per hour. The complainants also contended that they were refused the better-paying road jobs.

Of the forty-eight local drivers, only seven are white and five of these were promoted subsequent to the filing of the original complaint. There were twenty-five dock workers employed at this terminal, but only two of them were white and these were hired after the complaint was lodged against the company. It seems that the company found it more expedient to integrate the lower range of the job hierarchy by hiring a few whites than it did to hire Negroes as road drivers. Again, the sole Negro road driver was promoted to this job after the complaint was sub-mitted.

The EEOC investigated the case and subsequently notified the complainants that they would have to go to court to receive ade-quate relief. When the case went to court, the lawyers for the defendant did not even address themselves to the substantive matter of allegations, but rather argued that the court lacked jurisdiction. The firm's contention was that the EEOC had made no attempt whatsoever to eliminate the alleged discrimina-tion by mediation or other informal methods. This, they argued, was a necessary prerequisite before the filing of a formal suit.

The lawyers for the plaintiff requested that the court grant a preliminary and permanent injunction enjoining the defendant from the alleged practices and from interfering with the plain-tiff's rights. The plaintiff was also requesting back pay from the time of his alleged wrongful denial of equal employment opportu-nities. In denying these requests, the U.S. District Court, on

---

106. *Lee* v. *Observer Transportation*, C.A. No. 2145 (W.D.N.C.), dismissed 59 L.C. 9206, reversed by the Fourth Circuit Court of Appeals, 59 L.C. 9207, cert. denied by the Supreme Court on March 24, 1969.

January 25, 1968, ruled that conciliation was in fact a prerequisite to the plaintiff's right to file or maintain a civil action under Section 703 of the Civil Rights Act of 1964.

Upon appeal, however, the U.S. Circuit Court of Appeals for the Fourth Circuit reversed the decision of the Circuit Court when it held that conciliation per se was not a prerequisite to the plaintiff's right of civil action. The defendant appealed this decision to the U.S. Supreme Court, but the latter refused to hear the case. As of January 1970, the substantive issues of the case were being investigated by the lawyers of the plaintiff through discovery procedures.

Hairston v. McLean Trucking Company [107]

With its headquarters located in the Winston-Salem, North Carolina area, McLean Trucking has over 5,000 employees on its payrolls and sixty-five terminals located in twenty states. This complaint of alleged discrimination was filed by a Negro employed by the firm's wholly-owned subsidiary, Modern Automotive Services, Inc., which provides automotive services at the parent company's headquarters.

The complainant, a maintenance man in the tire department of the subsidiary company, maintained that the employer uses a hiring and promotion system which tends to exclude Negroes from the better-paying jobs. There were no Negroes in the body, paint, trailer, automotive, or parts department. Aside from the management and clerical personnel working at the corporate headquarters, the Winston-Salem terminal has essentially three groups of employees: over-the-road drivers, local drivers, and maintenance men. Both categories of drivers are employed by the parent firm, while the maintenance men, although working at the same location, are employed by the subsidiary company. In turn, the Teamsters' local in the area is party to three distinct labor agreements: two with the parent company for local and over-the-road drivers respectively, and one with the subsidiary maintenance company.

Because the subsidiary company has a departmental seniority system, any Negro transferring to a different department would lose his seniority, and the complainant contends that this promotional system deprives him of opportunities for advancement. But

---

107. *Hairston* v. *McLean Trucking Company*, C.A. No. C-77-WS-68, (U.S.D.C., W.D.N.C.).

the firm's promotional policy in fact does not allow a man to transfer from one job classification to another, nor does it permit an employee to resign from one job and then reapply for another. When this policy is combined with the practice of hiring Negroes only as tiremen, minority members are locked into a dead end department (tire department) where promotional opportunities are nonexistent. The charging party, a member of this department, requested to be admitted to the company's driver training program.

The employer held that because the complainant is an employee of Modern Automotive Services, Inc. a charge against the McLean Trucking Company is not appropriate. Although the parent company negotiates the labor contracts of the subsidiary firm, and formulates and implements its hiring and upgrading policies, it argues that it should not be party to the case.

The defendant also argued that even if the charging party had been white, his request for a transfer would have been denied. While this contention might be true, there are no whites isolated in the lowest-paying jobs offered by either the parent or subsidiary companies. Moreover, virtually all the Negroes employed by both the companies are locked in these non-status, low-paying, dead end job categories.

McLean Trucking refused to answer some of the questions submitted by the lawyers for the plaintiff on the grounds that these questions were irrelevant and immaterial to the case at hand. For example, the defendant objected to having to provide the address of the company that hires employees for its subsidiary, Modern Automotive Services, Inc., which provides maintenance service for McLean's fleet. On November 12, 1968, the plaintiff asked the court to compel the company to answer all the questions submitted in the interrogation or discovery procedures. McLean countered this move by filing a motion requesting that the court deny the plaintiff the right to answer any and all questions he might submit. As of January 1970 neither the plaintiff's nor the defendant's requests had been decided by the courts.

James v. Braswell Motor [108]

This complaint, lodged against a southern terminal in Dallas, Texas was, unlike the former cases, the first claim under Title

---

108. *James* v. *Braswell Motor*, C.A. No. 3-2113 (N.D. Tex., May 1, 1968.)

VII involving any industry where the case was presented to a jury. The plaintiff asserted that Braswell Motor refused to promote him from the job of dockman to that of checker, despite its promise to do so. He further alleged that he was bypassed several times when the defendant promoted newly-hired white employees to the position of checker. This action on the part of the defendant was discriminatory, according to Title VII of the Civil Rights Act of 1964.

Inasmuch as dockmen were paid less than checkers, the plaintiff requested that the company pay him the difference in wages occasioned by this unlawful employment practice. The plaintiff also requested that the jury order the defendant to pay the fees of his attorney at the rate of $50.00 per hour. Although the defendant denied the allegations, the jury awarded the aggrieved Negro $1,800, plus six percent interest, which represented the difference in pay he would have received had he been promoted to the position of checker. The defendant was further ordered to pay the plaintiff's lawyer fee of $750.00.

The defendant's motion for a new trial asserted that the court erred in requiring the jury to make its determination on inadequate facts. Moreover, the court allegedly erred because Title VII only permits back pay for lost wages and not because a man was not promoted. The defendant requested that the court order a stay of any proceedings to enforce the judgment entered in favor of the plaintiff, pending the defendant's motion for a new trial. Like the cases noted above, this one is waiting a final verdict.

The above cases are prototypes of alleged claims of discrimination lodged against four distinct trucking companies. While the firms involved were different, the cases themselves manifest certain similar characteristics:

1. All the complaints arose because of hiring or upgrading practices pursued by terminals located in the South.

2. Although one of them was initially filed with the EEOC as early as September 1965, all of these cases are still being litigated.

3. In all the cases the defendants have questioned procedural questions of law, besides the factual data submitted by the aggrieved.

Bradshaw v. Associated Transport, Inc., and United States v. Associated Transport [109]

Associated Transport employs some 8,000 people throughout its operations, but these complaints arose when two Negroes sought employment at its Burlington, North Carolina terminal. The total number of people employed at this location was approximately 530, of which 200 were road drivers, but there were no Negroes in this latter job classification. Two distinct complaints were filed simultaneously, but only one of them is unique enough for a detailed discussion.

The Negro filing this particular complaint alleged that he was denied employment as a road driver because he failed to meet the two-year experience standard stipulated by Associated. When he told the party who conducted the interview that he was willing to pay his own tuition and attend the North Carolina Driving School in Raleigh, he was told that the company's policy was not to employ drivers graduated by this school.

Although the original complaint was filed in September 1965, the case is still pending. The defendant is not questioning the allegation made by the complainant that the company's employment standards were different for Negroes, but rather is arguing that the court lacks jurisdiction because the case was not presented to the federal district courts within the time span allowed under Title VII. Again the plaintiff is confronted with substantiating a point of law, and as yet has not been able to raise the question of the presence of discrimination.

On August 6, 1968, the Department of Justice filed a suit independent of the individual complaint and alleged that Associated Transport was guilty of perpetuating a "pattern and practice" of discrimination. With two distinct charges lodged against the company, the courts ordered the lawyers for Bradshaw (the original plaintiff) and the Department of Justice to consolidate their investigating activities. On May 14, 1969, however, the Department of Justice arrived at a conciliated agreement with Associated Transport. The original case which arose because of a singular alleged claim of discrimination is still pending.

---

109. *Bradshaw* v. *Associated Transport, Inc.,* C.A. No. C-245-G-67 (U.S.D.C., E.D.N.C.) ;*United States* v. *Associated Transport,* C.A. No. C-99-G-68 (U.S.D.C., E.D.N.C.).

United States v. Roadway Express [110]

After receiving nineteen complaints of alleged discrimination, the EEOC requested the Department of Justice to take action against Roadway Express, the fourth largest and one of the more profitable trucking companies in the nation. Roadway, with corporate offices in Akron, Ohio, operates in twenty-four states.

Among its approximate 9,000 employees Roadway employed only 288 Negroes, the EEOC discovered, and no Negroes were found among its 2,100 road drivers or its 1,300 managers, professionals, and sales workers. Of Roadway's 1,043 office and clerical employees, only two were Negroes. The remaining 286 Negroes were employed as garage workers, dock workers, pickup and delivery drivers, checkers, and service workers.

This case is unique in that it marked the first time the federal government brought suit against a company's nationwide operations, rather than a single plant or facility. With the Negro-white employment profile established, the Justice Department claimed that Roadway "pursued and continues to pursue policies and practices that discriminate against Negroes and which deprive them of employment opportunities or adversely affect their status as employees because of race." [111] In implementing these policies and practices Roadway was accused of: (1) failing or refusing to hire Negroes on the same basis as whites; (2) always assigning Negroes to the lower-paying jobs; (3) perpetuating separate lines of progression based on race; and (4) refusing to promote Negroes according to the same criteria used for white employees.

The suit seeks an injunction to end discrimination and requests that Roadway be compelled to take the necessary steps to modify its practices so that Negroes will be treated equitably. As are all the other cases noted above, this one is still in litigation. Because of the size of the firm and the scope of the case, this will no doubt set precedents for other civil rights cases in the area of employment.

110. *United States* v. *Roadway Express*, C.A. No. C-68-321 (U.S.D.C. N.D. Ohio).

111. *United States* v. *Roadway Express*, C.A. No. C-68-321 (U.S.D.C. N.D. Ohio).

*United States v. Central Motor Lines, Inc. and Locals 71, 391,
and 710, International Brotherhood of Teamsters* [112]

Central Motor Lines employs in the neighborhood of 1,500
people throughout its system and operates terminals in at least
eight states. The Department of Justice claims that the company
employs 73 Negroes and 544 whites at its Charlotte terminal,
and 25 Negroes and 63 whites at its Greensboro location. Of
greater significance is the fact that Central employs no Negroes
among its some 300 over-the-road drivers and only two Negroes
are local drivers among the 76 such employees working at the
Charlotte and Greensboro terminals.

Similar to the Roadway case, the federal government argued
that Central Motor Lines has failed to take adequate affirmative
steps to correct the continuing effects of discriminatory practices
and, therefore, this constituted a "pattern and practice" of resistance to the full utilization of Negroes. In this case, however,
the Attorney General also filed suit against three Teamster locals, namely, Local 71, Charlotte, N.C.; Local 391, Greensboro,
N.C.; and Local 710, Chicago, Illinois. The charge against the
Teamsters contends that the collective bargaining agreement with
Central Motor Lines contributes to the perpetuation of racial discrimination. Since the contract provides for seniority determination on the basis of separate job classifications (separate lists for
local and long-haul drivers) rather than length of service at a
particular terminal, Negroes—so claims the Department of Justice—are not promoted to over-the-road jobs. In a decision handed down by the United States Court of Appeals for the Fourth
Circuit, it has been decided that total service at a location, regardless of time on a job, should determine who is promoted
provided the employee has the ability to perform the job. [113] The
complexity of the Central case and past experience suggests that
it will take several years of litigation before it can be determined
whether the rationale of the above [114] case applies here.

Against this background of protracted litigation over the application of Title VII, in particular cases the trucking industry

---

12. *U.S.* v. *Central Motor Lines, Inc. and Locals 71, 391 and 710, International Brotherhood of Teamsters,* as reported in *Daily Labor Report,*
August 13, 1969.

13. *United States* v. *Local 189, United Papermakers and Paperworkers, et al.,*
282 F Supp. 39 (E.D. La. 1968); affirmed, —— F 2d —— (5th Cir.,
1969).

14. *Ibid.*

has been urged continuously by the Post Office Department to
hire more Negroes. The industry is aware, however, that Title
VII, although subject to judicial interpretation, might well prove
to be the strongest antidiscrimination weapon at the govern
ment's disposal. The NAACP's Legal Defense and Education
Fund, which usually represents the plaintiffs in Title VII cases
is aware that a whole body of decisions is necessary before the
government can expedite any civil action that must be taken
against discriminating employers. Until this happens, it is un
likely that the trucking industry will change its past practice
and hire more Negroes, unless the government exercises its au
thority under Executive Order 11246 and prosecutes companies
found in violation of the Order.

In May 1968, a trucking firm, namely B and P Motor Express
of Pittsburgh, Pennsylvania, was one of five companies formally
notified by the OFCC that the latter was contemplating barring
them from government work. These companies, if they failed to
request formal hearings, were to be declared automatically in
eligible for further contracts and any existing contracts could be
terminated. Although this is the first such instance of such
notice, the OFCC has stepped up its practice of conducting in
formal conferences with representatives from individual truck
ing companies. It seems that the OFCC has decided that con
ciliation and persuasion have not convinced the industry as a
whole of its obligation to hire Negroes in the better-paying job
classifications. It is too early to tell whether OFCC's increased
use of informal private conferences will be sufficient or whether
formal methods will be necessary before truckers alter their em
ployment practices.

ADMINISTRATIVE PROBLEMS IN CIVIL RIGHTS ENFORCEMENT

The progress toward equal employment opportunity in the in
dustry, according to industry spokesmen, has been hindered by
the jurisdictional overlap of the OFCC and the Post Office De
partment with the Equal Employment Opportunity Commission
which was created under Title VII of the Civil Rights Act of
1964. Generally, the industry preferred the Post Office inspectors
because it found that Department's compliance examiners rea
sonable in their requests when they conducted investigations at
the various firms' headquarters or terminal facilities. Most truck

ers found them much more understanding than the staff personnel of the EEOC. One company representative attributed this fundamental difference in attitude and approach to the fact that most of the compliance examiners employed by the Department were former officials of the United Federation of Postal Clerks. Nagle had been administrative vice president of this union and recruited his staff from among its ranks. Their previous experience in dealing with people, the company representative claimed, made them more sensitive to the numerous human problems arising when a firm attempts to integrate its work force.[115]

The industry's initial impression of the Department's compliance examiners still prevails. When the author questioned representatives of the interviewed sample firms about the ability, understanding, and attitude of the Department's compliance examiners, the general response was: "They have a job to do and they are doing it." From the employer's point of view, in 1968 only one compliance examiner seemed to be making unreasonable demands of them at specific terminal locations. Incidentally, when the author mentioned this to the Department's Washington staff, he was told that this particular examiner was as effective as the others in encouraging employers to hire more Negroes.

The industry found the Equal Employment Opportunity Commission's examiners much more aggressive and less understanding of their problems. Having come from other agencies, these investigators, as one employer stated, want "the letter of the law upheld regardless." [116] Unlike the Post Office Department, the EEOC was not interested in the spirit of the law. This same employer contended that the EEOC examiner usually "wants to know nothing from anything about conciliation." [117]

Not only were the truckers censorious of the contradictory differences in attitude and approach between the EEOC and the Department, but they soon had reason to criticize the absence of interagency cooperation at both the federal and state level.

We find that when you say Gimbel's doesn't tell Macy's, as well as Macy's not telling Gimbel's—the same thing is true with the Post Office Department and the EEOC. They'll rehash the same facts and we'll tell them

---

115. *Applying Equal Employment in Trucking, Proceedings of the 16th Annual National Forum on Trucking Industrial Relations* (Washington: American Trucking Associations, Inc.), p. 182.

116. *Ibid.*

117. *Ibid.*

"go to the other department" and they'll say, "Well, we'll do this, we get in touch with them." But as a matter of fact, this doesn't happe We'll square away with the Post Office Department and on the identic facts the EEOC will come in and rehash the thing, and they'll find charge. They'll go through the entire thing, and if they just manage find just a little something wrong with you, they'll review your enti company situations.[118]

Needless to say, the companies found these duplications tim consuming, burdensome, and expensive. The first time one com pany learned that a complaint had been lodged against it wa when it was disclosed by the *Wall Street Journal.*[119] The com pany complained to the government because it had not been not fied of the discrimination charge. Nevertheless, the company ulti mately was visited by the Ohio Civil Rights Commission, th EEOC, the Post Office Department, the National Labor Relation Board, and the local chapter of the National Association for th Advancement of Colored People. Investigations by numerov agencies because of a single complaint prompted a represent tive from the Southwestern Area Motor Carriers Labor Relation Association to offer the rather caustic observation that, "Th number of people that will staff the bureaucracy grows in the i verse order of the problem,"[120] and that he could "envision th day when the staffs of the numerous agencies would be large than the unemployed." [121] Anticipating that management's pro lem in dealing with many agencies would not subside, one trucke recommended that the other companies follow his example: wri to congressmen from the states where they have terminal facil ties.[122]

In an effort to prevent several government agencies from i vestigating the same complaint, the Post Office Department pr posed to the EEOC that the OFCC should be given priority ove the complaint cases, but the EEOC would not agree with thi Insisting that it exercise its statutory authority to the fulles the EEOC intended to handle all complaints submitted to it. I 1966, the EEOC and OFCC adopted a joint poster directing th allegedly discriminated party to write either to EEOC or OFCC

118. *Ibid.*

119. The article, "Bias in the Cab," in the March 31, 1966 issue of th *Wall Street Journal* disclosed the name of this particular company.

120. *Ibid.*, p. 208.

121. *Ibid.*

122. *Ibid.*, p. 211.

In practice, many complainants submitted their case to both agencies. After one agency had conducted a complaint investigation and found no violation, it was not unusual for the other one to question the employer about the same complaint. Rather than inducing companies to assume nondiscriminatory practices, this procedure merely irritated them, as it has in other industries.

There is, of course, another side of the issue—that is, the relative opposition to civil rights in the industry. Only one firm, Bekins Van and Storage Company, joined Plans for Progress in the early stages of the affirmative action doctrine.[123] Few other trucking companies have been leading protagonists of the Civil rights Act or other such measures.

THE ROLE OF THE AMERICAN TRUCKING ASSOCIATIONS

It took less than a year from the promulgation of Executive Order 11246 for the Post Office Department to conclude that the larger trucking firms were not receptive to the objectives of the order. The Department then turned to the American Trucking Associations (ATA) to see if a voluntary trade association could assume a position of leadership regarding equal employment.

The American Trucking Associations, founded in 1933 prior to passage of the Motor Carrier Act, today is a national federation of fifty independent state trucking associations and twelve autonomous conferences representing the various types of carriers. As it endeavors to coordinate the activities of these sixty-two distinct bodies, the ATA's Washington staff also provides member companies with information and data about such topics as the current status of the industry's labor relations problems, federal highway regulations, and operating statistics of the various carriers. The ATA, moreover, is one of the most powerful and sophisticated lobbying agents on Capitol Hill. Individual firms that are close to their respective state trucking associations "can do anything, at any time they may desire, with respect to headquarters and staff." [124]

---

123. For the Bekins story, see Stephen Habbe, *Company Experience with Negro Employment*, Studies in Personnel Policy, Vol. 1, No. 201 (New York: National Industrial Conference Board, 1966), pp. 82-86.

124. *National Organization of the Trucking Industry in the United States*, revised ed. (Washington: American Trucking Associations, Inc.).

Among the twelve conferences are those established to satis
the needs of certain types of carriers, such as automobile move
private carriers, regulated carriers, and household movers. Ea
of these conferences maintains its own staff in Washington, re
resenting the specialized interests of their different kinds
carrier members. A greater degree of power is vested in t
state associations, the progenitors of the ATA itself. A trucki
company belongs to the ATA only after joining one of the a
filiated state associations, which can include all types and class
of carriers. The state associations usually do not engage in c
lective bargaining at the local level. Their primary function
to represent motor carriers before their state governments, chie
on regulatory matters.

Prior to the realization in 1964 of "Hoffa's dream"—the sig
ing of the first National Master Freight Agreement (coveri
mostly carriers of general commodities)—the industry was re
resented at collective bargaining sessions by distinct areawide e
ployer bargaining units. Hoffa's drive to broaden the geograp
cal scope of the contract forced the industry to establish a co
parable national bargaining team. Eventually more than thir
regional labor relations associations were amalgamated into o
national bargaining unit, Trucking Employees, Inc. (TEI). T
has the authority to bargain on all issues, but defers the ba
gaining of regional conditions to the regional units. This giv
rise to the numerous supplementary agreements now append
to the National Master Freight Agreement. Separate but simil
multi-employer labor agreements are bargained by labor relatio
associations or groups covering carriers of special commoditie
such as liquid bulk, auto-haul, etc.

If a motor carrier is not affiliated with a regional or sta
labor association, the IBT sends the company two copies of t
newly negotiated agreement, requesting it to sign and exped
tiously return one copy. A few companies refuse to join the
state associations in the belief that their operating conditio
require separate or special terms when they settle with t
Teamsters.

The state or regional groups also deal with the union on
day-by-day basis. Believing that they always may be fleeced b
the Teamsters, these groups are extremely cognizant of the co
of arousing the IBT's ire. While the ATA may be more symp
thetic to the Department's nondiscriminatory goals, as an agenc
which does not bargain, it can only urge the firms in the i

dustry to take positive steps regarding equal employment opportunities. This function is necessarily limited to working out complaints brought under the grievance procedure of the labor agreement.

Powerless to represent the industry at the bargaining table, the ATA's Industrial Relations Committee provides member firms with information and data relative to all aspects of trucking labor relations. The Committee sponsors an annual forum on such matters as how to handle grievances, motivating middle management, profit-sharing and incentives for trucking employees, and personnel practices in the trucking industry.

The Industrial Relations Committee's 1966 forum was devoted exclusively to the full spectrum of the significance of EEO in the industry. Representatives from the OFCC, EEOC, the Post Office Department, and Department of Justice have addressed these annual meetings. A spokesman for the ATA claims that these annual meetings have provided company representatives with the opportunity to understand the government's most current goals and have served a needed educational function.

CHAPTER VII

Concluding Remarks

It now seems apparent that genuine equal employment of Negroes in the trucking industry is far from a reality. Are there any indications that the future holds promise for the entry of Negroes into the better paying jobs of the industry?

There is some indication, based on a few carefully selected interviews, suggesting that since early 1969 some of the larger carriers have quietly hired or upgraded an increasing number of Negroes. The Teamsters' Union, moreover, has begun to cooperate with the federal government and the IBT now has given its support to a driver training program. The results to date are reputed to have been effective.[125] It is therefore possible that future government, union, and industry cooperation in the area of training may assist Negroes to a greater degree than manpower programs have in the past.

No doubt the several individual complaints of alleged discrimination filed under Title VII of the Civil Rights Act of 1964 and the two pending "pattern of discrimination" suits filed by the U.S. Department of Justice have had some impact upon the industry's former intransigency. Recent studies of the paper and tobacco industries in this series indicate that such litigation can be very effective in situations where union-management attitudes and relationships are antagonistic to the requirements of the Civil Rights Act of 1964.[126] The importance of this judicial prodding is epitomized by one authority who commented, apropos of the Civil Rights Act:

It seems strange, but those who come to evaluate Title VII ten years hence are more likely to find the answers in the files (or lack of them)

---

125. Fred H. Schmidt, "A Repair Shop for Unemployables," *Industrial Relations*, Vol. VIII (May 1969), pp. 280-285.

126. Michael I. Sovern, *Legal Restraints on Racial Discrimination in Employment* (New York: The Twentieth Century Fund, 1966), p. 102.

of the Justice Department than in those of the Commission of Equal Employment Opportunity.[127]

What was stated about Title VII of the Act is no doubt true of the contract compliance program. The degree to which the government enforces (or can enforce) the most recent Executive Order is likely to determine the trucking industry's employment of Negroes in the future.

We must concede that there is no reason to believe that the industry is so adverse to providing equal employment opportunities that it desires to engage in permanent conflict with the government. Once the seriousness of the government's purpose is well established, we can expect to witness an increased willingness on the part of the industry, and the Teamsters as well, to take a positive and cooperative position in regard to the hiring and the training of Negroes and other minorities. Hopefully, it will not be necessary to resort to that less-than-perfect vehicle, the rule of law, to resolve the extremely volatile and emotional problem of equal employment in this industry.

Although the legal posture of the Civil Rights Act of 1964 is more certain than the legality and latitude of Executive Order 11246, it has been the latter as implemented by the Office of Federal Contract Compliance and the Post Office Department that has been of greater significance in promoting equal employment in the trucking industry. In fact, the Post Office Department "stands out among federal agencies for its compliance efforts." [128] Indeed, there are some serious legal problems associated with the very concept of affirmative action, but many employers, fearing the worst, have begun to accept equal employment as a necessary corporate responsibility. Even in the absence of legal benchmarks, truckers have come to the realization that should the government be compelled to test the latitude of Executive Order 11246, their industry might well be the one chosen for such a showdown. Because there are so many firms in the industry and because most of the better-paying jobs require a minimal amount

---

127. See Herbert R. Northrup, *The Negro in the Paper Industry*, Report No. 8 (Philadelphia: Industrial Research Unit, Wharton School of Finance and Commerce, University of Pennsylvania, 1969); and Herbert R. Northrup, *The Negro in the Tobacco Industry*, Report No. 13 (Philadelphia: Industrial Research Unit, Wharton School of Finance and Commerce, University of Pennsylvania, 1970).

128. United States Commission on Civil Rights, *Jobs and Civil Rights*, prepared by the Brookings Institute, Clearing House Publication No. 16 (Washington, D.C.: U.S. Government Printing Office, 1969), p. 143.

of training, a debarment procedure against a single firm would not reduce significantly the transportation services provided by public motor carriers.

This study began by noting that in 1967 some Negro youths in Cincinnati blocked the passage of white drivers when they noticed that there were relatively few Negroes possessing these coveted jobs. The forming of this barricade by these Negro youths was a contributing factor to the racial confrontation that subsequently occurred.

In his classical exposition of *An American Dilemma*,[129] Gunnar Myrdal maintained that there was a disparity between the dictates of what he referred to as the American Creed of equality of opportunity and the manner in which whites treated Negroes. He believed that eventually there would be a bridging of the gap between the espoused principles of equality and the actual implementation of these principles. Theoretically, the wedding of ideal and action would take place when a tortured white conscience could no longer live with this inherent contradiction between ideal and action. Events have demonstrated that the Negro will wait no longer to see whether the white community will change its attitude toward him. What the youth in Cincinnati did demonstrates a singular incident in which Negroes have taken power into their own hands and have therefore made clear that they are capable and willing to accelerate the rate of social change and adaptation.

If power, therefore, be the vehicle by which the Negro is to gain the full exercise of his rights, including equal employment opportunities, then hopefully power channeled through existing governmental institutions is, in the long run, capable of aiding the Negro in his quest for equality. From the known to the unknown is a valid inference—we can infer that only with continued governmental efforts will the Negro find the trucking industry's doors always and everywhere open to him.

---

129. Gunnar Myrdal, *An American Dilemma* (New York: Harper & Row, 1944); also Arnold Rose, *The Negro in America* (New York: Harper and Row, 1948), p. 312. The second work offers a succinct comment on Myrdal's major thesis.

Appendix A

SAMPLE SELECTION

The 3,397 individual firms comprising the total population of this study must annually report to the Interstate Commerce Commission the number of people on their payrolls. The most recent published source from which these employment data could be obtained was *Trinc's Blue Book of the Trucking Industry* (1966 edition), and not the ICC Reports. These employment data were taken from this former publication. These employment data, in conjunction with 1960 census data were the bases upon which a representative sample of the 3,397 firms was selected. A detailed explanation of the criteria employed in the aggregation process, and of the statistical methods used in the selection of the sample firms is presented below.

1. Using a specially designed card, pertinent information about each of the 3,397 companies was systematically catalogued. Included on these cards was such information as: the name of the carrier, the type of carrier, total number of hourly employees, and the location of the firm's corporate headquarters.

2. The forty-six Standard Metropolitan Statistical Areas, with the largest total population according to the 1960 Census, were listed in an array. The choice of these forty-six SMSA's was predicated upon the fact that the 1960 Census reported nonwhite male truckdrivers and deliverymen for these areas only. It initially was assumed that these nonwhite data were relevant in the research, but this assumption proved to be wrong. Numerous trucking companies are headquartered in Winston-Salem and Greensboro, North Carolina. Therefore, the population criterion was relaxed, as was the availability of data relevant to nonwhite truckdrivers and deliverymen, and the SMSA's located in North Carolina were included in this study. Although the 1960 Census lists the Winston-Salem and Greensboro SMSA's independently, they were treated as one SMSA in the study. As a result, the geographical area, or the labor markets comprising the total population of the study consisted of forty-eight selected SMSA's. According to the 1960 Census, these forty-eight contain 42.3 percent of the nation's total population, and 9,559,240 or 46.6 percent of the nonwhite population.

3. Companies were separated according to the SMSA's in which their corporate headquarters fell. Consequently, 1,548, or 45.6 percent, of the 3,397 Class I and II carriers claimed one of the forty-eight SMSA's as the area in which their corporate headquarters were located. In 1965, these 1,548 firms employed 46.3 percent or 274,115 of the hourly personnel on the payrolls of all Class I and II carriers. The remaining 1,349 or 54.4 percent of the carriers which employed 305,502 or 53.7 percent of the hourly employees were not considered in the study.

4. The country was then divided into four geographical regions. Several factors were considered in determining the geographical scope of these four regions. First, an effort was made to include in each specific area those states possessing somewhat homogeneous attitudes regarding the racial problem. Second, the cost associated with having to interview firms in noncontiguous areas was seriously weighed. Third, these areas were determined so as to obtain a reasonable distribution of the employees in each of the four areas. Tables A-1 through A-4 show the particular SMSA's found in each of the areas, and the number of employees accounted for by both large and small firms having their corporate headquarters in these same SMSA's.

5. Once the total number of employees for each SMSA was determined, the SMSA's were listed in a descending order according to the total number of employees reported by firms with corporate headquarters in the respective SMSA's. For example, in the Northeast area the SMSA's were listed in the following order: New York, Philadelphia, Boston, Pittsburgh, Newark, Baltimore, etc. Then, these employment statistics were cumulated, and a random sample of SMSA's was selected in such a way that the probability of an SMSA being included in the sample was proportional to the industry's total hourly employment. Sample SMSA's for each region were randomly chosen so that the selected sample areas included approximately 50 percent of the industry's total number of hourly workers employed by the firms having their corporate headquarters located in each of the broad geographical areas. The sample SMSA's are shown in Table A-5.

6. After the sample SMSA's, thirteen in number, were chosen in a random manner, it was necessary to select sample firms with headquarters located in each of the SMSA's. To prevent selecting a disproportionate number of large firms, the companies in each SMSA were clustered into two distinct groups. All com-

TABLE A-1. *Trucking Industry*
Total Hourly Employees by Size of Firm
10 SMSA's, Northeast Region, 1966

SMSA	Total Firms	Total Hourly Employees	Number of Large Firms	Hourly Employees Large Firms	Number of Small Firms	Hourly Employees Small Firms
New York	113	23,406	20	19,062	93	4,344
Philadelphia	93	12,862	19	10,377	74	2,485
Boston	66	7,078	16	5,243	50	1,835
Pittsburgh	57	6,564	13	5,357	44	1,207
Newark	33	3,203	7	1,023	26	2,180
Baltimore	23	3,126	8	2,582	15	544
Jersey City	42	2,439	4	1,427	38	1,012
Buffalo	21	1,700	4	1,138	17	562
Washington	15	895	2	405	13	490
Rochester	6	321	—	—	6	321
Total	469	61,594	93	46,614	376	14,980

Source: *Trinc's Blue Book of the Trucking Industry*, 1966 Edition (Washington: Trinc Associates, Ltd., 1966).

TABLE A-2. *Trucking Industry*
Total Hourly Employees by Size of Firm
15 SMSA's, South Region, 1966

SMSA	Total Firms	Total Hourly Employees	Number of Large Firms	Hourly Employees Large Firms	Number of Small Firms	Hourly Employees Small Firms
Winston-Salem Greensboro	13	11,198	7	10,943	6	255
Dallas	22	7,917	9	7,470	13	447
Charlotte	18	5,805	8	5,217	10	588
Atlanta	20	4,738	5	4,142	15	596
Houston	23	4,288	7	3,671	16	617
Birmingham	19	3,078	8	2,600	11	478
Memphis	17	2,909	3	2,352	14	557
Tampa	8	2,056	4	1,845	4	211
San Antonio	7	1,633	4	1,558	3	75
El Paso	5	1,442	4	1,400	1	42
Miami	8	1,055	2	878	6	177
Louisville	13	790	3	314	10	476
Fort Worth	7	743	2	518	5	225
Norfolk	11	627	1	428	10	199
New Orleans	8	486	1	384	7	102
Total	199	48,765	68	43,720	131	5,045

Source: *Trinc's Blue Book of the Trucking Industry*, 1966 Edition (Washington: Trinc Associates, Ltd. 1966).

TABLE A-3. *Trucking Industry*
Total Hourly Employees by Size of Firm
12 SMSA's, Midwest Region, 1966

SMSA	Total Firms	Total Hourly Employees	Number of Large Firms	Hourly Employees Large Firms	Number of Small Firms	Hourly Employees Small Firms
Chicago	146	27,976	39	23,560	107	4,416
Detroit	52	13,597	27	12,866	25	731
Akron	22	11,672	11	11,307	11	365
St. Louis	57	7,904	22	6,721	35	1,183
Cleveland	43	8,331	19	7,332	24	999
Minneapolis-St. Paul	38	6,975	18	6,168	20	807
Columbus	18	6,781	9	6,457	9	324
Milwaukee	33	4,084	11	2,983	22	1,101
Cincinnati	22	3,590	11	3,115	11	475
Indianapolis	20	3,479	5	2,636	15	843
Toledo	11	1,082	3	688	8	394
Dayton	8	377	—	—	8	377
Total	470	95,848	175	83,833	295	12,015

Source: *Trinc's Blue Book of the Trucking Industry, 1966 Edition* (Washington: Trinc Associates, Ltd., 1966).

TABLE A-4. Trucking Industry
Total Hourly Employees by Size of Firm
11 SMSA's, West Region, 1966

SMSA	Total Firms	Total Hourly Employees	Number of Large Firms	Hourly Employees Large Firms	Number of Small Firms	Hourly Employees Small Firms
San Francisco	61	21,703	14	20,031	47	1,672
Los Angeles	134	15,736	29	12,105	105	3,631
Denver	36	9,690	12	8,840	24	850
Kansas City	32	8,535	12	7,847	20	688
Seattle	34	3,590	8	2,483	26	1,107
Oklahoma	15	3,410	5	3,010	10	400
Portland	34	1,905	8	988	26	917
Tulsa	14	1,309	3	795	11	514
Phoenix	15	1,027	2	514	13	513
Omaha	13	798	2	402	11	396
San Diego	6	205	—	—	6	205
Total	394	67,908	95	57,015	299	10,893

Source: *Trinc's Blue Book of the Trucking Industry, 1966 Edition* (Washington: Trinc Associates, Ltd., 1966).

TABLE A-5. *Trucking Industry
Sample SMSA's by Region*

Region	Sample SMSA's	TotalNumber of Hourly Employees	Percent of All Employees in Region
Northeast	1. Philadelphia	12,862	20.88
	2. Boston	7,078	11.49
	3. New York	23,406	38.00
	Total	43,346	70.37
South	1. Winston-Salem Greensboro	11,198	22.90
	2. Charlotte	5,805	11.91
	3. Birmingham	3,078	6.31
	4. Atlanta	4,738	9.71
	Total	24,819	50.83
Midwest	1. Chicago	27,976	29.10
	2. St. Louis	7,904	8.24
	3. Detroit	13,597	14.18
	Total	49,477	51.52
West	1. San Francisco	21,703	31.96
	2. Denver	9,690	14.27
	3. Los Angeles	15,736	23.17
	Total	47,129	69.40

Source: Data in author's possession.

Note: The SMSA's are arranged in the order they were randomly selected. Because Philadelphia and Boston accounted for only 32.4 percent of the total number of employees in the Northeast area, it was necessary to select another SMSA. In so doing, New York was chosen and therefore the total number of employees in the three samples exceeds the 50 percent criterion initially established. A similar situation arose in the West.

panies reporting 100 or less workers employed throughout the
operations were in one group, while firms with 101 or more er
ployees were included in the second group. Using employme
data as the criterion, the firms in each group were listed in
descending array, and then these employment statistics we
cumulated. After the firms were collated into two distinct clus
ers, and the firms employment statistics cumulated, a rando
sample of firms was selected in such a way that 20 percent of :
firms having 101 or more employees were chosen, and 10 perce
ers, and the firms, employment statistics cumulated, a rando
The 10 and 20 percent limits established for small and lar;
firms respectively were not rigorously adhered to in those cas
where the total number of firms in each cluster was less than te
The total number of large and small firms found in the select
SMAS's, as well as the number of firms chosen in the samp.
are shown in Table A-6. Mention is made in the text of tho
instances where the firms initially selected refused to coopera
in this study, and when, therefore, resampling was necessary.

TABLE A-6. *Trucking Industry*
Total and Sample Firms by Firm Size
Selected SMSA's

SMSA	Total Number of Large Firms	Number of Large Firms in Sample	Total Number of Small Firms	Numbe of Sma Firms i Sampl
Philadelphia	19	4	74	7
Boston	16	3	50	5
New York	20	4	93	9
Winston-Salem Greensboro	7	2	6	2
Charlotte	8	2	10	2
Birmingham	8	2	11	1
Atlanta	5	2	15	2
Chicago	39	8	107	10
St. Louis	22	4	35	4
Detroit	27	5	25	3
San Francisco	14	3	47	5
Denver	12	3	105	3
Los Angeles	29	6	24	10
Total	226	48	602	63

Source: Data in author's possession.

Appendix B

EXPANSION OF THE EMPLOYMENT DATA AND DETERMINATION OF THE COEFFICIENT OF VARIATION FOR FOUR GEOGRAPHICAL AREAS

Four statistical procedures were used to adjust the original employment data and determine the coefficient of variation. The first three of these procedures expanded the data in such a manner that Negro-white employment data are presented on the bases f four distinct geographical areas. First, the racial employment tatistics are reported on the bases of thirteen SMSA's. It was hen possible to expand the SMSA data so that they represented ne racial employment profile for four distinct geographical reas. (See Appendix A for details.) Third, the data were aggregated to reflect the percentage of Negroes employed by the rucking industry in forty-eight SMSA's. The exposition below ses either small or large firms in its examples, but it was necessary to follow the identical procedure for both large and small rms in all instances.

Adjusting the data for the thirteen selected SMSA's

The sample small firms in each SMSA were selected in proportion (10 percent) to the number of small firms in each SMSA, nd the original data were expanded according to:

$$\frac{\text{Total Number of Firms in the SMSA}}{\begin{array}{c}\text{Total Number of Selected Sample}\\\text{Firms in the SMSA}\end{array}}$$

This ratio then was multiplied by the original data obtained r each job classification. After doing this for all the job classifications and for large and small firms, the adjusted statistics r large and small firms were summarized. This statistical ethod of adjustment was used in compiling the employment ita for each of the sample SMSA's.

Adjusting the data for four distinct broad geographical areas

The sample SMSA's for each of the four broad regions were ndomly chosen so that the selected SMSA's included approximately 50 percent of the industry's total number of workers in each of the four geographical areas. The original employment data were expanded according to the ratio below:

$$\frac{\text{Total Employees for All the Small Firms in the Region}}{\text{Total Employees for All Small Firms in Each Sample SMSA}}$$

The ratio was multiplied by the number of employees in each job classification, as derived by the method explained above. This methodology was employed in adjusting the data for each of the sample SMSA's in the four broad regions. To obtain the regional totals, the further expanded data were summarized. For example, the number of Negro and white local drivers employed by small firms in Boston, New York, and Philadelphia were aggregated, making it possible to ascertain the percentage of Negro local drivers in the Northeast.

3. Procedure used to determine the Negro-white employment profile for forty-eight SMSA's combined

The aggregating of the employment data for forty-eight SMSA's was facilitated because statistical adjustments were made at the SMSA and broader geographical levels. The four combined regions contained a total of forty-eight SMSA's and an employment profile reflective of race was attained by adding the number of employees in each of the four regions. This was done on the bases of large and small firms, according to specific job classifications, and total statistics were obtained by adding the large and small firm adjusted employment data.

4. The determination of the coefficient of variation

After expanded employment data were determined, the estimated number of Negroes and the coefficient of variation associated with it was then computed. The coefficient of variation was computed for the four broad geographical areas only, and for the expanded adjusted statistics of both the large and small firms. These results are presented with the appropriate tables in the text proper.

Appendix C

POST OFFICE DEPARTMENT GUIDELINES ON AFFIRMATIVE ACTION UNDER EXECUTIVE ORDER 11246

"Affirmative Action" as defined in Section 202 (1) of Executive Order 11246 is a relatively new concept in contract management. The attached material has been prepared to acquaint Government contractors with this requirement.

Definition

Affirmative action means positive, firm or aggressive action as opposed to negative, uncertain or passive action. Affirmative action encompasses the steps necessary to insure that a contractor puts into practice his stated policies of equal employment opportunity without regard to race, color, creed or national origin.

Application

Employment (hiring); upgrading; demotion or transfer; recruitment or recruitment advertising; layoff or termination; rates of pay or other forms of compensation; and selection for training (on the job), including apprenticeship.

Examples

1. Publication and dissemination of written policy of equal employment opportunity.

2. Appointment of equal employment policy officer charged with responsibility of securing compliance and advising corporate officials of progress.

3. Establishment of system of control and feedback to assure application of policy at all levels.

4. Orientation lectures for all supervisory personnel as well as employees to insure familiarity with policy.

5. Inclusion of policy statement in all employee-management publications (newsletters, magazines, etc.).

6. Notification in writing to all recruitment sources that the contractor, as an Equal Opportunity Employer, *solicits* referral of qualified applicants without regard to race, color, creed, or national origin.

7. Secure statement in writing from employee bargaining representatives (unions) indicating that their policies and practices are consistent with the provisions of the Orders.

8. Post SF-38 (Notice to Unions) in conspicuous areas of plant.

9. Modify existing collective bargaining agreements, where necessary, to include nondiscriminatory clause and eliminate restrictive barriers established by:

    a. Dual lines of seniority based on race;

    b. Dual rates of pay based on race; and

    c. Dual lines of promotion or progression based on race.

10. Discontinue use of employee referral system as sole source of recruitment unless proven to be administered so as to assure reasonable racial mix of applicants.

11. Broaden recruitment sources to include referrals of qualified minority group applicants.

12. Insure that employment prerequisites are administered equitably. (Education and/or testing factors should not create disadvantage for minorities.)

13. Re-evaluate qualifications of lower echelon minority group employees to insure equal consideration for job progression based on standards and qualifications which should be no higher or no lower than those established for white employees.

14. Solicit directly the support of responsible and appropriate community agencies to assist in recruiting efforts.

15. Solicit cooperation of academic and vocational schools to establish curricula which will provide the skills and education necessary to fulfill manpower requirements.

16. Consider establishing new training program and classes in facilities where outside programs are inadequate or unavailable to minority groups.

17. Invite minority groups to tour facilities and receive explanation of Equal Employment Opportunity program.

18. Seek, employ and develop minority group personnel, as well as others, in white collar classifications.

19. Eliminate segregated washrooms, cafeterias, smoking areas, locker rooms, drinking fountains, time clocks, pay lines, contractor-sponsored recreational programs, etc.

20. Display EEO posters in conspicuous areas throughout the plant.

21. Use of approved slogan, emblem or statement in all recruitment advertising media.

22. Remove all reference to race, color, creed or national origin from *pre-employment* applications.

23. Maintain racial identity in post-employment files separate and apart from active personnel folders or records.

Index

PART FOUR

THE NEGRO
IN THE URBAN TRANSIT INDUSTRY

by

PHILIP W. JEFFRESS

TABLE OF CONTENTS

LIST OF TABLES

CHAPTER I

Introduction

A number of factors make the urban mass transportation industry significant in a study of Negro employment opportunities. It is, first of all, important because of its role as a primary source of employment in many cities throughout the country. In this context, urban transportation is similar to other major industries, making comparisons possible and feasible. In addition, the service of local and interurban transportation involves the broader problem of getting people to and from their jobs no matter what industry provides the employment. This is often a basic problem for Negroes as a group. In many cities, Negroes are the largest customer group of transit lines. Thus urban transit assumes a dual role in the study of Negro employment—directly as a potential employer and indirectly as a transporter.

The urban transit industry contains a number of features which facilitate a study of the economic, institutional, and behavioral factors determining racial employment patterns. Since urban transit employment declined steadily for a number of years before 1967, a study of this industry and comparisons with others where employment is declining or rising provide some insight into the effects of changing levels of employment on Negro job opportunities. Meaningful intraindustry comparisons can also be made. Regional comparisons are possible since transit companies serve medium- and large-sized cities throughout the country. It is also important to compare the policies of publicly owned firms to those under private control. In the former Negroes can exercise political as well as economic power. Since Negroes generally have greater political than economic power, the influence of government is a basic determinant of racial policies which can be considered in the context of the urban transit industry.

Although relatively small numbers of workers depend on urban mass transit for employment directly, many thousands ride a common carrier to and from work. This role of transporting people to and from their jobs is not new for mass transit. But many people ascribe a "new role" to mass transit by calling it

TABLE 1. *Urban Transit Industry*
Sample Companies by Urban Area, Ownership, and Type of Service
August 1968

Urban Area	Company Name	Type of Ownership	Type of Service
Atlanta	Atlanta Transit System	private	bus
Boston	Massachusetts Bay Transportation Authority	public	bus rapid transit trolley
Chicago	Chicago Transit Authority	public	bus rapid transit trolley
Cincinnati	The Cincinnati Transit Company	private	bus
Cleveland	Cleveland Transit System	public	bus rapid transit
Detroit	Department of Street Railways	public	bus
Houston	Rapid Transit Lines, Inc.	private	bus
Los Angeles	Southern California Rapid Transit District	public	bus
New Orleans	New Orleans Public Service, Inc.	private	bus trolley
New York	New York City Transit Authority	public	rapid transit bus

	Manhattan and Bronx Surface Transit Operating Authority (affiliate of New York City Transit Authority)	public	bus
	Port Authority Trans-Hudson Corporation	public	rapid transit
Philadelphia	Philadelphia Transportation Company	private [a]	bus, rapid transit, trolley
	Philadelphia Suburban Transit Company (Red Arrow Lines)	private [a]	bus, rapid transit
Pittsburgh	Port Authority of Allegheny County	public	bus, rapid transit
San Francisco	San Francisco Municipal Railway	public	bus, rapid transit, trolley, cable
St. Louis	Bi-State Transit System	public	bus
Washington, D. C.	D. C. Transit	private	bus

Source: Author's interviews, 1968.

[a] Philadelphia Transportation Company (PTC) was purchased by the Southeastern Pennsylvania Transportation Authority (SEPTA) in October 1968 and thus now operates under public ownership. Likewise, Philadelphia Suburban Transit Company was purchased by SEPTA in late 1969.

the key to many social and economic problems. Because of segregation in the housing market [1] and the suburbanization of many industrial plants, transportation is vital if Negroes are to compete for jobs. We shall consider the significance of this aspect of transportation in Chapter II.

SCOPE AND METHODOLOGY

This study concerns opportunities for Negro employment in the transit industry in the United States. Most of the industry data were supplied by the American Transit Association, which represents 85 to 90 percent of all urban transit operations in the country. Data from the Equal Employment Opportunity Commission are also utilized, to a limited extent. Since publicly owned transit systems are excluded from coverage of Title VII of the Civil Rights Act of 1964, they are not required to file racial data with EEOC. Moreover, few transit companies, public or private, are government contractors and therefore most do not file data with federal agencies pursuant to the various executive orders governing such contractors. A further limitation is that EEOC data include other than transit industry employees. Hence, EEOC data are included largely to supplement industry and company data.

Company Data

To answer certain questions concerning racial employment policies in urban transit companies, unstructured interviews were conducted with officials of 18 urban transit companies in 15 cities. Although an unstructured interview technique was used to obtain freer response from the interviewees, a general checklist insured a similarity of the general topics probed. Companies included in the survey are listed in Table 1. These companies were not chosen at random, but were deliberately selected from urban areas which satisfy the following criteria as closely as possible: (1) the largest urban areas by population, (2) urban areas with the largest numbers of workers employed in urban transit, (3) urban areas with the largest percentages of travel by transit, (4) urban areas with the largest percentages of consumer spending for urban transportation, (5) urban areas with the largest

---

1. See John F. Kain, "Housing Segregation, Negro Employment, and Metropolitan Decentralization," *The Quarterly Journal of Economics,* Vol. LXXXII (May 1968), pp. 175-197.

numbers of daily trips by urban transportation, and (6) urban areas differentiated by geographical location, type of transit service, type of ownership, and employee organization.

The first criterion was used to include the greatest possible number of people potentially affected by urban transit policy, and simply because major transit companies are concentrated in the largest metropolitan areas. The second criterion measures the importance of the transit company as an employer. Choosing the companies with the most employees enlarges the total sample with a given number of companies. Criteria three, four, and five measure the relative importance of urban transit as a means of transportation. The discretionary differentiation of companies by region, type of service, type of ownership, and employee organization is done to isolate the effects of these factors on the industry's Negro employment policies. A final survey of large systems was conducted in mid-1970 to give added currency to the findings.

Interviews were also conducted with officials of human relations and civil rights groups in those areas where the transit companies were located. These included representatives of the Urban League, the National Association for the Advancement of Colored People, the Opportunities Industrialization Commission, state commissions against discrimination, and other federal, state, and local action groups. These organizations provided information regarding employment problems on a local level.

The data collected from these combined sources are presented and analyzed after a discussion of industry structure in Chapter II. The next three chapters contain a chronological account of the development of racial employment patterns from the early beginnings of the industry to the present. The determinants of industry policies regarding Negro employment opportunities and the future of the Negro in the transit industry are discussed in Chapter VI.

CHAPTER II

The Urban Transit Industry

The origin of urban mass transportation as an industry can be traced back to the 1850's when companies in Brooklyn, Boston, Philadelphia, Baltimore, Cincinnati, Pittsburgh, and Chicago built horse-car lines and firmly established transit operation as an industry. Mass transportation in later years has been provided by cablecars, trolley coaches, electric subway and elevated trains, and motor buses. In 1922, the first motor buses were used, and by 1928 the trolley coach had been introduced, giving the country each major type of transit service in use today.[2]

NATURE AND DEFINITION

For purposes of this study the urban transit industry fits in the specific terms of the Standard Industrial Classification (SIC) system. The industry classification relevant to this study is SIC 4111 and the definition is as follows:

> Major Group 41—Local and Suburban Transit and Interurban Highway Passenger Transportation
>
> Group No. 411—Local and Suburban Passenger Transportation
>
> Industry No. 4111—Local and Suburban Transit
>
> Companies or systems primarily engaged in furnishing local and suburban mass passenger transportation over regular routes and on regular schedules. Such transportation may involve use of one or more modes of transportation. Companies primarily engaged in furnishing passenger transportation by automobile or bus to, from, or between airports or rail terminals over regular routes are included in this industry.[3]

---

2. American Transit Association, *Transit in America* (Washington: The Association, 1962), pp. 1-7.

3. U.S. Bureau of the Budget, *Standard Industrial Classification Manual* (Washington: Government Printing Office, 1967), p. 203.

The transit industry is commonly divided into three categories: electric railway, trolley coach, and motor bus companies. As shown in Table 2, the overwhelming majority of companies provide bus service exclusively, while the rest operate some combination of the various types of transit service.

TABLE 2. *Urban Transit Industry Operating Companies by Type of Service 1968*

Service	Number
Railway exclusively	3
Trolley coach exclusively	0
Motor bus exclusively	1,078
Railway and motor bus combined	7
Railway, motor bus, and trolley coach	4
Trolley coach and motor bus	2
Total	1,094

Source: American Transit Association, *'69-'70 Transit Fact Book* (Washington: The Association, 1969), p. 1.

PROFITABILITY AND STRUCTURE

It has been estimated that as many as 18 million families depend on public transportation by trolley coach, motor bus, and subway or elevated lines. Measured by annual revenues, the transit industry is the largest public passenger carrier engaged in ground transportation. Transit revenues of $1,478.5 million in 1966 represented roughly twice that collected from railroad passenger service, and three times the revenues accumulated by intercity bus operations.[4] This view of mass transportation, however, may be somewhat misleading because it ignores many problems which exist in the industry. Thus Owen notes:

Rising costs and declining patronage have led to a succession of fare increases and further reductions in service. In many cases it has been impossible to set aside necessary allowances for depreciation of equipment, and the industry as a whole has been unable to attract sufficient

4. Wilfred Owen, *The Metropolitan Transportation Problem* (Washington: The Brookings Institution, 1966), p. 67.

capital to renew, modernize or extend its services for the nearly eight billion riders per year who depend on public carriers.[5]

New York City's system is an extreme example of this trend. In 1948, this system carried 2 billion passengers and recorded an operating deficit of $30.7 million on a 5 cent fare. In 1969, the New York system carried only 1.3 billion passengers and suffered an operating deficit of $85 million despite a 20 cent fare. For 1970, estimates indicate a further passenger drop of 100,000 and an operating deficit of $120 million at the 20 cent fare.[6] The graph below summarizes the overall fare and patronage dilemma of the industry.

TRANSIT TRENDS

Fares Up . . .   Patronage Down . . .

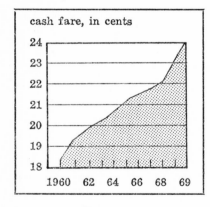
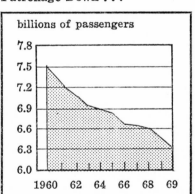

Source: *Philadelphia Evening Bulletin,* July 15, 1970.

The data in Table 3 further emphasize the cost and revenue problems of the industry. Thus, although operating revenue has increased by only 14.3 percent since 1945, operating expenses have climbed by 50.9 percent, resulting in a net revenue deficit in 1968.

Since 1963 the transit industry has experienced a deficit, largely because of deficits in the operation of the transit systems in

5. *Ibid.,* p. 4.

6. *Philadelphia Evening Bulletin,* July 15, 1970.

TABLE 3. *Urban Transit Industry*
Selected Operating Statistics
1935-1968

Year	Operating Revenue	Operating Expenses[a]	Net Revenue	All Taxes	Operating Income	Operating Revenue as a Percent of		
						Operating Expenses[a]	All Taxes	Operating Income
	Millions of Dollars							
1935	681.4	534.9	146.5	50.5	96.0	78.5	7.4	14.0
1940	737.0	598.0	139.0	62.7	76.3	81.1	8.5	10.4
1945	1,380.4	1,067.1	313.3	164.5	148.7	77.3	11.9	10.8
1950	1,452.1	1,296.7	155.4	89.0	66.4	89.3	6.1	4.6
1955	1,426.4	1,277.4	149.0	93.3	55.7	89.6	6.5	3.9
1956	1,416.1	1,271.4	144.7	89.1	55.7	89.8	6.3	3.9
1957	1,385.6	1,261.6	124.0	87.4	36.6	91.0	6.3	2.6
1958	1,349.5	1,265.9	83.7	77.1	6.6	93.8	5.7	0.5
1959	1,376.4	1,266.1	110.3	84.7	25.6	92.0	6.2	1.9
1960	1,407.2	1,289.9	117.4	86.7	30.7	91.7	6.2	2.2
1961	1,389.7	1,295.7	93.9	77.2	16.7	93.2	5.6	1.2
1962	1,403.5	1,306.1	97.5	77.8	19.7	93.0	5.5	1.4
1963	1,390.6	1,312.6	78.0	78.9	—0.9	94.3	5.7	—
1964	1,408.1	1,342.6	65.5	77.9	—12.4	95.3	5.5	—
1965	1,443.8	1,373.8	70.0	80.7	—10.6	95.1	5.6	—
1966	1,478.5	1,423.8	54.7	91.8	—37.1	96.3	6.2	—
1967	1,556.0	1,530.9	25.1	91.7	—66.6	98.3	5.9	—
1968	1,578.3	1,609.8	—31.5	98.5	—130.0	101.9	6.2	—

Source: American Transit Association, *'69-'70 Transit Fact Book* (Washington: The Association, 1969), p. 4.

a Includes depreciation.

the major cities of the country. New York City, for example, currently experiencing large annual deficits from its transit operations, accounts for roughly 20 percent of all transit revenues, and one-fourth of the total traffic. This kind of concentration tends to make national figures misleading in some respects. Losses have generally come in cities with long histories of inflexible fares, large investments in rail and rapid transit, and a high population density in the central city area. Since this group of cities accounts for so large a share of the transit business, the true financial structure of the industry may be somewhat hidden by the unqualified use of national figures. Of the 35 transit companies of major importance, 23 showed profits in recent years and others experienced only minor deficits. Furthermore, deficit financing has become accepted by public transit authorities as a means of support for the transit systems over which they have jurisdiction.

Nevertheless, the precarious financial position of many transit systems is significant. It means curtailed service where Negroes require that service to obtain and to hold jobs; and it means fewer jobs in an industry in which Negroes are a large portion of the work force.

Ownership Concentration

Initially, many transit companies were owned by electric utilities, a natural development since early transit vehicles ran on electric power. As buses replaced trolley cars, and as transit profits declined, most utilities disposed of their transit properties. Today, despite the size of the industry, only one predominantly transit concern, National City Lines, with headquarters in Denver, Colorado, is listed among *Fortune's* fifty largest transportation companies, ranking twenty-eighth in 1969. National City, a holding company, now owns about twenty transit systems in whole or part, and has disposed of several others. It also is active in several other businesses.[7] Other large privately owned transit companies are those in Washington, D.C. and in New Jersey. The latter, until recently one of the few still controlled by an electric and gas utility, was being purchased by a syndicate formed for that purpose in mid-1970.

_____

7. *Fortune*, Vol. LXXXI (May 1970), pp. 210-211. *Moody's Transportation Manual* (New York: Moody's Investors Service, Inc., September 1969), pp. 1603-1604.

MANPOWER

As can be seen from Table 4, since 1945, the number of employees required by the urban transit industry has been declining steadily. The total number of employees in all forms of transit service has fallen from 242,000 in 1945 to 143,590 in 1968, a drop of 40.7 percent. For the period of 1935-1968, employment fell by 31.3 percent. As shown in Table 5, this decline has occurred in each separate type of service as well, although the number of surface railway employees required has dropped most severely.

TABLE 4. *Urban Transit Industry*
Employment, Earnings, and Payrolls
Selected Years, 1935-1968

Year	Average Number of Employees	Payroll (Thousands)	Average Annual Earnings Per Employee
1935	209,000	$ 321,000	$1,536
1940	203,000	360,000	1,773
1945	242,000	632,000	2,612
1950	240,000	835,000	3,479
1955	198,000	864,000	4,364
1956	186,000	852,000	4,581
1957	177,000	840,000	4,756
1958	165,000	831,000	5,036
1959	159,100	832,000	5,229
1960	156,400	857,300	5,481
1961	151,800	856,400	5,642
1962	149,100	878,100	5,889
1963	147,200	892,300	6,062
1964	144,800	916,900	6,332
1965	145,000	963,500	6,645
1966	144,300	994,900	6,895
1967	146,100	1,055,100	7,222
1968	143,590	1,109,500	7,727

Source: American Transit Association, *'69-'70 Transit Fact Book* (Washington: The Association, 1969), p. 10.

The Negro in the Urban Transit Industry

TABLE 5. *Urban Transit Industry*
Employment by Type of Service
1943-1968

Year	Employees				
	Rapid Transit	Surface Railway	Trolley Coach	Motor Bus	Grand Total
1943	38,000	99,000	8,000	94,000	239,000
1945	33,700	95,500	8,500	104,300	242,000
1950	39,400	51,500	15,400	133,700	240,000
1955	41,000	25,000	16,000	116,000	198,000
1960	35,100	11,400	9,400	100,500	156,400
1961	34,800	8,900	8,600	99,500	151,800
1962	35,000	8,200	7,600	98,300	149,100
1963	34,400	.... 112,800			147,200
1964	34,800	.... 110,000			144,800
1968	37,930	.... 105,660			143,590

Source: Data provided by the American Transit Association.

Even though this trend in employment is in part a reflection of changing technology, discontinued service rather than capital intensification apparently is the major cause of the reductions in labor usage. This view is supported by data shown in Table 6. The ratio of passengers to employees has been relatively stable since 1935 with the exception of the war and postwar years. Using this as a measure of productivity indicates that manpower requirements in the industry have not changed significantly over the years in relation to passenger demand. There has been a slight drop in the passenger to vehicle ratio despite the fact that many smaller rail cars and buses have been replaced with larger ones. The number of employees per vehicle may perhaps be viewed as a rough estimate of the capital-labor ratio. In 1935 it took an average of 2.8 employees per vehicle operated, and by 1968 this ratio was 2.3 employees per vehicle. Although this minor decrease is evident for the past few years, the greatest part of the decline can be explained by examining the data by type of service. On the average since 1945, it has taken 4.0 employees for each rail car in operation on surface railway lines,

TABLE 6. *Urban Transit Industry Productivity Ratios 1935-1968*

Year	Total Transit Passengers (Millions)	Total Transit Vehicles	Average Transit Employees	Passengers Per Employee	Passengers Per Vehicle	Employees Per Vehicle
1935	12,226	74,844	209,000	58,498	163,335	2.8
1940	13,098	75,464	203,000	64,522	173,566	2.7
1945	23,254	89,758	242,000	96,091	259,074	2.7
1950	17,246	86,310	240,000	71,858	199,815	2.8
1955	11,529	73,089	198,000	58,227	157,739	2.7
1956	10,941	70,373	186,000	58,823	155,472	2.6
1957	10,389	69,971	177,000	58,695	148,476	2.5
1958	9,732	67,149	165,000	58,982	144,931	2.5
1959	9,557	65,780	159,100	60,069	145,287	2.4
1960	9,395	65,292	156,400	60,070	143,892	2.4
1961	8,883	64,012	151,800	58,518	138,771	2.4
1962	8,695	63,045	149,100	58,317	137,917	2.4
1963	8,400	62,189	147,200	57,065	135,072	2.4
1964	8,328	61,679	144,800	57,514	135,022	2.3
1965	8,253	61,717	145,000	56,917	133,723	2.3
1966	8,083	62,136	144,300	56,015	130,086	2.3
1967	8,172	62,069	146,100	55,934	131,660	2.4
1968	8,019	61,930	143,590	55,847	129,485	2.3

Source: American Transit Association, *'69-'70 Transit Fact Book* (Washington: The Association, 1969), pp. 6, 10, and 12.

but only 2.1 employees for each bus in operation.⁸ This sheds some light on an employee-to-vehicle ratio which is declining for the industry as a whole. Although employment in the bus companies has been relatively stable, the surface railways have experienced a marked decline in employment. Since most of the total decline in service has come in surface railways which have typically required more employees per vehicle, it is not surprising that the number of employees per vehicle has decreased for the industry as a whole.

Occupational Distribution

Employees in the transit industry are divided roughly into five departments: (1) transportation; (2) garages, shops, and car houses; (3) maintenance of way; (4) electric power supply and distribution; and (5) all others. Table 7 shows the departmental distribution of personnel, from 1960 to 1966. The transportation division, where about 66 percent of all employees work, is comprised mainly of those who run the vehicles—bus and trolley coach drivers, streetcar operators, and rapid transit motormen. Supervisory employees make up approximately 5 percent of this department.

Maintenance employees are found mainly in two groups: the shop or garagemen and those who maintain right of ways. The former, comprising about 17 percent of the work force, include automobile mechanics, electricians, carpenters, painters, tire and body repairmen, and others. The latter, who include about 6 percent of the total labor force, work to maintain right of ways and facilities where the system operates on other than public highways or has special facilities (tracks or wires) on highways. A third group—about one percent of the total—operates and maintains electric power facilities for the few systems that operate or generate their own power.

The remaining 10 percent of the industry's labor force include managers and the small number of professionals, specialists, and clerical forces now utilized in the industry. Among these are planners, engineers, personnel and labor relations experts, accountants, advertising and public relations specialists, and purchasing agents. Secretarial, stenographic, and clerical personnel round out today's general manpower needs in most transit companies.

---

8. Table 5 and American Transit Association, *'69-'70 Transit Fact Book* (Washington: The Association, 1969), p. 12.

TABLE 7. *Urban Transit Industry*
Employment by Department
1960-1966

Year	Transportation	Shops, Car Houses, and Garage	Maintenance of Way	Electric Power	Miscellaneous	Total
1960	101,000	27,000	9,800	2,400	16,200	156,400
1961	99,100	26,400	8,600	2,400	15,300	151,800
1962	96,000	26,200	9,100	2,500	15,300	149,100
1963	96,400	26,000	7,500	2,000	15,300	147,200
1964	95,500	25,500	7,400	2,000	14,900	145,300
1965	95,500	25,000	7,500	2,000	15,000	145,000
1966	95,480	24,000	7,900	1,920	15,000	144,300

Source: American Transit Association.

Note: These data have not been available since 1966.

Table 8, showing the occupational distribution of employees for six transit companies, more clearly demonstrates the manpower requirements of the industry. Only 5.7 percent of all these employees are included in the three top-ranking categories. Office and clerical personnel account for 10.1 percent of the employees. Close to three-fourths (72.3 percent) of all employees of these companies are in semiskilled or unskilled occupations. Adding skilled craftsmen to this group brings the total percentage in the lower four categories to 84.2 percent.

Unlike many other industries, urban transit has a large proportion of jobs at the lower skill levels. This is significant in that laborers can qualify for a vast majority of the transit jobs without having skills, ruling out the justification for the exclusion of blacks from the industry on the grounds that "they cannot qualify."

Also worthy of note is the fact that there is such a small proportion of supervisory and management jobs. Most of the personnel in the top positions have been employees of their respective companies for many years, having worked up through the ranks. This means that chances for promotion into supervisory positions exist only for a select few. Some of the methods used in the selection of upper-level personnel will be discussed in a later chapter.

Earnings and Unionization

One statistic which has run contrary to the declining nature of the transit industry is wages (Table 9). The industry payroll and average annual earnings per employee have been steadily increasing. Hourly wage scales of unionized local transit operating employees averaged $3.52 on July 1, 1969, in cities of 100,000 population or more. Using 1957-1959 as a base of 100, the U.S. Bureau of Labor Statistics index of union wage scales in transit stood at 168.6 as of July 1, 1969. The average hourly scale was higher ($4.04) for operators of elevated and subway equipment than that ($3.67) for operators of surface equipment who accounted for about 90 percent of all workers covered by the survey. These wages do not reflect overtime or fringe benefits.[9]

Most urban transportation properties are unionized; the majority of operating employees are members of either the Trans-

---

9. Data from U.S. Bureau of Labor Statistics. Chicago and New York account for nearly seven-eighths of the elevated and subway equipment operators, but for only one-fourth of the surface car and bus operators.

TABLE 8. *Urban Transit Industry*
Employment by Occupational Group
Six Companies, 1968

Occupational Group	Company						Total	Percent of Total
	A	B	C	D	E	F		
Officials and managers	416	59	37	107	318	22	959	3.8
Professionals	124	13	—	32	29	—	198	0.8
Technicians	93	6	—	133	60	—	292	1.1
Sales workers	—	—	2	—	—	—	2	*
Office and clerical	1,604	277	69	244	321	74	2,589	10.1
Total white collar	2,237	355	108	516	728	96	4,040	15.8
Craftsmen	1,464	339	70	537	548	106	3,064	11.9
Operatives	7,582	1,672	579	2,591	4,060	281	16,765	65.4
Laborers	520	112	37	195	227	64	1,155	4.5
Service workers	410	53	4	58	81	—	606	2.4
Total blue collar	9,976	2,176	690	3,381	4,916	451	21,590	84.2
Total	12,213	2,531	798	3,897	5,644	547	25,630	100.0

Source: Data in author's possession.

* Less than 0.05 percent.

TABLE 9. *Urban Transit Industry*
Average Hourly Wage Rates of Unionized Operating Employees
July 1, 1969

City	Average Hourly Rate
Atlanta, Georgia	$3.16
Boston, Massachusetts	4.20
Chicago, Illinois	4.10
Cleveland, Ohio	3.66
Cincinnati, Ohio	3.14
Detroit, Michigan	3.90
Houston, Texas	3.05
Los Angeles, California	3.75
New Orleans, Louisiana	3.25
New York, New York	4.13
Philadelphia, Pennsylvania	3.66
Pittsburgh, Pennsylvania	3.97
San Francisco-Oakland, California	4.11
St. Louis, Missouri	3.61
Washington, D. C.	4.16

Population Group	Average Hourly Rate
Population Group I (1,000,000 or more)	4.03
Population Group II (500,000-1,000,000)	3.80
Population Group III (250,000-500,000)	3.29
Population Group IV (100,000-250,000)	2.98

Source: U.S. Bureau of Labor Statistics, *Local-Transit Operating Employees, July 1, 1969 and Trend 1929-1969*, Bulletin No. 1667, p. 6.

port Workers Union of America (TWU) or Amalgamated Transit Union (ATU). The Transport Workers Union was first organized in 1934, mostly among New York City subway workers. Until 1936, attempts were made to join with the Amalgamated Association of Street, Electric Railway and Motor Coach Employees, the streetcar union of the American Federation of Labor. In 1936, the International Association of Machinists admitted it as Lodge No. 1547. Then in 1937, the TWU was taken into the CIO under its longtime, late president, Michael J. Quill. By the next year the TWU reported ". . . a national membership of 80,000, of which 34,000 are in the New York subway system." [10] Other estimates of the union's national membership in 1938 range from 27,200 [11] to 55,000.[12] By 1962 the union had grown to an estimated 80,600 members.[13] Its membership now is probably about 80,000, and includes air transport and railroad personnel as well as transit employees.

The Amalgamated Transit Union is the larger of the two primary transit unions. Strictly a transit organization, it originated as the Amalgamated Association of Street, Electric Railway and Motor Coach Employees during the early years of the transit industry. By 1938 it had approximately 79,000 members and today membership is estimated at just over 100,000. The ATU spread throughout the industry and has locals in cities in all areas of the country. By comparison, the TWU organization is concentrated in New York, Philadelphia, and a few other eastern cities. In other areas, ATU is the dominant union. Two notable exceptions are the TWU locals in Houston and San Francisco.

Other unions with transit employees as members include some of the railroad brotherhoods and a few craft unions. One of these, the Brotherhood of Railroad Trainmen (now the United Transportation Union) long had a racial restriction in its constitution. Craft unions such as the International Association of Machinists and the International Brotherhood of Electrical Workers have locals at some of the larger transit properties. Mechanics and skilled craftsmen are often organized by these craft

---

10. Benjamin Stolberg, *The Story of the CIO* (New York: The Viking Press, 1938), p. 228.

11. Leo Troy, *Trade Union Membership, 1897-1962*, National Bureau of Economic Research, Occasional Paper 92 (New York: Columbia University Press, 1965), p. A23.

12. Stolberg, *loc. cit.*

13. Troy, *op. cit.*, p. A27.

unions instead of ATU or TWU. In the following chapters, further attention will be given to the influence of these unions on the industry's racial employment policies.

INDUSTRIAL LOCATION

The location of the industry is significant to the study of the Negro in urban transportation. Many other industries have a larger work force with larger annual payrolls, but few offer job opportunities in as many different locations. In 1966 there were transit systems in over 1,000 different cities scattered throughout the 50 states.

In terms of location, the urban transit industry is certainly accessible to Negroes. This does not stem solely from the fact that the industry is well dispersed geographically. The location of the systems within their respective urban areas also is significant. Many cities have industrial parks in the outer fringe away from the downtown districts which lure industry from center city. Other industries must locate outside of cities. For example, "testing and product requirements lead most aerospace companies to locate away from center city and thus away from the Negro population concentrations." [14] This is not true for the transit industry. In most of the major cities where transit systems are well established, the business headquarters are located in or near the central business district. In most cases in which the transit system is publicly owned, the offices are in government buildings located in the central city. Business location should therefore be a factor aiding Negro job applicants.

The location of transit workers is also beneficial to Negroes once they are hired. In addition to having business locations near the central business districts, transit companies generally have stations, divisions, garages, or car barns interspersed throughout the city. This makes jobs available at a reasonable proximity to all residential areas including those with high concentrations of Negroes.

We now turn to the factors which influenced racial employment patterns in the early years of the transit industry. The following chapter deals with the Negro in the transit industry to the end of World War II.

---

14. Herbert R. Northrup, Richard L. Rowan, *et al., Negro Employment in Basic Industry*, Studies of Negro Employment, Vol. I (Philadelphia: Industrial Research Unit, Wharton School of Finance and Commerce, University of Pennsylvania, 1970), Part Three, pp. 143-144.

CHAPTER III

The Negro in the Transit Industry
through 1945

With minor exceptions, the transit industry remained generally closed to Negro employment except in menial and dirty jobs until the last years of World War II and immediately thereafter. This chapter traces racial employment practices in urban mass transportation through 1945, and analyzes the developments which subsequently led to more and better jobs for Negroes in the industry. First, attention will be focused on the historical flow overall including the conditions and developments most common within the industry. Then, consideration will be given to the experiences in several cities where there were special efforts to improve the hiring and upgrading policies of the respective transit companies.

OVERALL PICTURE IN TRANSPORTATION

The urban transit industry was not unique in its exclusion of Negroes from key jobs prior to the 1940's. All transportation industries followed the policy of hiring Negroes only for menial tasks and did not permit them to be upgraded. Negroes were not allowed to become conductors or engineers on the railroads; the maritime industry excluded them from serving as masters, mates, pilots, or chief engineers; airline pilots were all white; and only a few Negroes were employed in over-the-road trucking.[15]

Transportation unions, especially railroad-oriented ones, stood out as the most adamant in their opposition to Negro members. Marshall points out that ". . . almost all the unions with formal race bars were associated with the transportation industry." [16] In 1930 Spero and Harris listed eleven AFL-affiliated unions

---

15. See the other studies of Racial Policies of American Industry in this series pertaining to transportation.

16. Ray Marshall, *The Negro Worker* (New York: Random House, 1967), p. 58.

which barred Negroes by provisions in their constitutions or rituals, and thirteen independent unions with similar provisions.[17] All but two of the AFL affiliates and all of the independents were transportation industry unions. The independents included "the 'Big Four' railroad transportation unions, the Brotherhood of Locomotive Engineers, the Order of Railway Conductors, the Brotherhood of Locomotive Firemen and Enginemen, and the Brotherhood of Railroad Trainmen" which had ". . . always limited their membership to white persons." [18]

Railroading Mores

The railroads had a significant impact on the rapid rail urban transit systems. McGinley speaks of "railroading mores" [19] accepted by management in the transit industry. These racial practices which were common to companies and unions of the railroad industry influenced transit policy considerably. Major similarities can be found between the railroads and rapid rail transit, with many practices spilling over into urban bus and trolley operations.

What were these "railroading mores" which influenced urban transit? First, as already shown, the major railroad unions had bars against Negro membership in their constitutions. The Brotherhoods, with the exception of the Trainmen, were begun as social and fraternal societies, and not as trade unions. Since membership would have given Negroes symbolic social equality, they were excluded from membership.

In the South Negroes were employed as firemen and trainmen, but almost never promoted to engineer and conductor. Since Negroes' wages were less than wages for whites for the same work, southern railway management found in the Negro a convenient tool with which to fight unionism and depress wages.[20] Conditions before and during World War II were described by Northrup as follows:

---

17. Sterling D. Spero and Abram L. Harris, *The Black Worker* (New York: Columbia University Press, 1931), p. 57.

18. Herbert R. Northrup, *Organized Labor and the Negro* (New York: Harper & Brothers, 1944), p. 49.

19. James J. McGinley, *Labor Relations in the New York Rapid Transit Systems, 1904-1944* (New York: Columbia University Press, King's Crown Press, 1949), p. 253. The discussion of railroading mores is drawn from Northrup, *Organized Labor and the Negro, op. cit.*, pp. 48-101.

20. *Ibid.*, pp. 48-49.

The Negro railroad worker is in an anomalous position. He is denied a voice in the affairs of nearly all railway labor organizations; yet collective bargaining on the railroads has received wider acceptance than in almost any other American industry. He is, for the most part, ineligible for promotion although promotion in the industry is based almost exclusively upon seniority. And he frequently receives lower pay than white men when doing the same work . . . .[21]

This "railroading philosophy" carried over into urban transit through union influence, company policy, and employee attitudes. At least one major railroad union, the Brotherhood of Railroad Trainmen, represented workers in urban rapid transit as well. In the South, separate local unions were maintained to segregate whites and blacks. As noted in a later section, the practice of not allowing Negroes to advance beyond the job of porter was common throughout the industry. Transit companies in the South made good use of the cheap labor provided by Negro employees in laborer and service worker positions. Moreover, since the operating jobs in urban transit were similar (in some cases identical) to those on the railroads, white employees were opposed to having their jobs "degraded" by allowing Negroes to perform them.

THE EARLY PUSH FOR BETTER TRANSIT JOBS

Efforts to improve the occupational position of Negroes in the transit industry were not simply a result of war-bred labor shortages. Although the shortage of workers focused light on the discriminatory practices of many transit companies, attention had already been given to the problem. In his book, *All Manner of Men,* Ross states,

For many years Negroes in the big Northern cities had been actively restless at being restricted to maintenance jobs on traction lines. They belonged to the unions. White members monopolized the higher-paid platform jobs of motorman and conductor.[22]

Given this history of attempts at better jobs for Negroes, what were the catalysts which allowed for the minor success achieved by the end of 1945?

---

21. *Ibid.,* p. 48.

22. Malcolm Ross, *All Manner of Men* (New York: Reynal and Hitchcock, 1948), p. 85. Mr. Ross served as chairman of the wartime President's Committee on Fair Employment Practice.

Three basic factors influenced Negro employment in the transit industry through 1945: (1) the nature of the work, (2) the conversion of some companies from private to public ownership, and (3) the efforts of government agencies such as the War Manpower Commission and the President's Committee on Fair Employment Practice (FEPC).[23]

Nature of Transit Work

The nature of transit work made companies in that industry susceptible to attempts by Negroes to obtain improved treatment. For several of the same reasons that attention is focused on discrimination in the building trades today, the lack of job opportunities for Negroes in the transit industry was an issue during the war years. In the first place, transit employment expanded in the years prior to World War II. In addition, many Negro transit employees were in menial jobs, and this contact brought into sharp focus those related and more prestigious jobs which had very few or no Negroes, as in the construction industry.[24] The platform jobs of motorman and conductor were good jobs clearly visible to all, but especially visible to the Negroes who did related work. Although little skill was required to operate a bus or trolley, the responsibility was large and the platform jobs were strategic positions with high wages and attractive benefits. Furthermore, since supervisory jobs were most often filled from the operators ranks, the position was viewed as a stepping stone.

The same reasons which made platform work attractive to Negroes often hindered their chances of obtaining these jobs. Since they were good positions generally, they were well guarded by the whites who held them. Although the skill requirements were relatively low, the operation of any type of equipment, especially in the South, was considered "white" work. Moreover, these jobs required employees who could deal with (and in some cases exercise authority over) the general public. At that time, public sentiment was quite obviously against allowing a Negro to perform these tasks which were simply not considered to be "Negro" jobs. The continued exclusion of Negroes throughout the war years and during a period of labor shortage was not only outrageous, but clearly an insult to the Negro community.

---

23. Particularly the second FEPC which was established on May 27, 1943 by Executive Order No. 9346 of President Franklin D. Roosevelt.

24. Marshall, *op. cit.*, p. 64.

Early Impact of Public Ownership

Most of the progress which was made in getting better transit jobs for Negroes before 1940 was the result of a change in the ownership of transit lines. In at least three cities (Detroit, San Francisco, and New York) some of the transit properties had been sold by private owners to the city prior to that date, while Cleveland acquired ownership of its transit system in 1942. Municipal ownership and operation brought hiring and upgrading under the provisions of the respective civil service plans. The effects on Negro employment were quite apparent. Table 10 shows employment data for transit operations in fifteen major cities in 1943. Only 6.7 percent of transit employees in these cities were nonwhite. Of the 56,171 operators reported by these transit companies, only 2,450, or 4.4 percent, were Negro.

The picture is worse for the industry as a whole when it is noted that of the 2,450 Negro operators, 1,336 (54.5 percent) were employed in Detroit alone. New York, Cleveland, Detroit, San Francisco, and Chicago were the only cities in which Negroes were employed as operators, the latter having only one. After the rules of civil service were introduced into hiring and upgrading procedures, it became possible for Negroes to obtain some of the higher paying jobs, but this was not an automatic cause and effect relationship. According to Ross, even "back in Hoover days the Negroes on the municipally owned lines in Detroit and New York had begun a successful fight for platform jobs." [25] The civil service regulations encouraged efforts to obtain equal job opportunities for Negroes because it was becoming more and more difficult, in the North, for a public body to deny jobs to Negroes while private companies were hiring them.

Table 11 shows that by 1945 Negroes held some platform jobs and other upgraded positions in several cities, but most Negroes in such jobs—78.1 percent—were in Detroit or New York. The only southern city where Negroes had been upgraded was Winston-Salem, where Safe Bus Company, a unique line which is owned and operated by Negroes, employed forty Negro bus drivers, eight clerical workers, three assistant traffic supervisors, a maintenance supervisor, twelve mechanics, and a traffic supervisor in 1945.

---

25. Ross, *op. cit.*, p. 86.

TABLE 10. *Urban Transit Industry*
Total and Nonwhite Employment by Principal Occupation
Selected Cities, December 1943

City	All Employees			Operators			All Other Employees		
	Total	Nonwhite	Percent Nonwhite	Total	Nonwhite	Percent Nonwhite	Total	Nonwhite	Percent Nonwhite
Baltimore	3,745	166	4.4	2,022	—	—	1,723	166	9.6
Boston	9,029a	76	0.8	4,297	1b	—	4,732	76	1.6
Chicago	21,554	186a	0.9	13,236	—	*	8,318	185	2.2
Cincinnati	2,172	83	3.8	1,270	—	—	902	83	9.2
Cleveland	4,931	345	7.0	3,287	197	6.0	1,644	148	9.0
Detroit	7,354	1,898	25.8	4,874	1,336	27.4	2,480	562	22.7
Kansas City	3,127c	99	3.2	960	—	—	2,167	99	4.6
Los Angelesd	3,295	170	5.2	1,670	—	—	1,625	170	10.5
New York	35,711	3,371	9.4	12,554	862	6.9	23,157	2,509	10.8
Pittsburgh	3,240	64	2.0	1,986	—	—	1,254	64	5.1
Providence	1,335	—	—	852	—	—	483	—	—
San Francisco	3,410	55	1.6	2,455	54	2.2	955	1	0.1
Seattle	1,773	5	0.3	1,115	—	—	658	5	0.8
St. Louis	4,231	231	5.5	2,716	—	—	1,515	231	15.2
Washington	5,196	616	11.9	2,877	—	—	2,319	616	26.6
Total	110,103	7,365	6.7	56,171	2,450	4.4	53,932	4,915	9.1

Source: Data provided by the American Transit Association.

* Less than 0.05 percent.

a As of June 1942.

b Increased to 140 operators by August 1944.

c As of March 1943.

d Reported employing Negro operators as of 1946.

TABLE 11.   *Urban Transit Industry*
Negro Platform Operators and Other Employees
Selected Cities, January 1945

City	Negro Platform Operators			Negroes in Other Significant Jobs[a]	Total
	Total	Men	Women		
Boston	2	2	—	71	73
Buffalo	50	44	6	94	144
Chicago	161	161	—	—	161
Cleveland	204	191	13	115	319
Detroit	1,150	1,000	150	50	1,200
Flushing, L. I.	6	6	—	—	6
Los Angeles	57	37	20	—	57
New York	1,118	939	179	705	1,823
Phoenix	1	1	—	—	1
Philadelphia	18	18	—	882	900
San Francisco	53	53	—	—	53
Syracuse	1	1	—	—	1
Toledo	20	20	—	—	20
Tulsa	23	23	—	—	23
Winston-Salem[b]	40	40	—	25	65
Total	2,904	2,536	368	1,942	4,846

Source: President's Committee on Fair Employment Practice, Division of Review and Analysis.

[a] Such as mechanics, mechanic helpers, bus placers, clerical workers, traffic supervisors, maintenance supervisors, and others.

[b] Owned and operated by Negroes.

INDIVIDUAL CITY EXPERIENCES

The following sections analyze specific examples of attempts to obtain better job opportunities for Negroes in the transit industry during this period. Both public and private systems in all regions of the country are considered.

New York City

In New York [26] both public and private transit systems were in operation. McGinley reports,

---

26. This section draws heavily on McGinley, *op. cit.*, pp. 253-255.

28 *The Negro in the Urban Transit Industry*

For years, rapid transit in New York had its "Negro job"—porter—due to managerial acceptance of railroading mores, to lack of union interest, and to Negroes' inactivity in their own behalf.[27]

By 1944, however, Negroes filled positions as operators, motormen, and supervisors in a wide variety of rapid transit occupations. How this change came about is best explained in the context of the total New York City transit operation.

Prior to 1940, three separate rapid transit systems operated subway trains in New York City. The first two, Brooklyn-Manhattan Transit (BMT) and Interborough Rapid Transit (IRT), were private companies, while the third, Independent Subway System (ISS and later IND), was operated by the Transportation Board of the City of New York. In 1940, after the private companies went bankrupt, unification of the three separate companies was accomplished under the same Transportation Board, establishing the publicly owned New York City Transit System.

"On IRT the vast majority of porters were Negroes, and Negroes were not employed in capacities above porter until receivership." [28] At the time of receivership, eight Negroes had been made quasi-station agents, dividing their time between agent and porter. This first break in a long tradition was aided by a "civic association" [29] and not by a bargaining agent. In September 1939, partially because of pressure from the Transport Workers Union, Negro platform men acted as station agents during vacation periods, and there were at least two Negro conductors (called trainmen at that time). The former were appointed in 1938 and the latter, all of whom had been porters with IRT for many years, were promoted in April 1939. All were active TWU members.

The experience of Negroes with Brooklyn-Manhattan Transit was very similar over the years. Although one Negro transferred to ISS in 1933 with two years experience in a supervisory shop position, porter was definitely the Negro job on BMT.

Compared to the private lines, ISS made great progress in opening all jobs to Negroes. When it first began hiring in 1932, ISS took on numerous Negro porters and 30 Negroes were hired as station agents. All these agents, however, were assigned to certain restricted stations in Harlem. Realizing the significance

27. *Ibid.*, p. 253.

28. *Ibid.*

29. *Ibid.* (McGinley does not give the name of the civic association.)

of this segregation, a number of Negro employees appealed to the Board of Transportation, whereupon two more stations were declared "open." A decision by the Board of Aldermen in 1934 finally declared that all stations would subsequently be opened by the normal techniques of vacancies and seniority.

In 1935 the ISS appointed its first Negro conductor. As of January 1935, 15 Negroes had passed the open competitive civil service examination through which appointments and promotions were determined. Later 11 of these qualified as switchmen. By 1939, just prior to the formation of NYCTS, Negroes held the following ISS positions: one assistant station supervisor, 289 porters, 66 station agents, 63 conductors, and 20 motormen-conductors. In nontransportation departments during 1939, the following positions were filled by Negroes:

. . . two airbrake maintainers, one assistant foreman (track), twelve car maintainers, one foreman (car and shops), one laborer, one light maintainer, twenty-seven maintainers' helpers, two power maintainers, two structure maintainers, four trackmen, and one ventilation and drainage maintainer.[30]

In addition, there were Negro architectural draftsmen, clerks, junior electrical engineers, mechanical draftsmen, stenographers, and structural draftsmen all on the staff of the New York City Board of Transportation.

Because of the increased opportunity for Negro employment on ISS relative to that of IRT and BMT prior to unification, the greatest number of Negroes worked in the IND (as ISS was called after unification) division immediately subsequent to the merger. But the way had been opened under civil service for similar advancement in IRT and BMT divisions as well. McGinley places heavy emphasis on personal initiative by Negroes and the civil service system as major factors enabling blacks to fill permanent positions in the New York City Transit System. Under private management the job of porter was a dead end for practically all Negroes. But under civil service the Negro did rise above porter, ". . . and brought his Pullman porter talents to bear on jobs of platform man, conductor, and motorman—successfully." [31] McGinley adds,

The change was not due in any appreciable degree to union assistance, nor to public opinion. It was due to diligent effort on the part of Ne-

30. *Ibid.*, p. 254.

31. *Ibid.*, p. 255.

groes made articulate in the presence of civil service rules and competitive examinations.[32]

Detroit

Detroit stands out as the first property where Negroes were
employed to any significant degree. In 1922 the transit operations in Detroit were bought by the city, and the Department of
Street Railways was given jurisdiction over the system. As a department of the city, DSR came under civil service rules and
appointments were made in accordance with open competitive
examinations. After 20 years of experience under civil service,
the Detroit Department of Street Railways reported that almost
26 percent of its operators were Negroes. (See Table 10.)

The Detroit experience is clearly not representative of the entire transit industry for the period through World War II.
More typical were those cities where Negroes were not hired in
very large proportions, and only as porters, janitors, and laborers when employed at all. Accounts of the developments in some
of these cases follow.

Los Angeles

Hearings conducted before the President's Committee on Fair
Employment Practice in 1944 revealed a situation in Los Angeles
quite different from that in Detroit. The Los Angeles Railway
Company (LARY) and the Los Angeles Motor Coach Lines
(LAMC) were the principal companies engaged in mass transportation in Los Angeles. The combined total of trolley and bus
operators and conductors for these two companies was 2,096
employees, 1,844 of whom were male and the remaining 252 female. No Negroes were employed as operators or conductors on
either of the properties. Table 12 shows a listing of jobs held by
Negro men and women. There had been no efforts on the part
of either company to upgrade Negro employees, and as a result
Los Angeles Negro newspapers began a "campaign of protest." [33]
Negro civic groups joined the fight as did the president of the
Amalgamated local at LARY.

---

32. *Ibid.*, p. 253.

33. President's Committee on Fair Employment Practice, "In the Matter of
    Complaints of Alfonso Edwards *et al.* v. Los Angeles Railway Corpora-
    tion," *Proceedings*, Case No. 66, August 1944.

TABLE 12. *Urban Transit Industry*
Negro Employment by Occupation and Sex
Two Companies, Los Angeles, 1944

Occupation	Los Angeles Railway Company			Los Angeles Motor Coach Lines		
	Negro Employees	Male	Female	Negro Employees	Male	Female
Coach cleaner	27	27	—	21	8	13
Car cleaner	136	—	136	—	—	—
Matron	2	—	2	—	—	—
Janitor	32	27	5	2	2	—
Car repairer	1	1	—	—	—	—
Sander	2	2	—	—	—	—
Scrubber	16	16	—	—	—	—
Paint mixer	1	1	—	—	—	—
Tire man	—	—	—	1	1	—
Yard man	11	11	—	—	—	—
Cleaner foreman	6	2	4	—	—	—
Total	234	87	147	24	11	13

Source: President's Committee on Fair Employment Practice, "In the Matter of Complaints of Alfonso Edwards *et al.* v. Los Angeles Railway Corporation," *Proceedings*, Case No. 66, August 1944.

After Amalgamated lodged complaints with the Federal Conciliation Service against LARY, the War Manpower Commission and FEPC stepped in to arrange a meeting between management and union officials in January 1943. During this meeting the Amalgamated president pointed out that Negroes working in the car barns had developed driving skills and could be upgraded into operators' positions. He also stated that at least 100 blacks were qualified to be upgraded to mechanics, a skilled job, and that in many cases Negroes had been used to train whites who, having completed training, were immediately classed as mechanics.

Another union official, however, was violently opposed to the policies of the liberal president. This official began an organization in opposition to the upgrading policies. Although the role of his supporters is not clear, when the first two Negroes were upgraded in February 1943, there was a work stoppage by some 80 white employees. Company officials went back on their plans for upgrading Negroes, and in a subsequent union election, the liberal president was beaten up during the campaign and defeated at the polls.

For the ensuing months until August 1944, when FEPC hearings began, the union and the company took no action despite protests by the Mayor, the Chamber of Commerce, regional councils of both AFL and CIO, and other interested parties. At the FEPC hearings, LARY stood by its policy of discrimination, and said that upgrading had not been accomplished because of a threatened walkout by many of the white employees. One union official had testified that 87.5 percent of one division had threatened to quit if Negroes were upgraded.

The fact that the country was in the midst of a war intensified the arguments of both Negroes and whites. First, there was a definite manpower shortage in the Los Angeles Railway Company. Buses which should have been operated—especially during peak hours—were sitting idle for lack of drivers. Negroes used this opportunity to demand employment in all jobs in general, and upgrading into platform and operative positions specifically. They insisted that this hiring and upgrading should be done in the interest of providing the best service possible during wartime.

On the other hand, the pressures of wartime were brought to bear by those who threatened a work stoppage in the event Negroes were upgraded. Management and union leaders alike cited the particular seriousness of a work stoppage during wartime as being reason to continue to exclude Negroes from platform and other nonmenial jobs. A union counsel stood on the antidiscrimination clause in the constitution of the international union (Amalgamated Association of Street, Electric Railway, and Motor Coach Employees of America, now the ATU). But union leaders feared a work stoppage and testified that their possibilities for action had all been exhausted.

Although included in the fears of white workers, seniority was not a real issue. Seniority rules dictated a combination companywide and departmental seniority whereby men could gain company seniority, but use departmental seniority for picking runs, for example. The positions of those already in the platform division were not threatened by the prospects of Negroes being upgraded into that division. Some of the platform men stated simply that they would feel their ". . . jobs had been downgraded if women or Negroes were hired to perform them." [34]

After the public hearing in Los Angeles, the FEPC wisely brought the company and the union together for informal negotiations. The parties asked the committee to issue a directive at once and promised to act promptly. This was done. By March 20, 1945, 74 Negroes had been employed as operators and Negroes were being upgraded in the garages and shops without discrimination. No incidents of work stoppages occurred. [35]

Oakland: Key System Transit Lines

The success of the FEPC as the catalyst for Negro employment in Los Angeles was not repeated in Oakland, although Negroes had been employed for some years in the municipal system of nearby San Francisco. According to testimony in the Proceedings of the President's Commission on Fair Employment Practice, [36] the major factor opposing Negro employment in the Key System Transit Lines of Oakland was union exclusion. Local Division 192 of Amalgamated Association of Street, Electric Railway, and Motor Coach Employees excluded blacks both when referred to the division for membership and when transferred from other divisions.

---

34. *Ibid.*

35. President's Committee on Fair Employment Practice, *Final Report* (Washington: Government Printing Office, 1947), p. 15.

36. *Ibid.*, p. 17; and *id.*, "United States v. Key System and Division 192 Amalgamated Association of Street, Electric Railway and Motor Coach Employees of America," *Proceedings*, Case No. 81, March 1945.

Each prospective union member was examined by a union subcommittee on the basis of his union record, honesty, and ability to perform the job. The subcommittee would then recommend membership or exclusion for the candidate. If it was thought that the person would be objectionable to the general union membership, the recommendation would typically be for exclusion. Said one subcommittee member, "I know my membership. They would not accept a Negro." [37] Therefore, quite apart from the three criteria outlined as governing the judgment, Negroes were excluded because they were black. This was even more obvious in light of the fact that whites were allowed to begin working prior to the subcommittee vote. Negroes were not allowed this right, and in fact never began work because of union exclusion.

The company officials stated that they would otherwise have employed Negroes, but had failed to do so because of the history of union exclusion of Negroes. Public hearings failed to accomplish what they had in Los Angeles. The war ended and the life of the FEPC expired without Negroes being hired on the Key System; in fact, change did not occur until the 1950's.

Philadelphia

In Philadelphia the upgrading of Negroes became a major issue in a three-way union struggle. The result was three years of inaction by Philadelphia Transportation Company (PTC) officials finally culminating in a week-long strike.

Management dominated all employee organizations of PTC from 1911 to 1937. Control was established primarily through the Cooperative Association, management's answer to a union, and the Cooperative Wage Fund, an enforced savings scheme which led PTC employees to "regard themselves primarily as stockholders and only secondarily as workers." [38] As a company union, the Cooperative Association was outlawed in 1937 and replaced by the Philadelphia Rapid Transit Employees Union (PRTEU), a new independent.

In a bargaining election in March 1944, employees were offered a choice among three different unions. One was the independent PRTEU. The second possibility was the Amalgamated union

---

37. *Ibid.*

38. Joseph E. Weckler, "Prejudice Is Not the Whole Story," *Public Opinion Quarterly*, Vol. IX (Summer 1945), p. 128.

(AFL), and the CIO Transport Workers Union was the third candidate. TWU won the election securing about 55 percent of the vote, the remainder was shared about equally by the PRTEU and Amalgamated.

It is against this background of interunion struggle that the problem of discriminatory hiring and upgrading should be viewed. The PRTEU and management had been fighting a delaying action against rising demands from Negroes for equal treatment. In 1943 the FEPC had stepped in and ordered affirmative action by management and union officials. Instead of complying with this order, PRTEU bitterly attacked the FEPC officials and accused them of trying to destroy the seniority system of PTC.[39] Officials continued to hide behind a clause in the union contract concerning seniority which referred neither to Negroes nor to upgrading.

When this contract with PRTEU was voided by the new election, FEPC again asked PTC officials to proceed with upgrading, expecting help from the more progressive TWU. The deposed independent union leaders used the race issue to build up sentiment against the new TWU local union. The old propaganda about destruction of the seniority system was revived, mainly through posted signs urging PTC employees to "protect the seniority of their fellow workers in the armed services by refusing to work with Negro operators." [40]

The bitter fighting between TWU officials and those who wanted to force them out of Philadelphia culminated in the strike on the morning Negroes were first to operate transit vehicles. TWU denounced the strike at the beginning, and its stewards exerted every effort to get the strikers back to work. PTC management, however, was passive, at no time appealing for the strikers to return. Only when the army moved in did the workers return, and Negroes begin to operate buses.

The experience in Philadelphia was clearly one of discriminatory hiring and upgrading practices by the transit company, continually upheld and perpetuated by union struggles. When all else seemed right for a progressive change to more liberal hir-

39. The extreme attitude of these independent union officials and the position of the FEPC are found in *Hearings Before the Special Committee to Investigate Executive Agencies*, U. S. House of Representatives, First and Second Sessions (Washington: Government Printing Office, 1944), Part 2, pp. 1854-1926.

40. *Ibid.*, and Weckler, *op. cit.*, p. 132.

ing and upgrading policies, the labor-management relations were such that change was impossible, again until government pressure compelled the acceptance of change.[41]

Chicago

The experience in Chicago was quite different from that in Philadelphia. The three private companies providing transit service there had resisted "the campaign for Negro platform jobs" which had been carried on for ten years.[42] Unlike the Philadelphia experience, however, the upgrading of Negroes in Chicago occurred without undue delay and serious stoppages once the President's Committee stepped into the picture.

The Chicago office of FEPC was opened in September 1943, amidst a growing campaign by Negro newspapers and civic groups which prompted "mass meetings and excited public discussion." [43] Interviews with each of the transit companies were conducted almost immediately. The general manager of Chicago Surface Lines had expressed the fear that Negro upgrading would lead to unpleasant public reaction and that the white platform workers might strike. Nevertheless the company was willing to upgrade Negroes, and by the end of 1944 over 100 of its platform employees were Negro. The management of Chicago Rapid Transit Lines was equally willing to elevate the position of their Negro employees, and proceeded at once to open the position of trainman and other platform jobs to Negroes. The Chicago Motor Coach Company asserted that it had always had an open door policy for all levels of skill, but that it had never had any applicants. When Negroes later applied, those who passed the tests were hired, trained, and assigned runs.

Not only was management agreeable to the proposals of FEPC, but the local labor leaders also took charge to see that they received general cooperation. The head of the local AFL Amalgamated union refused to allow debate on the subject of Negro hiring and upgrading at one of the local's meetings. He obtained general agreement from the rank and file on his stand that all union members regardless of color had the right to job opportunity.

---

41. Weckler, *op. cit.*, p. 138; and President's Committee on Fair Employment Practice, *Final Report, op. cit.*, pp. 14-15.

42. Ross, *op. cit.*, p. 86.

43. *Ibid.*

The urging of the President's Committee on Fair Employment Practice seems to have had primary influence in the Chicago experience. A decade of campaigning by private groups had produced no visible progress. Although the same result might have followed their continued efforts, the aid provided by the FEPC seems again to have been the catalyst necessary to action.

Other Northern Cities

Although no formal hearings were conducted before FEPC concerning the Indianapolis Street Railway, the power of the Presisdent's Committee was used to integrate platform jobs there also.[44] Sixty Negro men had applied for jobs as operators, conductors, trainmen, and traffic checkers with the Indianapolis Street Railway Company. The company admitted that denial of employment for these men was solely because they were black. The reason for excluding Negroes, according to the company, was the fear that they would not be granted membership into the union, Amalgamated Association of Street, Electric Railway, and Motor Coach Employees of America. The union did not have a race bar in its constitution, nor had it barred any Negroes holding other positions from membership. Nevertheless the company felt that local members would not accept Negroes.

Company representatives contacted the President's Committee and in effect asked for a directive from them to upgrade Negroes into platform jobs. They reasoned that this directive would assure them of employee and union cooperation which they might not have otherwise. The FEPC met and considered the facts, but never formally held a hearing or issued a directive. It did write a "stipulation"[45] which stated its authority in the matter and which recognized that discrimination outlawed by the 1943 Executive Order had been the policy of Indianapolis Street Railway. On the basis of this "stipulation" the company revised its policy and implemented steps to upgrade Negroes.

In New Jersey, results of pressure during the war yielded neither the upgradings of New York City nor the violence of Philadelphia. Public Service Coordinated Transport hired no Negro bus or trolley operators until 1946, insisting, as a vice-president

---

44. President's Committee on Fair Employment Practice files, National Archives, Washington, D.C., correspondence concerning Indianapolis Railway, Inc.

45. *Ibid.*

wrote one stockholder in 1943, that it would "continue employing
qualified Negroes doing the work for which we need them and *for
which we think they are qualified."* [46] The company held to this
position until after the war and the passage of the New Jersey
antidiscrimination law when peaceful integration was accomplished. Buffalo, on the other hand, moved rapidly into integration during the war,[47] and Albany, New York employed its first
Negro bus driver in 1944.[48] By a few years after the war, most
major cities in the North, Midwest, and Pacific Coast states had
integrated their platforms.

Washington, D. C.: The Border State Situation

Few, if any, Negroes were employed as anything but laborers
or porters in border state transit facilities prior to World War
II. Moreover, the FEPC failed to change that situation in one of
its most important cases—Capital Transit Company.

Transit platform jobs in the nation's capital had historically
been a preserve of white persons. As Washington's population
was swelled by World War I governmental expansion in 1917,
the Capital Transit Company found itself in need of several hundred workers, but Negroes who applied were turned away.[49]
Again in 1934, with the New Deal of President Franklin D.
Roosevelt attracting thousands of new residents to the capital,
the transit concern was required to expand. Attempts by Negroes to obtain platform jobs were thwarted by the threat of the
local of the Amalgamated union to strike "if a single Negro
were employed." [50] The formation of the President's Committee
on Fair Employment Practice was, not surprisingly, a signal for
Negroes to try again.

46. Emphasis supplied. The stockholder was Dr. Herbert R. Northrup. He
    also provided the author with a manuscript describing the New Jersey
    fight to employ Negroes as bus drivers.

47. See Table 11; and John A. Davis, "Employment of Negroes in Local
    Transit Industry," *Opportunity*, Vol. XXII (April-June 1944), pp. 63-65,
    100.

48. "League Affiliate Aids in Placing Transit Employees," *Opportunity*, Vol.
    XXII (Summer 1944), p. 131.

49. Constance McLaughlin Green, *The Secret City: A History of Race Rela-
    tions in the Nation's Capital* (Princeton: Princeton University Press,
    1967), p. 186.

50. *Ibid.*, p. 228.

The first Roosevelt-appointed committee received a charge of discrimination in 1942.[51] Capital Transit had filed a job order with the United States Employment Service (USES) calling for only whites as streetcar conductors. Capital Transit blamed white employee opposition for this policy, but retracted the discriminatory job order in December 1942, after it was ordered to employ Negroes by the FEPC. In early 1943 a Negro was hired for training as a streetcar operator. When he reported to begin on-the-job training, the white operators refused to instruct him and eight of them stopped work in protest. The company then withdrew the Negro trainee from the operator's program and offered him a job as janitor, which he refused. The work stoppage ended.

Meanwhile, Paul V. McNutt, Director of the War Manpower Commission, under whose aegis FEPC then operated, canceled scheduled FEPC hearings on railroad discrimination, an act which put FEPC in an almost inactive status. He also tried to solve the Capital Transit problem by addressing a mass meeting of its operators. The meeting "wound up with insults to the featured speakers and a confirmation in the minds of Capital Transit workers . . . that they were in the saddle." [52]

After a number of attempts to resolve the problem, the second Roosevelt FEPC scheduled a hearing on Capital Transit, but postponed it so that an "expert" could work with the company to "educate" the white employees (prepare them for the subsequent hiring of Negroes). This "education" resulted in little more than an attitude survey the findings of which were used by company officials to reinforce fears of a walkout if they hired a Negro. The company continued to accept applications from Negroes, but none were hired.

All this was happening in a time of acute manpower shortages. Capital Transit Company was picketed in a protest against its seeking white women employees and its concurrent refusal to accept Negro men. The company had taken other special steps to reduce the severe shortage of labor. It spent money to convert two-man cars to one-man cars. It advertised extensively and not

---

51. This summary of the Capital Transit case is based on President's Committee on Fair Employment Practice, "Capital Transit Company," *Proceedings*, Case No. 70, January 15, 1945; *id., Final Report, op. cit.,* pp. 15-17; Green, *op. cit.,* pp. 258-260 and 285; and Louis Ruchames, *Race, Jobs and Politics: The Story of FEPC* (New York: Columbia University Press, 1953), pp. 49-50, 55-56, 59, 132, 152-153.

52. Ross, *op. cit.,* p. 157.

only employed white women but persuaded the regular male operators to forego seniority in order to allow women to operate the
most desirable runs. With such evident manpower problems, the
company found its hiring policies more and more difficult to
justify. In one case, it employed a Negro woman who "passed"
as white. She worked successfully as a bus driver until her color
was discovered and she was discharged.

The FEPC finally held hearings on Capital Transit in January
1945 and directed it to employ Negroes in April of that year.
By then, armed victory was near and interest in fair employment
had dwindled; the directives were ignored.

The government had one last chance to alter Capital Transit's
bigoted hiring policies before emergency legislation ended. On
November 21, 1945, the Amalgamated struck the company in a
wage dispute. Pursuant to the War Labor Disputes Act, President Truman seized its facilities. The FEPC then asked the
President to alter the transit system's racial policies to obtain
conformance to what the government was requiring of other employers. He demurred on the grounds that the War Labor Disputes Act required property so seized to "be operated under the
terms and conditions of employment which were in effect at the
time possession of such plant, mine, or facility was so taken" by
the government. In protest, the late distinguished Negro lawyer,
Charles H. Houston, resigned from the FEPC which soon passed
into oblivion. Capital Transit's platform men remained lily-white
until 1956 when new franchise owners reversed the system's racial policies and integrated the operators without incident.

In retrospect, it is apparent that the FEPC, beset by congressional criticism and wary of disruptions in wartime Washington,
moved too cautiously. The appearance of Mr. McNutt at a public
meeting served to reinforce the power of mass bigotry and the
postponement of the hearing for an attitude survey now seems in-
explicable. Moreover, the failure of President Truman to enforce equal opportunity after the system was seized was both
out of character for him and based upon an application of the
War Labor Disputes Act not elsewhere followed.[53]

---

53. For example, after the coal mines were seized, the government negotiated
    a welfare fund based on per ton mined royalty, a totally new departure
    in industrial relations at the time.

The South

In the South for the period through 1945 (and beyond) Negroes were employed only as laborers and service workers. It was a common practice for southern transit companies to bargain separately with Negroes and whites. Labor contracts and local unions remained segregated. This involved not only the Amalgamated, but also the Houston, Texas local of the TWU, which adopted a southern posture with segregated locals and seniority rosters. Many companies and unions had formal provisions limiting Negro employment to service and laborers positions. Separate seniority rosters precluded Negroes from obtaining platform or cleaner jobs. These provisions lasted until the late 1950's and early 1960's, when civil rights action and other factors led to abolishment. (See the discussion of southern job desegregation in Chapter IV.)

Table 13 indicates that proportionally, Negroes were better represented in the South than in other sections of the country in 1940. (Compare with Tables 10 and 15.) The percent Negro employment was greatest in the Deep South. For example, the border states, Kentucky, Maryland, Missouri, and Oklahoma had relatively fewer Negro employees than did Mississippi, Alabama, Georgia, North and South Carolina, and Florida. The cities in the North where Negroes held upgraded transit jobs were mainly those where public control or public pressure through the FEPC had opened the doors. In the South, where segregation was more institutionalized and Negro political power was very weak, ownership, control, and pressure did not make that difference. The Negro continued to be relegated to menial labor for two more decades. A study of union relations among urban transit employees in the South, published in 1949, did not contain a single reference to race,[54] apparently because the racial status quo there seemed too obvious and permanent to be noted.

SUMMARY

In summary, several factors were evident in the development of racial employment patterns through 1945. First, the nature of the transit work made the industry attractive to Negroes. Many jobs requiring little or no special skills were visible to Negroes,

---

54. Frederic Meyers, "Organization and Collective Bargaining in the Local Mass Transportation Industry in the Southeast," *Southern Economic Journal*, Vol. XV (April 1949), pp. 425-440.

TABLE 13. *Urban Transit Industry*
Employment by Race and Sex
Southern and Border States, 1940

State	All Employees			Male			Female		
	Total	Negro	Percent Negro	Total	Negro	Percent Negro	Total	Negro	Percent Negro
Alabama	1,632	184	11.3	1,562	174	11.1	70	10	14.3
Arkansas	1,012	97	9.6	963	95	9.9	49	2	4.1
Florida	2,045	243	11.9	1,938	230	11.9	107	13	12.1
Georgia	1,894	177	9.3	1,799	165	9.2	95	12	12.6
Kentucky	2,345	114	4.9	2,231	109	4.9	114	5	4.4
Louisiana	2,340	171	7.3	2,266	166	7.3	74	5	6.8
Maryland	4,049	153	3.8	3,888	146	3.8	161	7	4.3
Mississippi	772	89	11.5	720	85	11.8	52	4	7.7
Missouri	6,998	197	2.8	6,727	193	2.9	271	4	1.5
North Carolina	1,807	234	12.9	1,728	230	13.3	79	4	5.1
Oklahoma	1,529	106	6.9	1,459	102	7.0	70	4	5.7
South Carolina	563	66	11.7	531	64	12.1	32	2	6.2
Tennessee	2,581	327	12.7	2,474	318	12.9	107	9	8.4
Texas	5,408	365	6.7	5,219	350	6.7	189	15	7.9
Virginia	2,868	237	8.3	2,744	225	8.2	124	12	9.7
Total	37,843	2,760	7.3	36,249	2,652	7.3	1,594	108	6.8

Source: *U. S. Census of Population: 1940*, Vol. III, *The Labor Force*, Parts 2-5, Table 18.

especially since many of them rode buses and trains. Second, the influence of public ownership and civil service rules was beneficial to Negroes seeking transit employment. This was especially true outside the South where the increasing political power of Negroes worked in their favor. Third, the efforts of the President's Committee on Fair Employment Practice were particularly effective during World War II, when labor shortages were most severe. Indeed, the FEPC probably had as much, or even more, success in upgrading the transit work force than it had in any other industry, despite its failures in Washington, Oakland, and New Jersey.

In addition to these factors, union attitudes proved significant in a number of cities. Locals of Amalgamated restricted membership to whites or otherwise catered to pressure or prejudice of whites in some cities. Amalgamated allowed its locals more autonomy in racial matters than did the Transport Workers Union, but it should be noted that the TWU was not active in as many diverse situations. TWU also followed local practice in Houston where it permitted segregated locals and seniority rosters. In Philadelphia, an independent union fanned the fires of prejudice and led a violent reaction to the upgrading of Negroes.

CHAPTER IV

From 1945 to 1960 — The Negro in a Declining Industry

During the years immediately following the Second World War, transit operations reached a peak. Employment was 19 percent higher in 1945 than it had been in 1940, but by 1950, it had begun to fall slightly. Although total operating revenue continued to grow, fluctuating around $1.4 billion in the 1950's, operating income declined drastically after 1945, primarily because of rising expenses. During this period, however, when total employment in the industry was declining, the number of Negroes in urban transit increased absolutely and relatively.[55] The period of the 1950's was especially important in that some of the barriers to integration began to crumble in the South as well as in border cities and in the North where they still existed.

This chapter contains a discussion of the factors which influenced Negro employment in transit jobs from 1945 to 1960. Much of the discussion is based on census data which are used to show changes in Negro employment throughout these years of declining overall employment.

THE PICTURE FROM 1940 TO 1960

Table 14 shows Negro employment increasing as a percentage of total employment between 1940 and 1960. The greatest percentage increase came between 1950 and 1960, when Negro employment increased by 62 percent while total employment was falling by 9 percent. This represents a change in Negro propor-

---

55. This is an exception to the general conclusion that in declining fields Negro males lose employment at a more rapid rate than whites. This is the conclusion found in Dale L. Heistand, *Economic Growth and Employment Opportunities for Minorities* (New York: Columbia University Press, 1964), pp. 110-111. We have found also that Heistand's observation is not valid for shipbuilding. See Lester Rubin, *The Negro in the Shipbuilding Industry*, The Racial Policies of American Industry, Report No. 17 (Philadelphia: Industrial Research Unit, Wharton School of Finance and Commerce, University of Pennsylvania, 1970).

TABLE 14. *Urban Transit Industry*
Employment by Race and Sex
1940-1960

Year	All Employees			Male			Female		
	Total	Negro	Percent Negro	Total	Negro	Percent Negro	Total	Negro	Percent Negro
1940	202,670	6,101	3.0	194,363	5,846	3.0	8,307	255	3.1
1950	323,965	20,836	6.4	297,992	19,059	6.4	25,973	1,777	6.8
1960	288,488	31,321	10.9	256,191	28,661	11.2	32,297	2,660	8.2

Source: *U.S. Census of Population:*

1940: Vol. III, *The Labor Force,* U.S. Summary, Table 76.

1950: Vol. II, *Characteristics of the Population,* Part 1, U.S. Summary, Table 133.

1960: PC(1) 1D, *U.S. Summary,* Detailed Characteristics, Table 213.

tion of total employment of from 6.4 percent to 11.5 percent during this decade.

The tabular breakdown by sex (Table 14) indicates that very few transit jobs were filled by women, and that Negro women comprised roughly the same percentage of all female employees as the ratio of Negro males to all male employees. Perhaps because of the labor shortages caused by the war, Negro women gained more new jobs in the decade from 1940 to 1950 than from 1950 to 1960. Total female employment increased in both of those decades.

On the other hand, total employment of males in the transit industry increased from 1940 to 1950, then fell in the subsequent decade. Employment of Negro males increased by 11,570 during the latter ten-year period when overall employment of males was falling. Several reasons for this increase in Negro employment may be cited.

Population Movements

Population movements between 1945 and 1960 influenced Negro employment in urban transit in at least two ways. First, Negro migration from the South to other parts of the country (particularly the North) accounts for some of the increase in Negro employment in those areas. Moreover, the population movement within the cities left Negroes in greater percentages in the central cities where urban transit was concentrated. Migration was also significant because the Negro's increasing political power as he migrated made it possible for him to bring pressure on public bodies to open up public as well as private jobs.

In 1940, 77 percent of all Negroes in the United States lived in the South (Table 15). By 1960, only 60 percent of all Negroes remained in the southern states. The percentage of Negroes living in the North increased from 22 percent to 34 percent between 1940 and 1960. Migration of Negroes extended into both the northeast and north central sections of the North, and into the West as well. Since doors were open to Negroes for jobs above the menial level in many areas outside the South during this period, the migration of Negroes was from an area where certain jobs were unattainable to areas where they were. The increasing Negro population in northern cities therefore partially accounts for the increasing levels of Negro employment there.

Table 15 shows that Negroes not only migrated to metropolitan areas in this period, but also shifting population left the Negroes

TABLE 15. *Negro Population Distribution
by Region and Area Location, 1940-1969*

	1940	1950	1960	1966	1969
Percent distribution by region					
Northeast	11	13	16	17	19
North Central	11	15	18	20	21
South	77	68	60	55	52
West	1	4	6	8	7
Total	100	100	100	100	100
Percent of total population by region					
Northeast	4	5	7	8	9
North Central	4	5	7	8	8
South	24	22	21	20	19
West	1	3	4	5	5
Total	10	10	11	11	11
Population by area location (millions)					
Central cities	n.a.	6.5	9.7	12.1	11.3
Urban fringe	n.a.	1.9	2.5	2.7	2.7
Smaller cities, towns, and rural	n.a.	6.7	6.6	6.7	6.5
Percent distribution by area location					
Central cities	n.a.	43	52	56	55
Urban fringe	n.a.	13	13	13	15
Smaller cities, towns, and rural	n.a.	44	35	31	30
Total		100	100	100	100

Source: U.S. Bureau of the Census, *The Social and Economic Status of Negroes in the United States, 1969,* Current Population Reports, Series P-23, No. 29 (also BLS Report No. 375), pp. 2, 4, 6, and 7; and No. 24 (BLS Report No. 332), pp. 5, 8, and 9.

in the central city area both North and South while whites moved to the suburbs. The percentage of all Negroes living in metropolitan areas (central cities and urban fringe) increased from 56 percent to 65 percent between 1950 and 1960. Likewise the percentage of Negroes living in the central cities increased from 43 percent to 52 percent during the same period. But the percentage of Negro population residing in the urban fringe remained constant at 13 percent. These figures are particularly significant for the urban transit industry.

The major concern of urban mass transportation has traditionally been to transport people into and out of the downtown areas of the cities. Hence the central city becomes the center of urban transit operations. With the center of its business in the same general area as Negro population centers, urban transit and Negroes have been brought together. This location factor has brought Negroes to transit as consumers (riders) and as employees, with the increase in the former encouraging the utilization of Negroes in the latter capacity.

This point deserves further emphasis. While Negroes were migrating to the cities and utilizing transit facilities more and more, whites were moving to the suburbs and traveling by private automobile or by commuter train. The transit industry moved toward being a service utilized largely by blacks in many cities— a development which continued at a rapid pace in the 1960's. As this occurred, the industry lost appeal to white workers who took advantage of expanding opportunities elsewhere. To Negroes, however, the transit industry continued to be attractive because of its high wages and urban location. Thus in the 1950's, principally as a result of population movements, began the movement in customer and employee racial orientation that led to the remark in an interview in 1968 by an official of one large transit system that the transit industry in large cities is "slowly becoming a black organization for service to blacks."

Continued Switch from Private to Public Ownership

During the 1950's, 25 transit systems were sold by their respective private owners to the various city or county transit authorities. These included large systems such as Chicago Motor Coach Company, California Street Cable Railroad Company in San Francisco, and three independent companies in Los Angeles. Smaller companies were also sold to public authorities. The change from private to public ownership was not concentrated in any one region of the country. The list includes cities in California, New York, Texas, Florida, Indiana, and Illinois.

The importance of public ownership as a factor in Negro employment has been noted in the previous chapter. In many of the cases where public authorities acquired transit properties in the 1950's, civil service rules took effect governing hiring and upgrading policies. In cities where civil service was not applicable to city employees, or where, for whatever reason, transit employees were not brought under civil service, public ownership still had its effect. Much of the public acquisition of transit property has come about as a result of "transit authorities" created by legislative act of their respective states. In creating a transit authority, the legislatures wrote nondiscrimination policies into their charters. In many of the cases of municipal ownership, the same kind of policies were adopted. It was growing more and more difficult for a public body to continue to discriminate—especially in the North.

This is not to say that the mere statement of a policy of nondiscrimination by a legislature absolved the management of the further responsibility to execute that policy. Nor is it to imply that the statement of a policy of nondiscrimination guaranteed the Negro an equal opportunity. Nevertheless, public ownership did in many cases provide the first step toward a changing policy in the hiring and upgrading of Negroes. At least the statement of nondiscrimination policy was made where no such statement had existed previously. Since people apply for jobs they expect to be able to obtain, if nothing else, this encouraged an increasing number of Negroes to apply for transit jobs.

REGIONAL DIFFERENCES IN NEGRO EMPLOYMENT 1940-1960

Table 16 shows employment in the transit industry by region. Negroes comprised a larger percentage of the total transit work force in the South than in other regions for each of the three census years. These figures may, however, be somewhat misleading. Negro population was concentrated in the South, especially in the earlier years of this period, thus partially explaining their presence in transit jobs. It should also be noted that the census definition of the South includes Maryland, the District of Columbia, and Delaware, thus overstating the proportion of employees in the South. Another qualification must be made in that the

TABLE 16. *Urban Transit Industry*
Employment by Race and Sex
Four Regions, 1940-1960

Region	Year	All Employees			Male			Female		
		Total	Negro	Percent Negro	Total	Negro	Percent Negro	Total	Negro	Percent Negro
Northeast	1940	79,187	1,961	2.5	75,884	1,897	2.5	3,303	64	1.9
	1950	118,312	7,349	6.2	110,551	6,943	6.3	7,761	406	5.2
	1960	102,121	10,040	9.8	94,275	9,344	9.9	7,846	696	8.9
North Central	1940	64,194	966	1.5	61,611	926	1.5	2,583	40	1.5
	1950	89,400	4,701	5.3	82,690	4,370	5.3	6,710	331	4.9
	1960	68,000	6,474	9.5	60,585	6,162	10.2	7,415	312	4.2
South	1940	35,373	2,891	8.2	33,857	2,775	8.2	1,516	116	7.7
	1950	78,586	7,447	9.5	70,990	6,531	9.2	7,596	916	12.1
	1960	81,053	12,959	16.0	70,270	11,414	16.2	10,783	1,545	14.3
West	1940	23,916	283	1.2	23,011	248	1.2	905	35	3.9
	1950	37,667	1,339	3.6	33,761	1,215	3.6	3,906	124	3.2
	1960	37,314	1,848	5.0	31,061	1,741	5.6	6,253	107	1.7

Source: *U.S. Census of Population:*

1940: Vol. III, *The Labor Force*, Table 77.

1950: Vol. II, *Characteristics of the Population*, Part 1, U.S. Summary, Table 161.

1960: PC(1) 1D, *U.S. Summary*, Detailed Characteristics, Table 260.

employment of the Negro in transit jobs in the South prior to 1960 in the great majority of cases occurred in the lower level jobs of the unskilled variety. Buses were not integrated in most southern cities until the middle and late 1950's, and not until after integration were Negroes considered by transit companies in the South as suitable operators. Most Negro operators of urban buses in the southern states were hired after 1960.

In the North, the hiring and upgrading of Negroes had, as noted, occurred in several cities before 1945. In addition, between 1940 and 1960 Negro employment increased in the North in absolute terms and as a percentage of total employment. By 1960, many northern Negroes were operators and filled other platform jobs. A number of companies which had fought integration finally accepted it in the post-World War II era, often as a result of the action of newly constituted state fair employment practice commmissions. Thus, as we have noted, following a complaint to the New Jersey Division Against Discrimination in 1946, Public Service of New Jersey employed its first Negro drivers and gradually thereafter moved to full integration. In the same period, investigations by the Massachusetts Commission Against Discrimination found that the transit system of Springfield, Massachusetts had never employed Negroes except as janitors. As late as 1960, transit systems of Columbus and Cincinnati, Ohio employed only a token number of Negro drivers—5 of 419 in Columbus and only 3 of a larger total in Cincinnati. In Cleveland, however, 25 percent of the drivers were then black. Thus, despite great gains, there were still pockets of discrimination in the North.[56]

As a percent of all employees, fewer Negroes were employed in the West than any of the other regions. In the major cities such as Los Angeles, San Francisco, Oakland, and Seattle, the color line had been broken before 1960 for positions including platform jobs. Perhaps the lower ratio of Negroes to other employees is a result of the fact that fewer Negroes lived in the West than in other regions. Table 17 shows relative changes in Negro employment in the four regions between 1940 and 1960.

---

56. Data from files of New Jersey Division Against Discrimination, Massachusetts Commission Against Discrimination, and Ohio Civil Rights Commission. See also the discussion in the previous chapter.

TABLE 17. *Urban Transit Industry*
Relative Changes in Negro Employment
Four Regions, 1940-1960

Region	Percent Negro			Change	
	1940	1950	1960	1940-1950	1950-1960
Northeast	2.5	6.2	9.8	+3.7	+3.6
North Central	1.5	5.3	9.5	+3.8	+4.2
South	8.2	9.5	16.0	+1.3	+6.5
West	1.2	3.6	5.0	+2.4	+1.4

Source: Table 16.

The Special Case of the South

In the urban transit industry of the South lay all the outward
reminders of inequities and indignities of segregation for the
Negro. Negroes rode the buses in large numbers, but they rode
"in the back of the bus." Seats reserved for whites were not to
be used by Negroes even if no whites were present and all other
seats were filled. Seats in the unreserved section could be occupied by Negroes unless whites filled their reserved section and
demanded that Negroes surrender them. Not only were Negroes
not employed as bus drivers, they often suffered discourteous
treatment from the white drivers. The inequities of segregation
and the attitudes of whites toward Negroes were hardly ever
more visibly practiced and openly displayed than on urban buses
in the South.

In this period of the 1950's, Negroes began to protest their
plight. Transit became the focal point of these protests in several places and the results were significant for the whole civil
rights movement generally and for Negro employment in transit
specifically.

The events surrounding the bus boycott led by the late Dr.
Martin Luther King, Jr., in Montgomery, Alabama in 1955 and
1956 reflected conditions which existed throughout the South.
On December 1, 1955, Mrs. Rosa Parks, a Negro seamstress,
boarded a Montgomery bus and took a seat in the first row of
the unreserved section. Subsequently she was ordered along with
three other Negroes to stand and surrender her seat to boarding

white passengers. The other Negro passengers stood, but she refused. "The result was her arrest." [57]

Other Negroes had been arrested for violation of Montgomery's segregation laws. A few months before the Parks incident a fifteen-year-old Negro girl had been arrested for refusing to give up her seat on the bus. She was convicted with a suspended sentence.

With the arrest of Mrs. Parks, the necessary elements for a protest fell together. The buses were ridden by large numbers of Negroes who had experienced the unequal and discourteous treatment. Negro leaders were aware that a bus boycott had been successful in Baton Rouge, Louisiana and since approximately 75 percent of the riders in Montgomery were Negro, they decided a boycott would be effective there.

Three requests were made by the leaders of the protest: (1) that the bus company grant first-come, first-served seating on buses with Negroes loading from the rear and whites from the front, (2) courtesy from the drivers, and (3) employment of Negro drivers on predominantly Negro routes. Concerning the third request, King stated,

The bus company admits that seventy-five percent of its patrons are colored; and it seems to me that it would be good business sense for the company to seek employees from the ranks of its largest patronage.[58]

Negroes knew that they possessed the skills necessary to drive a bus. They also knew that they were excluded from jobs which provided service mainly for their own people. But under southern segregation it would be illogical to think that a Negro would have been allowed to drive a bus before he could sit in the front seats of these same buses.

Bus desegregation came in Montgomery in December 1956. Negroes were allowed to sit where they chose, and were guaranteed courteous treatment by drivers.[59] The third of their requests was not granted immediately. The company agreed to take applications from Negroes, but the first Negro operator was not hired until the 1960's.

---

57. The account of the Montgomery bus boycott is drawn from Martin Luther King, Jr., *Stride Toward Freedom* (New York: Harper & Brothers, 1958). The quotation is from page 43.

58. *Ibid.*, pp. 110-111.

59. *Ibid.*, p. 183.

The Montgomery experience is an example of general conditions in the Deep South. Segregation was institutionalized, and as a result Negroes generally had neither economic nor political power. The desegregation of buses was the first step toward an end to the exclusion of Negroes from transit jobs above the menial level. This upgrading came mainly in the early 1960's and is discussed in the following chapter.

NEGRO EMPLOYMENT IN SELECTED URBAN AREAS 1950 AND 1960

Negro employment in the transit industry varied considerably from one city to another. It is not only useful to compare one urban area with another, but also to note the differences in urban transit and other industries in regard to Negro employment. This is not to imply that Negroes were equally distributed throughout all skills, nor that this distribution would be the same for all industries. Nevertheless, for absolute employment figures, comparisons can be made based on data presented in Table 18.

It is useful to compare the percentage Negro employment in the transit industry with the percentage Negro employment in all industries and with the percentage Negro population. Noting that the latter two percentages are roughly equal for all the SMSA's included, these comparisons may be made simultaneously. In 1960, the following SMSA's had a smaller percentage of Negro employees in transit than the percentage of Negro population and Negro employment in all industries respectively: Atlanta, Cincinnati, Houston, New Orleans, Philadelphia, Pittsburgh, and Washington, D. C. In St. Louis, Negro employment in urban transit was proportional to Negro population and employment in all industries. For the remaining SMSA's, Boston, Chicago, Cleveland, Detroit, Los Angeles, New York, and San Francisco, the percentages of Negro employment were greater for the transit industry.

Some of the variation in employment from one SMSA to the next can be attributed to the differences in population ratios. In Boston, for example, the fact that a small proportion of transit employees was Negro can be explained largely by the relatively small (3 percent in 1960) Negro population there. On the other hand, the cities with the largest proportion of Negroes to whites employed in urban transit did not necessarily have the largest relative Negro populations. Atlanta, Houston, New Orleans, and Washington, D. C. all had populations which were at least 20 percent Negro in 1960. Only about 10 percent of all transit employees in those cities were Negro. Figures in Table 19 have been adjusted to allow for population differences from one SMSA to another. In Chicago, Cleveland, Detroit, and New York, Negro employment was greater than 15 percent of the total transit industry work force (Table 18). As noted in Chapter III, transit firms in these cities began hiring Negroes in platform jobs relatively early (at least by 1945). In all of these cities except Chicago there was a relatively high percentage of Negro employees by 1950.

Data in Table 18 also show the downward trend in employment for the transit industry in the decade from 1950 to 1960. Except in the Atlanta SMSA, total employment declined between 1950 and 1960. In five, both total and Negro employment decreased.[60] In all the other SMSA's Negro employment increased while total employment fell.

Furthermore, among the SMSA's with declining total employment, in all but one (Houston) the rate of decline was slower for Negroes than for whites. Thus the percentage Negro employment was greater in 1960 than in 1950 in all but one of the SMSA's studied. It should be noted again that while transit employment was declining generally, Negroes were gaining in the proportion of jobs which they filled.

The proposition that "the burden of short-time layoffs and unemployment will fall disproportionately on workers, such as nonwhite workers, who are members of minority groups," [61] has not been generally true in the transit industry. Negroes have not usually been "the first ones fired" as a result of the layoffs associated with declining business. Part of this may be accounted for in that

... differences in aggregate unemployment rates are not necessarily the result of differential hiring and firing of nonwhite workers. Instead, such differences may be accounted for by some characteristics of the nonwhite labor force which also produce higher unemployment rates for subgroups of the white labor force. Nonwhite workers, for instance,

---

60. Cincinnati, Detroit, Houston, Pittsburgh, and Washington SMSA's. In Detroit, however, while total employment fell by about 3,600, Negro employment fell by only 60.

61. Harry Gilman, "Economic Discrimination and Unemployment," *American Economic Review*, Vol. LV (December 1965), p. 1077.

TABLE 18. Urban Transit Industry
Employment by Race and Sex
Selected Standard Metropolitan Statistical Areas, 1950 and 1960

SMSA	Year	All Employees			Male			Female			Percent Negro in SMSA	Percent Negro Employed in All Industries in SMSA
		Total	Negro	Percent Negro	Total	Negro	Percent Negro	Total	Negro	Percent Negro		
Atlanta	1950	1,612	153	9.5	1,493	141	9.4	119	12	10.1	24.6	25.4
	1960	1,783	169	9.5	1,640	154	9.4	143	15	10.5	22.7	21.4
Boston	1950	10,279	109	1.1	9,496	104	1.1	783	5	0.6	2.2	2.2
	1960	7,344	116	1.6	6,904	116	1.7	440	—	—	3.0	2.9
Chicago	1950	24,931	1,300	5.2	23,499	1,247	5.3	1,432	53	3.7	10.7	9.6
	1960	16,863	3,053	18.1	15,715	2,955	18.8	1,148	98	8.5	14.3	11.8
Cincinnati	1950	2,952	114	3.9	2,768	93	3.4	184	21	11.4	10.5	9.6
	1960	1,871	93	5.0	1,756	77	4.4	115	16	13.9	11.9	10.9
Cleveland	1950	5,520	744	13.5	5,002	662	13.2	518	82	15.8	10.4	9.6
	1960	3,916	792	20.2	3,479	749	21.5	437	43	9.8	14.3	12.6
Detroit	1950	8,465	1,399	16.5	7,897	1,375	17.4	568	24	4.2	11.9	10.6
	1960	4,862	1,339	27.5	4,210	1,308	31.1	652	31	4.8	14.8	12.8
Houston	1950	2,237	215	9.6	2,080	206	9.9	157	9	5.7	18.5	19.9
	1960	2,197	182	8.3	1,464	140	9.6	733	42	5.7	19.8	19.2

Los Angeles—Long Beach	1950	9,262	594	6.4	8,392	521	6.2	870	73	8.4	5.0	5.2
	1960	8,509	799	9.4	7,147	744	10.4	1,362	55	4.0	6.9	6.4
New Orleans	1950	2,265	151	6.7	2,083	113	5.4	182	38	20.9	29.1	27.0
	1960	2,182	175	8.0	2,067	149	7.2	115	26	22.6	30.8	26.9
New York[a]	1950	47,775	5,730	12.0	45,571	5,398	11.8	2,204	332	15.1	8.6	8.8
	1960	46,419	8,086	17.4	44,238	7,516	17.0	2,181	570	26.1	11.4	11.5
Philadelphia	1950	14,967	941	6.3	13,466	904	6.7	1,501	37	2.5	13.1	11.9
	1960	10,553	1,019	9.7	9,451	956	10.1	1,102	63	5.7	15.4	14.6
Pittsburgh	1950	5,985	125	2.1	5,636	119	2.1	349	6	1.7	6.2	5.3
	1960	3,786	104	2.7	3,530	101	2.9	256	3	1.2	6.7	5.7
St. Louis	1950	4,722	248	5.3	4,471	241	5.4	251	7	2.8	12.8	11.2
	1960	3,501	433	12.4	3,207	413	12.9	294	20	6.8	14.3	11.8
San Francisco	1950	7,375	494	6.7	6,593	471	7.1	782	23	2.9	6.6	5.8
	1960	6,000	716	11.9	5,091	687	13.5	909	29	3.2	8.5	7.0
Washington, D.C.	1950	6,117	598	9.8	5,755	567	9.9	362	31	8.6	23.1	24.1
	1960	5,362	578	10.8	4,693	487	10.4	669	91	13.6	24.4	24.5

Source: *U. S. Census of Population:*

    1950: Vol. II, *Characteristics of the Population*, State Volumes, Tables 34 and 83.

    1960: PC (1) 1D, *Detailed Characteristics*, State Volumes, Tables 96 and 129.

Note: Data include interurban bus line employment.

[a] New York portion of New York-Northeastern New Jersey SMSA.

TABLE 19. *Urban Transit Industry*
Negro Employment Relative to Negro Population
Selected Standard Metropolitan Statistical Areas, 1950 and 1960

SMSA	Year	Negro Employment in Transit	Negro Population	Participation Rate[a]
Atlanta	1950	153	165,591	0.09
	1960	169	230,737	0.07
Boston	1950	109	51,568	0.21
	1960	116	77,753	0.15
Chicago	1950	1,300	586,598	0.22
	1960	3,053	889,961	0.34
Cincinnati	1950	114	95,059	0.12
	1960	93	127,713	0.07
Cleveland	1950	744	152,118	0.49
	1960	792	257,258	0.31
Detroit	1950	1,399	357,800	0.39
	1960	1,339	558,792	0.24
Houston	1950	215	149,286	0.14
	1960	182	246,118	0.07
Los Angeles— Long Beach	1950	594	218,770	0.27
	1960	799	464,112	0.17
New Orleans	1950	151	199,527	0.08
	1960	175	267,303	0.07
New York	1950	5,730	820,227	0.70
	1960	8,086	1,224,590	0.66
Philadelphia	1950	941	480,075	0.20
	1960	1,019	670,939	0.15
Pittsburgh	1950	125	136,285	0.09
	1960	104	160,845	0.06
St. Louis	1950	248	215,436	0.12
	1960	433	294,715	0.15
San Francisco	1950	494	147,223	0.34
	1960	716	237,428	0.30
Washington, D.C.	1950	598	337,757	0.18
	1960	578	485,117	0.12

Source: *U. S. Census of Population:*

    1950: Vol. II, *Characteristics of the Population,* State Volumes, Tables 34 and 83.

    1960: PC (1) 1D, *Detailed Characteristics,* State Volumes, Tables 96 and 127.

[a] Negro employment in transit as a percentage of the Negro population.

are employed disproportionately in the occupations in which unemployment rates for white workers are highest in level and in the absolute size of the cyclical swings.[62]

In urban transit a very large percentage of the jobs are entry level jobs, the greatest number of those being operators. Naturally, during a decline in general employment the number of operatives would tend to fall. Personnel managers reported in interviews that there is also a relatively high rate of turnover among operators, especially during the early months of driving. They also reported that in most of the large urban areas there is a growing percentage of Negro applicants for these entry level jobs. As was already noted, whites have found these jobs less desirable, Negroes more desirable.

We shall comment on some of the factors related to this in the next chapter. In the 1950's, however, the most significant were undoubtedly the poor prospects of the industry and the ability of whites to find employment elsewhere. Thus, while some Negroes may have been laid off because of declining general employment, the increasing proportion of Negroes hired to fill positions opening up because of natural attrition has led to a greater overall proportion of Negroes in the industry. As the next chapter will show, this trend has not only continued, but has accelerated.

---

62. *Ibid.*

CHAPTER V

From 1960 to Present—Changing Trends

The period of the 1960's has been one of change for urba transit, but except for the South, the trends of the 1950's ex tended into the early 1960's. Nothing changed significantly i those first few years. Companies continued to switch from pr vate to public ownership, population movements continued, ger eral employment continued to fall, and the Negro's share of urba transit jobs continued to rise as did the proportion of Negr users of transit facilities. Then in 1964 two vitally importan pieces of legislation altered the outlook for transit industr employment.

The first was Title VII of the Civil Rights Act of 1964, whicl went into effect in 1965, barring discrimination in employmen because of race, color, religion, national origin, or sex. The sec ond was the Urban Mass Transportation Act of 1964, aimed a reinvigorating the urban transit industry. Although the latte does not deal directly with employment discrimination, there ar important implications for employment which grew out of thi legislation. Both of these acts of Congress shall be considere along with other factors which caused the 1960's to be significan for urban mass transit.

EMPLOYMENT IN THE 1960's

Since 1970 industrial census data are not yet available, data comparable to our 1950 and 1960 figures do not exist. For many of the industry studies in this series, it has been possible to utilize 1966 data published by the Equal Employment Opportunity Commission to indicate changes which occurred in the first half of the 1960's. Data analysis for any industry which compares census and EEOC data must, of course, be made with extreme care. Whereas census data are based upon individual responses to questionnaires, EEOC data are compiled from employer payroll data submitted to the commission.

In the case of urban transit, however, more serious obstacles exist. Publicly owned concerns, unless government contractors, need not submit data to the EEOC. This eliminates most of the large systems from coverage, which are in turn among the largest employers of Negroes. In addition, EEOC data are compiled on a two digit basis so that the data include besides urban transit facilities (SIC 4111), privately owned charter and school bus concerns, taxi cab companies, terminal and freight facilities, among other activities. It is believed that the percentage of Negroes in these activities not included in our study is considerably less than in urban transit. Finally, the 1966 EEOC data exclude companies with less than 100 employees. Such transit concerns as fall within this category are found in small towns and are likely to have few black employees. Their combined employment total is, however, quite small.

By far the most serious limitation of the 1966 EEOC data is its exclusion of the large publicly owned systems. In 1966, the American Transit Association reported 144,300 employees in the industry (Table 4). The EEOC data, which include a sizeable number of nontransit employees, report only 122,160 for the same year (Table 20). The publicly owned systems excluded are, as noted, among the largest employers of Negroes. What is striking, therefore, about the data in Table 20 is that the proportion of Negroes—15.9 percent—is considerably higher than that recorded by the census for 1960 when 10.9 percent of the employees were found to be black (Table 14). Obviously Negroes continued to increase their share of jobs in the industry despite continued declining employment. It is also clear that if the large public systems were added to the EEOC data, the percentage of Negroes would have been much larger than 15 percent, and probably at least 20 percent in 1966, a figure almost double the 1960 percentage.

The 1970 Large System Sample

In order to supplement the incomplete EEOC data and to examine the racial employment trends in large systems, the Industrial Research Unit made a field survey of nine major systems in mid-1970—Atlanta, Chicago, Detroit, Houston, Los Angeles (Southern California Rapid Transit District), New York, Philadelphia (Southeastern Pennsylvania Transportation Authority), St. Louis (Bi-State Transit System), and Washington. Of these, Atlanta, Houston, and Washington are private and Philadelphia

TABLE 20. Urban Transit and Related Industries (SIC 41)
Employment by Race, Sex, and Occupational Group
United States, 1966

Occupational Group	All Employees			Male			Female		
	Total	Negro	Percent Negro	Total	Negro	Percent Negro	Total	Negro	Percent Negro
Officials and managers	5,753	101	1.8	5,654	101	1.8	99	—	—
Professionals	571	14	2.5	554	14	2.5	17	—	—
Technicians	1,251	44	3.5	1,223	42	3.4	28	2	7.1
Sales workers	7,499	725	9.7	6,131	613	10.0	1,368	112	8.2
Office and clerical	9,867	347	3.5	5,180	176	3.4	4,687	171	3.6
Total white collar	24,941	1,231	4.9	18,742	946	5.0	6,199	285	4.6
Craftsmen	21,630	1,122	5.2	21,518	1,118	5.2	112	4	3.6
Operatives	59,317	11,870	20.0	58,258	11,766	20.2	1,059	104	9.8
Laborers	5,626	2,129	37.8	5,346	1,978	37.0	280	151	53.9
Service workers	10,646	3,013	28.3	10,199	2,859	28.0	447	154	34.5
Total blue collar	97,219	18,134	18.7	95,321	17,721	18.6	1,898	413	21.8
Total	122,160	19,365	15.9	114,063	18,667	16.4	8,097	698	8.6

Source: U.S. Equal Employment Opportunity Commission, Job Patterns for Minorities and Women in Private Industry, 1966, Report No. 1 (Washington: The Commission, 1968), Part II.

Note: See text for discussion of the limitations of these data and their probable underestimation of Negro employment.

was private until 1968. Hence these latter systems are presumably included in the 1966 data, but the others are not. The data for these cities, as set forth in Table 21, show a very different picture than do those in Table 20—a Negro employment proportion of 40.3 percent as compared with 15.9 percent. The reasons seem quite clear.

In the first place, the data in our large system sample are for a period four years later than those in Table 20. All indications, including our field observations and interviews, point to a continued expansion of Negro employment in the industry. New accessions in some cities are overwhelmingly black. Generous retirement provisions, particularly in New York City, have hastened the retirement of whites, and their places have been taken by Negroes or other minorities, particularly Puerto Ricans in

TABLE 21. *Urban Transit Industry Employment by Race and Occupational Group Nine Large Systems, 1970*

Occupational Group	All Employees		
	Total	Negro	Percent Negro
Officials and managers	2,447	240	9.8
Professionals	1,045	65	6.2
Technicians	1,262	114	9.0
Sales workers	2	—	—
Office and clerical	7,811	3,229	41.3
Total white collar	12,567	3,648	29.0
Craftsmen	8,614	1,894	22.0
Operatives	47,988	21,290	44.4
Laborers	3,163	1,847	58.4
Service workers	1,980	1,251	63.2
Total blue collar	61,745	26,282	42.6
Total	74,312	29,930	40.3

Source: Data in author's possession.

Note: Systems are Atlanta, Chicago, Detroit, Houston, Los Angeles (Southern California R.T.D.), New York, Philadelphia (SEPTA), St. Louis (Bi-State), and Washington.

New York. Opportunities in what are considered more desirable industries, as well as violence and crime in the cities have caused whites to look elsewhere for work. The increasing percentage of black riders (based upon population movements) and the same problems of the cities have accentuated the changing employment trend.

Another factor which has increased the proportion of Negroes in the industry is the trend for bus companies in smaller cities to cease operation. Between January 1954 and December 1969, 175 transit concerns in 167 cities went out of business and were not replaced. Of these, 162 served areas with less than 50,000 population.[63] The bulk of the employees in companies in small cities and towns are white. Hence small company abandonment increases the weight of the larger cities in the industry data. With Negroes concentrated in the large city systems, the effect of small bus company abandonment is to raise the proportion of Negroes in the industry.

The transit industry is thus likely to continue to become an industry serving blacks and operated by blacks in major metropolitan areas. In terms of employment, this has already occurred in Detroit where a majority of the transit labor force is Negro. In New York a majority of the workers are Negro or Puerto Rican, with more than 40 percent black. In Houston and Washington, the Negro employment ratio exceeds 40 percent; in Chicago and Los Angeles, it is in excess of 30 percent; and in Philadelphia, about 25 percent. It is likely that for the industry as a whole, approximately 30 percent of the employees were black in 1970.[64]

The 1968-1970 Matched Sample

The increasing trend of black transit employment is illustrated by a comparison of Tables 22 and 23 which combine data for transit systems in six large cities for 1968 and 1970. In these cities, Negro employment rose from 29.9 percent in 1968 to 33.6 in 1970, while total employment was almost stationary, rising by about 270 persons. Of special note is the increase from 11.2 percent to 14.4 percent in the proportion of Negro salaried employ-

63. Data from American Transit Association. Discontinuance of service has continued in 1970, with such towns as Peoria and Joliet, Illinois losing bus lines.

64. Data in author's possession.

TABLE 22. *Urban Transit Industry*
Employment by Race, Sex, and Occupational Group
Six Large Systems, 1968

Occupational Group	All Employees			Male			Female		
	Total	Negro	Percent Negro	Total	Negro	Percent Negro	Total	Negro	Percent Negro
Officials and managers	1,040	70	6.7	1,034	70	6.8	6	—	—
Professionals	222	10	4.5	217	8	3.7	5	2	40.0
Technicians	310	15	4.8	297	13	4.4	13	2	15.4
Sales workers	1	—	—	1	—	—	—	—	—
Office and clerical	3,297	450	13.6	1,758	191	10.9	1,539	259	16.8
Total white collar	4,870	545	11.2	3,307	282	8.5	1,563	263	16.8
Craftsmen	3,514	597	17.0	3,442	595	17.3	72	2	2.8
Operatives	18,394	6,515	35.4	18,375	6,511	35.4	19	4	21.1
Laborers	1,192	574	48.2	1,162	565	48.6	30	9	30.0
Service workers	669	343	51.3	641	325	50.7	28	18	64.3
Total blue collar	23,769	8,029	33.8	23,620	7,996	33.9	149	33	22.1
Total	28,639	8,574	29.9	26,927	8,278	30.7	1,712	296	17.3

Source: Data in author's possession.

Note: Systems are those in Atlanta, Chicago, Detroit, Los Angeles (Southern California), Philadelphia (two large concerns, now part of SEPTA), and Washington, D.C.

TABLE 23. *Urban Transit Industry*
Employment by Race, Sex, and Occupational Group
Six Large Systems, 1970

Occupational Group	All Employees			Male			Female		
	Total	Negro	Percent Negro	Total	Negro	Percent Negro	Total	Negro	Percent Negro
Officials and managers	1,045	92	8.8	1,038	92	8.9	7	—	—
Professionals	219	13	5.9	213	11	5.2	6	2	33.3
Technicians	586	79	13.5	570	75	13.2	16	4	25.0
Sales workers	1	—	—	1	—	—	—	—	—
Office and clerical	3,183	542	17.0	1,667	248	14.9	1,516	294	19.4
Total white collar	5,034	726	14.4	3,489	426	12.2	1,545	300	19.4
Craftsmen	3,279	575	17.5	3,268	575	17.6	11	—	—
Operatives	18,565	7,380	39.8	18,548	7,375	39.8	17	5	29.4
Laborers	1,291	592	45.9	1,267	583	46.0	24	9	37.5
Service workers	742	428	57.7	720	414	57.5	22	14	63.6
Total blue collar	23,877	8,975	37.6	23,803	8,947	37.6	74	28	37.8
Total	28,911	9,701	33.6	27,292	9,373	34.3	1,619	328	20.3

Source: Data in author's possession.

Note: Includes same concerns as Table 22, with two Philadelphia companies merged into SEPTA.

ment. The high proportion of Negroes among the few salaried workers in the industry is a further indication of the locational factors favoring Negro employment.

OCCUPATIONAL DISTRIBUTION

The transit industry is overwhelmingly a blue collar industry. The 1966 EEOC data found about 94 percent of the Negro employees in blue collar jobs as compared with about 80 percent of all workers (Table 20). Nineteen percent of all blue collar jobs were filled by Negroes, but they held only 5 percent of the white collar jobs. The largest single occupational group for Negroes was the operatives classification, also the largest occupational group for the entire industry. Sixty-one percent of all Negro employees worked as operators in 1966. Another 27 percent worked as laborers and service workers.

Again our 1970 large city sample shows a radically different picture (Table 21). Negroes in these cities comprised nearly 30 percent of the white collar employees and 42.6 percent of the blue collar workers as compared with 40.3 percent of all employees. Although overrepresented in the lowest categories and underrepresented in the top white collar and craftsman categories, they held 41.3 percent of the clerical jobs and 44.4 percent of the operative (operators and trainmen) jobs. Moreover, even where underrepresented in organizations in terms of their overall employment, Table 21 shows that Negroes held a large share of the jobs in all categories.

Officials, Managers, Professionals, and Technicians

In 1966, the EEOC sample reported that only 101 of 5,753, or 1.8 percent, of the officials and managers were Negroes (Table 20). Most of these were foremen, traffic supervisors, maintenance supervisors, and other white collar employees. Very few Negroes held middle or upper management jobs.

This lack of Negro officials and managers reflects not only the deficiencies of the sample, but also the fact that in earlier years Negroes were barred from promotion past certain menial levels. Most transit officials and managers had advanced through the ranks, often having begun as operators or trainmen. Negro employees were not allowed to advance. In more recent years, for much of the industry, the lines of promotion have been opened to Negroes. But by 1966, whites in the companies reporting to the

EEOC generally remained in superior positions with regard to seniority. Furthermore, the absolute number of supervisory jobs was small, so the percentage of Negro officials and managers has continued to be small.

Table 21 again shows quite a different picture for the nine-system 1970 sample. Many of these systems have had a long record of employing Negroes so that a much larger percentage had been promoted to supervisory jobs by 1970, particularly as retirements accelerated. Thus Table 21 shows 9.8 percent of the officials and managers to be black. Most of these probably are supervisors, but the industry has some Negroes in higher management jobs as well.

Transit companies employ relatively few professionals and technicians. The 1966 EEOC sample included only 1,822 in these classifications, of whom 58 (3.2 percent) were black. Our 1970 large system sample included 2,307 of whom 179 (7.8 percent) were black. Larger, publicly owned systems employ more such personnel than do smaller ones, and Negroes obviously are being utilized in such capacities. Given the shortage of Negroes so trained and educated, the transit industry in the nine cities covered by our sample has made real progress in these categories.

Sales, Office, and Clerical Workers

Since transit companies deal in a service, it is difficult to distinguish between their "sales workers" and other office personnel. Although the employment data in Table 20 are kept separate as reported by the companies, it is more meaningful to combine the two categories for comparisons with other jobs.[65] Negroes held only 1,072 of the 17,366 sales, office, and clerical jobs in the EEOC data for 1966. This 6.2 percent also reflects the late start in the hiring of Negro clerical workers, and the late start in upgrading Negroes into white collar jobs. Of the total white collar positions in the 1966 data, almost 5 percent were held by Negroes. Although not high, this is a superior representation to many industries for 1966 and reflects the locational advantage of the transit industry relative to the Negro population even without the inclusion of the publicly owned major city facilities.

---

65. There is no uniform method by which transit companies distinguish sales workers from others. Some companies report all as office and clerical personnel. Comparisons of separate categories would be open to question. Few, if any, "salesmen" are found in transit operations.

The 1970 large city sample emphasizes the locational advantages of the transit industry for Negroes and the disinclination of whites to accept employment therein. It is unlikely that a comparable sample in any other major industry would show a Negro clerical employment as high as the 41.3 percent shown in Table 21.

Craftsmen

The 1966 EEOC data showed no significant difference in the percentage Negro employment in white collar jobs and that in jobs requiring skilled craftsmen. Only 1,122 of 21,630, or 5.2 percent of transit's skilled craftsmen were Negro in 1966. The craftsman category was second largest (after operatives) in terms of number of employees. These jobs requiring special skills remained "white" jobs over the years for several reasons. Proportionately Negroes did not possess the necessary skills for these jobs to the same degree as whites because of inferior educational and work-training opportunities. Also, the craftsmen held upgraded jobs from which Negroes who did have the necessary skills were barred until recent years. As a result of the absence of company apprentice programs, transit craftsmen traditionally came from other industries where they had been trained, or were workers with previous experience as laborers who had been upgraded and trained. Since Negro craftsmen have traditionally been denied these opportunities, and upgrading of Negroes came generally after World War II, Negro craftsmen remained scarce in the transit industry in 1966. This was true even in the larger publicly owned systems.

By 1970, however, considerable progress obviously had been made. The shortage of craftsmen forced companies to train and to upgrade Negroes. Other Negroes were placed in these jobs as whites retired. The 22 percent Negro proportion of craftsmen in the nine-system sample for 1970 is an indication that, over a period of years, these jobs too may well be manned by a majority of Negroes. Given the shortage of those trained as craftsmen, however, this will not occur nearly as rapidly as is the case with less skilled jobs.

Other Blue Collar Workers

In other blue collar categories, Negroes held a relatively greater percentage of the jobs in 1966. In the operatives category, one-fifth of the jobs were held by Negroes according to the EEOC data. Roughly one-third of all unskilled laborers and service workers in 1966 were Negro. These figures reflect the increased hiring of Negroes in entry level positions requiring little or no special skills. Almost 19 percent of all blue collar jobs were filled by Negroes according to the 1966 EEOC data.

In contrast, the 1970 nine city sample shows that 44.4 percent of the operatives (platform men, operators, and trainmen) and about 60 percent of the lower rated employees were black. Negro bus drivers and subway trainmen are undoubtedly already a significant force in all large cities and soon may dominate the labor force there. Before examining some of the implications for company and union policies of this development, regional differences will be assessed.

NORTHERN CITIES IN THE 1960's

In the North, as already noted, the general pattern throughout the 1960's found Negroes continuing to increase their share of jobs. Thus, as we have already noted, a majority of the work force in Detroit, more than 40 percent in New York, about one-third in Chicago and Los Angeles, and one-fourth in Philadelphia were black by early 1970. Boston, where the Negro population percentage is small, lagged.

We have found that a feature of Negro employment in these cities has been the substantial gains made by Negroes in white collar jobs, especially office and clerical work. Here, undoubtedly, location has been a major factor, as we already noted. The situations in New York, a leading employer of Negroes, and in Boston, where black employment has not progressed nearly as rapidly, are discussed below.

New York City

The New York City transit system now has a black-Puerto Rican employee majority. Moreover, the black employees are exerting considerable pressure to increase their numbers in policy making positions.

It will be recalled that Negroes were first employed as trainmen and operators on the New York system in the early 1940's. By the end of 1967, one source claimed that there were over 12,000 Negro transit employees in the Metropolitan Transportation Authority (MTA).[66] In the early part of 1968, however, Negro legislators, political leaders, and transit employees began a ". . . campaign to have Negroes appointed to policy-making or other top administrative posts with the new Metropolitan Transportation Authority." [67] The campaign was led by the Associated Transit Guild (ATG) a mainly Negro fraternal organization of 3,000 MTA employees.

Of the 38,000 MTA employees, 12,660 were Negro, according to Authority reports released by the Guild. (This was probably an understatement.) There were 4,700 supervisory positions, however, with fewer than 300 Negroes filling them. Reports by the ATG said that of 116 noncompetitive positions, Negroes had been appointed to four jobs.[68] Two held the rank of superintendent of buses and shops, and one worked as an authority attorney. The other was a labor relations assistant. (Our data show substantial improvement in Negro job holding since 1968.)

In February 1968, the Associated Transit Guild held a career development conference supported by legislators, civic leaders, and Guild members. The resulting proposal included an appeal by Dr. Thomas Matthew, a noted neurosurgeon who headed the National Economic Growth and Reconstruction Organization (N.E.G.R.O.), urging Governor Rockefeller and Dr. William J. Ronan, Transportation Board Chairman, to involve Negroes in planning and policy roles of the transit authority. Dr. Matthew pointed out that the minority communities should be consulted to determine the greatest need for adequate transit facilities and where transit facilities may best serve the public.

A specific goal of ATG is to have a Negro appointed to the Board of Transportation or a general management position. Of the 32 commissioners and general managers, none are Negro. Negroes expressed the feeling that since the transit authority would serve some two and one-half million Negroes, they should

66. On March 1, 1968, the MTA took control of the facilities of the New York Transit Authority, Manhattan and Bronx Surface Transit Operating Authority, Long Island Railroad, Triborough Bridge and Tunnel Authority, and Staten Island Rapid Transit Railway Company. The data were reported by the Associated Transit Guild.

67. Emanuel Perlmutter, "Negroes Seeking Top Transit Jobs," *New York Times*, February 17, 1968.

68. Associated Transit Guild, "Conclusions and Recommendations of Transportation Career Development Conference," mimeo., New York, February 24, 1968.

have a voice in the policy making concentrated in the nine-man board.

Formal recommendations of the ATG conference for "Negro inclusion in New York transportation management" were as follows: [69] (1) community involvement in planning, (2) enforcement of equal employment opportunity clauses, (3) use of Afro-American banks as depositories, (4) positions in the State Department of Transportation, (5) positions on the Bi-State and Tri-State Commissions, (6) positions on the Consolidated Board of the MTA, (7) heads of operating entities, (8) operating sub-department heads, and (9) staff and auxiliary positions.

The push for greater representation in skilled and supervisory jobs in New York characterizes similar attempts in other northern cities. One of the major problems of upgrading for Negroes in some cities is their relatively brief duration in positions from which promotion would normally come. Whites with greater seniority have continued to move up more rapidly even in areas where formal bars against Negro upgrading have been erased. The drive for greater Negro representation in policy making is being directed toward the union leadership as well as toward the transit authorities, as will be noted below.

In New York, the union actually quite accidentally opened the door to Negro promotions on a very large scale. In 1968, the Transport Workers Union won a retirement plan which would bankrupt most companies and may indeed be doing just that to New York City—retirement at age 50 or above after twenty years service at one-half pay based on the individual's last year's wages. The rush to retirement has been rapid particularly among transit employees who had worked considerable overtime in 1969, and thus received higher pensions, but also among all city employees to whom the standard was extended. For new applicants, many of whom are black and Puerto Rican, upgrading has been rapid with Negroes advancing to supervisory and white collar positions as well as to operating jobs.

Indeed, upgrading may have been too rapid for proper training of operators, black or white. New York subways have been plagued by a series of accidents since late 1969, and in some cases

---

69. Associated Transit Guild, "New York Mass Transportation Management and the Afro-American," unpublished report, February 1968.

inadequate training has been blamed.[70] With many of the applicants poorly educated and with mass retirements creating a shortage of trained personnel, greater, not less training is required, and the time and facilities given to such training have been subject to criticism.

Boston

In 1966, the Massachusetts Commission Against Discrimination (MCAD) made a study of employment practices in the transportation industry. According to that report, the percentage Negro employment was lower in bus and transit lines than in other types of transportation (trucking, taxicabs, railroads, and airlines).

Less than 1% of the work force is Negro in an industry where skilled jobs are few, beyond the ability to drive, or in some cases operate a typewriter. Not one Negro in this industry employing more than 2,000 people—outside the one large transit system in Boston—is filling a clerical or white collar job.[71]

According to the report, the Massachusetts Bay Transportation Authority (MBTA) serving the Boston area, employed 6,300 persons, but in 1966 only 96 of them were Negro, 94 of whom were either semiskilled or unskilled. In March 1968, MBTA and MCAD announced a joint plan of affirmative action. The plan involved providing training and facilities for economically disadvantaged persons to aid them in passing the MBTA's "operator-collector" exam. The plan took three directions—inauguration of improved recruitment and employment procedures, community relations programs, and institution of numerous training programs. As of March 1968, MBTA's personnel director reported that during an examination for operators in January 1967, its employment office worked closely with MCAD, the Division of Employment Security, and with community resource agencies to attract applicants with disadvantaged backgrounds. He further stated:

With respect to training of employees, the Authority has inaugurated a 50 percent tuition reimbursement plan for its employees and 19 members of minority groups have already taken advantage of this plan. Out of

---

70. "Four Transit Accidents Cited," *New York Times*, August 2, 1970, p. 50, includes a list of accidents. At least four involved faulty operating procedures.

71. Unpublished report of the Commonwealth of Massachusetts Commission Against Discrimination, June 28, 1966, p. 13.

some 100 employees who have finished courses in Cost Reduction and Methods Improvement held on company time, 27 are members of minority groups. Currently there are 14 members of minority groups enrolled for self-study programmed instruction courses in such areas as Shop Drawings, Practical Electricity, and Supervisory Principles.[72]

In addition, the proposal included plans for apprenticeship or preapprenticeship training. Attempts have been made to help disadvantaged persons pass aptitude tests for craft apprenticeship training. Also meetings have been held with representatives of MCAD, Action for Boston Community Development (ABCD), the Division of Employment Security of the Department of Labor, and Local 264 of International Association of Machinists and Aerospace Workers concerning plans for hiring ten additional apprentices in the fall of 1968.

Expanded efforts in community relations were carried out under the direction of a Negro employee elevated from his former position as an operator. These efforts included tours of MBTA properties for school children from underprivileged areas to develop interest in career planning, and the distribution of employment information to all local offices of the Division of Employment Security and approximately 50 neighborhood associations in the Roxbury, Cambridge, and Dorchester areas.

Negroes and Puerto Ricans, however, continued to experience great difficulty in obtaining jobs with the Massachusetts Bay Transportation Authority and in late 1969 Negro and Spanish-speaking job applicants brought a class suit to prohibit the Authority from continuing to use the General Aptitude Test Battery as a means of ranking applicants for positions. These nine tests measure aptitudes ranging from general intelligence to manual dexterity. They were being given by the Authority every two years. Jobs were then offered in the order in which applicants performed on the tests.

According to the court:

. . . of the total of 1,533 candidates that took the GATB test on September 7, 1968, approximately 300 of these were blacks. Out of that number only 60 achieved a score that put them within the top 1,000 on the rank list. This means that only 20 percent of the black applicants as compared with 75 percent of the white applicants were within the first two-thirds of those to be offered positions.[73]

72. Unpublished report of the Commonwealth of Massachusetts Commission Against Discrimination.

73. *Julius Arrington et al.* v. *Massachusetts Bay Transportation Authority,* U.S. D.C., Mass., Civil Action No. 69-681-G, December 22, 1969.

The court found that the method of selection combined relevant and irrelevant matters and "made a sound preliminary showing" of perpetuating a pattern of discrimination, particularly because of "the relative lack of racial imbalance in the present makeup of the list." [74]

This litigation continues. The Boston area remains one of the few in the North where Negroes have not made substantial progress in obtaining jobs as bus and subway operators.

SOUTHERN AND BORDER CITY PROGRESS

Most border cities desegregated their passenger service during World War II where it existed; southern cities did likewise in the middle and late 1950's. Employment integration, which the wartime FEPC was unable to accomplish in the nation's capital, did not occur to any substantial degree south of the Mason-Dixon Line (or in some cities such as Oakland or states such as New Jersey, north thereof) until after the war. Whereas by 1950, most northern cities of any substantial size had integrated their platform work forces, such integration occurred in border cities between 1950 and 1960, and in cities of the Deep South, in the 1960's.

Thus after the ousting of the southern financier, Louis Wolfson, from control of Capital Transit in 1956, Negroes made steady gains in that system's successor, D.C. Transit, and now comprise about 40 percent of the total work force there. By April 1966, 540 of the Baltimore Transit Company's 1,200 drivers—45 percent—were black,[75] and the proportion today probably exceeds one-half. In the St. Louis area, where a public agency took over transit operations, integration occurred in the principal former private company in 1953, as the following newspaper story stated:

The old Public Service Company, now part of the Bi-State Transit System, put on four Negro bus or street car operators in April 1953. By the end of the year they had 162 Negro drivers. The action opened up a new area of employment for the minority race in St. Louis.[76]

---

74. *Ibid.*

75. "Baltimore Bus Firm Upheld on Firing Klan Driver," *Pittsburgh Courier*, August 13, 1966.

76. *St. Louis Post-Dispatch*, June 13, 1963.

In the South, where passenger desegregation did not come until the 1950's, most of the employment of Negroes as drivers followed the passage of the Civil Rights Act of 1964. Thus, buses were desegregated in Houston in 1954, in Montgomery in 1956, and in Atlanta and New Orleans in 1958. The upgrading of Negroes was not achieved concurrently with bus desegregation. But the desegregation of buses, along with the earlier litigation to integrate public schools, resulted in changing Negroes' as well as whites' attitudes about practices in the South. One of the three demands in the Montgomery bus boycott, it will be recalled, was for Negroes to be hired to drive buses on routes through Negro neighborhoods. Although no Negroes were immediately upgraded or hired, they had focused attention on the problems of segregation in employment as well as segregation in seating, and following the Civil Rights Act of 1964, Negroes were employed as drivers.

There was some evidence of changing southern attitudes toward Negro employment earlier. In New Orleans "token" upgrading began in 1958 along with bus desegregation.[77] A consumer league composed of dissident Negroes threatened a boycott similar to the Montgomery experience. The settlement included an agreement by transit management to upgrade some of the Negro employees. It was not until 1964, however, that Negroes were first hired as operators, and the majority have been hired since 1965. In Houston prior to 1961, Negroes were employed only as service workers (bus cleaners and janitors) and mechanics. They could not be promoted according to the provisions of the bargaining agreement. In 1961 this provision was abolished, paving the way for upgrading. The following year, new equipment was purchased and the need for mechanics fell considerably. As a result, 14 Negro mechanics were promoted to drivers. Currently the company reports that about 45 percent of its drivers are black. This may be the largest proportion of Negroes in these jobs in any large city of the South, and is indeed one of the largest anywhere. In Atlanta, on the other hand, Negroes comprise less than 20 percent of the transit labor force.

It is likely that the Houston situation presages developments in other major southern cities. These cities find themselves with an increasing black population, many are at or close to a Negro majority. The passengers served by transit lines there are over-

---

77. Interview with George Rice, EEOC Regional Office, New Orleans, Louisiana, 1968.

whelmingly black. Expanding southern industrial development offers opportunities to whites more attractive than transit jobs. In southern cities, as in the North, the transit industry is likely to become more and more a black-operated industry serving primarily Negroes.

GENERAL FACTORS AFFECTING NEGRO EMPLOYMENT IN THE 1960's

In addition to regional differences, there are a number of factors which have affected Negro employment in transportation in the 1960's. A principal one, of course, has been the increased proportion of Negroes living in cities and the flight of whites to the suburbs. This in itself has resulted in an ever increasing proportion of Negroes applying for transit jobs. Moreover, the industry and its jobs no longer connote prestigious employment. With greater opportunities elsewhere, whites tend to avoid the industry for employment purposes. This is now, as noted, more true in the North than in the South, but this regional differential seems sure to lessen.

The Crime Problem and the Exact Fare

A major factor which has both reduced transit patronage and its lure for prospective job holders is the high rate of crime aimed at bus drivers, and sometimes passengers as well. Many of these crimes have taken place in slum areas where Negroes predominate, but certainly not only there. As a result, drivers began to refuse to serve certain areas in many cities and a number of strikes demanding better police protection were threatened.[78] Although these crimes were not racially oriented, several transit employers indicated their belief that they have had an especially strong impact in inducing prospective white employees to look elsewhere for employment.[79]

On June 1, 1968, after experiencing more than 500 robberies in one year, including the murder of a driver, the Washington system initiated an exact fare plan; today, nearly every major city and numerous smaller ones have followed suit. Drivers no longer make change; if the passenger does not have the correct

---

78. See, for example, the Victor Riesel syndicated column of December 18, 1967; and the *New York Times*, November 26, 28, and 29, 1967.

79. Interviews, 1968.

fare, he is given script redeemable at a few locations only. Crime against bus drivers has almost disappeared. In addition, the job of the bus driver has eased and the companies have been able to invest funds formerly needed to make change.[80]

In a survey of the exact fare program covering fifteen cities, the *New York Times* reported that, as a result of its installation, "transit and union officials also agreed that recruiting had been improved." [81] The president of the Washington, D. C. local of the Amalgamated Transit Union was quoted as follows:

Before the system went into effect . . . we were losing 20 good operators a month because of the danger. They were quitting and recruiting was almost impossible. Now that's all been reversed. Recruiting is much easier and the company is getting a better caliber of driver.[82]

Nevertheless, urban transit companies do have recruiting problems, and are likely to have more if the industry is expanded by an injection of government funds, as will be discussed below. A factor in this recruiting problem is the fear of many persons, black or white, to remain "downtown" at night. This fear reduces transit travel after evening rush hours, which causes transit curtailment, and the downward spiral continues. Many major facilities operate only skeleton crews and fleets at night—and still have difficulty obtaining personnel to handle them or finding riders to serve.

Manpower Policy Formulation

An interesting fact about the rise of Negro employment in transit operations is that it has occurred *without* any clear-cut, commonly accepted method of formulating manpower policy among the companies of the transit industry. While some transit firms make no attempt to project their future manpower needs, others attempt to make projections. However, these projections only range from seasonal predictions up to one year. Various departments are involved in satisfying manpower requirements. In most of the companies which were contacted, this responsibility rests with the personnel department with considerable direction from scheduling and planning departments. For one pub-

---

80. "Exact Fares Cut Robbery in Buses," *New York Times*, August 31, 1969, pp. 1, 45.

81. *Ibid.*, p. 45.

82. *Ibid.*

licly owned company the question was not so much "how many and what kind of employees will be needed?" but rather "will the state senate pass a tax bill necessary to support desired expansion?" [83] This seems to indicate for that particular firm that projections of future manpower needs would be made only in the case of expansion and not for the existing operation.

Formal manpower planning is not a common practice among urban transit companies. Among those companies contacted, there were no formal programs of manpower planning, and only two companies were giving serious thought to implementing such.

In light of the lack of formal programs to fill manpower needs, it is not surprising to find that most transit companies have only informal nondiscrimination programs. First, for public firms, the statements of nondiscrimination which have been made exist in the form of "catch-all" phrases included in the charter as drawn up by the legislature or the municipal government. Private companies have also made statements against discrimination in employment and upgrading. In most cases, however, these statements are superficial in that there is no formal communication of the policy from management to supervisors and foremen, and thus no formal methods for implementation of the policy at the lower levels or follow up to ascertain whether policies are being followed.[84]

Recruitment Policies

The methods by which companies attract and hire new personnel have a direct effect on the opportunities for Negroes to be included in the work force on an equal basis. Although employment has generally been declining for the transit industry as a whole, recruitment of new personnel has remained a high priority function of management. The great majority of transit jobs are entry level jobs—the operators are the most numerous. Furthermore, there is a relatively high turnover of operators, especially during the first months of employment when low seniority affords them little or no priority in picking runs.

---

83. Interview with the Director of Industrial Relations, July 3, 1968.

84. See Richard L. Rowan's discussion of company policy declarations in Herbert R. Northrup, Richard L. Rowan, *et al.*, *Negro Employment in Basic Industry*, Studies of Negro Employment, Vol. I (Philadelphia: Industrial Research Unit, Wharton School of Finance and Commerce, University of Pennsylvania, 1970), Part Four, pp. 320-322.

The source of new employees is an important indicator of recruitment policy. The list of different sources used by firms which were contacted includes walk-ins, employee referrals, state employment agencies, the National Alliance of Businessmen, civil service, and advertisements on radio and television and in newspapers, union magazines, and the buses and trains themselves. Those who walk in off the street and those referred by employees of the company or a state employment agency make up the majority of applicants. On the surface it may not seem to indicate any discrimination for a company to hire walk-ins and those referred to job opportunities by their friends. But, according to Marshall, Negroes ". . . rarely learn about jobs with few or no Negroes in them, and they apply for the kinds of jobs they know they can get. Since aspirations are conditioned by one's associates, few Negroes are motivated to apply for jobs from which they have been excluded." [85] As long as Negroes were excluded from transit jobs, it was not surprising that few Negroes were applying for jobs off the street or being referred by white workers. Nor is it surprising that even when some transit companies began to open their doors to Negroes, few Negroes responded. It was not because they did not want and need the jobs that they failed to apply, but probably because they were not aware that the job opportunities existed. Today, however, there are few areas where Negroes have any doubts that jobs exist. Bus drivers are too visible.

The experience in Boston serves as an example. A transit official stated, "We insist that we always had an open door, but no blacks came in." [86] Prior to 1967, most new employees were walk-ins or company referrals. In 1967 the Massachusetts Commission Against Discrimination began acquainting Negroes with the open competitive examinations given under civil service in Boston. Advertising the times and places of the examinations resulted in an increase in the number of Negro applicants, and subsequently the number of Negro employees, but as we have indicated, testing procedures still reduced those employed.

The reliance on state employment commissions or agencies may also reduce the probability that Negroes will be referred to transit companies if Negroes are not inclined (for whatever reason)

---

85. Ray Marshall, *The Negro Worker* (New York: Random House, 1967), p. 105.

86. Interview with the Director of Personnel, July 11, 1968.

to become acquainted with the employment service, or if that service is not inclined to be especially cognizant of its affirmative action duties. In Houston, a transit company official revealed that the Texas Employment Commission is the source of most new employees. There has been some effort to persuade the company to expand the recruitment efforts to areas of high Negro density. The official's response in regard to that idea was, "I don't think the responsibility should be ours to seek out these new sources." [87] This view was reflected in the statements of others who would refuse to accept the responsibility for the discrimination which might exist solely as a result of the particular source of applicants. The fact that Houston has so large a percentage of Negroes—45 percent—indicates little need for change, but elsewhere the situation may be different.

There have been a few changes in recruiting policy during the last several years. In addition to Boston, a few cities have initiated recruiting techniques which are more likely to give Negroes an equal opportunity at least to bid for jobs. Some companies did report connections with the National Alliance of Businessmen, other national organizations, and local human rights groups with the expressed purpose of getting Negro referrals. Some of the changes may or may not be effective from the Negro's viewpoint. In Dallas, for instance, a traveling office-bus is currently used to recruit personnel from outlying towns such as Terrell, Denton, Corsicana, Sherman, and Greenville. Officials of that company said that limited positions were available and only "qualified" men would be sought.[88] The office-bus is driven to one of these communities, parked in a downtown area, and used to interview prospective employees. Although this is not a direct attempt at affirmative action, it could be useful as such if it draws the attention of Negroes as well as whites.

Job Qualifications and Affirmative Action

Of equal importance is the policy governing which applicants (from whatever source) will actually be hired. The educational requirement in particular seems to be a primary factor in the ability of Negroes to obtain jobs. Traditionally, high school or equivalent education has been required for most entry level jobs

87. Interview, July 1968.

88. *Passenger Transport*, January 17, 1969.

among nearly all transit companies. Yet it is difficult to understand why such an educational requirement is pertinent. Recently, however, many companies, unable to attract high school
graduates, have relaxed this requirement and begun to accept for
employment those with less than a high school diploma. As a substitute for the twelve-year educational requirement, many of the
companies require that the prospective employee pass "simple
math tests" and other tests of I.Q. or mechanical aptitude. Furthermore, several companies indicated that passing scores on these
examinations have been lowered recently, not necessarily in order
to help the Negro, but because of the general shortage of labor.
Lower educational requirements should aid Negroes generally
because their median level of education is still below that of
whites. On the other hand, there is reason to believe that competitive examinations and testing can be detrimental to them, as
the Boston experience indicates.

Some companies have other requirements. The following "basic
requirements of applicants for position of Motor Coach operators" is a sample:

Minimum age of 23

Height: 5'5" no more than 6'4"

High school graduate or equivalent

United States citizen

Must possess a valid driver's license with no excessive violations and no drunk driving charges

Must not have been convicted of a felony (applicants are
fingerprinted)

Eyes cannot be less than 20/40 without glasses, and must be
correctible to 20/20

Must pass math tests

Must produce form DD 214, and/or valid draft classification
card

Previous employment references must be acceptable

Must pass physical examination

Even though the foregoing list is not universal, it is representative of the basic requirements throughout the industry.
Some companies using these criteria have reported that as many
as eight out of nine applicants fail to qualify, but in other areas

the ratio is not so high. Although many companies have had to relax their requirements to fill available jobs, this has usually stemmed from a shortage of labor rather than attempts at affirmative action.

Evidence of direct action to help the unemployed can be found among transit companies such as the Boston MBTA's work with the Massachusetts Commission Against Discrimination to attract qualified Negro employees. In San Francisco, close contact is maintained with community and human development centers such as Young Men for Achievement in Hunter Point and Bay View Youth for Service. These centers, as well as economic opportunity offices, screen applicants and make referrals.[89] In St. Louis a group called Work Opportunities Unlimited was contracted to furnish referrals to Bi-State Transit. It is likely that the industry will move strongly toward further direct action as a result of the injection of federal funds into urban transit. As qualifications are lowered, however, training capacity must be increased—and few companies have this capability. Moreover, inadequate training can lead to serious problems, as in New York City.

Apprenticeship, Upgrading, and Training Programs

The fact that Negroes are hired for entry level jobs does not dismiss the subject of job discrimination, since there have long been "Negro jobs"—jobs which were largely filled by Negroes and from which Negroes could not move. This raises the question concerning company policy toward the advancement of its employees.

Formal apprenticeship programs are almost nonexistent in the urban transit industry. Only one of the transit companies interviewed, Chicago Transit Authority, has an apprenticeship training program which is registered by the Bureau of Apprenticeship Training. Training programs which do exist for operators and mechanics generally consist of on-the-job training both in the classroom and out in the shop or on a bus or train. The length of training varies with different companies and for different jobs, but usually lasts from four to eight weeks.

Seniority rules influence upgrading procedures significantly in most transit firms, except those few where the merit system under civil service determines promotions. Where seniority is a primary factor, seniority systems seem to be similar among com-

---

89. Interview with Employment Contract Compliance Officer, July 8, 1968.

panies in the industry. Separate seniority lists for Negroes and whites which used to exist in southern cities have now been combined.

An employee gains system seniority and departmental seniority. Departmental seniority is of primary importance to upgrading and promotion procedures as well as in picking runs. There are commonly regular departmental picks held quarterly and generally employees are allowed one system pick per year. Interdepartmental transfers are possible, but the employee loses his seniority in the department from which he transfers, and begins anew to establish seniority in the new department.

Separate departments tend to contain a full range of jobs into which an employee could move, the only segregation being between operating and nonoperating employees. Since an employee can move from low rated jobs to better jobs within his department, there is no reason to shift from one department to another at the cost of losing departmental seniority. Some departments contain operating employees and others contain nonoperators, but each has a full range of low, middle, and high rated jobs.

Since the disappearance of segregated seniority rosters, seniority rules have not generally worked against upgrading for Negro employees. Only in the sense that the majority of Negro employees have been hired in recent years, giving them less seniority generally, does the seniority system act as an overt barrier to their job advancement.

Northrup states that generally a broad seniority district works to the advantage of the Negro employee in upgrading, but to his disadvantage in times when employment is falling.[90] In times of decreasing employment, bumping has indeed made seniority a significant influence on the relative position of the Negro in the transit industry. Negroes tend to be vulnerable to bumping since they are newly hired relative to other employees, and since they are disproportionately concentrated in lower jobs. Furthermore, since the transit industry has experienced declining employment while most other industries have prospered, Negroes have not gained seniority as quickly as they otherwise might have. (This has not been the case in New York, where a sudden wave of retirement has occurred.) Thus, advancement requiring seniority

---

90. Herbert R. Northrup, Richard L. Rowan, *et al.*, *Negro Employment in Basic Industry, op. cit.*, Part Three, pp. 183-184.

has come more slowly than it might have if the transit industry had been expanding.

Although seniority systems do not overtly bar Negroes from upper level jobs, they do not guarantee that Negroes will be treated fairly. Seniority and merit systems alike are implemented by supervisors and foremen who may or may not execute anti-discriminatory policy. Merit systems under civil service, a boon to Negro employment especially in the early years, do not absolutely guarantee fairness in upgrading. Promotions are made and vacancies filled through open competitive testing, but "fill-ins"—temporary replacements—are chosen by supervisors. When jobs become permanently vacant, and examinations are given to determine a replacement, those who have already performed the duties of the job have a definite advantage over those who have not. This was brought to light by a Negro who had worked his way up from a bus operator into an office position with one of the major transit companies. In the presence of other company officials he stated that although a policy of nondiscrimination was formally adopted in 1942, it was not until recent years (within the last decade) that this policy was actually implemented by supervisors. It was his opinion, however, that at present the Negro has chances not only for employment, but also for advancement within that same company.[91]

THE UNION IMPACT

In relative terms, unions have had only minor influence over racial employment policies in urban transportation. There are no union hiring halls, and the unions which have been most powerful in the industry have not flagrantly barred Negroes. Although segregated local unions existed in the South until recently, it is not evident that the unions prevented companies from hiring Negroes when the companies might have otherwise.

This is not to deny the racial exclusion practices of some transit unions which have been historically significant. Union conflict obviously took on racial overtones in the Philadelphia strike (see Chapter III). Some unions in the industry, although not those with the largest memberships, quite obviously barred Negroes from membership in their bylaws. The influence of many transportation unions, and especially the railroad brotherhoods, though not pervasive, has been felt in the urban transit

---

91. Interview, 1968.

industry. In the large cities, where rapid rail systems have operated for several years, unions such as the Brotherhood of Railroad Trainmen (BRT) and the Brotherhood of Locomotive Engineers (BLE) organized many of the trainmen, and pursued the
discriminatory policies which they followed on the railroads. Both
these unions excluded Negroes by constitutional provision until
quite recently.

As already noted, the two leading unions representing urban
transit workers are the Transport Workers Union of America
(TWU), and the Amalgamated Transit Union (ATU), both affiliated with the AFL-CIO. The Transport Workers Union, affiliated with the CIO before the merger, shared in the generally
good image the CIO had in the Negro community. In 1950 the
Eleventh Constitutional Convention of the CIO resolved "that
each CIO affiliate create a Civil Rights Committee, or Department
of Fair Practices within its respective organization." [92] The
Transport Workers Union was one of several bodies which did
so. [93]

The "fair practices" machinery has not always guaranteed fair
practices. Many local unions in the South remained segregated
until the early 1960's. In Atlanta, Amalgamated Transit Union
Local No. 732 had no Negro members until 1962. A separate
laborers division representing the Negro employees had separate
offices and separate meetings. Similar conditions existed in Houston, where operators were organized by Transport Workers
Union. Negroes were not upgraded into platform jobs until
1961, so the local naturally had no Negro members prior to that
date.

Although we have cited some differences in the policies of the
two primary unions, a further distinction should be made. The
AFL's Amalgamated union, whose locals were distributed throughout the country, was established well ahead of TWU so that most of
the bus and trolley operators who belonged to any union before
1933 were members of the Amalgamated. Because of the wide
dispersion of its locals, and because collective bargaining is on
a local basis, the national union officials did not exercise much
control over the actions of local unions regarding discrimination.
Many Amalgamated locals evidently practiced equal treatment of
Negroes, but in all of those cases save one which were brought

92. Marshall, *op. cit.*, p. 28.

93. *Ibid.*

before FEPC hearings during World War II charging a union with discrimination, locals of the Amalgamated were the offenders. The exception was the Philadelphia independent, now defunct.

On the other hand, the national organization of TWU, the CIO union, seemed to take a more aggressive stand. It is not perfectly clear, however, that the policies of the TWU were vastly different from those of the Amalgamated. The real difference may be in the fact that a great majority of TWU membership was among the large cities in the East, where Negroes were more readily accepted. The existence of segregated locals in Houston is evidence that even with a more aggressive national policy, TWU was not without its local inconsistencies.

Some transit properties remained unorganized. In New Orleans, for example, collective bargaining associations have been formed to speak for labor rights and there is only token Negro membership at best.[94] Somewhat different is the situation in San Francisco, where the Transport Workers Union represents employees, but not under a union contract.

Since the segregated locals in the South have largely disappeared, union discrimination in the urban transit industry has become less of a problem. This is not to say, however, that unions are guiltless in all current practices. The recent experiences in New York and Chicago illustrate how changes in the work force can affect internal union affairs, and conversely, how union rules may lag behind the needs of a changed work force.

We noted earlier in this chapter that Negro groups in New York were attempting to pressure the transit authorities to employ a larger number of Negroes in top jobs. In addition, in 1969 Negro transit workers there were challenging their white union leaders to end discrimination and "invigorate the complacent labor bureaucracy."[95] Under the leadership of Joseph Carnegie, a black subway conductor, a Negro caucus collected signatures on petitions for a representation election among employees of the transit agency. Hoping to take representation rights from the Transport Workers Union, the group needed 9,000 signatures to force a new representation election. Although they were unable to obtain a new election, their movement remains active as the "Transit Workers Union."

---

94. Field data, New Orleans, June 1968.

95. Damon Stetson, "Negro Members Are Challenging Union Leaders," *New York Times*, June 29, 1969.

Mr. Carnegie stated that rank and file Negro employees feel that the TWU has failed them. He claims that the TWU election procedures "deprived workers of a real voice in the operation of the union." [96] He also charges that the union allowed the pay of transit workers to fall below that for comparable work in the city, a questionable charge indeed. His third objection is that the union has neglected to stress safety measures on the subways. This claim has gained force as accidents have occurred.

Actually, what appears to have occurred in the New York transit industry is similar to that which is common elsewhere. The ethnic composition of the labor force has changed, but that of the union leadership has not. The New York local of the TWU continues to be Irish led and dominated, but the Irish are no longer entering the system in large numbers. Indeed, because the TWU has won pensions which encourage retirement, there has been a mass exodus of Irish and other European ethnic groups in recent years. Yet a picture of New York Local 100's strike committee on December 31, 1969, showed few blacks in positions of authority.[97] (In fact, 12 of the 32 executive board members of Local 100 are black.) If the racial composition of the New York subways continues to change, a black-dominated union could take over. More likely, however, Negro officers will take over Local 100 because the rank and file are not likely to change to a new union for fear of losing very advantageous benefits.

The TWU's rival, the Amalgamated Transit Union, is facing perhaps even stronger pressure from the black members of its Chicago local. That local has remained almost exclusively in the hands of whites, although Negroes comprise nearly one-half of the union's 8,500 working members. The ruling body, a 28-man executive board, had only four Negro members until 1968, when disgruntled Negro employees formed a group called the Concerned Transit Workers (CTW). The CTW attacked a union rule which allows retired members to vote in elections.[98] Since the retired members are almost 100 percent white, this provision has severely restricted the voice of Negroes in union affairs. When the voting rule issue was not allowed discussion at union meetings, the CTW

---

96. *Ibid.* See also the Victor Riesel column dispatched November 20, 1969.

97. Damon Stetson, "Negotiators Race Against Deadline in Transit Talks," *New York Times,* December 31, 1969, p. 12.

98. This is apparently a nonracial technique aimed at keeping incumbents in office. For example, the United Mine Workers has a similar rule.

resorted to two wildcat strikes in attempts "to bring pressure on the union" (and on management for improvements in working conditions).[99] After the second strike, one which reduced bus transportation during the Democratic Convention, the courts ordered the strikers back to work, and Chicago Transit Authority fired over 100 of the dissident drivers.

The Concerned Transit Workers, according to Wayman Benson, one of the leaders who had been fired, ". . . had run into a stone wall." [100] They decided to campaign for support to form an independent union. Considerable progress was made toward that end in the form of signatures of workers (3,000, according to CTW count) who agreed to name CTW as their bargaining agent in the event of an election victory over ATU. Subsequently, the campaign for an independent union suffered from legal problems. The National Labor Relations Board does not have jurisdiction over public employees, and Illinois has no state agency or law to resolve public employee representation questions. Consequently, any election would have to be by consent of the Chicago Transit Authority which is apparently satisfied with existing arrangements.

The Chicago experience is evidence that unrest among Negro members exists over their representation in union governing positions. At least some Negro members appear to believe that the *status quo ante* is being unfairly maintained. At the time of the strikes in Chicago in 1968 the following statement was presented by the Concerned Transit Workers: "The men with us today have reached their present posture because of labor's steadfast refusal to represent black workers and its repressive opposition to internal union democracy." [101]

A study of utility industries (which included urban transit) in New Jersey conducted in 1965 reported that "There are no Negro officers or members of negotiating committees in any utility union in the state." [102] Moreover, except for a water utility, all reports indicated that "the union had 'little or no effect' on encouraging Negro employment." [103] It is this apparent lack of Negro repre-

---

99. *Wall Street Journal*, November 29, 1968.

100. *Ibid.*

101. *Cincinnati Enquirer*, October 10, 1968.

102. Myron J. Levin, *Survey of Equal Employment Opportunities in New Jersey Investor-Owned Public Utilities* (Trenton: Division of Civil Rights, Department of Law and Public Safety, 1966), p. 50.

103. *Ibid.*

sentation in union leadership ranks and lack of positive interest of union officials in Negro job problems which adds to the gulf between the white union leadership and the black rank and file. It is possible that unions not overtly opposed to black membership may continue to be a factor in racial discrimination. As the composition of a work force changes, union rules originally instituted for purposes completely apart from racial matters may gradually take on racial implications. If labor, as well as management, is to represent the Negro community fairly, those rules, as well as policies purposely biased, should be changed and Negro representation included in the local ruling hierarchy.

In another sense, union policies have a profound effect on racial employment policies of the industry, and this effect may well have grown with increased government ownership. The fact that the urban transit industry offers a service that cannot be warehoused has long put it at a disadvantage in union negotiations. Strike resistance is weak when losses cannot be recouped. Like the railroad industry, the urban transit industry has seen unions win high wages and extensive benefits despite economic ill-health. Governmental operation of the transit industry may well weaken what opposition exists to further large gains.[104] Certainly, the experience of government-owned transit systems offers no indication of a slackening of union gains.

High wages and expensive benefits mean a better income for those employed. They also mean higher costs. Offsetting costs by fare increases reduces ridership appeal and subsequently employment. This is the classic syndrome of the industry. To the extent that union power accelerates costs and reduces patronage and employment, it means fewer jobs in the industry for Negroes or whites.

GOVERNMENT IMPACT

Federal and state legislation has been influential in changing employment patterns for Negroes in the transit industry. Beginning with the impact of the merit system in cities like Detroit and New York, going on to the already described activities of President Franklin D. Roosevelt's Committee on Fair Employment Practice, the transit industry's racial policies were liberalized

---

104. The Urban Mass Transportation Administration, Department of Transportation, is funding an Industrial Research Unit study which examines the impact of government ownership on mass transportation collective bargaining systems and resultant settlements.

prior to World War II and thereafter to a large extent by government policies. Indeed, as was made clear, the visibility of urban transit made it a special target for FEPC action during World War II, and that same visibility and political vulnerability have made municipal and state owned systems move toward more equalitarian policies.

In the years between World War II and the passage of the Civil Rights Act of 1964, federal executive orders did not especially affect the transit industry since few concerns in the industry are government contractors. Major systems, however, have been subjected both to state laws against discrimination and to special requirements included in the laws that permitted them to purchase previously private systems, as well as to state civil service regulations. The actions of the Massachusetts Commission Against Discrimination in regard to the Massachusetts Bay Transportation Authority provide a good example of positive state action.

Federal action again became significant in the mid-1960's, first with the passage of the Civil Rights Act of 1964, which outlawed both employment and accommodation discrimination, and with the passage during the same year of the Urban Mass Transportation Act. Although publicly owned transit systems are excluded from coverage under Title VII of the Civil Rights Act of 1964, they come within the purview of the Urban Mass Transportation Act, undoubtedly the most significant legislation ever enacted in behalf of the transit industry and its employees.

Urban Mass Transportation Act of 1964

The decline of the urban transit industry has, as noted, resulted in the demise of more than 170 companies in the last fifteen years. In addition, falling revenues and higher costs have forced many companies to postpone expansion of their facilities, to reduce service, and in many cases, to be unable to replace obsolete capital equipment for lack of funds. One transit official stated that a large company operating profitably usually was offering poor service. The injection of federal monies into transit has allowed companies to plan expansion of existing facilities and thus gives the promise of providing better service. Even though grants are not made to pay labor costs or other operating costs, the capital expansion now possible has direct implications for employment in the industry.

Under the Urban Mass Transportation Act, the Department of Housing and Urban Development (HUD) was authorized to provide grants to public agencies for purchase of vehicles and equipment, construction, and improvement of facilities. A reorganization in 1968 transferred the capital grant program to the Urban Mass Transportation Administration of the U.S. Department of Transportation (DOT).

In addition to the capital grants program, the 1964 act as amended in 1968 provides for urban mass transportation demonstrations, managerial training, university research and training, and technical studies. Thus federal grants are available for studies as to how to improve transit service in an urban area; for the training of personnel employed in managerial, technical, and professional positions; for research in transit methods; and for testing and demonstrating new ideas and methods for improving mass transportation methods and systems.

Table 24 shows the grants approved by the Urban Mass Transportation Administration as of March 31, 1970. Capital grants have assisted communities to purchase failing concerns, to buy busses for private or public concerns, to help to build new systems such as the Bay Area Rapid Transit in the San Francisco area and the Cleveland airport transit project, and to add

TABLE 24. *Urban Transit Industry*
Grants by Urban Mass Transportation Administration
March 31, 1970

Type of Grant	Number of Grants Approved	Estimated Federal Cost When Completed
Capital equipment purchases	130	$610,354,201
Demonstration	99	64,980,497
Research and development	49	9,398,480
University research and training	21	1,677,000
Technical studies	88	13,510,350
Managerial training	54	186,262

Source: Urban Mass Transportation Administration, Department of Transportation.

great varieties of equipment to large and small systems. Demonstration grants permit, among other things, the testing of new equipment and procedures including fare collection devices, smog control busses, test marketing techniques, computer usage, and the operation of bus routes designed to aid the disadvantaged in obtaining transportation to work. Research contracts are designed to develop new methods, new materials, new concepts, new products, and new usage of existing technology. University programs aim to increase the number of qualified professionals and others who might aid a revived industry.

The 1964 legislation, clearly a boon to urban transit, also has important implications for Negro employment in the industry. First, the federal aid increases the potential of the transit industry as an employer. After the passage of the 1964 act, employment in transit increased for the first time since the 1940's, although it has subsequently declined. With the expansion of facilities comes additional jobs. Companies which now receive grants for new equipment are better able to hire the necessary manpower to operate it. Also important is the fact that the federal grants are made only to public agencies, or to private companies participating through contractual arrangements with a public agency, since it has been shown that throughout the industry public ownership has aided the Negro in getting equal opportunities for employment. Federal aid to transit systems which have been least discriminatory improves the Negro's chances to gain a proportional share of any additional jobs which might be created. DOT's regulations implementing Title VII of the Civil Rights Act of 1964 provide that

. . . no person in the United States shall on the ground of race, color, or national origin be excluded from participation in, be denied the benefits of, or be subjected to discrimination under any program or activity receiving Federal financial assistance.[105]

Furthermore, a provision for bidding requires that affirmative steps to increase minority representation in employment must be included in all contracts. Thus, federal aid to transit is likely both to offset somewhat the job decline in the industry and to improve the Negro's chances for equal treatment in bidding for the jobs.

---

105. "Capital Grants for Urban Mass Transportation," U.S. Department of Transportation, Urban Mass Transportation Administration, July 1968, p. 7.

Urban Transportation—Its New Role

The significance of the federal grants to transit extends to Negroes outside the industry as well. Part of the rationale for federal aid to urban transit stems from its role in transporting workers to and from their jobs. New emphasis has been attached to urban transit systems as one possible solution to the problem of urban unemployment. As already noted, several cities have begun to study methods for improving transit service to low-income areas, or have been given grants to experiment with such service. In Seattle, 700 to 1,000 central-city youths in the Summer Youth Employment Program were transported to job opportunities in suburbs not previously served by existing transit facilities. Low-income, unemployed persons were hired and trained as drivers for the service. After completing their training, they were to be qualified for positions with the Seattle Transit System which has had an increasing recruitment problem.[106]

Programs to transport low-income workers to and from their jobs have been implemented in such cities as Atlanta, Boston, Los Angeles, Baltimore, St. Louis, Buffalo, and Flint, Michigan with varying degrees of success. In Flint, Michigan, for example, transit service which went so far as to pick up riders at their doors has failed to attract even a modest customer following.[107] Likewise, in suburban Long Island, New York, a "member's" service folded after two years because it could not attract enough passengers away from private cars.[108] On the other hand, Atlanta is apparently operating a successful shuttle bus from a slum area to job locations in cooperation with the Model Cities Program.[109] Other attempts, such as in the Harlem area of New York, the Watts area of Los Angeles, and in Baltimore have yet to attract a solid customer following despite heavy subsidy.[110]

---

106. *Passenger Transport,* August 2, 1968.

107. Raul Ramirez, "Luxury Transit Service," *Wall Street Journal,* September 4, 1969. One may well question whether Flint was a wise choice to pick for a bus subsidy in view of its complete domination by the automobile industry and the car psychology.

108. Roy R. Silver, "Minibus Project on Long Island is Failure," *New York Times,* January 4, 1970.

109. *New York Times,* December 15, 1969.

110. For summaries of these programs, see John Herbers, "Post-Riot Bus Projects," *New York Times,* March 29, 1970, and *Wall Street Journal,* May 26, 1970.

Yet transit needs are substantial for the low-income population, among whom Negroes are disproportionately represented. Inadequate service compounds the problem of domestics, low-wage service employees and those with marginal incomes or jobs, and those trying to obtain jobs.[111] Certainly, urban transit is needed both to serve the transportation needs and to provide jobs in so doing.

The political scale is still weighted in favor of highways. The government finances 90 percent of interstate highway construction, but only two-thirds of the cost of transit equipment. The Federal Highway Administration employs 5,000; the Urban Mass Transportation Administration, 55.[112] Behind the former are the well-endowed construction unions, the Teamsters, the country's largest union, the construction industry, and construction equipment manufacturers. No such potent group leads mass transit.

Nevertheless, the new, expanded interest in improving mass transportation is beginning to bear fruit. Massive injections of government money are needed to revive the industry and there are signs that increasing amounts will become available. Whether the funds will be adequate remains to be seen; at least federal spending promises to be many times greater in the 1970's than in the previous decade. If whites continue to avoid seeking work in transit or dwellings in the cities, and if transit companies in smaller communities, where whites are employed, continue to cease operations, Negroes are likely to obtain an ever increasing share of the job opportunities whether the industry declines or revives.

---

111. See, e.g., the story on the bus service and strike in Atlantic City, New Jersey, *New York Times*, August 24, 1969; or the story in *id.*, May 27, 1970, entitled "Newark: Ghosttown after 7."

112. Albert R. Karr, "Mass Transit: A Little Late Arriving," *Wall Street Journal*, July 24, 1970.

CHAPTER VI

Policy Determinants and the Future

Negro employees have played a major role in the urban transit industry for several years. Having moved first into the large proportion of unskilled and semiskilled jobs, Negroes are now making progress toward a larger share of skilled and white collar transit jobs.

We have noted that many factors have influenced the policies toward Negro workers in urban transit. It will be useful to review them here and then conclude with some brief comments on what the future may bring.

LABOR DEMAND AND THE CHARACTER OF THE WORK

As in most industries, Negroes made very significant gains in the transit industry during the labor shortages of World War II. In later years they made significant progress in spite of falling demand for labor—an almost unique situation which can be understood only by examining such factors as the image of the industry, industrial location, the availability of other jobs for whites, and government action.

The character of the work encouraged Negroes to apply for jobs in urban transit. Most—indeed the overwhelming number—of the jobs require at best only modest training although responsibility is often great. Yet the jobs are well paid. At the same time, the declining demand for transit encouraged whites to look elsewhere for jobs so that even though declining demand may have slowed progress for Negroes, it apparently discouraged whites even more. This left a greater share of the smaller job pool to blacks. The proportion of Negroes has increased also because of the trend for transit companies in smaller communities to go out of business, but for companies in larger communities to be purchased and operated by public bodies. With Negroes concentrated in the large urban centers, these trends tend to enhance the black proportion in the industry.

INDUSTRIAL LOCATION

The transit companies, almost by definition, are urban oriented and located. As Negroes flocked into the cities and whites into the suburbs, the locational factor tended to increase the propensity of Negroes to enter the industry and whites to look elsewhere. Again, only the companies in larger cities seem likely to survive.

Problems of violence and disorder undoubtedly accelerated this trend. In many areas of our cities, operating a bus or a train had become "hazardous duty." The fares collected and carried on urban buses invited robbery and mugging, especially in isolated sections of the cities at night. The severity of the problem has been considerably lessened especially by the use of "exact fare" plans, and by two-way radios and increased police protection. Yet it is evident that all this has made driving a bus less attractive. It is not unlikely that these events have greatly decreased white interest in transit employment, and this will probably continue unless a severe general job decline alters the situation.

MANAGERIAL POLICY

The transit industry does not appear to have produced the type of dynamic management which one associates with novel affirmative action programs. Indeed, given years of declining fortunes, one would not except that. The industry has generally allowed government to exert leadership and has been content to meet government requirements. Of course, there have been exceptions. Nevertheless, managerial policy has neither been particularly forward looking nor obstructive. The industry has a large percentage of Negro employees and may be expected to expand that percentage and to improve its occupational distribution, given the labor market and working environment in large urban centers. Spurred by government grants and policies relating thereto, as well as by existing availability of black, in contrast to white labor, management may well take a more direct and affirmative role in the future. Training needs of disadvantaged persons will undoubtedly also require more advanced personnel policies.

UNION POLICY

Union policy has been mostly localized and passive. Obstruction and discrimination by locals were frequent in the pre-World War II period. The Amalgamated Transit Union leaves authority to locals to a large extent. Although nondiscriminatory in principle, it could not control local actions; its officers always supported an open door for blacks without penalizing locals which did not comply.

The Transport Workers Union has always given heavy attention to its policies of nondiscrimination, but it too did not interfere with local union discrimination. Today both ATU and TWU are faced with rising discontent among black members who want a greater share of union offices and more black representation at the top. Like many union officials long in power, the officers of these unions face a strident rank and file, and in this case, a generation gap magnified by the racial issue. Finally, union policy undoubtedly will continue to push for higher wages and benefits at the expense of jobs, a fact which government aid has not fully offset to this date.

GOVERNMENT POLICY AND THE FUTURE

With government directly or indirectly in control of most key transit systems, government policy will continue to be, as it has in the past, a key, if not *the* key, determinant of racial policy. Civil service rules, state laws, federal grant regulations, and federal laws all will require continued and affirmative employment of minorities. This fact will insure a high proportion of Negro employment, especially in conjunction with the industrial location factor and the tendency of jobs in this industry to be ever more concentrated in the large metropolitan areas.

Moreover the changes which are occurring in the industry promise to have a salutary effect both on the number of Negroes employed and on the nature of their employment. Of prime importance is the general renewal of public interest in mass transportation systems. Federal and state legislation is evidence of this increasing concern. Federal grants to public transportation are being made for capital construction and equipment, managerial training, technical studies, and demonstration projects.

These federal assistance programs are helping the industry to overcome many of the financial problems of the past which contributed to declining service and employment. There will be a massive increase in federal spending in the future, as much as $3.1 billion in the next five years of a total $10 billion recently voted by the House. This should insure our prediction of greater Negro employment, particularly since the money will be concentrated in the most densely urban states (as much as 15 percent of any year's grants could go to New York alone).[113] Small town, small population centers, where few Negroes are employed, will not be greatly affected by such spending, and therefore their transit systems can be expected to continue to decline and go out of business.

Partly as a result of federal funds, employment in the industry has showed signs of reversing the declining trend which we have noted. In 1965 employment rose from the previous year's level for the first time since 1946. Then, after another off year in 1966, the industry employment levels turned upward again, only to decline again in 1968. Since Negro employment has increased during the long period of overall decline, it is reasonable to assume that Negroes will successfully bid for a significant share of any new jobs which may be created in the industry, again in view of the industry's urban role and concentration.

Technological change is also evident in transit. The Department of Transportation has recently hired the Jet Propulsion Laboratory to manage development of an experimental transit system.[114] Implementation of management techniques and engineering skills from the aerospace industry should speed up development and demonstration programs. Bay Area Rapid Transit (BART), scheduled to operate in the San Francisco-Oakland area by 1971, provides a notable example of technological improvements. Much of that new system will be automated with labor-saving equipment. BART is not likely to replace the other transit operations, however, so the overall effect will be additional transit jobs. Furthermore, new and expensive transit systems planned for other cities in coming years are not likely to be built without federal assistance. This means that federal regu-

---

113. Christopher Lydon, "House Approves $10 Billion Plan for Mass Transit," *New York Times*, September 30, 1970.

114. Robert Lindsey, "Aerospace Lab to Assess New Mass Transit Ideas," *New York Times*, October 4, 1970.

lations will be in effect to protect against discrimination where needed.

As we have repeatedly noted, the changes within urban transit reflect a new attitude toward the role of transportation. The industry is already providing some improved transportation services to disadvantaged urban dwellers and to other disadvantaged groups, often under federal subsidy. In some instances, the slum residents themselves are being trained to drive the buses. Programs of this nature are likely to have positive effects both in the transit industry, and in other industries as well. Not only are changes occurring which make transit favorable for Negro employment opportunities, but also many existing conditions indicate equal treatment in the future. Nevertheless, change will come slowly and new facilities will not be created rapidly.

Seniority rules have presented a barrier to Negro promotion because Negroes have been employed for a relatively short period of time compared to whites. Since separate seniority lists in the South have been abolished, however, Negroes can expect to advance as they gain experience in transit work. Rapid retirement is now encouraging promotion. In most cities outside the South, platform jobs have been open to blacks for a long enough time that many now have sufficient seniority to bid for supervisory job vacancies. Whether the lines of promotion will be kept completely free in every case is another question, but with added voice in jobs, this is likely to be less of a problem.

In large northern cities, Negroes have moved into all types of transit jobs. The efforts there are being directed toward upper management jobs, and to political appointments to commissions, governing boards, and public authorities. In addition to this, Negro transit employees are striving for better union representation. In Chicago and New York, for instance, increasing numbers of Negroes are likely to increase their power with both the companies and the unions.

In the South the number of Negroes holding supervisory jobs is relatively smaller than in the North. They have held platform jobs for a shorter period of time and generally have less seniority. Thus, even given nondiscriminatory lines of promotion, the southern Negro transit workers will find it difficult to advance to a significant degree in the near future.

On the other hand, greater industrialization of the South will likely produce a more active labor market. A combination of changing attitudes and scarce labor contributed to the hiring of Negroes in the North during the war and afterward, and in some southern cities in the 1960's. With federal Civil Rights legislation as a framework, the move toward job equality for Negroes is likely to continue in the South as well. Throughout our major population centers, the urban transit industry seems likely to become increasingly a black-operated industry serving a predominant black clientele except where it brings suburban commuters back and forth to center city.

Index

PART FIVE

CONCLUDING ANALYSIS

by

Herbert R. Northrup

TABLE OF CONTENTS

LIST OF TABLES

Concluding Analysis

The four transportation industries studied in this volume [1] have much in common, yet many different characteristics in terms of racial employment policies. All the industries initially followed the railroad industry mores of limiting Negroes to service and heavy labor jobs and denying them positions of responsibility or skill. In more recent years, this legacy of discrimination has been difficult to overcome on the railways where severe employment cutbacks have occurred, in air transport where skill and safety requirements inhibit rapid progress, and in trucking where a strong union and weak, fragmented managements appear for the most part reluctant to alter the status quo. In urban transit, the situation is radically different, as this industry moves toward a predominately black labor force serving a predominately black clientele.

This chapter compares and contrasts the racial employment situation in the four industries and summarizes our findings in the light of the fourteen hypotheses set forth in Volume I of our Studies of Negro Employment. [2] Before so doing, however, we believe it useful to examine the significance of the four industries in terms of black employment and of the nation's racial employment policies.

THE SIGNIFICANCE OF TRANSPORTATION EMPLOYMENT

In 1969, total employment in the four transportation industries exceeded two million persons, comprising approximately 10 percent of all manufacturing employees and 3 percent of total industrial employment. [3] Despite the precipitous decline in railroad employment and the drop in urban transit concerns and workers, increases in trucking and air transport jobs have kept

---

1. The maritime industries, which are not included here, will be the subject of a forthcoming volume in this series.

2. Herbert R. Northrup, Richard L. Rowan, *et al.*, *Negro Employment in Basic Industry*, Studies of Negro Employment, Vol. I (Philadelphia: Industrial Research Unit, Wharton School of Finance and Commerce, University of Pennsylvania, 1970), Part One, Chapter I; Part Eight, Chapter I.

3. *Employment and Earnings*, Vol. 16, No. 9 (March 1970), Table B-2.

transportation employment at high levels. Nevertheless, both in terms of the percentage of total employment and in actual numbers, employment remains below that of the early decades of this century when railroad employment alone was almost equal to the current total of the four industries.

These four industries are significant for racial employment policies beyond their importance in numbers of employees. They are employers in all sectors of the country. The work is generally well paid, and in many cases, prestigious as well. Employees of transportation companies are highly visible, in regular contact with the public, with other employees, and with industry and government personnel. Whether they lead or lag in fair employment can thus influence attitudes and performance in a considerable segment of the economy.

DEMAND FOR LABOR

Regardless of the avowed policies of a management or of an industry, the state of the labor market and the need for labor relative to supply affect the extent to which racial employment policies can be made operative. Thus in the railroad industry, the need for unskilled laborers prior to 1920, and to a lesser extent during World War II, led to the recruitment of large numbers of Negro laborers and service workers. Except during World War II, however, the period since 1920 has been one of secular decline in railroad employment, recently at a precipitous rate. The historic antipathy of white railroad workers to the employment of Negroes, except in menial or subservient capacities, has been materially strengthened by job insecurity. Not only did whites oppose improvement in the lot of the black railroad workers, but in addition they made determined, and largely successful, efforts to take over former "Negro jobs," especially as the working conditions and pay of such jobs improved. Insensitive management, often up from the ranks and sympathetic to the white workers' aspirations, usually agreed with the latter's demands, especially after racial wage differentials were eliminated. In more recent years, as management moved to comply with federal laws and regulations pertaining to civil rights, the sharp drop in railroad jobs put a brake on what could be accomplished.

Projections for the future do not indicate any rise in railroad employment. Indeed, it may well not have bottomed out. The industry's aging labor force and sizeable turnover, however, assure a large demand for labor in future years. Unfortunately, the experience of Negro workers during the fifty years prior to the passage of the Civil Rights Act of 1964, the continued hostility of many railroad unions toward black employees, the slowness of the industry to adopt modern personnel techniques, and the precarious financial situation, particularly of the eastern carriers, all tend to induce the most qualified black workers to seek employment elsewhere even when they are actively recruited by the railroads. A substantially increased demand for labor (which is most unlikely) would further the railroads' capacity to employ an increased proportion of Negroes, but it would not by itself ensure the accomplishment of that goal.

Like the railroads, the airlines originally confined Negroes to unskilled and menial jobs. Moreover, a smaller proportion of such jobs are found in air transport than in railroading. When the civil rights pressures of the 1960's arose, however, the airlines were blessed with an increased demand for labor. As a result, substantial progress was possible. Some of this progress, however, is now threatened by the heavy cutbacks and layoffs which have occurred in the industry since mid-1969. Moreover, even an increased demand for such key personnel as pilots and mechanics did not substantially increase the proportion of Negroes employed because of their historical exclusion and the consequent lack of available, trained blacks. Nevertheless, in the high turnover jobs, particularly among stewardesses and reservation clerks, the progress should continue.

In terms of the demand for labor criterion, the trucking industry would seem to offer great potential for Negro employment. It is a growth industry, employing largely semiskilled workers. Yet in 1968, only 7.6 percent of all operating employees, 2.4 percent of the road drivers, and 10.9 percent of the local drivers in our sample were black.[4] The high wages paid in the industry attract a large pool of whites. The typical firm is relatively small and decidedly anxious not to tangle with its white employees and their strong union. Moreover, Negro drivers are concentrated in the smaller firms, especially the local ones. As a result of a massive wage increase foisted on the industry by the Teamsters' Union in 1970, combined with the

---

4. See Table 11 in the trucking study, above. In 1969, the EEOC reported that only 6.3 percent of the employees in the industry were black. (Data from EEOC.)

decline in business at that time, a large number of small firms, particularly those engaged in local or short haul work, have gone out of business.[5] Thus Negroes are concentrated in the sectors of the industry which are most vulnerable to competitive pressures and largely excluded from the most remunerative jobs in the over-the-road sector which is likely to continue to grow.

The urban transit industry is one of the two studied in our Racial Policies series in which the percentage of Negroes has increased while employment has declined.[6] The increasing concentration of the industry in the major cities while these cities have been losing white population and gaining blacks is, of course, a major factor in this situation. Another has been the great increase in robberies and violent crimes in the cities and the perpetuation of such crimes against bus drivers and subway employees. The exact fare system has reduced such crimes to a bare minimum, but crime in the cities remains a great problem. With the greater proportionate education and employment opportunities of whites, and their increasing likelihood to dwell outside of the cities, they have tended to cease applying for urban transit jobs since the early 1950's, despite the relatively high wages and fringe benefits paid in the industry.

Another factor contributing to this inverted demand in Negro employment relationship is the declining social prestige of the urban transit industry. This is, of course, closely aligned with the population shifts between city and suburbs. The city is no longer a prestigious place to dwell unless one is quite wealthy and it is increasingly the home of the very poor. Likewise riding the city bus or subway has become heavily the mark of the poor while others use private cars, and to a lesser extent commuter trains, for transportation. Urban transit jobs prior to World War II were prestigious blue collar jobs barred to Negroes in many cities; today, despite high pay, they attract few white applicants in the large cities where the bulk of the industry is found.

---

5. Terry P. Brown, "Many Small Truckers Go Out of Business; Costly Labor Pact and Recession Blamed," *Wall Street Journal*, February 24, 1971, p. 32.

6. Shipbuilding is the other industry in which this has occurred. See Lester Rubin, *The Negro in the Shipbuilding Industry*, The Racial Policies of American Industry, Report No. 17 (Philadelphia: Industrial Research Unit, Wharton School of Finance and Commerce, University of Pennsylvania, 1970).

The transportation industries thus afford significant exception to the belief that there is an almost automatic correlation between a strong demand for labor and high or increasing black employment. Certainly, we have found in our manufacturing industry studies that where labor demand is increasing, as in electrical [7] or drug manufacturing,[8] it is easier to expand black employment; and that where increased demand is acute, as in automobiles,[9] textiles,[10] or paper converting,[11] black employment is likely to expand at a rapid rate; or conversely, where employment is declining, as in steel, rubber tires, or petroleum,[12] it is much more difficult to expand Negro participation. But we have also found an industry—shipbuilding [13]—which had an inverse relationship of demand and Negro employment similar to, although less dramatic than, that of urban transit; and we have noted many factors which offset or limit the impact of the demand factor. We conclude for the transportation industries studied herein that the demand factor is certainly very significant, but seemingly less so than in many other industries. Especially noteworthy is the failure of Negroes to gain jobs with the growth of the over-the-road trucking industry, and prior to 1960, their failure to share substantially in the growth of air transport, and their significant proportional employment increase in urban transit while that industry has lost 100,000 jobs since 1950—a decline of more than 40 percent. On the

7. Theodore V. Purcell and Daniel P. Mulvey, *The Negro in the Electrical Manufacturing Industry*, The Racial Policies of American Industry, Report No. 27 (Philadelphia: Industrial Research Unit, Wharton School of Finance and Commerce, University of Pennsylvania, 1971).

8. F. Marion Fletcher, *The Negro in the Drug Manufacturing Industry*, The Racial Policies of American Industry, Report No. 21 (Philadelphia: Industrial Research Unit, Wharton School of Finance and Commerce, University of Pennsylvania, 1970).

9. Northrup, Rowan, et al., *Negro Employment in Basic Industry*, op. cit., Part Two.

10. Herbert R. Northrup and Richard L. Rowan, *Negro Employment in Southern Industry*, Studies of Negro Employment, Vol. IV (Philadelphia: Industrial Research Unit, Wharton School of Finance and Commerce, University of Pennsylvania, 1971), Part Five.

11. *Ibid.*, Part One.

12. Northrup, Rowan, et al., *Negro Employment in Basic Industry*, op. cit., Parts Four, Five, and Six.

13. Rubin, *op. cit.*

other hand, the demand factor has been very significant in railroads, and in the 1960's, in air transport as well.

NATURE OF THE WORK

The nature of the work, or qualitative aspects of demand, greatly affects the extent of Negro employment. The occupational mix, the attractiveness of the work, and the pattern of job progression are all significant factors in this regard. Although none of the four transportation industries now deliberately divide jobs on a racial basis, past practice was altered such a few years ago that it still affects racial occupational job patterns.

Occupational Mix

Because of past employment practices and years of discriminatory educational opportunity, Negro workers in all industries are overconcentrated in the lower paying jobs. Consequently, it would be expected that the industries which require the largest concentration of unskilled and semiskilled jobs would employ the largest percentages of Negroes; and conversely, that those in which the higher skills predominate would employ a smaller percentage of Negroes. This was found generally the situation in manufacturing industries,[14] and presumably would be true also in all other industry until the effects of past employment and educational discrimination are eliminated.

The data set forth in Tables 1 and 2, however, do not demonstrate this close correlation between occupational mix and the percentage of black employment. To be sure, air transport, which has the lowest percentage of Negroes (5.4 percent) has also the largest percentage of white collar employees (55.8 percent), more than double that of each of the other three industries. Yet trucking, railroads, and urban transit, in which the overall occupational mix is very similar, have quite different percentages of Negroes. Railroads in 1969 reported a black percentage of 7.8, substantially below prior years when the industry employed large numbers of Negro track laborers and service workers. The urban transit data in Tables 1 and 2 show a Negro complement of almost 20 percent; if the large public

---

14. See Northrup, Rowan, *et al., Negro Employment in Basic Industry, op. cit.,* Part Eight, pp. 723-728.

TABLE 1. Four Transportation Industries
Employment by Race and Occupational Group
United States, 1969

Occupational Group	Railroads (SIC 40)			Air Transport a (SIC 45)			Trucking (SIC 421)			Urban Transit b (SIC 41)		
	Total	Negro	Percent Negro	Total	Negro	Percent Negro	Total	Negro	Percent Negro	Total	Negro	Percent Negro
Officials and managers	31,108	150	0.5	24,608	200	0.8	36,695	342	0.9	5,784	221	3.8
Professionals	7,079	38	0.5	46,474	179	0.4	3,642	67	1.8	1,036	59	5.7
Technicians	7,856	49	0.6	8,946	112	1.3	2,793	63	2.3	1,246	128	10.3
Sales workers	6,817	106	1.6	55,885	2,202	3.9	8,744	83	0.9	8,951 c	2,653 c	29.6
Office and clerical	118,229	3,021	2.6	46,180	1,708	3.7	61,717	1,722	2.8	10,167	731	7.2
Total white collar	171,089	3,364	2.0	182,093	4,401	2.4	113,591	2,277	2.0	27,184	3,792	13.9
Craftsmen	209,460	6,258	3.0	64,887	1,670	2.6	45,503	2,223	4.9	24,598	2,128	8.7
Operatives	142,296	8,135	5.7	32,168	3,890	12.1	213,467	12,821	6.0	53,155	12,941	24.3
Laborers	79,036	23,698	30.0	10,768	3,688	34.2	53,985	8,414	15.6	6,146	2,187	35.6
Service workers	14,453	6,910	47.8	36,601	4,082	11.2	10,335	1,939	18.8	7,052	2,055	29.1
Total blue collar	445,245	45,001	10.1	144,424	13,330	9.2	323,290	25,397	7.9	90,951	19,311	21.2
Total	616,334	48,365	7.8	326,517	17,731	5.4	436,881	27,674	6.3	118,185	23,103	19.6

Source: Equal Employment Opportunity Commission, 1969.

a As noted in Part Two, some airlines classify stewardesses as service workers, but most as sales workers. This tends to inflate the former figure and deflate the latter. It also, of course, inflates the percentage of blue collar relative to white collar employees.

b Data excludes several large publicly owned systems which we estimate would increase Negro percentage to 25-30 percent.

c An obvious misclassification. Virtually no sales workers exist in the industry.

TABLE 2. Four Transportation Industries

Percentage Distribution of Employees by Race and Occupational Group
United States, 1969

Occupational Group	Railroads (SIC 40)		Air Transport[a] (SIC 45)		Trucking (SIC 421)		Urban Transit[a] (SIC 41)	
	All Employees	Negro Employees	All Employees	Negro Employees	All Employees	Negro Employees	All Employees	Negro Employees
Officials and managers	5.0	0.3	7.5	1.1	8.4	1.2	4.9	1.0
Professionals	1.2	0.1	14.2	1.0	0.8	0.3	0.9	0.2
Technicians	1.3	0.1	2.8	0.6	0.7	0.2	1.0	0.5
Sales workers	1.1	0.2	17.1	12.4	2.0	0.3	7.6	11.5
Office and clerical	19.2	6.3	14.2	9.7	14.1	6.2	8.6	3.2
Total white collar	27.8	7.0	55.8	24.8	26.0	8.2	23.0	16.4
Craftsmen	34.0	12.9	19.9	9.4	10.4	8.1	20.8	9.2
Operatives	23.1	16.8	9.8	22.0	48.9	46.3	45.0	56.0
Laborers	12.8	49.0	3.3	20.8	12.3	30.4	5.2	9.5
Service workers	2.3	14.3	11.2	23.0	2.4	7.0	6.0	8.9
Total blue collar	72.2	93.0	44.2	75.2	74.0	91.8	77.0	83.6
Total	100.0	100.0	100.0	100.0	100.0	100.0	100.0	100.0

Source: Derived from Table 1.

[a] See notes, Table 1. Except for sales employees, which are misclassified in the EEOC data, the distribution of total and Negro employees is not materially different for the six large urban transit systems. See Part Four, Table 23.

systems were not excluded from these data, that figure would probably be 25-30 percent.

The trucking data show only a 6.3 black percentage; if local trucking were excluded, it would be considerably less. This is only one percentage point above air transport; yet three-fourths of trucking employees, but only 44 percent of those in air transport, are blue collar workers.[15] Obviously other factors besides the occupational mix are pertinent, particularly location in urban transit, declining employment and past discrimination by carriers and unions in railroads, and continued management-union discrimination in trucking.

Within each of the four industries, the occupational distribution of Negroes is less favorable than that of all employees. It is less so in urban transit than in the others, and perhaps less so than in almost any industry studied in this series, which is of course a function of its unusually high overall black complement. In air transport, the disparity between total and black employment distributions is the greatest. Yet also in air transport is found the highest percent of black white collar employees —a percentage approximately equal to the overall distributions of employees in the other three industries. Like its counterpart in manufacturing, aerospace,[16] air transport has a relatively small percentage of Negroes in salaried positions. Yet in terms of number and distribution, it is far ahead of competitive industries in employment of such personnel.

The Negro Female Transportation Worker

Until the advent of air transport, female employment in any transportation industry was not significant. The clerical staff in railroads, for example, was once heavily male. Table 3 shows female employment by race in the four industries. Except in air transport, the great bulk of female employees are found in the office and clerical group, although railroads has a sizeable number of black female laborers. In railroads, the evidences of

---

15. If stewardesses were classified as sales workers by all airlines, and not by some as service workers, the percentage of salaried employees would be somewhat larger in air transport.

16. In 1966, the aerospace industry's black professionals comprised only 0.8 percent of its total professional staff. Yet 21 major concerns in this industry employed 40 percent of all Negro professionals in manufacturing concerns reporting to the EEOC. See Northrup, Rowan, *et al., Negro Employment in Basic Industry, op. cit.*, Part Eight, pp. 726-727.

TABLE 3. *Four Transportation Industries*
Female Employment by Race and Occupational Group
United States, 1969

Occupational Group	Railroads (SIC 40)			Air Transport (SIC 45)			Trucking (SIC 421)			Urban Transit (SIC 41)		
	Total	Negro	Percent Negro	Total	Negro	Percent Negro	Total	Negro	Percent Negro	Total	Negro	Percent Negro
Officials and managers	131	....	....	1,432	12	0.8	742	3	0.4	122	2	1.6
Professionals	148	2	1.4	1,837	26	1.4	114	2	1.8	44	1	2.3
Technicians	158	....	....	1,101	15	1.4	112	1	0.9	64	12	18.8
Sales workers	256	2	0.8	33,824	1,560	4.6	239	6	2.5	1,257	162	12.9
Office and clerical	30,032	780	2.6	24,783	712	2.9	35,303	927	2.6	4,886	377	7.7
Total white collar	30,725	784	2.6	62,977	2,325	3.7	36,510	939	2.6	6,373	554	8.7
Craftsmen	145	11	7.6	294	13	4.4	154	4	2.6	314	13	4.1
Operatives	421	67	15.9	331	67	20.2	447	106	23.7	1,310	317	24.2
Laborers	1,621	905	55.8	703	482	68.6	292	128	43.8	876	184	48.9
Service workers	780	239	30.6	24,060	668	2.8	265	98	35.1	508	138	27.2
Total blue collar	2,967	1,222	41.2	25,388	1,230	4.8	1,158	331	28.6	2,508	652	26.0
Total	33,692	2,006	6.0	88,365	3,555	4.0	37,668	1,270	3.4	8,881	1,206	13.6

Source: Equal Employment Opportunity Commission, 1969.

discrimination are clear when it is noted that about 90 percent of all females are clerical workers, but among Negro women, the number of laborers exceeds that of clericals.

Air transport provides the most opportunities for women generally as well as for black women. The large number of reservation clerks and agents and stewardesses as well as traditional clericals give this industry a female work complement more than twice that of any of the other transportation industries, despite the fact that in total employment, air transport is substantially below railroads or trucking. Since 1960, airlines have recruited strenuously to obtain black women for these positions. As a result, Negro women have made the greatest progress in this industry.

Character of the Work

Besides occupational mix, black employment is affected by other aspects of work nature. For example, traditionally Negroes were utilized primarily in service and laboring jobs. The southern railroads used hired slaves to construct their right of ways and lay the trackage. For many years thereafter, the maintenance of way departments all over the country employed thousands of blacks and many were also employed to labor in the shops and around stations. The work was heavy, often unpleasant, and low paid. Similarly, passenger services used Negro porters, waiters, baggage handlers, etc. These were "Negro jobs." When mechanization, declining freight, and disappearing passenger service greatly reduced such work, the Negro railroad worker felt the greatest impact.

The locomotive fireman in the South was originally a laborer who shoveled coal to keep the steam boiler operating. Automatic stokers, then the diesel, plus declining employment altered the job and encouraged white workers to covet and to claim the work. Similarly, the attempts to utilize black porters as brakemen or black helpers as mechanics clashed with the white worker's concept of what was his work, and always the white worker seemed to win. Until the Civil Rights Act of 1964 became law, all skilled, responsible, and prestigious jobs were white men's work. Dirty, heavy, menial or service tasks were left for the black man. The railroads hired a large complement of Negroes because the nature of the work was sufficiently unpleasant or menial as not to fit the concept of white jobs.

Airlines had relatively few of the traditional type "Negro jobs." The redcap came over to airports as a skycap, but the black porter's place was taken by the white stewardess. Negro laborers worked around airports and overhaul bases doing the heavy, menial work as on the railroads, but far fewer such jobs existed. Again, prior to the early 1960's, the responsible, skilled, and prestigious jobs were traditionally for whites only.

Over-the-road trucking jobs carried prestige, responsibility, and later high pay. Negroes were either denied opportunity, or pushed aside by white worker competition and employers anxious to avoid problems. In urban transit, the "platform workers" were historically white, serving the public and accepting responsibility for the commuting public. But their visibility, the replacement of the trolley car by the bus, and the obvious ability of Negroes to drive busses, combined with the World War II assault on inequality at a time of labor shortage, led to a breakdown of the exclusionist and discriminatory patterns.

More recently, urban transit, like the cities which the industry serves, has lost its prestigious job flavor. Crime and population shifts have led whites to look elsewhere. Bus and transit positions in major cities are more and more looked upon by white workers as "Negro jobs" serving the Negro community. With few white job applicants, black predominance is likely to occur quite rapidly.

Pattern of Occupational Progression

The occupational progression pattern—the manner in which employees move from job to job up the occupational ladder—makes change very difficult in the railroad and air transport industries. For sound reasons, interdepartmental transfers are discouraged. A railroad shop craftsman cannot take his seniority into an operating job because his skills and experience do not qualify him as an engineer or conductor. In both railroads and airlines, the progression follows narrow lines from bottom to top. Experience in one department does not provide competence in another. Hence where Negroes were employed only in departments requiring no skills, they lacked the opportunity to learn the better jobs. When the opportunity arose for equal employment, qualifications were often absent.

The railway and airline seniority systems are not per se discriminatory. What was discriminatory in the past was hiring policies which channeled persons to jobs and/or departments on the basis of race. Now that such practices are illegal, those employed on a discriminatory basis remain victims of past practices. Moreover, while these practices were in effect, ambitious blacks were discouraged from qualifying because jobs were not available. The situation of airline pilots is an extreme, but quite valid, illustration of the vicious circle of qualification and opportunity. For many years, it was almost impossible for Negroes either to become qualified or to obtain jobs as pilots. Then the armed services barriers were broken; finally the airlines opened up. But the small number of black military and civilian pilots today is clear proof of the slowness of change and of the difficulty of overcoming past practice. The current progression from military training to civilian jobs makes rapid change virtually impossible.

In addition to employing personnel on a discriminatory basis, the railroads perverted the natural upgrading and learning progression for operating crews by denying Negroes promotion to engineer or conductor. Positions of such responsibility were beyond the pale for a black man. By paying Negroes less for performing the fireman and brakeman functions, the southern railroads more than made up for the extra cost of having to train engineers and conductors who had not previously worked in the fireman and brakeman jobs. When government and unions equalized the wages of black train crews, their usefulness was limited to railway management and the stage was set for their elimination.

One often forgotten fact should be noted here. Southern railroads, for all their discriminatory practices, did over the years employ large numbers of Negroes in their train crews. Those in the North and West did not discriminate in this manner; they completely excluded Negroes, which is, of course, far worse.

In the trucking industry, Dr. Leone found that separate seniority lists for local and over-the-road drivers tend to inhibit transfers. The local driver who desires a job in the better paying long distance sector must go to the bottom of the seniority list in the latter if he transfers. In view of the overt opposition of white drivers to black driver utilization in these jobs, Leone found considerable evidence that Negroes were inhibited from taking the risks involved in such transfers. Moreover, there appears to be little movement from warehouse or dockmen's jobs to over-the-road driver.[17]

---

17. See Part Three above, pp. 53-61.

The failure of Negroes to gain substantial employment in the top operating jobs in railroad, air transport, or trucking substantially reduces their opportunities to work into management jobs. Historically, these are the areas in transportation from which promotion out of the bargaining unit has frequently occurred, especially into lower management positions. In all three industries, former operating personnel have achieved executive positions as well. The effect of this lack of participation is thus far reaching since upgrading goes beyond the unionized employees.

In urban transit, the progression system is not as significant, nor is it now an inhibiting factor on black worker advancement. Some 60 percent of the employees in the industry are operators. With the large black complement in the industry, Negroes are moving strongly into lower management and white collar jobs, and are likely to increase their representation therein in the future.

TIME AND NATURE OF INDUSTRY DEVELOPMENT AND COMMUNITY MORES

The railroad industry dates back to the days of slavery, and its employment policies maintained the community mores of the nineteenth century far into the twentieth. The air transport industry grew out of World War I experience. The 1920's was marked by a resurgence of Jim Crow, often in very invidious aspects. Negroes were denied opportunities in new technologies and in elite areas of work. The transportation employment mores precluded the utilization of blacks in responsible jobs and air transport, as the elite of the group, had few thoughts of admitting blacks to the fraternity.

Urban transit, like railroads, had its origins in the nineteenth century. As electric and later gasoline powered vehicles came into use, jobs were "naturally" reserved for whites. The migration of Negroes to northern cities, their successful use in a few cities under civil service regulations, and the equalitarian concept engendered by World War II brought to a head the clash of old prejudices with current facts. This once bastion of white employment began its change into a citadel of black jobs.

Trucking is a relatively new industry which did not initially command social prestige. Gradually, however, one of the country's most powerful unions has made over-the-road driving an epitome of prestige blue collar work. In such a system, no place was reserved for the black driver. Craft exclusionism, like that of skilled construction workers, permeates the industry to limit most opportunities to whites.

A factor which encourages exclusionism in the railroad, air transport, and trucking industries, and once did also in urban transit, is the close cohesion of operating employees and operating management. Many of the latter, as already noted, are up from the ranks. They have a deep empathy for the feelings of the white rank and file; indeed many still share these feelings. The employment of "outsiders" arouses a shared antipathy. Moreover, both labor and management are likely to have spent their entire working lives in the particular industry in which they are now employed. A change in the pattern of employment involves new problems inconsistent with their experience. Not surprisingly, resistance to change is common.

A significant community more which has historically—and in trucking still does—inhibited the utilization of black operating crews is the long held belief that white and black personnel would not, or should not, or could not be made to room together. Truck drivers bunk on the job and often in special hostels. Segregated facilities in the South took care of the problem for train crews, but in the North, the easiest solution was not to employ Negroes. The opposition of white drivers to having a black partner remains a factor in the slow progress of integration in trucking.

Another aspect which slowed integration in the transportation industries was the existence of enforced segregation in the South. Until that was ended and public place discrimination outlawed, air transport officials worried about sending black personnel into southern cities, not desiring to offend either employees or the local public. Simply refraining from hiring Negroes for such jobs was formerly the principal way in which this potential problem was "solved."

CONSUMER ORIENTATION AND IMAGE CONCERN— TRANSPORTATION AS SERVICE

We have noted in previous volumes of this Series that companies which sell their products to consumers are likely to be more concerned with public reaction to their racial employment policies than are those which deal primarily with other companies.

Consumer oriented concerns frequently were found to work hard to avoid offending majority opinion, often trying to seem "reasonably progressive," but not too far out in front. The obvious reason is that racial unrest "can alienate a group, alter buying habits, and is generally bad for business." [18]

Certainly consumer attitudes were a significant factor in altering the policies of the urban transit industry. Fears that the public would object to black bus drivers were easily demonstrated to be groundless during the World War II period. Later, the Montgomery bus boycott showed the power of the black customer.

The airlines were quite fearful about customer reaction to black stewardesses, station agents, and plane crews. Undoubtedly this greatly delayed integration; yet the reaction has been mostly nonexistent.

For years only white truck drivers sold or delivered to the home. It was felt that white customers would not tolerate Negroes in such jobs. Even today, whites comprise most of the dwindling home delivery force, but Negroes are breaking into the work without customer complaint.

The railroad and trucking industries are not consumer oriented. Dealing as they do primarily in freight service, their public and customer relations are not generally affected by worries over consumer reactions. Companies in these industries are led primarily by operating and financial personnel whose concern is immediate problems, not the long range impact of racial employment policies. Moreover, it cannot be easily demonstrated that a greater concern for such problems would alter operating results. On the other hand, white employee unrest over integration could be immediately costly.

Likewise, "image concern" is foreign to the railroad or trucking industries. One finds little or no effort on the part of executives in these industries to publicize themselves as "socially minded" or "forward looking." On the other hand, in air transport, with passenger service the main business, public and customer relations executives abound, projecting their images as concerned citizens and in turn being, in many cases, genuinely as well as publicly concerned to improve their minority posture. The turnabout of the air transport industry's racial policies in

---

18. Northrup, Rowan, *et al.*, *Negro Employment in Basic Industry*, *op. cit.*, Part Eight, p. 734.

the 1960's was greatly aided by this top executive interest—and in a few companies seriously impeded by the lack thereof.

Urban transit is, of course, also in the passenger business, but its poverty, decaying image, and increasing public ownership leave it little "executive image" concern. In terms of black employment, of course, it has little need thereof.

Transportation exists to provide a service. Railroads and trucking seem to view themselves as primarily service businesses for business, despite the passenger operations of the railroads; airlines are, and see themselves as primarily service businesses for passengers—direct consumers. Although it is most difficult to separate the various factors affecting equal employment, undoubtedly the seemingly greater interest of air transport companies in that subject and in effectuating improvement stems at least in part from their desire to present a good image to all segments of society since all are potential passenger-customers.

MANAGEMENT ETHNIC ORIGIN

We found no evidence that ethnic origin had any particular influence over racial policies in the firms studied. One prominent executive each in the air transport and railroad industries, and several in the trucking industry were of the Jewish faith, and several others in the trucking industry were of southern or eastern European background. Our observation—and it is only that—was that all followed industry practice without discernible difference between them and Anglo-Saxon Protestant executives. We made no observations in the urban transit industry, but believe that the conclusions would be the same.

COMMUNITY CRISES

In studying manufacturing industries, we have found that integration in plants was often affected by community crises which tend to call attention to deficiencies in industry practice or to call for renewed efforts to bring citizens together and to give minorities a greater stake in the success of local plants or enterprises. Most transportation industries, however, do not seem to have been affected to such an extent by local crises. Their employees are less concentrated, more scattered throughout a region, or even the country, and their policies are less affected by local crises.

On the other hand, the urban transit industry is a local one. The boycott led by the late Martin Luther King, Jr., in Montgomery, Alabama, dramatized still existing exclusionist hiring policies, and ensured their eventual elimination. To be sure, the final settlement of the Montgomery boycott did not obtain jobs for Negroes as bus drivers, but it eliminated segregated seating. Like the lunch counter sit-ins, and the drives for equal rights in schools and in public accommodations, such desegregation was a necessary prelude to employment desegregation. And of course, this is applicable to all industry, as well as to urban transit.

IMPACT OF TECHNOLOGY

The substitution of machines for men or the substitution of a new technology for an old has often adversely affected Negro employment. Nowhere is that more apparent than in the railroad industry. Thousands of Negroes have been replaced as machines took over work in the maintenance of way departments; others lost their jobs as the introduction of the diesel, plus improved or altered methods, eliminated the need for shop laborers or helpers; and of course, the diesel introduction aided the unconscionable efforts of the operating brotherhoods to drive Negro firemen from their jobs.

At the same time, thousands of Negroes lost jobs as trucks took over freight hauling from railroads and airlines became the leading passenger carrier. The latter, of course, meant that the all Negro railroad porters were replaced by the one time all white, and now predominantly white airline stewardesses.

In one instance, technological change aided black employment. It was once argued that trolley car operation could not be mastered by the black workers. As busses replaced trolleys, this argument was difficult to sustain in the face of the black applicant driving to the employment office in his automobile. Overall, however, the impact of technology on the railroads and the loss of business by railroads to competitive carriers meant heavy job losses to black transportation employees.

INDUSTRIAL LOCATION

Generally speaking, the location of the transportation industries tends to be favorable to the employment of Negro workers. Located nationwide, the industries tend to concentrate in or near large cities, and thus near the centers of Negro population. Location is probably the major reason for the high black complement of the urban transit industry. Railroad yards and terminals tend to be easily accessible to the bulk of the black population, and for many years, rural dwelling Negroes found railway maintenance of way departments one of their few nonagricultural employments.

For airlines, the situation is mixed. Central offices of some are in cities, others in outlying airport areas. Likewise some airports are reasonably accessible; others are difficult to reach for inner city residents. Where the latter is the case, the locations are unfavorable to Negro employment, and have tended to inhibit black employment.

Truck terminals also offer a mixed situation. More and more, one sees them located in the cities' outskirts where land is available and maneuverability possible. Many are, however, located near Negro neighborhoods, and in addition, local trucking concerns employ their personnel within the cities. Trucking involves some locational problems for Negroes seeking employment, but there is little evidence that these problems are the significant ones which have precluded an expansion of black employment.

NATURE OF UNION ORGANIZATION

Even in the construction industry, union policies have not had such negative effects on black workers as they have had in transportation—and this, of course, is primarily the responsibility of the railroad unions. Virtually all unions which once barred minorities from membership were entirely railroad organizations, or had jurisdiction over railroad workers and employees in other industries.[19] But railroad unions did not stop with exclusion. Induced in part by their fraternal character, but largely by craft conciousness, job competitiveness, and management use of Negroes as strikebreakers and low wage competitors, and spurred on by lagging employment, the operating brotherhoods worked for nearly a century to drive Negroes out of their jurisdictions. Although some of the litigation still continues, there is little doubt that they succeeded. The fact that the industry is now employing black engineers and conductors does

19. See Herbert R. Northrup, *Organized Labor and the Negro* (New York: Harper and Brothers, 1944), Chapters I and III.

not reduce the enormity nor the invidious character of this discrimination.

In nonoperating crafts and classes, Negroes were "kept in their place" by unions, confined to nonvoting "auxiliaries," negotiated out of jobs, and misrepresented by their bargaining agents. The story, as summarized in Part One, is fortunately without parallel in American industrial relations, and repugnant in most of its aspects. Moreover, in reiterating this fact, we do not imply any exoneration of the unsavory collaboration of carrier management or federal government agencies in the situation, as will be noted below.

In the air transport industry, union policies have been less significant. For the most part, this is less because of an equalitarian union approach than because the industry itself took a discriminatory approach, one confining Negroes to a minor role prior to the 1960's. More recently, unions in the air transport industry have not interfered with managerial moves toward improving the industry's civil rights posture and performance, but have not aided integration either.

In trucking, the Teamsters' Union has a poor record despite some efforts to enhance its civil rights image outside of the key over-the-road driver area. It has given funds for social causes in collaboration with the Alliance for Labor Action, and it has participated in training the disadvantaged,[20] but it has done little or nothing to increase the opportunities of Negroes as over-the-road drivers, despite its great strength in the industry. Until that occurs, the Teamsters can lay little claim to an equalitarian position. Indeed, it bears a key responsibility for the low proportion of Negroes in the industry.

Unions in the urban transit industry tend to leave racial policies to local determination. This led to much discrimination in the past, but now the problems revolve around who shall control the unions. Despite the heavy black percentage in the industry, Negroes hold few union positions. This situation has given rise to a number of separate black rival union attempts which have so far been unsuccessful in winning bargaining rights. In the Amalgamated Transit Union, white control in a number of locals is furthered by permitting the pensioners, who are very heavily

---

20. Much publicity, for example, accompanied the training program known as "Tri-Faith Trucking Terminal Employment Project" in Chicago. Here union, companies, and the Chicago Conference on Religion and Race trained disadvantaged to be dock workers. No driver jobs were involved.

white, to vote. As the percentage of blacks continue to increase, it seems likely that Negroes will take over the top positions in the transit unions, first in the large locals, and probably in the internationals as well.

Before leaving this subject, it is well to note that union officials, as elected leaders, reflect their constituencies and cannot flout their wishes. Often a strong civil rights position is unpopular and politically disasterous. Yet democracy requires more than doing the wishes of the majority; it requires protection of the minority against majority tyranny as well. It is one thing to explain why unions act as they do. It is equally important to report that this does not excuse or condone invidiously discriminatory practices.

Finally, we emphasize again, as has been done in the volumes of this Series previously published, that where employment is a management function, as it is in the four transportation industries included herein, it is the companies that establish employment practices. Prime responsibility must therefore rest with them for the racial policies.

ROLE OF GOVERNMENT

In nearly all of the industries examined, government policies have been found to be a crucial factor in improving black employment opportunities. In the last decade, this has been the situation in the transportation industries. But prior to that time, particularly in regard to the railroad industry, the role of the government included strong negative and indeed, unsavory aspects.

Actually there is little in the relations of a government agency with some of its citizens that is as shameful as the part played by the National Mediation Board and the National Railroad Adjustment Board in aiding the discrimination against Negro railroad workers and even in eliminating them from their jobs. The Mediation Board has defined bargaining units which forced Negroes to be represented by unions which did not admit them to full membership; it has promulgated rules which deny employees the right to vote effectively against representation; its staff has conducted representation elections in a questionable manner; its members have participated and signed agreements designed to eliminate Negroes from jobs; and it has yet to give evidence of a belief in the "fair representation" doctrine enunciated by the U.S. Supreme Court more than a quarter of a century ago.[21]

The record of the National Railroad Adjustment Board is equally poor. Its decisions turning over black porter-brakemen jobs to white brakemen are as blatently unfair as they are unconscionable for this has been done without giving the affected Negroes notice or a right to be heard. Moreover, Negroes with grievances have no recourse from this board on which the offending parties sit and control.

Other branches of the federal government have attempted to right the balance, with modest successes. President Roosevelt's Committee on Fair Employment Practice, although rebuffed, did first call attention to the railroad situation. More recently the Post Office Department, the Equal Employment Opportunity Commission, and the Department of Justice have endeavored to effectuate the current law and policy, but they are greatly hampered by the declining employment in the industry. Prior to the current situation, various state antidiscrimination commissions, particularly the New York one, maintained pressure for reform in the industry.

Despite the extraordinary opinion of the district court in the *Jacksonville Terminal* case and some appellate court decisions in the porter-brakemen dispute (which, as Mr. Risher noted in Part One, do not appear to grasp the invidious nature of the discrimination involved), the federal courts, following the *Steele* case, have been the most consistent defenders of justice for black railroad men. A number of cases are now pending which could well improve the lot of Negro railroad workers, but even such progress will be slow because of the employment situation.

The air transport industry has also felt the discriminatory policies of the National Mediation Board, particularly in bargaining unit determinations wihch both aided discriminatory unions to gain a foothold in the industry and ignored their policies and rules in consigning workers to their jurisdictions. Such policies were, however, less significant than in the railroad industry because of the paucity of Negroes employed.

Government interest in fair employment in air transport stems from the work of the state antidiscrimination agencies, again particularly that of New York, which first achieved breakthroughs in key jobs. Since 1960, government interest and legislation has

---

21. *Steele* v. *Louisville & Nashville Railroad Co.*, 323 U.S. 192 (1944).

been a key factor in the improvement of Negro job opportunities in air transport.

Government interest in fair employment in trucking consisted only of state commission actions prior to 1960, and they were not on a broad scale. Since then the Post Office Department, the Equal Employment Opportunity Commission, and the Department of Justice have all been active. As Dr. Leone pointed out in Part Three above, there are a number of key cases in court. In one, *Roadway Express, Inc.*,[22] a consent decree has been signed which commits the Teamsters' Union and the company to cease using the union hiring halls as the exclusive sources of applicants and requires the company to seek out and to train Negro applicants not only for drivers, but also for its management training program. Furthermore, Roadway, a major carrier, is committed to do this at all of its terminal locations. The decree also sets up a monitoring system to see that Negro applicants and candidates for promotion are given a fair opportunity. In addition— and a key provision—"all city drivers at Baltimore/Washington and Dallas regardless of race, may request, in writing, consideration for transfer to a road driver position," and such applicants must be considered as openings arise in order of seniority. Furthermore, other city drivers who unsuccessfully sought over-the-road driving jobs at Memphis, if qualified, had to be offered such jobs in order of their city driving seniority as vacancies occur, and be given seniority over those drivers dispatched since January 18, 1968. Such city drivers who qualify received over-the-road seniority as of that date.

This case, which was decided after the trucking study in Part Three was completed, in effect involved the application of the "rightful place" doctrine to the trucking industry.[23] It involved a company which has more than 10,000 employees and terminals in 28 states. Prior to the consent decree, it had no Negroes among its 2,000 road drivers nor among its like number of white collar personnel.[24] As the first trucking case brought to a successful conclusion, it should be a constructive precedent in the

---

22. *United States* v. *Roadway Express, Inc.*, U.S. D.C., N. Dist. Ohio, Civil Action No. C-68-321, September 1, 1970.

23. For an analysis of this doctrine and of the cases in which it arose, see Northrup and Rowan, *Negro Employment in Southern Industry, op. cit.*, Part One, pp. 95-104; and Part Three, pp. 77-84.

24. U.S. Department of Justice, Press Release, September 1, 1970.

necessary task of bringing the industry and the Teamsters' Union to a more respectable compliance posture.

In urban transit, government policy has long been a constructive factor for fair employment. The first fair employment procedures developed in the publicly owned systems prior to World War II. The wartime FEPC made urban transit a special target, and had considerable success. Most transit concerns in the North not integrated by the end of World War II quickly became so, sometimes with pressure from state antidiscrimination commissions. Finally, the Civil Rights Act of 1964 led to the integration of the final group in the South.

Overall, governmental policy is now a positive influence. But the pernicious effects of the two railroad labor agencies continue to be felt, and these agencies themselves have yet to indicate an interest in equal employment opportunity by deed or word.

MANAGERIAL POLICIES

Managerial policies do not seem to have played a strong equal employment role in the transportation industries, at least prior to the air transport industry's commitment of the 1960's. This industry had several strong executives, men who built their airlines from tiny mail and passenger carriers. None, however, was a Henry Ford or Harvey Firestone who was willing to challenge existing mores and racial employment policies.[25] Perhaps that is asking too much of a company that is so easily hurt by employee or customer reactions.

In the railroad industry, management policies were formulated in earlier years and change and break with tradition do not come easily. Moreover, railroad management, except for a World War II interim, has been in financial difficulties, and has been beset by strong unions anxious to eliminate, not to employ Negroes.

Trucking management is also not strong. Many carriers are financially unable to withstand economic pressure, and are reluctant to act in the face of worker or union opposition. Trucking management is still heavily up from the ranks and concerned with basic operations and finances. It may well take additional

---

25. For the story on these two titans' role in Negro employment, see Northrup, Rowan, *et al.*, *Negro Employment in Basic Industry, op. cit.*, Part Two, pp. 55-58 and Part Five, pp. 401-402, 405-406.

cases like that involving Roadway Express before the significance of the civil rights issue is perceived and greater emphasis placed thereon.

Management in urban transit is now heavily a public trust. The issue of Negro employment has long been resolved by governmental pressure and labor market and locational factors. In most areas, the problem is now one of selection and training of blacks, with few whites applying.

In conclusion, it should be noted that some innovative steps have been taken by a few managements in the transportation industries. The airlines, especially, in the 1960's broadened their approaches to the problem. Now they too are mired in financial difficulties. The economic health of our transportation system has, of late, obviously been poor. This does not auger well for black employment. Even if it recovers, however, innovative management is necessary to solve critical civil rights problems. For the airline industry, this will mean a resurgence and improvement of the progress of the 1960's; for railroads and trucking, it will require breaking more sharply with the past. For urban transit, Negro employment has long since ceased to be a critical issue, but white led unions and management are certain to need to open their leadership ranks to their black labor force.